THE POETRY OF
DYLAN THOMAS

LIVERPOOL ENGLISH TEXTS AND STUDIES 60

THE POETRY OF DYLAN THOMAS UNDER THE SPELLING WALL

JOHN GOODBY

LIVERPOOL UNIVERSITY PRESS

First published 2013 by
Liverpool University Press
4 Cambridge Street
Liverpool
L69 7ZU

Copyright © 2013 John Goodby

The right of John Goodby to be identified as the author of this book has
been asserted by him in accordance with the Copyright, Designs and Patents
Act 1988.

British Library Cataloguing-in-Publication data

A British Library CIP record is available

ISBN 978-1-84631-876-4 cased

Typeset by Carnegie Book Production, Lancaster
Printed and bound by CPI Group (UK) Ltd, Croydon CR0 4YY

Contents

Acknowledgements

My thanks are due to Anthony Cond of Liverpool University Press whose enthusiasm and consistent support for this book have made its appearance possible, and to the AHRC for providing a Research Fellowship in 2005–06 during which the bulk of the work on it was completed. Thanks are due also to Swansea University for a semester-length sabbatical in 2010 during which the work was completed.

Some of the material in this book has appeared, in earlier form, in the following publications: *Swansea Review*, *New Welsh Review*, *Notes and Queries*, *The Locations of Literary Modernism*, *Dada and Beyond: Dada and its Legacies*, *The Cambridge History of English Poetry*; my thanks are due to the editors for allowing me to use this material, in heavily revised form, in the present study, as they are to the following organizers of conferences and invited lectures at which draft versions of some of the material was road-tested: Patrick Crotty (Yeats International Summer School), Fran Brearton (Queen's University Belfast), Alex Davis and Lee Jenkins (University College Cork), Ann Heilmann (Hull University) and Guy Cuthbertson (University of St Andrews). I should also like to thank my colleagues and former colleagues in the English Department at Swansea, James A. Davies, Neil Reeve, Steve Vine and M. Wynn Thomas, and my undergraduate, MA and PhD students, in particular Chris Wigginton, Victor Golightly and Rhian Bubear, all three of whom taught me at least as much about Thomas's poetry as I did them. I am also grateful to Andrew Duncan and Richard Chamberlain, who read through the manuscript and made shrewd suggestions for its improvement, and the two Liverpool University Press readers, whose advice was invaluable.

None of the work I have carried out could have been accomplished without the dedications of librarians, and I hereby acknowledge my debts to: Swansea City Library; the National Library of Wales; the Inter-Library Loans staff at Swansea University Library; the staff of the Department of Manuscripts at the British Library at St Pancras; the staff of the Manuscripts Section of the Library at the Harry Ransom Humanities Research Center at University of Austin, Texas; Michael Basinski and his team at the Special Collections section of the Lockwood Memorial Library at SUNY Buffalo.

Dylan Thomas's legacy remains a living and potent one in Swansea and its environs, and among those who are active in the many activities it generates I would like to record my thanks to Jeff Towns, to the members of Dylan Thomas Society of Great Britain, and to Dave Woolley, director of the Dylan Thomas Centre until 2010, for their advice, friendship and encouragement.

Any infelicities of style or errors of fact which remain after all the help and advice I have received are entirely my own. The biggest debt of gratitude – as ever – is due to Nicola, George and Kate, for their patience and affectionate understanding while this book was being written.

I had intended to dedicate this book to Stan Smith, who, despite his own avowed Audenesque propensities, has been an encourager of what I must, by this stage, call the Dylan Thomas 'project', from its very inception at the *Under the Spelling Wall* conference in Swansea in 1998. However, without at all minimising recognition of that debt, the tragic deaths of Victor Golightly, in November 2006 and Aeronwy Thomas in July 2009 forestalled this intention. Vic was well-known in Wales as a scholar and editor of rare distinction and quiet passion, and the dying of his light came far too early for the many who knew, admired and loved him. In the last months of his life he was reading the first draft of this work, and offering characteristically friendly yet cogent advice; indeed, at that stage he was the only person who had read it through. Aeronwy was the child of Dylan and Caitlin Thomas who did most to represent the family, and worked hardest at publically honouring and preserving her parents' memory and her father's literary legacy. An accomplished memoirist herself, she also inherited Dylan's intelligence, curiosity and keen wit, and was well aware of his ambivalent status in Welsh literary studies. When we last met, not long before her death, she asked whether Swansea University had promoted me yet and, on being answered in the negative, drily replied: 'You must still be working on my father's poetry then.' I wish both Victor and Aeronwy had lived to see this book, and I dedicate it to their joint memory: 'There shall be corals in your beds, / There shall be serpents in your tides, / Till all our sea-faiths die'.

The author and publishers wish to thank the following for permission to use copyright material:

The Dylan Thomas Estate, for extracts from *Collected Poems, Collected Stories, Collected Letters* and *Under Milk Wood* by permission of J. M. Dent and David Higham Associates and New Directions Publishing Corporation; Penguin Books Limited for permission to quote 'Epitaph for François' by Paul Celan; Ian Duhig for 'Aeronwy's Song'; and Drew Milne for 'Foul Papers'.

Every effort has been made to trace copyright holders; if any have been inadvertently missed, the author and publisher would be pleased to come to an arrangement with them at the first opportunity and note them in future editions of this book.

Preface

In 1977, Roland Barthes announced the death of the author in a celebrated essay of the same name.[1] Those who feel that it is high time that his work deserves to be read at a healthier distance from the force-field of his life than is now generally the case could be forgiven for feeling that there is, perhaps, no twentieth-century author who could have benefitted more from such a death than Dylan Thomas, whose actual demise in a New York hospital in November 1953 at the age of thirty-nine – from medical malpractice, not alcoholic 'insult to the brain', as legend still has it – set the seal on a popular reputation, which remains high to this day, buoyed as it is by a fascination with an exuberant life and seemingly exemplary bohemian dissolution.[2] Almost all of Thomas's work is in print over half a century later, and his status as a cultural icon, burnished to a high gleam during the 1960s, has diminished only a little since its heyday. Yet this popular reputation is almost wholly at odds with the one that Thomas enjoys among academics, critics, literary historians and literary journalists.

Thomas was – with W. H. Auden – one of two outstanding poets to emerge in Britain during the 1930s. He became the most influential young poet of the 1940s and was the last British poet to have an impact on both American and world poetry. For twenty years after his death, he was regarded as, if not a 'major' poet in the league of Eliot, Yeats, Stevens and Pound, then certainly an important one in the tier below this exalted rank. Yet despite the evident magnificence of his most celebrated poetry, since the mid-1970s, critics have largely avoided any prolonged engagement with it.

With a growing awareness of the significant and unique achievements of their own poetry, especially of the post-war period, critics from the United States (US) understandably grew less interested in a poet whose impact – however sympathetically registered at the time – could be viewed as a final manifestation of the deference of the American literary world to that of Britain. Less healthy, however, were the reasons for neglect in Britain itself. Samuel Hynes's *The Auden Generation*, published in 1976, set the fashion for most accounts of 1930s writing – the decade in which Thomas published two-thirds of his poetry – to more or less expunge him from the record. It was matched by the redefinition of Thomas as a solely 'Forties poet'; poor recompense, since the Movement's judgement of it as the 'dire decade' is still largely the standard stance. As a result, Thomas was made historically homeless, marginalised both by tunnel vision and guilt by association, robbed of the contexts that might justify further investigation of his work.

The Movement revolt against Thomas's work and the excessive idolisation of his memory – understandable as certain aspects of that revolt were – stemmed from, and often indulged in, a long-standing and far more dubious animus against his exuberance (in life and work), his showmanship and his refusal to know his place, and it has continued to exist as a critical position long after the Movement ceased to exist in literary terms. Equally, the moralising link that F. R. Leavis and *Scrutiny* had drawn between presumed excess in life and an excessive writing was prolonged after Leavisism had faded from view; the advent of theory did not annul British academia's puritanism, Anglocentricity or upper-middle class hauteur. Even the radical, countercultural poetic current, which emerged in the wake of the Movement and embraced Thomas as a forerunner, gradually waned in its allegiance; the avant-garde, in particular, underwent a 'post-1960s revulsion from the marketplace', from which Thomas, who was regarded by some as having capitulated to it, can be said to have suffered.[3] As a result, driven by theory and a taste for thematics and identity politics over questions of form, literary studies over the last three decades have had little to do with Thomas. They have, however, made it possible to frame a new set of questions about him. These have to do with the nature of the twentieth-century lyric; with whether he is a modernist poet, and what the nature of that modernism might be if he is; with the extent to which his writing practice can be called political or gendered; with the inadequacy of terms such as Welsh, Anglo-Welsh, English and British to describe him; with the vexed relationship between avant-garde and mainstream, and their relationship with a figure like Blake.

As this suggests, since the 1970s, Thomas has become an embarrassment to twentieth-century poetry criticism, almost a scandal. To avoid tackling the kinds of questions listed above – questions which threaten vested interests in canon formation and approved lines of literary succession – the figure of the public entertainer has largely supplanted that of the serious poet. Thomas is presented as kind of cliché Celtic bard, a literary-historical sport or a dead-end. At best an appealing figure, he is now widely regarded as irrelevant to the way that poetry developed after his death ('influence' being a key determinant of academic interest). There is, of course, an element of snobbery in this: Thomas's continued popularity with the general reading public is seen simply as evidence of his work's vulgarity. Condescending acceptance of this almost invariably involves avoiding the poetry. Thus, Philip Hobsbawm opined in 1995 that: 'One thinks how limited Dylan Thomas would seem if we did not have his stories and *Under Milk Wood* to dwell on'.[4]

If part of the problem in England has been Thomas's Welshness, the nature of that Welshness has similarly been one of his problems in Wales. Thomas is unavoidably the central figure of the Anglo-Welsh canon and is un-ignorable in this respect – no-one else comes near, although efforts have been made, rather desperately at times, to put forward possible alternative candidates, ranging from Henry Vaughan to Idris Davies and (the usual contender) R. S. Thomas. It is right and proper, of course, that Thomas should not be allowed to overshadow the richness and variety of other Welsh writing, as he once tended to, particularly in terms of its reception outside Wales. Yet, this necessary correction made, the aversion displayed towards Thomas by leading figures in Welsh Writing in English (henceforth 'WWE') studies – as Anglo-Welsh literature is now called – is unusually marked. Thomas's anomalousness within the tradition, un-amenable to a preferred focus on issues concerning national identity, is taken as justification for ignoring him (reflected in the fact that it is an Englishman with a research background in Irish poetry, a relative newcomer to the field, who is currently editing the new centenary edition of Dylan Thomas's *Collected Poems*). Remarkable as it will seem outside Wales, there are no Welsh-born WWE critics under the age of seventy specialising in Thomas.

One result of English and Welsh neglect is that Thomas criticism is largely innocent of the theory revolution in English studies. Studies in a contemporary critical idiom have been made by English, Israeli, French and Canadian, but not Welsh, critics. A great deal of previously uncollected material by Thomas appeared in the 1980s and 1990s, but it did not provoke much in the way of reappraisal, let alone feminist, New Historicist, psychoanalytic, Marxist, poststructuralist or postcolonial rereading.[5] Thus, while WWE criticism is currently awash with poststructuralist paradigms, its most deconstructive and hybrid writer has not been reread in this light or, better, the limited application of such paradigms has been ignored, and no engagement with Thomas's challenges to the discipline has been made. As ever, he is neglected, but refuses to go away.

In Thomas criticism, Arnoldian Celticism and the Leavisite slippage from the work to the man find one of their last redoubts, and even good critics succumb. Neil Corcoran, for example, shrewdly noted in his *English Poetry since 1940* that: 'The way the world is read through, or dreamed across, the human body in this poetry surely makes Thomas overdue for a contemporary Bakhtinian reassessment'.[6] But this 'reassessment' never arrives; rather, within a few short sentences, we are told that the sources of Thomas's poetry are a 'heady brew', that it is 'almost entirely selfish' and suffers from 'psychological regression', a 'mesmerised and self-obsessed narcissism' and 'glandular compulsiveness'.[7] The stereotypes compulsively resorted to are, it would seem, the predictable, un-illuminating ones of drunkenness, wizardry and infantilism. That the last epithet comes, unacknowledged, from a Geoffrey Grigson attack made a generation earlier shows the degree to which such responses have become automatic and how hard the legend has made it to separate the bundle of accident and incoherence that sits down to breakfast from the deliberative artist.

Because of the legend's burr-like ability to stick to the life – and of both to stick to the art – in what follows, I shall offer the bare minimum of biographical information required to understand why Thomas's work – with its emphasis on the materiality and evasiveness of the signifier, its foregrounding of the body, sex and gender, its manipulation of Freudianism and myth, its gothic-grotesque hybridity, its focus on elegy and mourning and its proto-ecological strain – has not attracted more sustained and insightful attention in recent years. Why is the default position one of presumed pathology, rather than, say, calculated subaltern role playing and textual *jouissance*? The answer to the lack of serious engagement with Thomas's poetry, I shall argue, has less to do with laziness or personal and poetic provocation, than with the inadequacies of the standard narratives of twentieth-century poetry. The attacks on Thomas certainly prove that he triggers national, 'racial, cultural and class tremors', but they also show him to be a kind of lightning rod, by which tensions generated by repressions and lacunae within the official narratives of British poetry discharge themselves (*SP1*, xvi).

By 'official narratives', I refer to those which endorse the dominant anti- and ante-modernist strain in British poetry, even where, as more recently, they attempt to borrow some of the radical clothes of modernism. The classic analysis of this strain is Andrew Crozier's essay of 1983, 'Thrills and frills: poetry as figures of empirical lyricism'.[8] According to Crozier, the fundamental premise of such poetry is that perception validates an integral, expressivist self and its object-world or, as Anthony Mellors has put it more recently: 'The self that stands at the centre of this writing may be transformed by epiphany and chastened by irony, yet it is always a stable, controlling presence. *In absentia*, it personifies landscapes and animals, and claims inside knowledge of other human beings, reducing them to similitudes or exposing their "real" identity'.[9] (It is not that this lyric 'I' is innately outmoded, as the work of, say, Denise Riley or Frank O'Hara show; rather, that it is bound to be so, if it lacks a sufficiently modernist-derived sense of the subject as an entity that it 'builds and confounds itself', and the very process of doing so.)

These basic parameters apply to the different shades of mainstream verse, from recreations of 'romantic conceptions of self-expression and communion with nature', to the kind which allows that poetry took an interesting detour through modernism, but holds that it then: 'returned to its wellsprings in a revision of the Wordsworthian ideal of "a man speaking to men"'. This latter variety – dominant since the early 1990s – invokes 'the democratic voice' and 'pluralism', but these invariably follow the model of a market-defined 'choice'. It can accommodate difference in niche and identity terms (black, lesbian, working-class, etc.), but not contemporary experimental poetry, and its canon runs from Hardy, Edward Thomas, mid-Auden and Larkin to Heaney, Raine, Duffy, Armitage and Paterson. It reigns supreme in the world of poetry prizes, festivals, broadsheet reviews, the poetry lists of large London publishers and journals and most academic criticism.

At the outset of Thomas's career, the literary sphere was characterised by a much greater range of poetic tastes and intermingling of them than exists today. Georgian, Imagist, New Country, modernist and surrealist poetries each had their own journals and claques, but invariably overlapped in certain mid-range journals, such as *John O'London's* and *Time & Tide*.[10] In its first twenty years of existence, Faber & Faber signed up poets as varied as Ezra Pound, Lynette Roberts, Henry Treece and Walter de la Mare. A wide variety of critical voices – Geoffrey Grigson, Middleton Murray, Sir John Squires, Edith Sitwell and Herbert Read – debated the nature of modern poetry in literary journals and newspapers such as the *Morning Post* and the *Sunday Times*. The contrast with today's review section of, say, the *Observer*, or with the current Picador poetry list, is stark indeed. To some extent, this can be said of the presumed opposition between Thomas and Auden. In fact, their responses to the crisis of 1931–3 were similar: an apocalyptic manner and the utilisation of traditional verse forms, even if Auden reinstated the stable lyric ego after *The Orators*, while Thomas continued to charge his traditional forms with modernistic disruptiveness. In the 1940s, the spirit of national unity demanded even more convergence. Yet the fragmentation of the cultural sphere accelerated in that decade, too; by its close, the general literary journals had vanished, and criticism had become more professionalised and uniform. In the 1950s, the academic canonisation of the 'Men of 1914' and the Movement's divorce from them in the realm of contemporary practice installed many of the rigid divisions which still obtain. The 'New Gen' poets of the early 1990s signalled a change of sorts, but one in which the mainstream domesticated certain of the more superficial aspects of modernism, rather than giving ground to genuinely avant-garde poetics.

It is, of course, all too easy to exaggerate the differences between different kinds of poetry and simplify the histories of exclusion (thus, the leaders of a powerful countercultural 'British Poetry Revival' scene contributed mightily to its marginalisation in 1977 during a bitter struggle for control of the National Poetry Society, as Peter Barry has shown).[11] The last decade has seen the rise of non-mainstream poetry imprints, such as Salt, Carcanet and Bloodaxe, the erosion of metropolitan power by the worldwide web and new print technologies, greater assertiveness by alternative poets and a greater degree of curiosity on the part of critics and academics. Above all, there are those poets who expose the ultimately unsustainable nature of the division by problematising it from, say, Edwin Morgan, Peter Reading and Ken Smith, to Medbh McGuckian, Roy Fisher, Geoffrey Hill, Zoë Skoulding and John Kinsella.[12] Yet if the general assumption of a cut-off point for high modernist experimentation at 1930 or 1939 looks increasingly untenable, divisions continue to run deep in British literary culture; indeed, 'respect for the great modernists, accompanied by unwavering contempt for "foreign" experiments carried out by British poets', still prevails and is directly relevant to the critical constructions of the 1930s and 1940s.[13] These are not immutable; cracks in the monoliths are beginning to show; but they still prevail.

This is where Thomas comes in. He has not been neglected because he was an avant-garde or modernist-influenced poet, although he could play at being the former and was certainly an example of the latter. Rather, as the author of both 'Fern Hill' and 'Altarwise by owl-light', of Welsh-English modernist masterpieces and Anglo-Welsh pastoral classics, he is avoided by critics because, if taken seriously, he would threaten a set of heavily entrenched positions. In a polarised poetry scene in which loyalty oaths and identity politics tend to rule, he has proved non-recruitable. And while he is not the only poet to have written for avant-garde and mass audiences, he is the only one to have done both in such an un-ignorable and public way. Thus, he holds the key to a major rethinking of British poetry.

In what follows, and because it has been so fraught, I begin with a history of the critical reception of Thomas's poetry. This establishes basic terms, traces the gradual understanding of the co-ordinates of his work and suggests new ways in which it might be read. It clears the ground for six chapters, chronologically arranged, spanning Thomas's poetic development from 1930 until his death. Because Thomas's poetic is based on interconnectedness and hybridity, however, it is almost impossible to discuss him in terms of separate themes or phases: body, language, sex, Wales and Anglo-Welshness are continually being collapsed into each other. More than this, Thomas's poems often begin as if from first principles, recapitulating and incorporating their predecessors. 'Fuse' is a recurring key term and concept – a reminder that the simultaneity which is a theme of Thomas's poetry is part of its very nature. Premised on defiance of paraphrase, overdetermination, boundary-breaking and 'excess' are not so much what the poems are 'about', but what they *are*. Nevertheless, I take what seems to me to be a central aspect of the poetry in each of its phases, drawing on the letters, fictions, film- and radio-scripts where necessary. I suggest fresh discursive contexts for the poetry, but try to avoid the Cultural Studies tendency to ignore the specificities of literary writing in favour of 'themes' and the flattened discursive spaces of 'texts'. And while one of the main reasons for writing this book is to bring Thomas's work into contact with it, I apply theory eclectically, allowing what seems to me to be the specific qualities immanent within particular poems to give me my cue.

Chapter 1, for example, unravels the mélange of sources which fed the explosive development of the trademark 'process' style. It teases out the implications of Martin Dodsworth's claim that Thomas's poetry: 'should be seen at least as an extension of modernist practice in English as much as a revival of something called Romanticism', viewing that 'extension' as both excessive and exaggerated – an outcome of belatedness and Welsh liminality.[14] I identify the components of the process style precisely as these were tested during the summer and autumn of 1933 and suggest that it can be called 'mannerist modernist' – a gothic-grotesque, hybrid, biomorphic poetry of cosmogenesis, which nevertheless avoids atavism. If Thomas owed much to Lawrence, in his mythopoeic work 'identity formation is more crucial than identity description', so that while it is concerned with essentialism 'its interest [is] in problematic formations or processes of identity'.[15] The early process style is also read as part of the response to Eliot's criticism, which we associate with the work of William Empson; an attempt to incorporate modernism via the literary canon and close reading, but with poems which tests this to its limits.

In Chapter 2, I explore the nuts and bolts of Thomas's process style, using ideas drawn from structuralism and poststructuralism. Thomas's love of the linguistic 'remainder', to use Jean-Jacques Lecercle's term, is unexampled in English poetry of the time, and unleashed a gleeful, despairing linguistic excess, by way of response to various forms of determinist threat and, above all, generational fears of world war, so creating a kind of revolutionary and materialist mysticism at odds with the Left's usual social realist response and the discursive style and instrumental language use that it required.[16]

Chapters 3 and 4 take their cue from this linguistic materialism to explore the specific bodily, gothic-grotesque and Welsh forms taken by processual energy and linguistic *jouissance*. Chapter 3 traces the materiality of Thomas's language to its origins in the body; here, the body of, and in, the texts, and its sexual and cyborg qualities, are read partly through 1930s histories and theories concerning the body, glands and hormones. Something, too, is said about the relationship between the body and mind and Thomas's self-chosen role as a 'Freudian exemplar'.[17] Hybrid monstrosity and the nature of Thomas's Welshness is the subject of Chapter 4, which also makes the case for him as a surrealist poet. 'Altarwise by owl-light' is discussed as a trickster-inhabited apotheosis of a kind of regional surrealist or *surregionalist* mode, with Thomas viewed as having arrived at the limits of this style in 1937, seeking to mix it with more conventional poetic strategies from 1938 onwards.

In 1939, as the position of the social realist poets crumbled, Thomas became the exemplary poet for the times, during which his modernism was tempered by the common struggle to win not just the war, but also a just peace. Chapter 5 deals with *Deaths and Entrances* (1946), examining poems which pit the generative principle against wartime deaths, reflecting involvement in film propaganda and the need to find a public idiom, while at the same time registering a fear of silencing, the unspeakable outrage of civilian death (symbolised by the burning child) and the death of the concept of childhood. Immediately after the war, I argue in Chapter 6, Thomas tried to negotiate a new relationship to a fragmenting literary-cultural sphere. Pastoral – placing the complex into the simple – is seen as the governing genre and tactic of all the later work, influencing both its style and language as profoundly as its subject matter. Thomas made compromises with the stereotyping and simplifying pressures of the mass media in some of this work, but the best of it is a salutary ethical (as opposed to ethnic or nationalist) response to the Cold War and the threat of atomic annihilation.

In the Conclusion, I return to the point that in his paradoxically popular and marginalised condition, Thomas rests on and highlights crucial fault-lines within, and between, British, Welsh, Anglo-Welsh and English poetry and that we therefore ignore him at the risk of misunderstanding not just mid-twentieth century, but contemporary poetry. I attempt to uncover his influence on poetry since 1953, setting aside, insofar as it is possible, the legend that he helped create as a vehicle of his literary ambition (and which later served as a means for dealing with fame) and the myth that it became, which eventually elbowed aside the poetry.[18] Inevitably, this 'return' involves revisiting material from the Introduction, but, by this point, I hope readers will agree with me that the most remarkable fact relating to Thomas is ultimately not his reception, but his authorship of the 'fabulous curtain' of his poetry – something no amount of myth or legend can ever account for or should be allowed to occlude (*CP*, 38).

Notes

1 Roland Barthes, 'The Death of the Author', transl. Stephen Heath, *Image-Music-Text* (London: Collins, 1977), pp. 142–8.
2 The phrase 'an insult to the brain' does not appear on Thomas's death certificate. The story that he drank eighteen straight whiskies is unfounded. Research strongly suggests a medical cover-up around the doctor called to treat Thomas in his room at the Chelsea Hotel, Morton Feltenstein, who failed to diagnose pneumonia and administered the large amount of morphine sulphate on the morning of 5 November, which sent Thomas into the coma in which he remained until his death around 1.00 pm on 9 November. This is not to say that Thomas was innocent of gross contributory negligence in his own death. See David N. Thomas and Simon Barnes, *Dylan Remembered: 1935–1953* (Bridgend: Seren, 2004).
3 John Wilkinson, 'Frostwork and the Mud Vision', *The Cambridge Quarterly*, 31: 1 (2002), p. 94.
4 Philip Hobsbawm, review of Michael Longley, *The Ghost Orchid*, *Thumbscrew*, 3 (Autumn / Winter 1995), p. 61.
5 These books include Barbara Hardy's *Dylan Thomas: An Original Language* (2000),

James A. Davies's *A Reference Companion to Dylan Thomas* (1998), John Ackerman's *A Dylan Thomas Companion* (1991) and Walford Davies's *Dylan Thomas* (1986). The exception is Eynel Wardi's *Once Below A Time* (2000), and the Thomas portion of Chris Wigginton's *Modernism from the Margins* (2007).

6 Neil Corcoran, *English Poetry since 1940* (London: Longman, 1993), p. 43.

7 Neil Corcoran, *English Poetry since 1940*, pp. 42–5.

8 Andrew Crozier, 'Thrills and Frills: Poetry as Figures of Empirical Lyricism', ed. Alan Sinfield, *Society and Literature, 1945–70* (London: Methuen, 1983), pp. 199–33.

9 Anthony Mellors, *Late Modernist Poetics: From Pound to Prynne* (Manchester: Manchester University Press, 2005), pp. 17–18.

10 R. George Thomas, 'Dylan Thomas and Some Early Readers', *Poetry Wales: Dylan Thomas Special Issue*, 9: 2 (Autumn 1973), p. 14. '[F]rom 1920 until the war-time '40s there existed many magazines and reviews that published a good deal of poetry … on the assumption that poetry was part of the tasteful entertainment of the average reader'. In many of these publications: 'the personal taste of the editorial board could be indulged with considerable latitude before the charge of "long-haired" … was raised against them in the interests of the "common" … reader'. They included such long-defunct journals as *John O'London's, Time and Tide* and *The Sunday Referee* (a sporting paper with a poetry corner, in which Thomas's 'The force that through the green fuse' first appeared).

11 See Peter Barry, *Poetry Wars: British Poetry of the 1970s and the Battle of Earls Court* (Cambridge: Salt, 2006). All the terms involved in this discourse are inadequate, and I use 'mainstream' and 'alternative' with some reluctance to characterise very broad and often intermingling poetic currents and critical stances. Terms such as 'experimental', for example, do not preclude 'mainstream' work (see Paul Muldoon's *Madoc* or *The Annals of Chile*), while 'linguistically innovative' begs a similar question. 'Postmodernist', rather differently, means different things at different times and in different places; simply 'after modernism', in Charles Olson's usage, dizzyingly playful and relativistic in the work of the US New York School poets, and a mannerist veneer on the empirical lyric in the case of the English Martian poets and their successors. Much of the debate centres on the question of what happened after high modernism in the 1920s. Ian Gregson and John Wilkinson usefully distinguish 'neo-modernist' as its continuation, while Anthony Mellors prefers 'late modernism': the attempt to rescue the totalities of modernist poetry from its reactionary matrices after WWII. This, he describes as: 'antithetical to postmodernism, which [destroys immanence] discloses myth as ideology and treats the "self" as a construct, not as an organic unity'. The most wide-ranging and least splenetic account available is John Matthias's review article, 'British Poetry at Y2K'. See Ian Gregson, *Contemporary Poetry and Postmodernism: Dialogue and Estrangement* (Basingstoke: Macmillan, 1996); John Wilkinson, 'Frostwork and the Mud Vision', *The Cambridge Quarterly*, 31: 1 (2001), 93–105; Anthony Mellors, *Late Modernist Poetics: From Pound to Prynne* (Manchester: Manchester University Press, 2005), p. 23; John Mathias, 'British Poetry at Y2K', http://www.electronic-bookreview.com (2000).

12 Desktop publishing and print on demand technology have been exploited by alternative poetry presses to create products, which, in sophistication of packaging and sales, now rival those of Picador, Faber and Cape. Between 2003 and 2005, *Poetry Review* operated a more inclusive editorial policy (and *Poetry Wales* has

been doing so since 2007). Collected poems by J. H. Prynne, Barry MacSweeney and Tom Raworth have appeared from Carcanet and Bloodaxe, while Salt and Shearsman have published not only scores of titles by poets rejected by the mainstream publishers, but numerous critical studies and anthologies. Much of the new activity has occurred via the worldwide web, through discussion lists and e-zines such as *The Lyre* and *Jacket*. The result has been a huge expansion of the sphere in which encountering, publishing and theorising about alternative poetries can take place.

13 As Mellors drily notes: 'No one doing the police in different voices is likely to pass muster with the judges of today's T. S. Eliot Prize'. Anthony Mellors, *Late Modernist Poetics*, p. 118.

14 Martin Dodsworth, 'The Concept of Mind and the Poetry of Dylan Thomas', ed. Walford Davies, *Dylan Thomas: New Critical Essays* (London: Dent, 1972), p. 120. As Dodsworth observes: 'Thomas's obscurity is bound up with [a modernist] attempt like Eliot's to short-cut the reason, by bringing the mind to bear upon a representation of reality which is resistant to a reduction to the mind's own reasonable terms'.

15 Chris Wigginton, *Modernism from the Margins: The 1930s Poetry of Louis MacNeice and Dylan Thomas* (Cardiff: University of Wales Press, 2007), pp. 108–9.

16 Jean-Jacques Lecercle, *The Violence of Language* (London: Routledge, 1990), Chapter 1, pp. 7–54.

17 Stewart Crehan, '"The Lips of Time"', eds. John Goodby and Chris Wigginton, *Dylan Thomas: A New Casebook* (London: Palgrave, 2001), p. 59.

18 Roland Barthes, 'Myth Today', selected and transl. Annette Lavers, *Mythologies* (London: Paladin, 1989), pp. 117–74. In Barthesian myth, 'Dylan Thomas' is a naturalised cultural construct, the signifier whose signified is gratuitous linguistic excess, irrationality, inauthenticity and primitivism, constituting a metalinguistic sign or 'signification' within the discursive formation of 'the English poetic tradition'.

Abbreviations

TB	*Dylan Thomas: The Broadcasts*, ed. Ralph Maud, London, Dent, 1991.
CP	*Collected Poems 1934–1953*, eds. Walford Davies and Ralph Maud, London, Dent, 1989.
CL	*The Collected Letters*, ed. Paul Ferris, 2nd edn., London, Dent, 2000.
CS	*Collected Stories*, ed. Walford Davies and intro. Leslie Norris, London, Dent, 1983 (repr. 1993).
DJ	*Dylan Thomas: The Poems*, ed. and intro. Daniel Jones, London, Dent, 1979.
EPW	*Early Prose Writings*, ed. and intro. Walford Davies, London, Dent, 1971.
LVW	*Letters to Vernon Watkins*, intro. Vernon Watkins, London, Faber / Dent, 1957.
NP	*The Notebook Poems 1930–1934*, ed. and intro. Ralph Maud, London, Dent, 1990.
PM	'Poetic Manifesto', *Texas Quarterly* 4 (Winter 1961), 45–53.
QEOM	*Quite Early One Morning*, New York, NY, New Directions, 1960.
TCSP	*Dylan Thomas: The Complete Screen Plays*, ed. John Ackerman, New York, NY, Applause Books, 1995.
SP1	*Dylan Thomas: Selected Poems*, ed. and intro. Walford Davies, London, Dent, 1993.
SP2	*Dylan Thomas: Selected Poems*, ed. and intro. Walford Davies, London, Dent, 2000.
UMW	*Under Milk Wood*, ed. Ralph Maud and Walford Davies, intro. Walford Davies, London, Dent, 1995.

INTRODUCTION

The critical fates of Dylan Thomas

> I do know that persons ... prefer to read about poets than read what those bleeders write.
>
> – Dylan Thomas[1]

Answers to the question of how the poetry of Dylan Thomas is regarded today are likely to perplex. Among the general reading public, Thomas is one of a small handful of widely recognised modern poets. His *Collected Poems* have been in print since 1952 and half a dozen or so Thomas poems are still anthology staples. Their popularity is boosted by his best-known work, *Under Milk Wood*, of course, but his other writings – stories, notebook poems, film scripts, radio plays and letters – have also been published and remain in print.[2] Yet among academics and literary critics, the story is very different. Very little research effort is now expended on Thomas – over the last three decades, more PhDs have been written on those other Thomas-poets, R. S. and Edward – and he barely figures in histories and critical discussions of mid-twentieth century poetry. Although articles on Thomas still appear with some regularity, as the LION database attests, these are invariably traditional and small-scale: thematic, allusion-hunting or close readings, generally of the better-known poems. More ambitious theory-based or more general considerations of Thomas's place within twentieth-century poetry are very rare. In poetry journals and among broadsheet reviews of poetry, the situation is much the same, and, although calls for a re-valuation of his poetry occur with some regularity, these never seem to materialise. All of which suggests that Thomas is a kind of embarrassment on just about every level of the mainstream poetry world. His work is powerful and won't fade away, and it appears that something needs to be said about it; but, for some reason, it cannot be made to fit the standard narratives and so nothing gets done. That Thomas doesn't seem to influence later poets is often taken as justifying the lack of attention;

literary historians like to trace lines of influence, causes and effects. At best, among those who determine the canon in its various forms, Thomas is viewed as a stylistic dead-end and a loveable literary curio; at worst, he is seen as a sham or pseudo-poet, all posturing and adolescent-sounding brass. Whether positively or negatively appraised, however, in this world, he is a decidedly minor figure.

The contrast with the valuation that ruled from the time of Thomas's death in 1953 until the mid-1970s could scarcely be greater. Between 1954 and 1976, around twenty studies of Thomas's work were published – more than on almost any other modern poet. In addition, there were two poem-by-poem glossaries, a biography, at least three book-length memoirs, an edition of the notebook poems, two selections of the letters, six miscellanies of prose, poetry and broadcasts, two bibliographies, a concordance, four collections of critical essays, at least four journal special issues, and scores of book chapters and journal articles. He drew sustained and approving attention on both sides of the Atlantic, from critics of the calibre of Raymond Williams, John Bayley, William Empson and J. Hillis Miller. Both of F. R. Tolley's standard histories, *The Poetry of the Thirties* (1975) and *The Poetry of the Forties* (1985), included separate chapters on Thomas's work, and he was frequently used as an example in studies of poetics (several textbooks featured his 'Poetic Manifesto' of 1950, for example).[3] Thomas's importance was attested to by fellow-poets as diverse as Louis MacNeice, Robert Lowell, John Berryman, e. e. cummings, Ted Hughes, Sylvia Plath and W. S. Graham. In almost every way, he was central to critical understanding and literary history. Indeed, despite some heavyweight opponents – among them Geoffrey Grigson, Donald Davie and F. R. Leavis – a consensus seemed to have emerged, by the time of J. B. Kershner's magisterial guide to the plethora of material, *Dylan Thomas: The Poet and His Critics*, in 1976. In his introduction, Kershner noted that: 'Thomas at last seems ready to take his place in the literary continuum, in meaningful relationship to other writers. His originality is no longer in question but, in the perspective of some twenty years since [his] death, neither is the fact of his position in the literary pantheon'.[4] If he was not a 'major' poet, he was certainly deemed to be on a par with, say, MacDiarmid or Crane, Moore or Bishop (as Thomas once self-mockingly put it, he was: 'top of the second eleven').[5] Most readers, at this time, could have been forgiven for thinking that his place in the 'literary pantheon' was assured.

In retrospect, however, Kershner's *summum* can be seen to mark the end of the golden age of Thomas criticism – that is, of engagement with his work by critics working with some knowledge of the latest critical thinking. From this point on, his reputation in academia swiftly collapsed. Since 1973, there have been just three critical studies of the poetry, two of which are introductory works of around 130 pages.[6] The best of the criticism that appeared in the 1980s and 1990s was lucid and usefully expository (especially on the poet's Welsh contexts), and it addressed crucial textual and editorial matters. But it was invariably couched in a critical idiom innocent of the revolution in English studies then taking place, from the re-valuations of modernism to feminist and postcolonial theory, and was largely editorial and consolidatory. In this sense, superb though some of it was, it merely reinforced the impression of critical stagnation. There is, of course, almost always a decline in an author's reputation immediately after their death, and one could argue that, in Thomas's case, this decline was artificially postponed for two decades, first by the wave of sympathy and interest caused by his untimely death and then by the way in which both his work and legend resonated with the libertarian temper of the 1960s and early 1970s (Thomas, at this point, became the cultural icon that he remains, with a particular appeal for rock and film stars). Even so, the collapse since then has been unusually long and deep, with only a few signs, in the last decade or so, of a possible recovery.

How did the huge gap between popular and academic-critical reputations open up and how has it remained so wide? One reason is that, during the 1970s, most critics and poets of Thomas's generation – or at least those identifying most closely with his work – reached retirement age and began to die off. But this doesn't explain why they had no successors. It is significant that one or two potential replacements *did* appear in the late 1960s, only to disappear after their initial contributions to Thomas studies. Another reason may be that the particular appeal Thomas had for the New Critics, in terms of their penchant for close reading and the teasing out of ambiguities, was held against him as Anglo-American academia also began to embrace theory in the 1970s. Yet when they turned to twentieth-century poetry, Yale poststructuralists focused on late Romantic poets, such as W. B. Yeats, Wallace Stevens, Hart Crane and John Ashbery, and Thomas had surely been of their company. He was passed over, however, despite having been the subject of a brilliant chapter by the pre-poststructuralist J. Hillis Miller in 1966. It may be that the legend doused any flickering of serious interest, but this does not explain the depth of hostility towards Thomas. Only a structural aporia can account for the number of theory-savvy critics who lapsed into *ad hominem*-ism when faced with poetry so aware of its linguistic medium, so body centred, so psychoanalytically self-aware, and hence so amenable to the insights of Barthes and Derrida, Bakhtin and Kristeva.

Kenneth Rexroth had foreseen, as long ago as 1949, a backlash against how 'terribly unBritish' Thomas seemed.[7] Thomas was resented by many during his lifetime for his combination of stylistic exuberance, roaring boy reputation and common touch. This resentment is tapped by George Steiner's characterisation of him in 1960 as an 'impostor' peddling bardic excess 'with the flair of a showman to a wide, largely unqualified audience [which] could be flattered by being given access to a poetry of seeming depth' – an outburst which makes it clear that, as higher education and BBC cultural outputs expanded, Thomas came to symbolise the threat of the middle-brow to many of the more mandarin and snobbish cultural arbiters, especially in England.[8] But, equally, there were also several commentators in Wales who disliked Thomas for his lack of Welsh (and his lack of guilt regarding this lack), his anti-nationalism and his consistent use of Welsh stereotypes. When a new edition of the poems appeared in 1971, Gabriel Pearson noted: 'Thomas lies in critical limbo … despite the traditional scholarly embalming, he retains a flavour of tainted meat, of matter over-hung, over-high, and subtly off … the reception has been almost blatantly cool. I take this to mean that Thomas's legend is charged and dangerous and potent enough to make critics edge away when they see it making towards them'.[9] Even so, it was not until the 1970s that this opposition to Thomas outweighed the support, when a seismic shift occurred in the way that English and Welsh (and 'British') poetry discursively constituted themselves.

One way of defining how Thomas is 'dangerous' is to ask whether his poetry best belongs in the 1930s or the 1940s. Nowadays, it is treated as Forties poetry, shunted into a decade which Movement-influenced poetry criticism still has little time for. And yet, two-thirds of Thomas's published poetry had already appeared by 1939, including his most explosive and innovative work. Why is it, then, that the standard works on 1930s writing say so little about Thomas? Or, put differently, one might ask *where* he belongs: Wales or England? The most common answer would probably be 'Wales', yet this raises the vexed issue of how Wales and England and the relationship between their literary traditions are defined. Thomas was regarded in his lifetime as belonging within the English poetic tradition – a poet who happened to originate from Wales (and had a 'Welsh' tone, whatever that was), but who was of larger, British and international significance. Since the 1960s, of course, devolutionary forces have created an increased awareness of the way in which the 'English' label has been (and still is) used to subsume other nationalities within the archipelago, naturalising English dominance over them, and how 'Britain', too, may co-opt Welsh, Scottish and Northern Irish identities within a greater England. However, to attach too many conditions to these identities is to miss how 'British' can expand, as well as narrow, horizons. While he emphasised his Welsh border inheritance, for example, Raymond Williams nevertheless insisted on setting it within the context of a British working-class culture, which, in certain crucial ways, transcended intra-British nationalisms based on blood and birthplace and offset their tendencies towards essentialism. As the other major 'English' poetic voice beside Auden in the 1930s and the dominant one of the 1940s, Thomas's work has a similarly British dimension. Too powerful to be confined to a literary region which defines itself over-narrowly, it also refuses to be confined to a single decade, confounding decade-as-style divisions. An outsider and interloper, but one secure in his multiple identities and talent, Thomas turns the kinds of questions I am considering back on his interlocutors: where do contemporary notions about 'English' and 'British' poetry originate and why? How are periods, canons and national identities defined and by whom? Unease at such provocation, genially but stubbornly offered by Thomas's work and the sheer un-ignorableness of his presence, informs the 'recurrent and strangely vindictive' attacks on his reputation.[10] In this sense, Pearson's comments point not just towards some innate ambiguity, but also towards the scandal and improper excess of the work and a difficulty in 'placing' Thomas which exceeds the distractions of the legend. So 'charged' have the attempts to address this become, that some account of the history of Thomas's critical reception is required before dealing with the poetry itself.

* * *

From its first appearance in a national journal in May 1933, Thomas's poems attracted a great deal of critical attention. They also tended to strongly polarise that attention. While the majority of the reviews for the six books of poetry published in the UK during his lifetime were positive, this polarisation was a constant. Frequently, the problems centred on Thomas's 'difficulty' and how justified it might be. On the one hand, the clear break with the Audenesque style represented by *18 Poems* (1934) was welcomed, because it returned a Jacobean colour, concreteness and rhythmical vigour to the English lyric in a mature and astonishingly authoritative manner. But it was also clear from the outset that it was not in the nature of this poetry to be fully understood and, in excess of the license usually granted to poetry to resist prose, paraphrased. There was, therefore, a continual uncertainty over its nature – were its impressive local effects part of a larger vision? To what extent were they intended by the poet? And what precisely did they mean? Although a few early readers, such as Desmond Hawkins (in a review of *18 Poems* of 1935), gave some idea of how the poems worked, others – most notably Edith Sitwell and Herbert Read – took the sonorously authoritative tone as a cue to defend them as an 'absolute' poetry written in accordance with first and last things – creation, conception, birth, orgasm, death – which, by their nature, were never fully knowable.[11] Read's assertion, in a review of *The Map of Love* (1939), that 'these poems cannot be reviewed; they can only be acclaimed' is a classic example.[12] Taken out of context from a piece which actually contained praise based on a shrewd insight into the poems, this phrase was made to serve as evidence of the lack of critical standards of Thomas's admirers. As early as 1936, Geoffrey Grigson – albeit he was nursing a personal grudge against Thomas – could declare that 'twenty-four twenty-fifths' of *Twenty-five Poems* (1936) were 'pathological nonsense'.[13] More representative of the general response were the poets associated with *New Country* (1933) (hereafter 'New Country poets'), who were impressed by Thomas's command of the language of dreams, the unconscious and pre-rational states, but felt that he presented these in a formless, passive way; wrongly, they took the inchoate nature of what was being described and the dense imagery and syntax to be signs of indiscipline and splurge. Stephen Spender, for example, claimed that: 'Thomas's poetry is turned on like a tap; it is just poetic stuff with no beginning or end, shape, or intelligent and intelligible control'.[14] While laudable for its rebellious, Freudian instincts, they felt that Thomas's poetry was too much in thrall to them, and they tended to regard it as a dark, subjective complement to their own more fully, because conscious, revolutionary work.[15] The 1936 edition of Cecil Day Lewis's *A Hope for Poetry* updated the 1934 first edition by recognising the new arrival, but it distinguished between the two kinds of poetry in an either / or way, using binaries of classicism versus romanticism, mind versus body and male versus female, in which the Thomas-associated term was the subordinate one. Defined in terms of a reaction against New Country, Thomas was thereby taken to register its primacy, together with a small group of other young poets at the time – George Barker and David Gascoyne being the best-known – in a manner which was thoroughly ideological; that is, determined by upper-middle class English attitudes towards lower-middle class and 'Celtic' writers.[16] As Spender later admitted: 'we patronized them, but we were afraid, really, of dirty boots on the carpet'.[17]

While the responses I have sketched were ostensibly opposed to each other, they were also complementary, insofar as they both missed Thomas's conscious and painstaking craft; strange as it now seems, most 1930s critics barely mentioned the strict syllabic metres and nets of pararhyme which Thomas forged, even in his early poems. He was regarded in an either / or way, as a romantic reaction against Auden, which one either agreed or disagreed with; as nature, in short, as opposed to culture. In truth, as Pearson shrewdly observed, Auden and Thomas were actually fellow-members of the same 'spiritually orphaned generation', which felt itself to be trapped between two wars, both responding to the crisis of 1929–33 in a 'vein of nervy apocalyptic jokiness'. Indeed, they were arguably 'the sundered halves of the great modernist poet that English poetry, after Eliot, failed to throw up'.[18] However, as the younger poet, Thomas borrowed from New Country, as well as high modernism, combining the traditional stanza forms, rhyme schemes and standard syntax of the one with the depth, leaps between images and verbal play of the other, adding to both a Blakean religiosity. The fusion of these unlikely elements baffled contemporaries; only Hawkins really grasped the extent of Thomas's originality, and it is only since the 1980s that it has been possible to theorise the modernist element in this mix as our understanding of modernism as a unitary phenomenon – the single-handed creation of lone artists, which had run its course by 1930 – has now unravelled. Thomas now appears within a plurality of competing, geographically diverse (often peripheral), alternative modernisms, to be envisaged as 'less ... a progression of ruptures with their climax in 1922 than as a series of 'traces, false starts, successive waves ... the joint output of a multinational cast of collectives and coteries'.[19]

Nevertheless, by the late 1930s, the intellectual climate had changed sufficiently for the intentions and craft of Thomas's work to be discerned more clearly, and he certainly made his difference from Auden apparent in his contribution to the issue of *New Verse* published to celebrate Auden's thirtieth birthday in late 1937, praising 'the mature, religious, and logical fighter', but deprecating his 'boy bush-ranger' aspect and adding that his poetry was: 'a hygiene ... a sanitary science and a flusher of melancholies'.[20] In letters written to Pamela Hansford Johnson in 1933–5, Thomas had already described his accomplishment in terms of a 'process poetic'; that is, one with an uncompromising focus on ultimates, first and last things, which linked body and cosmos and understood the universe from a post-Darwinian, Einsteinian perspective as absolute flux: time and space, energy and matter, growth and decay, birth and death were all equally interchangeable, implicit and active within each other in this vision of things – aspects of the same 'force' in which potential and actual events were indistinguishable. The literary antecedents for the micro- and macrocosm trope reached from Joyce's giant Finnegan back to medieval thought. The points of maximum bodily change – orgasm, conception, gestation, birth, adolescence and death – were necessarily those on which Thomas focused, conflating inner and outer 'weathers', blood, body, soil and nebulae to lend a pathos and dignity to the human condition, one which was not without its blackly humorous and grotesque aspect.

Thomas's 'process' vision demanded a corresponding processual handling of language, in which – as he said several times over the course of his career – he created poems from words and their interactions, from word-clusters and wordplay, rather than by trying to find the words that fitted an already existing thought or narrative: 'I think [the poem] should work from words, from the substance of words and the rhythm of substantial words set together, not towards words. Poetry is a medium, not a stigmata on paper' (*CL*, 208). Conflating 'word' and 'image', he described this radically compressed, mobile poetic practice, in a letter of 23 March 1938 to Henry Treece. This contrasted his 'How shall my animal', which '*needs* a host of images, because its centre is a host of images', with a typical New Country poem, which '*need[s]* no more than one image' and '[moves] around one idea, from one logical point to another, making a full circle'. Against this, Thomas's decentred practice began with an image or word-cluster being allowed to prompt and 'breed' others, which conflicted in their turn, thus producing new 'images' and conflicts:

I make one image, – though 'make' is not the word, I let, perhaps, an image be 'made' emotionally in me then apply to it what intellectual & critical forces I possess – let it breed another, let that image contradict the first, make, of the third image bred out of the other two together, a fourth and contradictory image, and let them all, within my imposed formal limits, conflict. Each image holds within it the seed of its own destruction, and my dialectical method, as I understand it, is a constant building up and breaking down of the images that come out of the central seed, which is itself destructive and constructive at the same time.

Reading back over that, I agree it looks preciously like nonsense. To say that I 'let' my images breed and conflict is to deny my critical part in the business. But what I want to try to explain – and it's necessarily vague to me – is that the *life* in any poem of mine cannot move concentrically round a central image; the life must come out of the centre; an image must be born and die in another; and any sequence of my images must be a sequence of creations, recreations, destructions, contradictions. I cannot, either – as Cameron does and as others do, and this primarily explains … their writing round the central image – make a poem out of a single, motivating experience; I believe in the single thread of action through a poem, but that is an intellectual thing aimed at lucidity through narrative … Out of the inevitable conflict of images – inevitable, because of the creative, recreative, destructive, and contradictory nature of the motivating centre, the womb of war – I try to make that momentary peace which is a poem. I do not want a poem of mine to be, nor can it be, a circular piece of experience placed neatly outside the living stream of time from which it came; a poem of mine is, or should be, a watertight section of the stream that is flowing all ways; all warring images within it should be reconciled for that small stop of time. … [E]ach of my earlier poems might appear to constitute a section from one long poem; that is because I was not successful in making a momentary peace with my images at the correct moment; images were left dangling over the formal limits, and dragged the poem into another; the warring stream ran on over the insecure barriers, the fullstop armistice was pulled & twisted raggedly on into a conflicting series of dots and dashes (*CL*, 328–9).

This remarkable passage reveals that, for Thomas, writing a poem involved creating the linguistic equivalent of cell mitosis or nuclear fission: the poem's 'life' came 'out of a centre' or core, which was not a single 'image', but rather a zone of metamorphosis, in which images (or words and phrases) were born, warred and died. Its product would be synthetic and summatory, not epiphanic or anecdotal – there is no 'single, motivating experience' (and, therefore, no singular, wholly stable self) behind it.

Treece published this passage in an essay of 1938, and it became one of the keys to critical understanding. Many of Thomas's concerns are evident in it, from its Great War imagery, to the poem's immersion in relativistic 'living stream of time'. One central aspect of the description is its pullulating biomorphic aspect. Later in the 1930s, as war loomed and civilisation seemed threatened with total destruction, more and more artists would use images drawn from the one irreducible factor of human existence – the body – to express a hope for human survival. In literary terms, Thomas was well ahead of the times; in 1933–4, the closest equivalent of his process style was the work of biomorphic visual artists, such as Hans Arp, Max Ernst and André Masson. In this poetry, a deep biological determinism is pitted against an electrifying verbal performance, which is thereby paradoxically charged with melancholia and an exuberant, self-spending energy. By the late 1930s, this early style began to mellow as Thomas became increasingly reconciled to the 'seedy' cycle of birth, growth, reproduction, decay and death. Rather than being a snapshot of aesthetic coherence wrested from – and yet embodying – the flux of process, poems came to be conceived, almost antithetically, as: 'a weapon against process, a rival creation impervious to time'.[21]

In the Treece letter, the agency of the self which presides over the writing of the poem seems uncertain ('I let, perhaps, an image be made … it's necessarily vague to me … I try to make'), and this is reflected in Thomas's definitions. Thus, while 'momentary peace' seems to describe traditional lyric closure, 'a watertight section of the stream that is flowing all ways' is a calculated paradox – the mobility of 'stream' is enhanced by the pun on 'all ways' / always and conflicts with the 'watertight' arrest. Thomas seems to be describing a poetry which is at once both open-ended and closed. The earlier poems 'dangle' over their 'formal limits' into others, while it is implied that, in later ones, the 'warring images' are brought to reconciliation. Throughout his career, however, Thomas would construct seemingly resounding conclusions, which were anything but conclusive. James Balakiev notes that 'the "ambiguous climax" was Dylan Thomas's way: he was a master of the open ending', but this needs to be qualified by adding that Thomas often sought to engineer a conflict, for those who looked closely enough, between 'open endings' and the rhetorical finality in which they were presented.[22]

No longer seen as unintelligible and formless, Francis Scarfe noted in *Auden and After* (1942) that Thomas's poetry was not obscure because of its lack of meaning, but rather because of its *excess* of it. He saw that it was a 'process of discovery', rather than 'what [the poet] knows he has found', and that it displayed an underlying 'sexually dynamic' 'philosophy'.[23] In succession, Robert Horan (1945), Linden Huddlestone (1948) and David Aivaz (1950) all made the same point, linking it to Thomas's unusual language use: the verbal 'process' of pun, renewed cliché, appositive clauses, and so on, enacted his 'basic theme'.[24] Aivaz spelt this out: 'Process is unity in nature; its direction is the cyclical return; the force that drives it is the generative energy in natural things. Like the "motivating centre" of a Thomas poem it is "destructive and constructive at the same time"; so that not only do life and death imply each other ... but they are, in Thomas's mind, in essence the same' and 'both art and faith ("nightingale and psalm") are illusory when they deny process.'[25] The violent, gnomic and grotesque aspects of 'process' were seen to distinguish it from Romantic pantheism or idealism, its particular flavour deriving from what Empson identified as Thomas's 'chief power as a stylist ... to convey a sickened loathing which somehow at once (within the phrase) enforces a welcome for the eternal necessities of the world'.[26]

Following Auden's departure for the US in January 1939, Thomas's existential humanist focus on death and (im)mortality, the fact that he had already invented a poetic language for the apocalyptic times and his recognition of the importance of the religious sense all established him as the leading figure in the efflorescence of a modernistic, visionary neo-Romanticism.[27] Poetry of the 1940s (except that by Eliot, Auden, Douglas and a handful of others) is today routinely denigrated or ignored, but this is largely a legacy of the bad press that the decade received from the Movement and its ideologues, periodically re-activated since the Movement's demise. Several members of the younger generation – W. S. Graham, David Gascoyne, Lynette Roberts, J. F. Hendry and Thomas himself – produced brilliant and original poetry, and women poets – Edith Sitwell and H. D., as well as Roberts – produced their best work in the 1940s. Dormant older poets, such as David Jones, T. S. Eliot and Edwin Muir, were re-energised. The decade was also notable for the advance of the regions against the metropolitan centre, with Scotland, Wales, Northern Ireland and the English North all experiencing poetic renaissances. In general, the period was remarkable (unlike the 1950s) for the variety of poetry it allowed to flourish. Under these conditions, 1930s poets, such as Spender and MacNeice, came to recognise, and pay tribute to, the structure and discipline of Thomas's work.

Nevertheless, in his journal *Polemic* (1945–7) and *The Harp of Aeolus* (1948), Geoffrey Grigson kept up 1930s-style attacks on Thomas; in a piece in *The Harp of Aeolus*, a bogus stanza made up of eight unrelated lines from 'There was a saviour' was passed off as the real thing, with the deception being revealed later in the essay, with the aim of catching Thomas's acolytes out.[28] Thomas was also attacked in F. R. Leavis's *Scrutiny* – the most influential post-war literary-critical journal; Wolf Mankowitz's review of *Deaths and Entrances*, for example, was among the most abusive it ever printed.[29] Leavis's manner of formulating observations assumes a commonsense account of the nature of communication, such that discourse is intelligible 'primarily as a revelation of the qualities of the mind of its individual author or speaker' and invariably elides the material text in its 'recurring slide from text to author', as Catherine Belsey has noted.[30] He also assumes an intimate relationship between the English language and English forms of experience, such that using it for non-English experience amounts to driving 'a dangerous wedge between signifier and signified' – hardly a belief likely to lead to a positive assessment of an Anglo-Welsh poet dedicated to the autonomy of the signifier.[31] Most damagingly, it is Leavis's essentially moralistic, character-based, expressivist critical model which still tends to be the default position for critics when they encounter the Thomas myth.

By the early 1950s, a reaction against neo-Romantic and Modernist poetry had begun in earnest. The Movement, in particular, defined itself against Thomas, as the leading figure of the predecessor generation, their animus exacerbated by the long drawn-out mourning which followed his death in November 1953 and the fulsome nature of many of the tributes. The Movement's ideological underpinning was established in the *Purity of Diction in English Verse* (1952) by Donald Davie, who argued for neo-Augustan clarity and rationality in poetry and against the model for poetic and personal behaviour set by the 'bardic' poets of the 1940s. Although he would later reconsider his anti-modernism, Davie always granted canonical centrality and legitimacy to plain-style, empirical poetry in 'the English tradition' (the definitive article is revealing) that he traced from Thomas Hardy to Philip Larkin, excluding Thomas. Davie resumed his attack in *Articulate Energy* (1955), in which Thomas was identified as a symptom of 1940s poetry's failings; the 'pseudo-syntax' of 'Altarwise by owl-light' was described as 'radically vicious' and signifying nothing less than a 'loss of confidence in the intelligible structure of the conscious mind and the validity of its activity'. The charge – in a pattern that would become commonplace – was based on a misquotation of a passage which was perfectly construable in the original.[32] Thus, in his 1955 Clark Lecture at Cambridge, Robert Graves attacked Eliot, Pound,

Yeats, Auden and Thomas, claiming that: 'Dylan Thomas was drunk with melody, and what the words were he cared not', identifying a 'defect in sincerity' and asserting that 'professionally-minded English poets ban double-talk ... and insist that that every poem must make prose sense as well as poetic sense on one or more levels'.[33] If Thomas was treated more leniently than the other four in this respect, and Graves admitted that 'the poems show every sign of an alert and sober intelligence', he miscalculated in calling the opening stanza of Thomas's 'If my head hurt a hair's foot' 'nonsensical' and offering a £1 note to anyone who could explicate it; it was a relatively transparent work, and a member of the audience, M. J. C. Hodgart, was able to provide a reasonable gloss with ease (Graves, however, refused to pay up).[34]

But Graves's was more an opposition to academic canonisation than to Thomas *per se*; the Movement's antagonisms were far deeper and more ideological in scope. The poetry in its defining anthology, *New Lines* (1956), edited by Robert Conquest, was selected on the grounds that it 'submits to no great systems of theoretical constructs nor agglomerations of unconscious commands' and is 'free from both mystical and logical compulsions and ... empirical in its attitude'.[35] While some Movement poets, like Larkin, cherished a secret liking for some of Thomas's work, they now repudiated his bardic afflatus and excess in public. Kingsley Amis was an obsessive and life-long Thomas-hater, devising fictional characters based on Thomas and attacking him openly in verse: 'They call you "drunk with words"', he wrote, 'but when we drink / And fetch it up, we sluice it down the sink. / You should have stuck to spewing beer, not ink.'[36] Seeking stable selves, realism and a plain-style, instrumental approach to language, the Movement represented an insular response to the post-war decline of Britain and the levelling down, as they came to view it, of the welfare state.

The dislike of Thomas found in both Grigson and the Movement reached its apotheosis in David Holbrook's *Llareggub Revisited* (1962; repr. 1964) and *Dylan Thomas: The Code of Night* (1972), but in a psycho-analytic mode alien to previous attacks. Holbrook interpreted Thomas's writing in a purely symptomatic way, as an expression of narcissism, oralism and schizoid inability to display 'real' love.[37] Literature, for Holbrook, was a form of unknowing self-analysis that permitted diagnosis of the artist and a moral judgement of him via his work, and Thomas's character disorders were made to bear the blame for most of the faults, as Holbrook saw them, of contemporary English poetry. As so often happens with such approaches, the source of the alleged flaws was not convincingly established; ultimately, Thomas's alleged moral and literary failings were said to derive from a failed pregnancy that his mother had suffered seven years before his birth, but, as Holbrook freely admitted, he could find no factual proof for this claim.

Tendentious reasoning and dubious methods of argument aside, what Holbrook's assaults chiefly revealed was the readiness with which the Thomas legend lent itself to representations of his work as involuntarily regurgitated psychic raw material, rather than as considered literary structures which manipulated such material for aesthetic ends. Holbrook's is a classic instance of the syndrome identified by Shoshana Felman: the critical compulsion to dismiss a writer as minor with such 'loud and lengthy negations' that one effectively testifies to his or her actual centrality.[38] This, she notes, resembles the paradoxical 'psychoanalytic negations' offered by patients undergoing psychoanalysis. After all, if Thomas was such a poor poet, why bother with him? From a historical point of view, the overkill found in Holbrook and others is a reminder that they belong to a tradition of literary-critical moral panics that includes *The Edinburgh Review* assault on Keats, Buchanan's on the 'Fleshly School' and those on Sylvia Plath.[39] Whatever else, it was clear that Thomas's work possessed the power to temporarily deprive commentators of the most elementary critical faculties. Geoffrey Johnston, for example, would claim in 1954, that: 'Over Sir John's hill' was 'a loose association of impassioned words trusting to luck and chance alliteration for psychological linkage with the reader', although the regular form of the poem is visible at a glance (in fact, its five 14–line stanzas maintain an intricate regular syllable count of 5, 6, 14, 16, 5, 1, 15, 5, 14, 5, 14, 14 and an *aabccbdeaedd* pararhyme scheme).[40]

Behind the assaults lay Thomas's anomalousness in an English (and, to a lesser extent, British) poetry culture, which increasingly distrusted not only rhetoric, excess and experiment, but whatever it was that distinguished poetry from prose in the first place. After the 1940s, it was US critics, with their stronger modernist and bardic allegiances, who led Thomas criticism, as a comparison of Henry Treece's rather ramshackle *Dylan Thomas – Dog Among the Fairies* (1949) and Elder Olson's *The Poetry of Dylan Thomas* (1954) shows. On the one hand, Thomas's relish of conceit, ambiguity, symbol, paradox and lyric autonomy perfectly suited New Criticism and genre criticism (*The Heresy of Paraphrase* by Cleanth Brooks might be said to encapsulate Thomas's definition of poetry).[41] Thomas was keen on the poet-critics Allen Tate, Robert Penn Warren and John Crowe Ransom, as well as Richard Wilbur, Robert

Lowell and Theodore Roethke, whom he had brought to the attention of students in Oxford during 1946–9. In addition, Thomas's (rare) critical pronouncements often uncannily resemble those of the New Critics – those of R. P. Blackmur, for example.[42] As the 1950s wore on, Thomas's 'image-clusters' – marine, to do with symbolic journeys, death and rebirth and so on – also proved amenable to US critics pioneering Jungian criticism, such as Lita Hornick.[43] Yet Thomas was also steeped in Whitman and stylistically resembled Hart Crane, while his electrifying readings and anti-authority stance appealed equally to the bardic tradition that the Beat and West Coast poets were about to resurrect. It is characteristic of all critics of the period, however, that they should measure the poems against a model of integratedness and wholeness (whether using Jungian, Laingian or New Critical models) and that they should try to 'explain' them fully. Olson's 1954 analysis of 'Altarwise by owl-light', in terms of no less than six separate levels of symbolism unified by the Hercules legend is perhaps the classic case of over-exposition.[44] Yet Olson, like other US critics, treated Thomas as serious artist. When *Letters to Vernon Watkins* appeared in 1957, it offered conclusive proof of his painstaking craftsmanship, and US reviewers interpreted it in this light, as a corrective to the personal and emotive accounts of Thomas given in John Malcolm Brinnin's *Dylan Thomas in America* (1956) and Caitlin Thomas's *Leftover Life to Kill* (1957). British reviewers, however, focused only on Thomas's alleged bad character.

However, not all English responses were negative. John Bayley's *The Romantic Survival* (1957) gave the first detailed analysis of Thomas's language use – his working 'from' rather than 'towards' words and treatment of them as a material medium. Bayley admired Thomas's risk-taking in this regard and accepted that poems might legitimately resist making 'prose sense', at least immediately, because they were themselves often their own subject: 'in the words of Wittgenstein, "that which expresses *itself* in language we cannot express by language"'.[45] His reservations centred on Thomas's penchant for mimicry and jarring stylistic heterogeneity: 'it is as if the attitudes to language of Donne, Blake, and Swinburne were all to be encountered in the same poem'.[46] This organicist preference for consistency reflected contemporary critical priorities, although Bayley managed to strike a tentatively hopeful note overall: 'the real uncertainty which must still be felt about Thomas's real status as a poet arises from the fact that we still do not know whether language is capable of what he tried to do with it … whether the consciousness of the reader can adapt itself to such a variety of linguistic uses and such a multiplicity of verbal stimuli. Probably it can'.[47]

Partly by way of response to that 'probably', perhaps, Winifred Nowottny's thorough and exemplary decoding of 'There was a saviour' in *The Language Poets Use* (1962) revealed not just the poem's subtle exploration of the master-slave dialectic in a shifting imagery of buildings and rooms, locks, chains and keys and so on, but also a string of hitherto unsuspected allusions.[48] Nowottny showed that the 'peculiarity of the [poem's] language compels us to construct a meaning for it' by way of moving us towards his vision of the love which can shatter the deadened sensibilities responsible for war.[49] Yet while the allusions could be said to reinforce the poem's general drift, for Nowottny, their concealment raised the question as to whether readers might be 'reasonably' expected to detect them.[50] In the following year, Ralph Maud's *Entrances to Dylan Thomas's Poetry* (1963) provided the classic summing-up of the work begun by Aivaz and Horan on the 'process poetic'. Maud highlighted Thomas's skill in presenting the inseparability of creation and destruction, reading Thomas's poems via their positive and negative terms (signalled as '(+)' and '(-)' in stanza two of 'I see the boys of summer'):[51]

> These boys of light (+) are curdlers in their folly (-),
> Sour (-) the boiling honey (+);
> The jacks of frost (-) they finger in the hives (+);
> There in the sun (+) the frigid threads
> Of doubt and dark (-) they feed their nerves;
> The signal moon (+) is zero in their voids (-). (*CP*, 7)

This helps us grasp how the two poles of expectation established in the opening line ('summer' and 'ruin'), developed over a series of images of fecundity and waste, provide a 'short cut to the symbolic level (along with the hypnotic rhythms)', which allows us to follow the basic sense and movement of the poem before grasping its details. As Maud notes, this first section of the poem ends by hinting at the dual nature of the boys' darkness, and the second section finds weirdly creative energies in it. Part three, in turn, presents a 'dynamic balance' of these forces.[52] Yet, as he also notes, the poem is not so much polarised, as it is radically ambiguous. For example, the first section ends: 'There from their hearts the dogdayed pulse / Of love and light bursts in their throats. / O see the pulse of summer in the ice', an example, as he points out, of the positive … submerged in the apparently negative'. In fact, the imbrication of the two goes further, if, like Walford Davies, we read 'love and light' as ironic (and negatively), as 'conventional morality' (*SP1*, 97). 'Bursts', too, doubles back on itself; literally, it is an aneurism, metaphorically, it is ecstasy. Is it rupture or rapture (this may be a submerged pun)? Even according to his own account then, Maud's 'balance' seems rather inadequate. Rather, what we seem to have is a highly unstable stand-off between mighty opposites and, simultaneously, a near-inextricable tangling of them, left deliberately unresolved in the poem's final line: 'O see the poles are kissing as they cross'. The 'warring images' are 'reconciled' only for that 'small stop of time'. The kissing poles unify north and south, birth and death, in an affectionate gesture, but, equally, they could indicate anger (being 'cross' with someone), deletion, betrayal or crucifixion. The context that the poem has constructed forces us to keep several radically opposed possibilities simultaneously in play.

Just why Thomas's poems might require such heterogeneity, allusiveness and violent ambiguity was never really explained. Nor, as the 1960s wore on, were these questions even posed with much urgency. Partly, this was because the cultural climate became more accepting of Thomas's libertarian qualities and, partly, because the quantity and quality of explicatory work appearing distracted from them. This included two glossaries, by Clark Emery and William Tindall (1962), monographs, by Ralph Maud (1963), H. H. Kleinman (1963), Jacob Korg (1965), William Moynihan (1966) and Annis Pratt (1970), Constantine FitzGibbon's edition of the letters and biography of Thomas (1965), Maud's edition of the notebook poems (1967), Walford Davies's edition of *Selected Early Writings* (1971), the Daniel Jones edition of the poems (1971) and three collections of essays (by Brinnin, C. B. Cox and Davies [1960, 1966 and 1972, respectively]). But, in the main, it was because Thomas's kind of poetry asked existing criticism to do what it was not equipped to do. The New Critical penchant for ambiguity was ultimately about the ironic balancing of extremes; it reflected the dilemma of the liberal intellectual faced with the conflicts of the Cold War era. Thomas's poetry often presented irresolvable paradoxes and asked for a level of exegesis far in excess of that required for the ambiguous poise that it was presumed all lyrics aimed at. In this sense, it exposed New Criticism's limitations.[53]

This is shown by the most sophisticated reading of the period in J. Hillis Miller's *Poets of Reality* (1966). Miller's phenomenological approach allowed him to grasp that 'process' raised the issue of subject-object relationships, of a 'new space [in which] the mind is dispersed everywhere in things and forms one with them', with peculiar intensity. 'Again and again', Miller argued, 'Thomas invents phrases which assert the reciprocal participation in one another, as activities, of what would ordinarily be thought of as isolated objects'.[54] The 'world of metamorphosis' that he apprehended went beyond more static senses of a creative-destructive 'force' and directly to the heart of the post-1938 work, in which such 'discontinuity becomes a law of continuity', and 'God is an anonymous totality of being ... a dark fluid background against which [all things] surge into being and which they negate by being specific objects rather than the inclusive *I am*'.[55] In the later poems, Thomas is said to view things 'from the perspective of their death', because this is the only way in which they can be 'recaptured in their vitality, and, paradoxically, saved from death'. Miller echoes Heidegger's claim that authentic being-toward-death liberates Dasein's individual self from its 'they-self', freeing it to re-evaluate life from the standpoint of finitude, making it possible to see Thomas as a phenomenological-existential writer; likewise, his claim that 'discontinuity becomes a law of continuity' in Thomas suggests that both Mikhail Bakhtin and Georges Bataille might shed new light on Thomas, too.[56]

Still, Miller's analysis, brilliant as it is, is limited in certain crucial ways.[57] First, it lacks a theory of the composite nature of the verbal sign (and thus of its contradictions) and of the paradoxical nature of language as both symbolic system and object in the world; the nature of the word, perceived as an integral entity, and its relationship with the world tends to be mystified. Words, Miller believes, can be firmly attached to concepts. Second, the concern with the poetry's phenomenological content, viewed as an isolated, timeless, organic entity, excludes a historical dimension, whether of Thomas's own development or in terms of the mediation of the external world in his language. There is no sense that, rather than looking for keys to the poems, it might be better to attribute indeterminacy to the free-play of the signifier or that there might be any socio-historical dimension to Thomas's poetic and linguistic strategies.

Similar points could be made about Thomas's allusiveness and intentionality. In this regard, the Bakhtinian concept of intertextuality, as developed by Julia Kristeva in the late 1960s, seems more relevant than any monological idea of 'influence' and thus to offer a way of understanding Thomas's ventriloquism – the point being that *how* he uses 'sources' may be as important as *what* they are.[58] Unlike Eliot, Thomas concealed, rather than framed, his source materials, hinting at and erasing their origins. As I discuss in Chapter 2, he culled his materials collage-style, but subordinated them to syntactical norms, in order to create the appearance of narrative flow. The result is the creation of poems that are 'a mosaic of quotations', but whose parts are often impossible to distinguish, because of the degree to which they have been involved in 'the absorption and transformation of another'.[59] This was a response to Eliot's case for the necessary 'difficulty' of modern poetry, but one which deceptively smoothed over the ruptures of high modernist collage; a poetic correlative, in effect, of the contemporary criticism of William Empson – effectively resisting close reading, but teasing readers with its arcane delights, wrapping its purloined letters of poetic authority in flagrantly overdetermined difficulty.[60]

Before such ideas could be pursued, however, Thomas criticism was ensnared by the requirements of the identity discourses which emerged during the 1970s. As I have argued, the English literary-academic establishment renewed its hostilities with Thomas and his work in the mid-1970s. Auden's death in 1973 was the catalyst for a thoroughly Anglocentric rewriting of the 1930s as the 'Age of Auden' – the last era of English literary greatness – in a kind of little-England act of cultural compensation for national decline (what Hugh Kenner in 1980 called the 'sinking island syndrome'), and this had the effect of augmenting the long-standing suspicion towards modernism.[61] Peter MacDonald noted in 1991 that: 'Few better examples could be found of the "hidden agenda" of much apparently "literary" criticism … than the English myth of the 1930s.'[62] In the same year, Adrian Caesar observed: 'Since about 1975, critics and literary historians have often agreed to define Auden by the use of the words "the 1930s" or vice versa.'[63] Little has changed since. Auden's semi-beatification was elaborated in Samuel Hynes's *The Auden Generation: Literature and Politics in England in the 1930s* (1976) and his canonical profile established in Edward Mendelson's *The English Auden* (1977). The year before Hynes's book appeared, A. T. Tolley's *The Poetry of the Thirties* had devoted an entire chapter to Thomas. In Hynes's 400 pages, however, Thomas managed just 'three fleeting appearances, one in brackets'.[64] It set the pattern of airbrushing the biggest threat to Audenesque hegemony from the 1930s record. One result was that, by the 1980s, amnesia had set in. It became possible to airily generalise about Thomas, without having read Korg, Moynihan, Kershner, Maud or Davies and without the close reading that was so essential to understanding how the poetry worked. It was accompanied by a return to the earlier *ad hominism* of Graves, Grigson and Amis.[65] Via the legend, lazy phrase-making substituted for critical analysis – as with Michael Schmidt's 'flamboyant idleness' and Chris Baldick's 'flamboyant irrationalism' – often betraying the casualness of the name-calling in the generic similarity of the adjectives deployed.[66] The culmination of the trend was Valentine Cunningham's *British Writers of the Thirties* (1988), which, although it challenges Auden-centricity, studiously excludes the biomorphic, Blakeian, apocalyptic strain in 1930s writing which Thomas originated and is hostile to experimental modernism more generally. It manages to avoid quoting one extract from a Thomas poem in its 500–odd pages, and the single Thomas work mentioned (though only in passing) is *The Death of the King's Canary* – a co-authored prose skit, unpublished in its author's lifetime. For Cunningham, clearly, Thomas did not possess what he calls: 'the ironic tone necessary in an English context'.[67] Given the recourse to earlier subjective, slipshod and impressionistic critical practices, one of the favoured terms of dismissal – 'regressive' – was unwittingly ironic. Thomas now suffered from both inverted elitism – a mainstream opposition to modernist difficulty outside the chronological period allotted to it – and the traditional kind displayed by the keepers of the canon with their abhorrence of the taint of populism (Cambridge University Press, for example, has twice turned down a Dylan Thomas title for inclusion in their Companions to Literature Series over the course of the last decade).[68]

In Wales, predictably, Thomas's legacy is even more contested than elsewhere. His reputation there during his lifetime is something I shall discuss in detail in Chapters 4 and 6 and will return to in my Conclusion. Here, I shall merely sketch his critical relationship to Wales and say something about the central, but highly anomalous, position he has been accorded in the Anglo-Welsh poetic canon and his role as a kind of floating signifier for WWE.

Thomas's attitudes to Wales, like those of his first Welsh critics, were based on a complex inheritance. He grew up in an industrial town on the edge of a rural hinterland, where modern and older modes of Welsh life met. He was the child of Welsh-speaking parents who did not hand down the language, feeling that it would restrict his future life chances (a common belief at the time), and, like many of the post-WWI generation, he was deeply suspicious of patriotism and any form of nationalist rhetoric. He was the leading member of the 'First Flowering', the first Anglo-Welsh generation of writers to achieve distinction – a generation which was shaped by the hostility of the likes of Saunders Lewis, the leader of Plaid Cymru, who sweepingly dismissed them as un-Welsh (of the 'Anglo-Welsh' Thomas Saunders disdainfully observed in 1937 that 'there is nothing hyphenated about him – he belongs to the English'). Thomas himself felt that, as a label,

'Anglo-Welsh' was an 'ambiguous compromise', but refused to see Wales in simplistic, polarised, Anglo-versus-true-Welsh terms; his hybridity was the source of his poetic originality and power. He did not, therefore, feel a sense of loss, let alone show any guilt at his lack of Welsh or his relatively limited knowledge of the 'matter of Wales'. In 1946, he claimed: 'There is a number of young Welshmen writing poems in English who, insisting passionately that they are Welshmen, should by rights be writing in Welsh, but who, unable to write in Welsh or reluctant to do so because of the uncommercial nature of the language, often give the impression that their writing in English is only a condescension to the influence and ubiquity of the tyrannous foreign tongue. I do not belong to that number' (*QEOM*, 97). Although the label of 'uncommercial' too easily elides the painful history of the decline of Welsh, Thomas's aim is to prevent literary-aesthetic value being made dependent upon spurious judgements concerning 'Welshness': 'Welshmen have written, from time to time, exceedingly good poetry in English. I should like to think that is because they are good poets, rather than because they are good Welshmen' (*TB*, 32). Thomas criticised Welsh artists who sold out in London as much as those who agonised over-much about their Welshness, and this reflects his own uncertainty, his relish for living in Wales and his simultaneous compassionate mockery of certain aspects of it. It was a pragmatic solution to the unavoidable and insoluble conflict of interests, and this has been distorted by the legend (the quip 'Land of my Fathers, my fathers can keep it' is well-known, but it is forgotten that, in his film-script *The Three Weird Sisters*, Thomas put this phrase in the mouth of the villainous rentier Owen Morgan-Vaughan).[69] Ultimately, however, he believed that the true artist has no home.

Thomas's ambivalence was shared, albeit to a lesser degree, by Anglo-Welsh fellow writers of the 1930s, Glyn Jones and Gwyn Jones, even though both were Welsh speakers (and Glyn Jones was also a practising Nonconformist).[70] Glyn Jones's *The Dragon has Two Tongues* (1968) – the founding text of Anglo-Welsh literary studies – indirectly makes the case for Thomas's central position in the Anglo-Welsh canon and is forthright about his status as one of the greatest poets of his time. Jones claims that Thomas's best poems have a quality of 'pure sensation', adding: 'I believe this ... to represent the highest – not the only – value of lyric poetry, and those who are able to provide it I regard as the greatest lyric poets.'[71] But he has reservations, too. On the one hand, while he sees in Thomas's writing 'a sincere, almost an agonised attempt to make ... poems out of [potent and beautiful] words and phrases' he has accumulated, following the Mallarméan dictum that 'poetry isn't a matter of ideas, it's a matter of words', on the other hand he feels that there is a problem, insofar as 'words themselves are in a way ideas, or they stand for ideas' and that some of 'Dylan's famous obscurity' arises from confusion as to this very point: while the words *qua* words are 'usually marvellous', 'too often they are the wrong ones to convey the ideas he wants them to convey'.[72] Jones praises verbal autonomy in the poem, but then draws the line at how far it should go more restrictively than Thomas (though he admits that if he could understand some of the poems better, he would have fewer reservations). He is also critical of Thomas's lack of interest in Wales, feeling that this left him unable to draw on Welsh communal solidarity, language and religion when he most needed bedrock of support. Traditionally, as he noted, Welsh poets were *bardd gwerin* (poets of the people), and, by this measure, Thomas's poetry could be considered un-Welsh. But Jones does not push this very hard; he is sure that Thomas articulates a valid Welsh experience and that he might not have been an exceptional poet if he had been different; in any case: 'No writer ought to be judged by the extent to which he recognises his roots'.[73]

Less qualified in his praise, Gwyn Jones could simply claim that Thomas 'was Welsh as a leek or a Teifi coracle. Welsh, let us say, as a *cwydd* or *englyn*'.[74] Jones reflects the attempt to counter attacks on Thomas's non-Welshness more strenuously than Glyn Jones. The Welsh language poet-critic Bobi Jones, for example, had argued, two years before, in 1955, that: '[Dylan Thomas's] exuberant but irresponsible concoction of verbal cleverness ... [and] ... undisciplined decorative flaccidity has not gone unnoticed in England ... With all the advantages that we have in Wales of a living traditional community and literature it is incongruous that we should spy so cravingly on such a decadent pretence at literature'.[75] Ironically, the eulogies often lapsed into the clichés that Thomas himself invoked in order to undermine. At the other end of the Anglophone spectrum from Gwyn Jones is this Amis-style outburst by the Cardiff-based critic Terence Hawkes in 1962, for example:

> Whether we like it or not, Dylan Thomas's *Collected Poems* sit unblushing on the bookshelves of hundreds of suburban semis, rubbing shoulders with the other inevitable pillars of the literary landscape, Shakespeare, Tennyson, and Betjeman. His pages are simpered over by the lovers of 'beautiful words', the image-bibbers, Rhiwbina romantics and Sketty scholars who know that poetry is somehow connected with magic, and that the streets of South Wales ring nightly to the (beautifully sung) extempore verses of poets going

home from the pit … The plain fact is that of Dylan Thomas's ninety extant poems, well over half are meaningless, and less than a dozen are worth reading, let alone preserving.[76]

Hawkes here adapts the Movement's English class snobbery to the Welsh scene ('image-bibbing' comes from 'ruin-bibber' in Larkin's 'Church Going'). Even so, the positive appraisals cancelled out the negative ones in Wales at this time. Thus Ancirin Talfan Davies' short study, *Dylan Thomas: Druid of the Broken Body* (1964), argued for the influence of Welsh metrical techniques and claimed that the poetry moved towards a eucharistic marriage of Celtic nature worship and Christian symbolism. Indeed, Thomas's life was often presented as a kind of progression towards a saint-like reverence in the face of the created world. John Ackerman, a Welsh former student of F. R. Leavis, set such an idealized version of Thomas even more firmly within his Welsh contexts in *Dylan Thomas* (1964) and *Welsh Dylan* (1979).

Between the 1960s and the 1990s, Aneirin, Walford and James A. Davies, John Ackerman, Paul Ferris and Ralph Maud all advanced Thomas studies greatly, via close reading, coupled with a new alertness towards his Welshness. They wrote in a lucid, expository, warily empirical manner, systematically glossing the poems' difficulties, explaining Thomas's procedures and contexts, gathering, editing and publishing his work and resisting both critical hyperbole and the toxic legend.[77] Unlike, say, Hillis Miller, they did not link Thomas to broader intellectual developments, or relate him to any emerging trends in critical theory and literary studies. They viewed his career and work teleologically, as a kind of prodigal son-like progression from London-based modernist solipsism and stylistic obscurity to his return to Wales and the adoption of mainstream clarity and humane, quasi-communal values – expressed, however, in national, not nationalist, terms.

Since the 1950s, however, the balance of power between the two main competing master-narratives of Welsh identity – nationalism and socialism – had been shifting. The inexorable decline of socialism's industrial South Welsh heartland produced a turn to a more active nationalism by the Welsh intelligentsia, anglophones included. This would alter the already complex terms of Thomas's reception. Anglo-Welsh writers and critics of the 1950s already had to contend with the way in which Thomas distorted external expectations of what Welsh writing ought to be, impeding their task of trying to generate interest in other splendid Anglo-Welsh writers. As, in the 1960s, an ambitious new generation tried to create a publishing and journal base within Wales, Thomas also seemed to symbolise the nation's long dependence on the London literary world, even though he had achieved his reputation there largely on his own terms (Stephen Spender rightly compared Thomas to Lloyd George; he had been a 'vertical invader' from the provinces taking the centre by storm, to use Ortega y Gasset's term).[78] On top of this, the pressure from Welsh-Wales, such as that registered by the poet-critics Roland Mathias and Raymond Garlick, was increasingly making itself felt in anglophone criticism. It was a sign of future trends that the 1954 Dylan Thomas memorial issue of the journal *Dock Leaves*, edited by Garlick, already contained criticism of Thomas along the communitarian lines as defined by the likes of Saunders Lewis and Bobi Jones.

'Community' is a favourite, yet insufficiently examined, positive term in WWE criticism. It signifies a collective spirit, and has an objective basis insofar as it reflects the relative classlessness and sporadic cohesiveness of Welsh society. The real problem is the way that this is valorised vis-à-vis England, since the urge to distinguish Wales from England can easily lead to exaggeration and untenable assumptions (for example, statements to the effect that Methodism and industrial valleys are unique to Wales, or that English society knows nothing of small, isolated communities and is a Hobbesian wilderness of dog-eat-dog individualism). What is reflected is a psychological need, rather than a sociological reality, one fuelled by the evidence of linguistic and industrial decline, and expressing the idealistic hankering after the pre-1920 Nonconformist-Liberal hegemony (and its projection into a future of unification and independence) of a certain kind of nationalism.[79] As a result, community can appear little more than a 'cult ... of the culture of belonging' and 'supposed rootedness', which is 'assiduously fostered by the Nonconformist establishment' and other authorities.[80]

M. Wynn Thomas notes that 'Welsh-language culture tends strongly to assume that many of the key events of Welsh history ... are in the keeping of the language, which thereby becomes custodian of that past which alone may help the nation make full sense of its present'.[81] Despite its recent extension to encompass working-class South Wales, the critical discourse surrounding 'community' derives from a backward look and ruralism, and is thus inextricably interwoven with a belief in Welsh language primacy, whose vehicle (or stalking horse) it has often been in Anglo-Welsh literary criticism and politics. This is not, it should be stated, a question of opposing the Welsh language. There is absolutely no doubt that its preservation and advance is wholly to be desired, nor that it is an unalloyed good that its rate of decline has slowed, that Welsh has legal parity with English and has gained a foothold in some formerly monoglot anglophone urban areas. The problem is the *way* in which Welsh may be advanced – that is, the tendency to treat it as the unquestionable and essential core of true Welshness, when four-fifths of the population, mainly working-class and South Walian, do not speak it. In these circumstances (most evident in the field of education), the language is allotted the role once played by religion in the older Welsh nationalism, namely that of the transcendent and unchallengeable ideological glue which holds it together. Assumed to be the sole repository of Welshness, it cannot be expressed as such, because an idealized concept of the nation is strictly irrelevant to many fields in which this presupposition may be brought into play, such as Welsh literature in English. It is therefore smuggled into a cognate concept like 'community' in mysticised form. Commitment to 'community' can still just about be justified as a test for the although that has to rely on the heavily sociological category of 'relevance'. Behind this, in turn, is concealed an essentialistic, Welsh-Wales judgement of the writer in terms of his or her relation to the Welsh language, one which echoes the extirpatory Anglophobia of earlier ideologues.[82] Noting its distorting effect in the critical discourses around Raymond Williams and making a case for Williams's Britishness, as well as his Welshness, in a debate with Daniel G. Williams in *Planet* in 1996, the distinguished historian Dai Smith coined the useful term 'linguistic culturalism' to describe the phenomenon.[83] (It should be noted that the bias against Welsh anglophones is often opposed by Welsh-speakers themselves, as was the case with Glyn and Gwyn Jones.)[84]

The Welsh anglophone poet-critic whose work most revealingly wrestles with these issues has been Tony Conran. In an article in the *Anglo-Welsh Review* in 1960, Conran followed linguistic culturalist predecessors by describing Thomas as 'an outsider, a man shut in by his own soul, lacking a community'.[85] In an introduction to a revised edition of his masterful anthology of Welsh poetry translations, *Welsh Verse* (1967), he revealed that a major reason for the creation of this anthology had been to redress the way that 'My English-speaking countrymen in Wales were being treated [by Welsh Wales] as if they were immigrants in their own country, potential Englishmen and women.'[86] It was a stark expression of the plight of the nationalist anglophone Welsh writer: they may want to engage with their Welsh inheritance, but Welsh-Wales ideology, locating ultimate worth in the Welsh language, ensures that they will only ever be partially accepted and only then on pain of being perpetually reminded that Welsh writing in English, by (assumed) definition, will always be inferior to what is written in the Welsh language. The situation is complex, and these pressures could be resisted to a degree; thus, the founder of *Poetry Wales* in 1966, Meic Stephens, stated that he 'could not help but make [it] a nationalist publication', given the nationalist resurgence, but suggested that R. S. Thomas's 'brooding on rural decay and the spineless attitudes of his countrymen' would prove 'an emotional dead end'.[87] In Stephens's case, however, this came with an insistence on the need to narrate the nation in narrowly empirical, plain-style terms (Stephens deplored poets who lived outside of Wales and claimed that the only way for Anglo-Welsh poets to prove their Welshness was to write on emphatically Welsh themes; the result, for this 'Second Flowering', was a mediocre and inward-facing poetry.

Conran's *The Cost of Strangeness* (1982), his seminal first full-length critical account of Anglo-Welsh poetry, contains two essays on Thomas. The first suggestively links him to Symbolism and its status as the poetic movement of the era of finance capitalism. However, it soon turns into an extended comparison of Thomas with Betjeman. A minor resemblance between two very dissimilar poets (both liked suburbs!) becomes a literary period – 'The Age of Betjeman and Thomas'.[88] The effect is to anglicise Thomas by association – to distance him from the Welsh fold. The second essay, on 'After the Funeral', reads it illuminatingly as an example of the Welsh praise poem (*gorhoffedd*) genre, but concludes disappointingly by valuing it because of 'the reality you can touch in it from time to time'.[89] Again, Conran finds it hard to deal with Thomas if he cannot link him to some external, sociological Welsh world.

If, in 1982, Conran was reflecting some of the bitterness of the failed Devolution Referendum of 1979, fifteen years later, in *Frontiers in Anglo-Welsh Poetry* (1997), he perhaps anticipated the expanded cultural horizons made possible by that year's vote in favour of a Welsh Assembly.[90] He returned to the notion of Thomas as post-Rimbaudian *voyant*, developing it with some élan and relating his style in *18 Poems* to the Jacobean soliloquy, the Welsh grotesque and town-dwellers' fear of the *buchedd* (the communal ethos of rural Wales).[91] Thomas's version of 'schizoid modernism' is related to Eliot's, and expressivist and liberal humanist readings are rightly rejected: 'their reluctance to come clean is not a fault of *18 Poems* but a condition of their being'.[92] The trouble is that Conran does not get beyond this one collection; he detects a lack of 'dramatic presence' in the poetry between 1934 and 1944, and the failure of 'poems on his own career as a poet, poems on his childhood – even, I

should say, the poems on the London blitz' – before the 'luminous clarity
of a great artist', which was reached in the late poems.[93] If there is a
grain of truth in the charge that some mid-career poems are laboured,
this skips far too much poetry with far too little justification. What has
happened, perhaps, is that Conran is happy when he can give Thomas
a fairly stable identity – Welsh grotesque modernist *voyant* or pastoral
elegist – but does not like the heterogeneous work in between so much;
that is, Thomas as the laureate of Anglo-Welsh hybridity.

A clue to this appears elsewhere in *Frontiers*: 'Anglo-Welsh poetry
differs from other poetry in the English language', Conran claims,
'[because] it has, in its background, a different civilisation – it is like
English poetry written by Irishmen or Indians'.[94] While there is some
validity in the first comparison, the second is an exaggeration. It seems
to reflect a desire to find, at whatever cost, some grounds of cultural
distinction between Wales and England – grounds which cannot be (or
cannot be admitted to be) those of language, because the critic does
not write in Welsh. It is feared that if these can't be found, there is, or
shortly will be, nothing to distinguish Wales from England: national
oblivion. As already noted, the acceptance of Welsh-Wales's claim for
the priority (in all senses) of the Welsh language means that the crisis
being suffered by Welsh is internalised by anglophone critics and is
projected in disguised forms as valorised 'community' or 'different
civilisations'; 'disguised', since Anglo-Welsh writing cannot rationally
be criticised for being what it is not – that is, in Welsh – although this
is the true reason for Welsh-Wales opposition. Intellectually, Conran
understands the illogicality of the requirement, but, at another level,
he concedes that it is the necessary price for Anglo-Welsh acceptance
by, and engagement with, a Wales which conceives of itself as a unified
national entity. This is how he comes to ask us to believe that the cultural
difference between two Caucasian populations, sharing a common
Christian culture and roughly the same level of material development
and living in geographically adjacent zones on the same island in the
same corner of north-western Europe over a millennia and a half is of
a 'civilisational' magnitude, greater than that between one of these and
the population of the Indian subcontinent 8,000 miles distant, with its
eighty-plus languages, four major religions and numerous racial groups.
Unfortunately for Conran, while Bangor and Birmingham are different
places, Bangor is not, therefore, more like Bangalore. Although he is too
honest a critic to tap the glamour of postcolonial victimisation, the effort
of proving that he is not to be thought of as a 'potential Englishman' has

a distorting effect. What is notably not discussed, despite the reference
to Ireland, is the success of other anglophone nations in distinguishing
themselves from England. The intense historical imbrication of Wales
with England, which has been one of the obstacles to this (the intense
inwardness of the Welsh reaction to it is another), is ignored, negatively
naturalised, because it takes linguistic culturalist form, rather than being
examined openly.

This complex and notoriously tricky subject is handled with more
nuance, if less boldness, by the other leading critic in the field, M. Wynn
Thomas.[95] Like Conran and unlike Ackerman, Maud and Davies, his
insights into Dylan Thomas derive from long involvement with Wales's
dual literary tradition, but are informed by a greater awareness of critical
theory. In *Corresponding Cultures: The Two Literatures of Wales* (1999), a
bravura reading of *A Portrait of the Artist as a Young Dog* proposes that it
'could, in fact, be subtitled, "A Guide to Modernist Art"' – one in which
a 'colourful', but 'hyperbolical', populist realism critiques the practice
and pretensions of Thomas's earlier modernism.[96] With similar acuity,
he observes, of the Welsh response to *Under Milk Wood*, that 'in the
Welsh context "Dylan Thomas" is more than the sum of his work, being
a socially constructed figure that enables two rival cultures to image
both themselves and each other'. Thomas is understood as an interstitial
distorting mirror, which Welsh language culture has used to demonise
anglophone culture, just as anglophone culture used it to critique the
inhibition and hypocrisy of Welsh-speaking Wales – a figure 'kept in
being at the very point where two opposite and equal stereotypes meet'.[97]

Usefully invoking Homi Bhabha's assault on 'pure' culture,
Corresponding Cultures claims that the often unacknowledged ground
shared by Wales's two literary cultures is reflected in Thomas's hybrid
qualities.[98] Unfortunately, Thomas's poetry is not tackled at all, nor are
the consequences of making a hybrid writer the basis of the Anglo-Welsh
canon. More than this, hybridity is used in a way that avoids its
more radical structural implications. What, for Bhabha, disturbs the
metropolitan centre most are those identities that are seen as shams,
those which, in the act of imitating, disturb the fixed and binary
categories of identity politics, of them / us and self / other: 'Hybridity's
threat ... comes from the prodigious ... production of conflictual,
fantastic, discriminatory "identity effects" in the play of a power that is
elusive because it hides no essence, no "itself"'.[99] Crucially, this involves
more than just the inversion of the binary terms of a relationship;
'Hybridity represents that ambivalent "turn" of the discriminated subject

into the terrifying, exorbitant object of a paranoid classification … it is not a third term that resolves the tension between two cultures'.[100] Yet *Corresponding Cultures* is predicated on the desire to find such 'third terms', to place the 'exorbitant' Thomas, without saying much about 'identity' as an 'effect' created through subversive mimicry, parody and the deployment of stereotypes.

However, despite their incomplete and somewhat cymrocentric readings, Tony Conran and M. Wynn Thomas were the first critics since the 1970s to discuss Thomas in something approaching a contemporary critical idiom. To say this is not to condemn Davies, Maud, Ackerman or Paul Ferris (Thomas's biographer and the editor of his *Collected Letters*) for not having done so, of course; indeed, they pressed the case for Thomas with admirable steadfastness and intelligence at a time when he was career-damagingly unfashionable. They were not responsible for the lack of interest on the part of younger critics, for his being ring-fenced as an Anglo-Welsh writer, or for the alarming degree to which the legend continued to fill the knowledge gap which persisted for want of a more thoroughgoing re-evaluation.[101] One common limitation, however, was that they shared the mainstream, empirical, anti-modernist views on the nature of poetry and the canon as Thomas's Anglocentric critics. To fully deal with their attacks, it was necessary to embrace Thomas's innovative excess, rather than skate over it, and to do so with an eye to alternative canons and new critical approaches.[102]

From around 2000, as with Irish criticism nearly two decades before, the postcolonial paradigm came to dominate Anglo-Welsh criticism. Its most forceful expression has been Stephen Knight's comprehensive *A Hundred Years of Fiction* (2004). Here, one might say, can be found the opposite problem to that on display in the work of Maud, Davies and Ackerman, namely that of the single theoretical insight inflexibly applied. Persuasive and insightful local readings of texts tend to conflict with a rigid overview, which fits all Welsh fiction into the master-narrative of rapacious English capitalist colonialists who despoiled Wales and left it a de-industrialised Third World basket-case. So, Thomas's early stories are suggestively read as 'a sort of Welsh gothic deriving … from Poe, the French romantics and the … surrealists', 'a powerful Welsh version of literary modernism, a projection of D. H. Lawrence's interest in a sentient world in a more rigorous and indeed Rimbaud-like form.'[103] But this is as far as it goes, because Knight wrongly attributes Thomas's change of style in *A Portrait* to pressure to conform to 'colonial' English literary tastes and seems unaware of the inner stylistic logic that had exhausted this mode of writing by 1937. The stories of *A Portrait* are not discussed; instead there is a heavy-handed attack on the slight television piece 'A Story' as a 'colonial entertainment ... in which the South Wales industrial world is reduced to a sort of black and white minstrel show for an English radio audience for English consumption'. The complexities, even of this very minor piece, unsettle Knight's procrustean coordinates, however, and he makes no less than four errors of fact in the very sentence with which he dismisses it.[104]

Like Tony Conran's, Knight's rather mechanical sociological model of Anglo-Welsh writing does not allow for the autonomous dynamics of literary styles; writers always write as they do because of some external pressure. But Knight's postcolonialism does at least mention Thomas. Kirsty Bohata's *Postcolonialism Revisited* (2004), a more theoretically sophisticated exploration of the Bhabha-esque 'Third Space' of translation and negotiation – the in-between space which carries the burden of the meaning of culture in WWE studies – and a work which is properly sceptical of the blanket use of the postcolonial paradigm, does not discuss him at all. This means that the most intelligent and insightful analysis of hybridity in Anglo-Welsh writing fails to tackle its most hybrid figure. This means, in turn, that the major challenges that Thomas poses to it – concerning the monstrous aspects of his hybridity, the tendency of certain nationalist positions to merely invert colonial structures, nationalism's preference for coherent, nationally representative selves and realist styles and so on – are not addressed.[105]

This, indeed, is the larger problem that Thomas poses to the construct of WWE studies, and it accounts for the way most theory-aware critics have avoided Thomas or treated him only partially, in a skewed way. Extreme discomfort with Thomas's manipulation of national and narrative stereotypes remains the norm, and there is the tendency to avoid examining these by acting as if even to use them is to capitulate to them. When Katie Gramich, for example, in a 1998 vote among Welsh critics for the greatest Anglo-Welsh writer of the century, opted for R. S. over Dylan Thomas, because Dylan was 'our clichéd bard, the poetic equivalent of *How Green Was My Valley*', this vital level of critical discrimination was what eluded her and led her, ironically, to judge Thomas in a 'clichéd' way. It should have been difficult to even conceive of bracketting 'Altarwise by owl-light' with *How Green Was My Valley*; to do so was to be guilty of a category error.[106]

In general, then, it seems a little theory is a dangerous thing in WWE studies. It is deployed to signal that Anglo-Welsh criticism has come of age, but its anti-foundational thrust means that it must be severely curtailed, in order for linguistic culturalist and other shibboleths to be preserved. Thomas is disturbing because his work activates this aspect of theory in its most lethal form. If he is taken to be 'Welsh', then Welshness becomes something other than an identity based ultimately on the primacy of Welsh and community. The attempt to overcome the visible self-division of 'Anglo-Welsh Literature' inscribed within 'Welsh Writing in English' unravels, revealing the incompleteness of its critique of essentialism. The non-correspondence between linguistic culturalism and an incorrigibly mongrel Anglo-Welsh poetry, whose innumerable links to English poetry are indicative not of civilisational difference, but of an uneven, transcultural, dynamic productive of hybridity, is thrown into relief. Daniel Williams has noted that the problem for those attempting to construct a canon is that, while Thomas is 'a dominant [figure] within ... [his] literary tradition', his writings are 'paradoxical', in that they 'are particularly resistant to being read as national allegories and thus frustrate attempts at placing them within the safe confines of a national literary canon', unlike equivalent figures in other national literatures.[107] But it all depends upon what you mean by 'national allegories'. The wholesome, integrative kind is being assumed here (though Williams is not necessarily endorsing these). Yet there are others, and Thomas's work certainly offers them. As an allegory of Wales's abjection as a metropolitan colony and the grotesque psychic deformations inflicted by Nonconformist repression, after all, Thomas's early work would be hard to beat. Likewise, his later work's subversive interweavings of the English Romantic canon with Welsh place and musicality could be said to playfully deconstruct the claustrophobic impactedness of Wales and England in exemplary fashion. The problem, then, is not that Thomas fails as a national allegorist, but that he does not offer allegories which are comfortable to some kinds of nationalist *amour propre*. Not facing the implications of this means that WWE critics rarely dig very deep: trailing the historians and taking in their own critical washing, far too many are content to be what Thomas dubbed the 'giants in the dark behind the parish pump, pygmies in the nationless sun'.[108]

Thomas's reputation today is stuck between a Welsh criticism unable to furnish an adequate context for re-presenting him to the world and an English criticism largely accepting of the Audenary account of the 1930s and Movement dismissal of the 1940s. This means that nothing much prevents the new reader reading Thomas through his legend, from feeling that they know the meaning of the work before actually encountering it. In Thomas's case, the presumption of direct author-reader communication often seems confirmed by the urgent tone of the poems. In such circumstances, lack of immediate comprehension, far from acting as a deterrent, can increase intensity of identification. Either transference or rejection can result, but, in both cases, the poetry is assumed to be an 'expression' of the imaginary figure of the legend. The aim of criticism is to prevent this transference, but those best equipped to do this are often in thrall themselves. To take one fairly recent example, it is disappointing to find such a normally iconoclastic critic as Terry Eagleton trashing 'A Refusal to Mourn the Death, by Fire, of a Child in London' in his *How to Read a Poem* (2007). Eagleton claims that it is a poor poem, because it 'has little to say about the burnt child' as an 'actual person' and because Thomas 'go[es] to extraordinary lengths to say very little'.[109] But can the critic complaining about lack of meaning-content and 'actuality' *really* be the arch-theorist, who, in *Literary Theory: An Introduction*, stated that 'meaning is not simply something "expressed" or "reflected" in language: it is actually *produced* by it'? Or the one who endorsed Jakobson's claims for poetry's uniquely non-instrumental qualities and warned that, in Wittgenstein's famous phrase: 'a poem, even though it is composed in the language of information, is not used in the language game of giving information'?[110] In a rare capitulation to conservative critical platitudes, Eagleton performs a series of ideological somersaults by reading 'A Refusal' as if it should be 'ordinary speech' or mere reportage to be judged banally by its factual content and 'for the sake of the thoughts [it conveys]'; effectively, language as commonsense's conveyor-belt.[111] Equally telling, he misses what the poem *does*, in fact, empirically 'say': its glancing allusions to the Holocaust ('Zion', 'synagogue'), news of which was breaking when it was being written, and to the London Underground shelters ('stations of the breath') memorialised by Henry Moore's drawings, the monumental abstraction of which, like Thomas's poem, reflect a concern not to violate the dignity of any 'actual person'. This lapse illustrates the distorting power of the legend, yet it is also an example of Thomas's power to read the unexamined prejudices of his readers. Eagleton is just one of many exposed by the poet he presumes to expose, trapped by the legend within the transferential structures of a Thomas poem, caught out in his own fiction of interpretative mastery. By moralising, rather than analysing, he contributes, rather unflatteringly, to the continued 'stunning ... disagreement regarding [Thomas'] achievement'.[112]

Fortunately, the last twenty-five years or so have seen some promising attempts to break out of these vicious circles. Perhaps the first to suggest that contemporary theory might find a worthy subject in Thomas's hybrid, mannerist modernism was the Canadian critic Don McKay. In two essays of 1985 and 1986, 'Crafty Dylan and the Altarwise Sonnets' and 'What Shall We Do with a Drunken Poet?', McKay focused on impropriety and language use. Thomas's language, McKay saw, was not so much a 'problem' to be 'solved' through ever more detailed explication, so much as itself a specific mode of writing – a case of linguistic surplus or *jouissance*. Tackling charges of 'showmanship' and 'intellectual fake[ery]' head-on, rather than attempting the futile task of assessing 'sincerity', he divined in the poetry's excess evidence of a consciously self-subverting rhetoric, doubleness and 'willed grotesquerie' of craft, exemplified by pun.[113] Thomas could be 'pompously oracular', he argued, because 'the trickster's tongue is in the poet's cheek'.[114] The poem's 'extreme fancy-work', he added in a nod to Derrida, was an exemplary instance of apparently marginal material, 'as often in recent criticism ... turning out ... to function as the unsung matrix or ground-work for the whole'.[115]

McKay's second essay wittily imagined the Julia Kristeva of *Revolution in Poetic Language* prizing Thomas's ability to unsettle the identity of meaning and the speaking subject and considering how she would reverse the judgement of anthologists by valorising poems from the 'outlaw territory' of his oeuvre ('Today, this insect', rather than 'Fern Hill', say).[116] He proposed a 'trickster', 'rogue' Thomas, who demanded to be read in accordance with his mixed style – irreverent, thieving, deliberately vulgarising and over-subtilising – and whose work ran counter to modernist-derived requirements of unity. For McKay, indeed, Thomas's language anticipated and enacted the struggle that later appeared in criticism as one between avant-garde 'material anarchy' and shaping mainstream modernist-style myth. Indeed, what made him so difficult to place was his apparent shift in allegiances from poem to poem and line to line, from one mode to another and to several points in between them. John Bayley's charge of 'ventriloquism' was explicable, in this reading, not as a lack of control, but as a stylistic tactic.

Important as they were, however, McKay's essays were largely suggestions as to how Thomas might be read. It was left to Stewart Crehan, in the essay '"The Lips of Time"' published in 1990, to put suggestions into practice.[117] Crehan drew on Marxism, Freudianism and Anthony Easthope's *Poetry as Discourse* (1983) to argue that Thomas's verbal play and autonomy foregrounded the arbitrary nature of the link between signified and signifier for the individual subject, returning readers to the liberation of spontaneous pleasure in linguistic manipulation. By identifying the commonsensical repression of language's innate anarchic energies as a source of the moralising in much of Thomas criticism, Crehan presented a positive psychoanalytic interpretation of those energies. Moreover, since identity and power were encoded in the restraints of the Symbolic Order, he argued that this made Thomas's stylistic challenge a potentially far-ranging and, ultimately, political one. Thus 'The force that through the green fuse', for Crehan, enacted a dialectical conflict between repression and rebellion – in effect, a psychic 'permanent revolution' – which mediated the stalled historical moment of the early 1930s. This theorised the link between Thomas's socialism and his apparently apolitical style and endorsed Pearson's claim for Thomas and Auden as twin products of the early 1930s crisis – a crucial point in re-placing Thomas within a history of 1930s poetry and re-examining the nature of the New Apocalyptic, neo-Romantic 1940s.

Crehan's essay led to mine and Chris Wigginton's critical labours on Thomas, beginning with a conference held in Swansea in 1998. Its outcomes – a collection of the conference papers offering new readings (feminist, linguistic, postcolonial and others using Blanchot and Bakhtin), a chapter in an essay collection on non-metropolitan modernisms and a title on Thomas in the New Casebook series – have yielded Wigginton's *Modernism from the Margins*, a novel reconsideration of Thomas's engagements with modernism, monstrosity and surrealism, and this study, which further extends the attempt to engineer an encounter between Thomas, his historical contexts and some elements of modern literary theory.[118] In the meantime, a new psychoanalytic reading of Thomas's poetry, Eynal Wardi's *Once Below a Time: Dylan Thomas, Julia Kristeva, and Other Speaking Subjects*, appeared in 2000.[119] All of these efforts assume that it is increasingly possible to do justice to the complexity and beauty of Thomas's poetry in ways which were not possible forty years or more ago.

The slow reappraisal of Thomas has occurred within the context of the growing sophistication of Anglo-Welsh literary criticism already mentioned. But it has also been spurred on by a better understanding of the plural nature of modernism and of the course of twentieth-century British poetry more generally. The dominant readings of 1930s and 1940s poetry and the short-circuiting of Thomas criticism through his myth can increasingly be understood as part of a long struggle over how to respond to *The Waste Land*, which has been going on in British poetry since around 1930. The contours of this struggle have become much clearer during the last decade, following illuminating studies by, among others, Keith Tuma, Andrew Duncan, Anthony Mellors and James Keery.[120] Keery's series of ten essays, collectively titled 'The baby and the bathwater', published in *P.N. Review* between 2002 and 2006, are unique in fully elucidating what is at stake: namely that reappraising Thomas entails a major reappraisal of the standard accounts of 1930s and 1940s poetry. They do so by meticulously documenting, for the first time, the process of Thomas's marginalisation within critical, histories, the nature of his relationship with the New Apocalypse poets and the fate of these and 1940s poetry.[121] But Keery's research also makes a compelling case for a native visionary poetic modernism concerned with issues of (im) mortality, co-originated by Gascoyne, Barker and (chiefly) Thomas in 1933–4, which reached its peak in the mid-1940s and was sufficiently vital to be a seminal influence for Geoffrey Hill, Sylvia Plath, Roy Fisher, Ted Hughes, W. S. Graham and others into the 1950s. It confirms, again, Gabriel Pearson's claims for Thomas and Auden as apocalyptic 'twins', make it clear that an Apocalyptic style was pervasive and powerful throughout the 1940s and prove the wrongness of trying to 'save' Thomas from association with it.[122] More recently still, as 1940s fiction has begun to receive its critical due, studies such as those by Leo Mellor and Marina MacKay have strengthened claims for this poetic strain as a 'modernism beyond the Blitz'.[123]

* * *

Such criticism, finally, highlights the problems that Thomas continues to cause by having written outstanding poems of kinds so different that they are usually held to be mutually incompatible, thereby revealing, if not their occult kinship, then the fact that they are not exactly as pure and distinct from each other as their proponents would like to believe. This has a significant bearing on our understanding of the current divisions within British poetry and the difficulty involved in incorporating Thomas within mainstream and late modernist accounts of the way that it has developed over the last eighty years. For if he embarrasses an empirical poetics, Thomas also cocks a snook at the avant-garde: if he believed that a poem changed the world, he had little regard for claims that poetry could revolutionise consciousness.[124] More, his work resists the current critical trend to reconfigure poetry as sociological forms to be 'interrogated' for their ideological content. At once solemn and mocking, alternately flaunting and concealing its sources, authoritative-seeming yet unstable, it confounds standard distinctions and haunts the histories in which it is un- or misrepresented. A gnawing sense of this is what makes Thomas a constant absent presence, the elephant in the drawing room of British poetry around which everyone tiptoes – an example of what Pierre Macherey calls the silence which speaks.

In approaching Thomas's work afresh, however, we might do worse than recall that it was coeval with the poems and criticism of his friend William Empson, as I noted earlier. Both Empson and Thomas responded to Eliot's essays as much as to *The Waste Land*, and *18 Poems* (1934) can be read as a critical document as much as a poetry collection; like *Seven Types of Ambiguity* (1930), it mediates Eliot's influence by celebrating the beauty of the effects of polysemy. If, as Jacob Korg stated, '*18 Poems* is formidably Empsonian', that is because Thomas belonged to a specifically British response to high modernism, which tended to take literary-critical, rather than avant-garde, forms, as I discuss in Chapter 1, with Thomas pushing his own brand of polysemy beyond close reading's limits. The complex hybridity fuelling this tactic is precisely what makes it so hard to consistently apply a theoretical model to the work, although if one had to settle for a single term, it would probably be 'overde-termined'. Appropriately, since Thomas made himself a kind of Freudian exemplar in his work, the term was first used by Freud to describe those features of dreams caused by multiple factors, from the 'residue of the day' to the 'potent thoughts' of deeply repressed traumas and desires.[125] It was taken up by I. A. Richards to explain the importance of ambiguity in literature and, later still, by Louis Althusser as a way of thinking about the multiple forces active in any political situation without falling into a simplified notion of them as merely 'contradictory'.[126] Thomas's poetry, likewise, is an unstable conjunction of the several powerful forces I have outlined – the tension between 'high' and 'low' art, coterie taste and mass-audience fodder, Welsh-Wales and Anglophone Wales, parodic modernism and romanticism, linguistic surplus and constraining stanza forms, biological determinism and relativity – which intensify its contradictions to a paradoxical point, at which the judicious balancing of liberal ideologies break down. Thomas dedicated the poems in his fourth and final notebook, of September 1933–April 1934, 'To others caught / Between black and white'; the uniqueness of his work, as I shall attempt to show, stems from the fact that while it contains an unparalleled range of conflicting antinomies, it strives at all points to avoid the compromise of grey.

Notes

1　Paul Ferris, *Dylan Thomas* (London: Penguin, 1977 [repr. 1978]), p. 302.

2　The fiftieth anniversary of Thomas's death in 2003 saw the publication of a new glossary of the poems by Ralph Maud, a new biography (the third since 1965) and the first of two volumes of archive material held by the National Library of Wales. The *Collected Poems*, *Under Milk Wood* and *Collected Stories* have been in print since 1952, 1954 and 1983, respectively. A Dent *Selected Poems* of 1974 (reprinted six times) was revised and re-issued in 1993 and 2000, while another selection (from Faber, edited by Derek Mahon) appeared in 2003. The 1995 Dent edition of *Under Milk Wood* was re-issued as a Penguin Classic in the same year. Paul Ferris's edition of the *Collected Letters* (1985) was republished in 2000. *The Notebook Poems 1930–1934*, edited by Maud and first published as *Poet in the Making* in 1968, has been available in paperback since 1989. Memoirs and coffee-table books continue to appear. By any commercial or cultural measure, Thomas remains an astonishingly popular and successful poet.

3　Perceptions of Thomas's importance can be seen in the inclusion of his 'Poetic Manifesto' (as 'Notes on the Art of Poetry'), ed. James Scully, *Modern Poets on Modern Poetry* (London: Collins, 1966), together with pieces by Eliot, Pound, Hopkins, Moore, Yeats, Stevens, David Jones, e. e. cummings, Frost, Crane, Olson, Williams, Ransom and Lowell. The piece also appears in Graham Martin and P. N. Furbank, eds., *Twentieth Century Poetry: Critical Essays and Documents* (Milton Keynes: Open University Press, 1975), accompanying articles by Hardy, Pound, Eliot, Yeats, Auden, Brecht, MacDiarmid, Larkin, Lowell, Hughes and Plath. The Martin and Furbank volume also includes Empson's essay 'The Poetry of Dylan Thomas'.

4　J. B. Kershner, Jr., *Dylan Thomas: The Poet and His Critics* (Chicago, Illinois: American Library Association, 1976), p. 107.

5　Quoted in Constantine FitzGibbon, *The Life of Dylan Thomas* (London: Plantin, 1987), p. 49.

6　By Walford Davies (1986), Eynal Wardi (2000) and Barbara Hardy (2000); the studies by John Ackerman (1991) and James A. Davies (1997) are 'companions'.

7　Kenneth Rexroth, ed., *The New British Poets* (New York, NY: New Directions, 1949), p. xviii.

8　George Steiner, 'The Retreat from Word', *Kenyon Review*, XXIII (Spring 1961), p. 207.

9　Gabriel Pearson, 'Gabriel Pearson on Dylan Thomas', *The Spectator Review of Books*, 20 November 1971, p. 731.

10　Derek Mahon, ed., 'Introduction', *Dylan Thomas: Poems Selected by Derek Mahon* (London: Faber, 2004), p. vii.

11　Although she initially attacked Thomas in her *Aspects of Modern Poetry* (1934), Sitwell reviewed *18 Poems* positively in the *London Mercury* and *Life and Letters Today* and lavishly praised *Twenty-five Poems* in *The Sunday Times* on 15 November 1936: 'The work of this very young man ... is on a huge scale, both in theme and structurally ... [it is] nothing short of magnificent ... I could not name one poet ... of this ... generation who shows so great a promise and even so great an achievement'. See Ferris, *Dylan Thomas*, p. 210. Likewise, Cyril Connolly's review of the *Collected Poems: 1934–1952* in *The Sunday Times* on 9 November 1952 claimed that: 'he distils an exquisite, mysterious, moving quality which defies analysis as supreme lyric poetry always has'. See Andrew Lycett, *Dylan Thomas: A New Life* (London: Weidenfeld & Nicolson, 2003), p. 340.

12 Read reviewed *The Map of Love* in *Seven* in Autumn 1939, concluding: '... It is the most absolute poetry that has been written in our time, and one can only pray that this poet will not be forced in any way to surrender the subtle course of his genius'.

13 Geoffrey Grigson, review of *Twenty-five Poems*, in *Poetry* (Chicago), November 1936; cited in Paul Ferris, *Dylan Thomas* (London: Penguin, 1978), p. 133, fn. 2.

14 Quoted in R. B. Kershner Jr., *Dylan Thomas*, pp. 121–2.

15 Louis MacNeice, for example, did find 'meaning', but had other New Country reservations: the 'cumulative effect' of Thomas's 'nonsense images' 'is usually vital and sometimes even seems to have a message', he wrote, it is 'wild and drunken speech, but with the saving grace of rhythm'. See R. B. Kershner Jr., *Dylan Thomas*, p. 122.

16 Adrian Caesar places Thomas in a mini-'generation', which included George Barker (1913–91) and David Gascoyne (1916–2001). All three were from lower, not upper-middle class backgrounds, the products of grammar, rather than public, schools, 'unencumbered by a university education', less 'English' than New Country and rejecting sociological and analytical attitudes to poetry and language in favour of an organicist vision. Their work replaced the figure of poet-as-analyst with that of the poet-as-prophet, and this entailed the use of rhetorical, emotive and metaphysical materials rejected by the New Country poets. All three were initially published by the small, private Parton Press, run by David Archer. Barker's and Gascoyne's first collections, *Thirty Preliminary Poems* and *Roman Balcony and Other Poems*, were published in 1933, just before Thomas came to prominence. See Adrian Caesar, *Dividing Lines: Poetry, Class and Ideology in the 1930s* (Manchester: Manchester University Press, 1991), pp. 177–200.

17 Cited by Robert Fraser, *The Chameleon Poet: A Life of George Barker* (London: Pimlico, 2002), p. 46.

18 Gabriel Pearson, 'Gabriel Pearson on Dylan Thomas', p. 731.

19 Anne Fogarty, 'Yeats, Ireland and Modernism', eds. Alex Davis and Lee M. Jenkins, *The Cambridge Companion to Modernist Poetry* (Cambridge: Cambridge University Press, 2007), p. 127. The seminal study of the subject is Peter Nicholls, *Modernisms: A Literary Guide* (London: Macmillan, 1995).

20 The letter to Grigson containing his contribution concluded irreverently: 'P.S.: Congratulations on Auden's seventieth birthday' (*CL*, 298). Writing to James Laughlin, he described the issue as: 'devoted entirely ... to gush and pomp about [Auden]. He's exactly what the English literary public think a modern English poet should be. He's perfectly educated ... but still delightfully eccentric. He's a rebel (i.e. an official communist) but boys will be boys so he is awarded the King's Medal [for Poetry, in 1938]; he's got a great sense of Humour; he's not one of those old-fashioned escapist Bohemians' (*CL*, 346).

21 Ralph J. Mills, Jr., 'Dylan Thomas: The Endless Monologue', *Accent*, XX (Spring 1960), p. 130.

22 Balakiev, James J., 'The Ambiguous Reversal of Dylan Thomas's "In Country Sleep"', *Papers on Language and Literature*, 32: 1 (1996), 21.

23 Francis Scarfe, *Auden and After: The Liberation of Poetry 1930–1941* (London: Routledge, 1942), p. 114. The Thomas material is reprinted in *Dylan Thomas: The Legend and the Poet*, ed. E. W. Tedlock (London: Heinemann / Mercury Books, 1963), pp. 96–112.

24 See Linden Huddlestone, 'An Approach to Dylan Thomas', *Penguin New Writing*, XXXV (1948), pp. 123–60: '[T]he universe is sexually dynamic; bird, beast and stone share the same (sexual) life with man ... for ever conscious of a sense of sin, Thomas conveys this as something terrible ... His universe is dynamic, frighteningly active and alive ... But, in consequence, death itself appears not as a negation, but as an equally dynamic force'; Robert Horan, 'In Defense of Dylan Thomas', *The Kenyon Review*, VII: 2 (Spring 1945), pp. 304–10; and David Aivaz, 'The Poetry of Dylan Thomas', *The Hudson Review*, VIII: 3 (Autumn 1950) [repr. E. W. Tedlock, ed., *Dylan Thomas: The Legend and the Poet* (London: Heinemann / Mercury Books, 1963)], pp. 186–210.

25 David Aivaz, 'The Poetry of Dylan Thomas', p. 200.

26 William Empson, *Argufying*, ed. John Haffenden (London: Hogarth Press, 1988), p. 394.

27 A sense that Auden's versified cultural commentary missed a crucial aspect of the era is expressed in Robert Horan's 1945 'In Defense of Dylan Thomas', p. 305: 'There is a kind of subject matter currently passing for profound and personal content among both younger and older poets. Auden ... has evolved a cryptic, Noel Coward shorthand, cautiously glamorous, flattered by his own sensitivity like a public-school prodigy. Saturated by self-consciousness, more and more poems appear from the tomb of Henry James or the bier of Freud. These are gratuitous identifications with tradition, distinctly "literary subject matters", apathetic and indulgent, conditioned by an attitude towards experience that begins to sound professional, as if it were lived through in order to be written about. Thomas has escaped this contagion, this small and anxious form of exploitation, even if at the cost of publication in the *Atlantic Monthly*'.

28 The stanza makes no grammatical sense; as Walford Davies notes, we are left wondering 'what sort of helpless audience Grigson had in mind whom he could expect either to fall into the trap and blush from embarrassment, or wink in approval at such a ploy', as well as being struck by the lengths that Grigson was prepared to go to frame Thomas and his readers. See *SP1*, p. xiv.

29 'Dylan Thomas', *Scrutiny*, XIV: 1 (Summer 1946), pp. 62–7. Mankowitz claims: 'Mr. Thomas is playing at games' with his poems consisting of 'rotten tissues ... falling apart', 'tedious demonstration of self-pity', 'poetic pseudo-statement' and 'Clever-boy pranks in verbal gymnastics and "*ersatz*"'.

30 Catherine Belsey, *Critical Practice* (London: Methuen, 1980), p. 12.

31 Terry Eagleton, *Heathcliff and the Great Hunger*, p. 269. Francis Mulhern, *The Moment of Scrutiny* (London: Verso, 1979), p. 257. As James A. Davies has noted, *Scrutiny* castigated Thomas for, among other things, his alleged 'immaturity of adolescence', 'self-indulgent religiosity', bardic gesturing and 'a downright disgusting self-righteousness'. James A. Davies, 'Questions of Identity: The Movement and

"Fern Hill"', John Goodby and Chris Wigginton, eds. *Dylan Thomas: A New Casebook*, p. 158.

32 Donald Davie, *Articulate Energy* (London: Routledge & Kegan Paul, 1955), pp. xii, 125–7, 129. For a discussion, see Walford Davies, *Dylan Thomas* (Milton Keynes: Open University Press, 1986), pp. 103–5.

33 Robert Graves, 'These Be Your Gods, O Israel!', the sixth and last of the Clark Lectures on Professional Standards in English Poetry delivered at Trinity College, Cambridge, Michaelmas Term, 1954–5 (repr. *Essays in Criticism*, 5 (1955), pp. 148–9). Graves's ambivalence towards Thomas is clear in the Clark lecture: 'He could put on the *hwyl* like any Rev. John Jones, B.A., Bangor, albeit in English as spoken in Langham Place; and, when I listened to him broadcasting, I had to keep a tight hold of myself to avoid being seduced. As when once, in 1916, I listened to a war speech given by Lloyd George …'. Graves acknowledged, in *The Crowning Privilege*, that Thomas was a poetic prodigy, but described these as: 'monstrous and ill-omened'. Ironically, as critics have noted, Thomas's work exemplifies the bardic qualities championed by Graves in *The White Goddess* to a far greater degree than Graves's own restrained and classical verse.

34 See R. B. Kershner Jr., *Dylan Thomas: The Poet and His Critics*, pp. 204–5.

35 *New Lines*, ed. Robert Conquest (London: Macmillan, 1956), p. xii. Conquest's assumption that empiricism was not a 'theoretical construct' was itself, of course, a 'theoretical construct'.

36 *A Case of Samples: Poems* (New York, NY: Harcourt Brace, 1957), p. 53. Thomas is also the model for Gareth Probert in Amis's novel *That Uncertain Feeling* (1955) and Bryden, the dead Welsh poet-as-tourist-attraction, in *The Old Devils* (1986).

37 Psychoanalytic criticism before 1950 tended to psychoanalyse the individual author, uncovering a latent text that somehow yields up the psychology of the author. As Shoshana Felman notes, this invariably reveals more about the critic than the author, however, and matches the way that Thomas's poems, approached via his myth, tend to read the critic. Thereafter, authors tended to be seen as representative of collective, rather than individual, morbidity. Holbrook combines both approaches with those of W. F. Winnicott and R. D. Laing. See David Holbrook, *Llareggub Revisited: Dylan Thomas and the State of Modern Poetry* [1962 repr. *Dylan Thomas and Poetic Dissociation* (Carbondale, IL: Southern Illinois University Press, 1964)]; *Dylan Thomas: The Code of Night* (London: Athlone Press, 1972).

38 Felman notes the coexistence of high acclaim and 'violent disclaim[ing]' in the critical reception of Poe, observing the unanimity concerning his 'genius effect', his ability to wring confessions of his work's 'magnetism', 'magic' and so on, even from detractors. As she observes, these 'seem to be unaware … of the paradox that underlies their enterprise: it is by no means clear why anyone should take the trouble to write – at length – about a writer of no importance … The elaborate written denials of Poe's value, the loud and lengthy negations of his importance, are therefore very like psychoanalytic negations … The fact that it so much *matters* to proclaim that Poe *does not matter* is but evidence of the extent to which Poe's poetry is, in effect, a poetry that matters'. The attacks partake in the nature of an 'analytical effect'. Like Poe's, Thomas's psychoanalytic critics fall into two broad camps: those who see his work as the expression of a unique pathology and those who see it as a shared one ('the unthinkable and unacknowledged but strongly felt community of … sexual drives'). Felman notes that these are two sides of the same

coin: the second simply replaces uncontrolled utterance and disease by control and health. Neither accounts for the 'dynamic interaction between the unconscious and conscious elements of art'. Using Lacan's seminar on Poe's 'The Purloined Letter', she argues that: 'what is repeated in the text is not the content of a fantasy but the symbolic displacement of a signifier through the insistence of a signifying chain'. Here we come close to a basic point on which I elaborate in this study: that language writes back and that Freud's most important insight, with regard to Thomas at least, is that: 'significance lies not just in consciousness but, specifically, in its disruption'. If the signifier can be analysed in its effects without its signified being known, then 'what calls for analysis is the insistence of the unreadable in the text'. It is crucial, in short, to recognise the irreducible textuality of the text and the fact that poetry 'is precisely the effect of a deadly struggle between consciousness and the unconscious; it has to do with resistance and with what can neither be resisted nor escaped'. Shoshana Felman, 'The Case of Poe: Applications / Implications of Psychoanalysis', *Jacques Lacan and the Adventures of Insight: Psychoanalysis in Contemporary Culture* (Cambridge, MA: Harvard University Press, 1987), pp. 30–2, 38, 44, 48.

39 Although Thomas was more assured and less anxious, the parallels between the attacks on him and those on Keats, as discussed by Marjorie Levinson in *Keats's Life of Allegory: the Origins of a Style*, are particularly striking. Levinson directly confronts the discourse of sexual disgust surrounding the reception of Keats ('profligate', 'unclean', 'puerile', 'onanist', 'piss-a-bed', 'miserable Self-polluter of the human mind', 'nonsense') and the critical troping of his poetry as masturbatory exhibitionism. According to Levinson, the established literary powers were substantially correct, from their point of view, in judging Keats's 'aggressively *literary* style' 'not just "not Literature" but, in effect, "*anti*-Literature: a parody"'. She views the true virtue of Keats's poetry to be not some 'capacious, virile, humane authenticity' belatedly offered in compensation by twentieth-century critics, 'but its subversion of those authoritarian values'; it is the poetry's self-knowing egregiousness, which makes a virtue of its anxious necessities and of its appropriations and flauntings of the 'literary', a 'triumph of the double-negative'. See Marjorie Levinson, *Keats's Life of Allegory: The Origins of a Style* (Oxford: Basil Blackwell, 1987), pp. 3–5.

40 Geoffrey Johnston in E. W. Tedlock, ed., *Dylan Thomas: The Legend and the Poet*, p. 220.

41 See, for example, Monroe C. Beardsley and Sam Hynes, 'Misunderstanding Poetry: Notes on Some Readings of Dylan Thomas', *College English*, XXI (March 1960), pp. 315–22.

42 This is Thomas in 1946: 'A good poem is a contribution to reality. The world is never the same once a good poem has been added to it. A good poem helps to change the shape and significance of the universe, helps to extend everyone's knowledge of himself and the universe around him' (*QEOM*, 192–3). This is R. P. Blackmur in the late 1930s: 'The art of poetry is amply distinguished from the manufacture of verse by the animating presence in the poetry of a fresh idiom: language so twisted and posed in a form that it not only expresses the matter in hand but adds to the stock of available reality'. Cited in John Berryman, *Love & Fame* (London: Faber, 1971), p. 27.

43 Lita Hornick's ground-breaking thesis identified clusters linked by the 'ideational core' of process with three main themes: 'the dying and resurrected god' (figured

in the vegetable cycle, reproduction and tumescence / detumescence), creation and genesis and time and mortality (often imaged in 'the motif of death by water or fire'). These manifested themselves in an 'imagery of circular motion, upward motion, sea-voyages, of music under the sea, of vegetable growth, birds, wind, and scarabs'. It is a sophisticated account of the superstructural forms generated by process and still sheds useful light on Thomas's cosmos and use of religious motifs – Everyman as Christ, Adam, Attis and Osiris, continually undergoing death and rebirth. See Lita Hornick, 'The Intricate Image: A Study of Dylan Thomas', PhD dissertation, Columbia University, 1958.

44 Elder Olson, *The Poetry of Dylan Thomas* (Chicago, IL: University of Chicago Press, 1954 [repr. 1955]), pp. 63–89. As Hornick drily notes, Olson is: 'ingenious in his speculation, but presents no objective evidence to support his debateable theories'. Lita Hornick, 'The Intricate Image: A Study of Dylan Thomas', p. xi. It should be said that Olson's book is otherwise a very good one.

45 John Bayley, *The Romantic Revival: A Study in Poetic Evolution* (London: Constable, 1957), p. 218.

46 John Bayley, *The Romantic Revival*, p. 194.

47 John Bayley, *The Romantic Revival*, p. 196.

48 *The Language Poets Use* (London: Athlone Press, 1962 [repr. 1965]), pp. 187–222.

49 Nowottny, *The Language Poets Use*, p. 187. Among the unsuspected sources of the poem, Nowottny identifies Eliot, Marvell, Brooke, Stein and Keats.

50 In 1948, the poet Nicholas Moore noted that: 'Mr Thomas's first poems are positively silly with hints and references, and one could spend a whole essay on the analysis of a few lines (any few lines)'. Nicholas Moore, 'The Poetry of Dylan Thomas', *The Poetry Quarterly* (1948), p. 231.

51 Ralph Maud, *Entrances to Dylan Thomas' Poetry* (Pittsburgh, PA: University of Pittsburgh Press, 1963), pp. 20–1.

52 Ralph Maud, *Entrances to Dylan Thomas' Poetry*, p. 39.

53 C. B. Cox, *Dylan Thomas: A Collection of Critical Essays* (London: Prentice-Hall, 1962 [repr. Englewood Cliffs, NJ: Prentice-Hall, 1966]), p. 69, fn. 9.

54 J. Hillis Miller, *Poets of Reality: Six Twentieth Century Writers* (Cambridge, MA: Harvard University Press, 1966), p. 198.

55 J. Hillis Miller, *Poets of Reality*, pp. 199, 201, 203.

56 J. Hillis Miller, *Poets of Reality*, p. 214.

57 See Martin Dodsworth, 'The Concept of the Mind and the Poetry of Dylan Thomas', ed. Walford Davies, *Dylan Thomas: New Critical Essays* (London: Dent, 1972), p. 111.

58 Although what they are is of interest, of course. I discuss Thomas's reading and influences in Chapter 1; here, I simply note that Thomas denied knowing work of which he was well aware (surrealism, for example), in order to shape the reception of his work by laying false trails – or out of sheer perversity. Daniel Jones, Thomas's closest friend, claimed that he had no interest in any studies 'with names ending in -ology, -onomy, -ography, osophy, -ic, -ics or, even, to a large extent, just -y (history, botany)', but this is controverted by other friends, who speak of his interest in popular science. Jones adds: '[he] did not know by heart The Koran, the Zend Avesta, the Upanishads, the Lun Yu, and had no access to the Kabbala', which confirms the point about the unsuspected extent of Thomas's reading, since we know that Jones himself gave Thomas a copy of The Koran for Christmas in 1933.

See Daniel Jones, *My Friend Dylan Thomas* (London, Macmillan, 1978), p. 57, and *CL*, p. 91.

59 Kristeva notes: 'The notion of *intertextuality* replaces that of intersubjectivity, and poetic language is read as at least *double*'. See Julia Kristeva, 'Word, Dialogue and Novel', ed. Toril Moi, transl. Seán Hand and Léon S. Roudiez, *The Kristeva Reader* (Oxford: Basil Blackwell, 1986 [repr. 1989]), p. 37; also Julia Kristeva, *Revolution in Poetic Language*, transl. Margaret Waller (New York, NY: Columbia University Press, 1984), pp. 59–60.

60 An excellent discussion of the Eliotic and Empsonian aspects of Thomas's work is given by Edward Larrissy in 'Languages of Modernism: William Empson, Dylan Thomas, W. S. Graham', ed. Neil Corcoran, *The Cambridge Companion to Twentieth Century English Poetry* (Cambridge: Cambridge University Press, 2007), pp. 131–44.

61 Hugh Kenner, *A Sinking Island: the Modern English Writers* (Baltimore, MD: Johns Hopkins University Press, 1988 [repr. 1989]).

62 Peter McDonald, *Louis MacNeice: The Poet in his Contexts* (Oxford: Clarendon Press, 1991), p. 1.

63 Adrian Caesar, *Dividing Lines: Poetry, Class and Ideology in the 1930s*, p. 2.

64 James Keery, 'The Burning Baby and the Bathwater', *P.N. Review* 156, 30: 4 (March-April 2004), p. 40. Keery adds: 'Check it out: *Garden Revisited*, *A*, Lehmann, John, p. 75; *Professor, The*, Warner, Rex, p. 311; *Sign of the Fish, The*, Quennell, Peter, p. 26. *18 Poems*? Hmm. Thomas, Dylan? P. 153: "two others (Dylan Thomas and David Gascoyne) aligned themselves more vaguely with revolution" in a survey conducted by Grigson, Geoffrey (pp. 113, 153, 158–9, 167, 197, 202, 296, 348–9). Not a line of Thomas's verse is cited, not so much as a title to his name. As "a surrealist story" in "the first issue of *Contemporary Poetry and Prose*", "The Burning Baby" *just* misses out on a name-check; and Thomas's influence is sarcastically acknowledged, if only on "undergraduates"'.

65 Michael Schmidt is a perfect example of how empiricist exasperation with Thomas operates. First, work and life are conflated. This is followed by an attack on figurative language ('[It] mean[s] "I was born" – after five stanzas of lurid gestation – and "I shall die"'), followed by Arnoldian stereotypes ("Thomas weaves spells"). The whole procedure is informed by a misconception of the relationship of language with the object world: 'he has not engaged experience but *only* language' (emphasis added) – as if poems were made of something other than 'language' or 'experience' was not always mediated by it. Michael Schmidt, ed., *An Introduction to Fifty Modern British Poets* (London: Pan, 1979), p. 58.

66 Chris Baldick, *The Oxford English Literary History, vol. X, 1910–1940, The Modern Movement* (Oxford: Oxford University Press, 2005), p. 108.

67 Valentine Cunningham, *British Writers of the Thirties* (Oxford: Oxford University Press, 1988), p. 402.

68 Commercial grounds were cited as the reason for the lack of interest on both occasions. However, while Thomas is not taught on university courses, his broad appeal would seem to make him a more saleable proposition than, say, the titles on Ben Jonson and Fanny Burney. This may reflect a general Cambridge attitude: in a recent appreciation of Andrew Crozier, Peter Riley notes, in passing, that: 'like everyone else from Cambridge [he] undervalued Dylan Thomas'. Peter Riley,

'Review of Ian Brinton (ed.) *An Andrew Crozier Reader*', *Cambridge Literary Review*, 3: 6 (Easter 2012), p. 154.

69 Although the lengths to which Morgan-Vaughan is permitted to go suggests that Thomas was indulging his own animus, too: 'Huh! How vile was my valley! I'm sick of all this Celtic claptrap about Wales. My Wales! (mockingly) Land of my Fathers! As far as I'm concerned, my fathers can keep it. You can tell a Welshman by the lilt in his voice. Huh, little black back-biting hypocrites, all gab and whine! Black beetles with tenor voices and a sense of sin like a crippled hump. Cwmglas! Full of senile morons and vicious dwarfs, old poles of women clacking at you like blowsy hens, self-righteous humbugs with the hywl, old men with beards in their noses cackling at you, blue gums and clackers. Oh the mystical Welsh – huh! About as mystical as slugs!' Dylan Thomas, *The Complete Screenplays*, ed. John Ackerman (New York, NY: Applause Books, 1995), p. 299.

70 Glyn Jones (1905–95), leading Anglo-Welsh poet, novelist and critic. Gwyn Jones (1907–99), Welsh novelist, academic, editor and outstanding Norse scholar.

71 'What I first experienced when I first read "Light breaks where no sun shines" seemed to me an almost identical emotion to that aroused by the high strings in the first movement of *Eine Kleine Nachtmusik* – a sort of transport of ecstasy'. Glyn Jones, *The Dragon has Two Tongues* (Cardiff: University of Wales Press, 2000), p. 173.

72 Glyn Jones, *The Dragon has Two Tongues*, p. 183.

73 Glyn Jones, *The Dragon has Two Tongues*, p. 173.

74 Gwyn Jones, 'Background to Dylan Thomas: The First Forty Years', ed. Gwyn Jones, *Background to Dylan Thomas and Other Explorations* (Oxford: OUP, 1992), p. 95. *Cwydd* and *englyn* are intricate Welsh metrical forms.

75 Bobi Jones, 'Imitations in Death', *Welsh Anvil*, 7 (1955), pp. 85–6. Jones's comments derived from his belief that England was 'decadent' – 'the inevitable development of a language and society that have lost their creative distinction'. He assumes Welsh superiority and exceptionalism based on this belief, and this underwrites his valorisation of community. See Kershner, p. 180. There is a spirited and intelligent discussion of the issue in M. Wynn Thomas, '"He Belongs to the English": Welsh Dylan and Welsh-language Culture', *Swansea Review: Under the Spelling Wall*, Special Dylan Thomas Issue, eds. Glyn Pursglove, John Goodby and Chris Wigginton, 20 (2000), p. 123.

76 Terence Hawkes, 'Review article', *Anglo-Welsh Review*, 12: 30 (1962), p. 69. Rhiwbina and Sketty are suburbs of Cardiff and Swansea, respectively.

77 Their work included editions of Thomas's notebook poems (Maud, 1967 [rev. and repr. 1989); stories, criticism, broadcasts and miscellanea (Walford Davies, 1971); fiction (Walford Davies, 1983); letters (Ferris, 1985); radio broadcasts (Maud, 1991); film-scripts (Ackerman, 1995); and a part-annotated *Collected Poems 1943–1953* (Maud and Walford Davies, 1988), plus two companions (Ackerman 1991; James A. Davies 1997), a third poem-by-poem guide (Maud, 2003) and an annotated *Under Milk Wood* (Walford Davies, 1995). Ralph Maud was born in Yorkshire and has lived in the US and Canada since 1949, but is 'of Welsh ancestry', according to the Literature Wales's Writers of Wales website.

78 Cited by John Berger when describing Picasso's emergence on the Parisian art scene in *The Success and Failure of Picasso* (London: Writers and Readers Publishing Co-operative, 1980), p. 40.

79 From the 1880s until around 1920 when the Labour Party and the First World War broke its grip, Wales was ruled by an alliance between the Welsh Liberal Party and the Nonconformist chapels. What this means is that, as Andrew Duncan has explained, a major strand in contemporary nationalism is 'not a creative and modernising and self-conscious formation [but] a disenfranchised former ruling class', which formerly ruled 'a single-party country'. Andrew Duncan, *Centre and Periphery in Modern British Poetry*, p. 227.

80 Caradoc Evans, *My People*, ed. and intro. John Harris (Bridgend: Seren, 1987), p. 20. M. Wynn Thomas, *Corresponding Cultures*, p. 157.

81 M. Wynn Thomas, *Corresponding Cultures*, p. 149. This diplomatic formulation is spelt out more trenchantly in Tony Bianchi's description of the resurgent Welsh-speaking middle class of the post-WWII period. He argues that it displays: 'a hostility to science and urban life as unWelsh; an elevation of rural values; an essentialist or ahistorical notion of nationalism, based on a selective view of the past and notions of an organic tradition; a belief in the importance of an elite in defending this ideal, of which the Welsh language is the embodiment; a view of the English-speaking Welsh as alienated and needing to align themselves with these values in order to overcome [it]; and above all, the elevation of culture, literature and even "taste" as a surrogate religion which informs these convictions'. See Tony Bianchi, 'R. S. Thomas and his Readers', ed. Tony Curtis, *Wales: The Imagined Nation* (Bridgend: Poetry Wales Press, 1986), p. 84.

82 The Lloyd George-era Nonconformist Liberals pursued a strategy of lobbying for Welsh interests at the imperial centre and did not promote separatism or the Welsh language. However, the post-WWI collapse in religious belief meant that the Welsh language became the core value of their successor, Plaid Cymru, founded in 1925. Plaid's leader, Saunders Lewis, asserted that Welsh nationalists: 'cannot … aim at anything less than to annihilate English in Wales … It must be deleted from the land called Wales: *delenda est Carthago*'. Gwyn A. Williams, *When Was Wales?*, p. 281.

83 Dai Smith, 'Textual Tales and True Life Stories', *Planet*, 116 (June 1996), p. 104. M. Wynn Thomas, *Corresponding Cultures*, p. 149. Linguistic culturalists tend to assume that the relationship between the two languages of Wales is a zero-sum one – in Linden Peach's words: 'Welsh writers who write in English do so because of what has been denied Welsh language speakers'. This is to foist guilt by association on monoglot anglophones and requires that Anglo-Welsh poets admit not just linguistic deprivation, but psychic incompleteness. Lyndon Peach, *The Prose Writing of Dylan Thomas* (Basingstoke: Macmillan, 1988), pp. 8–9.

84 See, for example, Glyn Jones's poem 'Y Ddraig Goch' / 'The Red Dragon', which warns against assuming that a Welsh state run on purist, *völkisch* nationalist lines would avoid the errors of other such states: 'The language of Llanrhaeadr and Pantycelyn / Shall be used for the utterance of her cruelty, her banality, her lies'. Glyn Jones, *Selected Poems*, p. 81.

85 Tony Conran, 'The English Poet in Wales II: Boys of Summer in Their Ruin', *Anglo-Welsh Review*, 10: 26 (1960), p. 12.

86 Tony Conran, *Welsh Verse* (Bridgend: Seren, 1986), p. 13.

87 Meic Stephens, 'The Second Flowering', ed. Cary Archard, *Poetry Wales: 25 Years* (Bridgend: Seren Books, 1990), p. 26.

88 There is an essay to be written about Thomas and suburbs and why his suburban-ness offended the likes of George Steiner and Terry Hawkes so intensely (and I discuss the subject in passing in Chapter 6). However, positing him as a spokesman of 'the professional and managerial classes' asserting themselves against 'the big bourgeoisie' is bizarrely wide of the mark. Tony Conran, *The Cost of Strangeness: Essays on the English Poets of Wales* (Llandysul: Gomer Press, 1982), pp. 178–9.

89 Tony Conran, *The Cost of Strangeness: Essays on the English Poets of Wales*, p. 186.

90 Saunders Lewis's policies were Catholic-feudal and fascist-inclined. In ditching him as leader in 1945, Plaid was able to detach itself from the toxicity of his inter-war politics. It was much-revivified by the rise of Cymdeithas yr Iaith Gymreig (the Welsh Language Movement) in the 1960s, which led to the passing of the Welsh Language Act in 1967, which gave Welsh parity with English in many areas of public life. Although anglophone working-class South Walians remained distrustful of Plaid and thwarted Plaid's efforts to win devolution in 1979 (it was rejected by a 4–1 majority), Thatcherism, multiculturalism and New Labour brought about new alignments. In the 1980s, the aspiration to bilingualism became the new orthodoxy for all political parties, while the reaction against Tory hegemony and Labour's moribund state led Plaid to some electoral successes. Since 1997, the Welsh Assembly has partially defused some of the cultural and linguistic polarisation and created the space for more generous definitions of Welsh identity.

91 Tony Conran, *Frontiers in Anglo-Welsh Poetry* (Cardiff: University of Wales Press, 1997), p. 120.

92 Tony Conran, *Frontiers in Anglo-Welsh Poetry*, p. 128.

93 Tony Conran, *Frontiers in Anglo-Welsh Poetry*, pp. 133–4.

94 Tony Conran, *Frontiers in Anglo-Welsh Poetry*, p. 1.

95 As noted in the preface 'Anglo-Welsh Literature' has been supplanted as a label since the late 1990s, following the rise of postcolonial theory in academia, by the clumsier, but more strictly accurate, 'Welsh Writing in English'. Labels matter greatly in Wales, starting with 'Wales' and 'Welsh', which derives from the Anglo-Saxon *waelsc*, meaning 'foreigner'; Stephen Knight, for example, in *A Hundred Years of Fiction* (2004), prefers *Cymraeg*, 'the language's name for itself', and also claims that: '"Anglo-Welsh" is found unacceptable by most authors … on the grounds that it refuses Welsh status to Welsh people who, not speaking *Cymraeg*, nevertheless do not feel at all English'. While I endorse some of these sentiments, in this book, I shall vary my use of 'Anglo-Welsh', 'Welsh anglophone' and 'Welsh writing in English' for stylistic and historical reasons, as long as there is no danger of my being misunderstood. 'Anglo-Welsh' is a specific period term, while, as Knight himself points out, 'Welsh writing in English' is a 'clumsy phrase'. Authors may be 'Anglo-Welsh', because, in some contexts, 'Welsh' would wrongly suggest 'Welsh language', but no feeling of Englishness is thereby imputed to them. I also use 'Welsh', rather than *Cymraeg*, without intending what Knight calls 'a damaging mockery' of either the language or authors using it; this usage, I feel, will be the least confusing to the majority of this book's readers (not all of whom will be Welsh-speaking critics of WWE). To use *Cymraeg* instead of 'Welsh' if you do not speak Welsh seems to me to run the risk of patronising those who do and criticising those who do not. Where it is a question of a Welsh word which is more accurate than its English equivalent or has no adequate English equivalent – as 'bro', 'gwerin', 'hywl' or 'hiraeth', for example – I naturally use the Welsh.

See Stephen Knight, *A Hundred Years of Fiction: Writing Wales in English* (Cardiff: University of Wales Press, 2004), p. xv.

96 M. Wynn Thomas, *Corresponding Cultures: The Two Literatures of Wales* (Cardiff: University of Wales Press, 1999), pp. 75, 79.

97 M. Wynn Thomas, *Corresponding Cultures: The Two Literatures of Wales*, p. 59.

98 M. Wynn Thomas, *Corresponding Cultures: The Two Literatures of Wales*, p. 49.

99 Homi K. Bhabha, *The Location of Culture* (London: Routledge, 1994), p. 90.

100 Homi K. Bhabha, *The Location of Culture* (London: Routledge, 1994), p. 113.

101 Not all of Thomas's main advocates avoid the dangers posed by the legend. Perhaps because he shows little appreciation for the poetry, Paul Ferris's thorough, meticulous and clearly-written biography and comprehensive edition of the letters are strangely disfigured by constant petty sniping at Thomas's personal foibles, both real and imagined.

102 Thus, Walford Davies's Introduction to his first *Selected Poems* tackles the 'weird misrepresentation' of Thomas by English critics in a brilliant, yet measured, manner, by rebutting the falsifications and sloppiness of those who indicted his craftsmanship (Davie, Grigson, Graves, Steiner) and remarking the double standards of those who impugned Thomas's 'drunkenness and … scrounging', while overlooking 'facts morally far more intolerable known about the likes of Larkin, Eliot and several other poets' ('blatant racism … an obsession with pornography'). It is, however, a statement of the case for Thomas's seriousness as a writer (against which there is no real case to answer) and an *ad hominem* defence against *ad hominism*. That is, it does not explain the structural reasons for the demonisation of Thomas and the collapse in his critical reputation, or explain what a critically aware student of poetry might find in his work in 1993 (*SP1*, xvi-xviii).

103 Stephen Knight, *A Hundred Years of Fiction: Writing Wales in English*, p. 124.

104 Stephen Knight, *A Hundred Years of Fiction: Writing Wales in English*, p. 124. 'A Story' is (a) set in West, not South, Wales; (b) located in a rural, not an industrial, area; (c) was first broadcast on television, not radio; and (d) was first broadcast to a Welsh, not an English, audience. Before Knight, the same non-target had been chosen by the critic Jeni Williams to convict Thomas of infantilism, misogyny, lack of communal feeling and a host of other heavy sins; see Jeni Williams, 'The Place of Fantasy: Children and Narratives in Two Short Stories by Kate Roberts and Dylan Thomas', ed. Tony Brown, *Welsh Writing in English: A Yearbook of Critical Essays*, 6 (2000), p. 56. For a discussion, see my 'Eight Ways of Looking at Welsh Writing in English', *New Welsh Review*, 51 (December 2000), pp. 57–61.

105 The Indian Subaltern Studies Group, from whom Bhabha took his cue, regards the very idea of nationality as one which was transferred to the colonies by imperialist ideology. The coloniser's ideology was adopted and turned back on upon the imperialist by the colonised, in order to conceptually justify their own struggle against the metropolitan centre, but the result is a postcolonial world of nation states, which structurally and practically imitate their former oppressors.

106 Katie Gramich's comments come from *New Welsh Review*, 40 (Spring 1998) and are cited in Daniel Williams, 'Beyond National Literature? Dylan Thomas and Amos Tutuola in "Igbo masquerade"', *New Welsh Review*, 60 (Summer 2003), p. 9.

107 Daniel Williams, 'Beyond National Literature? Dylan Thomas and Amos Tutuola in "Igbo masquerade"', p. 9.

108 Two terms from recent Irish literary studies can be usefully brought into play in

this regard. First, the term 'metropolitan colony' is applicable to Wales as both subordinated nation and part of the imperial centre which imposes British imperial power. Wales was not, and is not, a colony, in the sense that, say, India was, and this has implications for a more nuanced sense of national hybridity. Second, there is Colin Graham's pinpointing of the need to go beyond 'colonial structures [seen] purely in terms of division ... easily pinned down and dichotomised' in a seminal article on Irish writing of 1994 and his use of the term 'impacted' to describe the long, complex and claustrophobic nature of the relationship between the entities we call 'English' and 'Irish', together with the fact that postcolonialism must deconstruct, not only colonial discourse, but also the reliance of cultural (or linguistic or other) nationalist discourse on 'Englishness'. See Colin Graham, '"Liminal Spaces": Post-Colonial Theories and Irish Culture', *The Irish Review*, 16 (Autumn / Winter 1994), p. 41.

109 Terry Eagleton, *How to Read a Poem* (Oxford: Blackwell, 2007), p. 75.

110 Terry Eagleton, *Literary Theory: An Introduction*, pp. 60, 99. As Eagleton so eloquently notes elsewhere: 'what is truly regressive is realism's pleasure in its fixing of the object which is the "imaginary"'. See Terry Eagleton, *Walter Benjamin* (London: Verso, 1981), p. 85.

111 As with most debates about Thomas, we have been here before. Thus, in 1940, Julian Symons claimed in *The Kenyon Review*: 'What is said in Mr. Thomas's poems is that the seasons change; that we decrease in vigour as we grow older; that life has no obvious meaning; that love dies. His poems mean no more than that. They mean too little'. Julian Symons, 'Obscurity and Dylan Thomas', *The Kenyon Review*, 2: 1 (Winter 1939/40), p. 71. In response, John Berryman observed that Symons had ignored the material, rhetorical and performative aspects of the poetry by summarising its general meaning and then 'proving' its banality by condemning the banality of his own précis. 'Evidently it is necessary to point out to Mr Symons, what is elementary, that a poem means more than the abstract, banal statement of its theme; it means its imagery, the disparate parts and relations of it, its ambiguities, by extension the techniques which produced it and the emotions it legitimately produces. A poem is an accretion of knowledge, of which only the flimsiest part can be translated into bromide'. John Berryman, 'The Loud Hill of Wales', *The Kenyon Review*, 2: 4 (Autumn 1940), pp. 482–3.

112 Dylan Thomas, *Selected Poems*, ed. Walford Davies (London: Dent, 1993), p. xi.

113 Don McKay, 'Crafty Dylan and the Altarwise Sonnets: "I Build a Flying Tower and I Pull it Down"', *University of Toronto Quarterly*, 55 (1985 / 6), p. 377.

114 Don McKay, 'Crafty Dylan and the Altarwise Sonnets', p. 376.

115 Don McKay, 'Crafty Dylan and the Altarwise Sonnets', pp. 377–8.

116 Don McKay, 'What Shall We Do with a Drunken Poet?: Dylan Thomas' Poetic Language', *Queen's Quarterly*, 93: 4 (1986), p. 796.

117 Stewart Crehan, '"The Lips of Time"', ed. Alan Bold, *Dylan Thomas: Craft or Sullen Art* (London / New York, NY: Vision Press, 1990).

118 See Glyn Pursglove, John Goodby and Chris Wigginton, eds., *The Swansea Review: Under the Spelling Wall*, 20; John Goodby and Chris Wigginton, '"Shut, too, in a Tower of Words": Dylan Thomas' Modernism', eds. Alex Davis and Lee Jenkins, *The Locations of Literary Modernism* (Cambridge, Cambridge University Press, 2000), pp. 89–112; John Goodby and Chris Wigginton, eds., *Dylan Thomas: New Casebook* (Basingstoke: Palgrave, 2001); Chris Wigginton, *Modernism from the*

Margins: The 1930s Poetry of Louis MacNeice and Dylan Thomas (Cardiff: University of Wales Press, 2007).

119 While Eynal Wardi's monograph is a *tour de force*, it follows David Holbrook in using Thomas's work to psychoanalyse him, replicating the 'slide from work to author', which my book eschews. As Wardi admits: 'Holbrook's analysis has been useful to me for a variety of reasons. In the first place, his psychoanalytic approach is very close to my own, and allows him to discern issues of textuality and intersubjectivity which will be the focus of this chapter'. A Lacanian / Kristevan reading of the early poetry, which does not use the poetry to psychoanalyse Thomas, is Rhian Bubear's '"The World of Words": A Post-Freudian Rereading of Dylan Thomas's Early Poetry', unpublished PhD thesis, University of Swansea, 2011.

120 Keith Tuma, *Fishing by Obstinate Isles: Modern and Postmodern British Poetry and American Readers* (Evanston, IL: Northwestern University Press, 1998); Andrew Duncan, *The Failure of Conservatism in Modern British Poetry* (Cambridge: Salt, 2003); *Centre and Periphery in Modern British Poetry* (Liverpool: Liverpool University Press, 2005); *Origins of the Underground: British Poetry between Apocryphon and Incident Light, 1933–79* (Cambridge: Salt, 2008); *The Council of Heresy: A Primer of Poetry in a Balkanised Terrain* (Exeter: Shearsman, 2009); *The Long 1950s: Morality and Fantasy as Stakes in the Poetic Game* (Bristol: Shearsman, 2012); Anthony Mellors, *Late Modernist Poetics: From Pound to Prynne* (Manchester: Manchester University Press, 2005).

121 As I discuss in Chapter 4 and the Conclusion, Keery challenges the Movement-derived double-bluff concerning the 1940s 'whereby the Apocalypse [poets of the 1940s] could be denied intrinsic interest yet identified with an entire decade', with the only legitimate critical task being to retrieve a few individuals from the rubble. See James Keery, 'Menacing Works in my Isolation', eds. John Kerrigan and Peter Robinson, *The Thing About Roy Fisher* (Liverpool: Liverpool University Press, 2000), p. 78, fn. 11.

122 For a brief account of the variety and achievements of 1940s poetry, see Goodby, 'Dylan Thomas and the Poetry of the 1940s', ed. Michael O'Neill, *The Cambridge History of English Poetry* (Cambridge: Cambridge University Press, 2010), pp. 858–78.

123 See Marina MacKay, *Modernism and World War II* (Cambridge: Cambridge University Press, 2007); Leo Mellor, *Reading the Ruins: Modernism, Bombsites and British Culture* (Cambridge: Cambridge University Press, 2011). The phrase is MacKay's. I gratefully acknowledge a debt to Leo Mellor for his generosity in making a copy of his ground-breaking study available to me.

124 Thus, Tony Lopez goes to great lengths to minimise the links between Thomas and W. S. Graham (even though Graham made no secret of them) in his pioneering study, *The Poetry of W. S. Graham* (Edinburgh: Edinburgh University Press, 1989).

125 Stewart Crehan, '"The Lips of Time"', eds. John Goodby and Chris Wigginton, *Dylan Thomas: A New Casebook*, p. 59.

126 Louis Althusser, 'Contradiction and Overdetermination', ed. Louis Althusser, *For Marx* (London: Verso, 1985).

CHAPTER ONE

'Eggs laid by tigers': process and the politics of mannerist modernism

The social importance of lyric poetry ... may not focus directly on the so-called social perspective or the social interests of the work of their authors. Instead, it must discover how the entirety of a society, conceived as an internally contradictory unity, is manifested in the work of art, in what way [it] remains subject to society and in what way it transcends it. In philosophical terms, the approach must be an immanent one.

– Theodor Adorno.[1]

The appearance of Dylan here seems to be an unintegrated tradition.

– Jeffrey Ganz.[2]

'The Rimbaud of Cwmdonkin Drive'? Becoming a modernist

Dylan Thomas famously exploded onto the London literary scene with the publication of 'The force that through the green fuse drives the flower' in *The Sunday Referee* on 29 October 1933. A month later, Sir Richard Rees, the editor of *The Adelphi*, would write to the nineteen-year-old Thomas to inform him that poems he had submitted were too good for his journal and that he was passing them on to T. S. Eliot, via Herbert Read, for possible publication in *The Criterion*. William Empson later recalled that 'What hit the town of London was the child Dylan publishing "The force that through the green fuse" ... from that day he was a famous poet', adding: 'Thus began the Dylan Thomas revolt against the political poetry of the thirties, with Auden as its most brilliant exponent, in favour of a poetry of magic, religion, guilt or a world of personal relations'.[3] 'The force' was followed by the publication of 'Light breaks where no sun shines' in *The Listener* in March 1934, which drew enquiries to the editor about its author from Eliot and

Geoffrey Grigson (and, in a sign of things to come, complaints from readers about its 'obscenity'). It confirmed Thomas's arrival on the scene, and eight more poems in the same strange and forceful style appeared in national journals over the course of 1934. On 11 December, Thomas's first collection, *18 Poems*, appeared from the Parton Press. Between this date and the appearance of *Twenty-five Poems* (1936), Thomas would establish himself as the leading voice of the youngest 'mini-generation' of British poets, although his work and its sources would remain little understood.[4] As Glyn Jones put it: 'Dylan's "influences", whatever they were, did not reveal themselves at all in his first book ... At twenty he seemed fully-equipped, entirely original, completely mature stylistically and indebted to no-one.'[5] To use his own mocking self-description, he appeared to literary London, as he did to Jones and other Anglo-Welsh writers then emerging, to be a voice from nowhere – 'the Rimbaud of Cwmdonkin Drive' (*CL*, 548).

Cwmdonkin Drive, in the Uplands suburb of Swansea, was where Thomas had been born on 27 October 1914, the second and last child of Florrie and John (D. J. or 'Jack') Thomas. He grew up in this suburb and was educated at the local grammar school, where his father was Head of English. D. J. Thomas was a thwarted poet, who read Shakespeare aloud to his son from an early age and gave him the run of his extensive personal library. The paternal example meant that Thomas was hooked on poetry early, starting to write it as a seven year old and continuing to do so throughout his years at school. Of this verse, Thomas said in 1951: 'I wrote endless imitations, though I never thought them to be imitations but, rather, wonderfully original things, like eggs laid by tigers'. He listed his models, somewhat self-deprecatingly, as 'Sir Thomas Browne, de Quincey, Henry Newbolt, the Ballads, Blake, Baroness Orczy, Marlowe, Chums, the Imagists, the Bible, Poe, Keats, Lawrence, Anon., and Shakespeare', noting elsewhere that the works which had most inspired him to write were 'nursery rhymes and folk tales, the Scottish Ballads, a few lines of hymns, the most famous Bible stories and the rhythms of the Bible, Blake's *Songs of Innocence*, and the quite incomprehensible magical majesty and nonsense of Shakespeare heard, read, and near-murdered in the first forms of my school' (*CL*, 43; *EPW*, 156–7). The *Swansea Grammar School Magazine*, which he edited in the late 1920s, is full of his accomplished verse, usually comic or commemorative of the First World War dead. It was a sample of this early rhymed poetry which Thomas sent to Robert Graves when he was about sixteen; Graves later noted, 'I wrote back to say that they were irreproachable, but that he would eventually learn to dislike them. Even experts would have been deceived by the virtuosity of Dylan Thomas's conventional and wholly artificial early poems.'[6]

At fifteen, bored by formal education and convinced of his calling as a writer, Thomas left school. It was around this time that his most intense efforts to become a poet began. From April 1930 until April 1934, he started to fair-copy and date what he considered to be his best poems in a series of school notebooks. These poems marked a break with the 'conventional' juvenile verse he had perfected; four rhymed poems in the first notebook were crossed out and the notebook was titled 'Mainly Free Verse Poems'. Between July 1931 and December 1932, he worked as a cub reporter with the *South Wales Evening Post*, but his late teens were preoccupied by his writing, which included short stories, as well as poems (a single notebook filled with these stories survives). This period was uneventful, although his father's diagnosis of cancer of the mouth in late 1933 had a strong impact on his son and left its mark on the poems in the fourth notebook. However, drastic treatment (radium needles inserted into the tumour) saved D. J. Thomas, who lived for another twenty years. By November 1934, with both poems and stories beginning to appear regularly in London periodicals and the publication of *18 Poems* imminent, Dylan Thomas's occasional trips to the capital in search of work and contacts became a semi-permanent move.

In 1967, the four surviving notebooks, containing almost 200 poems, were published by Ralph Maud as *Poet in the Making*.[7] 'Eggs laid by tigers' is really a better description of these remarkable documents than of the earlier verse, recording, as they do, the stages in Thomas's poetic self-making between the ages of fifteen and nineteen, and the growth of the extraordinary *18 Poems* style. Notebooks one and two run concurrently from 27 April 1930 to June 1932, breaking at December 1930. Another notebook, now lost, covered the period from July 1932 to January 1933. The third and fourth notebooks run from February 1933 to August 1933 and from September 1933 to April 1934; it is in these that the process poetic was fashioned, between April 1933 and April 1934. This record exists not only because, unlike most poets, Thomas did not destroy his apprentice work, but also because he frequently returned to it after 1934, sometimes to retrieve entire poems for minor overhauls, but more often to quarry phrases and ideas out of which new poems were generated. This process did not finally come to an end until 1941, when Thomas sold the notebooks.[8] As well as the notebooks, much of the correspondence from this period between Thomas and a number of friends who were fellow writers (Trevor Hughes, Glyn Jones and Pamela Hansford Johnson) has also survived. In these, we find Thomas discussing his poetry in a candid way; the letters to Johnson, for example, written between September 1933 and April 1934, are particularly informative and frank and account for ninety pages of the *Collected Letters*.

It would be natural, given the unusual wealth of material dating from the most crucial period of development, to expect that it would be relatively easy to shed a good deal of light on the origins and development of Thomas's distinctive style and his 'process poetic'. But, in fact, it is surprisingly difficult to do so. The poems entered in the notebooks before spring 1933 are impressive for the age of their author, but not for much else. Between April 1930 and April 1933, the development in technique is noticeable, but not great. The three years of poetry opened up some of the veins of imagery which would be intensified and fused together in the earliest, most rudimentary process poems, which date from April and May 1933, but many of the definitive original features developed in the months after mid-1933 and, even then, often in ways which are not immediately apparent, if at all. Similarly, while the letters tell us a lot about Thomas's beliefs and what he thought he was trying to say in his poems, they don't show him consciously identifying, seeking out and integrating the distinctive components of *18 Poems* – biomorphism, Joycean wordplay, post-Einsteinian and Darwinian viewpoints, surrealism, the gothic-grotesque, literary sources such as the Bible, Bunyan, Blake, Caradoc Evans, the Metaphysical poets, D. H. Lawrence and the rest. His discussions of his character-istically overdetermined style occur after innovation has occurred and are too broad-brush or too minutely-focused to shed much light on the whys and wherefores of evolution; sadly, there are no sketches of aims or intentions. One result of this is that there has been very little critical discussion of the most crucial phase of Thomas's poetic development.[9]

Glyn Jones's point about 'influences' requires some qualification at this point. In the first two notebooks, Thomas's models are actually clear enough. The poems reflect a slightly dated, nineteen-teens notion of modernism written largely in short-line irregular *vers libre*, generally unrhymed and take as their models the Imagists, early Yeats, Richard Aldington and Sacheverell Sitwell. Writing to Henry Treece in 1938, characterising *all* of the notebook poems, Thomas found in them 'the Elizabethans and George Peele, Webster, and, later, Beddoes, some Clare (his hard country sonnets), Lawrence (animal poems, and the verse extracts from The Plumed Serpent), a bit of Tennyson, some very bad Flecker and ... bits from whatever fashionable poetry – Imagists, Sitwells – I'd been reading recently' (*CL*, 343) – that is, very few of the models which Thomas spoke of as imitating as a child and young teenager, quoted above. The notebook poems were initially light and rather whimsically decadent in tone – usually about imaginary love affairs and mythological subjects – but, in mid-1931, they acquired a darker, brooding, more subjective tone, although this did not cause any stylistic alteration. By February 1933, a new social-satirical strain had arrived, which Thomas attempted to conjoin with the brooding, sexually charged one. Near the end of the second notebook, Thomas had begun to use rhyme more often (its title, also 'Mainly Free Verse Poems', was crossed out, perhaps because of this). By 1933, he was using rhyme extensively, although the irregular *vers libre* metrical template was still standard. Then, from April 1933 onwards, he also started – tentatively at first – to use regular stanza forms.

This is the point at which the development of the process style really begins. The first poem to have the characteristic concerns *and* the formal compression of the process poems was 'And death shall have no dominion', which is undated, but sandwiched between poems dated 2 and 16 April (as I discuss below, we also know the circumstances under which it was composed). For the next three months, Thomas continued the free verse-based blends of social and subjective styles which had been in place in February, but also attempted further traditional-shaped lyrics, which try to repeat the success of 'And death shall have no dominion' – the best being '"Find meat on bones"' of 15 July. These poems further developed aspects of the process poetic before the next wholly successful lyric in the mode – 'Before I knocked and flesh let enter' – appeared on 6 September. Such fully accomplished poems now appeared at shorter intervals – 'My hero bares his nerves' on 17 September, 'The force that through the green fuse drives the flower' on 12 October, 'When once the twilight locks' on 11 November, 'Light breaks where no sun shines' on 20 November and so on. In all, thirteen of the poems of *18 Poems*, dating from between 6 September and 30 April 1934 – the date of the last poem entered in it ('If I were tickled by the rub of love') – derive from the fourth notebook.[10]

As Thomas's poetry became darker in tone from mid-1931 onwards, new literary influences made their mark. The social realist, political style, announced in Michael Roberts's trend-setting anthologies *New Signatures* (April 1932) and *New Country* (April 1933), had an influence on the appearance of social themes, while the Bible, Welsh Nonconformist hymns and pulpit oratory informed a series of anguished enquiries into faith in 1932–3. A list of books at Cwmdonkin Drive drawn up for Johnson around Christmas 1933 shows the impressive range of resources that Thomas had immediately to hand at this stage; his father's library was 'full of all the accepted stuff, from Chaucer to Henry James; all the encyclopaedias and books of reference, all Saintsbury, and innumerable books on the theory of literature. ... My books, on the other hand, are nearly all poetry ... I have the collected poems of Manley Hopkins, Stephen Crane, Yeats, de la Mare, Osbert Sitwell, Wilfred Owen, W. H. Auden, & T. S. Eliot; volumes of poetry by Aldous Huxley, Sacheverell & Edith Sitwell, Edna St. Vincent Millay, D. H. Lawrence, Humbert Wolfe, Sassoon, and Harold Munro; most of the ghastly Best Poems of the Year; two of the Georgian Anthologies, one of the Imagist Anthologies, "Whips & Scorpions" (modern satiric verse), the London Mercury Anthology, the Nineties Anthology ... ; a volume of Cambridge Poetry [including Empson] & Oxford Undergraduate Poetry [including Auden and Spender]; most of Lawrence, most of Joyce, with the exception of Ulysses, all Gilbert Murray's Greek translations, some Shaw, a little Virginia Woolf, & some E. M. Forster' (*CL*, 93–4). To these could be added the many authors referred to in his letters – James Thomson and Francis Thompson, Swinburne, Dreiser, Wolfe, Whitman, Christina Rossetti, e. e. cummings, Gertrude Stein, Wyndham Lewis, Pound and others.

Many of these appear, at times, to hover around the work; I say 'appear' because when we read *18 Poems*, what we feel is that, as Nicholas Moore put it as early as 1948, 'Mr. Thomas's first poems are positively silly with references, and one could spend a whole essay on the analysis of a few lines (any few lines)', but these are hard to specify or pin down.[11] Allusions are approximate – by rhythm only, perhaps – or are disguised by their unusual contexts. Thomas's voice – one of the most distinctive in twentieth-century poetry – seems to dissolve under close inspection into any number of not-quite-definable components. This may be because he 'bulldozed' his way through literature in an unorthodox way: 'The thin erudition of the previous [Auden] generation, the result of judicious schooling and back numbers of *The Criterion*, seem[s] idle stuff beside his wolfing down of books', as Kenneth Rexroth put it.[12] It may also be because of the influence of non-literary material: popular science, religious writing, myth and legend, philosophy, jazz and film magazines and film itself. Something of the uncertainty is crystallised in the debate, never resolved, as to whether (or when) Thomas had read Rimbaud and the French symbolist poets, the surrealists, Hopkins and Hart Crane, or if he was aware of the traditional Welsh metrical forms collectively referred to as *cynghanedd*.[13] All have been adduced as sources for Thomas's style, and Thomas denied all of them at some point or another. The only thing it is safe to say is that if it seems he knew about something, he probably did, and that critics have habitually underestimated the range of his reading.

But there is more to Thomas's precocious development than unorthodox and copious reading. Reading, for a start, is not writing, let alone the creation of an original style. More importantly, it is not the 'sources' or 'influences' themselves so much as Thomas's *manner* of using them which is truly distinctive. As we have seen, Thomas played along with the modernist game of parading influence, but in ways which sent both it, and himself, up. His poetry does something similar. We would recognise, say, *The Merchant of Venice* when 'All all and all' mentions a 'pound of flesh', but the poem also has a 'pound of lava' and its 'flesh' is 'mechanical', making us wonder how Shakespearean concerns with justice and mercy might feature, if at all (*CP*, 29–30). Similarly, the line 'Light breaks where no sun shines' echoes Wilfred Owen's 'Foreheads of men have bled where no wounds were' (from 'Strange Meeting'), but this adds to the poem's resonance in ways which are not easy to discern (*CP*, 23). 'The hand that signed the paper felled a city' adapts Jonathan Swift's line 'The hand that sign'd the mortgage paid the shot' in his 'An Elegy on the Much Lamented Death of Mr Demar, the Famous Rich Man', yet knowing this adds nothing essential to an understanding of Thomas's poem; more to the point, who knows the Swift line? (*CP*, 51) Thomas's approach to literary property and propriety is both defensively subaltern and brazenly authoritative and gives a new twist to Eliot's famous dictum that 'Immature poets imitate; mature poets steal; bad poets deface what they take, and good poets make it into something better ... . The good poet welds his theft into a whole of feeling which is unique, utterly different from that which it was torn.'[14] As with the buried allusions to Keats, Stein, Brooke and others in 'There was a saviour', as identified by Winifred Nowottny and mentioned in the Introduction, it is the mixture of blatancy and obscurity – of the blatantly obscure and the obscurely blatant – which is of the essence. Thomas's poetry seems unusually intertextual, murmurous with other works that we cannot quite identify or identify all too easily, emphasising the fact that texts exist at the intersection of other texts. Yet, at the same time, it sounds strikingly original, and the unnerving blend of secondhandness and originality is reflected in the way that it seems at once both highly confessional and mythically impersonal.

This helps to explain why its first readers found *18 Poems* impressive, yet hard to place. However, it only begins to touch on the other aspects of the process poetic that I have mentioned and wish to explore further in this chapter. Hitherto, explanations for the emergence of the process style in the summer of 1933 have been confined, more or less, to biography – to a response to surroundings and a desire to escape provincialism. They tell us next to nothing about how Thomas moved from 'And death shall have no dominion' in April 1933 to stylistic take-off in late August and early September and how he then further developed the process poetic between September 1933 and April 1934, let alone in the period between the end of the notebooks and the publication of *18 Poems*. If, as Walford Davies claims, 'And death shall have no dominion' was the first process poem, and an effective and memorable one at that, (it was Thomas's first publication in a national journal, appearing in the *New English Weekly* on 18 May), why was it excluded from *18 Poems*? Conversely, why *did* Thomas include it, with some other poems of March to August 1933, in his second collection, *Twenty-five Poems*? To turn this question round: why does Ralph Maud think that it was *not* the first process poem and that that honour should go to the later '"Find meat on bones"' of 15 July 1933? Another crucial issue – the answer to which bears on the treatment of 'And death shall have no dominion' – concerns establishing precisely when the *theme* of process entered the language of the poems and became their *substance*, as wordplay, pun and so on.

In attempting to answer these questions, I do not pretend to be able to give complete or definitive answers. Although his poetic self-making was a major subject of the notebook poems, this self-making also involved Thomas covering his tracks, at which task he proved to be very good indeed. Much of what happened has to be inferred. However, it is now possible to use new models of modernism and Thomas's social, cultural and historical contexts to offer a more coherent explanation of what happened in the third and fourth notebooks than has hitherto been possible. In what follows, I discuss the parallel crises of high modernism and the Great Depression and Thomas's response to them, before describing how various components of the process poetic were tested out. There is particular emphasis on stylistic matters, since, for all the talk of Thomas's 'craft', the question of the valorisation of craftsmanship, the *ideology* of form, we might say, has been almost wholly neglected. I then discuss Thomas's relationship to New Country poetry and Eliot's criticism – two of the most salient contemporary components of his style. I shall try to show that attention to the development of Thomas's 'dialectical method' in the evolution of his process poetic leads to a qualification of Empson's claim that he was in 'revolt against' political verse. Rather, in paring the lyric back to its generic essentials, Thomas reinscribed the political at the level of language and the embodied mind, so that its apocalyptic-prophetic mood cut to the quick of its times, and its textual toughness matched a moment when historical causality itself had suddenly grown menacingly opaque.

Mannerist modernism

In 'Modern Poetry', an essay published in the *Swansea Grammar School Magazine* in 1929, the fifteen-year-old Dylan Thomas had presciently observed: 'No poet can find sure ground; he is hunting for it, with the whole earth perturbed and unsettled about him. To-day is a transitional period' (*EPW*, 85–6). He identified the difficulty facing a young poet in search of a modern style between 1929 and 1933, namely the impossibility of avoiding, and the hopelessness of emulating, the achievements of high modernism. As modernist formalism intensified during the late 1920s in the hands of a few established practitioners (notably in *A Draft of XXX Cantos* and *Work in Progress*), their succession seemed to founder.[15] The most appealing of the high modernists to the young, D. H. Lawrence, died in 1930, which was the year that sealed Eliot's turn to conservatism in poetic form with the poem of his conversion to Anglicanism, *Ash Wednesday*. Auden's *Poems*, also of 1930, offered a model for young poets, but he was not yet as influential as he would become. The Georgians had dissipated as a coherent grouping, but individual survivors – including Walter de la Mare and Robert Graves – were still active and respected. On the one hand, several versions of the avant-garde were available, from the sound poetry of Edith Sitwell's *Façade* (1927) to Gertrude Stein and the surrealists, while, on the other, Kipling was still active (he did not die until 1936). To further complicate the transition between high modernist and New Country styles, Yeats had recently published *The Tower* (1928) and was at the height of his powers.

The outcomes of this poetic flux were profoundly shaped by the deepening social and political crisis. The Wall Street Crash of October 1929 brought about a crisis in global capitalism and worldwide political instability. While Soviet Russia offered the alternative of a planned economy, it was apparent to many sympathisers with the aims of 1917 that the revolution was beginning to devour its own children and that freedom of thought and expression were, in fact, being suppressed. In Britain, between 1931 and 1933, unemployment rose to a historic high of three-and-a-half million. The first majority Labour Government was split by Ramsay MacDonald's defection to form a National Government and means testing of the dole was introduced; there were even protests in the British navy, leading, at one point, to outright mutiny, over pay cuts. In the US, where the economic situation was even worse, the immediate literary response was not social realism, as we retrospectively tend to believe, but a hybrid and uncertain style, which Marjorie Perloff has dubbed 'mannerist modernism':

> The shift that takes place at the turn of the decade is one from the modernist preoccupation with form – in the sense of imagistic or symbolist structure, dominated by a lyric 'I' – to the questioning of representation itself. Discourse now becomes increasingly referential, but reference does not go hand in hand with the expected mimesis. Rather, the boundaries between the 'real' and the 'fantastic' become oddly blurred. The taste for the 'natural', as in Pound's insistence that 'the natural object is always the adequate symbol', gives way to artifice and a marked taste for abstraction and conceptualisation. In the same vein, irony – so central to modernist poetics – gives way to the parodic, but even parody is not often sustained, with abrupt tonal shifts and reversals in mood becoming quite usual. Indeed, this 'time of tension' … exhibits a mannerist style as distinct from its modernist antecedents as from the socialist realism to come.[16]

This form of modernism is one of the 'alternative modernisms' complicating traditional 'Men of 1914' and 1922-centred accounts, which I mentioned briefly in my Introduction, and it has British equivalents, it seems to me, in the Auden of *The Orators: An English Study* (1932) and the Thomas of *18 Poems* (1934). Following Gabriel Pearson, it makes sense to regard Auden and Thomas as fellow-members of the same 'spiritually orphaned generation', responding to its likely historical fate with 'nervy apocalyptic jokiness'. Where the two differed was in their formal response and attitude to high modernism. In England, a modernist moment had already occurred in the wake of *The Waste Land* (1922). Attempts to replicate its innovative techniques in the later 1920s by younger poets were unconvincing, but under the impact of the early 1930 crisis, modernism's radical attitude to form seems to have exerted a final, fleeting attraction on emergent poets. Auden, however, soon abandoned experimentalism, and it was the more discursive aspects of his early style which were absorbed by the poets around him in both *New Signatures* and *New Country*.[17] The New Country style and its three chief modes, as listed by MacNeice in 1935 – 'the topical, the gnomic, the heroic' – were established as *the* 'modern' poetic mode by 1934–35, ending the stylistic hiatus.[18] It was soon widely regarded as the only appropriate response to crisis and looming catastrophe; as Perloff notes, 'Pound's "make it new!" could hardly be the watchword of a poetic generation ... that understood that the "new" was by no means equivalent to the true, much less the good and the beautiful.'[19]

For the New Country poets, this meant adopting traditional verse forms, which could be infused with radical social content and made to carry an argument, analysis or allegorical narrative more unambiguously than modernist parataxis and collage. A greater subordination of the medium to the message was suddenly required. As MacNeice again noted in 1938: 'Most of the younger generation [of English poets] ... returned to more regular forms [than Eliot's] while trying to be their masters, not their slaves.'[20] Modernist radicalism was thus absorbed by these poets, largely as a *thematics* of modernity. Auden claimed: 'For gasworks and dried tubers I forsook / The clock at Grantchester, the English rook' and read *The Waste Land* as 'a directly political statement – a *literal* account of contemporary Britain', while Cecil Day Lewis described it as a 'social document'.[21] But MacNeice's 'trying' honestly registers the problems that the divorce between form and content required. On the one hand, the new straightforwardness could not embody the fractured disjunctiveness of the contemporary scene as faithfully as high modernist techniques, while, on the other, the 'more regular forms', as they came to be applied as a matter of course, increasingly made their users 'slaves' to their formal banality.

At first sight, the teenage Dylan Thomas would seem to have been damagingly isolated from these English developments, hampered by his position on 'the furthest peaks of the literary world' (*CL*, 41). Because of the very recent emergence of Anglo-Welsh literature, by 1930 Welsh literary modernism had only occurred in the fiction of Caradoc Evans, and it had seemed to pass Wales by completely during the 1920s. There was potential for a poetic modernism in Wales, however. From the beginning of his notebooks, Thomas was committed to *vers libre* as the sign of poetic modernity, but if this embrace of the formal possibilities of modernism was more timid than could have been found elsewhere, he nevertheless had greater scope than in those places where modernism was regarded as passé. His marginal location gave him free rein to forge a mannerist modernism, which mapped the turbid and involuted condition of his own adolescent subjectivity (he was seven years younger than Auden and MacNeice, ten years younger than Day Lewis) onto the literary interregnum and early 1930s social crisis – this being intensified in Wales by the collapse of the half-century-old Nonconformist-Liberal party alliance in the 1920s. The overdetermined complexity of the layerings of self, language and literary discourses which resulted were what raised Thomas's work above the provincial or post-pubertal and gave it far greater resonance, significance and appeal.

Already, in late 1931, the notebook poems were beginning to reflect Thomas's exploration of the Nonconformist imaginary, with its repression and displacement figured in poems concerning faith, illness, heredity, sex, suicide and death. During 1932, he began to yoke this glowering, gothic strain to the growing social crisis, following the example of the Auden-influenced poets. The political scene at the time was one of near-total reaction and paralysis as already noted. The defining moment for the younger generation, in politics, as in poetry, was Hitler's seizure of power in Germany on 30 January 1933. This was when, as Thomas's contemporary Francis Scarfe put it, they realised that they had been 'born into one war and fattened for another'.[22] For the New Country poets, it required a renunciation of individualism and experiment; for Thomas, lacking upper-middle class guilt, living where the 'bourgeois' subject was still, in any case, a problematic entity (who and what were the 'Anglo-Welsh', who were only now finding their literary voice?), something differently apocalyptic was required. His response, both more full-blooded and more oblique, arose from the understanding that, suddenly, the only certainties were 'bodily existence and its answering state of mind', both of which were threatened with destruction.[23] His work accordingly bypassed the dominant poetic response as superficial and sought out the deeper linguistic-somatic roots of the self, attempting to recreate the frozen dialectic of history at the level of poetic form in a poetry of process.

Of course, the need for this response was not immediately obvious. Thomas's initial instinct was to define the alienated protagonists of his poems in relation to the social world, although the gap between their sense of looming apocalypse and society's obliviousness made retreat, madness and suicide seem the only authentic actions: 'The suicides parade again, now ripe for dying', as a poem of late February 1933 concludes (*NP*, 135). This passive and marginalised subject, who views society in abject, derivative terms as he fends off insanity, is the speaker of 'That sanity be kept' (August 1933):

That sanity be kept I sit at open windows,
Regard the sky, make unobtrusive comment on the moon,
Sit at open windows in my shirt,
And let the traffic pass, the signals shine,
The engines run, the brass bands keep in tune,
For sanity must be preserved.

Thinking of death, I sit and watch the park
Where children play in all their innocence,
And matrons, on the littered grass,
Absorb the daily sun.

The sweet suburban music from a hundred lawns
Comes softly to my ears. The English mowers mow and mow.

I mark the couples walking arm in arm,
Observe their smiles,
Sweet invitations and inventions,
See them lend love illustration
By gesture and grimace.
I watch them curiously, detect beneath the laughs
What stands for grief, a vague bewilderment
At things not turning right.

I sit at open windows in my shirt,
Observe, like some Jehovah of the west,
What passes by, that sanity be kept. (*NP*, 226–7)

Reviewing *18 Poems* in 1935, Desmond Hawkins would remark that one of its major achievements was its fusion of the two leading poetic voices of the time, but in terms favourable to Thomas:

> [T]he Audenesque convention is nearly ended; and I credit Dylan Thomas with being the first considerable poet to break through fashionable limitation and speak an unborrowed language, without excluding anything that has preceded him. ... He is a grateful heir to Eliot's magical sense of the macabre and to Auden's textual firmness, but by inheritance rather than by imitation ... Airmen and pylons are no longer stewed to a smooth fluency. ... [Mr Thomas] is at present obsessed with the vocabulary of physiology in its more sinister aspect, and he is apt to repeat certain block-phrases of a private code of thought. These are minor faults, however, and they vanish in the achievement of fusing metaphysical poetry into sensuous terms.[24]

Hawkins was perfectly correct concerning the originality and authority of Thomas's 'fusing', even if he underestimated the longevity of

'Audenesque convention'. However, 'That sanity be kept' strikes the reader forcefully now, precisely because it is *not* such a 'fusing'. On the contrary, it presents a sorry domesticated version of the gaze of Auden's 'helmeted airman' and abjectly echoes Eliot's 'Morning at the Window'. Its mannerist modernism, we might say, is merely derivative, its textures and rhythms flaccid and unconvincing. It contains several of the basic ingredients of the process poems of *18 Poems* – appearance versus reality, sexual angst, fear of death and madness, suicidal gloom – but Auden's 'firmness' and Eliot's 'macabre' are inertly juxtaposed.[25] In 'That sanity be kept', Thomas is still clearly a too-'grateful heir', whose materials have not yet melded in his parodic, morbidly exultant and verbally playful signature style. The final self-deprecatory identification with 'Jehovah' – so different from the powerful biblical identities of poems such as 'Before I knocked' – acts to emphasise dependency. To Pamela Hansford Johnson, Thomas apologetically opined that his Jehovah-pose was 'really odd', adding 'if I were some Apollo it would be different' (*CL*, 40). His discomfort confirms the sense that the poem's real subject is the figure of the marginal writer 'of the West' gazing towards the metropolis, seeking recognition from the 'English mowers', the New Country poets at their 'sweet suburban music' making lyrical hay while the sun shines and he looks impotently on. The very idiom of his weak protest is indebted to them.

Yet, since April 1933, Thomas, we know, had been writing poems which did precisely 'fuse', to some degree, Auden's 'firmness' and Eliot's 'magical sense'. Indeed, just seven weeks after 'That sanity be kept' appeared in *The Sunday Referee* on 3 September, the same journal would publish 'The force that through the green fuse drives the flower', in which Eliot's 'hanging man', Auden's driving rhythm and shapely form, together with much else, conjoined in one of the master-lyrics of the decade. Flaccid confessionalism was replaced by a gleefully bleak *performance* of abjection in a parodic appropriation of the very verse forms that Thomas had previously renounced in defining himself as a modern poet. What he had come to grasp over the summer of 1933 was a way of recreating the modernist lyric by stripping off its social surfaces and its encrustations of superficial signs of the 'modern', drawing on the sophisticated primitivism of Lawrence and Joyce's verbal energy. In this work, the bodily and psychic drives bypassed the social realm to rediscover their connection to what Allen Ginsberg – another Blakean poet – would call 'the ancient heavenly dynamo' of the earth, water, vegetative and cosmic cycles.[26] The knowledge lacked by the grammar school-educated, suburban, petit bourgeois Thomas, cut off from his parents' Welsh language and culture and from the public school- and university-educated metropolitan literary world, was rendered superfluous as he forced his entry into the hegemonic English literary culture which had been chosen for him, and even personified, by his father. Necessity became a virtue, marginality reconfigured as advantage and belatedness turned into an asset by the fusion of current styles. Irony and satire were replaced by the gothic-grotesque as a mode of critique, modernist disjunction compressed within traditional forms, these forms rendered in an exaggeratedly punctilious syntax and a language as mutable as the processes it described.

Thomas's relationship to modernism meant that he had a keen sense of its innately parodic aspect and clearly understood what Rainer Emig calls 'the greatest structure of all, the modernist myth of itself'.[27] 'A Letter to my Aunt, Discussing the Correct Approach to Modern Poetry' is a versified DIY manual of modernism sent to Johnson in 1933, which breezily mocks, among others, Pound, Lawrence, cummings, Gascoyne, Auden and avant-garde fashions, offering advice on 'how to scale and see the sights / From modernist Parnassian heights', before concluding:

> Remember, too, that life is hell,
> And even heaven has a smell
> Of putrefying angels who
> Make deadly whoopee in the blue.
> These things remembered, who can stop
> A poet going to the top? (*CL*, 86)

This is modernism as tourist spectacle, blending careerist knowingness with fascination at the decay of high modernism. 'Deadly whoopee' perfectly sums up the calculated morbidities and *lèse-majestés* – the reverence for modernism's authority *and* mocking appropriation of its aura – of *18 Poems*.

A good example of these parodic tactics is 'Now', written in 1935. Thomas told Vernon Watkins that 'so far as he knew, [it] had no meaning at all', but rejected his friend's suggestion that it should be dropped from *Twenty-five Poems*: 'Let them [the reviewers] have a bone', he replied (*LVW*, 16).[28] The first stanza runs:

> Now,
> Say nay,
> Man dry man,
> Dry lover mine
> The deadrock base and blow the flowered anchor,

Should he, for centre sake, hop in the dust,
Forsake, the fool, the hardiness of anger. (*CP*, 45)

This stanza hints at Dada, *zaum* and nonsense poetry, and Thomas's friend Trevor Hughes took it to be a burlesque in the style of Gertrude Stein. But, like Watkins, Hughes was wrong to assume that it was written 'with little serious intent', and it certainly had 'a meaning', despite Thomas's dismissal.[29] 'Now' is a cod avant-garde poem, which mimics experimental form and transrationalism. The main verbs – 'say', 'mine' and 'forsake' – are disguised. Once this is grasped, the poem reads as the soliloquy of a Hamlet-like figure trying to argue himself into turning his suicidal anger outwards against the world. The speaker adjures his potentially suicidal self (the 'dry lover') to 'Say nay' to his aridity ('dry') and 'mine' (blow up) 'the deadrock' self (a play on 'bedrock'). This will allow 'the flowered anchor' (hope, the life-giving ocean) to 'blow' (blossom), should the negative 'he' of line six (a superego figure) lose his temper and hop (like Rumpelstiltskin) in the dust 'for centre sake' (that is, for the sake of his tyrannical self-centredness). 'Forsake', he reiterates, the 'fool'-self and his inner-directed, self-destructive anger. In the second stanza, the use of 'handsaw' confirms the figure of Hamlet as a clue to the speaker's state of mind. Thomas's parodic stance is chiefly apparent in the odd-looking stanza, which closer examination shows to be impeccably conventional at heart: if added together, the first four lines make a single iambic pentameter, yielding a regular quatrain (of alternate ten- and eleven-syllable lines) rhyming 'anchor' / 'anger'.

Nothing reveals the value of formal patterning to the development of Thomas's poetry more clearly than this witty manipulation of readerly expectations. 'Now' offers a lively simulacrum of avant-garde style, which is at once a mockery and tribute to it; it is a parody of an avant-garde poem and an avant-garde poem *as* parody. It is a reminder that Edmund Wilson, announcing the end of high modernism in *Axel's Castle* (1931), had declared that: '[i]t is not merely that these modern novelists and poets [Yeats, Proust, Valery, Eliot, Joyce, Stein] build upon their predecessors, as the greatest writers have in all times, but that they have developed a weakness for recapitulating them in parodies'.[30] Similarly, Thomas Mann's fictional composer, Adrian Leverkühn, would proclaim that modern art must, of necessity, be made out of creative parody. In the summer of 1933, Thomas learnt how to exploit that 'weakness' or 'of necessity' in various ways as part of his process vision – itself a parodic version of the more elaborate constructs (the gyres of *A Vision*, Joyce's Viconian cycles, etc.) of his modernist predecessors.

Many elements produced Thomas's process poetic, but they entered his work at different times and with differing emphases. The body-centred death-hauntedness appeared as early as 1932, for example, but did not rise above adolescent morbidity until it was given a social dimension in the first half of 1933. It then had to slough off this social aspect for a cosmic-apocalyptic one between April and July 1933, in order to realise its full potential in a more universal vision of the human predicament. Developed still further, it imparted a gothic-grotesque twist to Thomas's brand of modernist metaphysical lyric, trespassing on surrealist territory as it flowered in his most experimental work from 1935 to 1937. Similarly, in the second and third notebooks, it is possible to discern the tentative emergence of an interest in the materiality of words and, 'working from' them, an interest in wordplay and pun, desultory at first, then becoming structural, focusing and intensifying several strands of the poems from September to October 1933 at the start of the fourth notebook. In summer 1933, Thomas had already begun to *perform* the self, creating dramatic scenarios and confrontations, in order to obtain a vantage point beyond conventional Romantic confessionalism. This wrestling with the lyric 'I' – so central to modernism – can be linked, in turn, to the gothic-grotesque and hybrid Anglo-Welsh aspect of Thomas's modernism and finds an outlet in a fascination with origins – of the self, the body and the poem – and with the question of mortality and immortality. Religion interested Thomas, because he was in revolt against its Welsh form, Nonconformism. Yet as the poems of autumn 1933 show, this was not so much because he was a believer, as because he believed in belief. He refused a purely mechanistic atheism, using Christ as a symbol for human potential. Several popular scientists of the day – some of whom, like Alfred North Whitehead, were certainly read by Thomas – tried to reconcile the paradoxes of religious faith with those of determinism and the relativism of contemporary science. Thomas, it seems to me, was not interested in a faith-based reconciliation so much as the possibility of a fusion of the material and spiritual, especially as it could be figured microcosmically, the human body as the universe. I will now sketch out how these elements appeared and became part of the process style, focusing first on the role of traditional form in the breakthrough of April to September 1933 and then on the year or so following it in the fourth notebook and afterwards, when that breakthrough was further developed in more ambitiously biomorphic, surrealist and linguistically playful works.

The process poetic I: the first three notebooks

It is a striking feature of Thomas's process style that some of its elements were sounded very early indeed; this was why he was able to return so often to the notebooks. By December 1930, for example, in the prototype of 'How shall my animal', reworked in the mid-1930s, we find a poem about poetry (*NP*, 59–60). By May 1932, in the second notebook, Thomas was so adept in this vein, that he could record the first version of 'The hunchback in the park' substantially similar to the final version of 1941, but directly linking (in the line 'It is a poem and it is a woman figure') the hunchback and the poet (*NP*, 110). As noted above, the anatomy of Nonconformist repression started early, too – around July 1931. A key moment in the turn away from the filigree, rather fey style of the first notebook is the second notebook's 'XLIX' of 26 October 1931:

> Never to reach the oblivious dark
> And not to know
> Any man's troubles nor your own –
> Negatives impress negation,
> Empty of light and find the darkness lit –
> Never is nightmare,
> Never flows out from the wound of sleep
> Staining the broken brain
> With knowledge that no use and nothing worth
> Still's vain to argue after death;
> No use to run your head against the wall
> To find a sweet blankness in the blood and shell,
> This pus runs deep.
> There's poison in your red wine, drinker,
> Which spreads down to the dregs
> Leaving a corrupted vein of colour,
> Sawdust beneath the skirts;
> On every hand the evil's positive
> For dead or live ... (*NP*, 99)

The Beddoes-tinged, existential dramatic tenor of these lines is effective, because it is compelling in its comprehensiveness; adolescent angst and sexual obsession hint at the larger forces of Nonconformist repression and an ingrown society. But it is not just the negativity that is notable; negation as such – the nothing which is a something, 'never' as a noun, the double negative – also fascinates Thomas, and it was to become the basis of the rhetorical structure of many later poems. There is even a hint of the later penchant for wordplay in the anagrammatic 'live' / 'evil' of the last two lines. Similarly, 'XLI' (of 12 September 1931) opens with the kind of parodic Donnean catechism (mocking the intellectual desire to 'know' natural mysteries) which would feature in 'My world is pyramid' and 'Altarwise by owl-light' in 1934–5:

> Why is the blood red and the grass green
> Shan't be answered till the voice is still
> That drieth the veins with its moan
> Of man and his meaning ... (*NP*, 94)

Yet for all this development of basic themes and sophisticated self-reflex-iveness, the poetry of 1931–2 usually lacks conviction and impact. It is, of course, probably asking too much of any seventeen-year-old to expect writing more accomplished than Thomas was producing at this time. The point, however, is that – as developments eventually showed – a major reason for the weakness was the absence, at this stage, of any equivalent of his thematic and aesthetic advances at a formal level.

Form is always more than the organisation of content in good poetry; it is intimately related to the demands of the material it helps to organise. In the poems of the first two notebooks and much of the third, there is a disconnect between aesthetic sophistication and the *vers libre* technique in which it was being realised. *Vers libre* increasingly failed to articulate the growing urgencies – personal, political, linguistic – in Thomas's writing. The fact that so little has been said about this also touches on a much broader issue in English literary studies; the way in which, in reaction against New Criticism's over-concentration on technique, it has been the fashion for several decades to downplay the role of form, preferring to map poems onto contexts or modes of production in a drive to extract textual meaning. Form, however, is always ultimately a mode of perception; poems articulate 'new kinds of social and political sensibility *through* their apparently "physical" or relatively ahistorical features such as rhythm, phonetic form and textual inscription' (or rhyme) and to miss this is to overlook the history of verse styles, the 'social potentials' embedded in them and how 'structures of form are also structures of feeling' (think of the political charge of Keats's 'Cockney couplets').[31] Literature is always 'simultaneously a form of knowledge and a knowledge of form', and this is most true of poetry.[32] Although lip service is often paid to Thomas's 'craftsmanly' verse-forms, the extent to which his use of form makes meaning has been under-appreciated.

Following the gap in the notebooks' record between July 1932 and January 1933, we find that rhyme firmly established itself in Thomas's poems, although his *vers* remained metrically *libre*. A typescript poem from late 1932 – later to be 'Especially when the October wind' – rhymes throughout, before trailing off towards the end, and also displays a vague anticipation of the stanzaic organisation of the later version, before its final long verse paragraph (*NP*, 121–2). Like other poems in this typescript, it also contains some of the most explicit descriptions to date of a recognisable social world, reflecting the impact of *New Signatures* on Thomas in the missing notebook. This trend was well established by the time of the opening poems of the third notebook, in poems such as 'Four', dated 6 February 1933, the Spenglerian gloominess of which is exacerbated by mass unemployment and recent events in Germany:

> Before the gas fades with a harsh last bubble,
> And the hunt in the hat stand discovers no coppers,
> Before the last fag and the shirt sleeves and slippers,
> The century's trap will have snapped round your middle,
> Before the allotment is weeded and sown,
> And the oakum picked, and the spring trees have grown green,
> And the state falls to bits,
> And is fed to the cats,
> Before civilisation rises or rots
> (It's a matter of guts,
> Graft, poison, and bluff,
> Sobstuff, mock reason,
> The chameleon coats of the big bugs and shots),
> The jaws will have shut, and life be switched out. ... (*NP*, 127)

Pararhyme is not simply imposed here, but works within the verse texture, hinting at how it might be given greater cogency. It also tends to reinforce other forms of repetition. Thus, wishing us to notice the ingenuity of 'bubble' / 'middle', 'coppers' / 'slippers', Thomas exposes them at the end of (rough) hexameters in the first four lines. But the short fifth line shows a sudden resistance to metrical regularity – something he still treats, instinctively, as conservative. Lines seven to ten are pararhymed with monosyllabic end-rhyme, but 'bluff', following them, changes the principle of repetition by rhyming on the vowel of 'guts', rather than on the consonantal cluster. Thomas then returns to hexameters and an unrhymed end-word ('reason'), before the final return of vowel-plus-*ts* pararhyme in line thirteen with 'shots'. The result is heterogeneous – a testing of the value of rhyme and regular metre, with the agglutinative effect of rhyme suggesting the potential value of increased verbal condensation.

The apocalyptic *zeitgeist* of 'Four' is the subject of a poem from 16 and 17 February 1933, which enumerates prematurely aged youth, 'weak before we could grow strong', specimens of 'The Western man with one lung gone', 'cancerous' women, lovers 'turning on the gas' and 'Exsoldiers with horrors for a face'. It concludes with: 'We ... who have no faith' crying 'Believe, believe and be saved' (*NP*, 130–2). Over the next two months, other poems of the same kind, such as 'Fourteen' ('I have longed to move away', 1 March), 'Seventeen' ('See, on gravel paths under the harpstrung trees', 31 March) and 'Twenty' ('The ploughman's gone, the hansom driver', 28 March) oscillate rapidly between subjective intensity and external images of social crisis and between consistent and sporadic use of rhyme and a metrical norm, unable to settle on a single mode or settled formal structure. It was in this context of metrical fluidity and a poetry trying to integrate its social with its subjective concerns that, in early April 1933, Thomas took part in a competition with his friend Bert Trick to see who could write the best poem on the theme of immortality.[33]

This was poem 'Twenty Three' – 'And death shall have no dominion' – a poem which suddenly crystallised the flirtation with traditionalism and temporarily reversed the trend towards social commentary. Several critics have rightly described it as the first process poem, but none have added that its success is due to its regularity of form, albeit Ralph Maud notes that it is: 'the first poem in this notebook in regularly rhymed stanzas' (*NP*, 258). Yet this is the crucial issue, it seems to me. Although the reason for this choice is unclear – was Thomas mimicking Trick's taste for regular form? – the switch from a purist commitment to *vers libre* to the constraint of regular stanzas, refrain and consistent rhyme scheme was what gave the poem its propulsive force and lyrical sweep. Typically, as if trying to distance himself from the un-modern mode he was using, Thomas pushes it to the verge of parody; the declamatory bardic tone, exaggerated religiosity, not one, but two refrains per stanza, thumping rhythms, crashing alliteration and driving rhythms are all at the other end of the scale from the subtle, if ineffectual, waverings of his *vers libre*. But this exaggeration, too, is part of the poem's unprecedented success.

Its original version, and Thomas's revision of it, shed light on his tangled motives and the poem's unexpected outcomes. The first stanza, both in notebook form and as it appeared on 18 May 1933 in the *New English Weekly*, ran:

And death shall have no dominion.
Man, with soul naked, shall be one
With the man in the wind and the west moon,
With the harmonious thunder of the sun;

When his bones are picked clean and the clean bones gone,
He shall have stars at elbow and foot;
Though he fall mad he shall be sane,
And though he drown he shall rise up again;
Though lovers be lost love shall not;
And death shall have no dominion. (*NP*, 146)

In this version, 'Man' is tested and tortured in the first stanza, but assured that he 'shall not die' in the second. In stanza three, his oneness after death with the wind, moon and stars is emphatically asserted. A fourth stanza, later dropped before it was collected in *Twenty-five Poems*, follows:

And death shall have no dominion.
Under the sea or snow at last
Man shall discover all he thought lost,
And hold his little soul within his fist;
Knowing that now can he never be dust,
He waits in the sun till the sun goes out;
Now he knows what he had but guessed
Of living and dying and all the rest;
He knows his soul. There is no doubt.
And death shall have no dominion. (*NP*, 147)

As this shows, the poem originally read as an expression of faith. There is ambiguity, because of the forcefulness with which a pantheistic vision is expressed, but it can reasonably be taken to support the fourth stanza's assertion of bodily resurrection.[34]

Thomas's exaggerated parodic inversion of his usual technique for this single poem led him to deploy not just regular stanzas and rhyme, but iambic rhythms characterised by heavy stresses, end-stopping and parallel caesura, all of which were reinforced by alliteration, assonance and consonance well in excess of his usual style. In a manner owing something to Welsh hymn-singing and the *hwyl* of chapel sermons, these effects encourage a 'primitive' identification of the rhythms of the sea and the cosmos, on the one hand, with those of the physiological bases of verse rhythm in pulse, heartbeat and sexual arousal, on the other.[35] Without consciously intending to create a template, Thomas had hit upon a matching of form and content; tight and repetitive structure lends an apocalyptic-mythic register to the theme of the conflict-in-unity of life and death drives and a sense of generational entrapment. More than this, the highly charged rhetoric also encouraged him to increase the poem's innate ambiguity, when he revised it in February 1936. The fourth stanza, with its message of resurrection, vanished, as did 'shall not die' in stanza two and stanza one's 'soul', with its assumption of a Christian form of immortality.[36] 'Man' became the more accurate 'dead men' and 'they' replaced 'he', making the poem less gender-specific. Other minor changes were made for the sake of sharper phrasing and the reduction of 'harmonious thunder'.

The result is that the poem now 'affirms ... the indissolubility of the general fact and principle of Life, [but] not any promise of individual Christian resurrection', in Walford Davies's words. The Bible texts, on which it is based (and on which the poet-preacher improvises), remain present in the refrain, but the poem's pantheism no longer supplements it; rather, it makes it seem 'puzzling how [the positive tone] is accomplished'.[37] The uplifting *effect* of the rhetorical apparatus, which Thomas leaves intact, remains at odds with a message which is both anti-humanist and non-consolatory (the subtext is the slang phrase 'pushing up the daisies' for 'dead'). It thereby simultaneously tests, and testifies to, the power of language to make us believe, and raises questions about its relationship between authorial sincerity and reader manipulation. The poem uses negatives to say two incompatible things at once, revealing the unavoidably rhetorical nature of language. As Terry Eagleton puts it: 'Literature may appear to be describing the world, and sometimes actually does so, but its real function is performative; it uses language within certain conventions in order to bring about a certain effect in a reader. It achieves something in the saying; it is language as a kind of material practice in itself, discourse as social action.'[38] It is this *performative* status of literature – the understanding that poetry could be a material practice and discursive social action without necessarily 'describing the world' – which Thomas displayed in his revision of 'And death shall have no dominion' in early 1936, and it came to him as he sought to discover and replicate what had made the poem a success during the summer of 1933.

Huge poetic vistas lay before Thomas at this moment. Traditional stanza form, plus refrain and repetition, rhyme, emphatic rhythm, double negatives, pun, simultaneity effects, the interpenetration of growth and decay, pantheism and the detachment of the lyric ego from its confessional limitations – all pointed to a style in which traditional form, far from being reactionary, would embody a modernist poetry of apocalyptic, cosmic flux. Why, then, was 'And death shall have no dominion' omitted from *18 Poems*? There were, perhaps, a number of reasons. First, it is invariably the fate of the prototype to be weaker than its offspring, and this is true, here, in certain crucial respects. The poem is a rather simplistic statement of a subject that Thomas would expound with much greater subtlety a few months later. Second, as he further developed the process poetic, language was made to enact the theme of process more closely than in this first attempt. When he came to revise the poem in early 1936, it was at this linguistic level of the process poetic that he tried to beef it up. 'Windily', a pun, spun from 'windings of the sea', is added to stanza two and is developed in 'blew' and 'blow' in stanza three through an associative play on 'nails' and 'hammer' and puns on 'break' and 'characters'. But this may not have been enough to satisfy him; Vernon Watkins records that he was still unwilling to include it in *Twenty-five Poems* (*LVW*, 16). Yet, as of April 1933, even in its original form, this poem was, by some way, the most impressive that Thomas had ever written, and he knew it.

This, of course, was the problem. After many years of apprenticeship, he had just written his best poem – a minor masterpiece – and it turned out to be a sport in a form that he still considered un-modern. As a result, he initially had some difficulty accepting it and grasping its implications and was uncertain as to how to build on it. The rest of the third notebook, from April onwards is thus the record of a *re*-discovery – a working-out, in a more systematic way, of what precisely made 'And death shall have no dominion' so powerful.

The following poem reveals the problems that Thomas had to overcome. 'Twenty Four', 'Within his head revolved a little world' (16–20 April 1933), is a long rambling poem of 104 lines in the same social-discursive style as 'Four'. It charts the breakdown of its protagonist, who is at odds with a world of 'non-stop dancing', 'tinned music' and women 'With serpents' mouths and scolecophidian voids / Where eyes should be', cut off from his soul and faith. So extreme is his alienation, that it is imaged as crucifixion: 'He, too, has known the agony in the Garden, / And felt a skewer enter at his side ... [has] seen the world at bottom rotten' (*NP*, 148–9). Pushed to the brink of madness, he can only preserve his psychic unity in isolation: 'he has found his soul in loneliness', and the cure seems as bad as the disease (*NP*, 150). The outlook of the sociopath is common in Thomas's early stories, but there its deviancy is placed and relativised by the fictional frame of narrative. In a poem such as 'Within his head', nothing similar mitigates the absolute alienation of the protagonist, who seems purely pathological as a result – too close to the madness that he fears. In addition, the pantheistic unity he claims to attain only superficially resembles that of 'And death shall have no dominion':

Now he is one with many, one with all,
Fire and Jordan and the sad canal ...
I see him in the crowds, not shut
From you or me or wind or rat
Or this and that. (*NP*, 150)

Here, the oneness of self and world is stated, rather than established; as Thomas informed Johnson, eight months later: '[b]y the magic of words and images you must make it clear ... that the relationships are real. If you are one with the swallow & one with the rose, then the rose is one with the swallow ... show ... how *your* flesh covers the tree & the tree's flesh covers you' (*CL*, 95–6).

Yet Thomas was beginning to extend, albeit tentatively at first, his mastery of regular metrical and stanza forms, developing the means by which a vision of process could be realised. 'Pass through twelve stages' of 23 April considers process in biological terms, anticipating the simultaneity of youth and age in 'The force that through the green fuse' and other more accomplished poems of later 1933. Although finally dissolving in metrical irregularity, it contains a passage on determinism which would later be incorporated into 'From love's first fever to her plague' (*NP*, 154). Then, after a three-week gap, in 'First there was the lamb on knocking knees' (13 May 1933), Thomas tried to encapsulate the simultaneity of process in a larger seasonal cycle. Although metrically somewhat knock-kneed itself, this piece compresses its theme – the implacable round of breeding, birth and death – by returning to pararhymed stanzas. Puns ('First there was calf love which grew a cow') and phrasings anticipate *18 Poems*: 'First there was innocence and then desire, / A maggot in the veins; there's nothing now' (*NP*, 156).

By this point, regular stanza forms had begun to predominate. 'No man believes', of 23 May, offers part of the solution to the impasse of 'And death'. Not quite regular (two stanzas of six lines, one of five and one of seven using pararhyme and mixing octosyllabics with iambic pentameters), its importance lies in the way its formal compression lends rhetorical force to the use of the double negative. In Thomas's work, double or multiple negatives are often used to affirm a qualified positive, so that it remains entangled in the complications, doubts and self-interrogation from which it has emerged.[39] Truth can only be arrived at by indirection; it has to be looked at askance, if it is to be seen. The subject, in this case, is religious faith, which, it is claimed, can only be maintained by being negated:

And this is true, no man can live

Who does not bury god in a deep grave
And then raise up the skeleton again,
No man who does not break and make,
Who in the bones finds not new faith,
Lends not flesh to ribs and neck,
Who does not break and make his final faith. (*NP*, 161)

This claim applies to the principle of contradiction in the natural and human world, thus: 'No man believes ... Who feels not coldness in the heat, / In the breasted summer longs not for spring ... who, young / And green, sneers not at the old sky' (*NP*, 161). Like the boys of summer, who claim that 'seasons must be challenged', youthful rebellion is part of the natural order of things. Thomas's formulation is Hegelian-Marxist; as he put it in a letter to Johnson: 'Out of the negation of the negation must rise the new synthesis' (*CL*, 185). Blake was also a source for his search for truth through paradox, cancelled cancellations and contradictions: 'I like things that are difficult to write and difficult to understand; I like "redeeming the contraries" with secretive images ...', he would tell Charles Fisher in February 1935, quoting Blake's description of his own notion of poetry in *Milton*: 'There is a Negation, & there is a Contrary: / The Negation must be destroy'd to redeem the Contraries' (*CL*, 208).[40] Far more than mere inversion or gainsaying, multiple negatives lent themselves to complex shades of qualified assertion and refusal. Double logic – a form of rationality which rejects the self-identical concept as irrational – began as part of a Blakean critique of New Country positivism, but would become a permanent part of Thomas's repertory.

Another – this time, longer – gap in the notebook, between 23 May and 1 July, reflects the continuing struggle for poetic synthesis, both in thematic and formal terms. But now Thomas made a series of important breakthroughs. 'Thirty Seven', 'Why east wind chills', dated 1 July, and 'Thirty Nine', 'In me ten paradoxes make one truth', dated 7 July, restate the paradoxical intuitions of the May poems: 'And never shall the roots bear to bear fruit / Till life and death shall cancel out' (*NP*, 165). More significantly, in 'Forty One', 'Praise to the architects', Thomas explicitly rejected a poetry of overt social critique, ironically praising the social realist poets, for whom: 'A pome's a building on a page; / Keatings [a brand name] is good for lice, / A pinch of Auden is the lion's feast ... Empty, To Let, are signs on this new house' (*NP*, 167). As Ralph Maud notes: 'Audenesque poetry is likened to radio and poster advertising; promising much, giving little, mere surfaces, a Barmecide's feast'.[41] 'We have the fairy tales by heart', of 14 July, uses New Country phraseology and sentiments in claiming 'Half of the old gang's shot, / Thank God, but the enemy stays put', yet its subject matter centres on the difficulty of rationalising away the irrational (listed as 'fairy tales', 'a bishop's hat', 'ghosts', 'fairies' and 'furies') and the permanence of death and evil in the face of logic. A day later, Thomas made another advance with '"Find meat on bones that soon have none"'. For Maud, this, and not 'And death shall have no dominion', is the first true process poem. In the form of a father-son debate (two aspects of the poet, but also reflecting the relationship between Dylan and D. J. Thomas), its eight-line stanzas display elements of pantheism, and the paradoxical negation of the negation, as the older voice tells the younger to follow him in slaking sexual appetite and 'rebelling' against natural limits – of sun, moon, sea, night and day, the body and death itself: '"War on the destiny of man!"'. But this nihilistic counsel is rejected:

> 'The maggot that no man can kill
> And the bird no bullet sting
> Rebel against the reason's wrong
> That penetrates the drum and lung
> And cataracts the soul.
> I cannot murder, like a fool,
> Season and sunlight, grace and girl,
> Nor can I smother the soul's waking. ...' (*NP*, 171)

It concludes '"Night and day are no enemies / But one companion"'. Though the limits of mortality and the universe oppress the first speaker, the second accepts them, because they 'rebel against the reason's wrong'. What truly destroys 'the soul' (understood as spirit or imagination, rather than in a Christian sense) is the 'revolt' of would-be dominative-will against such limits. To deny death, which is inextricably bound up with life, is to deny process and unity. Thomas revised '"reason's wrong"' as '"my father's dream"' and lines four and five as '"That out of a bower of red swine / Howls the foul fiend to heel"', emphasising that our embodied nature should not attempt to call 'to heel' the forces of the universe. '"Find meat on bones"' succeeded, if not quite as memorably, in re-activating the supercharged rhythm, rhyme and alliteration of 'And death'.

A sign of Thomas's new-found ease with traditional form is 'Forty', also of 7 July, which has the subtitle: 'After the performance of Sophocles' Electra in a garden. Written for a local paper'. Although too occasional and conventional to be collected, and distinct from the exploratory impulse driving the proto-process poems around it, it has a control of tone, atmosphere, diction and music beyond that which Thomas had yet attained in those pieces:

> A woman wails her dead among the trees,
> Under the green roof grieves the living;
> The living sun laments the dying skies,
> Lamenting falls. Pity Electra's loving
>
> Of all Orestes' continent of pride
> Dust in the little country of an urn,
> Of Agamemnon and his kingly blood
> That cries along her veins. ... (*NP*, 166)

'Forty' was perhaps entered in the third notebook as Thomas's model to himself of what he wanted to achieve in the different, riskier mode. The third notebook culminates in 'Forty Eight', 'The Woman Speaks' – a soliloquy in which a woman laments her lover (or son) killed in battle, extending the 'pity' for the Electra of 'Forty' in a grim monologue that draws on Sophocles, the Medieval Welsh *Heledd Cycle*, Rimbaud's 'Le dormeur du val' and Wilfred Owen. It brings together elegy, a fascination with bodily decay, disease, fear of war, graves, greenness, the cosmos (as moon and stars), blood, bones, marrow, pun ('ordured bed'), grief, love, youth and age, and 'the mortal miracle' – so much, in fact that like 'That sanity be said', but in a more impressively original way (and despite being in iambic pentameters), it refuses to cohere. If this makes it appear to strive too hard to assemble all that Thomas had learned in the previous months, the lyrics of the fourth notebook would now show that the ground was being cleared for another major advance.

The process poetic II: the fourth notebook and after

Listing the basic features of his poetry to Johnson in a letter of October 1933, Thomas commented 'Rhythm, certainly. It's as essential to poetry as it is to music', adding afterwards: 'Rhyme, certainly, but with qualification. I've been under the impression that I have defended form in my recent letters and spat me of the sprawling formlessness of Ezra Pound's performing Yanks and others' (*CL*, 49). Confirming his abandonment of *vers libre*, the confidence of this claim was based on a number of recent lyrics, which matched and, indeed, surpassed the achievement of 'And death shall have no dominion'. Between 6 September, when he copied 'Seven', 'Before I knocked and flesh let enter', and 20 November, when he entered 'Thirty', 'Light breaks where no sun shines', Thomas composed seven of the poems in *18 Poems*, bringing the process poetic to its first phase of perfection. After a pause of just over a month, he wrote a further seven between 'Thirty Five', 'A process in the weather of the heart', of 2 February 1934 and 'Forty One', 'If I were tickled by the rub of love' (30 April) – the final notebook poem. In this phase, Thomas advanced from fairly simple lyric forms to more complex, dialogic structures and multi-part poems, such as 'Our eunuch dreams' (March 1934) and 'I see the boys of summer' (April 1934).[42] Overall, it was a burst of lyric invention which bears comparison with any for which records exist; for, in these poems, Thomas managed, at last, to fuse all of the varied parts of his new poetic, including the action of process in linguistic form.

A new audacity marks the poems of this phase. 'Before I knocked' (6 September) is not only in the voice of an embryo, but also of Christ, who foresuffers his conception and the pains of the flesh and crucifixion, before his incarnation and birth. The fact that Christ existed before his conception by Mary is used as the vehicle for the process notion that all human beings exist as part of an unending and ceaseless cycle of birth, death, dissolution, reincorporation and rebirth. Unitarianism – from which this idea partly derives – holds that Christ is everyman, and every man has the potential to be Christ-like, and these are grounds for faith and hope. But Thomas's account, set in a neutral universe, in which God and Christ (because never fully human) 'doublecross' Mary's 'womb', is an almost wholly malign one, in which all human beings are at once alive and fodder for the fires of process, effectively dead men walking 'born of flesh and ghost [but] neither / A ghost or man, but mortal ghost' (*NP*, 187). Yet, as Maud notes, 'the stage is set in this poem for Thomas's distinctive organic imagery', in which the universe-as-Logos is re-begun each time conception occurs (as 'Fifteen' provocatively puts it: 'In the beginning was the three-eyed prick'), and each embryo is a recapitulation of cosmic growth, the ascent of man and the emergence of language and consciousness, as in 'Twenty Four' and 'Twenty Six' – 'From love's first fever to her plague', in which this is charted in a series of numbers, which multiply exponentially like the fertilised egg: one, two, four, a score, a million (*CP* 22).

The signature lyric of the new mode was poem 'Twenty Three', 'The force that through the green fuse drives the flower', of 12 October:

> The force that through the green fuse drives the flower
> Drives my green age; that blasts the roots of trees
> Is my destroyer.
> And I am dumb to tell the crooked rose
> My youth is bent by the same wintry fever.

The force that drives the water through the rocks
Drives my red blood; that dries the mouthing streams
Turns mine to wax.
And I am dumb to mouth unto my veins
How at the mountain spring the same mouth sucks.

The hand that whirls the water in the pool
Stirs the quicksand; that ropes the blowing wind
Hauls my shroud sail.
And I am dumb to tell the hanging man
How of my clay is made the hangman's lime.

The lips of time leech to the fountain head;
Love drips and gathers, but the fallen blood
Shall calm her sores.
And I am dumb to tell a weather's wind
How time has ticked a heaven round the stars.

And I am dumb to tell the lover's tomb
How at my sheet goes the same crooked worm. (*CP*, 13)

The implications of pantheism are pushed to the extreme point of Blake's visionary 'world in a grain of sand' and Shelley's radical monism, beyond the idealist version of pantheism found in Coleridge or in, say, Wordsworth. The speaker grasps his identity with the processual flow, in terms of vegetable growth, the water cycle and the elements of earth, water, air and fire, before considering the relationship between time, love and sex. The 'force' which drives (and 'dries') all of these does the same to him; the engulfment threatens selfhood, yet, at the same time, has a sublime aspect, because it is a liberation from the prison of individual consciousness. However, the fact that the speaker can grasp this unity paradoxically separates him from the natural world, which has no such self-consciousness. This realisation renders him 'dumb' ('unable', but also 'stupid' for attempting it) to 'tell' of their kinship, returning him to his separation from nature and his imprisonment in human time. Again and again, the poems of the next few months would explore this separation-in-unity, conflating body and universe and representing process in microcosmic terms. In doing so, Thomas drew on the medieval and renaissance notions of 'correspondences' that he found in John Donne (his *Devotions* and 'I am a little world') and Sir Thomas Browne, but also in Blake's Albion, Whitman's union of 'kosmos' and ego and, above all, the giant Finnegan of Joyce's *Work in Progress*. As Thomas explained to Pamela Hansford Johnson and Trevor Hughes in November 1933 and

January 1934: 'Every idea ... can be imaged and translated in terms of the body, its flesh, skin, blood, sinews, veins, glands, organs, cells, or senses'; 'the earthquakes of the body' can 'describe the earthquakes of the heart' and because 'it is impossible for me to raise myself to the altitude of the stars', he must 'bring down the stars to my own level and ... incorporate them in my own physical universe', in order to prove 'that the flesh that covers me is the flesh that covers the sun, that the blood in my lungs is the blood that goes up and down in a tree' (CL, 57, 108). In the same month, he informed Glyn Jones that his obscurity stemmed from a 'preconceived symbolism derived ... from the cosmic significance of the human anatomy' (CL, 122). 'The force that through the green fuse' is exemplary in linking the body to planetary 'forces', while a poem like 'Thirty', 'Light breaks where no sun shines', of November 20 incorporates the universe into the organic cycles of the body; as Andrew Duncan claims, it is 'probably the ideal biomorphic poem':[43]

> Light breaks where no sun shines;
> Where no sea runs, the waters of the heart
> Push in their tides;
> And, broken ghosts with glow-worms in their heads,
> The things of light
> File through the flesh where no flesh decks the bones. (CP, 23)

The use of regular stanza form, metrical scheme and rhyme scheme give the poem's narrative a structure, with stanzas one (quoted above), two and five offering successive images of growth and decay and stanzas four and five, respectively, dealing solely with life and death. Syllabically regular stanzas (lines of 6, 10, 4, 10, 4, and 10 throughout), and complex end-pararhyme and internal rhyme patterns, bind the stanzas together, even as they explore dissolution. Far from seeming too rigid, the strict organisation compresses imagery and narrative elements to the point at which they overlap and grow fluid, leaking into each other and containing aspects of their opposites (not: 'Are the "things of light" spermatozoa or charnel worms?', but 'To what extent are spermatozoa always already charnel worms, and vice versa?').

In the poems of autumn and winter 1933 to 1934, we can follow a rapidly evolving symbolic language pertaining to sleep, tidal and blood flows, genesis and conception, sex, bodily growth and decline, night and day and inner and outer weathers, in which apparent antitheses are shown to grow out of, and be implicit in, the opposite term, 'nor fenced nor staked' (CP, 24). The human subject that they outline is seemingly asocial, simultaneously terrified and exalted in realising its at-one-ness with a universe swept by vast, primordial forces. The realisation has a primarily negative aspect; mortality has, for Thomas, a Jacobean presence and pungency (and the treatment of his father for cancer of the mouth in September 1933 must have surely exacerbated this).[44] Not only do life and death imply each other in these poems, they are, essentially, the same thing. The growing embryo is already dying and, 'crouched like a tailor', sews its fleshy winding-sheet or, as Thomas's 'lovely Beddoes' has Wolfram – a character in *Death's Jest-Book* – express it: 'But dead and living, which are which?'[45] (*CP*, 81). Though death is understood intellectually as a dynamic force, as humans forced to inhabit the illusion of temporality, we are haunted by time's passing and the foreknowledge of our demise. Unity with some vast eternal recurrence is cold comfort when 'Cadaver' relentlessly pursues us on the 'cinder death' running-track we call life (*CP*, 19–21).

In 'Thirty Five', 'A process in the weather of the heart', dated 2 February 1934, we find Thomas using the word 'process' in a poem which is virtually a template for the style – a summation of what had been assembled since the previous April:

A process in the weather of the heart
Turns damp to dry; the golden shot
Storms in the freezing tomb.
A weather in the quarter of the veins
Turns night to day; blood in their suns
Lights up the living worm.

A process in the eye forewarns
The bones of blindness; and the womb
Drives in a death as life leaks out. ... (*CP*, 10)

Like so many of the poems in *18 Poems*, there is an emphasis on the vigour of the deathly aspect of process ('*Drives in* a death'), which contrasts forcibly with the passivity of its aspect as the life force ('life *leaks out*'). In the more complex 'The force that through the green fuse' or 'Light breaks where no sun shines', however, Thomas's language confronts process-as-loss much more actively, allying its protagonists to process as unity in nature. As William Walton Rowe notes, the negativity has much to do with 'an underlying anxiety about loss and expenditure in sex and death', and several poems – 'Thirteen', 'My hero bares his nerves' (17 September 1933), is the classic instance – figure this as masturbation or involuntary nocturnal ejaculation. Whatever Thomas's attitude to these acts (though he is unlikely to have been morally disapproving), biologically, this is a form of waste – the death of potential – as in a deleted stanza from 'Twenty Nine', 'When once the twilight locks', of 11 November 1933:

> Crow on my heap, O living deaths;
> There is no horror death bequeaths
> I cannot number on this sleepy hand ... (*NP*, 208)

Such a passage, like the complexity of the treatment of this subject in a poem which *was* published, 'My hero bares his nerves', shows that the negativity is ultimately less important than the excess; existence as the tragic consciousness of self-expenditure, as opposed to an empirical and incremental balancing of life against death, with death always, inevitably, tipping the scales. 'The expense of spirit in a waste of shame', then; but also, as Rowe puts it, 'The force that through the green fuse' 'makes nonsense of the common-sense idea of life as an accumulation of experience. Life in Thomas's poem is sheer exuberant loss'.[46]

This excessive aspect of process, linked with the radically new models of the universe proposed by early twentieth-century science, is enacted at both intellectual and verbal levels in Thomas's poetry. Insofar as it recognises that there is (and always will be) a gap between what is known and what is knowable to human beings, and insofar as Thomas sometimes uses biblical material, it is liable to be viewed as religious mysticism. Yet it is more properly a recognition that human existence necessarily has a metaphysical dimension – one within which religious belief arises, but the understanding of which it by no means monopolises – and that this dimension is central to poetry's resistance to instrumental logic and paraphrase (one might compare it to Keats's concept of 'negative capability' – an active and creative assertion of unknowability). Thomas's grasp of what the new science entailed, in terms of the treacherousness of appearances and the need for the counter-intuitive, was thorough to the point where it could easily be material for humour. It would be wrong, however, to see his quip to Pamela Hansford Johnson in October 1934 that 'Life is only waves, wireless waves and electric vibrations', and the follow-up line describing her as 'my little radio programme from Battersea', as simply a jest. Like so much else in Thomas, the element of parody is strong, but Paul Ferris rightly glosses it with the note: 'Early in October [1934] a six-day international physics conference in London and Cambridge had prompted newspaper articles about the mysteries of the atom, including (to quote *The Times*) the fact that sub-atomic matter could "behave both as particles and as waves"' (*CL*, 195). We also know that Thomas read such books as *Science and the Modern World* (1926) by Alfred North Whitehead, a leading international physicist and popular science writer, who was the Stephen Hawking of his day.[47] Whitehead's metaphysical idealism was indebted to Platonism and Bergson's philosophy of change; he rejected Cartesian dualism and held that all truths were only ever half-truths. He was also one of the first British scientists to understand and expound Einstein's Theory of Relativity to a lay audience. What he would call his 'process philosophy' emerged in *The Concept of Nature* (1920), was expanded upon in *Science and the Modern World* and was fully set out in *Process and Reality* (1929).[48] This is a defence of theism, but Whitehead's God is highly unorthodox; just as the universe is in a state of constant flux, so God, as source of the universe, is viewed as growing and changing with it.

In fact, Thomas's ideas match Whitehead's in so many ways that it is unlikely that his use of 'process' was innocent of its scientific significance. Moreover, as I discuss in Chapter 4, it is not a large step from the Unitarian inheritance of the Thomas family, with its denial of Christian supernaturalism, to Whitehead's theism and monism. Thomas also refers to Einstein in his letters, and his radical sense of the atomic and sub-atomic flux underlying all solid appearances, and of the simultaneity of events and times, testify to an awareness of the propositions that matter is energy and that space and time are functions of each other (spacetime). The basic premise of the new physics – that events are 'relative' to the position of the observer – is also apparent in Thomas's rejection of being at 'right angles with the earth', only able to 'look only at things that are between the earth and the sky', 'much in the position of a reader ... who can only look at the middles of pages'. Humans, Thomas went on, 'see only a part of the tree ... what the insects under the earth see when they look upwards at the tree, & what the stars see when they look downwards at [it], is left to our imagination', and we would be wiser 'if we could change our angles of perspective as regularly as we change our vests', dispensing with 'prejudiced vision'.[49] As he explained to Johnson, this lay behind 'the conscious rapidity with which I [change] the angles of the images' in 'See, says the lime', and this rapid switching between stellar, cellular, insectile and human viewpoints and scales and angles reflects a considered artistic use of the new understandings of reality (*CL*, 99–100, 94).

Whitehead was joined in the late 1920s by two other astronomers keen to popularise the new physics – Sir James Jeans and Sir Arthur Eddington. Jeans claimed that the universe resembled more a great thought than a machine and that chronological time was an illusion:

'Time ... no longer ... involves change; it is merely a geometrical direction of our own choice ... . The pattern is not being continually woven ... but is spread before us complete in a continuum in which future events have just the same kind of existence as past events.'[50] In Thomas's process universe, what are normally distinct seasons and life-periods are frequently presented in ways which make it impossible to tell them apart; if linear time is an illusion, then conception, birth, the eruption of adolescence, sexual climax and death may all be understood as containing each other, and Thomas's poetry focuses on these states of maximum change, fluid identity and metamorphosis, because they exemplify the processual nature of existence. These states run together, presented in terms which apply to them all – 'When once the twilight locks', for example, deliberately evokes states which could be those of an embryo, baby or adolescent.

As well as championing relativity theory, like Whitehead, Eddington developed the first true understanding of stellar processes; he was associated with the idea that the bodies of human beings are made up of elements created in dying stars – or, as he put it in 1932: 'We are bits of stellar matter that got cold by accident, bits of a star gone wrong'.[51] 'I dreamed my genesis' directly alludes to this – the flesh of the speaker is said to have already 'filed / Through all the irons in the grass, metal / Of suns in the man-melting light', not just 'all flesh is grass', but we are made up of materials from the nuclear furnaces of stars and will return to them (CP, 26). As with Whitehead and Jeans, Eddington's writings would have appealed to Thomas not only because of the counter-intuitive propositions of modern science, but also because they tried to reconcile personal immortality and religious belief with the universe of relativity and quantum physics. If Thomas did not share their religious faith, the paradox that advances in materialism reinstated a metaphysical-spiritual dimension banished by Newtonian physics would have appealed to him as a follower of Blake.

Returning to the question of form, it is now possible to see more clearly how Thomas's style in late 1933 and 1934 developed in the ways that it did. In applying traditional form and increasing polysemy, he significantly advanced his modernist metaphysical lyric mode, using the stanza forms he had adopted to shape complex, conflicted and overdetermined personal material in order to absorb the more universal vision of process. It was a vision that gave the desperately polarised times a modernist lyric which recognised stark oppositions, yet was open-ended and subject to ceaseless change; one in which inner and outer, subject and object, organic and inorganic, dream and reality and life and death were always already infiltrating each other and in which time, as in so many modernist texts, was relative and biologistic, where different temporalities could 'overlap, collide, and register their own completion'.[52] The simultaneity of states and times is fundamental to Thomas's early poetry and informs such paradoxes as the 'fathering worm' and the Jesus of 'Before I knocked', who is both 'ungotten' and already crucified. In this world, time accelerates (as in time-lapse photography) and dissolves: 'The haring snail go[es] giddily round the flower' and Peter, in the short story 'The Visitor' (April 1934), watches animals live, die and decompose in mere moments (CP, 34).[53] In 'A Prospect of the Sea', from 1937, both temporal and spatial extension are abolished in 'an iron view' of the planet, which pierces down through civilisational layers to the Garden of Eden – all alive in a single moment and a single glance.[54] As Jacob Korg notes, 'Duration is laid out flat' in such works, so that 'the different conditions through which things pass are seen simultaneously, telescoped into a single composite entity ... There is no distinction between the potential and the actual'.[55]

The physiological bases of the process vision demanded concreteness of imagery, while its all-encompassing nature required that process operate at linguistic, as well as thematic, levels. This is reflected in a characteristic process vocabulary. 'Weather', for example, is a typical term for several reasons. First, it can simultaneously denote inner and outer states (as in 'the weather of the heart'). Second, it can be a verb, as well as a noun, so enacting the equivalence of both matter and energy. Third, it works punningly as 'whether' and 'wether'. It is also an apt metaphor for representing whatever resists order, signalling a universe of shifting contingency, which is conceptually related to the new physics.[56] (Although the sea, even more than the weather, is Thomas's favourite and most fruitful source of images and metaphors for the dynamic and complex flows and non-Euclidean geometries of the Einsteinian universe and Freudian psyche.) 'Process' terms include 'eye', 'flesh', 'worm', 'ghost', 'grain', 'bone', 'marrow', 'fork', 'wax' and 'green'; usually single-syllabled, concrete and charged with pun-potential, these terms can face in two or more directions at once, focusing the paradoxes of process. Thus, 'wax', as verb-noun in 'The force that through the green fuse', combines growth, but also the waxy flesh of the dead. Process terms may be combined: 'quicksand', in the same poem, is deadly swamp (and reinforces the 'lime' of three lines later as 'quicklime') and the sand hastening through an hourglass (a symbol of mortality); but it is also sand that is 'quick', instinct with life. 'Sheet', in the poem's last line, is a bed-sheet and a shroud or winding-sheet, but also – in a typical self-referential twist – the paper on which the poem is written. Sex, death and creation fuse in a single word. 'Seedy', from 'I see the boys of summer', might just be the perfect process word; literally, it means 'sexually mature, full of seed', but metaphorically, it has the sense of 'past it, down at heel, degenerate'. Thomas's insistence that his poetry be read 'literally' has much to do with the fact that we so often settle only for those meanings of words that are wrapped in stale metaphor (*CL*, 348). And, for all that the poems of embryonic growth, birth and decay and the impersonal 'force' that drives them are organicist and archetypal and elide the daily world, they nevertheless incorporate and reinscribe it through cybernetic and surreal collocations of organic and inorganic terms ('chemic blood', 'petrol face' and 'bronze root' are just a few of dozens of such usages that yoke together the modern-mechanical and archaic-organic) and in single words which also do this. The best-known example of such a usage is the word 'fuse' in 'The force that through the green fuse', where it is an archaic term for the stem of a flower, but also the fuse on a bomb and the circuit-breaker for an electrical grid, as well having the sense of 'a fusing'.[57]

Language's ability to enact process expanded in the later poems of the fourth notebook. Thomas used increasingly varied devices, from adapted cliché to leitmotifs (e.g. the several variants on 'death's feather') and word-and-sense mutation ('drives' to 'dries' in 'The force that through the green fuse'), to disguised verbs and heaped-up appositive clauses, which suspend grammatical resolution and create states of simultaneity and interconnectedness (as in the thirty-five clauses running over five stanzas and twenty-five lines of 'When, like a running grave'). In this way, the shifting energy of the 'force' was enacted, and language was seen to be active in generating the poem, working 'from' words themselves. Rhyme, too, grew more elaborate. In early November 1933, Thomas asked Johnson: 'But surely you haven't missed one of the biggest warps in my poetry. My melting pot is all sour. In two out of three of the poems I have sent you, there has been a steady scheme of consonantal rhyming. "The Eye of Sleep" is rhymed throughout. I never use a full rhyme but nearly always a half rhyme ... you may have noticed it all before, for it has a strange effect' (*CL*, 58). In the most elaborate case, 'I, in my intricate image' (which Ralph Maud rightly describes as 'the nineteenth process poem'), there are 'seventy-two variations in line-endings on the letter "l"' (*LVW*, 15). Being difficult to detect, pararhyme conveys an order which, in Paul Volsic's words, defamiliarises and 'is "perceived" as occult ... [Thomas's] poems are not amorphous, they are built around extremely complex, but in some ways asymmetric, "hidden" structures', in which end-rhyme is cut across by internal sound-patterning, such that their texture 'is deliberately and controlledly "frayed"'. Now disguised, now foregrounded, pararhyme (along with other sonic devices) means that Thomas's poems are never quite 'watertight', to use his own term, creating a sense of a breakdown within their tightly structured forms or a 'panic space', effectively casting doubt on the nature of the frame of the poem and an uncertainty within it concerning perspective: 'The text ceases to be an evidently stable space, with a privileged point of view established by an "I" who perceives. The text, like the world, is multiple, fragmented and metaphoric – not simply complex'.[58]

In 'All all and all', 'I dreamed my genesis', 'My world is pyramid' and 'When, like a running grave' – the four poems included in *18 Poems* which were written between the end of the fourth notebook in April 1934 and December of that same year – Thomas can be seen to be developing the process poetic still further. The first of the four sums up the volume and is relatively straightforward, but 'I dreamed my genesis' (which Thomas claimed was 'more or less based on Welsh rhythms') has a very unusual assonantal rhyme-scheme, while the last two poems reveal a new level of difficulty, largely because of the greater degree of strangeness of their images and the speed of transition between them (*CL*, 161–2).[59] Theodor Adorno once observed: 'The principle of montage was supposed to shock people into realising just how dubious any organic unity was'. Thomas, however, in these poems, deliberately presents collage-like discontinuity in a standard (if sometimes only just standard) syntax.[60] The conflict between appearance and actuality, exposed by particle physics, is given linguistic form. Rather than the discrete visual images which usually defines collage, Thomas's images are like Joyce's in *Finnegans Wake*, created by wordplay, as in this opening stanza of 'Grief thief of time' – a poem entered in the fourth notebook on 26 August 1933, but heavily revised in August 1935:

Grief thief of time crawls off,
The moon-drawn grave, with the seafaring years,
The knave of pain steals off
The sea-halved faith that blew time to his knees,
The old forget the cries,
Lean time on tide and times the wind stood rough,
Call back the castaways
Riding the sea light on a sunken path,
The old forget the grief,
Hack of the cough, the hanging albatross,
Cast back the bone of youth

And salt-eyed stumble bedward where she lies
Who tossed the high tide in a time of stories
And timelessly lies loving with the thief. (*CP*, 55)

The prose sense of the stanza is that the old tend to forget the miseries of youth – 'the seafaring years' – worn down and robbed of faith in the future by pain, sentimentalising ('salt-eyed') and stumbling towards the grave, where the 'she' of their youthful hope and promise now embraces 'the thief', death. From the first line, this notably complicates the straight-forward syntax of the early version of the poem – 'Grief, thief of time, crawls off / With wasted years …'. The lack of commas after 'grief' and 'time' now suggests that 'grief' *produces* 'thief' through rhyme, and, in a sense, it does. Having produced this conjunction alogically, Thomas now generates a narrative which will make apparent the logical sense of 'Grief thief' (in which 'grief' is an adjective). However, this is not done in order to normalise the 'grief thief' conjunction; on the contrary, the excess and *jouissance* which this fortuitous coupling embodies is viewed as an innate and irrepressible aspect of language, and it will keep re-erupting in the poem. To allow it, Thomas manipulates punctuation: to produce grammatically suspended appositive clauses, such as 'with the seafaring years', for example, which could refer backwards or forwards. As the stanza proceeds, wordplay (on 'time and tide [wait for no man]', on 'lean' [verb or adjective] and 'stood', 'light' [noun, adjective or adverb?], sonic parallelism ['*Ha*ck of the *cough*, the *ha*nging albat*ross*'] and so on) exploits linguistic accident and texture in order to create the poem, refusing to be a passive bearer of some pre-decided tale, but actively intervening, increasing interpretative possibilities to prevent the emergence of single fixed readings (my own is provisional and partial) and making the physical medium of the words themselves part of the poem's meaning. It is revealing that in sending some of his poems to Eliot in November 1933, Thomas asked him to 'corroborate or contradict' the label 'automatic writing' which had been attached to them by Richard Rees, claiming that '[t]he fluency complained of [by Rees] is the result of extraordinary hard work, and, in my opinion, the absence of "knotty or bony passages" is again the result of much energetic labour … and of many painful hours spent over the smoothing and removing of the creakiness of conflict' (*CL*, 75). This might amuse us – Thomas, of all poets, trying to *eliminate* 'knotty' passages! – but the emphasis is on removing 'creakiness', not 'conflict', and he is referring to his efforts to present collage-type material with the appearance of seamless flow. This is what Linden Huddlestone meant when he claimed that: 'Thomas is doing word for word what Eliot in *The Waste Land* was doing line by line'.[61] Quasi-surreal images, often disjunctive or linked by wordplay, are unnervingly presented in a syntax which belies radicalism. This is the style which reached the maximum extent of its bizarre richness in the period between early 1934 and the end of 1937 and was present in more attenuated form until 1941.

In the fourth notebook, Thomas learned how to adapt traditional form to give definitive shape to previously inchoate attempts to explore a growing crisis of faith, sexual repression, cultural unease and fear of war. The process poetic was based on terrifying premises – human beings are infinitesimal specks of consciousness in the non-human void, machines of flesh compelled by biological imperatives to mate and produce offspring who will shoulder them into the grave, creatures thirsting for spiritual significance, yet denied traditional religious comforts. But insofar as it extended its metaphysical premises into a language of unique and continual wit and inventiveness, it was not just the 'expression' of an anguished awareness of mortality, but also a form of resistance, of a brief moment in which the 'force' could be ridden, the outcome being 'a watertight section of the stream that is flowing all ways', where the 'warring images [are] reconciled for that small stop of time' (CL, 329). Process was Thomas's way of '[Singing] the sun in flight' as simultaneously 'meat-eating' and life-giving, which recast the traditional *topoi* of lyric – life, love, death, faith – in compressed and distorted form. As I shall show, its heroically self-spending struggle with determinism lends it political, even revolutionary, aspects, too. Before exploring this, however, I shall look at Desmond Hawkins's claim, quoted earlier in this chapter, that Thomas 'fused' Eliot and Auden, by way of illustrating the boldly original and complexly derivative nature of *18 Poems*.

Contemporary intertexts I: extra-Audenary Thomas

'And never hear their subaltern mockery.'

– W. H. Auden, 'XVII'.[62]

Constantine Fitzgibbon, Thomas's first biographer, claimed that: 'there is not a trace of [the so-called "thirties" poets], scarcely even of W. H. Auden, to be found in [Thomas's] own poems written [in 1931] or later'.[63] In this, he was probably reflecting Thomas's own opinion of the 'thirties' poets, exemplified by his young-doggish assessment of Auden in *New Verse* in 1937 and the even more waspish comments scattered throughout his letters about Louis MacNeice, Cecil Day Lewis, Stephen Spender and others.[64] Thomas was inclined to mock his contemporaries – this partly reflecting his social and educational insecurity – but the flyting usually wrapped some astute critical observation. His critique of the New Country poets was based on what he viewed as their 'bogus' radicalism, instrumental attitude to language and, implicitly, positivism and ironic evasion of fundamental existential questions (*CL*, 212). 'I like to read good propaganda', he told Glyn Jones in March 1934, 'but the most recent poems of Auden and Day-Lewis seem to me neither good poetry or propaganda. A good propagandist needs very little intellectual appeal; and the emotional appeal in Auden wouldn't raise the corresponding emotion in a tick' (*CL*, 121). Ticks must have flesh to feed on, and the swipe at Auden's cerebral bloodlessness was related, in a description of Spender in 1938, to the superficiality of New Country's politics: 'I find his communism unreal; before a poet can get into contact with society, he must, surely, be able to get into contact with himself, and Spender has only tickled his outside with a feather' (*CL*, 328). These criticisms were matched by a sharp eye for the facile aspects of Auden's cult of the new (Thomas may have been detecting Auden's own half-heartedness in this respect). Of 'Sir, no man's enemy', he asked Trevor Hughes in January 1934: 'Does one need "New styles of architecture, a change of heart"? Does one rather not need a new consciousness of the old universal architecture and a tearing away from the old heart the things that have clogged it?' (*CL*, 111). At the same time, the example set by the New Country poets' use of traditional form was crucial in creating the process poetic, and closer examination of Thomas's early work reveals the incorporation of some of its other elements.

Thomas's resistance to Auden, for example, went deep, but it had an important dialogic dimension. A version of Auden's line in *The Orators* – 'They give the prizes to the ruined boys' – is the opening line of *18 Poems* 'I see the boys of summer', within a stanza in which Stan Smith also detects an allusion to Auden's 'Hearing of harvests rotting in the valleys':

> I see the boys of summer in their ruin
> Lay the gold tithings barren,
> Setting no store by harvest freeze the soils;
> There in their heat the winter floods
> Of frozen loves they fetch their girls,
> And drown the cargoed apples in their tides. (*CP*, 7)

As Smith notes, these are just two of many Auden echoes (elsewhere, he discovers 'Consider this and in our time', 'Paysage Moralisé', 'Doom is dark' and *Paid on Both Sides*; there are numerous others). Auden is the most pervasive contemporary presence in *18 Poems*, and this extends to syntactic, thematic and structural similarities.[65] Thus, the tripartite structure of Thomas's poem and its debate form have affinities with 'It was Easter as I walked in the public gardens' and 'The Witnesses', and his habit of evoking landscapes of dereliction and menace is also Auden-influenced. For Smith, this is evidence that Auden and Thomas were both 'ruined boys' – arrested adolescents of the kind described by Cyril Connolly in *The Enemies of Promise*. Both shared secret affinities with the 'Old Gang' they denounced, as well as with each other, but the essence of their relationship was oedipal, and 'Thomas had to slay the poetic father; and that meant Auden'.[66] And yet it seems to me that Thomas's poem strikes the reader as a dialogue with the Audenesque, conducted by one who has outstripped its terms, consisting of affectionate (and not-so-affectionate) parody and pastiche – a kind of ingestion and disassembly of it for strikingly different purposes. It is not just that Auden's social discursiveness is lacking, although a narrative outline can be discerned. Thus, in part I, a speaker castigates the boys' negativity and wastefulness; once 'summer children' in the 'brawned womb', he tells them, they will eventually become 'men of nothing' (they are addressed as unborn *and* fully grown, in keeping with the simultaneity of process) (*CP*, 7). In part 2, the boys collectively defend themselves with some bravado – 'seasons must be challenged' – and, if they are 'dark deniers', 'comb[ing] the county gardens', only to produce a 'wreath', they nevertheless embody energy and change (*CP*, 8). The two parts of the poem present antagonistic positions, similar to those in '"Find meat on bones"', albeit in a far more dialectical, image-rich fashion. Part 3 – a single summatory stanza – resists anything but a provisional hazarding at its speakers and meaning to this day:

> I see you boys of summer in your ruin.
> Man in his maggot's barren.
> And boys are full and foreign in the pouch.
> I am the man your father was.
> We are the sons of flint and pitch.
> O see the poles are kissing as they cross. (*CP*, 8)

The end-stopping and sense of each line suggests that they are the utterances of, alternately, the boys' critic, the boys and a third speaker, who may be a chorus or fusion of both (the last line follows a formula established in the last lines of the first two sections), or completely new. As with other early Thomas poems, there is no guidance – not even Joyce's dashes, let alone speech marks – to indicate where speech begins or ends. Consequently, there is no way of being absolutely sure who is speaking. Like the poem's antinomies, its separate subjects have 'kissed' and blurred throughout the poem anyway, and the final image, agonised and yearning in tone, signifies both life *and* death, erasure *and* presence, summation *and* inconclusiveness, as well as the inter-involvement of these terms – a modernist parody of closure, in fact, like that of *The Waste Land*.

In the poem's archetypal-mythic aspects, lack of social reference, density and rapidity of image-shifts and uncertainties of tone and speaker, the differences which outweigh the similarities with Auden are made manifest. The Audenesque traces reveal not so much dependence as absorption into Thomas's processual flow and idiom. Thomas may even pastiche Auden; 'On the consumptives' terrace taking their two farewells' in 'I, in my intricate image', said by John Bayley to sound as if it 'might almost be a line from Auden', is a good example.[67] The last line of the opening stanza of 'I see the boys of summer' – 'They drown the cargoed apples in their tides' – is a different way of doing the same thing. Commentators on the poem have read it as a mythic-biomorphic representation of wasted fertility, missing a reference to the Depression-era practice of dumping agricultural produce in the sea in order to maintain market prices (Thomas referred to 'fish, wheat and coffee' being 'burnt by the hundreds of tons' for the same reason in a letter of January 1934) (*CL*, 105). This reminds us of the need to read literally, as Thomas insisted, and of his poetry's often overlooked social dimension. But perhaps its chief significance lies in the act of sleight-of-hand – the way the absorption of the Audenesque within the new style is both flaunted and hidden.

Smith's claim that Thomas 'assumes ... the parodic mantle of Auden's old boy', in order to turn it on Auden himself and particularly on the 'unitary ego of those cryptic, self-circling early Auden poems', is therefore a shrewd one. It is necessary to add, however, that this is because, for Thomas, the 'ego' is scarcely 'unitary', as it is in Auden. Auden would claim in 'In Memory of Ernst Toller' that 'we are lived by powers we pretend to understand', yet the self in his post-*Orators* poetry is never rendered in a manner which bears this claim out.[68] 'In Memory of Ernst Toller' frames but never actually embodies this insight; lack of control is asserted by a grammatically unruffled, sovereign and self-present subject, with whose magisterial judgement 'we', as readers, are presumed to identify. There is no sense that the logical outcome of 'pretend' would be a challenge within the poem to the illusion of the 'unitary ego' and its instrumental use of language. By contrast, Thomas's poetry breaks with the assumption that language is a transparent window on the object world and expressive of the self, and foregrounds its role as a collaborator in the 'breeding', conflictual interaction of world, word, body and psyche. The lyric 'I' relinquishes power in reality, rather than, as in Auden, tokenistically ceding it in order to bolster its authority. Thomas's poems riskily tap into the flux out of which the subject is constituted; Auden presents the ego as a settled fact. As a result, Thomas challenges the politics of representation, rather than, like Auden, the representations of politics.

The complex relationship with the New Country poets this suggests is evident in other aspects of *18 Poems*. One of its principle themes – conception, gestation and birth – can be found, I would argue, in Cecil Day Lewis's *From Feathers to Iron* (1931), a long sequence tracing the gestation and birth of the poet's son. It maps his embryonic growth and the feelings of his mother onto the changing seasons and the contemporary socio-political crisis – 'Suppose that we, tomorrow or the next day, / Came to an end …?' However, the tone is largely one of cherishing, wonder and an expectant optimism, in which birth is aligned with social renewal: 'So turn, my comrades, turn, / Like infants' eyes, like sunflowers, to the light'.⁶⁹ Unlike Day Lewis's humanistic allegory and pastoral *couvade*, Thomas's 'brawned womb's weathers' visit historical, religious and Darwinian terrors on his embryos, who fall from their antenatal Edens even before they are born, 'smel[ling]' the 'maggot[s] in [their] stool[s]' in 'Before I knocked', 'sunlight paint[ing] the shelling of their heads', in anticipation of a new Western Front in 'I see the boys of summer', their future loves and dooms projected, film-like, on the womb-wall (*CP*, 7, 12). Biological and historical destiny is always already glowering, and the betrayal of humanity begins in the womb, with no chance of the thaumaturges of Day Lewis's poetry leading it out into the light.

These differences are even clearer in Thomas's attitude to Stephen Spender's work as revealed in his *New Verse* review of Spender's *Vienna* – a book-length poem tracing a love affair set against the backdrop of the crushing of workers in Vienna by the clerical-Fascist Dolfuss Government in February 1934. In it Thomas argued that 'in a poem … the poetry must come first; what negates or acts against the poem must be subjugated to the poetry which is essentially indifferent to whatever philosophy, political passion, or gang-belief it embraces' (*EPW*, 169). Provocatively, he added: 'Dollfuss and Fey are nice words. Does it really matter if they are, or are not, nice men?' – admitting it to be a 'ridiculous' claim, were it not that 'Mr. Spender, working now away from words, regarded only the historic significance of these two men as being important and not the verbal context in which he placed the letters that make up their names'. In other words, 'historically emotional signif-icance' cannot make a poem successful and, therefore, 'as a poem *Vienna* leaves much to be desired; in the first place it leaves poetry to be desired; and, in the second, any real intensity of the propagandist mission'. It fails, for Thomas, in its *political*, as well as its *poetic*, ambitions. In poetry, the politics of language is inescapably the language of politics, and *Vienna* is not truly revolutionary, because it is not truly poetry.[70] Its well-meaning, but vacuous, final lines, which hymn 'Those burrowing beneath frontier, shot as spies because / Sensitive to new contours', and look to the masses to 'conjoin / Accomplished in justice to reject a husk' bear this out. All too clearly, these lines are couched in a dead jargon of pseudo-scientific objectivity and born of the desire to create 'instant myth' from historical events.[71]

This is one case where direct comparison can be drawn, since we know that Thomas also responded to *Vienna* by writing a poem, and that a few lines from it survive in 'My world is pyramid':

> My world is cypress, and an English valley.
> I piece my flesh that rattled on the yards
> Red in an Austrian volley.
> I hear, through dead men's drums, the riddled lads,
> Strewing their bowels from a hill of bones,
> Cry Eloi to the guns. (*CP*, 28)

It seems to me that these lines powerfully generate the resonance so unsuccessfully striven for by Spender through their forceful concrete imagery and weirdly convincing conflation of historical events ('Austrian volley' fuses the 1934 massacre with the assassination of Archduke Franz Ferdinand at Sarajevo and the First World War). England and Austria are linked, but the gesture of solidarity is not straightforward: 'cypress and an English valley' are part of a tradition of graveside lament, the gentleness of which seems far removed from the horrors of modern European history and part of the embalmed 'pyramid' world of the past that the poem is concerned with. The Christ-like sacrifices of the dead are part of a larger Western apocalyptic view of history, but they are problematic, too; a fragmented speaker identifies with the trauma, but wordplay makes the 'lads' who have been 'riddled' by bullets riddled in the sense of being 'questioned', also. As Stewart Crehan observes, the poem is an active, living, linguistic texture combining pun and allusion, assonance and alliteration to produce more than monologic statement; this is, ultimately, the chief difference between Thomas's style and that of much New Country poetry.[72]

Contemporary intertexts II: *Hamlet* and the imaginary burglar – Dylan Thomas Stearns Eliot

We do not readily associate Thomas with T. S. Eliot, whom he admired as 'a great man' and credited with 'a very splendid sense of form', but whose work he jokingly described as requiring 'an intimate knowledge of Dante, the Golden Bough, and the weather-reports in Sanskrit' (*CL*, 249, 141, 122). Yet Eliot almost published *18 Poems* at Faber; and Thomas knew Eliot's work thoroughly, relishing the gothic-surreal sanctioned by *The Waste Land*'s 'bats with baby faces' and crepuscular 'whisper music', and avidly absorbing the lessons of the essays contained in Eliot's *Selected Essays* (1932) and *The Use of Poetry and the Use of Criticism* (1933).[73] I shall argue that Eliot's essays, 'The Metaphysical Poets' and 'Hamlet and His Problems' in particular, had a greater impact on Thomas even than Eliot's poetry and that the date of publication of the *Selected Essays* and Thomas's references to Eliot in his correspondence points to its seminal role in creating the process poetic between late summer 1934 and spring 1934.

'The Metaphysical Poets' furnished Eliot's unimpeachable authority, as well as a modernist checklist for any young poet who needed it in the late 1920s and early 1930s. But it was especially supportive of the kind of modernist metaphysical lyric towards which Thomas was striving in the third notebook during late summer 1933. It justified, for example, a focus on metaphysical questions (as opposed to the social ones of the New Country poets). It also endorsed 'concentrated' poetry ('it appears likely that poets writing in our civilization, as it exists at present, must be *difficult*') and the taking of radical linguistic liberties (to '[form] new wholes' from 'disparate' experiences, the poet responds to the modern world by 'becom[ing] more and more comprehensive, more allusive, more indirect, in order to force, to dislocate if necessary, language into his meaning').[74] It confirmed a preoccupation with the body, sardonically noting that, while to 'look into our hearts and write' is all very well, to write truly modern poetry, 'one must look into the cerebral cortex, the nervous system, and the digestive tracts'; the 'dissociation of sensibility' between abstract and concrete, thought and feeling could only be overcome by contemporary metaphysical poets through the radical juxtapositions of collage.[75] Thomas gleefully extended this physiological emphasis, blasphemously upping the ante on Eliot's efforts with his more grotesque gothic: even 'the skull beneath the skin' seems tame beside Christ as a 'stiff', maggots in stools and 'bags of blood let[ting] out their flies' (*CP*, 16, 12, 9). Equally radically, he parodically healed Eliot's 'dissociation' at a stroke by abolishing the social sphere in which it existed, collapsing the gap between subject and object and interring it in a boneyard as unquiet as Stetson's garden. Body and cosmos were fused in a grotesque, profanely monistic and materialist version of the unified sensibility whose loss Eliot mourned. Of the collapsed, yet expanded, self which resulted, it may truly be said – more, indeed, than of the Donne in 'The Metaphysical Poets' – that its thought is an experience which 'modified [its] sensibility' as insistently, concretely and immediately as 'the odour of a rose' – albeit, in Thomas's case, a 'crooked', Blakeian one.[76] As I discuss in Chapter 3, while *The Waste Land* is a text of abjection which expels the flesh as 'waste', Thomas rubs our face in the flesh, restoring the grisly poetry of the body – its mucous, skin, teeth, blood, bone, gristle, semen and breast milk – as the body of poetry.[77] Eliot is understood and celebrated in a perversely literal way, and Maud Ellman's claim that *The Waste Land*'s opening lines reveal a 'sickening collapse of limits' points to *18 Poems* as an exemplary instance of the texts that crawled out of its 'citational abyss'.[78]

Eliot first appears in Thomas's correspondence in a letter to Glyn Jones in March 1934:

> Are you obscure? But, yes, all good modern poetry is bound to be obscure. Remember Eliot: 'The chief use of the "meaning" of a poem, in the ordinary sense, may be to satisfy one habit of the reader, to keep his mind diverted and quiet, while the poem does its work upon him. 'And again: 'Some poets, assuming that there are other minds like their own, become impatient of this "meaning" which seems superfluous, and perceive possibilities of intensity through its elimination.' ... The fact that a good poem is obscure *does* mean that it is obscure to most people, and its author is therefore ... appealing to a limited public (*CL*, 121–2).

Thomas was fond of Eliot's defence of obscurity, repeating it in his reply to a *New Verse* questionnaire in October 1934. In response to the question 'Do you think there can now be a use for narrative poetry?', he answered in the affirmative, adding: 'There must be a progressive line, or theme, of movement in every poem ... Narrative in its widest sense, satisfies what Eliot, talking of "meaning", calls "one habit of the reader". Let the narrative take that one logical habit of the reader along with its movement, and the essence of the poem will do its work on him' (*EPW*, 149). It is the 'widest sense' he found in Eliot's definition that Thomas intends here. Eliot's 'meaning' and Thomas's 'narrative' are, in fact, a kind of sleight of hand practised on the reader – what Eliot described as a way of 'satisfy[ing] one habit of the reader, to keep his mind diverted and quiet, while the poem does its work upon him: much as the imaginary burglar is always provided with a bit of nice meat for the house-dog'. The 'work' that the poem performs, while the conscious, rational, narrative- and meaning-seeking conscious mind is being distracted, occurs at the level of what Eliot calls elsewhere the 'auditory imagination' – that is, of the unconscious mind. It is there that poetry's 'primitive', non-rational effects of rhythm, repetition and 'colour of saying' make their impact.[79] This is discussed at greater length in Chapter 2; for now, it is worth adding that, for Eliot, the auditory imagination is a necessary part of all real poetry and the reason why 'genuine poetry can communicate before it is understood'.[80] Thomas regards himself as one of Eliot's poets who are legitimately 'impatient' of superfluous meaning, entitled to eliminate much of it, in order to maximise the appeal to the auditory imagination. In answering the second *New Verse* question in the negative – 'Do you wait for a spontaneous impulse before writing a poem ...?' – he therefore stressed the labour involved in making a space in which the auditory imagination can achieve its effects beneath the narrative flow. Writing, he said, was 'the task of constructing a watertight compartment of words, preferably with a main moving column (i.e., narrative) to hold a little of the real causes and forces of the creative brain and body' (*EPW*, 150). The 'moving column' is his standard narrative of the processual cycle, rhetorical rather than expository, which provides cover while the 'burglar'-poem acts on the somatic and affective roots of the self. Temporarily disarmed by it, the reader experiences 'the essence' of the poem – the reality of process in a language of 'sheer exuberant loss'. But the difference between Thomas's use of this ruse and Eliot's use of it is that he makes manifest, at the level of the narrative (that is in a thematic sense, too), what the 'auditory imagination' component is up to. Thus, 'Light breaks where no sun shines' generates an urgent, seemingly irresistible unfolding of events with a resonant conclusion, thematising the auditory imagination's aim of 'returning to the origin and bringing something back, seeking the beginning and the end'.[81] The final stanza runs:

Light breaks on secret lots,
On tips of thought where thoughts smell in the rain;
When logics die,
The secret of the soil grows through the eye,
And blood jumps in the sun;
Above the waste allotments the dawn halts. (*CP*, 24)

As in 'I see the boys of summer', Thomas offers a Depression-era scene on the literal level that we might miss at first reading – 'lots', 'tips' and 'allotments' as fate, spoil-heaps and self-sufficiency. But the larger process narrative is one in which the halted 'dawn' is death – a return to the elements and the new life emerging from them, as described in the poem's opening line. Beneath this 'meaning effect' of the cyclical narrative, however, the poem is working on the reader as a sombre and brilliant linguistic event, extravagant in both verbal surplus and slippage, with an unstable and fragmented lyric subject or 'eye' / I pierced by 'the secret of the soil'. *The Waste Land* – to which 'waste allotments' also refers – is famously discontinuous, too, yet its discontinuity is of a kind that encourages the reader to produce a metanarrative, in order to hold its parts together. In Thomas's poem, on the contrary, a narrative drive yields a coherent lyric unity, but the supremely assured unity is baffling: what, exactly, is the nature of the 'allotments' and the 'dawn' which 'halts' above them? Paradoxically, only by accepting the polysemousness, instability and open-endedness of process can we feel satisfied at the poem's close. In short, while Eliot backtracked on the radical implications of the auditory imagination, Thomas took him at his positive word with a calculated literalness that verged on the parodic, making the auditory imagination a foundation of his process style.[82]

Finally, it seems undeniable that Eliot's essay 'Hamlet and His Problems', in the *Selected Essays* published in 1933, deeply influenced Thomas's process poetic. Several critics – George Morgan, most recently – have noted that both Shakespeare and Hamlet haunt *18 Poems* and *Twenty-five Poems*. Shakespearean debts are present in a general way in Thomas's renovation of iambic pentameter, as are his unmodern vocabulary ('mark', 'morrow', 'unto'), allusions ('wheel of fire'), penchant for puns, and taste for the generic noun and generalising verb (*CP*, 48, 13, 29). More, the casting of so many poems in soliloquy form indicates the centrality of Jacobean drama in Thomas's poetic development of summer 1933. Dramatic stylisation of emotion (which also reflected Thomas's deep involvement in local theatre) gave him both a necessary distance from the material of his writing and forms such as the dialogic structure of '"Find Meat on bones"', the self-questioning of 'Was there a time' and the self-interrogation of 'I have longed to move away'. These reflect a specifically modernist take on the soliloquy. Tony Conran has argued that these efforts came to fruition a few months later, when Thomas worked out how to dramatise the symbolist *voyant*, the 'schizoid "I"' of modernism, and to refurbish 'the tragic soliloquy of Marlowe and Shakespeare'.[83] 'Schizoid' here refers to the new subjectivity of the era of finance capital, not Holbrook's attacks, and it is true that, from this point on, Thomas created in his poems 'a mental space, a kind of imaginary stage in which he attempts to reconcile the linearity of a discourse or plot and the spatial simultaneity of theatre', as the self-dramatisations, rhetorical questioning, interrogations and debates of poems such as 'Before I knocked', 'This bread I break' and 'If I were tickled by the rub of love' attest.[84]

The specific echoes of, and allusions to, *Hamlet*, moreover, are pervasive and reflect the play's special significance. Hamlet is mentioned by name in 'Today this insect' ('Death: death of Hamlet and the nightmare madmen') and 'I, in my intricate image' ('five fathomed Hamlet on his father's coral'), as well as in rhythmic echoes (compare 'And drown the cargoed apples in their tides' with 'And smote the sledded poleaxe on the ice') (*CP*, 38, 35, 7). Hamlet's obsession with 'words, words, words', sardonic wit and air of resignation in the face of oncoming doom also made him an appropriate surrogate for Thomas. Three *topoi* recur: Hamlet's consideration of the temptations of suicide in 'To be or not to be' (which Thomas invokes in phrases such as 'sweat of sleep', 'shuffled off' and 'creasing flesh' and allusions to Ophelia); his madness (and the ambiguity concerning its real or feigned nature); and his relationship with his father (*CP*, 24). All three are sexually charged, of course, and Thomas's 'If I were tickled by the rub of love' from Hamlet's 'Ay, there's the rub' sees him using Hamlet's frustration to intertextually distance and, at the same time, dramatise his own adolescent sexual angst.

Suicide is a major subject of Thomas's early work, constantly referred to in the notebooks, letters and poems and usually informed by the famous 'To be, or not to be' soliloquy. In existentialism, suicide appeared as the defining human act in an otherwise absurd universe. Thomas's concern with it distinguishes him from the New Country poets, insofar as it reflects his insistence on ultimate questions of being and his belief that poetry must attend to the spiritual aspect of existence, acting as a corrective to positivism and hyper-rationalism. Suicide faded from his poems in the late 1930s, as did the madness behind which Hamlet, like Thomas with his 'antic disposition' as trickster-poet, hid his methods.[85]

Eliot famously accused Shakespeare of failing to create an 'objective correlative' for Hamlet's mood and actions – that is, 'a set of objects, a situation, a chain of events which shall be the formula of that particular emotion; such that when the external facts, which must terminate in sensory experience, are given, the emotion is immediately evoked'.[86] But if Eliot saw Hamlet's behaviour as excessive in respect of its cause, Freud's disciple Ernest Jones argued that it was precisely and explicably the result of his incestuous Oedipal desire for Gertrude; Hamlet prevaricates in killing Claudius, precisely because this would clear the way to his mother's bed. Thomas incorporated Hamlet into his performance of the role of Freudian exemplar and used it as a way of figuring his relationship with his father, D. J. Thomas – the 'great reader-aloud of Shakespeare' to him as a child (CL, 751). Hamlet-Dylan's father lurks within the presence of the genetic 'warning ghost' of 'From love's first fever', and is elsewhere the deathly 'issue armoured of the grave' and 'the tapped ghost in wood'; he is 'An old mad man still climbing in his ghost, / My father's ghost … climbing in the rain' and 'My half ghost in armour … in death's corridor', who can, and perhaps ought, to be sent back where he came from: 'For we shall be a shouter like the cock / Blowing the old dead back' (CP, 21, 9, 46, 25, 33, 18). Old Hamlet's ghost's cap-à-pé armour may figure D. J. Thomas's rectitude, but the allusions also confirm the speaker's kinship with his phantom. The question of paternity as a fiction, so central to Ulysses, is also part of these poems' meaning: the son is always already the father in the world of process: 'I am the man your father was' or, more quizzically: 'Am I not father too, and the ascending boy … Am I not all of you?' (CP, 8, 42) But there is guilt, too, naturally enough; Hamlet's father's murder surfaces as 'He lying low with ruin in his ear / The cockerel's tide upcasting from the fire', his poisoning, purgatorial fires fading 'on the crowing of the cock' (CP, 45).

The 'brassy' 'hero' and the 'ghost', which we find in so many poems, enact the struggle between body and spirit, the mechanical and the organic, but also the agon with the father in an inner psychodrama representing the processes which gave rise to the poem. A Hamletian web captures Thomas's predicament as poet, son and member of a generation caught in 'the century's trap' in 'times … out of joint', who is seized by paralysis, while it also figures his relationship with English literature; Hamlet is its central canonical text, but its central character is Thomas himself as the outsider, trickster figure. For Morgan, the poems record the son's struggle to embody the father's ghost, and he becomes the 'five-fathomed Hamlet on his father's coral', who is transfigured into a Prospero, fulfilled in magic and song (*CP*, 35). Yet they also limn out a tale of the would-be poet-father who is usurped by his precocious son – a son who masters the maternal body of language and guiltily tries to make amends by paying tribute to his father's love of Shakespeare in his poetry. A Prospero-Thomas more at ease with himself makes an entrance, but not until 'After the funeral', with its 'cloud-sopped, marble hands' echoing Prospero's great speech of renunciation; that is, not until *The Map of Love* (1939), the same collection in which the youthful Hamlet-Thomas – in 'Twenty-four years', with its Hamletian 'flesh-eating sun' – takes a final bow.

Discussion of Thomas's response to Eliot must also be framed by the issue of his place within the larger British response to modernism. In this sense it is revealing that his response to Eliot's intimidating example closely resembled that of his friend William Empson, as Edward Larrissy has argued.[87] Early on, Empson grasped what Thomas was about, and his comments show that he saw him as a poet who exemplified his own critical procedures; in turn, Thomas's early poetry could almost have been written as a manual to illustrate the fusion of modernism and the Metaphysicals assumed by *Seven Types of Ambiguity* (1930). This blend can be related to the peculiarly literary critical form that modernism took in Britain in the early 1930s and which, to some extent, it has been bound by ever since. In an essay of 2007, Drew Milne argued that, for example, Eliot's criticism initiated a process of making the modernist poetic revolt thoroughly traditional and amenable to close reading. Eliot's approach is reflected in Robert Graves's and Laura Riding's *A Survey of Modernist Poetry* (1927) – the first study of 'modernism' to name it thus, and one which defensively domesticates avant-garde disruptiveness under the umbrella of the modernist label. *Seven Types of Ambiguity* (which acknowledged its indebtedness to Graves's and Riding's book) extended this process; and both studies, by effectively reading British modernism 'through the history of English poetry', began a discourse which thwarted 'the very possibility of what might make it "modern"'.[88] Eliot, for Milne, helped 'lock' British modernism into a double-bind, according to which the only viable forms of modernist poetry have seemed not to be experimental ones, but those which can be understood as 'inheritors of premodernist English poetry, [and most] notably … retrospective conceptions of the modernism of seventeenth-century poetry'.[89] Empson's fostering of a taste for ambiguity and structural complexity is thus to be seen as 'a major development of modernist poetics within criticism', the rewriting of earlier poetry according to Eliotic tenets becoming a way of 'writing modernist poetry by other means'.[90]

Milne's essay shrewdly identifies a crucial aspect of British 'mannerist modernism', although it is somewhat teleological in assuming that 'the reception of modernism in Britain is historically out of step with, say, French or American developments'. Equally, there is evidence of the power of the Thomas legend in the fact that Milne's list of those whose work challenges the mainstream's marginalisation of modernist poetry from 1930 to the present day does not include Thomas. Nevertheless, his argument unintentionally illuminates the contexts of Thomas's modernism. For it is precisely in Thomas's work that Empson's response to Eliot in 'ambiguity and structural complexity' was pushed beyond Empson's own limits. Thomas's poetry consciously aims to simultaneously satisfy and thwart the new clerisy of close readers, who were the core of his initial audience. He writes, that is, as if Empson were his ideal reader, yet, at the same time, as if he resented and was trying to resist the new tools devised by Eliot, Richards and Empson as threats to the autonomous world of the poem. We are enticed to exercise our decoding skills, but, at the same time, our belief that all poems must succumb to them is rebuffed. This is an important source of Thomas's reputation for "obscurity" and part of the explanation for why it is that, even eighty years after they were written, some of the poems resist critical summary. Paradoxically, then, the English domestication of modernism led to Anglo-Welsh poems, whose difficulty exceeded even that of more avowedly avant-garde writing of its time.

None of this detracts from Eliot's crucial importance; exaggerating aspects of the older poet's critical and poetic practices enabled Thomas to create his own kind of originality, while the appropriation and splicing of Eliot's 'magical sense' and Auden's 'firmness' allowed him to nullify the anxiety which the two might have been expected to create. More akin to Eliot than Auden in terms of his fundamental poetic principles, Thomas aimed 'to short-cut the reason, by bringing the mind to bear on a representation of reality which is resistant to a reduction to the mind's own reasonable terms'.[91] Yet his poetry also rejected modernism's elitism, outed its Romantic subtexts and undercut its reactionary ideologies. Teetering on an excess of derivation and an absence of influence, the process style embodies a subversive deployment of obscurity and continues to problematise the assumed succession from Eliot to Auden.

The total politics of process: 'All all and all ...'

The social-realist aesthetic which dominated mid-1930s writing rested on a separation of surface and depth; as Alan Wilde has noted, its chief paradox was 'the inevitable but unintended subversion of depth through a relentless attention to surface, undertaken in an attempt to change both self and word by rendering language transparent'. The waning of high modernism led 1930s writers to 'frequently superficial involvements', which left them bewildered, rather than heartened, all the more in that, unlike the modernists, they espoused a positivist faith that crisis could be solved. 'As a result', Wilde argues, 'the genuine paradox of the twenties gives way to apparent paradox, metaphysics to social science'.[92] Thomas's work resisted this surrender to social surfaces, valorising modernist depth by dramatising the genesis of the poem and articulating a powerful sense of cosmic, biological, political and socio-psychic determinism. As we have seen, it had its own ways of signalling interest in the modern world. Even so, the question remains as to why a poetry so resolutely devoted to first and last things, to the biomorphic, mythic and religiose (however it explores the grounds of faith, rather than expounding them) does not strike us as being reactionary – as an example, that is, of 'language ... absolutized as the voice of Being', to cite Adorno's criticism of Heidegger.[93]

As I have suggested, Thomas's work escapes this criticism, because of its status as a mannerist, hybrid and parodic modernism aware of its own procedures. The heterogeneity of its linguistic textures, with their Joycean and excessive self-spending, works to offset the reactionary aspect of the pessimism which might arise from a determinist worldview. This can be traced in 'The force that through the green fuse', where the self oscillates between determinism and self-assertion and identifies its growth and decay with that of the natural world to such an extent that it *is* the 'flower' – one who flows. The distinction between speaker and the natural world is blurred, and, in the first three stanzas, the speaker is dispersed into the natural world. At the same time, natural phenomena invade body and consciousness, creating an organic image of the place of the individual in the life cycle. Yet this movement is repeatedly checked by the refrain 'And I am dumb to tell' – a confession of the speaker's inability to inform the world of his intuition of their continuity. The fourth stanza seems to offer some respite: the 'lips of time' are those of the infant at the breast, with 'Love' – the mother – being made 'calm' by the child's feeding; they are also those of the poet, renewed at the 'fountain head' of inspiration by the cycle of nature; and they are those of a personified Time – the natural cycle itself – being renewed by 'fallen blood' in the endless process of growth and decay (more sexually, the lines may describe the male or female sexual organs seeking each other out). But if the peace of assuaged desire contrasts with blasted roots and the other negatives, dumbness reappears in its usual place in this penultimate stanza and in the final couplet-coda, which links the post-coital bed ('the lover's tomb') – both a literal one, and a literary one, since the 'sheet' is the paper on which this poem is written, and the 'crooked worm' is a finger, as well as a grave-worm or penis.

Despite defeat, however, the poem *has* 'told' something of the speaker's dilemma, and it has done so without foreclosing the natural cycle or moralising. Knowledge of the split between human consciousness and nature has halted it, but by refusing to 'express' a determinate truth by a self-identical speaker, the abjection of silence has been offset by the intransitive force of '*I* am dumb to *tell*', just as, in the later 'A Refusal to Mourn', a future that '*Tells* with silence' is imagined (although 'tells' contains 'tolls', too) (*CP*, 85). Typically, a positive has been created from a negative. Dumbness has reintegrated the ego after the acknowledgement of oneness dispersed it, making it an act of differentiation. A diastole-systole motion of absorption and self-definition enacts the dynamic relationship between consciousness and the creative-destructive 'process' which is the poem's subject.[94] In its fusion of human, natural and metaphysical properties, the poem displaces both the lyric ego and any omnipotent Other (God or Romantic Nature) which might have been assumed to lie beyond it. It thus refuses the usual traps of nature poetry, displaying a deep ecology in refusing to speak *for* nature. Mutual process is made to oppose the dominative logic of religions which rely on a father-figure, 'who enslaves all creation, human and non-human, on the basis of his own unimpeachable self-identity', including the Leader figures of the New Country poets.[95]

By contrast, J. Hillis Miller's argument (as discussed in the Introduction), which also has a 'deep ecological' aspect, assumes unified selves and texts, placing them beyond issues of genre, style, psychic structures, audience and history; the contradictions which generate the work become gaps to 'fill in' and harmonise in the process of constructing each text as internally consistent.[96] Thomas himself said that he aimed at 'the smoothing and removing of the creakiness of conflict', as I noted earlier, but his emphasis was on 'creakiness', not 'conflict' as such (*CL*, 56). The phenomenological aspects of process – its isolation of a pure authorial consciousness presented in concrete, dynamic and intuitional terms – is always countered in his work by the constant challenges to the unified self and closed text, as a fearful and exhilarated subjectivity struggles with eternal flux. The 'I' arising from, or sinking into, a 'dark fluid background' is never fully coherent; it is an 'intricate image' forever ghosted, doubled and 'fellowed', and its archaism is not atavistic in the manner of high modernist poetry nostalgic for tradition or blood-and-soil belongingness.

Naturally, this is reflected in language. Leslie Fiedler's claim that Thomas's poetry is devoid of 'all manufactured things more recently invented than ships' seems a plausible one, but is actually untrue: in reality, it contains macadam, celluloid, arc-lamps, drills, differential gears, carbolic soap, allotments, oil well 'gushers', periscopes, propellers, photographic stills, van (as vehicle), cyanide, solder, hangars, glands, hormones, slot-machines, radium and 78 r.p.m. records, not to mention the technology of modern warfare – barbed wire, fuses, high explosives and poison gas.[97] As Thomas told Treece: 'it is evasive to say my poetry has no social awareness … quite a good number of my images come from the cinema & the gramophone and the newspaper, while I use contemporary slang, cliché, and pun' (CL, 359). Thomas even described poetry in wartime terms, as a 'stream' brought to its conclusion by a 'fullstop armistice' (CL, 328). But as I showed in my discussion of 'I see the boys of summer', he subordinates such items to the processual flow of the verse, subsuming such indicators of modernity within its organicism, even enshrining the blend of blatancy and concealment in the cybernetic collocations mentioned earlier. These reflect a desire to subvert surface with depth at the linguistic level and, as Annis Pratt notes, bear a strong family resemblance to surrealist montage: '[t]he most striking trait of surrealist art was a weird mingling of object and subject, of machine and flesh in an expression of both acceptance and distaste for the modern age'.[98]

This valorisation of depth and difficulty amounted to a political act. Empson claimed that 'Thomas would not agree that he had no political opinions, but they were not at any rate the surface of what he was trying to say', and I take this to mean not just that Thomas did not set out to be an overtly political poet, but that his work's lack of 'opinions', which 'were … [its] … surface', did not stop them entering his poetry in other non-superficial ways.[99] The poetry's politics lie in its resistance to the 'subversion of depth' via its attempt to reinstate 'genuine paradox' in the form of the process poetic. 'Self and world', for Thomas, were not to be altered outwardly by realism and irony, but internally by absorbing dialectic and paradox and emphasising the materiality and historical nature of language. For Thomas, the faith in a merely exiguous rationalism was what crippled New Country poetry as poetry, and its plain style was invariably a concession to conservatism. Writing to Bert Trick in early 1935, not long after arriving in London, Thomas described 'intellectual communists' as 'hav[ing] no idea of what they priggishly call "the class struggle" ... They are bogus from skull to navel; finding no subjects for their escapist poetry, they pin on a vague sense of propagating the immediate necessity of a social conscience rather than the clear sense of expressing their own un, pro, or anti social consciousness. The individual in the mass and the mass in the individual can be made poetically important only when the status and position of both mass and individual are considered by that part of the consciousness which is outside both' (*CL*, 212). This 'part of ... consciousness' is evidently that which grasps its imbrication within the 'universal architecture' of process, and Thomas's comment makes it clear that he felt the processual, biomorphic and cosmic aspects of his poetry had profound political implications.

Depth and surface are thematised in the most pervasive form of technology in the poems, film – the definitive modernist art form and the one which, in its montage and simultaneity effects, best realises the process vision. Film mediates the surface-depth relationship in several poems, and its essentially illusionist nature also symbolises the operations of ideology. This is clearest in 'Our eunuch dreams', which sets the power of wish-fulfilment of Hollywood film beside the fantasies of sex-starved adolescence, yoking sex and violence ('the gunman and his moll, / Two one-dimensioned ghosts, love on a reel') and juxtaposing them with a midnight 'unhous[ing] [of] the tomb' – that is, masturbatory fantasy imagined as vampiric. Both are 'eunuch dreams', 'all seedless' in the light of day, which is that of sexual fulfilment and revolutionary transformation. In accordance with the 'real' / 'reel' pun that Thomas uses elsewhere, the poem asks:

> Which is the world? Of our two sleepings which
> Shall fall awake when cures and their itch
> Raise up this red-eyed earth?
> Pack off the shapes of daylight and their starch,
> The sunny gentlemen, the Welshing rich,
> Or drive the night-geared forth. (*CP*, 17)

Or, after the socialist revolution, when the 'red-eyed earth' of the working class is 'raised up' by suffering and socialist 'cures', which of the two eunuch dreams will 'fall awake' and become reality? Both should be disposed of by overthrowing 'the Welshing rich'; moreover, the 'night-geared' fantasies reinforced by the filmic 'shapes of daylight', 'one-sided skins of truth' and sexual and social repressions are functions of each other. Their oppressive false dreams are given in a vitalist version of Marx's notion that the tradition of all the dead generations weighs like a nightmare on the brains of the living: they are: 'The dream that kicks the buried from their sack / And lets the trash be honoured as the quick' (*CP*, 18). 'This is the world', he adds, 'Have faith'. Thomas is not necessarily dismissing fantasy or film; he does not know what the fate of the 'two sleepings' will be, and he certainly did not share the belief of those, like Leavis, who maintained that film induces 'surrender, under conditions of hypnotic receptivity, to the cheapest emotional appeals'.[100] What he is targeting, rather, is the falseness of the promises made by film and the fantasy that is based upon it. In other words, he is targeting the glamour or system of 'publicity' (we might say 'celebrity culture') which is based on envy, as it was defined by John Berger in *Ways of Seeing*: 'The pursuit of individual happiness has been acknowledged as a universal right. Yet the existing social conditions make the individual feel powerless. He lives in the contradiction between what he is and what he would like to be. Either he then becomes fully conscious of the contradiction and so joins the political struggle for a full democracy ... or else he lives, continually subject to an envy which, compounded with his sense of powerlessness, dissolves into recurrent day dreams'.[101] 'Our eunuch dreams' takes in more than sexual fantasy (though that is viewed as the most powerful kind) and thus explores the contradictions of trying to free oneself from it. This is nowhere more the case than in the final stanza, which, typically, has a positive, affirming tone – 'Praise to our faring hearts' – but is riddled by ambiguity (does the phrase 'Blowing the old dead back', for example, mean rejecting the dead or resurrecting them?) Certainly, no easy revolutionary fervour is endorsed.

A. T. Tolley notes that 'The political poetry of the early 1930s might be called *apocalyptic*', but this worked both ways; Apocalyptic poetry was now inevitably political, too.[102] Many of Thomas's contemporaries grasped the apocalyptic political unconscious of his poetry and the way it emerged as it did in resistance to socio-political surfaces. From his experience of outreach teaching to undergraduate societies and 'adult audiences in the Rhymney Valley', Thomas's contemporary R. George Thomas concluded that:

> The febrile grotesqueness of the decade between 1930 and 1940 was accurately mirrored ... in Dylan Thomas's verse. ... As many readers recognized then,

the confused and horrible images in the last verse of the poem ['The force that through the green fuse'] were acceptable not as good reportage but as an externalized expression of long suppressed fantasies and fears ... [about] unknown sources of physical suffering that must lie ahead of us, most probably in gas warfare or Guernica-like devastation. None felt uneasy about the macabre images ... though all detected the mixed attitudes of confident exhilaration and wry acceptance of fate that were conveyed ... There was a nightmare quality in the drift towards Hitler's War which was echoed more closely in Thomas's non-political verse than in any of the Home Guard poems of C. Day Lewis or the twisted agonies of Spender's more personal verse.[103]

Even so, an openly revolutionary socialist-sexual vision does not appear until the very end of *18 Poems* in the last stanza of 'All all and all'. This is one of three poems in the collection with a tripartite structure that mimics the thesis-antithesis-synthesis triad of Hegelian dialectics. It moves from the organic, but death-loving, 'dry worlds' to one in which a mechanical self is urged not to 'fear ... the working world' or the biological 'screws' which compel the body into sexual activity, concluding with the 'coupl[ing]' of a 'contagious man' with 'his shapeless people' – social renovation through the synthesis of 'people's fusion' and 'flame in the flesh's vision', or libertarian love:

> Flower, flower the people's fusion,
> O light in zenith, the coupled bud,
> And the flame in the flesh's vision.
> Out of the sea, the drive of oil,
> Socket and grave, the brassy blood,
> Flower, flower, all all and all. (*CP*, 30)

The poem's title reinforces the family resemblances between Thomas's visionary process poetic and Hegelian-Marxist dialectics – 'totality' being the 'organizing core of the dialectical method', in which the 'historically determined' whole is always implicit in the part, and the part always subsumed by the whole.[104] It draws together the other process poems in its 'flower', 'fusion', 'sea' and 'blood' and, for the only time in Thomas's poetry, refers to 'the people'. The combination of vitalism and death, the mechanical and organic, in the poem Thomas self-mockingly referred to as 'Bradawl, Nuttall & Bugger-all' are unsettling, too – 'socket and grave, the brassy blood' – in acknowledging schematic-parodic aspects, refusing to succumb to any levelling 'light in zenith' and thus unify depth and surface (*CL*, 184).

The space of a tactic

It used to be believed that 'after [1930] … certain elements of Modernism seem to be reallocated, as history increasingly came back in for intellectuals, as, with the loss of purpose and social cohesion, and the accelerating pace of technological change, modernity was a visible scene open to simple report'.[105] Recently, however, it has become evident that unitary accounts of modernism, which take 1930 (or even 1939) as their terminus, are inadequate. Rather, it is necessary to think of a 'plurality of competing and geographically diverse alternative modernisms that encompasses peripheries', viewing them 'less as a sudden rupture or as a linear progression climaxing in the achievements of the 1920s', than as a series of 'traces, false starts, successive waves'.[106] For many writers, the modernist vision was never as 'visible', 'open' or 'simple' as the social realists conceived it to be. This is the case with Thomas, who both rejected positivism and reaction in his resolution 'not to differentiate between what is called rational and what is called irrational, but to attempt to create, or let be created, one rationalism' (*CL*, 97–8). Traditional form was in Thomas's poetry to be estranged from itself by modernist content, and modernist disjunctiveness was to be undermined by organicist pseudo-coherence in the stroppily subaltern, Anglo-Welsh hybrid process mode.

This began as a tactic – an outsider's attempt to exploit and turn a period of literary interregnum to good account. It resulted in a shifting, slyly humble-assertive poetic voice which is very different from the impersonal-ironic, authoritative ones of Eliot or Auden. An abstract Everyman, 'at once mankind, Christ, newborn infant, and cadaver', it did not presume, on the basis of some symbolically representative vision, to offer a synoptic overview of modern society or human (and divine) nature.[107] Nor did the metaphysics of process claim the kind of essential truth offered by other synthesising philosophies of the era, although it adopts a stance of radical opposition to the gradualist liberalism in which crises are diplomatically resolved, and its discursive conventions (which included those of the 'bogus' revolutionaries of New Country).[108] The hour has passed, it instinctively knows, for such niceties.

In his essay '"Making do": uses and tactics', the theorist Michel de Certeau distinguished between the strategy of power and tactics – 'the art of the weak' – in a way which sheds light on Thomas's position and practice as a writer.[109] 'The space of a tactic', he points out, 'is the space of the other … it must play on and with a terrain imposed on it and organized by the law of a foreign power'. Although more mobile than centralised power, it has no base 'where it could stockpile its winnings, build up its own position, and plan raids. What it wins it cannot keep'. It can only operate in an opportunistic, guerrilla manner, which is availing itself of 'the cracks that particular conjunctions open up in the surveillance of the proprietary powers. It poaches in them. It creates surprises in them. It can be where it is least expected. It is a guileful ruse'.[110] Thomas, in these senses, is a peculiarly *tactical* poet, one whose success would give him no position and who was incapable of complying with, and operating from, entrenched positions; his major stylistic leap arose from the guileful exploitation of the 'cracks' created in a transitional period. As de Certeau notes, such 'trickery' operates through procedures that Freud makes explicit with reference to wit, which 'boldly juxtaposes diverse elements in order to suddenly produce a flash shedding a different light on the language of a place and to strike the hearer'.[111] Yet this *modus operandi*, 'taking advantage of opportunities, using comedy to subvert occasions, employing the know-how and make-do of "crosscuts, fragments, cracks and lucky hits"', is an exhausting one, insofar as it requires constant reinvention, is threatened at every moment with elimination and has no fall-back position, no reserves and no institutional basis.[112] It means that – as Thomas tended to do – the tactic or poem has to be reinvented every time that it is written; in sum, it has to contain everything.

'A tactic, in short, is the art of the weak', and this requires a more-than-usual level of trickery and rhetorical artfulness. Indeed, the more that the totality of process asserts itself, the more it is undermined by the intertextual, hybrid and playfully self-delighting aspects of its writing (albeit less strongly after 1938, as the poems acquired something of the status of rival creations, impervious to time, and less as embodiments of processual flow). At the same time, as a 'vertical invader' possessed of a style of unrivalled originality, Thomas seems supremely self-confident. The result is mixed, conflicting and difficult to describe, according to the standard taxonomy of literary development. So, Thomas does not destroy his notebooks full of teenage poetry, but sells them to a research library. He often buries his 'sources' beyond reasonable expectation of discovery, but, at times, he flaunts them in a brazen way. He does not 'progress' in the usual linear and incremental sense, but each poem attempts to recapitulate what the others have already established. He never abandons his pre-process style, which is eventually absorbed within his final, transparent style or, as Peter Riley observes: 'Thomas's writing did not develop steadily towards or away from difficulty, but was liable to lean either way at any time, until it reached a certain stability in his last poems'.[113] Their constant tactical manoeuvring means that while the early poems are often about the same basic things, as some critics complain, this does not lead to monotony: they are all distinct and unique verbal events. Not only is almost every poem an example of a verse form 'laboriously developed, perfected in that one poem, then dropped', but they are animated by a conflict between processual unity and linguistic dis-unity.[114] It is Thomas's main tactic in this regard – the tapping of linguistic *jouissance* in excess of both discursive requirements and the 'reasonable' requirements of pattern-making – and the extraordinary pains he took to realise it – which I consider in the next chapter.

Notes

1 Theodor W. Adorno, 'On Lyric Poetry and Society', ed. Rolf Tiedemann and transl. Sherry Weber Nicholson, *Notes to Literature, vol. 1* (New York, NY: Columbia University Press, 1991), p.39.

2 Jeffrey Ganz, transl., *The Mabinogion* (London: Penguin, 1976), p.97.

3 William Empson, *Argufying*, p.387.

4 See Introduction, fn. 16. *18 Poems* enjoyed a *succés d'estime* and was reviewed, generally favourably, in *The Listener, New Verse, Time and Tide, Criterion, TLS* and the *Spectator*. From 1934, Thomas was the most visible of this group, which also included George Barker and David Gascoyne. All three were represented in the definitive 1930s anthology, Michael Roberts's *Faber Book of Modern Verse* (1936).

5 The enigma of an original style without any obvious origins confronted all of Thomas's first readers. Thus, Jones, who first encountered Thomas in March 1934, asks: 'How was it that Dylan, a schoolboy, provincial, inexperienced, had come to write in that particular way, to evolve at so early an age a style of such power and originality?' Glyn Jones, *The Dragon Has Two Tongues: Essays on Anglo-Welsh Writers and Writing* (Cardiff: University of Wales Press, 2001), p.171.

6 Robert Graves, 'These Be Your Gods, O Israel!' This was the sixth and last of the Clark Lectures on Professional Standards in English Poetry delivered at Trinity College, Cambridge, Michaelmas Term, 1954. See Graves, *Essays in Criticism*, 5 (Oxford: Basil Blackwell, 1955), p.148 [repr. Robert Graves, *The Crowning Privilege* (London: Cassell, 1955)]; John Malcolm Brinnin, ed., *A Casebook on Dylan Thomas* (New York, NY: T. Y. Crowell, 1961).

7 Thomas told Geoffrey Grigson of 'innumerable exercise books full of poems' in Spring 1933, and there were evidently more notebooks, probably containing different kinds of poems to the 'Mainly Free Verse' ones, which Thomas was filling during this period (*CL*, 33). It is highly unlikely that they were more important than the extant notebooks, however, whose status is reflected in their continued use until 1941. See Ralph Maud, *Poet in the Making: The Notebooks of Dylan Thomas* (London: Dent, 1968 [North American edn. 1967]). A revised version of *Poet in the Making* appeared in 1989, complementing the Ralph Maud and Walford Davies edition

of the *Collected Poems* of 1988, as *The Notebook Poems 1930–1934* (London: Dent, 1989). This lacks the long introductory essay and the exhaustive textual annotations of the earlier edition. However, it increases the number of non-notebook poems, of which just twenty were previously included under the headings 'Early Rhymed Verse', 'Typescript Poems' (conjectured to be from the lost July 1932–January 1933 notebook) and 'Collateral Poems'.

8   See Chapter 5, fn. 4. Ralph Maud gives details of Thomas's use of his notebook poems in Ralph Maud, *The Notebook Poems* pp. viii-x. These show that, after *18 Poems*, Thomas used or drew on sixteen notebook poems for *Twenty-five Poems*, eight for *The Map of Love* and three for *Deaths and Entrances*.

9   Ralph Maud's *Poet in the Making* gives an invaluable notebook-by-notebook account of the development of the poems, locating them in a biographical framework. Walford Davies's analysis is literary-critical, as well as biographical, tying the notebook poems to Thomas's Swansea contexts James A. Davies makes valuable, if brief analyses of 'The Woman Speaks', 'Jack of Christ' and other notebook poems in James A. Davies, *A Reference Companion to Dylan Thomas* (Westport / London: Greenwood Press, 1998), pp. 107–24. Jon Silkin offers a fascinating analysis of the notebook version of 'The hunchback in the park'. Walford Davies, 'The Wanton Starer', ed. Walford Davies, *Dylan Thomas: New Critical Essays* (London: Dent, 1972), pp. 136–65; Jon Silkin, *The Life of Metrical and Free Verse in Twentieth Century Poetry* (London: Macmillan, 1997), pp. 242–70.

10 A fourteenth, 'Especially when the October wind', is a post-notebook revision of a poem presumed to come from the missing notebook of July 1932–January 1933; the other four poems in *18 Poems* were all written in full after the notebook poems ceased on 30 April 1934 (these were 'When, like a running grave', 'I dreamed my genesis', 'All all and all' and 'My world is pyramid').

11 Nicholas Moore, 'The Poetry of Dylan Thomas', *The Poetry Quarterly*, 10: 4 (1948), p. 231.

12 Kenneth Rexroth, ed., *The New British Poets: An Anthology* (New York, NY: New Directions, 1948), p. xx.

13 See, for example, Nathalie Wourm, 'Dylan Thomas and the French Symbolists', Welsh Writing in English Yearbook: A Yearbook of Critical Essays, 5 (1999), pp. 27–41).

14 T. S. Eliot, 'Philip Massinger', *Selected Essays* (London: Faber, 1932), p. 206.

15 'Seemed to', because, in the long run, modernist poetry (whether redescribed as 'late modernist' or 'neo-modernist') continued until the 1970s (after which a 'postmodern' period might properly be said to have begun). I follow Anthony Mellors and Marjorie Perloff in this, noting the appearance between 1939 and 1975 of such major modernist works as T. S. Eliot's *Four Quartets*, David Jones's *The Anathemata*, Basil Bunting's *Briggflatts*, Charles Olson's *The Maximus Poems*, Louis Zukofsky's *'A'* and William Carlos Williams's *Paterson*, not to mention modernism's extension in the work of Frank O'Hara, Jack Spicer, Robert Duncan, Paul Celan, Bernard Noël, Andrea Zanzotto, J. H. Prynne, Denise Riley, Allen Fisher and others. What occurred in the early 1930s was a succession crisis for 1920s high modernism, the temporary nature of which has been occluded by the valorisation of the decade's plain-style political poetry. Followers of Pound, such as Basil Bunting, Joseph Macleod (in *The Ecliptic*, 1930, described as: 'a synthesis of first-generation modernist poetry and English traditions') and the Auden of *The*

Orators did not generate a new 'dawn' for British modernism, as Keith Tuma has pointed out. However, as this book argues, the impact and daring of Thomas's work gave this 'dawn' a different (non-Poundian) form to that which Tuma seeks. See Keith Tuma, *Fishing by Obstinate Isles: Modern and Postmodern British Poetry and American Readers* (Evanston, IL: Northwestern University Press, 1998), pp. 120, 123–39; Anthony Mellors, *Late Modernist Poetics: From Pound to Prynne* (Manchester: Manchester University Press, 2005), pp. 17–23.

16 Marjorie Perloff, '"Barbed-Wire Entanglements": The "New American Poetry," 1930–32', *Poetry On & Off the Page: Essays for Emergent Occasions* (Evanston, IL: Northwestern University Press, 1998), pp. 53–4.

17 *New Signatures* included poetry by W. H. Auden, Julian Bell, Cecil Day-Lewis, Richard Eberhart, William Empson, John Lehmann, William Plomer, Stephen Spender and A. S. J. Tessimond; *New Country* also included Auden, Day-Lewis, Lehmann, Spender and Tessimond, plus Richard Goodman, Charles Madge, Rex Warner and Michael Roberts. Both anthologies included prose, as well as poetry.

18 Louis MacNeice, 'Poetry To-day', ed. Alan Heuser, *The Selected Literary Criticism of Louis MacNeice* (Oxford: Clarendon Press, 1987), p. 34. It is worth noting that MacNeice did not appear in Roberts's anthologies and was neither a member of the Auden group inner circle, nor an uncritical admirer of its literary style and politics.

19 Marjorie Perloff, '"Barbed-Wire Entanglements": The "New American Poetry," 1930–32', p. 53.

20 Louis MacNeice, *Selected Literary Criticism*, ed. Alan Heuser (Oxford: Clarendon Press, 1987), p. 141.

21 W. H. Auden, *The English Auden: Poems, Essays and Dramatic Writings 1927–1939*, ed. Edward Mendelson (London: Faber, 1989), p. 195; Samuel Hynes, *The Auden Generation: Literature and Politics in England in the 1930s* (London: Bodley Head, 1976), p. 155.

22 Francis Scarfe, *Auden and After: The Liberation of Poetry 1930–41* (London: Routledge, 1942), p. xiii.

23 Tony Conran, *Frontiers in Anglo-Welsh Poetry* (Bridgend: Seren, 1997), p. 137.

24 Desmond Hawkins, 'Poetry', *Time and Tide*, XVI: 6 (9 February 1935), pp. 204, 206.

25 Space prevents a full consideration of Thomas's indebtedness to modernist writers. Along with Eliot, Joyce was the primary influence. From Lawrence, he took sexual vitalism, inflected by their shared Methodism, regional origins and lower-middle class *ressentiment*. Thomas also seems to have found Wyndham Lewis useful for his 'mechanical' and inorganic qualities, approving of *Tarr* and *The Apes of God*. Of Pound's work, Thomas had definitely read *Cathay* and the shorter pre-*Cantos* poems.

26 Allen Ginsberg, *Howl and Other Poems* (San Francisco, CA: City Lights Books, 1956 [repr. 1971]), p. 9.

27 Rainer Emig, *Modernism in Poetry: Motivations, Structures and Limits* (London: Longman, 1995), p. 124.

28 See also Thomas's written denials of experimentalism: 'I'm not an experimentalist & never will be. I write in the only way I can write, & my warped, crabbed & cabined stuff is not the result of theorising but of pure incapability to express my needless tortuosities in any other way' (*CL*, 160). This, of course, does not explain why he should contrive to make 'Now' and other poems *appear* experimental.

29 While its significance may indeed 'come from its form and insistence on form', that insistence is not simply mechanical and certainly does not arise from a 'refus[al] to provide normal syntax', as Maud and Davies claim. (*CP*, 201) As with Eliot's defence of Edward Lear in 'The Music of Poetry', it can be said that 'his non-sense is not vacuity of sense: it is a parody of sense, and that is the sense of it'. See T. S. Eliot, 'The Music of Poetry' (1942), *On Poetry and Poets* (London: Faber and Faber, 1957), p. 29.

30 Edmund Wilson, *Axel's Castle: A Study in the Imaginative Literature of 1870–1930* (London: Collins, 1931 [repr. 1976]), p. 230.

31 Drew Milne, 'Flaming Robes: Keats, Shelley and the Metrical Clothes of Class Struggle', *Textual Practice*, 15: 1 (2001), 102; Raymond Williams, *Marxism and Literature* (Oxford: Oxford University Press, 1977 [repr. 1978]), pp. 128–35.

32 W. J. McCormack, *From Burke to Beckett: Ascendancy, Tradition and Betrayal in Literary History* (Cork: Cork University Press, 1994), p. 330.

33 Bert Trick was a radical socialist Labour Party member, influenced by Christian socialism, as well as Marxism, and under his tutelage and against the background of fascist activity in Swansea, Thomas became actively engaged with local socialist politics (see fn 99 below).

34 The texts are from Romans (6: 9) and Revelation (20: 13). Ralph Maud, *Where Have the Old Words Got Me?* (Cardiff: University of Wales Press, 2003), p. 38.

35 See John L. Sweeney: 'Chant and hymn were in his full-bodied music but the underlying rhythm was always simple. It was un-English and would not yield its cadence to slur or drawl. The syllabic beat was sharply defined'. Dylan Thomas, *Selected Writings*, ed. John L. Sweeney (New York, NY: New Directions, 1946), p. xii.

36 Trick's piece evinces an unequivocal faith in an afterlife: 'Moves a soul ... Like a fluttering bird ... To some high altitude / Where breathes a living God. / Then death is not the end!' See Paul Ferris, *Dylan Thomas* (London: Penguin, 1978), p. 83.

37 Walford Davies, *Dylan Thomas* (Milton Keynes: Open University Press, 1985), p. 88.

38 Terry Eagleton, *Literary Theory: An Introduction* (London: Blackwell, 1983), p. 118.

39 See Linden Huddlestone, 'An Approach to Dylan Thomas', *Penguin New Writing*, XXXV (1948), p. 134: 'through ... disruption and negation of life assailed by the intimidation of sexual disgrace and the diabolically active forces of sin, there are signs that something positive has been found – though *positive in the sense of a double negative*' (emphasis added).

40 'Milton', Book II, Plate VIII, ll. 32–3, eds. W. H. Stevenson and David V. Erdman, *William Blake: The Complete Poems* (London: Longman, 1972), p. 563.

41 Ralph Maud, *Poet in the Making*, pp. 23–4.

42 The poems that Thomas wrote during this period include: 'My hero bares his nerves' (17 September 1933), 'In the beginning was the three-pointed star' (18 September 1933), 'The force that through the green fuse' (12 October 1933), 'From love's first fever to her plague' (14–17 October 1933), 'When once the twilight locks no longer' (11 November 1933), 'Light breaks where no sun shines' (20 November 1933), 'I fellowed sleep' (5 October-27 November 1933), 'This bread I break' (24 December 1933), 'A process in the weather of the heart' (2 February 1934), 'Foster the light' (23 February 1934), 'Our eunuch dreams' ('March' 1934), 'Where once the waters of your face' (18 March 1934), 'I see the boys of summer in their ruin' ('April' 1934) and 'If I were tickled by the rub of love' (30 April 1934).

43 Andrew Duncan, *Origins of the Underground: British Poetry between Apocryphon and Incident Light 1933–79* (Cambridge: Salt, 2008), p.148. As mentioned in the Introduction, the parallels between visual art and Thomas's poetic practice are highly suggestive in this regard. In the early 1930s, when Thomas began visiting it, London was embracing modernist art for the first time. There were exhibitions of work by Picasso, l'École de Paris, Max Ernst and Joan Miró between 1931 and 1933, while Unit One, formed in 1933, was: 'introducing to a wider public styles such as Biomorphism, Abstraction and Surrealism'. The precursors of biomorphism, which was a major component of surrealism, included André Masson, S. W. Hayter, Joan Miró and Roberto Matta. See Jonathan Miles and Derek Shiel, *David Jones: The Maker Unmade* (Bridgend: Seren, 1995), p.179.

44 D. J. Thomas was first treated with radium needles for cancer of the mouth on 10 September; Thomas's poem 'Take the needles and the knives' is dated 12 September in the third notebook.

45 Thomas Lovell Beddoes, *Death's Jest-Book*, ed. and intro. Alan Halsey (Sheffield: West House Books, 2003), p.132.

46 William Walton Rowe, *Three Lyric Poets: Harwood, Torrance, MacSweeney* (Tavistock: Northcote House, 2009), p.7.

47 See David N. Thomas, ed., *Dylan Remembered, Vol. 1, 1914–1934*, interviews by Colin Edwards (Bridgend: Seren, 2003), p.145; W. Emlyn Davies records 'I do know definitely that he read Whitehead's *Science and the Modern World*.'

48 Alfred North Whitehead (1861–1947), philosopher and mathematician, taught at Cambridge University, University College London, Imperial College London and Harvard University. Whitehead published extensively and influentially on algebra, logic, the philosophy of science, physics and education. He was the author of a rival theory to Einstein's General Theory of Relativity and the co-author, with Bertrand Russell (his former student), of *Principia Mathematica*. He expounded his 'process philosophy' in, among other works, *The Concept of Nature* (1920), *Science and the Modern World* (1926), *Religion in the Making* (1926), *Process and Reality* (1929) and *Adventures of Ideas* (1933), propounding several ideas strongly echoed in Thomas's work. These include: nature as perpetual process ('nature is a structure of evolving processes. The reality is the process' and process, rather than substance, is the fundamental metaphysical constituent of the world); the interconnectedness of subatomic and cosmic events; simultaneity and perpetual potentiality ('Whatever is going to happen is already happening'); the impossibility of language as complete communication ('There is always a background of presupposition, which defies analysis by reason of its infinitude'); and profound scepticism towards ratiocinative logic ('Logic, conceived as an adequate analysis of the advance of thought, is a fake'). Whitehead's ideas shaped later literature and thought; Maurice Merleau-Ponty and Gilles Deleuze, for example, are indebted to him, and he is a key presence in the poetry of Charles Olson and Ted Berrigan. Thomas was one of several contemporary poets interested in the concept of process: William Carlos Williams felt that Einstein's discoveries implied a new conception of poetic form, and, for Muriel Rukeyser, the work of Willard Gibbs, a founder of thermodynamics, inaugurated: 'a language of process … of the kind of life that is not a point-to-point movement, but a real flow in which everything is seen as deeply related to everything else'. See Tim Armstrong, *Modernism* (Cambridge: Polity Press, 2005), p.120. Thomas would also have been aware of the vigorous

rebuttals of such philosophies of flux and simultaneity by Wyndham Lewis in *Time and Western Man* (1927).

49 Thomas's reference to 'the middles of pages' echoes J. W. Dunne's bestselling *An Experiment With Time* (1927) – one of the works which provoked Lewis's *Time and Western Man*. In it, Dunne argues that all time is eternally present, with past, present and future occurring together. Human consciousness experiences this simultaneity in linear form, but this ceases to be the case in certain dream states. The analogy that Dunne uses is of a book. The whole book exists in itself; at any given moment, we can only be reading one page at a time, but in dream, we can grasp both the linear and the simultaneous at once (somewhat as in Thomas's 'I, in my intricate image').

50 Sir James Jeans (1877–1946) taught at Princeton and Cambridge Universities and was the founder, with Arthur Eddington, of British cosmology. He made important contributions to quantum theory, the theory of radiation and stellar evolution; his proposal that the planets had condensed from material drawn out of the sun by a near-collision with a passing star was the dominant one from the 1920s until the 1960s. In 1928, Jeans was the first to conjecture a steady state cosmology. His popular science works include *The Universe Around Us* (1929), *The Mysterious Universe* (1930), *The Stars in Their Courses* (1931), *The New Background of Science* (1933) and *Through Space and Time* (1934).

51 Sir Arthur Eddington (1882–1944) was director of the Cambridge Observatory from 1914. He did much pioneering work on the nature of stars, and the natural limit to the luminosity of stars – the Eddington limit – is named after him. He was also famous for his work regarding the theory of relativity and played a major role in explaining the theory of general relativity to the English-speaking world; his expedition to observe the solar eclipse of 29 May 1919 yielded one of the earliest confirmations of relativity. His books include *The Internal Constitution of the Stars* (1926), *The Nature of the Physical World* (1928) and *Why I Believe in God: Science and Religion as a Scientist Sees It* (1930).

52 Tim Armstrong, *Modernism*, p. 9.

53 Because he is dead – although he does not yet know it – Peter witnesses fully the operations of process: 'No sooner did the cattle fall sucked on to the earth and the weasels race away, then [sic] all the flies, rising from the dung of the fields, came up like a fog and settled on the sides. ... Now the sheep fell and the flies were at them. ... It was to Peter but a little time before the dead, picked to the symmetrical bone, were huddled in under the soil by the wind ... Now the worm and the beetle undid the fibres of the animal bones, worked at them brightly and minutely, and the weeds through the sockets and the flowers on the vanished dead sprouted up with the colours of the dead life fresh on their leaves' (*CS*, 29–30).

54 The boy narrator of the tale 'saw every plough crease and beast's print, man track and water drop, comb, crest, and plume mark, dust and death groove and signature and time-cast shade, from icefield to icefield, sea rims to sea centres ... he saw through the black thumbprint of man's city to the fossil thumb of a once-lively man of meadows; through the grass and clover fossil of the country print to the whole hand of a forgotten city drowned under Europe; through the handprint to the arm of an empire broken like Venus; through the arm to the breast, from history to the thigh, through the thigh in the dark to the first and West print between the dark and the green Eden; and the garden was undrowned, to this next minute and for

ever, under Asia in the earth that rolled on to its music in the beginning evening' (*CS*, 93).

55 Jacob Korg, *Dylan Thomas* (Washington, DC: Hippocrene Books, 1965 [repr. 1972]), p. 32.

56 Tim Armstrong, *Modernism*, p. 121.

57 The third notebook's 'Twenty Six', 'The first ten years in school and park' (dated 22 April 1933), may be the source of the practice, with closing lines which run: 'That music understood, then there's another: / The music of turbine and lawn mower ... Blackbird and Blue Bird, moth and Moth' (*NP*, 153). What was originally meant as a conventional contrast between mechanised modernity and a Romantically conceived nature slips up on wordplay, first as 'blackbird', which gives Sir Malcolm Campbell's world speed record-breaking cars (all named 'Blue Bird') and then through a 'Gypsy Moth' biplane as a moth; both perhaps suggested how polysemy could incorporate modernity without falling into mimeticist representation.

58 Paul Volsic, 'Reason, Rhyme and Metamorphosis', *Les Années 30. Dylan Thomas* (Université de Nantes), 12 (Juin 1990), pp. 40–1.

59 The poem is, indeed, highly unusual; it maintains a strict syllable-count in each of its quatrains of 12, 7, 10, 8. A comma precedes the final word of the first three lines of each quatrain, producing a forceful enjambment. The assonantal rhyme scheme is elaborate, with the last, unaccented syllable of the first line of each stanza pararhyming with the last, accented syllable of the second line and lines three and four pararhyming on their stressed syllable.

60 Theodor Adorno, *Aesthetic Theory* (London: Routledge, 1984), p. 223.

61 Linden Huddlestone, 'An Approach to Dylan Thomas', p. 156.

62 W. H. Auden, 'XVII', *The English Auden*, p. 32.

63 Constantine Fitzgibbon, *The Life of Dylan Thomas* (London: Dent, 1965 [repr. Plantin Paperbacks, 1987]), p. 59.

64 See, for example, the letter to Henry Treece of 23 March 1938: '... I cannot accept Auden as head-prefect. I think MacNeice is thin and conventionally-minded, lacking imagination, and not sound in the ear; flop Day-Lewis; and Spender, Rupert Brooke of the Depression, condemns his slight, lyrical, nostalgic talent to a clumsy and rhetorical death' (*CL*, 328).

65 Stan Smith, '"The little arisen original monster"; Dylan Thomas's Sour Grapes', eds. John Goodby and Chris Wigginton, *Dylan Thomas: New Casebook*, pp. 26–8.

66 Stan Smith, '"The little arisen originary monster"', p. 33.

67 John Bayley, *The Romantic Survival: A Study in Poetic Evolution* (London: Constable, 1957), p. 207.

68 W. H. Auden, 'In Memory of Ernst Toller', *Collected Shorter Poems 1927–1957* (London: Faber, 1975), p. 144.

69 Cecil Day Lewis, *Poems of C. Day Lewis 1925–1972, vol. 1*, ed. and intro. Ian Parsons (London: Jonathan Cape, 1977), p. 81.

70 Thomas attacked *Vienna* in more conventional terms, too: 'Here we have a revolutionary poem published by Faber and Faber, i.e. published ... without the disapproval of the author of *The Rock* ... What sort of revolutionary propaganda would Mr. Eliot permit himself to publish? Obviously not that which would have any effect, but rather that of the stand-in-the-corner, pat-on-the-back young man who, by his insistence on the crudities of language and the tin thunder of his

images, sets himself up immediately as the communist-intellectual type, pigeon-holed by *Punch*' (*EPW*, 170).

71 Stephen Spender, *Vienna* (London: Faber and Faber, 1934), pp. 42–3.

72 Stewart Crehan, '"The Lips of Time"', p. 48.

73 Thomas initially offered his first collection to Faber; however, Eliot prevaricated for several months. On 1 November 1933 Erica Wright, Eliot's secretary, informed Thomas that Eliot 'hopes that you will not make any decision about the publication of your poems before hearing from him', but it was too late. Eliot later said that he regretted having been 'so fussy ... one ought to have accepted the inferior with the first-rate' (*CL*, 199–200).

74 T. S. Eliot, 'The Metaphysical Poets', *Selected Essays 1917–1932* (London: Faber, 1932), p. 289.

75 T. S. Eliot, 'The Metaphysical Poets', pp. 290, 288.

76 T. S. Eliot, 'The Metaphysical Poets', p. 287.

77 Maud Ellmann, *The Poetics of Impersonality: T. S. Eliot and Ezra Pound* (Brighton: Harvester Press, 1987), pp. 101, 93–7.

78 Maud Ellmann, *The Poetics of Impersonality*, pp. 94, 96, 95.

79 Eliot's definition of the auditory imagination describes it as: 'the feeling for syllable, rhythm, penetrating far below the conscious levels of thought and feeling, invigorating every word; sinking to the most primitive and forgotten, returning to the origin and bringing something back, seeking the beginning and the end. It works through meanings, certainly, or not without meanings in the ordinary sense, and fuses the old and obliterated and the trite, the current, and the new and surprising, the most ancient and the most civilised mentality'. T. S. Eliot, 'Matthew Arnold', *The Use of Poetry and the Use of Criticism* (London: Faber, 1933 [repr. 1934]), pp. 118–19. I discuss this at more length in Chapter 2.

80 T. S. Eliot, 'Dante', *Selected Essays*, p. 238. Eliot gives three justifications for obscurity: 'personal causes', sheer novelty and omission. He chiefly defends the second: 'The more seasoned reader, he who has reached ... a state of greater *purity*, does not bother about understanding ... at first. I know that some of the poetry to which I am most devoted is poetry which I did not understand at first reading; some is poetry which I am not sure I understand yet'. See T. S. Eliot, *The Use of Poetry and the Use of Criticism*, p. 151.

81 T. S. Eliot, 'Matthew Arnold', *The Use of Poetry and the Use of Criticism* (London: Faber, 1933), p. 118.

82 In 'Milton I', first published in 1936, Eliot recanted, attacking 'syntax ... determined by ... musical significance, by the auditory imagination, rather than by the attempt to follow actual speech or thought'. Linguistic autonomy was revoked to prevent a 'hypertrophy of the auditory imagination'. T. S. Eliot, 'Milton I', *On Poetry and Poets* (London: Faber, 1957), p. 142.

83 Tony Conran, *Frontiers in Anglo-Welsh Poetry* (Cardiff: University of Wales Press, 1997), p. 120.

84 George Morgan, 'Dylan Thomas and the Ghost of Shakespeare', *Cycnos*, 5 (Nice Cedex, France, 1989), p. 115. I am indebted to Morgan's insightful article throughout this section of the chapter.

85 Like the 'boy who slit his throat' in 'After the funeral', an uncollected poem sent in a letter to Treece reflects the fact that, by 1938, Thomas was able to distance himself from the earlier self who brooded on suicide. The poem starts 'O Chatterton and

others in the attic' and includes the mock exhortation 'Be a regular / Fellow with saw at the jugular' (*CL*, 353).

86 T. S. Eliot, 'Hamlet and His Problems', *Selected Essays*, p. 124.

87 Edward Larrissy, 'Languages of Modernism: William Empson, Dylan Thomas, W. S. Graham', ed. Neil Corcoran, *The Cambridge Companion to Twentieth-Century English Poetry* (Cambridge: Cambridge University Press, 2007), pp. 131–44. Larrissy argues that all three poets 'enact a Modernist emphasis on the poet as rational and impersonal craftsman with words. In their particular expression of this emphasis in terms of metaphor and wordplay capable of rational interpretation, they reveal their indebtedness to the revolution in poetics wrought by Eliot'.

88 Drew Milne, 'Modernist Poetry in the British Isles', eds. Alex Davis and Lee Jenkins, *The Cambridge Companion to Modernist Poetry* (Cambridge: Cambridge University Press, 2007), p. 153.

89 Drew Milne, 'Modernist Poetry in the British Isles', p. 154.

90 Drew Milne, 'Modernist Poetry in the British Isles', p. 156.

91 Martin Dodsworth, 'The Concept of Mind and the Poetry of Dylan Thomas', ed. Walford Davies, *Dylan Thomas: New Critical Essays* (London: Dent, 1972), pp. 119–20.

92 Alan Wilde, *Horizons of Assent: Modernism, Postmodernism, and the Ironic Imagination* (Philadelphia, PA: University of Pennsylvania Press, 1987), p. 4.

93 T. W. Adorno, *Notes to Literature*, Vol. *1* (New York, NY: Columbia University Press, 1993), p. 43.

94 For Richard Chamberlain, this paradoxical dumbness, which 'tell[s]', allows the self to 'rejoice in the [very] speaking of that silence … [i]n this way dumbness comes to invade that side of the poem which attempts to dissipate individuality, reinscribing an altered state of singularity there which is open and permeable to what surrounds it'. Richard Chamberlain, 'Fuse and Refuse: The Pastoral Logic of Dylan Thomas's Poetry', Dylan Thomas Boathouse at Laugharne, p. 2. See www. dylanthomasboathouse.com

95 Richard Chamberlain, 'Fuse and Refuse', p. 2.

96 Thus, Miller argues that, in 'Fern Hill', the word 'it' is the name for 'the undifferentiated substance which underlies all activities and entities': 'All the sun long it was running, it was lovely … it was air / And playing'. Stewart Crehan, however, sees 'it', more convincingly, as the id. As he points out, for Miller, words and certain concepts '[exist] not as a substance', but purely as metaphysical categories, ruling out a theory of language, as well as psychological entities. Words in Thomas, both polysemic and surcharged, are never so stable. Stewart Crehan, '"The Lips of Time"', p. 62.

97 Leslie Fiedler, 'The Latest Dylan Thomas', *Western Review* (Winter 1947), p. 105. Thomas's awareness of trench warfare would have been stimulated by the surge of First World War memoirs appearing from the late 1920s onwards. As he wrote to Johnson: 'The state was a murderer [in WWI], and every country in this rumour-ridden world, peopled by the unsuccessful suicides left over by the four mad years, is branded like Cain across the forehead' (*CL*, 54). See also James A. Davies, '"A Mental Militarist": Dylan Thomas and the Great War', *Welsh Writing in English: A Yearbook of Critical Essays*, vol. *2* (1996), pp. 62–81.

98 Annis Pratt, *Dylan Thomas' Early Prose: A Study in Creative Mythology* (Pittsburgh, PA: University of Pittsburgh Press, 1970), p. 130.

99 William Empson, *Argufying*, p. 387. Thomas picked up much of his politics from Bert Trick, whose beliefs were shaped by works such as John Cowper Powys's *The Religion of a Sceptic* (the Powys brothers were also favourites of Thomas's). At their evening discussions, he remembered, they would 'start on modern poetry and end up discussing the dialectics of Karl Marx'. Thomas published two Trick-influenced articles in the short-lived Left-wing *Swansea and West Wales Guardian*, edited by another friend, John Jennings, in 1934 (included in *CL*, 169–70, 176–8), and he wrote to Pamela Hansford Johnson: 'There is only one thing you and I … must look forward to, must work for and pray for … [as poets] … not only of our personal selves but of our social selves, we must pray for it all the more vehemently. It is the Revolution' (*CL*, 55). Thomas was, throughout his life 'a socialist … though a very unconventional one', as he described himself to Glyn Jones in April 1934 (*CL*, 121). In *New Verse* that year, he proclaimed 'I take my stand with any revolutionary body that asserts the right of all men to share, equally and impartially, every production of man from man and from the sources of production at man's disposal …' (*EPW*, 150) His desired political scenario closely resembled that of the I.L.P.: for an elected Labour Government to take the commanding heights of the economy into public ownership, while mobilising the working class to resist sabotage by the ruling class and the State machine (*CL*, 185).

100 Chris Baldick, *The Social Mission of English Criticism 1848–1932* (Oxford: Clarendon Press, 1987), p. 166, citing F. R. Leavis, *For Continuity* (1933).

101 John Berger, *Ways of Seeing* (London: Penguin / BBC Books, 1972 [repr. 1981]), pp. 146–9.

102 A. T. Tolley, *The Poetry of the Thirties*, p. 154.

103 R. George Thomas, 'Dylan Thomas and Some Early Readers', *Poetry Wales: Dylan Thomas Special Issue*, 9: 2 (Autumn 1973), pp. 4, 11–12.

104 Tom Bottomore, ed., *A Dictionary of Marxist Thought* (Oxford: Blackwell, 1988), pp. 479–81.

105 Malcolm Bradbury and James McFarlane, eds., *Modernism: 1890–1930* (Harmondsworth: Penguin, 1976), pp. 51–2.

106 Anne Fogarty, 'Yeats, Ireland and Modernism', eds. Alex Davis and Lee Jenkins, *The Cambridge Companion to Modernist Poetry* (Cambridge: Cambridge University Press, 2007), p. 127.

107 R. B. Kershner Jr., *Dylan Thomas: The Poet and His Critics* (Chicago, IL: American Library Association, 1976), p. 1.

108 As W. S. Merwin notes: 'the exultation of such marvellous poems as "Poem in October", "Fern Hill", "Poem on His Birthday" and "Author's Prologue" is not an exultation proper to the liberal humanist'. W. S. Merwin, 'The Religious Poet', ed. E. W. Tedlock, *Dylan Thomas: The Legend and the Poet*, p. 243.

109 Michel de Certeau, '"Making Do": Uses and Tactics', *The Practice of Everyday Life*, transl. Steve Rendell (Berkeley / Los Angeles / London: University of California Press, 1988), pp. 29–42.

110 Michel de Certeau, '"Making Do": Uses and Tactics', p. 37.

111 Michel de Certeau, '"Making Do": Uses and Tactics', pp. 37–8.

112 Michel de Certeau, '"Making Do": Uses and Tactics', p. 38.

113 Peter Riley, 'Thomas and Apocalypse', *Poetry Wales*, 44:3 (Winter 2008 / 09), p. 12.

114 William T. Moynihan, *The Craft and Art of Dylan Thomas* (Oxford: Oxford University Press, 1966), p. 8.

CHAPTER TWO

'Under the spelling wall':
language and style

Here words are not the polite contortions of 20th century printer's ink. They are alive. They elbow their way on to the page, and glow and blaze and fade and finally disappear.

> – Samuel Beckett on *Finnegans Wake*.[1]

Only the great masters of style succeed in being obscure.

> – Oscar Wilde, 'The Artist as Critic'.[2]

'Innumerable bananas': Dylan Thomas's style

'Have I ever told you', Dylan Thomas asked Pamela Hansford Johnson in a letter of 2 May 1934, 'of the theory of how all writers either work towards or away from words? Even if I have, I'll tell it to you again because it's true. Any poet or novelist you like to think of—he [sic] either works out of words or in the direction of them. The realistic novelist—Bennett, for instance—sees things, hears things, imagines things, (& all things of the material world or materially cerebral world), & then goes towards words as the most suitable medium through which to express those experiences. A romanticist like Shelley, on the other hand, is his medium first, & expresses out of his medium what he sees, hears, thinks, & imagines' (*CL*, 147–8). To Trevor Hughes in early 1935 he would report: 'I think [poems] should work from words, from the substance of words and the rhythm of substantial words set together, not towards words. Poetry is a medium, not a stigmata on paper' (*CL*, 208).[3] It was an axiom that he repeated throughout his life. Thomas's point was that, while most writers start with a fixed idea of what they want to say and then find ('work towards') the words for it, others started with a set of words and let these prompt the movement 'away from' them towards the finished verbal object. The second of these attitudes was, for Thomas, the only real way to write poetry. And no-one would dispute, I think, that the appeal of Thomas's work stems, to some degree, from the sense we get when reading it that words are being allowed to express themselves; why not be able to say 'once below a time' or 'a grief ago'? This is one reason why almost all his work possesses an unmistakeable signature style. Torqued syntax, novel collocation, daringly refurbished clichés, outrageous puns and wordplay, together with a whole gamut of devices, from anacoluthon to zeugma, resist and draw us in, expanding our sense of the possibilities of language itself and reminding us that poetry is the art form whose medium is language. Contrivance and pleasure coexist, just as they do in Thomas's description of himself as a writer of 1950:

> I am a painstaking, conscientious, involved and devious craftsman in words … I use everything and anything to make my poems work and move them in the directions I want them to: old tricks, new tricks, puns, portmanteau-words, paradox, allusion, paronomasia, paragram, catachresis, slang, assonantal rhymes, vowel rhymes, sprung rhythm. Every device there is in language is there to be used if you will. Poets have got to enjoy themselves sometimes, and the twistings and convolutions of words, the inventions and contrivances, are all part of the joy that is part of the painful, voluntary work. (*EPW*, 158)

This list of devices – though by no means complete, of course – nicely mimics the excess of the writing it describes. Tongue-in-cheek self-justification aside, it is also clear that the manipulation described above is viewed as both inescapable and as its own reward: the painstaking 'twisting' of words is an integral 'part of the joy' of the creative act. Poetry is a near-oxymoronic craft, at once 'painful' and 'voluntary', which requires the poet to be both 'conscientious' and 'devious'.

This passage reveals just how closely Thomas's tactics as a stylist are 'involved' with his conception of poetry, the role of the poet and a particular attitude to language. There are pleasures in writing – a positive feedback, as it were – but these are a by-product of, and may be proportional to, the effort involved in bringing to bear a battery of devices, which will 'make my poems work and move them in the directions I want them to'. Here, Thomas echoes the 'dialectical method' of his letter of 23 March 1938 to Henry Treece, which I quoted in the Introduction, describing how his poems arose from, and moved around, a 'host' of conflicting, breeding 'images', words or phrases – a decentred, Einsteinian (rather than Copernican) model – out of which the poem emerges.

In a Thomas poem, words and verbal units often play a role which is more active and structure-creating, less subordinated to a pre-existing end or goal than is usual, even in poetry. As David Aivaz observed:

> The generative method ... [in the early poems], is very often an unashamed and inexhaustible word-play. The transition from image to image is by means of the pun, the double meaning, the coined word, the composite word, the noun-verb, the pronoun with the double antecedent. And there is a larger machinery, verbal and syntactical: clauses that read both forward and backward; uneven images that are smoothed by incantatory rhythms, rhymes, word patterns, verse forms, by the use of commas in place of full stop punctuation; cant, slang terms and formal, general abstract wording juxtaposed in image after image, so that the agitation of each becomes the repose of the group.[4]

Working 'from words', then, involves permitting language's own capacity for play to advance the poem within the formal constraints of metre, stanza form, rhyme scheme and refrain, in order to produce the (barely contained) verbal object which is the poem. Language is treated as a material object – a 'medium', rather than abstract, 'stigmata' – and deployed according to its sonic echoes and patterns, its timbres, colours and connotations, rather than simply according to the dictates of its denotative content, with the poem emerging more from the promptings of these, than any predetermined argument or 'subject'.

Granting agency to language and the foregrounding of it as the medium of poetry is accompanied by a sense of its tremendous innate energy. Like the Joyce of *Finnegans Wake*, Thomas revels in the 'plurabilities' of language as process, in all the ways in which, exuberantly and promiscuously, it realises and spends itself, and this underscores the crucial differences between his attitudes to it and those of the dominant figures of poetic modernism. The linguistic scepticism traceable from Yeats's 'The Song of the Happy Shepherd', with its world-weary 'Words alone are certain good', to Eliot's claim in 'East Coker', fifty years later, that they are 'shabby equipment, always deteriorating', is resisted.[5] Avoiding such relished disillusion, Thomas credits language with innate creative powers, and, at his most extravagant, in a poem such as 'In the beginning', he blasphemously dramatises his status as poet-demiurge by appropriating the openings of Genesis and St John's Gospel, subsuming the Word within the poet-as-Christ's lowercase word. More often, he tries to release the power of language to renew our perception of the world through defamiliarisation. His aim is not just to speak of process, as we have seen, but to embody it linguistically. There is formal structure in abundance and nominal adherence to grammar (even the most challenging sentences are construable), but, within these restraints, the innate tendencies of language to slippage, mutation, self-contradiction and deferral are given full rein.

This is not, however, a matter of merely generating verbal pyrotechnics. In Thomas's wordplay, a crucial paradox of language is continually being raised: namely its dual nature, as both a symbolic system of representation, abstracted from, and standing over, the object world it represents, and as an object within that world. This word / world problematic is a high modernist one, which attracted the attention of members of the Prague Linguistic Circle in the 1930s, as well as William Empson and such successors of his as Veronica Forrest-Thomson in *Poetic Artifice* (1978), and it distinguishes Thomas's work from more straightforward versions of Symbolism and Imagism.[6] The Symbolists promoted verbal colour and music at the expense of denotative sense, by creating an atmosphere of ethereal vagueness and suggestiveness, which dematerialised the word. Equally, Imagism aspired to close the gap between word and thing, but it saw this as a purely mental operation; the physical, material nature of words was not acknowledged.[7] New Country and its successors – including much of today's 'mainstream' poetry – curbed what it saw as modernism's excesses of linguistic and metrical 'defamiliarisation' in an effort to make formal control of tension and ambiguity 'the cornerstone of a continuing humanist enterprise'.[8] Thomas, however, created the effects sought by the Symbolists through a concrete, rather than dematerialised, use of language, closing the gap between the word and thing in two ways: first, by eschewing abstractions and using language which was muscularly forceful and physical; second, by literally 'thinging' the word, through the use of forceful rhythms, alliteration, assonance, dissonance, consonance and onomatopoeic effects. It is as if he is attempting to reproduce his own experience of language, as he described it to Alastair Reid: 'When I experience anything I experience it as a thing and a word at the same time, both equally amazing'.[9] Thomas, then, reproduced the physicality of the world in verbal terms within the poem, aggressively countering the tendency to elide linguistic materiality, as he told Pamela Hansford Johnson in October 1934: 'I've got to get nearer to the bones of words, & to a Matthew Arnold's hell with the convention of meaning and sense' (*CL*, 195). This excess, though held within Thomas's own tight 'formal controls', is what sets his work apart from the *juste milieu* poetics of liberal humanism and allies it with the 'revolution of the word' and the move against signification found in Futurism, Surrealism, Expressionism and Dada, for all that his fascination with the avant-garde was tempered by defensive parody.[10]

Thomas's style and his attitudes to language were, naturally enough, shaped by his origins. Standard English in South Wales coexists beside a local dialect, as elsewhere in Britain. Unlike most other places in Britain, however, the dialect is shaped by a Welsh language substrate, and this is inflected, in turn, by the continued vigorous existence of the Welsh language. Non-Welsh speakers are continually being made aware of these Welsh language presences, whether subsumed or immediate; in anglophone Swansea in the 1920s and 1930s, it would have been impossible not to regularly encounter or overhear spoken Welsh or to miss it in the names of numerous buildings, institutions, parks, streets and areas of the town and its hinterland. Thomas had Welsh withheld from him by his parents, but the 'spider-tongued, and the loud hill of Wales' informs his English in many subtle ways (*CP*, 19).[11] Most importantly, perhaps, the presence of Welsh means that the existential status of English is always more problematic than it is in England. This, together with other Anglo-Welsh aspects of his situation – belatedness as a modernist, subaltern-suburban stroppiness, Nonconformist oratorical inheritance (with its reverence for the Word) and a sense of the Welsh poetic tradition – suffuse his attitudes to language. Even so, Thomas's importance lies not in these circumstances as such (as it would with a lesser poet), but in the very way in which they were used by him to figure the lyric genre's traditional, primal themes of love, birth, death and faith in a manner charged with mid-century crisis and the crisis of modernity more generally. 'Process', an extreme awareness of instantaneity, flowed from this, but the poetry's scope and authority was increased by the fact that the struggle for origin – the creative act itself – is so often a subject of these poems. Again, this has a Welsh aspect; Thomas's obsessive tracing of the birth of the poem lays bare the Nonconformist Imaginary, allegorising, in its own way, the struggle for national identity. But this is also part of a self-authoring and generational struggle, with the broadest implications, and these are extended by Thomas's style. Readers are enticed into identification with the sensuous dynamism of the poems and their mythic structures, encouraged by wordplay and fluid-speaking selves, and these are constructed so that readers enact the poems' own struggles with the roots of the self in language (but not wholly in it), often in the form of the mechanisms by which humans acquire language in the first place.

Infants initially encounter words as an abstract auditory phenomenon:

as non-signifying sound which is only later understood to be a form of communication. They respond to it accordingly, imitating adults and manipulating its material, aural properties, without relation to meaning, until they intuit links between sound and sense. The enchantment of language arises in the gap between sound and sense – a gap in which the potential sense of the word is still huge. Thomas's own account of this process of enchantment and acquisition identifies it as the origin of his urge to write:

> I wanted to write poetry in the beginning because I had fallen in love with words. The first poems I knew were nursery rhymes, and before I could read them for myself I had come to love just the words of them, the words alone. What the words stood for, symbolised, or meant, was of very secondary importance. What mattered was the *sound* of them as I heard them for the first time on the lips of the remote and incomprehensible grown-ups who seemed, for some reason, to be living in my world. And these words were, to me, as the notes of bells, the sounds of musical instruments, the noises of wind, sea, and rain, the rattle of milkcarts, the clopping of hooves on cobbles, the fingering of branches on a window pane, might be to someone, deaf from birth, who has miraculously found his hearing. I did not care what the words said, overmuch, nor what happened to Jack & Jill ... I cared for the shapes of sound that their names, and the words describing their actions, made in my ears; I cared for the colours the words cast on my eyes ... I fell in love – that is the only expression I can think of – at once, and am still at the mercy of words, though sometimes now, knowing a little of their behaviour very well, I think I can influence them slightly and have even learned to beat them now and then, which they appear to enjoy. I tumbled for words at once. And, when I began to read ... I knew that I had discovered the most important things, to me, that could be ever. ... [M]y love for the real life of words increased until I knew that I must live *with* them and *in* them, always. I knew, in fact, that I must be a writer of words, and nothing else. The first thing was to feel and know their sound and substance; what I was going to do with those words, what use I was going to make of them, what I was going to *say* through them, would come later. (*EPW,* 154–5)

Unashamedly relishing a word-besotted condition, this is also a shrewd analysis of the pleasure principle behind language acquisition. It registers the initial claim for the 'shape of sounds' and 'colour of words' over sense, based on their appeal as pre-signifying sounds, and suggests that, in being transferred to print form as he learned to read, his 'love' for them was increased, not diminished. In its first part, at least, this echoes Freud and anticipates later theories linking language, the unconscious and the pre-linguistic or Symbolic realm, particularly those of Jacques

Lacan and Julia Kristeva. Viewed in terms of Thomas's Anglo-Welshness, the process of infant language acquisition parallels the situation in which one language is succeeded by another; in such cases, the retention of speech patterns and grammatical forms from the first into the second language creates new forms and suggests further stylistic liberties – gives rise, that is, to a gusto which those wholly centred in either language dare not take.

Love for, and astonishment at, language, as well as a sense that its norms were fluid, were attributes that Thomas never lost. His best friend, Daniel Jones, recorded how, in their teens, he and Thomas collaborated to write hundreds of lyrics by an imaginary poet named Walter Bram (*bram* is Welsh for 'fart'), whose style he described as: 'bafflingly inconsistent … fragile, furious, laconic, massive, delicate, incantatory, cool, flinty, violent, Chinese, Greek, and shocking'. The pair also had word obsessions: 'everything at one time was "little" or "white"; and sometimes an adjective became irresistibly funny in almost any connection: "innumerable bananas", "wilful moccasin", "a certain Mrs Prothero"'. But, as he claimed: 'These word games, and even the most facetious of our collaborations, had a serious experimental purpose, and there is no doubt that they played an important part in Dylan's early poetic development'.[12] If infant, and even adolescent, logophilia is not so uncommon, Thomas was nevertheless unusual in consciously invoking it as part of his mature poetic style, making it part of a sophisticated modernist-style deployment of primitivism (the modernist derivation of his 'Manifesto' account is given away in the 'fingering of branches on the window-pane', which are those in Earwicker's dream in that most avant-garde and childlike of 1930s works, *Finnegans Wake*). By contrast, Louis MacNeice's 'When we were children words were coloured / (Harlot and murder were dark purple)' presumes a fond shared memory only; the quasi-synaesthetic appeal of words may lead us to poetry, but is essentially childish and not a significant part of a mature poetic practice.[13]

Yet Thomas's verbal exuberance is also qualified in certain ways. The process poetic was war- and suicide-haunted, and its relationship with modernism was a fraught one. He was anxious about its linguistic consequences from the start, protesting as early as May 1934 that 'My lines, all my lines, are of the tenth intensity. They are not the words that express what I want to express … And that's no good. I'm a freak user of words, not a poet' (*CL*, 130). The anxiety is reflected in stylistic heterogeneity. During his most experimental period, between 1933 and

1938, Thomas continued to occasionally write and even publish material in the pre-process notebook style, as if to disavow the avant-garde fetish of innovation for its own sake. *Twenty-five Poems* exemplifies this, at the level of the book; significantly, as if staging a provocation, it contains both his most difficult poems – 'I' in my intricate image' and 'Altarwise by owl-light' – and his most straightforward ones, such as 'The hand that signed the paper' and 'I have longed to move away'. Like a confession of linguistic guilt, the emergence of the process style was punctuated by images of solipsistic entrapment in the tower of the autonomous word, as in 'Ears in the turrets hear' and 'Especially when the October wind'. Gareth Thomas rightly notes that, for all its glitter and muscling bravado, the flip-side of his relish of language is a need to confess inadequacy, figured in lapses into inarticulateness and the haunting sense that meaningful communication is impossible, even futile: 'And I am dumb to tell' (*CP*, 13).[14] Like Hamlet, the young Thomas was pushed towards words partly by his own melancholy in a 'sort of narcissistic regression', while, at the same time, darkly revelling in his reversal of the fall of words into merely instrumental usage.[15] Refusing to make concessions, on the one hand, and fearful of a 'crabbed, elliptical density', on the other, by 1936, he was telling Vernon Watkins that 'I'm almost afraid of all the once-necessary artifices and obscurities, and can't, for the life or death of me, get any real liberation, any diffusion or dilution or anything, into the churning bulk of the words; I seem, more than ever, to be tightly packing away everything I have and know into a mad-doctor's bag, and then locking it up … What I fear is an ingrowing, the impulse growing like a toenail into the artifice' (*CL*, 249). Glancing back at the anxiety of the mid-1930s for Bob Rees in 1938, he would place this 'ingrowing' in a broader context:

> I don't know whether I was ever 'determined' – a slightly self-conscious word, especially if applied to the early, formative period of one's own writing … – to make 'a richer texture' than as so much English poetry (though I had, then, no idea of literary nationalism), but I think that I was always attracted to the idea of extremely concentrated poetry; I could never like the poetry that allowed itself great breathing spaces, tediums and flatnesses, between essential passages; I want, and wanted, every line to be the essence of the poem, even the flourishes, the exaggerations. This, naturally, I could never achieve, but it still remains an ideal for me … Later I realized that this essential writing, this writing without concessions – I say 'without concessions' for I think that the only person allowed, in a poem, to take time off, is the reader – could avoid dullness only if it was dramatically effective at the same time. (*SP1*, xxxvi)

No single new style ensued from this turning point. Rather, a changed set of tactics in 1938–41 meant that Thomas's poems became less static and marmoreal and more syntactically sinewy and mobile, with a tendency to frame aspects of his earlier modernism, as in 'After the Funeral' and 'How shall my animal'. This led to the greater use of what seems to be overtly biographical material. After 1944, Thomas's poetic style changed again, as if following the prose, yet differing from it in still ultimately working 'from', rather than 'towards', words. What Malcolm Bowie calls 'the speaking subject's riposte to the simple fact of being trapped inside a language that she/he did not create and whose rules she/he has no real power to affect or mitigate' is continued in these final works, albeit in a more attenuated form.[16]

Thomas's stylistic shifts can be described using Roland Barthes's distinction between two fundamental types of texts: what he calls the readerly (*lisible*) and the writerly (*scriptible*). The first applies to those which are grounded in a transmission theory of communication and confirm the split between writer (producer) and reader (consumer). The second, which perfectly describes Thomas's process style, is resistant to habitual reading, forces the reader to work to construct meaning and fulfils 'the goal of literary work (of literature as work) … to make the reader no longer a consumer, but a producer of the text'.[17] In the words of the Canadian poet-critic Steve McCaffery: 'The writerly proposes the *unreadable* as the ideological site of a departure from consumption to production, presenting the domain of its own interacting interior (Barthes's "magic of the signifiers") as the networks and circuits of an ultimately intractable and untotalized meaning'.[18] Precisely such 'sites' are offered by poems such as 'Altarwise by owl-light', before the concessions to a readerly style, in which a more determinate meaning is available – although, as I shall argue in Chapter 6, a better way of describing that style, with its mesmeric repetitions, is in terms of the 'paragram' or the patterned dispersal of sonic effects, as opposed to their concentration.

Barthes's distinctions nicely pinpoint the engagement we are forced to make with Thomas's trickier texts and confirm his mannerist modernist, liminal status. But they don't explain why he mixed process and plain-style writing at almost every point in his career, since his inconsistent and parodic relationship to avant-gardism cannot be fitted to a schema as rigorous as Barthes's. Thomas is distinguished not only by his resistance to précis, but by an unpredictable, heteroglossic switching between different modes – what John Bayley was referring to when he noted that 'It is as if the attitudes to language of Donne, Blake and Swinburne were all to be encountered in the same poem'.[19] Nor do Barthes's distinctions say anything specific about Thomas's writing strategies and his belief that a poem should be 'an event, a happening, an action perhaps, not a still-life or an experience put down, placed, regulated' (CL, 325–6).

One reason why Thomas's language use differs from that of most high modernists is because the 'revolution of the word' opposed their urge to impose order and did not shun psychoanalysis to the same degree. Thomas's response, albeit in a trickster spirit, was parodic: to make himself a 'Freudian exemplar', who unashamedly exploited Freud's conceptualisation of the unconscious through verbal manifestations, and his claim that *lapsus linguae* – slips of the tongue, dream-words, parapraxes – reveal the fears and desires which constitute it.[20] Thomas may have also taken Freud's point that children tend to 'treat words as things' and, conversely, that puns and jokes – the conscious construction and utilisation of verbal slips – serve the purpose of allowing adults to be childish without sanction, briefly escaping from adult restraints. More complex jests, Freud saw as 'releas[ing] pleasure even from sources that have undergone repression', and this suggests why, while Thomas did not pose as a thaumaturge, his language has a powerful liberatory charge.[21]

Pound and Eliot, of course, thought critically about language and recognised its unconscious aspects – Eliot, in particular, was haunted by 'the auditory imagination' as I discussed in Chapter 1 – but their main impulse was the traditionalist attempt to try to bring 'words' closer to 'things', to ensure that signifiers were tied to single signifiers and referents, and this required treating words as unified entities.[22] Thomas had no such urge and, accordingly, like Joyce, treated words as fissile bundles of signification, whose inherent slippery polysemousness and plurivocality it was the writer's duty to encourage and harness, not suppress.

The concern of writers with their own medium parallels the occurrence in the early teens of the twentieth century of what is known as the linguistic 'turn', according to which, rather than describing the world, language came to be seen as shaping it. Its structuralist and synchronic aspect was analysed in Saussure's *Course in General Linguistics* (1916), in which he separated the verbal sign into signifier and signified, stressed the arbitrary, unmotivated nature of the sign and held that words do not 'represent' the essences of their referents in the world, but create meaning relationally.[23] This strand of the structuralist 'turn' also included the

Russian Formalists, who read poetry for its use of the 'device' and 'defamiliarisation', laying the basis for later radical analyses of culture, such as Barthes's own. The other, organicist, diachronic and phenomenological aspect of the 'turn' was the one most powerfully represented by Martin Heidegger, which holds that human involvement in language is ultimately resistant to technical or external analysis. If, for Saussure, language users are produced by *langue*, Heidegger's famous formula 'die Sprache spricht' means something different; language 'speaks us' in a more primordial sense, and it falls to poetry to utter the mystery of Being beyond it, to invoke a pre-dualistic sensibility with a mythopoeic relationship to the world. Thomas's writing, which plays on the arbitrary nature of the sign *and* invokes its organic and irreducible 'magical' qualities, reflects both trends implicit in modernism.[24]

Words, device, syntax

Thomas's vocabulary has been considered the main difficulty for readers of his early poetry, although, as Emery notes, it would seem, at first glance, to be ordinary in the extreme.[25] Coinages ('morsing', 'cockshut', 'pickbrain') are few, as are exotic items ('hyleg', 'parhelion'), although there are a number of Egyptian and classical references (*CP*, 20, 28, 72). Dialect ('gambo', 'mitching') is very rare, and archaism ('sin-eater', 'unto', 'pickthank') and slang ('lammed', 'scrams') is uncommon (*CP*, 151, 74, 42, 13, 10, 47, 38). Yet simple words often seem teasingly unfamiliar through unusual compounding or collocation, or because the image they describe is a bizarre one. The core vocabulary consists of simple terms – 'seed', 'oil', 'fork', 'worm', 'cross', 'wax' and so on – but they are chosen for their polysemous, slippery ability to exacerbate and resolve the Blakean contraries of process.[26] 'Worm', for example, can have up to eight meanings in Thomas's poetry: grave-worm, parasitic worm, penis, glow-worm, umbilical cord, Satan, garden worm and the long worm-screw gears found in canal lock-gates (as in 'Where once the twilight locks'). Compounds – 'goblin-sucker', 'mothers'-eyed', 'wear-willow', 'moon-and-midnight', 'grave-gabbing' – are frequently odd, and sometimes surreal (*CP*, 51, 25, 144, 8, 25). A simple word, such as 'grave', may be made strange by being yoked to a host of epithets, which, in themselves, seem unexceptional: 'stallion', 'moon-drawn', 'corkscrew', 'running', 'savage', 'outspoken', 'country-handed' and 'gallow' (*CP*, 55, 34, 19, 27, 15, 48, 62). Words continually approach a potentially chaotic welter of signification, with ordinary items made contradictory or downright uncanny.

Scissors and knives, both *Struwwelpeter*- and medically-derived, signify castration, but also the severing of the umbilical cord and, hence, birth. The sea, so often used by Thomas, may symbolise the womb, death, our evolutionary past, voyages, the terrors and pleasures of the unconscious, or several of these at once, all within the same poem, as in 'I, in my intricate image', where the sea is the site of a symbolic death followed by rebirth. Indeed, the different resonances of these two sets of images reflect the fact that, while Thomas was a 'Freudian exemplar', the archetypal imagery of emergent Jungianism finds a place in his poetry, too.

Thomas's lexis changed with the development of his poetry. Many of the body-derived process items of *18 Poems* were supplanted by religious ones in *Twenty-five Poems*, these being augmented in *Deaths and Entrances* by a language of buildings and imprisonment – locks, keys, bolts, wards, chains, doors, stairs and windows. But the bodily-cosmic structure of process continued to underwrite the poetry, and at no point does Thomas's symbolic shorthand allow itself to be cracked like a code, once and for all; its lexis evades singular definition as contexts shift and parts of speech metamorphose into others: nouns regularly become adjectives ('cargoed', 'acorned'), and verbs ('Jacob to the stars'), and polysemous verb-nouns are legion: 'marrow' (bone-marrow, to marry, to transmit 'marrow' through sexual intercourse), 'reel' (film-reel, fishing-rod reel and the actions of these things) and 'gear' (clothes or mechanical gears, to put on clothes, make something mechanical) are just three examples (*CP*, 7, 95, 59). Peculiar verb-noun compoundings also occur, such as 'man-iron sidle', in which 'sidle' – a noun used to describe a sunset in Whitman's *Song of Myself* – describes a sidling movement, while homophonically evoking 'side' (*CP*, 33).[27] Such confusions of object and action, stasis and movement, being and becoming, are verbal equivalents of process, treating matter and energy as aspects of each other. The modern world is more obviously incorporated via cybernetic collocations of organic and inorganic items, such as 'chemic blood', 'motor muscle' and 'milky acid', as discussed in Chapter 1, these being ubiquitous in the first two collections. (The 'implacably opaque' 'petrol face' from 'I, in my intricate image', agonised over by both John Bayley and Alan Young, is of this kind.)[28]

Thomas 'makes strange' most obviously at the level of the device. Roman Jakobson – the theorist who links the Russian Formalists and the Prague Linguistic Circle – famously claimed that 'The poetic function projects the principle of equivalence from the axis of selection to the axis of combination', meaning, roughly, that, in poetry, words are not simply combined for their 'equivalence' in terms of the thoughts that they convey (their referential aspect), but with an eye to the patterns of similarity, parallelism, opposition and so on created by their sound, meaning, connotations and rhythm.[29] For Jakobson, poetry differed from other kinds of function, because in it language was placed in a certain kind of self-conscious relationship to itself – one which promoted the 'palpability of signs' and dislocated the usual bond between signifier and signified (what Jakobson called the 'referent') by making it evident, through the deployment of its various 'devices' (metaphor, asyndeton, alliteration, etc.), that they were not equivalent. Yet despite striving to separate language from the world in certain ways, by making it more opaque and by fostering the autonomy of the poem, literature was paradoxically given the power to alter our relationship with reality. Over time, the Formalists believed, there was a tendency for the relationship between signifier and signified to become automatic and lifeless. In setting language at a distance from it, literature was able to 'make strange' everyday reality, creating an estrangement effect (*ostraneniye*), which counteracted the debasement of the bond and thereby renewed our jaded perceptions of the world (as this shows, the Formalists' perception of the relationship between language and the world was an idealist one).

Up to a point, Thomas's work accords with Formalist analyses of the way in which literary language operates. His promotion of what Victor Erlich called the 'palpability of the signifier' and the device is reflected in his description of the 'work of words' and his ability to 'beat ... now and then' their 'sawn, splay sounds' to create the poem's 'hacked at' 'rumpus of shapes' (*CP*, 78, 106, 1).[30] As Thomas confessed in 'O make me a mask', he was 'lashed to syllables', both bound to his labour and flogged into a debris of phonemes (*CP*, 70). The poet's 'pencil' he described as an 'electric drill, breaking up the tar and concrete of language worn thin by the tricycle tyres of nature poets and the heavy six wheels of the academic sirs' – although if the pencil is decidedly phallic and the poem described as a 'womb of war', the poet's 'labour by singing light' is also that of childbirth, matching Thomas's many pre-natal subjects (*CL*, 208, 329; *CP*, 106). Language is presented as a body, not an abstraction, by exploitation of what Jakobson called poetry's 'distinctive combinatory strategies', including heavily stressed, repetitive rhythm, reinforced by alliteration ('There is *l*oud and *d*ark *d*irectly un*d*er the *d*umb *fl*ame') and consonantal and assonantal counterpointing ('F*la*voured of ce*l*lu*l*oid give *l*ove the *l*ie'; 'He wept from the crest of grief, he prayed to the *veiled* sky'). These declarative usages create a powerful impression of synthetic self-containment and illustrate, in almost textbook manner, the Formalist point about the self-referential nature of the 'poetic' (*CP*, 78, 17, 100).

At the same time, echoing Karl Kraus's sexualised version of the same Formalist idea, Thomas informed Trevor Hughes that 'Centuries of problematical progress have blinded us to the literal world; each bright and naked object is shrouded around with a thick, peasoup mist of association; no single word in all our poetic vocabulary is a virgin word, ready for our first love', while Pamela Hansford Johnson was told that 'It is part of a poet's job to take a debauched and prostituted word, like the beautiful word "blond", and to smooth away the lines of its dissipation, and to put it on the market again, fresh and virgin' (*CL*, 111–12, 43). Claiming to reject Joycean neologism and Steinian repetition as 'abstract patterns' made only from 'the bare and beautiful shells of the words' (but using both, on occasion), his letter to Hughes added 'we need to ... to make ... new associations for each word', and one can, indeed, find him generating such 'new associations' by displacing words from their usual contexts (the Egyptian group of 'pyramid', 'mummy', 'crocodile' and 'desert' is one example).

Thomas was also well aware of the prominence of these features in the intricately sound-patterned and syllabic metrics of the traditional Welsh verse forms collectively known as *cynghanedd*. As with the charge of Surrealism, he denied this influence, claiming that reproducing Welsh effects in English poetry 'succeeded only in warping, crabbing, and obscuring the natural genius of the English language'. But this was a smokescreen to cover genuine interest. As early as May 1934, in a letter to an editor at Jonathan Cape, Hamish Miles, he claimed that: 'I dreamed my genesis' was 'more or less based on Welsh rhythms', and examples of *cynghanedd*-style patterning can be found everywhere in his poems (*CL*, 161).[31] A line such as 'The lovely gift of the gab bangs back on a blind shaft' from 'On no work of words' (1938), for example, is one of the more elaborate of countless examples that could be adduced: mirroring alliteration ripples out on either side of the '*gab / ba*ng' chiasmus (l li g ft i g ab / ba g ba a bl a ft) to offer both a beautiful formal patterning and an enacting of the 'banging back' as the writer's block, and its overcoming, which is the poem's subject, finds verbal material form around the line's central plosive event. Such examples indicate a reverently tricksterish relationship to the spirit of Welsh poetry, rather than complete identification with it, although it is worth noting that, for Lynette Roberts, a friend and near neighbour from 1938–40, the same techniques were used more extensively still as the basis for a new avant-garde style. Andrew Duncan has usefully coined the term 'anglo-*hanedd*' to describe Roberts's effects, and the Welsh language poet Euros Bowen at this time described *cynghanedd* effects as a form of Symbolism's verbal autotelism *avant la lettre*.[32] Both the label and idea are applicable to Thomas, whose poetry is a good example of an 'archaic avant-garde' practice in action.[33]

Such effects produce what many see as one of Thomas's great strengths – his verbal mimeticism or onomatopoeia. This stanza from 'Ballad of the Long-legged bait' is a good example:

> Whales in the wake like capes and Alps
> Quaked the sick sea and snouted deep,
> Deep the great bushed bait with raining lips
> Slipped the fins of those hunchbacked tons. (*CP*, 127)

Here, the lines are heavily alliterated on 'w', 'k', 's' and 'p' and slip between high frontal vowel sounds and lower, more palatised ones, in order to mimic the slide from wave crests to troughs, realising the fisherman's sea-sickness, as well as the 'slipping' away of the bait from her 'hunchbacked tons'. And yet, Thomas's poetry often works on an opposite principle to this, as if in accordance with Saussure's claim that the verbal sign is not motivated.[34] As Walford Davies has noted, this is often because we just do not know the referents of his words; the third stanza of one of his more opaque pieces, 'How soon the servant sun', is an extreme case in point:

> All nerves to serve the sun,
> The rite of light,
> A claw I question from the mouse's bone,
> The long-tailed stone
> Trap I with coil and sheet,
> Let the soil squeal I am the biting man
> And the velvet dead inch out. (*CP*, 49)

Thomas exacerbates the disjunction between the verbal music and any onomatopoeic purpose, which we, as readers, cannot yet establish (although the poem is construable enough with a little effort).[35] The origin of a relish of words as sounds detached from meaning or onomatopoeic purpose is described in the 'Manifesto', as it is in a letter of 1934 to Pamela Hansford Johnson:

> I read in an old John O'London's ... several lists of favourite words, and

was surprised to see that the choice depended almost entirely upon the associations of the words. 'Chime', 'melody', 'golden', 'silver', 'alive', etc. appeared in almost every list; 'chime' is, to me, the only word of that lot that can, intrinsically, and minus its associations, be called beautiful. The greatest single word I know is 'drome' which, for some reason, nearly opens the doors of heaven for me ... 'Drome', 'bone', 'dome', 'doom', 'province', 'dwell', 'prove', 'dolomite' – these are only a few of my favourite words, which are insufferably beautiful to me. The first four words are visionary; God moves in a long 'o' (CL, 73).

Significantly, several of these items do not have a 'long "o"' and one, 'dwell', doesn't have an 'o' in it at all. It is the arbitrariness of the selection of the words, in terms of their meaning, that Thomas is at pains to stress; his list does not 'depend entirely upon associations'. But even if the appeal of words may not depend on meaning, there is considerable evidence for the iconicity of the verbal sign or onomatopoeia, and a naïve opposition to signifiers having 'innate' meanings may be just as limited as a naïve belief in the bond between sound and sense. Indeed, many systems of poetics have had a place for the link between the two. In fact, it appears that, while Saussure may have been right concerning the arbitrariness of the verbal sign, he was wrong about the phonemes and consonantal clusters that make them up – that is, a local 'lexical affinity' works against the general arbitrariness of *langue* as a system.[36] To consider, for example, 'snap', 'snitch', 'snort', 'snivel', 'snarl' and 'sneer' is to see that the consonant 'sn-' functions as what Benjamin Lee Whorf called a 'phonostheme' – a phoneme possessed of expressive meaning.[37] Onomatopoeia is a fact, and, since the phonetic shape of onomatopoeic words appears motivated, rather than arbitrary, they exert significant limitations on the doctrine of the arbitrariness of the sign. What Thomas does is exaggerate both arbitrary *and* motivated aspects of language; he produces bravura examples of onomatopoeia in one place and elsewhere weakens the grasp on semantic sense, such that the word-music is autonomous, unmotivated by signification – a groundless onomatopoeia, as it were. As with metaphor, discussed later in the chapter, he creates situations in which there is an apparent reversal of the normal terms applicable to such a device. The resultant shifting play between sonorous excess and semantic deficiency denies readers a secure relationship to the 'sound of shape' and 'shape of sound', as Thomas respectively terms them (CP, 61; EPW, 154). As is the case with many other examples, Thomas is exploiting contradictory tendencies within language itself, exploiting the ways in which, in

Jean-Jacques Lecercle's words 'phonemes are motivated by instinctual drives, relative (and sometimes absolute) motivation rules'.[38]

As far as more elaborate devices go, what is notable is their variety; false parallelism ('tallow-eyed' and 'tallow I', [*CP*, 61]), transferred epithet ('hissing shippen' [*CP*, 151]), hendiadys ('at long and dear last' [*CP*, 91]) *occupatio* and palinode ('A Refusal to Mourn' is both), periphrasis ('this four-winded spinning' for globe [*CP*, 8]), metathesis ('manwaging' and 'warbearing' [*CP*, 39]), spoonerism and transposition ('the man in the wind and the west moon' [*CP*, 56]), etymologies ('sullen' [*CP*, 106]) and what Thomas, referring to 'bellowing' and 'heroine', called 'stunt rhyme' (*CP*, 77; *CL*, 376). A standard epithet for a wind – 'rain-bringing' – becomes, through intensification, rhyme and a kind of paronomasia, 'rain wringing': a wind which wrings the rain out of the clouds (*CP*, 87). This distortion of stock phrase or cliché into new sense is a particular favourite. Examples, again, are legion: they include 'nicked in the locks of time', 'fall awake', 'dressed to die', 'the quick of night', 'up to his tears', 'jaw for news', 'happy as the grass was green' and 'lie down and live' (*CP*, 36, 17, 81, 99, 98, 58, 134, 111). These wittily refurbish their originals, partly by the greater immediacy created by their defamiliarising, *unheimlich* effect, but also because they insinuate an opposed concept, which, taken together with the original, produces a third one, namely that of 'life's paradoxical ambivalence', in Clark Emery's phrase. For example, the quick of the night refers to the fact that there is much sensitive life (particularly sexual) at the 'dead of night', and movement in the dark is often necessarily rapid (think of owls and mice). The two conceptions of night yield one which has to do with processual life-in-death and death-in-life, the 'quickness' of death and the death-orientedness of what is 'quick'. Some of these forms are particularising substitutions ('sins and days' for 'nights and days' in 'Unluckily for a death', for example), while others are simple shifts of meaning. But all, as Emery points out, 'have the effect of the *double-entendre*: two sets of words are heard and seen. Though they are not exactly puns, they have the same effect ... producing from opposed movements a third'.[39]

De/composing selfhood

Altered idioms testify to the origins of many poems in Thomas's 'working from words'. Although he often had recourse to, or created his own variants on, traditional stanza and metrical templates, he claimed that poetry should find its own form: 'Poetry finds its own form; form should never be superimposed; the structure should rise out of the words and the expression of them' (*CL*, 43). Accordingly, accounts of Thomas's methods of composition – his notion of how a poem should be organised (and organise itself) – shed much light on questions of form. They also tell us a lot about the degree and nature of the control that Thomas exercised over his poems and the degree of agency of the self, as both speaker and subject, as it appears within the poems.

Typically, it seems as if the process of a poem's composition would begin when some cluster of relatable verbal items attained a critical mass sufficient to trigger the image-breeding labour of the 'dialectical method'. Thomas was in the habit of recording and listing phrases, puns, reworked idioms and lines as they occurred to him and kept a list of usefully polysemous terms (this was probably what he described to Vernon Watkins as his 'Doomsday Book').[40] A poem would emerge from a 'lump of texture or nest of phrases', in Watkins's words 'out of which he created music, testing everything by physical feeling, working from the concrete image outwards'.[41] Because they were synchronous verbal fields, rather than causal narratives, the constitutive items often had to wait until they could be found a place within a 'lump'. (It was not until 1939, for example, that the 'youthfully made' phrase 'When I woke, the dawn spoke' yielded the poem 'When I woke, the town spoke'.)[42] Writing in 1946 to Harry Klopper – a poet who was working in English as his second language – Thomas spoke of the importance of 'the texture and movement' of words, in contrast to their 'meaning'; of the '*stuff* itself out of which poetry is made', as opposed to the sense-content 'that any poetry can convey' and 'which is common to all readers and writers in every language' (*CL*, 662). Some such 'stuff' would be literary, and I have discovered one example of Thomas directly sampling another text – Djuna Barnes's *Nightwood* – in order to acquire the lexical cluster he wanted:

> Night people do not bury their dead, but on the neck of you, their beloved and waking, sling the creature, *husked of its gestures*. And where you go, it goes, the two of you, your living and her dead, that will not die; to daylight, to life, to *grief*, until both are *carrion*. (My italics.)[43]

Compare this to the fifth stanza of 'If my head hurt a hair's foot':

> Now to awake husked of gestures and my joy like a cave
> To the anguish and carrion, to the infant forever unfree,
> O my lost love bounced from a good home … (*CP*, 80)

As with the examples found by Winifred Nowottny in 'There was a saviour', very few, if any, readers would catch the echo. Rather, it is another example of Thomas's attraction to the 'colour' of words (if, also, a coded homage to a favourite writer), to their power to evoke a desolate, yet paradoxical, emotional field, encoded in the abrupt *us* of 'husked' and 'unfree', the alliteration of 'gesture' and 'joy' and the assonance of 'carrion' and 'infant'.[44]

Far from his intuitive concept of intra-verbal relationships easing composition, Thomas's insistence on groping towards and piecing together his lyrics in this prehensile way – his *gestalt* poetic, as it might be called – often made composition immensely difficult. Many poets initially follow similar compositional procedures by accumulating verbal items, of course, but Thomas insisted on fusing his 'lines, phrases & hints' in their pure form, rather than using a few items to trigger larger amounts of 'ordinary' material, as he dismissively called it (*CL*, 139). Thus, as Watkins observes:

> His method of composition was itself painfully slow. He used separate worksheets for individual lines, sometimes a page or two being devoted to a single line, while the poem was gradually built up, phrase by phrase. He usually had beforehand an exact conception of the poem's length, and he would decide how many lines to allot to each part of its development. In spite of the care and power and symmetry of its construction, he recognized at all times that it was for the sake of divine accidents that a poem existed at all. (*LVW*, 17) [45]

Indeed, his need to grasp the poem as a whole meant that Thomas would often write it out again in full after even a minor alteration; hence the 200 or so worksheets for 'Fern Hill', to take an extreme example.

From his letters, it is clear that Thomas's idea of acceptable poetic 'music' was less smooth than Watkins's, closer to the oddity and sometimes gnarled textures of his germinative material: 'Before one gets to a truth in one's own mind one has to cut through so many crusts of self-hypocrisy and doubt, self-bluff and hypnotism; the polishing of phrases rubs off the sharp madness of the words and leaves only their blunt sanity', as he put it (*CL*, 98). And yet, as the general fluency of his poetry suggests, he eschewed the abrupt leaps of collage and parataxis, too, as shown by the letter to Eliot about "removing the creakiness of conflict" which I cited in Chapter 1.' (*CL*, 75). In March 1934, he would complain to Glyn Jones that: 'There seems to be an aversion today to poems which flow quite evenly along the pages; readers are always looking for knobbly, gristly bits of conflict in modern poems, apparently not realising that a poem can express the most complex of conflicts and yet show none of the actual conflicting gristle' (*CL*, 121). As David Aivaz noted in the passage quoted earlier, the poems contain 'uneven images that are smoothed by incantatory rhythms, rhymes, word patterns, verse forms, by the use of commas in place of full stop punctuation'. What this all indicates, as I argued in Chapter 1, is a stylistic paradox: the poems flaunt lyric fluency, but this fluency disguises their collage-like assembly from 'bony passages' and bits of 'conflicting gristle', of which the aleatory lift from *Nightwood* is an extreme example.

The syntax in a Thomas poem has to reconcile unusually heterogeneous source materials with a powerfully unifying narrative drive, and it has the simultaneity of process and the principle of non-identity as its conceptual correlates. In the early process poems, this means that the basic syntactic unit is the short, rhetorically coherent clause, encouraging the local construction of meaning.[46] The adjacent clauses are often disjunct, however, and this impedes meaning-construction at the larger levels of the sentence and the stanza. Often, Thomas interposes extended chains of such appositional (syntactically equivalent) phrases between the pronominal subject of the sentence and the verbs that it governs, complicating the syntax even further. Monstrously long sequences are constructed from these paratactical clauses, as in the opening sentence of 'Unluckily for a death'. This spills thirteen clauses over twenty-four lines, even though it pivots on its main verb – 'dedicate' – as early as line six.[47] For Ralph Maud, the purpose of this slow, periphrastic release of meaning is to 'distance the intimate' – the poems' often sexual material.[48] For William Moynihan, on the other hand, Thomas seeks to create emotional effects by 'holding the apprehension of grammar ... in suspense'. The problem is that Thomas often takes no pains at all to disguise the 'intimate', nor is there always an obvious reward of sense for the 'suspense' he creates.[49] If the mixture of the convoluted and blatant certainly enacts the conscious mind's attempts to censor the unconscious, Thomas seems keener to thwart hermeneutical efforts, making language resistant to the too-swift absorption of sense, as times, events and identities are collapsed in ways that recall the 'time theories' of Bergson, Whitehead and Dunne.

Syntax – the means by which a stable consciousness establishes itself through time – reflects the instability and multiplicity of the self in Thomas's work, and is derived from his modernist rejection of subjectivism and his decentred *gestalt* compositional process. It enacts the internally divided self of the process world, suggesting the inner divisions of the Freudian subject (id, ego, superego) and anticipating the self as 'en procès' or 'on trial' in Julia Kristeva's sense. Dispersed and refocused by the effects of polysemy, slippery syntax, uncertain deictics, puns ('I/ eye', 'there/their') and hard-to-track pronouns, the self often appears to go grammatically AWOL. The 'she' of the opening sentence of 'A grief ago' is a case in point:

> A grief ago,
> *She who was who I hold*, the fats and flower,
> Or, water-lammed, from the scythe-sided thorn,
> Hell wind and sea,
> A stem cementing, wrestled up the tower,
> Rose maid and male,
> Or, masted venus, through the paddler's bowl
> Sailed up the sun;
>
> *Who is my grief*,
> A chrysalis unwrinkling on the iron,
> Wrenched by my fingerman, the leaden bud
> Shot through the leaf,
> *Was who was folded* on the rod the aaron
> Rose cast to plague,
> The horn and ball of water on the frog
> Housed in the side. ... (*CP*, 47) (My italics.)

The ostensible narrative, italicised for emphasis, and typically elusive, though its sexual subject, the 'rose maid and male', and the fear of conception as a result ('the frog / Housed in the side') is clear enough and further confirmed by details such as the nervously jokey pun 'fats and flower' standing for the female body and sexual organ (with 'flower' / flour and 'fats' also suggesting baking, perhaps with an eye to the slang 'a bun in the oven'). Here, I simply remark on the tortuous phrasing of 'she who was who I hold ... who is my grief ... Was who was ...'. The second 'who' ought, grammatically, to be 'whom' ('she who was [the she] *whom* I hold') and is, in any case, superfluous to the meaning ('she who I hold' gives the sense). But Thomas wants to convey that the 'she' that the speaker holds *now* is not, strictly speaking, identical to the one he held a 'grief' (that is, a sexual act) ago. He also wishes to avail himself of the universalising sense, which goes with this kind of usage ('whoever at all'), or, in Maud's words: '"She who was who I hold" is the mysteriously estranged loved one'.[50] The reader is made remote from the specific sexual act and, at the same time, thereby given an insight into the external biological compulsions which drive sexual activity. Equally distancing is the separation of subsequent uses of 'she' and 'who' over a long and complexly unravelling sentence, which, with tense shifts, forces us to undergo the speaker's own problems in 'holding' onto his subject. The stretching of meaning enacts the compressions and extension of time experienced during the sexual act and makes us consider the provisionality of identity as it is constructed in time by memory. Eventually confronting this directly, the fourth stanza begins by asking: 'Who then is she?'

Using language using you: autonomy, surface

Thomas's work attempts to break linguistic boundaries and has been seen as perverse as a result. It is important to emphasise, again, that there are different levels at which this operates. 'The hand that signed the paper' has a neo-Augustan clarity and lack of radical ambiguity. But most of the early poems are far less transparent and several push at the furthest bounds of intelligibility. Comparison of 'To-day, this insect and the world I breathe' (1935) and 'How shall my animal' (1938) sheds light on Thomas's oscillation between avant-garde and modernist positions in this regard. The later poem traces the birth of the poem as a paradoxical struggle, which, in bringing an innermost essence to light, seems to destroy it (but actually results in the accomplished artwork).[51] It questions the Romantic notion of art as self-expression in a thoroughly modernist manner. In the earlier poem, however, what is problematised is the process of meaning-construction itself; it is a poem which remains radical today, almost as resistant as it was when it was first written:

> To-day, this insect and the world I breathe,
> Now that my symbols have outelbowed space,
> Time at the city spectacles, and half
> The dear, daft time I take to nudge the sentence,
> In trust and tale have I divided sense,
> Slapped down the guillotine, the blood-red double
> Of head and tail made witnesses to this
> Murder of Eden and green genesis.
>
> The insect certain is the plague of fables.
>
> This story's monster has a serpent caul,
> Blind in the coil scrams round the blazing outline,
> Measures his own length on the garden wall
> And breaks his shell in the last shocked beginning;
> A crocodile before the chrysalis,

Before the fall from love the flying heartbone,
Winged like a Sabbath ass this children's piece
Uncredited blows Jericho on Eden.

This insect fable is a certain promise.

Death: death of Hamlet and the nightmare madmen,
An air-drawn windmill on a wooden horse,
John's beast, Job's patience, and the fibs of vision,
Greek in the Irish sea the ageless voice:
'Adam I love, my madman's love is endless,
No tell-tale lover has an end more certain,
All legends' sweethearts on a tree of stories,
My cross of fables behind the fabulous curtain.' (*CP*, 38)

A poem which juxtaposes 'space, / Time' in its opening lines prepares
us for extreme relativism, and the identity of the poem's 'insect' is
ambiguous. 'Symbols', 'sentence' and 'sense' suggest that it is the poem
itself which is likened to an insect because it is segmented.[52] More
literally, too, 'insect' alludes to Genesis's plague of locusts. It also has
an archaic sense as the 'snake' and 'serpent' (and the Fall) figure in
stanza two, as does the insectile 'chrysalis' – the metamorphosis of
Old Testament Mosaic law, via the 'flying heartbone' of Christ into
the New Testament's gospel of forgiveness ('blow[ing] Jericho on [the
expulsion from] Eden'). But the energy that drives the poem is verbal
– a punning and playful riding of the slippage between signifiers and
an exploitation of pun, homophone and paragram. Thus, the opening
'to-day' is the activity of writing the poem-insect within 'the world I
breathe', being reflected upon at the point at which the poem's 'symbols'
have displaced ('outelbowed') the exterior world ('space') and 'time' in a
social and, even, limited way ('half'), as imaginative sense. The speaker
tells us that he has a divided sense about, and has divided his sense of,
'trust and tale', faith and fiction, describing his antithetical procedure,
but querying it, too. 'Sentence' suggests another way of putting this,
its juridical meaning supplementing the grammatical one to produce
an execution and 'guillotine'. 'Slapped down' reflects this ambivalence;
it signifies the guillotine blade falling *and*, in its idiomatic sense, 'gave
a check to' – another example of Thomas seeking out terms which
signify opposites and constructing contexts which enable these to occur
simultaneously. 'Trust and tale', according to the antithetical schema,
produce 'head and tail' – the 'blood red' physical 'double' of the more
abstract terms stemming from the tale / tail pun. 'Head' is equated with
'trust' grammatically, but is conventionally opposed to it (as rationality,

contrasted with the heart's association with faith), and this means the 'murder' of faith, represented as 'Eden and green genesis', which 'head and tail' – snakes seem to be all head and tail – have generated. This is an example of the manipulated cliché, too: to be unable to 'make head *or* tail' of something is to be unable to understand it, but 'head *and* tail' suggests that the cliché is too polarising and hints at a third position of undecidability and resistance to both faith in 'tales' and the head's rationalist dismissal of these.

The rest of the poem tends to confirm this reading, although, as usual, others lurk within and around it (one, naturally, is sexual: 'head' and 'tail' can both be applied to the penis, and the 'guillotine' introduces a narrative about castration anxiety and a serpent-phallus that induces a 'fall from love' into sexual knowledge). The second stanza refers us to the Fall, but only in order to signify the fall of belief in the Fall. This part of the poem is read by Ralph Maud as being simply about the 'violent' hatching of disbelief. However, the tale / tail is too densely presented to simply be about a loss of faith, and Maud's reading, in any case, reflects a critical tendency to personalise Thomas's poems. There is no evidence for a crisis of belief, and to assume an autobiographical 'explanation' goes against what we know of Thomas's procedure of 'working from words'. First, as I argue in Chapter 4, 'Incarnate devil', which precedes 'Today, this insect' in *Twenty-five Poems*, presents the Satan-serpent as a vivifying principle – a trickster who 'stings awake' the 'circle' of God-dominated stasis. It seems likely that he features here in the same role, being responsible for the *felix culpa*, but 'uncredited' for it (much like the donkey in G. K. Chesterton's poem of that name).[53] Thomas is more concerned with the way that fictions established as truths deconstruct themselves; the New Testament relativises the Old Testament, but is, in turn, relativised by it. Satan produces Christ's triumph, but, in grasping this, we establish a circular process of endless deferment, in which there is no place for absolute truth anymore. The gospels, making a fiction of Mosaic law, also become one of a number of supreme fictions – Revelation is levelled with *Hamlet*, Job with *Ulysses*, Genesis with *Don Quixote* – and with that, the promise of eternal life disappears.

This process is exemplified in the two oracular single-line refrains separating or segmenting the three stanzas, which emblematise the tension between the *lisible* and *scriptible*, worrying away at the meaning of 'certain' – a word which can be noun, adverb or adjective. What are we 'certain' about in this lyric? In the first line, 'The insect certain is the plague of fables', the chief meaning seems to be adverbial 'certainly': the poem plagues 'fables' such as that of Eden, since, for Thomas, a poem is the antithesis of dogma. However, like 'insect' and 'certain', 'plague' and 'fables' also have at least two potential meanings ('plague' can be a curse – as in Genesis's locusts – a bothersome thing, or simply a huge number of things; 'fables' are lies, fictions and, un-coincidentally, insect allegories *à la* La Fontaine or Joyce's Ondt and Gracehoper). The syntax permits various readings in addition to the one that I have given, among them: (a) the insect (poem) is certainly the huge number of fables; (b) the insect (poem) expressive of certitude is the curse of fables; and (c) the insect (poem) expressive of certitude is the huge number of fables. Of these, (b) seems to have the strongest presence, within what I take to be the dominant sense. So the poem deconstructs desirable, yet fixed fictions, but it is always already potentially one itself, and hence the certainty that the poem 'plagues' the 'fable' of Christian dogma must itself be challenged. As already noted, Thomas foregrounds the undecidability of, and resistance to, both faith in fictions and rationalist dismissal of them.[54]

The second inter-stanza line is a variation on the first: 'This insect fable is a certain promise' moves 'certain' along the line and makes it an adjective, applied to 'promise', which has displaced 'plague' from the line, while 'fable' has become the noun, for which 'insect' is now the adjective. Again, possible meanings multiply almost vertiginously, and the relationship of this line to its partner complicates things still further. Apart from the fact that, strictly speaking, 'insect fable' is tautologous, Thomas seems to be saying that the fabular (lying) poem replaces the absolute promises of Christianity with something which is a promise of certainty – a definite promise and / or a 'certain promise' (as in, 'a certain Mrs. Prothero'). The ironic, even oxymoronic, nature of the 'promise' suggests that death is the outcome of all the 'fibs of vision'. Yet, again, the one certainty in this relativistic universe is that there is no such thing as a certainty, and the 'madman' 'tell-tale lover' uttering the final lines paradoxically proclaims that his only certain end is the endlessness of his love for Adam – the original man, type of Christ and father of humanity. Death may be certain, but so, too, is desire – 'Though lovers be lost, love shall not' (*CP*, 56). In this sense, writing is also 'endless'; behind the curtain of fables which replaces fables of certainty is the poet (as Hamlet, Christ, Don Quixote and the rest all pining for their 'sweethearts'), whose crucifixion is a crucifiction, as Tindall puts it.[55]

Moreover, the 'generative method' of these final lines, magnificently conclusive as they seem, remains Aivaz's 'unashamed and inexhaustible word-play' – the 'fabulous curtain' of art. 'Certain' has drawn down this 'curtain', just as 'Adam I love; my madman's love' is a cross between anagram and palindrome, and the inter-stanza refrains ask to be read as musical permutations, at least as much as determinate meaning-bearing statements. 'Today this insect' pushes poetry towards a saturation point of linguistic meaning, testing the structural and organicist, arbitrary and motivated, aspects of language towards destruction. Yet the need for a style which embodies process only partly explains this. When J. Hillis Miller claims that 'The overlapping of mind, body, and world mean that language ... can be used by Thomas to describe all three simultaneously', it begs the question of what it is about language that means it 'can be used' in this way in the first place?[56] Or, better, what is it in language that allows Thomas to let it use him? Thomas identified a hesitation between conscious and unconscious agency when producing the poem in his March 1938 letter to Treece ('I make one image, – though "make" is not the word, I let, perhaps, an image be "made" emotionally in me and then apply to it what intellectual & critical forces I possess').[57] This describes the delicate balancing act between exerting mastery over language and submission to the linguistic unconscious which constituted Thomas's writing method, the poem dynamically oscillating between both, in order to reflect language's ambiguous status as both descriptive system and object in the world.

The answer to the question of what it is 'in language' is precisely this undecidable status – the curtain-like artifice of what purports to be 'certain'. It is the form that process takes (despite communicative appearances) in language, and, in more conventional terms, it can be seen as the conflict between a poem's latent impulse and its realisation in words. 'How shall my animal', for example, traces such a struggle between the desire to express an inner impulse and the fear of its betrayal in utterance, buried 'under the spelling wall': 'expression' as a contra-diction in terms. Linguistics-based criticism helps us understand such radical ambivalence by explaining the necessary paradoxes of language and the sign and improves on the explicatory approach (all obscurities can be resolved empirically) and intuitive approach (the poetry is only explicable on its own non-paraphrasable terms), albeit its Saussurean and Heideggerian incarnations incline towards one or other of these kinds of explanation. A fuller explanation would entail acknowledging the excess of language – that which grammar cannot account for – and the lack of authorial control over it, the surplus of the device over what is ostensibly required. In the stanza of 'How soon the servant sun', cited earlier, for example, narrative ambiguity makes it unclear whether 'nerves' is a verb or plural noun. 'I question' is a main verb, but 'Trap I' is more ambiguous – is this a verb, too, or does it belong with the 'long tailed stone', meaning that 'I' belongs with 'Let the soil squeak'? Is 'I am the biting man' speech or not? 'Trap' is probably a verb, but the uncertainty about sense increases the word's sonic autonomy and, with grammatical sense in short supply, this comes to supply much of the structure of the stanza (and the poem generally). The internal rhymes (nerve / serve, rite / light, etc.), pararhymes (sun / man, light / out, etc.), alliteration of /k/ and /s/ and arch inversion (of 'Trap I' – which lures the reader to construe 'squeal I' in the same way) all foreground a playful linguistic excess. The same could be said about the use of devices generally; for Thomas, the road of excess seems to have led to the palace of wisdom, since there is almost always a surplus which has no strictly mimetic purpose.[58]

It is this surplus, over and above the communicative function and even directed against it and thriving in its absence, which aligns Thomas with the idea that meaning is not just 'expressed' or 'reflected' in language, but actually produced by it. Language loses its apparent status as a self-effacing medium when the link between sign and referent is eroded or when we allow language's innate tendency to erode that link to operate. It is not just a question of releasing the sign from mere sense-transmission in order to increase its availability for manipulation as a sound value, for the sign itself is probed for suggestions as to how the bond can be loosened. Foregrounding linguistic materiality has been an avant-garde aim from Mallarmé to L=A=N=G=U=A=G=E poetry, of course, but the point is that it involves an exploitation of properties which are innate to language and poetry, rather than, as is commonly thought, innovation per se. Northrop Frye's critique of New Criticism stressed not only the lyric's linguistic autonomy, as Jakobson had, but its use of the verbal unconscious: 'what we think of as typically the poetic creation ... [is] an associative rhetorical process, most of it below the threshold of consciousness, a chaos of paronomasia, sound-links, ambiguous sense-links, and memory links very like that of a dream', this being responsible for lyric's 'oracular' and 'unconscious' priorities.[59] Acknowledging the nature of language, the poet may bypass, or at least appear to bypass, censoring and rationalising mechanisms. 'Appear to' because Thomas, like other poets, 'makes' it impossible to quantify the extent to which language is *spoken by*, or *speaks*, the poet. As Denise Riley puts it: 'Sound runs on well ahead of the writer's tactics. The aural laws of rhyme precede and dictate its incarnation – and this is only one element of an enforced passivity in the very genre where that irritating thing "creativity" is supposed to most forcefully hold court'. She adds: 'There seems to be very little which isn't driven by sound-association, maybe in the form of puns, maybe in the form of cadence, maybe in the form of half-realized borrowings'.[60]

We can link this to two aspects of Thomas's work. The first is his insistence that poetry be read aloud – something he reiterated almost as often as he did the need to work 'from words'. In *The Adelphi* in 1934, for example, he argued for a 'poetry that can be pronounced and read aloud, that comes to life out of the red heart through the brain'. He urged Pamela Hansford Johnson to declaim her work aloud and deplored contemporary poetry's 'lack of aural value and ... [its] debasing of an art that is primarily dependent on the musical mingling of vowels and consonants' (*EPW*, 166). In hearing a word, we initially register it as a sound, even if only fleetingly, before registering its meaning, although information transmission is almost invariably experienced as instantaneous. However, if this delay is prolonged by a context which foregrounds the signifier at the expense of its signified, the slide from signifier to signified is impeded (the prolongation briefly recreates the position of the infant Dylan overhearing 'those remote and incomprehensible grown-ups' in Thomas's 'Manifesto', quoted earlier). This, it seems to me, helps to explain Thomas's taste for reading aloud (and even his reading style); it is something that creates a delay in the process of meaning-absorption. Many of his lyrics, too, contain sentences so complex that they can only be comprehended by a reader; to *hear* the five stanza-long single sentence opening of 'When, like a running grave', for example, with its thirty-four appositive clauses and without having the text to hand, inevitably means experiencing an increase in the preponderance of the sonic over the referential dimension of the poem.

The second aspect is the visual equivalent of this, as noted by Peter Riley, who claims Thomas:

> pushed figuration beyond the bounds of rational location, and set up poetry as a meta-language, something which, like a painting or sculpture, uses materials of the world to create an entity which, stands independently, and which rather than a commentary on or reflection of, is 'an addition to the world.' ... The principal is that perception is arrested at the surface of the poem ... The halt at the linguistic surface eradicates anecdote or reportage, but allows perception to infiltrate an imaginative space. ... [A]t this particular juncture [the early 1930s] ... the imaginative space to which

the reader gains access is, perhaps for the first time, imbued with the features of the barrier, by which figures of language, while retaining traces of their representative function, become themselves objects of attention performing their own acts and creating their own theatre without becoming fixed as symbols. A 'constructed space' is formed which becomes fragmented and multi-faceted, in which the author's space and the spaces of the world are cast against each other without being conciliated into a depiction. Access to it is partial or momentary, and the degree of visibility may vary along the course of the poem between transparency and complete closure. You might often call it a tantalising space, but the movement of the text is so emotively bonded by urgency of address and poetic artifice that we are transfixed before this restless surface where metaphors of body, earth and language mix and collide with each other such that we cannot, will not, and no longer want to, know exactly 'where we are' in depictive, narrative or intellectual sense.[61]

Poetry, that is, confounds any straightforward naturalisation of its verbal material and is avowedly liminal in making us encounter language as a mediating threshold between our internal and external experience. Riley also reminds us, indirectly, that Thomas's poetry tends *not* to renew the verbal sign, according to the classic defamiliarising Formalist formula. If it 'promotes the palpability of the signifier', it does so with such a brusque sundering of signifier and signified that the integrity of the sign itself is altered. Rather than renewing language and, through it, the world, Thomas often 'renews' the signifier *at the expense of* the signified, cutting it off from any referent in the world. Rather than a more intensely experienced world, we get a more vivid, autonomous linguistic space. A line like 'The last angelic etna of the whirring featherlands' hardly renews our perception of the object world, since we cannot fully grasp what it refers to, initially at least; our first response is to relish its musical and weirdly suggestive richness for its own sake (*CP*, 78). We should eventually manage to paraphrase such a line within the poem's narrative, of course; but, initially, it 'makes strange' the verbal signs themselves, separating them from real-world referents and then splitting their signifiers and signifieds apart. What is renewed is not the world, but language itself in a defamiliarisation of defamiliarisation or meta-*ostrananiye*.

The interest in metalinguistic and metapoetic structures is equally evident in Thomas's use of metaphor.[62] The New Critics described metaphors as comprising a 'tenor' – the real-world part of the metaphor – and a 'vehicle' – the comparative term (in 'the sunshine of your smile', for example, 'smile' is the tenor, while 'sunshine' is the vehicle). Thomas manipulates metaphor with abandon: 'Where once the waters of your face', for example, inverts the tenor ('face') and vehicle ('waters') of its initial metaphor ('the face of the waters' from Genesis) to free the poem's signifiers from their signifieds:[63]

> Where once the waters of your face
> Spun to my screws, your dry ghost blows,
> The dead turns up its eye;
> Where once the mermen through your ice
> Pushed up their hair, the dry wind steers
> Through salt and root and roe. ... (CP, 14)

This poem is detached from reference to an object world, because the explicit metaphoric comparison it opens with (already an arbitrary product of wordplay) is used to 'breed' a series of *implicit* metaphors. In a standard metaphorical usage, we would eventually return to the 'real-world', to which 'your face' – the tenor – belonged. Here, however, 'waters' – the vehicle – becomes the tenor of a series of further metaphors, generating new vehicles – 'mermen', 'corals', 'tides', etc. – none of which are related back to the tenor of the initial metaphor. Thus, we end in the self-created metaphorical world in which we began:

> ... Dry as a tomb, your coloured lids
> Shall not be latched while magic glides
> Sage on the earth and sky;
> There shall be corals in your beds,
> There shall be serpents in your tides,
> Till all our sea-faiths die. (CP, 15)

The narrative, as Walford Davies notes: 'never had a real-world equivalent that could stand as referent [ie: tenor] in the first place'.[64] Yet it is not a case of simply inverting the metaphor. First, the 'waters of your face' may be metaphorical in the normal sense, as a conceit for tears (Crashaw's 'The Weeper' in Herbert Grierson's famous 1921 anthology of Metaphysical poetry metaphorises eyes as 'two faithfull fountaines; / Two walking baths ... Portable, and compendious oceans'). Second, while 'face' is metaphorical in 'face of the waters', if we take 'waters' as tears, it becomes metonymic in 'waters of your face'. Third, we may wonder whether referencing the 'real-world' is appropriate – even ordinary metaphor, let alone Thomas's, can have a tenor that is abstract or fictional ('the fires of love', for example). A more thoroughgoing destabilisation of metaphor seems to be occurring – one intended to make us uncertain about the poem's subject and its procedures. Is this a love poem, in which the loss of love is metaphorically illustrated by the dried-up waters? Or is it a nature poem, in which a dried-up foreshore is represented by amorous and religious symbols? If a love poem, how are we to take the blatantly sexual 'screws' and phallic 'serpents'? Questions are raised, but remain unanswered, instead we get an image with alternative meanings 'oscillating, suspended, and open', in Barbara Hardy's words, its sense 'not stably determined', but both 'sensuous and abstract, grotesque and rational'.[65]

Such confounding of distinctions between tenor and vehicle to create autotelic metaphor is common in the early fictions, as well as in the poems. In 'A Prospect of the Sea', the boy's imagining of a tree becomes the entire countryside: 'Every leaf of the tree that shaded them grew to man-size then, the ribs of the bark were channels and rivers wide as a great ship; and the moss on the tree, and the sharp grass ring round the base, were all the velvet coverings of green county's meadows blown hedge to hedge' (CS, 91). Here, metaphor 'nearly bursts [its] usual function', as Annis Pratt notes, nor is this unusual in the early stories.[66] Some poems offer the vehicle of a metaphor alone (the tenor being already implicit), occurring in a realm which is always already metaphorical. This is an example of a double 'genitive metaphor' – tenor becomes vehicle, which acts as the tenor for a further vehicle – as objected to by Christine Brooke-Rose in the line 'My fathers' globe knocks on its nave and sings' in 'I fellowed sleep'. For Brooke-Rose, the metaphorical relationship between 'fathers' and 'globe' is insufficiently clear for Thomas to proceed to a further metaphorical relationship between 'globe' and 'nave'.[67] She also points out that, if the candle is metaphoric for penis in the line 'Where no wax is, the candle shows its hairs', 'hairs' cannot be metaphoric with regard to the original tenor, the penis (CP, 24). What is happening in both cases, however, is that Thomas is identifying how a conceit works and intensifying it or making it negate itself. Blurring the frame which metaphor places between tenor and vehicle also leads to a levelling-out of phenomena and, hence, to a peculiar verbal density.

This is one source of Thomas's much-debated demand that he be read 'literally', as in his disputing of Edith Sitwell's explication of 'Altarwise by owl-light':

> Edith Sitwell's analysis, in a letter to the Times, of the lines 'The atlas-eater with a jaw for news / Bit out the mandrake with tomorrow's scream', seems to me very vague and Sunday-journalish. She doesn't take the literal meaning: that a world-devouring ghost creature bit out the horror of tomorrow from a gentleman's loins. She says the lines refer to 'the violent speed and the sensation-loving, horror-loving craze of modern life'. A 'jaw for news' is

an obvious variation of a 'nose for news', & means that the mouth of the creature can taste already the horror that has not yet come or can sense it coming, can thrust its tongue into news that has not yet been made, can savour the enormity of the progeny before the seed stirs, can realise the crumbling of dead flesh before the opening of the womb that delivers the flesh to tomorrow. What is this creature? It's the dog among the fairies, the rip and cur among the myths, the snapper at demons, the scarer of ghosts, the wizard's heel-chaser. The poem is a particular incident in a particular adventure, not a general, elliptical deprecation of this 'horrible, crazy, speedy life' (*CL*, 348).

What Thomas meant by 'literal' has taxed critics, because his explanations expand on, rather than explaining, the lines in question. They make perfect sense, however, if taken as a reference to the poem's metalepsis (frame-breaking) conflation of inside and outside, accomplished through the manipulation of the tenor and vehicle of metaphors. Jacob Korg's claim that 'The chief source of obscurity in [Thomas's] stories is the fact that imagined things are expressed in the language of factual statement instead of the language of metaphor', and that 'metaphor ceases to compare, and equates instead' makes a similar point.[68] With autotelic metaphor, nothing appears to be 'metaphoric', because everything is; conversely, everything is 'literal', because nothing is.

Word, world, wor(l)d

As we have seen, Thomas was keenly aware of the inter-involvement of world and word. At its most vatic, this meant appropriating the majestic rhythms and tones of John 1:1, itself an echoing of Genesis. Having audaciously rewritten the creation myth in his own processual terms in the first four stanzas of 'In the beginning', Thomas declared:

> In the beginning was the word, the word
> That from the solid bases of the light
> Abstracted all the letters of the void;
> And from the cloudy bases of the breath
> The word flowed up, translating to the heart
> First characters of birth and death. (*CP*, 23)

This is a physiological theory of the origins of language in 'the cloudy bases of the breath', emerging from microcosm and macrocosm simultaneously with the stars, the religious impulse, sexual energy and, what the final stanza calls, the universe's 'secret brain'. The 'word' is emphatically lowercase and originates in a universe already textualised, which 'translat[es] to the heart / First characters of birth and death'. World and word are born together, the universe is intended to be read and the word mediates between, and belongs to, both the inner self and external world.[69] Yet although it belongs to 'The ribbed original of love' (*CP*, 23), the nature of language and its relationship with the world and self is something to be anxious about, too. How might language fare, self-conscious of its object status, in a world of other objects? What does the world do to language under such circumstances? And how might this affect the sense of language use as a play between asemantic materiality and meaning, as we see it at work in poems such as 'Today, this insect'?

As the signifier within the verbal sign is detached from its signified, becoming autonomous, it becomes available for new forms of verbal play, but is, at the same time, cast worryingly adrift in the world of objects, to which it can only temporarily and ambiguously belong: 'The word is too much with us', Marlais notes in 'The Orchards'. The paronomasia of the wor(l)d updates Wordsworth's rejection of 'getting and spending' in a much later, more bewilderingly complex phase of capitalist society, and, from the far side of Symbolism, as the 'leaden spire' of his pencil falls and words disintegrate into mere phonemes: 'down fell the city of words, the walls of a poem, the symmetrical letters. He marked the disintegration of cyphers as the light failed' (*CS*, 44). Like other protagonists in the early fictions, Marlais has abandoned 'verbal princesses' and 'abstract fantasy' for a more tangible embodiment of his desire, and he now abandons signifiers which are only mental-conceptual in search of more tangible ones. On his quest, 'the "word" is a lively and autonomous entity which both accompanies and combats him', as Pratt observes.[70] Yet that quest, in a pattern repeated in the other stories, is frustrated, as world and word fail to wholly interpenetrate, and the signifier ultimately fails to escape its usual function within the sign. *Jouissance* turns to disquiet. '"Image, all image", cried Marlais, stepping through the window onto the level roofs', starting the 'indescribable journey' which will take him westwards to the sea, the orchards, the two sisters and the transformation of the one who embraced him, vampire-like, in his dream into 'the fork-tree breast, the barbed eye, and the dry, twig hand' (*CS*, 49). The dream-within-a-dream of 'The Orchards' – its deathly doubling of desire back on itself – reflects the self's entanglement in language and representation, an anxiety which takes the form in the early writing of continual re-runs of language as both origin and plenitude (the orchards) and fall (sexual disappointment). Because words cannot fully escape their referential function, however 'lively and autonomous', their anarchic corporeality and status as mere signifiers produces conflict.

The poetry explores the implications of the way in which words, which interiorise the world, also exteriorise the self. The world is continually being visualised as written, and writing is viewed as of the world, each imaged in terms of the other.[71] In the early poetry, this is radically disturbing; later, it will resemble the traditional trope of reading sermons in brooks and stones: 'I open the leaves of the water at a passage / Of psalms and shadows ... And read, in a shell, / Death clear as a buoy's bell ...' (CP, 143). As the writer conjures up his world in words, so the world 'spells', 'tells', 'signals' and 'writes' itself. A diastole-systole pulse is established, in which words circulate between self and world and back again. This is frequently likened to the circulation of the blood, which is 'syllabic' in 'Especially when the October wind'. Contrasting his position with Roy Campbell's in 1938, Thomas explained: 'I want my sentimental blood: not ... Campbell's blood, which is a red & noisy adjective in a transparent vein, but the blood of leaves, wells, weirs, fonts, shells, echoes, rainbows, olives, bells, oracles, sorrows' (CL, 326).[72]

The punning, 'in a transparent vein', emphasises the preference for a thickened language, which confuses worldly and wordy bodies. Writing to Johnson in May 1934, Thomas wondered: 'whether I love your word, the word of your hair ... the word of your voice, the word of your flesh, & the word of your presence' (CL, 164). More playfully, two months later, he greeted her 'Through the body of words', with 'a courteous salute under the chin' (CL, 180). The language is that of a reversed incarnational poetics of origin, which pulls the Word down to the level of word, exemplified in the 'Lotos-Eaters' chapter of Ulysses and Martha Clifford's rebuke to Leopold Bloom ('I called you naughty boy because I do not like that other world'), and thus reveals the slippages by which meaning is made.[73]

'Especially when the October wind', which is set in the month of Dylan Thomas's birth, probes the anxieties generated by the world-word, taking its cue from the reminder of mortality, which every birthday must signify. In the first stanza, a textualised perception of the world is received as the speaker walks 'By the sea's side' hearing 'My busy heart who shudders as she talks / Sheds the syllabic blood and drains her words' (CP, 18). The 'blood' is punningly sibylline, as well as 'syllabic', in keeping with its tidal surroundings, going forth into a world which is always textualised for the poet and balancing between word and world. In the second stanza, the textual aspect of the world is made clearer:

Shut, too, in a tower of words, I mark
On the horizon walking like the trees
The wordy shapes of women, and the rows
Of the star-gestured children in the park.
Some let me make you of the vowelled beeches,
Some of the oaken voices, from the roots
Of many a thorny shire tell you notes,
Some let me make you of the water's speeches. (*CP*, 18–19)

The isolated speaker has charted, in the first stanza (in 'noise', 'cough' and 'talks'), the external world's progression towards utterance, and he now sees his words enter a text-world of 'wordy shapes of women', 'star-gestured children' and speaking water and trees with 'vowels' (like those of the Welsh tree alphabet). In the third stanza, however, time also becomes textual ('the hour's word'), and his anxiety, hitherto balanced between word and world, increases, with the 'signal grass' '[breaking] through' his 'eye' (punning on 'I') threatening his identity with death and dissolution. 'Breaks' is a grotesque image in an increasingly menacing landscape:

Especially when the October wind
(Some let me make you of autumnal spells,
The spider-tongued, and the loud hill of Wales)
With fist of turnips punishes the land,
Some let me make you of the heartless words.
The heart is drained that, spelling in the scurry
Of chemic blood, warned of the coming fury.
By the sea's side hear the dark-vowelled birds. (*CP*, 19)

Thomas's insistence on language's status as an object in the world means that the world has acquired language-like powers – an ability to speak and construct meaning. Words become part of the world of real objects, and things reciprocate by signifying in a way which cannot be divorced from their simple physical presences. The problematisation of the signifier-signified bond is confirmed and, to some degree, justified for, to the extent that words are palpable, 'they do not (or cannot) simply stand in for the objects which they symbolise, but must become (or, rather, aspire to become) those objects in their own right: objects able to speak the real by being the real'.[74] Yet even as this is celebrated, anguish comes with the awareness of the threat that words pose to the self, which lies between word and world. With words unable to ever simply be objects-in-the-world, the confusion of world and word darkens the 'autumnal spells' of the poem. The ravens – descendants of

Poe's sardonic intruder in his eponymous poem – grow more ominous, and the speaker's repeated requests for permission to 'make' words real increasingly register language as loss, rather than as transformation, moving from a promise to a plea. In the final lines, words have escaped the speaker (they are 'let', like blood) to a dangerous degree; the image of them as blood, initially symbolising a life-giving influx of meaning into the world, now unnerves.[75] The heart pumping out the syllabic-sibylline word-blood that might have enabled the speaker to prophetically 'tell', 'spell' and 'make' the word-world is now 'drained' and abandoned in a bitter pun by the 'heartless' blood-words; the attempt to overcome isolation through language has failed.

Thomas's strenuous attempts, in devising a language of process, to 'get nearer to the bones of words' had a paradoxical effect; so, in his May 1934 letter to Johnson, he mockingly asserts, in classical modernist fashion, the existence of an *ur*-word, beyond all 'torture in words ... and in my knowledge of their inadequacy', gesturing towards the impossibility of grounding linguistic signification: 'All sentences fall when the weight of the mind is distributed unevenly along the holy consonants & vowels. In the beginning was a word I can't spell, not a reversed Dog, or a physical light, but a word as long as Glastonbury and as short as pith ... [which] ... speaks out everlastingly with the intonations of death and doom on the magnificent syllables' (*CL*, 164). Yet even as language strained and slipped it was pushed towards exceeding the usual orders of signification.

'Creep, crawl, flash, or thunder in': violence, economy and the pun

W. S. Merwin, John Berryman, W. H. Auden and Winifred Nowottny are among the many commentators on Thomas's poetry who have applied the adjective 'violent' to it. It is this feeling that informs John Bayley's claim that Thomas's 'oral vigour' is 'so amazing that one would scarcely believe that English was capable of it' and that his poetry can give 'the sensation ... that we are being assaulted by some other means than words'.[76] Among anglophone critics, 'violence' is a mark of excess and oddity, and it is a sign of the difference between anglophone poetic practice and that of most other Western literatures that, for Roman Jakobson, all literature, and poetry in particular, is necessarily 'a kind of organized violence committed on ordinary speech'.[77] Nevertheless, Jakobson maintained a belief in the communicative function of language, based on the assumption of stable, self-sufficient subjectivities existing prior to, and standing outside of, language, able, therefore, to intend and communicate a message *through* it. This assumption was not shared, however, by other twentieth-century theorists of language, such as Wittgenstein and Heidegger.

In his study *The Violence of Language*, Jean-Jacques Lecercle convincingly combines structuralism and certain aspects of these other contending traditions by explaining how violence is an innate aspect of the normal operations of the sign and that all language operates violent constraints on its users. As Lecercle sees it, linguistic exchange is a locus for relations of power; far from occurring in a co-operative vacuum (as structuralism assumes), it depends on historical conjuncture and often involves agonistic tactics. This makes the construction of stable, intending selves untenable: 'The speaker is the locus of two contradictory tendencies. He speaks language, i.e. he is the master of an instrument, and he is spoken by language, in other words it is language that speaks'.[78] Lecercle, who follows both Lacan in finding that the unconscious is structured like a language and Derrida in thinking that 'the conscious and speaking subject ... is constituted only in being divided from itself ... in temporizing, in deferral', argues that the stability of Saussure's *langue* is undermined by what he calls *lalangue* – the 'remainder', 'the part of language that is corrupted and that corrupts', a constitutive excess, which is reflected in solecism, pun, parapraxis and slippage and which exceeds the metalanguage of grammar – and that this is most notably the case when grammar believes it is most firmly in control.[79] In Thomas, I would argue, the subaltern and tricksterish subject is unwilling to presume itself to be the centre of consciousness and control, which a presumption of co-operation and intentional meaning requires. Thomas's 'dialectical' and 'generative' method both reveals and reverses the power relationships encoded in the inherent violence of language – his ambivalence is ambi*violence* – and also suggests that his use of language, while seeming anomalous, is, in reality, abnormally normal.

Indeed, for Thomas, the moments when the remainder manifests itself are precisely those for which a poem exists. 'Poems are pieces of hard craftsmanship ... made interesting ... by divine accidents: however taut, inevitably in order, a good poem may appear, it must be so constructed that it is wide open, at any second, to receive the accidental miracle which makes a work of craftsmanship a work of art', he argued in 1946 – a formulation echoed in Watkins's point that poems exist for the sake of such 'accidents', which is repeated in the 'Manifesto': '[t]he best craftsmanship always leaves holes and gaps in the works of the poem so that something that is not in the poem can creep, crawl, flash, or thunder in' (QEOM, 152). Craftsmanship, on its own, does not make art; it can only provide the conditions in which it may occur. The intricate formal structures of the poems exist as 'cages' – to use W. S. Graham's word – constructed so as to allow an unforeseen verbal surplus to emerge, which will bend or break the violence of discursive constraints. The paradoxical aim of the mastery exercised in the poem is to be rendered redundant, insofar as it will be usurped by the 'something that is not in the poem' – the anarchic promptings of language itself, Lecercle's *lalangue*. Only this excess, which cannot be planned in advance, is the mark of the true poem.

Another way of regarding this question is in the light of William Walton Rowe's point, cited in Chapter 1, that Thomas's verbal energy is shadowed by anxiety about 'expenditure in sex and death' and how he often presents life as 'sheer exuberant loss', rejecting 'the common-sense idea of life as an accumulation of experience'. This is informed by the idea of language as an economy, rather than a structure. Thus Steve McCaffery, adapting Georges Bataille, proposes two contrasting, but not exclusive, 'economies of writing' – the restricted and general. The restricted, as its name implies, values restraint, conservation, investment, profit, symmetrical balancing of line, stanza, rhyme and so on, accumulation and 'cautious proceduralities in risk-taking'.[80] Writing 'as a general economy', by contrast, is 'a non-utilitarian activity of excess, unavoidable waste and non-productive consumption'; McCaffery also links this to Barthes's later writings, which shift from a utilitarian understanding of reading (including the *scriptible* production of meaning by the reader) towards the concept of a *jouissance* of the text. Although McCaffery is discussing recent avant-garde poetry, his terms shed light on what happens in the typical Thomas poem or pre-1938 short story (and *jouissance*, of course, can be translated as 'sheer exuberant loss' in its sexual, as well as other, senses).[81] For the general economy is not proposed as a replacement to the restricted one; rather, as with Freud's parapraxes or Lecercle's remainder, it is a suppressed or ignored presence within the 'scene of writing' and of language more broadly conceived, which emerges by way of rupture, but which may be re-appropriated, covered up or repressed by the restricted economy.

The most consistently excessive device in Thomas, and the one that most resists appropriation in this way, is the pun; it is, in all its varieties, his master-trope.[82] Auden said that good poets have a weakness for bad puns, while Pope opined that 'he that would pun would pick a pocket', and the two reactions might be said to delimit the range of responses to Thomas's work. Encouraged by Joyce's example, Thomas grasped the possibilities of a pun and laboured to rescue it from the critical opprobrium in which, because it is so egregiously at odds with plain-style poetics and theories of language, it has been held since the late seventeenth century. Now, as then, pun has been viewed as incompatible with literary dignity, amounting to a childish abnegation of the duty to communicate lucidly. Yet pun continues to confound empirical and structural approaches to language and literature. While Saussure's linguistics make room for paronomasia and pun, for example, his claim that in discourse 'words acquire relations based on the linear nature of language' and insistence that signifiers have stable relationships with their signifieds, each existing in mutual interdependence 'like two sides of a sheet of paper', excludes the possibility of pronouncing two elements simultaneously.[83] Despite Saussure's best efforts, pun undermines his basic principles; for, more than a set of meanings articulated through a differential system, the meaning of pun is that meaning is a linguistic *effect*, not a presence within or behind language, and is inherently unstable and uncontrollable. This is the aspect grasped by Heidegger, for whom puns were: 'close to the essence of language, because they disclose that language is not reason and order but overpowering and uncanny, uncontrollable and wholly other ... they [stand for] waywardness or ambiguity, endless dissemination as against the placing of things in their proper categories or the subsumption of things within a total system'.[84] Puns, in other words, are instances of overdetermination in verbal forms and, thus, perfect for Thomas's purposes. As Derek Attridge notes, in pun: 'The material envelope of the sign ... [is] allowed to take the initiative ... [bringing] about a coalescence of otherwise distinct fields of reference', flouting the rule that 'phonemes and graphemes should be servants, not masters' and that 'the mere coincidence of outward similarity should have no bearing on the meanings within'.[85]

Thomas is not content to merely deploy words that have multi-directional and often antithetical themes, but often makes puns structural to his poems. The Blitz elegy 'Among those Killed in the Dawn Raid was a Man Aged a Hundred' begins 'When the morning was waking over the war' – a line which puns on 'mo(u)rning' and 'wake' to establish simultaneous narrative strands, which both grieve the death and affirm the resurgence of new life. Again, the lack of the expected hyphen in the title of 'Into her lying down head' makes present the lover's head lying on a pillow and, her down(y) head as that of a liar; solicitude and reproach are inextricably mingled. Thomas's method, then, is predicated on the ineluctable tendency of language towards instability, displacement and deferral of meaning. If, in his work, mind and world are brought together by words, then it is at the cost of splitting the linguistic sign apart: in this poetry, not only is the sign not equal with its referent, but it is often not equal with itself either, divided as it is between signified and a more or less autonomous signifier. In the period of refining his process poetic, pun became habitual to Thomas. Stuck in rainy Laugharne (pronounced 'Larne'), he informed Pamela Hansford Johnson:

> I am a Symbol Simon. My book will be full of footlights & Stylites, & puns as bad as that. Kiss me Hardy? Dewy love me? Tranter body ask? I'll Laugharne this bloody place for being so wet. I'll pun so frequently and so ferociously that the rain will spring backward on an ambiguous impulse, & the sun leap out to light the cracks of this saw world (*CL*, 163).

Such flights occur constantly in the letters, radio writings and conversation. Thus, Daniel Jones was reminded of their teenage friendship in a punning version of 'Love's Old Sweet Song' – '"just a song at twilight, when the lights Marlowe and the Flecker Beddoes Bailey Donne and Poe"' (after 'Just a song at twilight / When the lights are low / And the flick'ring shadows / Gaily come and go') (*CL*, 274). He told Vernon Watkins: 'You are right to write poems of all kinds: I only write poems of allsorts, and, like the liquorice sweets, they all taste the same'. 'Brainlessly I cut out drink', he informed another correspondent, Brains being a Cardiff-brewed beer (*CL*, 223). According to Brinnin, almost his last words involved a pun on 'roses' (flowers) and a Rose's (a brand of lime cordial) (*CL*, 336).[86] Thomas learnt to make puns inseparable from his understanding of the world, and they abound in his poetry to a degree unknown since that of the metaphysical Poets. From 'the shelling of their heads', referring to an embryo's delicately forming skull *and* artillery bombardment in the looming war, in 'I see the boys of summer' – the first poem in *18 Poems* – to the seagull's beaks 'Agape, with woe' (the two- and three-syllabled forms) and a 'prowed dove' in the 'Prologue' – his last completed poem – pun proved to be irresistible to Thomas. Its uses range from metaphysical wit ('down pelts [furs / throws] the naked weather') to the groaningly brilliant contrivance of 'Abaddon' (the Angel of the Pit and 'a bad 'un' in 'Altarwise') and the tragic 'dug' of 'Ceremony after a fire raid' (the breast of the earth-as-mother and the child's grave it has dug). Nor does it settle for just two meanings: 'scale' in 'I, in my intricate image' has four or five, depending on where it appears, appertaining to fish, climbing, weights, measures and music, sometimes combining several of these at once. Even the most outrageously compact and complex, however, enrich the poem: thus, in 'A grief ago', a mere five words – 'the rod the aaron / Rose' – combine, backwards as well as forwards, to generate the biblical Aaron's rod (also a D. H. Lawrence novel), the rose of Sharon and Arianrhod (the maiden who, in *The Mabinogion*, gave birth to Thomas's namesake – Dylan eil Ton / Dylan, Son of the Wave), all of them contributing to the poem's narrative and further charging it with resonance and interpretive potential.[87]

In multiplying the signifieds attached to each signifier, pun weakens the signifier-signified bond, making it more difficult to treat the signifier as a transparent vehicle of a fixed sense, arresting and slowing attention and so thickening the materiality of the signifier.[88] Its arbitrary quality also threatens standard symbolic or associative functions, undermining authorial dominance and equalising the relationship between poet and language; to enable puns, the poet must serve language, rather than the other way around, work to motivate linguistic signs and, as Jonathan Culler notes, forge contexts in which they will yield their additional semantic value, by responding to 'the call of the phoneme, whose echo tells of wild realms beyond the code and suggests new configurations of meaning'.[89] Far from being a minor form of wit, Culler describes pun as 'the foundation of letters, in that the exploitation of formal resemblances to establish connections of meaning seems the basic activity of literature', but one which simultaneously makes it clear that literature's foundations are shaky, manifest in the 'shifty relationship' between letter and sound.[90] Furthermore, pun – Thomas's work is happy to remind us – is an innate quality of language, a pressure point at which the violence of imposing monologic meaning on the verbal sign is revealed. Above all, it is a place where that 'something that is not in the poem can creep, crawl, flash, or thunder' into it. Attridge notes that pun can be used to enforce authorial control; an elaborately framed pun, as most are, signifies risk and the reassertion of authorial control, in contrast with the portmanteau words, which are a more destabilised cousin of pun deployed by Joyce in *Finnegans Wake*. However, it is arguable that the critical wrath Thomas often incurs is because his puns edge into the realm of Joycean portmanteau-style waywardness, in which meanings refuse to stabilise entirely, multiplying beyond the normal pair of signifieds. So often in Thomas's work, pun focuses the crucial paradoxes of a poem, but in a manner which is simultaneously centrifugal and centripetal. 'Before I knocked' offers a well-known example:

> You who bow down at cross and altar,
> Remember me and pity Him

Who took my flesh and bone for armour
And doublecrossed my mother's womb. (*CP*, 12)

The poem's theme – broadly, the mortal Christ's protest at the destiny imposed on him by God the Father – allows us to read 'doublecrossed' as 'twice-traversed', 'twice-crucified' and 'cheated' or as a combination of all three. It is impossible to specify exactly singular or simply-punning meaning. For a reader who demands one, this is bound to be a blemish, as Pamela Hansford Johnson thought and Barbara Hardy has argued since.[91] The counter-argument is that the grotesqueness and excess of meaning might be precisely the point in a description of the incarnation – an event said to be beyond mortal comprehension. Pun, in fact, is useful for not only multiplying the reach of language, but also suggesting that there is a place beyond language, even if that can only be said in language (as in Derrida's 'Il n'y a pas un *hors-texte*'). More characteristically, Thomas might have replied that he was simply following religious authority for mixing sacred matters of religion and profane wordplay, the Church having been founded on Christ's pun (*petrum* = rock) on the name of his disciple Peter, with Christ himself (as sun / Son) being a favourite opportunity for pun. In the same seriously witty vein, both 'doublecrossed' and 'roc(k)' (as Thomas uses it in 'Altarwise') present, with unparalleled economy, the meanings within meanings involved in a mystery, but are also a witty critique of that 'mystery'. In the first case, it is implied that the mystery is based on blood-sacrifice and cheating; in the second, as a poem like 'There was a saviour' elaborates, the firm foundation can represent an ossified, spirit-killing orthodoxy. Poetry may look like a game, as Heidegger noted, but yet it is not.

Because it short-circuits the usual flow of sense then, pun forces meaning to abandon the safe route from signifier to signified and makes it occur in the play of signifiers, giving the poet the freedom to exploit accidental phonic coincidences (again, the parallels with deconstruction hardly need labouring). It crystallises process in linguistic form, but simultaneously subverts a too-organicist, etymology-based and potentially reactionary approach to words (in this aspect, the variousness and mobility of Thomas's puns are decidedly un-Heideggerian). If mind and world were split apart without words and language (and the body) is the place in which they interpenetrate, pun ensures that language can make that less a monolithic fusion than a creative con-fusion.

Naturally, the implications of pun will be resisted, if the reader is seeking signs of progress towards transparency. In 'After the funeral', for example, we read that Ann's 'hooded, fountain heart once fell in puddles / Round the parched world of Wales' (*CP*, 73). Ralph Maud rightly notes that 'parched' here is a pun on the Welsh *parchedig*, 'priest', and hence a prod at Nonconformism. What he will not allow, however, is that it is active in the poem: 'I would maintain that the pun does not operate within "After the funeral". Perhaps it exists as a nod and a wink between author and an in-group of readers, but essentially outside the poem'.[92] That is, he prefers to read the poem as the utterance of a unified subjectivity bound by the rules of more or less realistically delivering its narrative, and he understands that the wayward energies of pun would threaten this.[93] The rather desperate attempt to explain away its metaleptic, frame-breaking force is revealing. To claim that the pun is not needed to 'make the poem work' and therefore does not deserve 'a permanent place', as Maud does, confirms conventional criticism's acceptance of 'the notion of the author as unquestionable and pre-given', determining how the text should be read, and its refusal to see how 'the author is a product or effect of the text'.[94] Denying the pun also misses its role in helping to represent the poem's fractured subject; the poet's younger self has just been ironised, and, immediately after the use of the term 'parched', the speaker attacks his current temptation to bombast. But it is also a question of genre; in the process poems, Maud has no problems with a pun. It is because 'After the funeral' seems to be a realist poem, using language more or less transparently, and the existence of pun would rupture this illusion, that he objects to it. It is precisely this quality which can make pun 'a scandal and not just an inconvenience ... the product of a context deliberately constructed to enforce an ambiguity ... to leave the reader or hearer endlessly oscillating in semantic space'.[95] In this poem, the 'oscillation' triggers self-interrogation, with the arbitrariness of pun paradoxically prompting a heightened degree of sincerity, intensifying the lament for Ann by folding authorial presence back upon itself.

'Colour of saying': the 1938 turn

The pun on 'parched' is radical in a new way for Thomas, since it occurs in a poem which is relatively *lisible*, by the standards of his previous work, and does not seem to proceed, at least overtly, by 'unabashed wordplay'. 'After the funeral', and *The Map of Love* more generally, record the start of an attempt from 1938 onwards to give more transparency, syntactical flexibility and variety to the sometimes marmoreal style of the process poetry. A transitional style, switching between the earlier opacity and a greater clarity of verbal texture, would prevail until 1941. In prose, however, the 1938 shift towards clarity was immediate and complete. The contrast between Thomas's final three 'process' stories – 'The Map of Love', 'In the Direction of the Beginning' and 'An Adventure from a Work in Progress' (written between 1937–8) – and those that he began to write in 1938 for *A Portrait of the Artist as a Young Dog* is immense. The first three are among his most daringly experimental work in any genre; 'The Peaches' – the first story in *A Portrait* – is, by contrast, a model of colourful realist prose.

Stephen Knight, as I noted in the Introduction, has denounced the shift as marking an enforced compromise with English 'colonial' demands. More often, it has been praised as a sign of maturity. Marriage, fatherhood and looming war, it is argued, ended experimentalism. John Ackerman voices a general relief in his mild denigration of the 'introspective intensities' of the pre-'turn' work and in the welcome he extends to Thomas's move 'outward to the world around him, both realistically observed and exactly recalled' (indeed, he regards his initial turn towards 'introspective intensities' in 1933 as 'regrettable, perhaps').[96] Others have demurred from this judgement, as far as the poetry is concerned, seeing the later work as less compelling. Very few, such as Knight and Pratt, have argued for the superiority of the pre-'turn' fictions, however. It is probably invidious to compare the earlier and later stories; both are excellent exemplars of their kind. However, there are good reasons for at least querying the grounds on which they are so often passed over. For one thing, biographical explanations – the dubious 'prodigal son' narrative, in this case – are almost always suspect. Second, while new responsibilities probably did alter Thomas's attitudes to his writing, to assume that realism was his only other option misses the choice he had of blending experimental and more straightforward styles. This, after all, was what he had done previously in *Twenty-five Poems*. Third, it is unlikely that he suddenly came to the conclusion in 1938 that his previous work was an error ('After the Funeral' and the *Portrait* stories ironically frame his younger modernist self; they don't renounce it). Rather, it seems more likely that Thomas felt he had reached a certain stylistic limit and had to change direction, because he could go no further. Indeed, the last three experimental stories, written between 1937–38 – 'The Map of Love', 'In the Direction of the Beginning' and 'An Adventure from a Work in Progress' – show him deliberately attempting to exhaust the possibilities of the early style. I shall briefly discus these, before tackling 'Once it was the colour of saying', which is usually taken to mark Thomas's farewell to his early writing.

All three stories use language pushed to extreme limits of verbal materiality and play, exacerbating the struggle between word and world found in the tales that precede them. They are fantastic, post-Symbolist fictions in a folktale and gothic-grotesque vein and take the form of quest narratives. The 'generative method' dominates the last two, which develop the quest for unity between a male and female 'character' established in 'The Map of Love'. 'In the Direction of the Beginning' is an almost implacably dense single-page-and-a-half long paragraph, in which we discern an Odyssean hero, 'born in the direction of the beginning', summoned to a sea-voyage by a woman's disembodied voice (*CS*, 117). What awaits him is a semi-surreal, ceaselessly shifting version of the eternal feminine:

> Which was her genesis, the last spark of judgement or the first whale's spout from the waterland? The conflagration at the end, a burial fire jumping, a spent rocket hot on its tail, or, where the first spring and its folly climbed the sea barriers and the garden locks were bruised, capped and douting water over the mountain candle-head? Whose was the image in the wind, the print on the cliff, the echo knocking to be answered? She was orioled and serpent-haired. She moved in the swallowing, salty field, the chronicle and the rocks, the dark anatomies, the anchored sea itself. She raged in the mule's womb. She faltered in the galloping dynasty. She was loud in the old grave, kept a still, quick tongue in the sun (*CS*, 118).

The story concludes with a fusion of the voices of the hero and the female figure in 'One voice', which 'travel[s] the light and water waves'. 'An Adventure from a Work in Progress' has a similar quest structure. As in 'In the Direction of the Beginning', the hero sails a boat with a mast of cedar, decorated and rigged out with beaks, shells, 'finned oars' and a 'salmon sail'. His journeying leads to two encounters – one on a tropical island surrounded by polar ice, the other at the summit of a mountain (where the woman he seeks *is* the mountain). As he reaches her, time 'falls', events become simultaneous and revelation seems at hand, but, on the first occasion, the 'waterfall' of her blood turns to 'fishdust and ash', and, on the second, she 'diminish[es] in his arms', growing younger and de-evolving: 'With his cries she caved in younger to a child. ... She dangled there with bald and monstrous skull, bunched monkey face and soaked abdominal tail. ... a white pool spat in his palm' (*CS*, 123). The fusion of voices of 'In the Direction of the Beginning' is not achieved.

Although their style is highly-wrought and the narrative threads are difficult to trace at times, it is sufficiently clear that the tales are a culmination of Thomas's many attempts to fuse apocalyptic narratives of origins and endings – literary, biological and sexual – probably written in prose, because the material was too inchoate to be shaped into metrical form. The boat of 'An Adventure' is drawn onwards (as in 'Ballad of the Long-legged Bait' of 1941) by a phallic anchor, and the masts of the boats in both stories are made of cedar, because it is the wood that most pencils are made from. Both stories, too, are suffused with references to script, writing and the production of sound. The orgasmic compression of imagery used to present an intensely sexual 'world happen[ing] at once' could scarcely have gone further, nor could the degree of punning and wordplay, which is less formally controlled and inhibited than in the poems, alternating as it does between external quasi-biographical allusion and purely inner dramas powered by linguistic excess. In Lecercle's terms, these stories suggest a kind of 'schizolinguistics', in which 'the remainder, far from being a residue, has now invaded the whole field' and '[t]he desire for rules … give[s] way to the rule of desire'.[97] The identification of language, body and desire reaches the limits of coherent selfhood, but, in doing so, threatens to collapse writing into an undifferentiated stasis.

Thomas's stylistic swerve of 1938 acknowledges his arrival at these limits. *The Map of Love* takes the title from the most experimental work it contains (it does not contain 'In the Direction' and 'An Adventure'), but it also includes poems that show the search for a new, less simultaneous and more discursive style. 'After the Funeral', with its interrogation of past and current writing selves, shows one solution; 'Once it was the colour of saying' of December 1938, rather differently, anticipates his self-description as 'the Rimbaud of Cwmdonkin Drive' by rewriting 'Voyelles' – the poem in which Rimbaud allocated the five vowels a set of colours, images and associations, according to a personal synaesthetic logic (one quite unlike the differential arbitrariness of Saussure's system).[98] Synaesthesia is akin to onomatopoeia, as another form of what linguistics calls 'phonetic symbolism'. It runs throughout Thomas's writing, and 'colour of saying' translates the French poet's *alchimie du verbe* into his own terms. Just as it defeats the usual demarcations of the senses, so the poem manages to seem more transparent than many of the poems around it and, at the same time, thwart full comprehension. Thomas's sonnet signals its imperfect fit with the French original by losing a line. It takes its cue not only from Rimbaud's vowels, but his notorious renunciation of poetry; how does the poetic prodigy renew itself if it is *not* going to give up writing?

> Once it was the colour of saying
> Soaked my table the uglier side of a hill
> Where a patch of black and white girls grew playing
> On a capsized field where a school stood still;
> The gentle seaslides of saying I must undo
> That all the charmingly drowned arise to cockcrow and kill.
> When I whistled with the mitching boys in the reservoir park
> Where at night we stoned the cold and cuckoo
> Lovers in the dirt of their leafy beds,
> The shade of their trees was a word of many shades
> And a lamp of lightning for the poor in the dark.
> Now my saying shall be my undoing
> And every stone I wind off like a reel. (*CP*, 74)

Curiously, although Thomas's renunciation seems to be of 'the colour of saying' of his 1933–7 poetry and prose, the extended conceit of the spilt ink 'capsized' onto the paper he wrote upon so precociously, overlooking the black-and-white-uniformed hockey-playing girls on the 'capsized' field (small as a schoolboy's hat, tilted like a sinking vessel), reminds us that these poems are pretty monochrome (green and red are just about the only colours). In fact, the obvious response to the farewell is that the later poems, this one included, are actually *more* colourful than the earlier ones. For Thomas did not give up an exuberant style for a chastened one; quite the reverse. The marine imagery of 'capsized', 'drowned', 'soaked' and 'gentle seaslides of saying', echoing 'colour of saying', has the sea giving up its dead as the poem's compass expands from table, to field, to the view beyond it. The 'capsized field' figures writing (styles) being overturned, as well as writing the hill-tilted playing 'field' / sloping writing table. 'Capsized' also conjures up a 'foolscap'-sized page and the later 'leaves'. What, then, is actually being renounced here?

Perhaps what is being confessed to is that Thomas once found colours where there seemed to be very few – 'The shade of their trees was a word of many shades' – and that now they will have to be presented more overtly. The 'seaslides' of a more average kind of saying ('gentle') will be released, with the result that personal memory (the 'charmingly drowned'), rather than the linguistic unconscious, will, in future, feature more heavily in the poetry – this amounting to a Peter-like ('cockcrow') betrayal of the inner linguistic self. Yet personal memories can be shaming, as that of the 'mitching boys' who stoned the lovers in the 'reservoir park' in Cwmdonkin suggests. Previously 'drowned', earlier selves will now 'arise': the sea of the past will give up its dead and the ambiguity of 'charmingly' ('using spells', as well as 'conventionally attractive') hints at the dangers of anecdote and memory as the basis for poetry. Writing may well be 'undone', as the graven 'stones' of new poems, episodes from his past life, are wound off like 'a reel', meaning both cast off like a thrown stone or an angler's cast and projected like a film-reel. The effect on his ability to write may be the same as the (surely prophylactic) effect of stoning on the lovers. The poem can be read, then, as an assessment of the cost of a poetry which may have to become more 'reel'-ist', thus expressing a fear that, to strengthen the 'I make' at the expense of the 'let be made' aspect of poetry, one may shed too much light on 'the dark' in which imagination breeds 'colours of saying', and stifle the rich linguistic subconscious which has hitherto been poetry's troubled taproot. In that case, 'saying' would be a paradoxical 'undoing'; the opacity of 'stones' become the transparency of a 'reel' (or Real) of the life.

Performance / deconstruction / psychoanalysis and the body

As his process style reached the limits of the linguistic intensity of which it was capable, so Thomas adapted it by allowing it to articulate more of the social world – a world in which, following marriage in 1937 (and fatherhood in 1939), the alignment of his life and writing had altered. The poems have greater emotional amplitude – and the emotions include jealousy and anger, as well as uxoriousness and tenderness – but they continue to be based upon the process vision and the 'generative method', even if Thomas now came to accept and celebrate being subject to supersession and dissolution into the continuum by its 'force'. The process of adaptation and evolution is reflected in the styles of the poems found in *The Map of Love* (1939) and *Deaths and Entrances* (1946), which are various, although without the almost aggressive heterogeneity of *Twenty-five Poems*.[99] In *The Map of Love*, we find Thomas attempting poems in the new style canvassed in 'Once it was the colour of saying'; they include 'After the funeral', 'If my head hurt a hair's foot', 'On no work of words now', 'How shall my animal' and 'A saint about to fall'. In *Deaths and Entrances*, the variety results from the mixture of poems in this transitional style and the simpler style of 1938–41, which emerged after a break of three years, in

1944–5. Throughout these shifts and silences, however, the fundamental nature of poetry for Thomas – that it be an embodiment of the process vision in verbal form – remained the same, alert to, and pushing at, the vanishing points of language (what Lacan calls 'the Real' or what lies outside the Symbolic Order), as I shall show in Chapters 5 and 6. The verbal embodiment of process in poetry was never simply a case of pressing language to the point of disintegration. As we have seen, Thomas exploits two aspects of Lecercle's remainder or *lalangue*. On the one hand, he takes advantage of the arbitrariness of the verbal sign – the way it can be wrenched away from its signifier to achieve status as a free-floating sonic object independent of sense. On the other, he exploits the occasions provided by puns and other devices to do the opposite, hyper-motivating the link between signifier and signified by multiplying it. If pun maximises the slippage between signifieds, we might say that other kinds of wordplay largely tend to maximise the slippage between signifiers. Both kinds, pushed to extremes, work in defiance of the 'social fact' of language. Yet, as Anthony Easthope (following Émile Benveniste) has pointed out '[a]s far as the social fact of discourse is concerned the bond of the signifier and signified ceases to be arbitrary; but it never ceases to be arbitrary for the subject'.[100] Thomas exploits the dual sense that we all have of language as both arbitrary and motivated. At the same time, he plays on the way in which language is both a meta-referential symbolic system purporting to stand above the object world and a material object in that world. Again, he switches between these functions, although, because we overwhelmingly use language instrumentally, he tends to emphasise the anarchic materiality of the signifier and its 'sculptural' qualities. This affects us, as readers, with the *scriptible* aspect of the writing drawing out the lag between visual recognition and comprehension. It also affects us as listeners, and Thomas's emphasis on performance exploits the fact that the lag between hearing and meaning-comprehension increases the potential for setting up wordplay. These lags and gaps match that which is always present in the Saussurean sign, in the sense that the signifier can never be unshakably fixed to, or fully comprehend, its signified. Their importance to his verbal play, together with Thomas's sense of poetry as *to-be-spoken*, suggestively anticipates certain key concepts of deconstruction, including, of course, 'slippage' and 'phonocentrism'.[101] The phenomenon of textual aporias – points at which language contradicts its ostensible meaning-content, allowing presuppositions and authority-claims to be prised apart – is exploited ceaselessly and consciously in Thomas's work. The opening *non sequitur* of 'A Refusal to Mourn the Death, by Fire, of a Child in London', 'Never until', for example, is a case in point; the specification of a future moment – 'until' – contradicts 'never', and the poem emerges in the aporia that this opens up.[102]

One might even say that, in the sense that Thomas thematises such aspects of language, he – like avant-garde writers – indicates the limits of deconstruction.[103] Such is the degree of differential play in the language of some of his poems, that to deconstruct them would be futile. Thomas also diverges from poststructuralism in his concern with the body and the unconscious of language – subjects about which deconstruction has little to say. Poetic labour, like the drives in Freud's theory of the subject, lies in this both / and (as opposed to either / or) zone of oscillation between the willed and the mediumistic, the ideational and the somatic – an interface which Freud traced in the way that the unconscious manifests itself in the conscious mind in the form of dream-words, slips of the tongue and parapraxes. Freud's analysis of *lapsus linguae* initially linked writing in which the emphasis was on relationships between signifiers themselves to the unconscious and the infantile in denial of the world of work. After the carnage of the First World War, however, he came to feel that the death instinct fuelled the reality principle's repression of the pleasure principle. This led him to alter his schema, and to view language's connection with the body as a positive thing. Such play, in Thomas's work, also has a critical force: linguistic 'excess', 'remainder' and 'violence' may be taken to reflect an age of mass unemployment, fascism and war-fears as much as direct allusions to, and descriptions of, these things. McCaffery observes that: 'Freud allows language … alternative relations with itself, based not on utility, consciousness and investment, but … on the grounds of their own radical contradictions. The linguistic subject shows itself to be a divided subject in desire whose conscious / unconscious dispositions reveal themselves in a graphic economy extending beyond written, grammatical marks into oneiric operations (substitution, displacement, condensation) and unconscious figurations (pun, homophony, paragram) where language emerges as a general force whose operation is no longer authenticated, nor controlled by, conscious instrumental reason and the intentional subject'.[104] From here, it is a short step to Lacan's post-Freudian model of the unconscious being structured as a language not wholly at the disposition of its user, but prone to erupt through fissures in conscious discourse. Or, to give it a more positive spin (as Thomas generally did): words are always late for the event, and explication always late for words; but, if saying always diverges from meaning, language generates new life in the mouth or the mind, begetting and issuing from a world that is no less real for the omission of the original, intended meaning.

Disrupting the normal functioning of the verbal sign problematises the role of language in constructing and socialising the self and forging the bond between the self (as signifier) and social authority (as signified). This was Thomas's aim, and it remains the aim of much contemporary experimental poetry, with its fondness for 'those varieties of wordplay [pun, homophony, palindrome, anagram, paragram, charade] which relate writing to the limits of intentionality and the Subject's own relation to meaning'.[105] To resist authority's interdicting of a 'regressive' pleasure in linguistic materiality is, accordingly, to challenge it. If the repeated avant-garde claim that overthrowing syntax will somehow smash state power invariably proves to be overstated, it is still only through the signifier that the cultural limits of the self – the subject – may become visible.[106] For all that Thomas's language use removes social world reference, it actually restores writing and reading to us as work, and thereby re-politicises it. The authoritative aura of the poems is undermined by the way in which their genetic textures force us to work, readers being turned into writers; the usually passive consumers of signs mobilised as their producers. What seems, at first, to be an exclusive authorial code, handed down *ex cathedra* to the recipient, turns out to be motivated by occasions when engagement with the writing's indeterminacies is positively demanded.

In short, Thomas's poetry dramatises the creation and interpellation of human subjects in language within the social order, but undermines the process by realising the *jouissance* latent within language. Thus, 'From love's first fever' stages the birth of linguistic subjectivity from primal, ungendered unity ('earth and sky were as one airy hill / The sun and moon shed one white light'), through the 'miracle of the first rounded word' to infantile acquisition of speech. The use of process terms that are interchangeable for infancy and adolescence mean that the poem doubles for the onset of sexual capability and the acquisition of a poetic voice, too:

And from the first declension of the flesh
I learnt man's tongue, to twist the shapes of thoughts
Into the stony idiom of the brain,
To shade and knit anew the patch of words
Left by the dead who, in their moonless acre,
Need no word's warmth.

The root of tongues ends in a spentout cancer,
That have but a name, where maggots have their X.

I learnt the verbs of will, and had my secret;
The code of night tapped on my tongue;
What had been one was many sounding minded. (*CP*, 22)

'Declension' wittily implicates language *and* body. As Crehan puts it, 'The dead generations bequeath words and their meanings to the living, who must re-tongue them and learn their meanings as the dead decreed, but it is through this very process of language acquisition that the "I", the human subject, is born ...'[107] Once again, we see the struggle between language speaking the subject and the subject speaking language fought out across the body. But although the linguistic legacy is a 'stony idiom', death (the 'maggots') is crucially without a language – it can only sign its 'name' like an illiterate, as a self-cancelling, maggoty 'X' – while the self, cast in language, is empowered by the 'verbs of will' (desire) and 'code of night' (sex). Unlike the subject of Louis Althusser's theory of 'interpellation' forever in thrall to ideology, the speaker of 'From love's first fever' celebrates his liberation in language – the move from primal unity to being 'many sounding minded'. Indeed, the very construction – 'many sounding minded' – grammatically enacts the excess that the subject feels as it goes on to proclaim: 'From the divorcing sky I learnt the double, / The two-framed globe that spun into a score; / A million minds gave suck to such a bud / As did condense'. (*CP*, 22)

More than Althusser, however, the thinkers that this passage will most remind us of are surely Mikhail Bakhtin and Julia Kristeva, whose ideas seem to be anticipated in certain ways by Thomas's 'Poetic Manifesto'. Like Bakhtin and Kristeva, rather than lamenting what is lost, absent or impossible in language, Thomas marvels at this other realm of the semiotic (bodily experience) that makes its way into language. Signification, for all three, is like a 'transfusion of the living body into language'.[108] Kristeva's description of the pre-Oedipal 'semiotic' state, linked to the Freudian 'primary' processes, is of a pre-linguistic condition that begins in the embryo's recognition of pulsional flows within the womb. After being born, the child imitatively babbles the sounds, rhythms, alliterations and stresses that s/he hears. In this state, like that described in the 'Manifesto', the child doesn't yet possess the necessary (verbal) linguistic signs, and there is thus no meaning for it in the strict sense of the term. Its melodies and babblings are an image in sound of its bodily instability, and, in this state, the endless flow of bodily pulsions is gathered up in what Kristeva calls the chora: 'a wholly provisional articulation that is … anterior to figuration and therefore also specularization, and only admits analogy with vocal or kinetic rhythm'.[109] Induction into the symbolic 'man's tongue' comes about with the Oedipal and mirror phases, when the individual becomes capable of articulation, as it has been prescribed.[110] Having fallen into the symbolic, however, Kristeva argues that traces of the semiotic remain within it, returning to disrupt its ordered surfaces, and that this is particularly the case for 'every type of creation'. The attempt to reach back to this semiotic phase of infantile babbling and grammarless articulation lies behind the innovative strategies of montage, parataxis and so on, pursued by modernist writers, such Mallarmé, Joyce and Artaud: the 'experience of the semiotic chora' is 'the source of all stylistic effort, the modifying of banal, logical order by linguistic distortions such as metaphor, metonymy, musicality'. Although the semiotic is neuter, the disruptions it causes are identifiable with the maternal body, through the mother's closeness to the child at that stage of his / her existence.[111]

Here, I think, it is possible to glimpse the striking similarities between Thomas's writing and Kristeva's post-Freudian, post-Lacanian concept of the body, 'babble' and poetic language, for he, too, in the 'Poetic Manifesto', tells of a time before the comprehension of words, during which it was enough 'to feel and know their sound and substance', to delight in the 'babble' of language as material, separate from the Symbolic Order, although first heard 'on the lips of … grown-ups' (*EPW*, 154–5). The musicality of words is likened to the 'miraculous' discovery of a new sense. But this is not a prelapsarian vision in the sense of being dominated by regret. Remarkably, as 'From love's first fever' shows, Thomas does not mourn a fall, but celebrates the continuing ability to tap into the 'colour' of words. Linguistic anxiety – ever-present in the material nature of language – does not rule out pleasure. The preservation of the utopian possibilities of the signifier against the sternly phallic Symbolic Order is, we might say, underwritten by his acknowledgement of the maternal (and therefore material) body of language itself. It is to the figuration of the material body *in* language – that is, for Kristeva, always and already there – that I turn in Chapter 3.

Notes

1 Samuel Beckett, cited on the flyleaf of James Joyce, *Finnegans Wake* (London: Faber and Faber, 1988).

2 Oscar Wilde, 'The Artist as Critic', ed. Richard Ellmann, *The Critical Writings of Oscar Wilde* (New York, NY: Random House, 1969), p. 434.

3 Thomas repeated versions of this, mantra-like, to various correspondents, thus: 'the structure [of the poem] should arise out of the words and the expression of them' (*CL*, 43). He also worked it into reviews; he noted approvingly of Ruth Pitter that: 'She is, primarily, a worker in words, a woman employed upon a job' (*EPW*, 176).

4 David Aivaz, 'The Poetry of Dylan Thomas', *The Hudson Review*, VIII: 3 (Autumn 1950) [repr. E. W. Tedlock, ed., *Dylan Thomas: The Legend and the Poet* (London: Heinemann / Mercury Books, 1963)], pp. 190–1.

5 T. S. Eliot, 'East Coker', *Four Quartets* (London: Faber & Faber, 1974), p. 31.

6 Thus, Jan Mukařovský analyses how the material and representational aspects of language interact problematically in poetic texts in *On Poetic Language* (1940). In poetry, language is said to be 'a *material*, like metal and stone in sculpture, like pigment and the material of the pictorial plane in painting', while it is 'in its very essence is already a sign', calling up associations that connect words both to other words in a self-contained poetic system and to words used in everyday communication; it is simultaneously *both* opaque material and transparent sign. Jan Mukařovský, *On Poetic Language* (New Haven, CT: Yale University Press, 1976), pp. 13–14. Forrest-Thomson argues that language is both continuous and discontinuous with the world. It is 'a thing that for the poet can be as plastic as transparent', allowing 'the realisation that we can shape, and are shaped by, the words we use'. Veronica Forrest-Thomson, *Poetic Artifice, A Theory of Twentieth Century Poetry* (Manchester: Manchester University Press, 1978), p. 118.

7 See Frank Lentricchia: 'The mainstream of aesthetic modernism … has primarily characterised itself not by its misleading propaganda against science and philistinism that the aesthetic world is a thing wholly apart, but by its claims that the aesthetic world plumbs the nature of things; and the pivot of this claim is the prior ontological claim for a natural bond between signifier and signified, and between sign and thing'. Frank Lentricchia, *After the New Criticism* (Methuen: London, 1983), p. 119. Pound's 'A Few Don'ts for an Imagiste' and 'Prolegomena' treat language as a transparent medium for registering objects and experiences apprehended by a subject, who is conceived as external to, and pre-existing, language. They subordinate signifier to signified and elide the materiality of language.

8 Alex Preminger and T. V. F. Brogan, eds., *The New Princeton Encyclopaedia of Poetry and Poetics*, (Princeton, NJ: Princeton University Press, 1993), p. 65.

9 Alastair Reid, *Dylan Thomas: The Legend and the Poet*, p. 54.

10 Thomas's own descriptions of his attitudes to language and poetic practice often resemble those of more avant-garde writers – for example, that of the Dada poet Hugo Ball, who claimed '[the] release of language from its normal transactional duties discloses the innermost alchemy of the word', leading to a rediscovery of 'the evangelical concept of the "word" (logos) as a magical complex image'. See Peter Nichols, *Modernisms: A Literary Guide* (Basingstoke: Macmillan, 1995), p. 225.

11 Thomas would have known many Welsh words and phrases as a result of growing up in Swansea and holidaying with Welsh-speaking relatives. One example of a direct lift from Welsh is the alteration of the line 'How time is all' in the *Sunday Referee* version of 'The force that through the green fuse'. A worksheet note shows that Thomas looked up the Welsh for 'time', 'amser' (whose two components, *am* and *ser*, mean 'around the stars') in *Spurrell's Welsh-English Dictionary* before

revising the line as 'How time has ticked a heaven round the stars'. See Ralph Maud, 2003, pp. 237–8.

12 Daniel Jones, cited in Constantine Fitzgibbon, *The Life of Dylan Thomas* (London: Dent, 1965 [repr. Plantin Paperbacks, 1987]), pp. 60–1.

13 Louis MacNeice, 'When we were children', *Collected Poems*, ed. E. R. Dodds (London: Faber, 1979), p. 214.

14 Gareth Thomas, 'A Freak User of Words', ed. Alan Bold, *Dylan Thomas: Craft or Sullen Art* (London / New York, NY: Vision Press, 1990), p. 84.

15 Sylvia Bigliazzi, 'Fable versus Fact: Hamlet's Ghost in Dylan Thomas's Early Poetry', *Textus*, 5 (1992), p. 61.

16 Malcolm Bowie, 'Lacan and Mallarme: Theory as Word-Play', ed. Michael Temple, *Meetings with Mallarme* (Exeter: University of Exeter Press, 1998), p. 79.

17 Roland Barthes, *S/Z*, transl. Richard Miller (Oxford: Blackwell, 1974 [repr. 1992]), p. 4.

18 Steve McCaffery, *North of Intention: Critical Essays 1978–85* (New York, NY: Roof Books, 2000), p. 143.

19 John Bayley, *The Romantic Survival* (London: Constable, 1957), p. 194.

20 See, in particular, Sigmund Freud, *Jokes and their Relation to the Unconscious*, ed. Angela Richards and transl. James Strachey (Harmondsworth: Penguin, 1991) and *The Psychopathology of Everyday Life*, ed. Angela Richards and transl. Alan Tyson (Harmondsworth, Penguin [repr.] 1991).

21 Sigmund Freud, *Jokes and their Relation to the Unconscious*, Vol. 6 Penguin Freud Library, ed. Angela Richards and transl. James Strachey (Harmondsworth: Penguin, 1991), p. 185.

22 In 'Swinburne as Poet' (1920), Eliot stated: 'Language in a healthy state presents the object, is so close to the object that the two are identified', contrasting this with Swinburne's 'morbid' fusion of the two, in which: 'the object has ceased to exist, because the meaning is merely the hallucination of meaning, because language, uprooted, has adapted itself to an independent life of atmospheric nourishment'. In 'Matthew Arnold' (1933), he returned to the subject, locating the poet's power to unify the archaic and modern in the 'auditory imagination'. As noted in Chapter 1, fn. 82 Eliot retreated from the implications of this in 'Milton I' (1936), attacking Milton (and Joyce) for 'hypertrophy of the auditory imagination at the expense of the visual and tactile, so that the inner meaning is separated from the surface and tends to become something occult'. But while Eliot convicts these poets of decadent language use, he remained aware – as later arbiters of British poetic taste often were not – that eliminating the auditory imagination would destroy poetry itself and that it must somehow be accommodated. See T. S. Eliot, *Selected Essays* (London: Faber, 1932), p. 327; T. S. Eliot, *The Use of Poetry and the Use of Criticism* (London: Faber, 1933), pp. 118–19; T. S. Eliot, *On Poetry and Poets* (London: Faber, 1957), p. 142–5.

23 According to Saussure, signs form the mental structure of a language or *langue* – the total system of the linguistic signs which make language self-contained, held together by communal agreement that specific words 'mean' specific concepts and also by 'the irrational principle of the arbitrariness of the sign' (Saussure, 1916, p. 133) Accordingly, as Rob Penhallurick observes, 'a language is not a piece-by-piece straightforward translation of the real world of objects into a linguistic world of names. Rather, [it] is a social, communal interpretation of the real world

which produces another virtual, symbolic reality which then impinges upon and changes our perceptions of the "real" world'. Rob Penhallurick, *Studying the English Language*, 2nd edn. (London: Palgrave, 2010), p. 107.

24 My considerations will focus on just one branch of linguistics-based analyses of style. However, I can equally imagine fruitful approaches based on the Sapir-Whorff hypothesis or George Lakoff and Mark Johnson's discussion of metaphor. Noam Chomsky's famous 'grammatical but meaningless' sentence: 'Colourless green ideas sleep furiously' has always sounded to me like a line from a draft of 'Altarwise by owl-light'.

25 Clark Emery, *The World of Dylan Thomas* (Miami, FL: University of Miami Press, 1962), p. 19.

26 The commonest words – not necessarily 'process' words – are those that we might expect of a lyric poet with Thomas's origins and mythical and processual interests: 'sea', 'man', 'love', 'sun', 'eye' and 'time', in that order. Clark Emery's is the best discussion of Thomas's diction; see *The World of Dylan Thomas*, pp. 10–27.

27 See John Goodby, 'Whitman's Influence on Dylan Thomas and the Use of "Sidle" as Noun', *Notes & Queries* (March 2005), pp. 105–7.

28 Other examples in *18 Poems* include: 'cemented skin', 'oil of tears', 'motor muscle', 'girdered nerve', 'ribbing metal', 'mechanical flesh'. This trope finds its apotheosis in 'All all and all', as discussed in Chapter 1.

29 Roman Jakobson, 'Closing Statements: Linguistics and Poetics', ed. Thomas A. Sebeok, *Style in Language* (Cambridge MA: MIT Press, 1960).

30 Victor Erlich, *Russian Formalism: History-Doctrine*, cited in Terry Eagleton, *Literary Theory: An Introduction* (London: Blackwell, 1983), pp. 98–9. The intensity of hermeneutical labour that they demand makes Thomas's 1930s writing the literary equivalent of the South Walian heavy industry that he is often said to have ignored. Hence the appositeness of Lawrence Durrell's description of his poems: '[they] rattled and banged away in the darkness like convoys of coal trucks. And you could always hear the sound of the rock-drill in the best of them'. See 'Lawrence Durrell', ed. E. W. Tedlock, *Dylan Thomas: The Legend and the Poet*, p. 36.

31 Thomas's comments show that he was aware of *cynghanedd* – a metrical system which is based on syllable-count and various patterns of vowel and consonant patterns (twenty-four in all), some of great complexity. 'I dreamed my genesis' has a regular stanza-form of 12, 7, 10 and 8 syllables, but, like most of Thomas's poems before the 1940s, it is built around stress patterns. Syllable count came to predominate in the later wartime poetry (for example, 'Poem in October'). Apart from its regular syllable-count, 'I dreamed my genesis' has one other unusual technical feature: the opening line of each stanza ends with a caesura after the tenth syllable, followed by a two-syllable word, which belongs grammatically with the next line. Unlike contemporary attempts to evoke a historical presence in this way – by the Irish poet Austin Clarke, for example – Thomas alludes to Welsh tradition without endorsing cultural exclusivity, invoking while qualifying it. For the argument that the poem is based on the *cynghanedd englyn unodl union* form, see Katharine T. Loesch, 'Welsh Poetic Stanza Form and Dylan Thomas's "I dreamed my genesis"', *Transactions of the Honourable Society of Cymmrodorion*, pp. 29–49.

32 Andrew Duncan, 'An Approach to the Poetry of Lynette Roberts', *Angel Exhaust*, 21 (Summer 2010), pp. 115–20.

33 The phrase is Terry Eagleton's, applied to the modernism of the Irish Literary Revival. See Terry Eagleton, *Heathcliff and the Great Hunger: Studies in Irish Culture* (London: Verso, 1996), pp. 273–319.

34 That is: 'phonemes are characterized not, as one might think, by their own positive quality, but simply by the fact that they are distinct … [they] are … opposing, relative, and negative entities'. Thus, '[w]hat differentiates /big/ from /pig/ is the sound, not the intention, of the speaker', and the signifier is only ever a physical entity (the signified, conversely, can only ever be a mental one). See Anthony Easthope, *Poetry as Discourse* (London: Methuen, 1983), p. 12. Saussure's claims, cited by Easthope, are from Ferdinand de Saussure, *Course in General Linguistics*, transl. Wade Baskin (New York, NY: Philosophical Library, 1959), p. 119.

35 For a plausible reading, see Ralph Maud, *Where Have the Old Words Got Me?*, pp. 116–17.

36 Alex Preminger and T. V. F. Brogan, eds., *The New Princeton Encyclopaedia of Poetry and Poetics*, pp. 860–3. Jakobson may have been mistaken in assuming that signifiers are naturally adapted to convey signifieds, but words which seem to have phonetic motivation exert significant limitations on Saussure's doctrine of the arbitrariness of the sign, too, even though it has been fashionable to disparage sound-symbolic effects. If the phoneme – as the basic unit of difference and hence of meaning-generation – is wholly determined by the system of *langue* and not by any innate qualities, it nevertheless can appear to possess meaningful properties. Indeed, it is impossible to ignore the fact that what poetry does in stressing the paradigmatic axis of language is often intended to foreground just such qualities.

37 Although, as is usually the case, one can think of counter-examples which reveal the onomatopoeic fallacy: 'snuggle', for example. See Jean-Jacques Lecercle, *The Violence of Language*, p. 88.

38 Jean-Jacques Lecercle, *The Violence of Language* (London: Routledge, 1990), p. 40.

39 Clark Emery, *The World of Dylan Thomas*, pp. 25–6.

40 Andrew Lycett, *Dylan Thomas: A New Life* (London: Weidenfeld & Nicolson, 2003), p. 120.

41 Dylan Thomas, *Letters to Vernon Watkins*, ed. Vernon Watkins (London: Faber / Dent, 1957), p. 13. John Malcolm Brinnin's recollection of Thomas's explanation of the process confirms Watkins's account: 'He began almost every poem merely with some phrase he had carried about in his head. If this phrase was right … it would suggest another phrase. In this way a poem would "accumulate." Once given a word or phrase or a line … he could often envision it or "locate" it within a pattern of other words or phrases or lines that … had yet to be discovered'. John Malcolm Brinnin, *Dylan Thomas in America* (Boston, MA: Little, Brown and Co., 1955), p. 126.

42 Equally, there might be more than one set of relationships between items going on in a given poem or a section of a poem. In stanza two of 'Especially when the October wind', for example, the dominant imagery and verbal textures have to do with the relentless passing of time: a church clock, a weather-cock and fading grass and flowers. However, the clock / cock rhyme sets off a series of sexual puns and double entendres which subvert and counterpoint this: 'flies', 'shafted', 'cock', 'wormy' and 'sins'.

43 Djuna Barnes, *Nightwood* (London: Faber, 2001), pp. 79–80. The novel contributed to the making of other poems at this time, including 'How shall my animal' and

'Into her lying down head'. Thomas read the entire 'Watchman, What of the Night?' chapter, from which this passage comes, on his American reading tours.

44 *Nightwood* may have appealed because the 'anguish' of the speaker in this passage, Matthew Dante O'Connor, is that of someone who absorbs his friends' suffering and who is also an abortionist – reflecting, perhaps, on the dilemma of the mother and child in the poem. For a fuller discussion, see John Goodby, 'Djuna Barnes as a Source for Dylan Thomas', *Notes & Queries*, 58: 1 (March 2011), pp. 127–30.

45 Or, in Thomas's more self-deprecating description, 'my method is this: I write a poem on innumerable sheets of scrap paper, write it on both sides of the paper, often upside down and criss cross ways unpunctuated, surrounded by drawings of lamp posts and boiled eggs, in a very dirty mess: bit by bit I copy out the developing poem into an exercise book: and, when it is completed, I type it out' (*CL*, 209).

46 In the later poems, the need for place, time and person to appear more consistent meant that the phrasal units were lengthened and the transitions between them grew less abrupt. In 'Fern Hill', for example, clauses also pile up in an apparently careless way, but are joined by excess, rather than a dearth of link elements. Energetic circularity and montage gave way to greater verbal fluency, but both sets of tactics disrupt temporal flows and undermine the usual subordination of the grammatical elements in a sentence.

47 Thus, in 'Hold hard, these ancient minutes', Thomas allows readers to understand the verb in the opening line to have its main clause successively in 'ancient minutes' or 'Under the lank, fourth folly' in line two or 'As the green blooms ride upward' in line three. Walford Davies, *Dylan Thomas* (Milton Keynes: Open University Press, 1985), p. 105.

48 Ralph Maud, *Entrances to Dylan Thomas's Poetry* (Pittsburgh, PA: University of Pittsburgh Press, 1963), pp. 81–101.

49 R. B. Kershner, Jr., *Dylan Thomas: The Poet and His Critics* (Chicago, IL: American Library Association, 1976), pp. 208–11.

50 Ralph Maud, *Entrances to Dylan Thomas' Poetry*, pp. 82–3, 90–4.

51 As I discuss in Chapter 3, this poem uses fishing to metaphorise the paradoxical process by which the inner animal (or 'anima') of the title is haled up to become the poem. As it emerges from the non-verbal, oceanic unconscious, it struggles for breath in the atmosphere of the conscious realm of language and expires 'under the spelling wall'. The final paradox is that, with the beast's death, the poem is mournfully, but magnificently, realised as an aesthetic object.

52 Thomas was adept at raiding the *OED* for etymologies; the 'divided sense' of the poem makes it clear that he knew that 'insect' derives from Pliny's loan-translation of the Greek *entomon* (insect) – Aristotle's term for this class of life, in reference to their 'notched' bodies.

53 Chesterton's once well-known lyric redeems the donkey from the scorn usually reserved for it as 'The devil's walking parody / On all four-footed things', by reminding the reader of its role in bearing Christ into Jerusalem. For the full text, see http://www.poetryfoundation.org/poem/177440

54 Sylvia Bigliazzi argues that the final stanza exemplifies the way in which the poem is: 'explicitly centred around the fable-versus-fact opposition and, more precisely, around the act of composition conceived as a boundary-displacing experience. ... The serpent kills the story and Hamlet too [in stanza two]'. However: 'death as opposed to and divided from life cannot be included in the undifferentiated horizon

of the fable, because [its] logic is not serial and asymmetrical but self-contradictory in that it reflects the omnipotence of thought on which magic is also based. ... [I]n spite of his announcement of Hamlet's death as well as the prevailing of fact over fable, Thomas actually remains totally immersed in his fabulous, obscure world to the last line: as the [linguistic] compression method demonstrates, the space-time co-ordinates continue to be absent from Thomas's universe as admitted ... in the first stanza'. See Sylvia Bigliazzi, 'Fable versus Fact: Hamlet's Ghost in Dylan Thomas's Early Poetry', *Textus*, V (1992), pp. 56–9. It is worth comparing this reading with that by Don McKay; whereas Bigliazzi discerns a fragmentation which just about pulls out of a Mallarméan language of 'desperate and unpenetrable obscurity', McKay is clear that the poem ends with a 'firm mythic structure' – the 'ageless voice's univocality rest[ing] upon the energies of many madmen' – and that it therefore suggests that: 'ultimately, order and anarchy belong to the same poetic and cosmological enterprise'. Don McKay, 'What Shall We Do with a Drunken Poet? Dylan Thomas' Poetic Language', *Queen's Quarterly*, 93: 4 (Winter 1986), p. 802.

55 Wiliam York Tindall, *A Reader's Guide to Dylan Thomas* (Syracuse, N.Y.: Syracuse University Press, 1996), p. 92.

56 Miller claims that this reflects Thomas's desire to create: 'structures of words which cannot be understood piece by piece, but only by a single leap which carries the reader into the uncanny', thus memorably describing language-as-process. The problem lies in his understanding of process as a 'theme' prior to language, which is at odds with Thomas's own sense of them as simultaneous. J. Hillis Miller, *Poets of Reality*, p. 195.

57 As David Aivaz points out: 'One point seems clear: Thomas's divided allegiance to the words "let" and "make" does not permit one to base on this statement generalisations about the degree of reasonableness in his poetry. Evidence must come from the poems'. David Aivaz, 'The Poetry of Dylan Thomas', Tedlock, p. 188.

58 The unusual subject matter, too, complicates understanding. According to Walford Davies: 'The early poetry closes ... the usual gap between thing and word ... isn't the "thinginess" of these words the result of our not quite knowing in the first place what the things are that they communicate? Isn't it the strangeness of the referents that gives such apparently autonomous life to the words?' See Walford Davies, *Dylan Thomas*, p. 103.

59 Northrop Frye, *Anatomy of Criticism* (London: Penguin, 1957 [repr. 1990]), pp. 271–2. See also Frye's positive take on 'babble': 'We remember that a good deal of verbal creation begins in associative babble, in which sound and sense are equally involved. The result of this is poetic ambiguity, the fact that ... the poet does not define his words but establishes their prowess by placing them in a great variety of contexts. Hence the importance of poetic etymology, or of the tendency to associate words similar in sound and sense'. Northrop Frye, *Anatomy of Criticism*, p. 334.

60 Denise Riley, 'Is there Linguistic Guilt?' *Critical Quarterly*, 39: 1 (Spring 1997), pp. 83, 92.

61 Peter Riley, 'Review of W. S. Graham, *New Collected Poems*', *Jacket*, 26 (October 2004). See http://jacketmagazine.com/26/rile-grah.html

62 There are, of course, different kinds of metaphor in Thomas. I focus on the autotelic variety in this discussion. For the argument that catachretic (mixed or excessive) metaphor is Thomas's definitive trope, see Don McKay, 'Crafty Dylan and the

Altarwise Sonnets: "I Build a Flying Tower and I Pull it Down"', *University of Toronto Quarterly*, 55: 4 (Summer 1986), p. 377. As McKay notes, Thomas is the source for the modern illustration of this trope in *The New Princeton Encyclopaedia of Poetry and Poetics* ('the sun roars at the sun's end' from 'Vision and Prayer'); like the autotelic variety, this is a kind of metaphor which flags up its own metaphoricity, resisting naturalisation.

63 Genesis I: 2: 'And the Spirit of God moved upon the face of the waters', *The Bible: Authorized King James Version*, intro. Robert Carroll and Stephen Prickett (Oxford: Oxford University Press, 1998), p. 1.

64 Walford Davies, *Dylan Thomas*, p. 114.

65 Barbara Hardy, *Dylan Thomas: An Original Language* (Athens, GA: University of Georgia Press, 2000), p. 47.

66 Annis Pratt observes, when Thomas writes of the girl in this story 'the heart in her breast was a small red bell that rang in a wave', that the metaphor cannot be grasped 'until one accepts the previous statement that the waves not only resemble but *are* a "white-faced sea of people" ... [the] girl herself *is* a wave, her heart a meeting place of men and mermen, land and sea'. Such 'metaphysical metaphors' (or 'meta-metaphors') 'are not literary tokens heightening realistic situations ... nor are they incorporated into the tales from an external system ... [but] juxtapose, blend and contain the several dominant themes' of the stories in which they occur. Annis Pratt, *Dylan Thomas' Early Prose: A Study in Creative Mythology* (Pittsburgh, PA: University of Pittsburgh Press, 1970), pp. 40–1.

67 Christine Brooke-Rose, *A Grammar of Metaphor* (London: Secker and Warburg, 1958), pp. 200–3. The metaphor seems wilfully obscure at first glance, but given that the poem stanza slangily presents a Nonconformist vision of heaven ('angelic gangs'), a little thought suggests that the line can be construed as something like: 'the globe or world/-view of my forefathers (shaped by, but also *like*, a Nonconformist chapel) knocks, to remind me of my religious inheritance, on its nave (the part of chapel in which the hymn-singing congregation is gathered) and sings – again, reminding me of my inheritance'.

68 Jacob Korg, *Dylan Thomas* (New York, NY: Twayne, 1965 [repr. Hippocrene Books, 1972]), p. 158.

69 'In the beginning' is also, as Martin Dodsworth notes, a good example of the way that the mind-body problem is reflected in Thomas's fascination with words involving two opposed points of view: 'one from which the world is seen as a medium of the visionary imagination – "... from the cloudy bases of the breath / The word flowed up, translating to the heart / First characters of birth and death" – and the other from which the word appears as a sign of the mind's division, as in "Especially when the October wind": "Shut, too, in a tower of words, I mark / On the horizon walking like the trees / The wordy shapes of women ..."'. Martin Dodsworth, 'The Concept of the Mind and the Poetry of Dylan Thomas', ed. Walford Davies, *Dylan Thomas: New Critical Essays* (London: Dent, 1972), p. 129.

70 Annis Pratt, *Dylan Thomas' Early Prose*, p. 132.

71 See, for a lucid discussion of this aspect of the poetry, Nathalie Wourm's 'Dylan Thomas and the French Symbolists', ed. Tony Brown, *Welsh Writing in English: A Yearbook of Critical Essays*, vol. 5 (1999), pp. 27–41.

72 In Thomas, the body and nature are animated by words and made up of them. In the story 'The Visitor', Peter, the dying poet, hears the voices of his friends

Callaghan and Rhiannon 'battle in his brain ... and tasted the blood of words'. (*CS*, 24) Poems are 'wordy wounds' in 'If I were tickled by the rub of love', wounds being at the interface between interior and exterior, body and world (*CP*, 16). In this sense, being wounded is painful and potentially deadly, but also empowering.

73 As Jeri Johnson points out, Martha has a preference for material signs, enclosing an actual flower with her letter to Leopold Bloom (whom she knows as 'Henry Flower'), just as Bloom's mind continually works to materialise language, striving to 'substantiate the ephemeral and incorporeal'. James Joyce, *Ulysses*, ed. Jeri Johnson (Oxford: Oxford University Press, 1998), pp. 74, 798. 'Calypso' concerns itself with incarnation, profanely reversing transubstantiation and casting doubt on insubstantial symbols or interpretations, just as Thomas insisted on being read 'literally'. 'Henry Flower' is also a Henry who *flows*, and Bloom's *nom de ruse* may have suggested a pun on flower in 'The force that through the green fuse'.

74 See Harri Garrod Roberts, '"Beating on the Jailing Slab of the Womb": The Alleged Immaturity of Dylan Thomas', *Embodying Identity: Representations of the Body in Welsh Literature* (Cardiff: University of Wales Press, 2009), Chapter 5. My thanks are due to Harri Roberts for allowing me to see his essay before its publication in book form.

75 See Jacob Korg, 'Imagery and Universe in Dylan Thomas's "18 Poems"', *Accent*, XVII: I (Winter 1957), p. 9: '"Syllabic blood" [in 'Especially when the October wind'] involves a comparison between blood and language. Language is made up of units, words, just as blood is made up of its little coin-like cells. In Thomas's view it performs for the spirit the life-giving function which the blood performs for the body'.

76 John Bayley, *The Romantic Survival: A Study in Poetic Evolution*, pp. 214–15. Bayley's examples are: 'the movement of "some dead undid their bushy jaws / And bags of blood let out their flies"' and 'the x and z sounds between the long u's in "Blew out the blood gauze through the wound of manwax"'.

77 Terry Eagleton, *Literary Theory: An Introduction*, p. 2.

78 Jean-Jacques Lecercle, *The Violence of Language*, p. 58.

79 Jean-Jacques Lecercle, *The Violence of Language*, pp. 224–64.

80 Steve McCaffery, *North of Intention*, p. 202.

81 Steve McCaffery, *North of Intention*, pp. 202–3.

82 The varieties of pun include: paronomasia (an intensification of consonance, in which the close resemblance of words denoting different things is foregrounded, for example: word / world); antanaclasis (where the same word bearing two different meanings is repeated, for example: 'I'll worm my way in with the worm'); syllepsis (now zeugma) – a structure in which a single form, not repeated, functions in two senses (Pope's 'Or stain her honour, or a new brocade' is the best example, notwithstanding his opposition to pun); anagram (Thomas was fascinated that 'evil' could become 'live'); homophone (the commonest type) and portmanteau words (for example, Thomas's 'cockwise').

83 Ferdinand de Saussure, cited in Frank Lentricchia, *After the New Criticism*, p. 60. The incompatibilities of pun with the fundamental Saussurean claim that signifier and signified enjoy an arbitrary relationship can be demonstrated simply enough: 'the link between the signifier "tree" and its signified is arbitrary' is a far more convincing statement than 'the link between the signifier "tree" and its signified is arbretrary'.

84 Gerald L. Bruns, *Heidegger's Estrangements* (New Haven, CT: Yale University Press, 1989), pp.145, 120.

85 Derk Attridge, 'Unpacking the Portmanteau or, Who's Afraid of *Finnegans Wake?*', ed. Jonathan Culler, *On Puns: The Foundation of Letters* (Oxford: Blackwell, 1988), p.143.

86 John Malcolm Brinnin, *Dylan Thomas in America: An Intimate Journal*, 5th edn. (New York, NY: Viking Press, 1957 [1964]), p.274.

87 Jeffrey Ganz, transl., *The Mabinogion* (Harmondsworth: Penguin, 1976), p.106.

88 While metaphor brings together two seemingly unrelated things in order to reveal their illuminating similarities-in-difference, pun (which includes 'paronomasia and paragram') works by creatively splitting what the signifier had promised as an integral, singular meaning.

89 Cited by Derek Attridge in 'Unpacking the Portmanteau or, Who's Afraid of *Finnegans Wake?*', p.3.

90 Jonathan Culler, 'The Call of the Phoneme: Introduction', ed. Jonathan Culler, *On Puns: The Foundation of Letters*, p.4.

91 Johnson's objection (not recorded) elicited this rejoinder from Thomas: 'There must be no compromise; there is always only the one right word: use it, despite its foul or merely ludicrous associations; I used "double-crossed" because it was what I meant' (*CL*, 43). Hardy's objection is based on what she sees as the adolescent attempt to shock readers (one sense of 'doublecrossed', as the language of Thomas's response to Johnson hints, is sexual: that Mary was cheated, because she did not experience pleasure on being impregnated by the Holy Ghost).

92 Ralph Maud, *Where Have the Old Words Got Me?*, p.8.

93 See, for example, Clark Emery's similar demurral on some of Thomas's puns: if it 'destroy[s] the continuity of the tone, the poet loses more than he gains'. Clark Emery, *The World of Dylan Thomas* (Coral Gables, FL: University of Florida Press, 1962), p.26.

94 Anthony Easthope, *Poetry as Discourse*, p.7.

95 Derek Attridge, 'Unpacking the Portmanteau or, Who's Afraid of *Finnegans Wake?*', p.141.

96 John Ackerman, *A Dylan Thomas Companion: Life, Poetry and Prose* (London: Macmillan, 1991), p.168.

97 Jean-Jacques Lecercle, *The Violence of Language*, pp.48, 50.

98 No-one has ever convincingly explained Rimbaud's attributions; Graham Robb's claim that the colours and vowels are arranged simply to 'produce a mellifluous, unobstructed line of sounds', for 'as Verlaine knew, there was no real distinction in poetry between a hoax and a revelation', is as good as any other and arguably captures something of Thomas's motivation, too. Graham Robb, *Rimbaud* (London: Picador, 2001), pp.136–7.

99 Just two of the sixteen poems in *The Map of Love* are in Thomas's densest early manner, 'I make this in a warring absence' and 'It is the sinner's dust-tongued bell'. The others are either fairly minor pieces reworked from the notebooks or transitional pieces.

100 Anthony Easthope, *Poetry as Discourse*, p.35. As Jakobson put it: 'Émile Benveniste in his timely essay "Nature du signe linguistique" (1939) brought out the crucial fact that only for a detached, alien onlooker is the bond between signans and signum [signified and signifier] a mere contingence, whereas for the native user of the same

language this relation is a necessity'. Roman Jakobson, 'Quest for the Essence of Language', eds. Krystyna Pomorska and Stephen Rudy, *Language in Literature* (Cambridge, MA: Harvard University Press, 1987), p. 417.

101 Robert Penhallurick, *Studying the English Language*, p. 179. Like Derrida, Thomas would agree that language is 'essentially wordplay, play between words', with slippage innate to its workings. Derrida expanded Saussure's claim that meaning (identity) is a function of difference, not some metaphysical 'presence' innate to the signifier. He radicalised Saussure by transposing his location of meaning in difference to *différance*; meaning being deferred as soon as difference generates it, preventing it from ever being self-present in the sign. Every attempt to ground the signifier in signified slips further along the signifying chain, and this 'slippage' means that there is no final resting place where the signifier yields up the truth of the signified. In a universe only accessible to us in textualised form, all meaning is therefore subject to ceaseless dissemination. It is *différance* which guarantees 'play' and 'undecidability' in the sign. Derrida also attacked phonocentrism, which denotes the privileging of speech over writing, based on the assumption that spoken language entails some peculiarly intimate relationship between words which are spoken and the intent of the speaker and makes written language secondary.

102 Similarly, when the speaker of 'In the White Giant's thigh' implores the poem's childless, but sexually vibrant, female presences to 'clasp me to their grains', we are aware, as Ralph Maud notes, that the context raises 'groins' within 'grains'. But there is no reason why Derridean 'dissemination' should stop there; 'grins' and 'groans', for example, also ghost the sense. See Ralph Maud, *Entrances to Dylan Thomas' Poetry*, p. 25.

103 Thus, Geoff Ward acknowledges that deconstructive methods can usefully disclose, say, unconscious erotic puns in early Henry James, but adds: 'how could one diagnose *lapsus linguae* in a poem like Schuyler's "The Dog Wants His Dinner", which so clearly knows that trick backwards? "The sky is pitiless. I beg / your pardon? OK then / the sky is pitted"'. In it, as he notes, the text: 'has shifted onto the level of what it signals as intentional meaning a whole stratum of signification that criticism would have located as the unconscious operations in, say, a Victorian novel'. Coincidentally, exactly the same pitted / pitied pun is used by Thomas in 'An Adventure from a Work in Progress'. Geoff Ward, *Statutes of Liberty: The New York School of Poets* (London: Palgrave, 2001), pp. 28, 30–1.

104 Steve McCaffery, *North of Intention*, p. 66.

105 Steve McCaffery, *North of Intention*, p. 58.

106 Ron Silliman, *The New Sentence* (New York, NY: Roof Books, 1987), p. 146.

107 Stewart Crehan, 'The Lips of Time', John Goodby and Chris Wigginton, eds., *Dylan Thomas: A New Casebook*, p. 49.

108 Kelly Oliver, ed., *The Portable Kristeva* (New York, NY: Columbia University Press, 1997), p. xx.

109 Julia Kristeva, *Revolution in Poetic Language* (New York, NY: Columbia University Press, 1974), p. 26.

110 Kristeva's account of the 'semiotic' and the 'chora', with its pulsional energies, as well as of the 'mirror stage', in which the infant achieves a moment of self-recognition and separation from the mother's body, is drawn from the psychoanalytic theory of Jacques Lacan, whom she effectively reads from a feminist-informed perspective. In Kristeva, the *chora* is anterior to everything; Lacan's Real in her system is a cross

between it and the Imaginary. The main point at issue here (since these ideas will be dealt with in more detail in Chapter 3) is the passage from a pleasurable order of 'babble' (the semiotic) to the world of 'normal', rule-bound language —a state that Lacan calls the Symbolic Order of the father. It is important to note that Kristeva does not merely valorise the semiotic and denigrate the Symbolic, although she sees the semiotic as responsible for the inventive disruption of standard modes of writing found in modernism: each is necessary for signification, because a dynamic interplay between both is necessary for it to take place.

III Equally, one might note François Fourquet's concept of the 'impact of the human subject with the thresholds of linguistic meaning' in writing, which has broken free of 'the historical purpose of summarizing global meaning' and opened itself up to 'an alternative "libidinal" economy which operates across the precarious boundaries of the symbolic and the biological and has its basis in intensities'. The major premise in libidinal economy is that language is possessed of a double disposition: one towards naming, logicalizing, predicating; the other towards an assertion of pre-linguistic gestures ... (the semiotic order) that push through but remain unattached to symbolic meaning'. See Steve McCaffery, *North of Intention*, pp. 153–4.

CHAPTER THREE

'Libidinous betrayal':
body-mind, sex and gender

Nothing is certain but the body.

– W. H. Auden, XXV, 'In Time of War'.[1]

'Meaty & metaphysical': body, language and mind

We often speak of the 'body' or 'corpus' of a writer's work, but in Dylan Thomas's case, the metaphor seems somehow tautologous, given the extraordinary prominence of the body and bodies within it. This is an outcome of the process poetic, with its microcosmic figuration of the macrocosm, according to which the body 'has roots in the same earth as the tree', such that '[a]ll thoughts and actions emanate from the body' and 'the description of thought or action – however abstruse it may be – can be beaten home by bringing it onto a physical level. Every idea, intuitive or intellectual, can be imaged or translated in terms of the body, its flesh, skin, blood, sinews, veins, glands, organs, cells or senses' (CL, 57). Thomas even claimed: 'I think in cells', adding 'Nearly all my images, coming, as they do, from my solid and fluid world of flesh and blood, are set out in terms of their progenitors' (CL, 38). From cell mitosis in the womb to the panorama of human evolutionary descent, such 'cells' and 'progenitors' are thought and set out in bodily terms in poem after poem.[2] This is particularly the case in *18 Poems* and *Twenty-five Poems*, in which human anatomy is vividly, viscerally realized in a kind of ghastly gothic anti-blazon of skin, eyes, teeth, ribs, bone, hair, blood, brain, nerves, womb, cock, nails, breasts, heart, 'manseed', sweat and other bodily fluids.

That blazon was, as I argued in Chapter 1, central to Thomas's Welsh gothic-grotesque modernism – a response to Eliot's call for poetry that was aware of 'the cerebral cortex, the nervous system, and the digestive tracts'. It rejected the prizing of mind over body, as found in New Country poetry, and accentuated the materiality of language itself as a kind of maternal body. This sets Thomas apart, not only from the New Country poets, but also from many high modernists (Joyce – author of the 'mamafesta' of *Finnegans Wake* – is the obvious exception). Moreover, as Peter Nicholls notes, modernist distrust of the body and its functions also had a strongly gendered aspect:

> For Eliot ... a decadent language is one which has become somehow 'bodily', a condition which prevents 'objectivity' and which is quickly marked as 'feminine'. So, for example, Virginia Woolf's 'feminine type' of language is one which 'makes its art by feeling and by contemplating the feeling, rather than by the object which has excited it or the object into which the feeling might be made ...' Mina Loy similarly 'needs the support of the image ... [otherwise] she becomes abstract, and the word separates from the thing.' Eliot's suspicion of forms of writing which make the word somehow self-sufficient – 'feminine' or narcissistic forms, because language has not there become a register of differentiation of self from other – are shared in various ways by Pound and Lewis ... [this indicates] the powerful association between a 'false' materiality and 'the intuitional, mystical chaos' which is the world of desire and the unconscious. The true modernist aesthetic is thus supported by a mechanism of reference and metaphor, and exhibits a related concern with outline and borders which protect against the 'chaos' of subjectivity.[3]

Allowing for the differences between Thomas's and Eliot's targets, it is possible to discern how the provocation of Thomas's work stemmed, at least in part, from its perceived 'false materiality' and 'feminine type' of language, its 'narcissism' and lack of bulwarks against 'the "chaos" of subjectivity'.[4] The same attitudes are displayed towards him by critics of his own generation, as well as more recent ones. From Grigson and Graves in the 1930s and 1940s to Holbrook and Corcoran in the 1970s and 1990s, 'references to materiality as a figure for some kind of deadly self-absorption produce a conception of poetic language as the record of successful objectification' and as the 'scrupulous' presentation of 'things as they are'. Thomas's lack of such objectification, of the 'armour' of style [to set] against the mere '"drift" of desire', has consistently been taken as proof of his lack of a 'strong and authoritative [version] of the self'.[5]

This anti-body, masculinist agenda, uncomfortable with the rebellious materiality of flesh and language and its resultant dissolving, fluid, 'female' threat is perhaps best regarded as one in a series of moral panics, which have periodically seized English poetry, from 'Z's' and Lockhart's assaults on Keats, and Robert Buchanan's denunciation of Swinburne and Rossetti in 'The Fleshy School of Poetry' in 1871, to the savaging of Sylvia Plath.[6] This, for example, is Grigson in 1957:

> While Mr Eliot's poems live tightly above the waist, those of Mr Thomas live, sprawl loosely, below the waist. Mr Eliot is a reasoning creature. The self in Mr Thomas's poetry seems inhuman and glandular. Or rather like water and mud and fumes mixed in a volcanic mud-hole … not to worry the metaphor too far, one would prefer a man's poetry to break out of the common fury like a geyser, at least with the force and cleanness of form, at least with the meaning of a pillar; and not with the meaningless hot sprawl of mud.[7]

Comic in his unwitting sexism, Grigson sets '[a] man's poetry' of the phallic 'pillar' – one with a 'force … [and] cleanness of form', against what his language suggests is a vagina-like 'volcanic mud-hole' – a 'meaningless hot sprawl of mud'. Thomas is gendered as 'female', because he is lacking in phallic definition, guilty of a promiscuous ('loose') and immature (non-'reasoning') life driven by desires that 'sprawl loosely, below the waist'. (For other attackers of the time, a similarly sexualised dislike of Thomas's bodiliness is noticeable; thus, Robert Graves's offhand comment that 'Thomas was nothing more really than a demagogic Welsh masturbator who failed to pay his bills' is charged with more than merely class and xenophobic animus.)[8] Thomas's combination of material language *and* all-too-solid flesh activated in Grigson the tradition of constructing the body as bad – a threat to spirit and mind – or, more accurately, of constructing the female body as romantic, fleshy, impure, sexually voracious and formless against the male body as classical, hard, pure, chaste and harmonious. Within this discourse, the mind is necessarily set above and beyond the messy anarchy of corporeal desires; what is feared, above all, is the challenge to the sovereign (male) ego, by what are perceived to be its base origins. 'Fleshy' poets are not only physically corrupt, but feminine, flashy imposters, like Sylvia Plath's Death in 'Death & Co.', who 'masturbate[s] a glitter', all pinchbeck and pasteboard, inauthentic.[9]

If Thomas's bodily and embodied poetic, his fleshiness and 'female' fluidity, were anathema to many mid-twentieth century critics, viewed more objectively, they display striking similarities with contemporary philosophical concerns. I argued in Chapter 1 that the heterogeneity of Thomas's work was ultimately at odds with the groundedness and essentialism of Heidegger's thought, yet there are distinct affinities between the anti-Cartesian thrust of Thomas's poetic and other, more decentred strains of phenomenology. Maurice Merleau-Ponty's claim that 'the body is not an object among objects to be measured in purely scientific or geometric terms, but a mysterious and expressive mode of belonging to the world through our perceptions, gestures, sexuality and speech' seems, for example, very much like the body in, and of, Thomas's writing.[10] The protagonist of 'The Peaches' tell us: 'I felt all my young body like an excited animal surrounding me, the torn knees bent, the bumping heart, the long heat and depth between the legs, the sweat trickling in the hands, the tunnels down to the eardrums, the little balls of dirt between the toes, the eyes in the sockets, the tucked-up voice, the blood racing, the memory around and within flying, jumping, swimming, and waiting to pounce. There ... I was aware of me myself in the exact middle of a living story, and my body was my adventure and my name'; this sense of the self as a narrative body conveyed in a material and muscular language is, if often less delightedly, that of many of the poems, too (CS, 137–8). As William Moynihan recognised: 'an important aspect of Thomas's rejection of convention is his elemental emphasis on the Keatsian maxim that truth should be proved on the pulse. His appeal for life is for a fully physical life ...'.[11] Thomas's writing reflects a fear of determinism, but his emphasis on the inextricability of body and mind anticipates the recent shift to 'embodied cognition' and 'feeling brain' paradigms, which reflect neurophysiology's confirmation of phenomenology's claims concerning how we experience 'belonging to the world'.[12] Science – and biology, in particular – was dominated in the first three-quarters of the twentieth century by Behaviourism, which dismissed internal mental states as irrelevant to objective truth-values. Today's consensus, however, is that, in Antonio Damasio's words: 'The mind exists for the body, is engaged in telling the story of the body's multifarious events, and uses that story to optimize the life of the organism' – that is, and with 'me myself in the exact middle of a living story, and my body ... my adventure and my name'.[13]

Modern aesthetics, from Shaftesbury onwards, can be said to have originated in the reaction against the Cartesian and scientific separation of mind and body and fed Sentimentalism and Romantic protests against it. Thomas, as a good Blakeian, clearly belongs to this tradition, although his brand of fevered corporeality reflects a revolt against Nonconformism – a revolt whose boldness is reflected in the fact that it could be derided by one Welsh critic as late as 1995.[14] This revolt, as I argue in Chapter 4, aligns Thomas with the body's more extreme manifestations in gothic-apocalyptic literature, as well as with the residual, subversive body of popular culture, as described by Mikhail Bakhtin in *Rabelais and His World*. Its use was complexly prompted by his marginality and the extremes of the process poetic; however, while his historical circumstances meant that, in his early work, any celebration of the body took place under the shadow of a fearful awareness of physical mortality. Confined to, not simply immersed in, the body, the speakers of *18 Poems*, *Twenty-five Poems* and the pre-1938 stories offer an exhilarated, terrified performance of embodied selfhood. In them, the grotesque body is intensified by an intense adolescent awareness of sex – physically urgent, yet confined to imagination and auto-eroticism, due to the 'dictat[ion] [of] a more or less compulsory virginity during the period of life when virginity should be regarded as a crime against the dictates of the body' (*CL*, 76). Rebelling against the traditional prohibitions laid on sex and using Blake, Whitman and Lawrence as exemplars for his revolt, Thomas filled the gap left by sin with a sense of biological terror. Sex, viewed objectively, is natural, clean and the ultimate expression of processual unity, he told Pamela Hansford Johnson in his correspondence of 1933–34; but, at the same time, it is the expense of spirit in a waste of biological shame – dissolution and spending, the flinging of each generation under the wheels of the juggernaut-like successor it has spawned.

This fearful side to his embrace of sexuality informs the carnal-charnel quality of Thomas's body-centredness, and he was well aware of the pitfalls of his 'hangman's morbidity' and of being too 'willy-minded'. Writing to Trevor Hughes in 1934, he bluffly counterpoised Pound's cynical sexual realism to what he felt was Auden's too-easy gestures towards modernity in 'Sir, no man's enemy':

> Does one need 'New styles of architecture, a change of heart?' Does one not need a new consciousness of the old universal architecture and a tearing away from the old heart of the things that have clogged it? Still our minds are hovering too much about our testicles, complaining
>
> ... In delicate and exhausted metres
> That the twitching of three abdominal nerves
> Is incapable of producing nirvana.[15] (*CL*, 111)

The 'old universal architecture' of the human body and its drives is commended, only for a qualification – 'Still' – to immediately appear, expressing a fear of the 'three abdominal nerves' or what he called, in a letter of the same time to Johnson, the 'succession of wearisome [visceral] similes' required to render the 'small, bonebound island' of the embodied self (*CL*, 38). Yet Thomas's insistence that death is inseparable from the life of all embodied beings is, it can also be argued, one of his great strengths, linking, as it does, his own personal and generational fears of destruction to a universal human sense of the impermanence of physical being. More than this, from the late 1930s onwards, the coordinates of this aspect of his writing were reset by marriage and the actual outbreak of war. At this point, from a vision of the sexual body as overawed by the death-instinct, Thomas's work came to acquire something of the amplitude of Eros.

In what follows, I explore these imaginings of the body, and also some of the terms of the interaction between the body and mind, or spirit. I shall try to show how these may be read in their broader contexts; for it was in the 1920s and 1930s that the history and perception of bodies came to be charted against the background of totalitarian politics, neo-Darwinian science and Freudian psychology. History, politics, science and psychology all promised an unprecedented understanding of minds and bodies, but, at the same time, they revealed archaic physical and psychic survivals lurking within both. Thus, the 'primitive' forces (the 'old universal architecture') laid bare by modernity 'aroused widespread fears of regression' as Tim Armstrong has noted and could easily 'destabilize relations between self and world'.[16] Thomas's fleshy, 'cybernetic', sexualised bodies bear witness, I shall argue, to a contra-dictory writing of the body-mind in a historical, not merely abstract or theoretical, way.[17] In such work, an inescapably embodied existence is seen to threaten, as well as empower; thus, the 'animal' of 'How shall my animal' is drawn up from the unconscious, its metamorphic power given corporeality as it '[leaps] up the whinnying light', only to find that it has 'dug [its] grave' in the speaker's breast (CP, 76).

It was against such a background that Thomas established a form of the dialectical relationship between text and body sought by the modernists, although in a manner which was antithetical to theirs. The ultimate resolution of the subject-object dichotomy in Thomas lay in the most extreme form of physical immediacy – that is, sex. And it is through sex that human beings, for Thomas, became most completely part of process. Sex is like death (the Renaissance conceit of orgasm as the 'little death' is ubiquitous in Thomas), insofar as it witnesses the continuity of being within individually discontinuous existences. Yet, unlike death, it allows at least the temporary overcoming of ego-isolation in the 'bone-bound island' of the body. In this aspect of his work, Thomas daringly confronted auto-eroticism as a species of writing through a kind of double dis-semination (the brilliantly articulated mixture of delicacy and crudeness in his lyric unravelling of this subject, unlike the criticism it has attracted, being neither prurient, nor evasive). As sexual intercourse, sex is first determinism – an archaic 'grief' dominated by the womb-tomb and penis-worm, the child as 'plague' and conventional Freudian scenarios – and then a disentangling of Eros and Thanatos, as a result of the growing acceptance of his place in the reproductory cycle, of the body and of death. Increasingly, Thomas realised, in his poetry, the feminised and fluid sense of sexuality implicit in process, complicating earlier 'urchin hungers' with his sense of being 'the time dying flesh astride' (where 'dying' also means the flesh 'kills' or 'stains' time) (*CP*, 15, 102). From the late 1930s, the poetry fully clasps to its grains the material, maternal body of language as the 'Freudian exemplar' modified his masculine part in the Freudian script, adopting more androgynous, dissolute forms of selfhood – ones which may be aligned with the philosophical tradition of the embodied self, as well as more explicitly feminist readings of bodies, selves and writing.

Although it treats body, spirit and mind as different entities, Thomas's poetry assumes, at every point, their interchangeability. Even as he defended the need for his 'anatomical' imagery in letters written between 1933 and 1934, he agonised over the nature of the relationship between the two, struggling to reconcile them without collapsing into mechanical materialism or sterile abstraction. The distinction is presented as one of perspective, rather than of kind, in a letter to Johnson on Christmas Day 1933, which argues that: 'the materialist can be called the man who believes only in the part of the tree he sees, & the spiritualist a man who believes in a lot more of the tree than is within his sight' (*CL*, 100). Preferring the latter, Thomas emphasised the need to 'change our angles of perspective' on the tree. In a previous letter to her, dated just four days earlier, he had also opposed materialism via a discussion of the merits of Aldous Huxley and D. H. Lawrence – viewed respectively as 'intellect' (or 'brain') and the material universe in the form of the body. Huxley, he told Johnson, 'preaches the sermon of the intellect; his god is cellular, and his heaven a socialist Towards', while 'Lawrence preached paganism … as the life by the body in the body for the body' – a doctrine which 'contents man with his lot … [and] defies the brain', although 'it is only through the brain that man can realise the chaos of civilization and attempt to better it' (*CL*, 87).

Both are seen as reductively scientist or sexual: if Huxley 'would condense the generative principle into a test-tube', Lawrence 'would condense the world into the generative principle'. It is Huxley who finally appears to get Thomas's approval, but this is a contingent judgement and flows more from political than aesthetic considerations – Lawrence, because he would make man 'content ... with his lot', must be reactionary. Taking this to its logical conclusion would lead Thomas to a New Country position – the poetry of the 'socialist Toward'.[18] But this doesn't happen; rather, he articulates a dilemma created by the polarising forces:

> The young writer, if he would wish to label himself at all, must class himself under one of two headings: under the philosophy (for want of a better word) which declares the body to be all and the intellect nothing, and which would limit the desires of life, the perceptions and the creation of life, within the walls of the flesh; or under the philosophy which, declaring the intellect and the reason and the intelligence to be all, denies the warmth of the blood and the body's promise. You have to class yourself under one heading – the labels might overlap a little – for the equilibrium between flesh and not-flesh can never be reached by an individual. While the life of the body is, perhaps, more directly pleasant, it is terribly limited, and the life of the non-body, while physically unsatisfying, is capable of developing, of realising infinity, of getting somewhere, and of creating an artistic progeny. (CL, 87)

The alternatives are presented as starkly as possible in an attempt to make them to undo themselves. So great is the difficulty of arriving at his definition of the nature of 'spirit' or 'mind' and thus achieving the 'equilibrium' he seeks between mind and body, that he is driven to use the terms 'not-flesh' and 'non-body'. What he attempts to do is to spiritualise the concept of the mind, to shed its most ratiocinative and body-negating aspects. As Martin Dodsworth notes, 'the "non-body" is ... endowed with spiritual qualities' and these contradict the 'mechanistic concept' of the mind-body relationship of Thomas's claim, made in a previous letter, that 'the description of a thought ... can be beaten home by bringing it onto a physical level' (CL, 57).[19]

Dodsworth attributes this ambiguity in Thomas both to the slipperiness of a term like 'mind' and to Thomas's saturation in Blake. Blake felt, on the one hand, that dependence on reasoning power had caused man to find the senses inferior and limiting; this made the body a kind of prison to the soul, with reliance on the body's senses and reasoning power alone reducing him to a mere 'natural organ subject to Sense'.[20] As a result, he argued that 'Man's perceptions are not bounded by organs of perception: he perceives more than sense (tho' ever so acute) can discover'.[21] Against this clear distinction between mundane and visionary sight, Blake also claims that it is merely dependence on reasoning power that has degraded the senses and that, as Dodsworth puts it 'to raise the status of the senses is [therefore] to strike a blow for the imagination' (*The Marriage of Heaven and Hell*, for example, envisages the millennium being brought about by just such 'an improvement of sensual enjoyment').[22] The first stage in this process is to destroy 'the notion than man has a body distinct from his soul'. Blake's apparent contradictions arise from his insistence that the physical world is merely an aspect of the spiritual one and that: '[b]ody and mind and spirit become interchangeable terms as a consequence'. Thus, when Thomas speaks of the 'non-body' capable of 'realising infinity', he is following Blake's doctrine of the supremacy of the imagination. Similarly, when he says that 'all thoughts and actions emanate from the body', he draws on the notion that the five senses are: 'the chief inlets of Soul in this age'.[23]

Thomas's understanding of Blake is mediated by his interpretation of Lawrence, whom he strips of his conservatism and (some of) his phallocentrism. Revealingly, given his qualms about him, the only Lawrence novel mentioned in his letters was one of the most avowedly primitivist, *The Plumed Serpent* (he tells of 'reading [it] for the hundredth time' in December 1933 and recalled the influence of its 'verse extracts' on his early work to Treece in 1938) (*CL*, 87, 343). The novel's heroine, Kate, recognises Mexico's 'ancient, inscrutable life of the senses' and appeals: 'Let me close my prying seeing eyes, and sit in still darkness ... They [Don Ramón and Cipriano] have got more than I, they have a richness that I haven't got ... The itching, prurient, *knowing*, imagining eye, I am cursed with it'.[24] The novel does not finally endorse total surrender to such a blood-philosophy; Kate maintains an element of self-conscious distance throughout. But her thoughts resemble Blake's better-known distrust of the tyranny of sight and its externalising, calculating tendency and, in particular, an anti-visualism drawn from both sources, which informs Thomas's poems. This is most explicit (or 'mechanical', in Thomas's self-deprecating account) in 'When all my five and country senses see':

> When all my five and country senses see,
> The fingers will forget green thumbs and mark
> How, through the halfmoon's vegetable eye,
> Husk of young stars and handfull zodiac,
> Love in the frost is pared and wintered by,
> The whispering ears will watch love drummed away
> Down breeze and shell to a discordant beach,
> And, lashed to syllables, the lynx tongue cry

That her fond wounds are mended bitterly.
My nostrils see her breath burn like a bush.

My one and only noble heart has witnesses
In all love's countries, that will grope awake;
And when blind sleep drops on the spying senses,
The heart is sensual, though five eyes break. (*CP*, 70)

Here, the speaker-as-embryo anticipates the time after birth when sight, currently its most undeveloped sense, will come to dominate and tyrannise the other four (Lawrence's play on 'eye, I', in the passage cited above, implies a similar critique of the role of the rational ego). (*CP*, 34) In the same way, it argues, love afflicted by the 'frost' of sight – the merely 'vegetable' eye – is diminished (the beauty of 'Husk of young stars and handfull zodiac' should not disguise the fact that this will be a diminution of the scope that the embryo now enjoys). Typically, Thomas conflates different periods and states of existence, shown here in the speaker's rather adolescent tendency to diminish 'love' to a merely visual reckoning of women. In a series of synaesthetic images, the various senses testify to their bondage; for example, 'lynx tongue' calls up, and is informed by, the conventional 'lynx-eyed'. Indeed, these now 'spy' on the true life of the body, in order to confine it; only the heart bears 'witness' to the 'sensual' plenitude experienced in the womb. The final quatrain states that in 'blind sleep', plenitude will be restored. However, this condition is not only achievable in 'sleep'. 'Country' love is sexual (Hamlet's 'country matters'), and our memories and dreams of the embryonic state are fulfilled in the oceanic bliss of adult sexual love, when sight is again temporarily deposed. The paradox of the awakening of true 'sensual' love in that most ethereal of organs, the heart, is only intensified by its being balanced by the coarsest concrete imagery, 'grope' surely being ironic at the expense of the 'noble heart'.

Bodies in history: glandular compulsions and cyborgs

'Flesh comes to us out of history; so does the repression and taboo that governs our experience of flesh.'

– Angela Carter, *The Sadeian Woman*.[25]

The 'countries' and 'spying' of 'When all my five and country senses' are reminders that Thomas's body-centredness within 1930s literature is not untoward in its contemporary philosophical, psychoanalytic, political, anthropological, historical and scientific contexts. The interwar years were – partly as a result of the rise of dictatorships – a time of unprecedented debate about the role and meaning of bodies. Thomas's work ambivalently resists and exploits the new discourses, in order to explore his own experience of the dilemmas of embodied cognition. Bodies mediate historical events – such as the rise of fascism – because, as the historian Dorinda Outram has pointed out: 'the physical body is at once our most intimate experience and our most inescapable public form. Because it is at once so inalienably private and so ineluctably public, it has also formed, in most western cultures, the most basic political resource'.[26]

Thus, in pre-bourgeois societies, the body was invested with dignity through the concepts of the body politic, the king's body and the sacralised body of Christianity – a religion based on the transformation of the suffering of one body into the redemption of the world, since Christ's suffering gave meaning to the suffering of believers, dignifying the painful gap between the desire for personal survival and the knowledge of death. The secular-democratic erosion of these forms raised difficult questions concerning the symbolic function of bodies, both for individuals and in relation to power. There were, and are now, few answers to these questions, beyond the satisfaction of basic symbolic and biological needs and the transmission of genetic material. More, the sacral concept of the body was dealt a huge blow by the First World War – so inter-involved, as we have seen, with the linguistic violence of the process poetic – in which slaughter on a vast scale exacerbated a more general sense of the worthlessness of the body, stemming from its helplessness in the face of technological progress. Whether or not they were augmented by it, technology weakened a belief in the significance of the body and its destiny; and, if faith in the resurrection of the body declined, so too did a sense of bodily integrity.

Yet, as Outram also argues, fascism temporarily altered the trajectory of this decline by offering a new set of attitudes towards the body characterised by an extreme focus on the public body, in the form of a charismatic leader and an extreme desacralisation of the individual body, the ultimate expression of which would be the death camps. The tendency to disciplined mass public displays of the body (of which the Nuremburg rallies were perhaps the best-known example) show how 'the body had become the prime area of public gesture as well as the prime location where the exercise of political control was demonstrated'.[27] But this was not confined to Germany, Italy or the Soviet Union; it was also a (lesser) feature of life in contemporary liberal-democratic societies, in the form of Busby Berkeley films, mass gymnastics displays and the broader communalisation of leisure. Economic and political activity saw the same massification and disciplining, from the spread of Fordist working practices to state-organised housing, education and health programmes. The interventionist attitude to bodies by state and industry further eroded their status as sites of spiritual value, since they now appeared as locations where the sovereignty of mass politics and culture was made manifest, rather than possessed entities over which individuals sought to realise the Victorian ideal of *self*-control.

Unease at this shift was reflected in works such as Freud's *Civilization and its Discontents* (1930), which discussed the integration of physical control and self-image within social norms, and the anthropological studies of Margaret Mead and Geoffrey Bateson on the problems of relationships between different cultures and of physical expression. But it was most directly reflected in sociology, as Max Weber's work on bodily restraint and capital accumulation was extended to other areas. The Nazi theorist Carl Schmitt, Mikhail Bakhtin (in *Rabelais and His World*, 1934–40), Elias Canetti, Wilhelm Reich (whose *The Mass Psychology of Fascism* applied Freud to politics), Georges Bataille and Norbert Elias, whose major work was *The Civilizing Process* (1939) – each of these very different researchers reflected the fact that physical violence had become a tool of politics and that racial and other 'bodily' legislation informed the policies of major European states, setting bodies at the heart of politics.

Although bodies were the basis of new political systems, the inevitably personal physical experience of the individual remained highly contested. Thomas's 'seek[ing] out [of] the inexplicable elements of human experience and bring[ing of] them face to face with the baffled "ratio"' in the form of antenatal existence, sex, death and the linguistic unconscious, therefore demands to be viewed in light of such developments, at least as much as personal-biographical ones (it could be argued, more radically, that the areas that Thomas focuses on are not 'experience' in the usual sense at all and that, in this sense, he is redefining the areas proper to poetry).[28] These 'inexplicable elements' resisted not simply the New Country 'ratio', but the broader, more threatening discourses of the body in circulation.

Something of Thomas's use of these bodily discourses can be seen indirectly, but all the more revealingly, in the epithet 'glandular', as applied to his work by Geoffrey Grigson (who used it not only in the passage already quoted, but on two other occasions, between 1935 and 1957, with growing spitefulness) and Neil Corcoran. Writing of the handful of later poems by Thomas which have become anthology favourites, Corcoran claims that they 'turn the mesmerised and self-obsessed narcissism of the earlier work outwards to a recognisable external world of action, event, suffering and relationship, though without losing the neural exacerbation which is the Dylan Thomas signature. ... [T]he pain Thomas wakes to in these poems is not his, or not his alone: they diffuse the glandular compulsiveness into the compunctions of lament and love'.[29] There is a lot wrong with this as an account of Thomas's poetry – the way it misses the impersonality of the early poetry, for example, or the questionable equation of a 'recognisable external world' with freedom from 'mesmerised and self-obsessed narcissism' – but it is Corcoran's use of Grigson's 'glandular' and its quality as an aporia or 'psychoanalytic negation', to use Shoshana Felman's term, which interests me here (something similar could be said about the rather loose use of 'narcissism').[30] As with 'adolescent', there is no attempt to define, through textual reference or other argument, what precisely is so deplorable about 'glands', either as a subject or as a purported style of writing. Doesn't everyone have them? The objection here seems to derive from the fact that something so uncontrollable and bodily can exercise such sway over the mind, and Thomas's too-ready capitulation to their compulsion, which, in turn, seems to mean that his poetry sometimes deals with masturbation. (But since it is in the nature of glands to compel the body to do things, isn't 'glandular compulsiveness' tautological in any case?)[31] The problem, once again, is not so much with the terms, as with their vagueness – an assumption that some physical facts are an unworthy poetic subject – and, as I shall show, a lack of critical curiosity.

The phrase 'glandular compulsiveness' does, indeed, identify some crucial aspects of the early poetry. Glands, and their effects, are undeniably prominent in Thomas's mental and physical internal worlds, while in an external one, just about discernible, woman features largely as the 'shades of girls' or a 'dam', a 'tufted axle' ruled by 'the brawned womb's weather', possessor of the breasts' 'galactic sea', with man a 'knobbly ape' dominated by his 'cockerel's eggs' and phallic 'mortal ruler' (*CP*, 17, 7, 51, 7, 9, 16, 50, 13). As in Picasso's paintings of Marie-Thérèse Walter from this period, the human figure appears reduced, both schematically and semi-surrealistically, to its orifices and sexual characteristics (breasts, buttocks, vagina, hips, penis, testicles, lips, eyes), when, that is, it is not being represented in foetal form. The ubiquity of the foetus shows that Thomas conflates adolescent 'glandular compulsions' with those of the other major period of glandular-hormonal bodily metamorphosis, and this is a vital clue to his intentions in using 'glandular' material. Moreover, the word 'gland' itself occurs twice in *18 Poems* and, on both appearances, sheds light on this trademark aspect of the work.

The first is in 'From love's first fever' – 'the rumour of manseed / Within the hallowed gland' (*CP*, 21) – and is applied to an infant self, moving from an ungendered identity (Freud's stage of 'polymorphous perversity') to that of a 'boy'. The lines following the first mention of the 'hallowed gland' describe the transition from a sense of ecstatic and wordless oneness with the world into the world of language, as in the 'Poetic Manifesto' passage cited in Chapter 2:

> And the four winds, that had long blown as one,
> Shone in my ears the light of sound,
> Called in my ears the sound of light … (*CP*, 21)

The second occurrence is in 'All all and all', which, as we have seen, offers a millenarian vision of sexual-social transformation in its final stanzas:

> How now my flesh, my naked fellow,
> Dug of the sea, the glanded morrow,
> Worm in the scalp …
>
> Flower, flower, the people's fusion,
> O light in zenith, the coupled bud,
> And the flame in flesh's vision. (*CP*, 29–30)

Here, 'glanded' is metaphoric and figures the new, youthful energies of the revolutionary future ('morrow') – social transformation as a rejuvenating gland-grafting operation. In either case, the aesthetic, structural and self-aware precision of the usage is quite at odds with a writing practice blindly capitulating to a thematics of 'glandular compulsion'.

In fact, 'glands' (and hormones, their chemical secretions) appear, in accord with the organic contexts of Thomas's process poetic, as part of a debate that the poetry conducts concerning the biological limitations on human existence. Glands were the main focus of the biological determinism informing contemporary Behaviourist models of the body and neo-Darwinian social paradigms – paradigms that Thomas strove to escape and subvert in the verbal wit and energy of his poetry. Thus, the 'horny milk' of 'My world is pyramid' not only brilliantly compresses Freud's theories of infantile sexuality and the sexual mother, but seems informed by the recent discovery that lactation is triggered by the sex hormone progesterone. There are, as this suggests, very powerful historical reasons why a writer coming-of-age in the early 1930s might have been 'glandular', and aware of glands other than his own. Quite simply, they constituted the new physiology of the day, the 1920s and 1930s being an age of 'glandular compulsion', when almost all of the the hormones produced by the glands, and their functions were discovered, and of pioneering glandular surgery – all of which was widely reported in the press. Information about these activities, which may lie behind Grigson's usages (but which Corcoran, writing later, has missed), cannot have escaped Thomas – a reader of books on popular science and science fiction, living in a household which took two daily newspapers (*The Times* and *The Daily Telegraph*) – any more than it is possible, today, to miss their equivalents: cloning, stem cells, IVF treatment, the human genome project, Viagra and surrogate motherhood (to name a few).[32] British scientists were at the forefront of gland and hormone research, with most of the major discoveries – widely reported in the press – occurring in the years immediately before the publication of *18 Poems*.[33] By the early 1930s, it had been discovered that all glandular activity was controlled by the mysterious pituitary gland, which became the subject of widespread speculation and debate. Even more spectacularly, these years saw clinical technology responding to such discoveries with hormonal and glandular implant treatments, many of which were also pioneered in Britain. Sexual surgery was unavoidably in the literary atmosphere at the time, if only because of Yeats's well-publicised 'Steinach operation' (vasectomy) of 1934.[34] It should be no surprise, then, that, given his body-awareness, Thomas should reflect the general interest in glands in his dealings with biological determinism. The third notebook's 'Pass through twelve stages' (April 23 1933), for example, has an old man trying to 'Retrogress' to youth and being ironically exhorted to:

… [step] back through medium of abuse,
Excess or otherwise, regain your fire.
Graft a monkey gland, old man, at fools' advice. (*NP*, 154)

The same discourses inform the short stories of the mid-1930s. In 'The School for Witches' (1936), for example, the doctor's daughter, who heads a coven, blends black magic with a then-current hormone treatment: 'she taught the seven girls how the lust of man, like a dead horse, stood up to his injected mixtures' – a reference to androsterone injections used to make penises 'stand up' in cases of erectile dysfunction (the 'dead horse' refers to the potency of the mixture and to trial experiments on animals)

(*CS*, 67). Similarly, 'The Lemon' features Doctor Manza – a Wellesian mad scientist – 'graft[ing]' an ovary into a dog, breasts onto birds and preparing to implant 'mastoids' in a ferret (*CS*, 56, 57). Genetics, heredity and biological discourses appear frequently elsewhere: in 'The End of the River', it takes the form of the end of 'Twelve generations of the Quincy family', while the 'synthetic prodigals' of 'The Map of Love' are exhorted to 'return to thy father's laboratory … and the fatted calf in a test-tube' (*CS*, 50, 112).

The swiftness with which Dublin gossip dubbed Yeats's 'The Gland Old Man of Irish Letters' indicates the public confusion over vasectomies, implants and injections. But the main point, as 'Pass through twelve stages' shows, is that these treatments were not held to be exclusively sexual in their effects; old age, too, it was felt, could be held at bay by them, senescence renewed by the vigour of youth. Furthermore, as sex and gender became increasingly viewed as chemically determined, the discoveries and therapies associated with them began to constitute a challenge to the notions of unchangeable and essential identities; alter the hormone balance, it was believed, and you could alter the person.[35] Thus, increased understanding of certain predetermined aspects of the chemistry of the human body paradoxically opened the door to an increasingly fluid sense of physical identity and selfhood. In its glandular-hormonal aspects, these discourses informed Thomas's early treatment of sex and were used to body forth, in biological determinist terms, his generational sense of socio-historical fatedness. But if he was less sanguine than many about the positive potential for bio-science, he was not alone; while hopes for transforming the human body (and human nature) lasted until the end of the decade, the sheer intractability of the subject was clear as early as 1930.

It was Aldous Huxley who, in *Brave New World* (1932), gave the most memorable literary expression of this ambivalence. Comparisons between Huxley and Lawrence in his correspondence the year before show that Thomas was keenly interested in Huxley's writing. To set the early poems beside the descriptions of the London Hatchery and Conditioning Centre or the Pregnancy Substitute is to see how much Thomas owed to *Brave New World*'s dystopian convergence of Fordist social regimentation, eugenics and 1930s gland and hormone science.[36] Our post-1945 abhorrence of eugenics means that *Brave New World* is now often misunderstood; it was intended as a satire of extremes, not of eugenics *per se*, since Huxley himself held eugenicist beliefs.[37] Thomas's democratic and hybrid nature rebelled against these, but, like many on the Left, he would have been well aware of their effects; one of the first acts of the Nazis in power had been to pass a Sterilisation Law.[38] He Blakeanly refused to accord bodily experience a merely mechanico-physical status, urging its claims against cerebralism and the reduction of imaginative consciousness to cold ratiocination, even as he resisted irrationalism. But he also registered the challenge of determinism and the fear and wonder generated by the new bio-technologies.

The process poetic embodies this at the most basic level through its collocation of organic with inorganic terms on the site of the body (e.g. 'chemic blood', 'mechanical flesh', 'motor muscle', 'girdered nerve'), as noted in Chapter 2. These signal Thomas's essential modernity, since the inorganic is not rejected in a merely reactionary-romantic way, but regarded as growing out of, and supplementing, the organic – the quick contain the dead, animal and vegetable, which are simultaneously mineral (but never simply reducible to chemistry). His attempts to represent the conflicted self implicit in this view, to 'square the mortal circle', are clearest in 'I, in my intricate image', which contains more cybernetic collocations than any other poem:

> I, in my intricate image, stride on two levels,
> Forged in man's minerals, the brassy orator
> Laying my ghost in metal,
> The scales of this twin world tread on the double,
> My half ghost in armour hold hard in death's corridor,
> To my man-iron sidle. (CP, 30)

Here, the self is 'Forged' (fused, but also counterfeit, because essentially divided) – a 'ghost in metal' or 'half ghost in armour', later described as a 'metal phantom', bringing spirit (ghost, phantom) and flesh (armour, metal) together. More, the writing itself embodies the split self, as the act of printing poetry is described as 'laying my ghost in [the] metal' of a printer's type (that the frame in which type was held was called a 'forme' is probably a submerged pun). The poem wrestles with Cartesian dualism in a complex narrative, which subjects the split selves of the 'intricate image' to a sea voyage, drowning and rebirth, but its very imagery reflects throughout the power of dualism to impose its either / or schemas and mind-body, organic-inorganic divisions. The image-clusters used to depict the self can be related to Elias's central notion that the growth of civilised behaviour in the West ('manners', etiquette, bodily control and so on) had led to a pathologically isolated personality type or form of selfhood, which he called *homo clausus* or the 'closed self'.

This rigidly defined sense of the self and body – the self as an unknowable, yet self-sufficient, 'black box' or 'ghost in the machine' of the body – was one which was developed over centuries of discipline and pedagogy. To quote Elias: 'If one grows up in the midst of such a group, one cannot easily imagine that there could be people who do not experience themselves in this way as entirely self-sufficient individuals cut off from all other beings and things. This kind of self-perception appears as obvious, a symptom of an eternal human state … The conception of the individual as *homo clausus*, a little world in himself … determines the image of human beings in general'.[39] As a result, the nature of the 'wall' between subjectivities and the world is hardly ever considered. To do so, as Elias also notes, is to problematise our sense of self, body and world: 'Is the body the vessel which holds the true self locked within it? Is the skin the frontier between "inside" and "outside"? What in the human individual is the container, and what the contained?'[40] The point concerning *homo clausus*, for Elias, is that, if we 'continue to see the human being as by nature a closed container with an outer shell and a core concealed within it', it will be impossible to 'comprehend the possibility of a civilizing process embracing many generations, in the course of which the personality structure of the individual human being changes without the nature of human beings changing'.[41]

Questions concerning 'personality structure' and the 'nature of human beings' are debated in the intense inwardness of Thomas's early writing, as well as in his imagery – the most traditional being that of the body-self as a suit, or clothing. This further elaborates on the classical image of the yarn of life, spun and cut by Atropos' shears in Greek myth, thus fulfilling the demands of process for simultaneity, since it allows the foetus to be imagined as a cross-legged tailor, hunched-up and sewing its suit of flesh for the life to come. So, in 'Twenty-four years', the embryo is 'In the groin of the natural doorway … crouched like a tailor', stitching together its glad-rags, in order to be 'Dressed to die' when 'the sensual strut beg[ins]' at birth, its 'red veins' like pockets 'full of money' or blood, like a young collier down for a Saturday night spree in Swansea (*CP*, 81). Similarly, in 'Once below a time', the body is 'my pinned-around-the-spirit / Cut-to-measure flesh bit / Suit for a serial sum' – a 'silly suit, hardly yet suffered for', sewed (and stitched up) by God as heredity and the evolutionary principle, the 'cloud perched tailors' master' with [that is, using] 'nerves for cotton' at work on the speaker, 'the boy of common thread' (*CP*, 109–10).

'Pinned-around-the-spirit' suggests the body's disposable and renewable nature through the round of pantheistic process, but, in more threatening mode, the 'suit' is more like Elias's armour than one cut from cloth. Often, therefore, Thomas figures the self as a creature with a hard carapace. Another representation of the problematic of surface and depth that has already been considered, this depicts the self as 'container', like that defined by Elias. Thomas's early work is full of images of the ego as carapace, mineral or animal: '[a]ll issue [is] armoured' and sports 'My Egypt's armour'; or it is the 'crabbing' self of 'Especially when the October wind', the 'turtle' of 'When, like a running grave' or the 'crocodile' which has to be 'clawed out' before self-realization can take place in 'I, in my intricate image' (*CP*, 9, 28, 18, 19, 36). Above all, it is an 'insect', belonging to an order which is defined by its exoskeleton. The carapace is a deathly covering, and man is 'Cadaver's masker, the harnessing mantle', who, in 'Today, this insect', finds he is 'A crocodile before the chrysalis' of rebirth who must '[break] his shell in the last shocked beginning' (*CP*, 38). The antithesis of the plated, armoured animal are invertebrates, which also slimily inhabit the poetry (although technically insects, too, are invertebrates). To be an octopus, however, as in 'How shall my animal', is to be vulnerable and 'flailed'. The snail – whorl-shaped, like the crouched embryo in 'Then was my neophyte' ('My sea hermaphrodite, / Snail of man in His ship of fires') – is perhaps closest to Thomas himself in its ambivalent combination of carapace and raw core, dionysiacally 'drunk' in a vineyard in 'How shall my animal' and tenderly realised in the description of 'the sea wet church the size of a snail / With its horns through mist' in 'Poem in October' (*CP*, 75, 57, 87).

This embodied self continually hovers between such extremes of petrification and vulnerability in Thomas, in an interplay between organic and inorganic, which William York Tindall refers to as his 'habitual confusion of metal and flesh'.[42] For, however vulnerable it may be, the self has to don some kind of armour or carapace, in order to have agency and function in the world. As Thomas, only half-jokingly, put it in a letter to Johnston: 'on goes the everyday armour, and the self, even the wounded self, is hidden from so many. If I pull down the metals, don't shoot, dear. Not even with a smile ...' (*CL*, 133). It would be an error to imagine that this is a situation in which there is a 'right' or 'wrong' state; Thomas is fascinated with the apparatus of self-protection, even if he senses that a 'wounded self' is necessary to his writing. The sculptural autonomy of his poems, growing in its protective elaboration, is itself a kind of 'cybernetic fantasy' and, in some of them – 'I, in my intricate image' or 'I dreamed my genesis' – as Ivan Phillips has observed, the speakers can seem 'nothing less than a cyborg':

> I dreamed my genesis in sweat of sleep, breaking
> Through the rotating shell, strong
> As motor muscle on the drill, driving
> Through vision and the girdered nerve ... (*CP*, 25)

The main point is that Thomas is attracted to the cybernetic trope and the figure of the cyborg, because these are ambivalent 'boundary figure[s]', between states, 'neither one thing nor the other'. Far from simply setting up an organic / inorganic split, as distinct from Lawrence, he seeks to deconstruct the dichotomy. Always, he senses that, as Phillips puts it: 'manufactured mechanisms of control and communication will always breach the walls – mental, epidermal – of the individual and fuse with what was thought to be inviolably natural. The constant slippage in [his] writing between external and internal physicalities, between a sense of the embodied and the disembodied, reflects a fundamental uncertainty about the limits of the self'.[43] Thomas presents the attractions of the autonomous 'cyborg' body, together with its threats and, as I shall show, the alternative of dissolution. Again, the anomalousness of the attempt to preserve some kind of self between forces, making either for fixity or liquidation in a decade striving for realist and psychological precision, is strongly marked. Certainly, the insistence on the claustrophobic and ineluctably embodied nature of the self sets this aspect of Thomas's work radically at odds with the largely futuristic, surface technologism of poems referring to airmen, pylons and express trains.

Sex: from masturbatory muse to libidinous betrayal

'Take me as I come – sounds like Onan – ...'

Dylan Thomas to Daniel Jones.

For Eliot, Pound and Wyndham Lewis, what most threatened to betray the 'armoured' masculine *homo clausus* into femininity, narcissism, false materialism and, ultimately, dissolute identity loss, is sexual desire. For New Country, by contrast, overt misogyny was cautiously reversed: the neuroses resulting from repression were acknowledged to require treatment, but in a way which cerebrally distanced the solution – Freudian insight, communal solidarity – from the body. As a result, the overcoming of repression is scarcely ever convincingly enacted.

In Thomas, however, as I have argued, the body, and particularly the sexual body, was central to process from the start. Yet how was sex to be represented, to be spoken of? Thomas's writing shows that he understood the repression of adolescent sexual energy to be a basis for the authority of state, family and church. However, his experience of sex was, to put it mildly, limited. As a 'Freudian exemplar', the analysand as much as the analyst, Thomas was concerned with presenting the inner turmoil, fantasy and desire that repression produced. When, in 'Answers to an Enquiry' – the *New Verse* questionnaire of 1934 – he claimed that his poetry was an attempt to 'cast light upon what has been hidden for too long', this did not signal acquiescence in the therapeutic New Country project; rather, it was the sanctioning of a controlled revelation of symptoms, through a 'dialectical' and associative treatment of images and language, which allowed the unconscious to break the surface (*EPW*, 150).

At one point in 'The Peaches', the narrator and his friend Jack find themselves in a tree they have climbed, looking down at 'the lavatory in the corner of the field'. They notice Gwilym inside, 'sitting on the seat with his trousers down … He was reading a book and moving his hands. "We can see you!" we shouted' (*CS*, 138). Since the stories of *A Portrait of the Artist as a Young Dog* often recapitulate the anxieties of his earlier work, holding them up for affectionate debunking, we are probably justified in reading this episode as a comic overview of the self-abuse which features in a more agonised manner in the early writing. Thomas might have joked about it in 1938, when 'The Peaches' was written, but he does so with a painful sense that the sexual restrictions of adolescence had been all too real. Rather than treating the subject as unmentionable, then, or simply as evidence of immaturity, its prominence in the early work is better viewed simultaneously as a sign of both painful honesty and provocation.[44] In one sense, that is, it can be read as sincerity; in another, it is calculated to expose the confessional limits of realist or Romantic poetics.

Thwarted energy is traced by Thomas in a symbolic language, which is both repressed and blatant, since, to the libidinally saturated body and imagination, almost anything is sexual provocation. In 'I see the boys of summer', the boys who 'lay the gold tithings barren' ask us to read a metaphorical harvest and sexualise it: 'lay' as 'have intercourse with' (*CP*, 7). Within their 'finger[ing]' of 'jacks of frost … in their hives', we hear the slang term for masturbation, 'jacking off'. 'Divid[ing] the day and night with fairy thumbs' sounds innocently childish, auto-erotic and homosexual all at once – it is a reminder that Freud's argument that children had a sexual nature was taken seriously by Thomas, and it can be seen running through all of his work, from this poem to 'In country sleep' and *Under Milk Wood*, twenty years later. The 'seedy shiftings', which make the 'boys' 'men of nothing', are louche verbal evasions, but they are also masturbatory flows. These may occur even where no 'fingers' or 'thumbs' are involved; other poems also allude to nocturnal seminal emissions. 'Our eunuch dreams', as its opening suggests, has to do with unfulfillable nocturnal sexual fantasies – a kind of 'sleeping' which 'suck[s] the sleeper of his faith / That shrouded men might marrow as they fly'; they deprive him, that is, of his aspiration of sexual fulfilment (*CP*, 18). 'I, in my intricate image' also mentions 'Shames and the damp dishonours', while the 'carcase shape' conjured up in wet dreams appears in 'When once the twilight locks' (*CP*, 35, 10). In 'My world is pyramid', the devilish speaker confesses:

> The loin is glory in a working pallor.
> My clay unsuckled and my salt unborn,
> The secret child, I shift about the sea
> Dry in the half-tracked thigh. (*CP*, 28)[45]

Yet, although he emphasises the sterility of masturbation, Thomas does not quite establish a straightforward equation of it with evil and an equal opposition with mutual sexual activity viewed as good and wholesome. The devil often has the best tunes in his work, and the energy and invention of the voice in part II of 'My world is pyramid', for example, cannot be entirely ignored. Similarly, in 'I see the boys of summer', the boys' response to the attack on them in part I is to declare, in part II, that they are 'dark deniers', because 'seasons must be challenged or they totter / Into a chiming quarter / Where, punctual as death, we ring the stars' – in other words, that even a negative challenge can break up ossified convention and is, therefore, justifiable (*CP*, 8). In general, it can be said that *18 Poems* associates masturbation with narcissism and deathliness. Yet it simultaneously covertly acknowledges it as a form of self-assertion and self-discovery; its presence in the book is a crucial aspect of the sexual tension between the boring suburban bedroom and the universe of process, explored with a nervous aplomb and melancholy wit, as a figure appropriate to outsiderness and literary belatedness.

As a symbol for repression and waste, as well as a form of illicit, yet pleasurable, self-knowledge, auto-eroticism receives its apotheosis in the astonishing 'My hero bares his nerves'. This unashamedly 'prais[es] the mortal error':

My hero bares his nerves along my wrist
That rules from wrist to shoulder,
Unpacks the head that, like a sleepy ghost,
Leans on my mortal ruler,
The proud spine spurning turn and twist.

And those poor nerves so wired to the skull
Ache on the lovelorn paper
I hug to love with my unruly scrawl
That utters all love hunger
And tells the page the empty ill.

My hero bares my side and sees his heart
Tread, like a naked Venus,
The beach of flesh, and wind her bloodred plait;
Stripping my loin of promise
He promises a secret heat.

He holds the wire from this box of nerves
Praising the mortal error
Of birth and death, the two sad knaves of thieves,
And the hunger's emperor;
He pulls the chain, the cistern moves. (*CP*, 13–14)

Beginning as a description of the act of writing and of the writer-as-hero, the poem soon insinuates its sexual dimension through a series of blatant double entendres ('head', 'ruler', 'proud', 'secret heat') playing on the slang of 'to pull one's wire', meaning 'to masturbate'.[46] The final line's detail 'pulls' the rhetoric of 'love', of 'Venus' and 'emperor', crashing down to earth.[47] Not for the last time – it is also the subject of 'In my craft or sullen art' – writing is recognised as isolated from, yet secretly kin to, sex – 'a secret heat'. That recognition is rehearsed as the difficulty of entering an adult world of sexual empowerment and authorship. The implicit wordplay informing the poem is that of the pen within penis, but rather than the phallic bullishness of the 'phallic pencil [that] turns into an electric drill', as Thomas described it in a letter to Trevor Hughes, this presents the entrapment of both sex and writing in a circle of incomplete, self-abusive identity formation (*CL*, 208). The conflation of auto-eroticism and writing is logical enough; just as Thomas disrupts the social bonds linking signifiers and signifieds, he also disrupts convention by refusing to acknowledge the socio-symbolic value of the sexual act – that is, as it is approved within the bounds of marriage and as potentially procreative.

The poem's honesty lies not just in its frankness, but also in its understanding that both writing and auto-eroticism promise a fulfilment or presence, which can never be granted. As 'Grief thief of time' puts it, Thomas is 'Jack my fathers' ('Jack' being his father D. J. Thomas's nickname), trying to father, auto-erotically, his own authority (CP, 55). But both literary and sexual forms of self-authentication deconstruct themselves in 'My hero bares his nerves'. The 'page' – as both writing paper and the receptacle for sperm – is 'lovelorn', because marked by an absent presence, with the 'unruly scrawl' of ink or semen 'telling' of the 'empty ill' of writing and masturbation. Yet the unnerving absence is also, of course, a disquieting plenitude (or 'praising'), for evidence of the 'secret heat' must be disposed of, as the last line makes clear. Like Jacques Derrida's notion of the 'supplément' – broached in his discussion of Rousseau's Confessions – the signs of the 'secret heats' ostensibly complete full presence, but, in fact, also mark its absence and unobtainability: '[a] terrifying menace, the supplément has not only the power of procuring an absent presence through its image; procuring it for us by proxy [procuration] of the sign, it holds it at a distance and masters it. For this presence is at the same time desired and feared'.[48]

Like the body, masturbation has a history, as chronicled by Thomas Laqueur, and this largely consists of its post-Enlightenment construction as pathology.[49] Laqueur notes that, before the eighteenth century, masturbation was disapproved of, but for transgressing a social and divine order, which regarded as sacrosanct God's order to 'multiply' (Onan is punished for practising contraception through coitus interruptus, not for masturbation, as such). But auto-eroticism came to trouble Enlightenment thinkers who were engaged in challenging the old order, because of its apparent threat to self-discipline and care of the newly-born modern self: 'it was secret in a world in which transparency was of a premium; it was prone to excess as no other kind of venery was; the crack cocaine of sexuality; and it had no bounds in reality, because it was the creature of the imagination'.[50] Masturbation endangered modern individualism by exposing its evil twins: solipsism and anomie, and the failure to regulate one's own desires; it was the wrong kind of engagement with the self – a kind of secular waywardness. Later, in the nineteenth century, it became the sign for almost all sexual threat – a source of madness, consumption, blindness, homosexuality and death – to be countered with threats of eternal hellfire, corporal punishment, scouting and the reinvention of the chastity belt. Although by Thomas's time, the work of Freud on infant sexuality and of sexologists such as Havelock Ellis (whom he dubbed 'Havelick Pelvis') had, to some extent, tempered opinion, masturbation was still regarded as dangerous, because it was a sexual 'stage' that one might be arrested in and had, therefore, to grow out of, its immaturity counterpoised, in an either / or way, to mature, mutual sexuality (*CL*, 253).

As we have seen, Thomas made concessions to, but also confounded, this binary opposition. 'My hero' completes its self-enclosed circuit of desire within the bounds of the singular body, eschewing the usual male impulse to deny desire and project its disturbance onto the female. The poem bears out Dorinda Outram's claim that 'the creation of the heroic male public persona is impossible to understand except as a simultaneous exclusion of an imputed female body', although it does so through private auto-erotic self-authoring; the 'hero' phallus is a symbol – *the* symbol – of the public world of male achievement.[51] The usual male detachment from the flesh is short-circuited, and the 'hero' is shown beset by crisis, self-doubt and dysfunction. The transcendental signifier of the phallus, as it is found in the psychological systems of Freud and Jacques Lacan, is fused with Derridean logocentrism, but in a manner which exposes the inadequacy of the conflation of the two which feminist critics have dubbed *phallogocentrism*. For if, in Simone de Beauvoir's terms, Thomas presents his body 'immanently' in 'My hero bares his nerves' by identifying it with the gross materiality of flesh and sex (that is, in a manner which has been stereotypically cast as 'female'), rather than as something to 'transcend', in the normal manner of male writers, this move is not related to any specific female presence.[52] Ruefully, wittily, Thomas articulates an impasse in articulating this absence and the failure of phallogocentric efforts to overcome it. For the present, he cannot move from the failure of the 'heroic male persona' towards the possibilities of a female one.[53]

In 1934, Thomas's treatment of sex shifted from the largely auto-erotic, locked, gothic modernist contexts presented in *18 Poems* and (to some degree) *Twenty-five Poems*, to the inevitably more complex questions about the body and self, as raised by sexual relationships with others. *Twenty-five Poems* also reflects an understanding that sex has a different meaning for women than it does for men and at a basic bodily level. Although a more empathic involvement in this reality occurred after 1937 – and, here, the biographical circumstance of marriage is partly, if not wholly, an explanation – fear of determinism initially gave it a selfish, morbid aspect: to have children is to release a 'plague', to make oneself disposable, to admit time and hasten death (*CP*, 20) or, as the third notebook poem 'Take the needles and the knives' (September 1933) has

it, 'a child might be my slayer / And a mother in her labour / Murder
with a cry of pain' (*NP*, 189).

'A grief ago', as I showed in Chapter 2, opens by exploring anxiety
about the identities of the speaker and his lover, in a series of puns and
periphrases for the sexual act which lead to just such a 'plague' – the
'frog / Housed in the side'. It continues:

> And she who lies,
> Like exodus a chapter from the garden,
> Brand of the lily's anger on her ring,
> Tugged through the days
> Her ropes of heritage, the wars of pardon,
> On field and sand
> The twelve triangles of the cherub wind
> Engraving going.
>
> Who then is she,
> She holding me? The people's sea drives on her,
> Drives out the father from the caesared camp;
> The dens of shape
> Shape all her whelps with the long voice of water,
> That she I have,
> The country-handed grave boxed into love,
> Rise before dark.
>
> The night is near,
> A nitric shape that leaps her, time and acid;
> I tell her this: before the suncock cast
> Her bone to fire,
> Let her inhale her dead, through seed and solid
> Draw in their seas,
> So cross her hand with their grave gipsy eyes,
> And close her fist. (*CP*, 48)

This is the scenario repeated in many of Thomas's poems. Human beings
are viewed as compelled towards self-extinction by their sexual drive,
victims of their genetic material's attempts to transmit itself. Thomas
both fears and obeys this as a kind of fatality: a letter to Johnson tells
of 'The chromosomes, the colour bodies that build towards the cells of
these walking bodies, have a god in them that doesn't care a damn for
the howls of our brains. He's a wise, organic god, moving in a seasonable
cycle in the flesh ...' (*CL*, 155). In sex, for Thomas, the partner's genealogy
is involved both genetically and literally. As Freud put it, four other
people, one's own and one's partner's parents, are always in attendance

on the sexual act; Thomas however, takes this to its logical extreme, since genes contain traces of all one's ancestors. Thus, dead forebears make a literal appearance in the story 'The Map of Love', for example, and, similarly, in 'Ballad of the Long-legged Bait', the speaker's fathers' 'cling to the hand of the girl / And the dead hand leads the past … / The centuries throw back their hair / And the old men sing with newborn lips' (*CP*, 130). The dead are raised, physically reborn, each time their genetic material is transmitted.

Aware of the 'plague', the male speaker not only considers the brevity of his sexual role, but imagines its outcome, too. The concern with the embryo does not read, however, as an actual anticipation of pregnancy. 'Plague' occurs because of process; the act of sex contains within itself simultaneous, because potential, conception, birth and death. Even at this point, however, it is the woman who is plugged into the genealogical continuum, not the man; she, alone, has 'tugged through the days / Her ropes of heritage' and may 'inhale her dead' into her womb in a world of mortality symbolised by the winds, whose cherub-like features (as they appear on old maps) resemble those of the embryo, and in whose forms the inextricability of death with life is punningly suggested by 'engraving going' – the child is 'going' grave-wards from the moment of conception.

The question opening stanza four registers the speaker's exclusion, as male, from these proceedings, potential or otherwise – 'Who then is she …?'. Biological priority now means that 'she' is no longer his possession ('she who I hold'), as he believed she had become through the sexual act. On the contrary, she submits to 'the people's sea' – the genetic inheritance – of crowding ancestors, who 'drive out' the 'father' from the 'caesared camp' of the womb, as 'the dens of shape / Shape all her whelps'.[54] Though the syntax is gapped, the last lines of this stanza may be glossed:

> [in order] that [the] she [whom] I have,
> [whom] The country-handed grave boxed into love,
> [May] Rise [pregnant] before dark [death].

Thomas objected to what he saw as Edith Sitwell's misreading of these lines: they did not, as she thought, 'make the grave a gentle cultivator'; on the contrary, he was 'a tough possessor, a warring and complicated raper rather than a simple nurse or innocent gardener. I mean that the grave had a country for each hand, that it raised those hands up and "boxed" the hero of my poem into love. "Boxed" has the coffin and the pug-glove in it' (*CL*, 348). The 'countries', it should be added, both the hugeness of death and its imperative to procreate, and are the genetic ones of the two sets of ancestors – that is, the threat of death, ancestral urgings and biological imperatives have all led the pair to their sexual encounter. The final stanza confirms masculine resignation to the female role: he 'lets' her seize the past, the 'gipsy' – fortune-telling and wandering – eyes / 'I's of the dead being 'close[d]' in 'her fist', as she hands them on to future generations, but necessarily excludes him.

The poems written after 1936 begin to show a further change in Thomas's treatment of sex. As usual, it is almost impossible to isolate this as a single aspect of the poetry, bound up, fused and extended as it is with many others, and it would be wrong to simply make it a consequence of his marriage in 1937 or the birth of his and Caitlin's first child, Llewelyn, in January 1939. The latent empathic aspects I mentioned were being explored in the first poem written after the publication of *Twenty-five Poems*, 'It is the sinner's dust-tongued bell' – a poem which draws on a drowned church image-cluster associated with mortality. Although the link of sex with conception and process is continuous, rather than specific or biographical, the unborn child – the 'urchin' implicit in the 'grief' of coitus – gets the last mention in this poem, and this new emphasis is borne out by the other poems in *The Map of Love*, through their further intensification of empathy in the realisation of this figure.

This collection also introduces the theme of sexual jealousy and antagonism; and the coincidence of the two shows Thomas shifting, as it were, his own position within the Oedipal triangle from that of child to father, while at the same time attempting to increase his identification with its other two positions, those of mother and foetus / child. This process is dramatised (not to say histrionicised) in 'I make this in a warring absence', which has antagonism and jealousy as its main subject. A critically unloved poem, it is, perhaps for this very reason, one of the very few which Thomas tried to 'explain' in his correspondence.[55] According to his own gloss, it charts a couple's temporary separation, exploring the husband-speaker's feeling that his wife's 'pride in him and their proud, sexual world has been discarded ... [it] ... seems, to him, to have vanished ... perhaps, to the blind womb from which it came', reduced, that is, to a foetal or childish state ('Bread and milk mansion in a toothless town') (*CL*, 313; *CP*, 68).

This 'seems, to him' is crucial to the poem's self-questioning mode, since Thomas's account of it for Hermann Peschmann specifies the woman to be 'the crucial character (or heroine) of the narrative' (*CL*, 313). The first stanza's images for her 'pride in him' – mast, fountain, tree – can therefore be seen to announce a phallocentrism whose lack of self-awareness will be gradually unpicked. The excessive quality of the initial deflation ('corner-cast, breath's rag, scrawled weed, a vain / And opium head, crow stalk, puffed, cut, and blown') smacks of self-pity, as the following shift to consider the 'contraries' of the beloved proves. Thomas explained that the poem was 'jealously made' as an exploration of 'the fear of … future unfaithful absences', and its overblown imagery is calculated to alert us to its speaker's deficiencies: by stanza five, he is a raging Samson, who 'make[s] a weapon of an ass's skeleton' (that is, not merely its jawbone, like the biblical Samson) to 'Cudgel great air, wreck east, and topple sundown …' (CP, 68). This air is hot, as well as 'great', and leads to his collapse under the weight of vengeful rhetoric and his 'sprawl[ing] to ruin'. The deflation of sexual pride has led him to a jealous rage, which, in striking out at the beloved, has brought about his own self-induced sexual death – a kind of psychic suicide.

The subsequent burial and rebirth – as in 'Altarwise', part IX – are expressed in Thomas's best cod-Egyptian mode. 'Ruin' is now the speaker's 'proud pyramid', a mausoleum for phallic pride:

> Ruin, the room of errors, one rood dropped
> Down the stacked sea and water-pillared shade,
> Weighed in rock shroud, is my proud pyramid;
> Where, wound in emerald linen and sharp wind,
> The hero's head lies scraped of every legend,
> Comes love's anatomist with sun-gloved hand
> Who picks the live heart on a diamond. (CP, 69)

But, dead now, he can at least be reborn; a harangue by his fellow-dead in the grotesque seventh stanza makes this point in imagery already familiar from pieces such as 'A grief ago', confirming that, since his bodily form came from process ("'His mother's womb had a tongue that lapped up mud'") and ancestral genetic material ("'See,' drummed the taut masks, 'how the dead ascend'"), his sexual self will be reborn too, for "'In the groin's endless coil a man is tangled'" (CP, 69). While this is not meant to be reassuring, as it is in 'When all my five and country senses see', synaesthesia, as often is the case in Thomas, announces new insight: 'These once-blind eyes have breathed a wind of visions', the speaker claims, and he is 'pardon[ed]' by his wife's 'cloud of pride'. Sexual death will be suffered again (she is already, cloud-like, gathering the next storm, and there are 'Prides of tomorrow suckling in her eyes'), but he can now accept future conflicts, proclaiming 'Yet this I make in a forgiving presence'.

The poem, then, dramatises the overcoming of phallic anger and pride. Its verbal difficulty stems from the fact that Thomas wants us to be able to read the narrative of the speaker's pride, death and rebirth simultaneously as one of coitus, detumescence, orgasm and conception (while most critics see the poem as being an account of the husband's overcoming of 'pride', as I have described it, others view it as 'verses on the child's conception'; but the point is that, given Thomas's penchant for polysemously fusing different life-stages, it is most likely to be both of these at once).[56] Despite its difficulty, 'I make this in a warring absence' is a step away from biological fatalism towards a more self-sacrificing, erotic love, in which death is accepted as part of the cycle of being, anticipating the poetic shift announced in 'Once it was the colour of saying'.

Related concerns can be seen in four of the most ambitious poems that Thomas wrote over the following two years, 'How shall my animal' (1938), 'A saint about to fall' (1938), 'Unluckily for a death' (1939) and 'Into her lying down head' (1940). Emotionally charged, highly elaborate, ode-like in form and virtuosically mixing syllabic with stress metres, these poems are among Thomas's greatest achievements, although their complexity means they have been somewhat neglected critically. Much that has been said above of 'I make this in a warring absence' can be applied to them, however. 'Unluckily for a death' is another marriage piece, emphasising the wife's achievement in saving the speaker from different kinds of false love, figured as the 'phoenix / Under the pyre ... of my sins and days' and the 'saint carved and sensual ... Of the wintry nunnery of the order of lust'. The pair stands for the renunciation of the flesh and opportunistic promiscuity, respectively, appearing as two sides of the same 'death biding' coin ('great crotch and giant continence') (CP, 91, 92). 'Death biding', both awaiting death and fixated by it, critiques the poems of the first two collections and stresses Thomas's shift to a less 'morbid' viewpoint. 'How shall my animal', rather differently, is both a poem about writing poetry *and* an address by a mother to her child (either poem or child may be the 'animal' of the title); specifically, it is the artistic pride of the speaker which is forced to acknowledge its limitations.

'Into her lying down head', like 'I make this in a warring absence', deals with male anger. This time, jealousy at adulterous imaginings grows vividly literal and falls between the couple. While the poem's origins may lie in a blend of Thomas's puritanism and jealousy – revealingly, its working title was 'Modern Love' – his description of it for Watkins suggests wider implications (it also closely echoes the 'Watchman, How Goes the Night?' chapter of *Nightwood* referred to in Chapter 2): 'All over the world love is being betrayed as always, and a million years have not calmed the uncalculated ferocity of each betrayal or the terrible loneliness afterwards. Man is destroying his partner man or woman and whores with the whole night, begetting a monstrous brood; one day the brood will not die when the day comes but will hang onto the breast and parts and squeeze his partner out of bed' (*CL*, 516).

What Thomas is initially interested in, therefore, as in 'Our eunuch dreams', is the mental baggage we bring to sex and the role of fantasies in it. But in contrast to the 'two sleepings' of that poem, this one shows a new awareness of the complexity of the subject in the intricacy of the stanza form – the most elaborate that Thomas ever created.[57] This is the first stanza:

> Into her lying down head
> His enemies entered bed,
> Under the encumbered eyelid,
> Through the rippled drum of the hair-buried ear;
> And Noah's rekindled now unkind dove
> Flew man-bearing there.
> Last night in a raping wave
> Whales unreined from the green grave
> In fountains of origin gave up their love,
> Along her innocence glided
> Juan aflame and savagely young King Lear,
> Queen Catherine howling bare
> And Samson drowned in his hair,
> The colossal intimacies of silent
> Once seen strangers or shades on a stair;
> There the dark blade and wanton sighing her down
> To a haycock couch and the scythes of his arms
> Rode and whistled a hundred times
> Before the crowing morning climbed;
> Man was the burning England she was sleep-walking, and the
> enamouring island
> Made her limbs blind by luminous charms,
> Sleep to a newborn sleep in a swaddling loin-leaf stroked and sang
> And his runaway beloved childlike laid in the acorned sand. (*CP*, 94)

The lack of a hyphen in the titular 'lying down' means that 'down' can function as both positional ('lying-down') and adjective ('downy'); in the latter case, 'lying' would mean 'telling lies', thus activating the ambivalently treacherous and innocent nature of sex which the poem will explore. The title's 'head' can also be 'maidenhead', whichever way we read it, making the 'encumbered eyelid' and 'drum of the hair buried ear' surrealistically vaginal and hymeneal, as well as cranial.

Opening *in media res*, we divine that the couple made love 'last night' ('whales' are synecdochal figures of sexual passion and for 'Wales', hence Thomas himself; the 'fountains of origin' are sperm [as in Sperm whale], and the male has taken the form of 'a raping wave' – an allusion to the source of the name 'Dylan' in Dylan eil Ton / Dylan Son of the Wave in *The Mabinogion*). Over the course of the poem, the woman's 'innocence' has been involved in histrionic, passionate fantasies – of him as 'Juan', 'Lear' and 'Samson', herself as 'Queen Catherine' (of Russia or Aragon) – and the male speaker now imagines her fantasies or dreams as his 'enemies' entering their bed. These are collectively symbolised in the figure of a seducer, who, utilising a pun on 'blade' (dashing and cutting), conflates sex and death, across lines 16 and 17, as 'sighing' and 'scythes' suggest 'scything' and the traditional image of Death harvesting the living. Typical of Thomas's work in this sense, it is also characteristic because, as in 'A grief ago', the woman has endured the sexual attentions of the male because of her deeper biological involvement in procreation (if not necessarily her commitment to it during each sexual encounter). She has imagined sex with this figure in post-coital sleep 'a hundred times' before the morning, her limbs made 'blind' to the violation, because sex potentially leads to conception. Typically, sex, conception and birth are present in 'swaddling loin-leaf', while the male 'stroke[s] and [sings]' the woman to a 'newborn' and 'childlike' sleep, and 'laid' also describes eggs being laid – the fusion of sperm and ovum. The numerous levels – sexual, fantastic, 'childlike' and biological – undercut complacent masculinity in a passage which is at once astonishingly tenderly protective, sorrowfully alienated and agonisingly aware of the biological imperatives that drive romantic love and sexual desire. Its urgencies acquire greater keenness from being mapped onto an anticipated 'burning' England (the Blitz had not yet begun when the poem was written in the summer of 1940), and it is significant that Thomas reverses the standard reactionary symbolisation of national territory as female.

The second stanza is dominated by the 'monstrous brood' of the woman's fantasies:

> There where a numberless tongue
> Wound their room with a male moan,
> His faith around her flew undone

And darkness hung the walls with baskets of snakes,
A furnace-nostrilled column-membered
      Super-or-near man
    Resembling to her dulled sense
    The thief of adolescence,
Early imaginary half remembered
    Oceanic lover alone
Jealousy cannot forget for all her sakes ... (*CP*, 95)

'Their room', both bedroom and womb entered by the male, is an echo-chamber for the 'numberless' tongue of male fantasy images (but also, presumably, the millions of sperm), with the contrast between single and collective lovers, individual and universal, conveyed in the lack of agreement between 'numberless' and 'tongue'. Thomas deals with sexual fantasy by allowing the imaginings their full grotesque force, while 'placing' the material subtly through hints and textural detail; thus, the cartoon-like Freudian obviousness of the phallic snakes and members is hinted at by 'Super-or-near man', its excessive quality enacted by the *rime riche* 'remembered' / 'membered'. This stanza sees the male part/ner, indeed, 'squeez[ed] out of bed' by 'vanished marriages in which he had no lovely part / Nor could share, for [that is, *because of*] his pride'. As the pun on 'lovely part' ('part' as 'share' and 'genitalia') shows, fantasy is not simply being condemned. However, the psychodynamics of sexual love in this poem lead to a peculiarly violent and violating intimacy of 'blood-signed assailings' – one which is reliant on 'oceanic' archetypes – and to the objectification of the lovers as a male 'trespasser' and female 'broken bride'. At one level, 'the thief of adolescence' is the artist Augustus John, by whom Caitlin was raped at the age of fifteen (she was still under his spell in 1936 at the age of twenty-three, when she met Thomas).[58] This partly accounts for the poem's violence; the distorted and thwarted sexual instincts and lurid fantasies of the woman are the result of a patriarchal assault. It is also one reason why physical love is viewed so negatively; for the woman, every subsequent sexual act, with whatever partner, no matter how mutual or loving, founders on this trauma (this is why the male agent is implicated by 'raping wave'). But, as this also suggests, we do not need to know the biographical circumstances, in order to make sense of the poem; sex is a penetration of the male by the female, patriarchy is fixated on the phallus and, in this sense, the sexual act always has the potential to brutally elide the female.

In what seems like a move to counter this violence, the poem sets the mutuality of betrayal against a larger backdrop and salvages a sense of the woman as less guilty than the man; as the third stanza will insist: 'she lies alone and still / *Innocent* between two wars' (added emphasis). The couple are located within nature, viewed first as 'sand grains together in bed', but singly lying 'with the whole wide shore' – that is, promiscuously engaged with all the other grains. More, the 'bed' is covered by sea, which is 'nightfall with no names' – the dark, anonymous reservoir of those who appear in sex, dream and fantasy. Out of nature, a 'voice in chains declaims / The female, deadly, and male / Libidinous betrayal' (*CP*, 96). The point of this adaptation of 'the female of the species / Is deadlier than the male' is that, while one can be guilty of betrayal, it is impossible to be guilty of deadliness. The female's 'betrayal' is actually part of her altruistic subservience to biological process for the good of the species. When the 'she bird sleeping brittle by / Her lover's wings' calls to the 'treading [mating] hawk' above, even as she 'sleep[s] brittle by / Her lover's wings', this worst-of-all betrayals arises from her inability to separate the sexual act from its genetic purpose (*CP*, 96). She makes of it 'the seconds to perpetuate the stars', and this, ultimately, makes her 'innocent'.[59] With this growing realisation, the man's mourning at being supplanted by his 'incestuous secret brother' is alleviated. It may seem that the woman has been exculpated at the expense of being equated with nature, but this does not happen in the usual way, by making culture a male monopoly. True to its female-centred poetic, the poem enacts the dynamic movements of desire in both male and female, and its achievement lies in managing to preserve 'the dangerous irrationality' of the speaker's initially feverishly jealous state of mind, while also carrying its subject away from the vindictive feelings of those origins.

Some light is shed on Thomas's attempt to be true to raw, and often ugly, emotions by the ideas of Wilhelm Reich in *The Mass Psychology of Fascism* (1933). Reich reordered Freud's self of id, ego and superego as a 'biopsychic structure' of three layers: a surface layer, which is social (reserved, polite, compassionate, responsible, conscientious); a layer beneath it, corresponding to the Freudian unconscious ('that which is anti-social in man', 'a secondary result of the repression of primary biologic urges'); and, deeper in the biological substratum of the 'human animal', a 'biologic core' (which, under favourable social conditions, made her or him 'an essentially honest, industrious, co-operative, loving, and, if motivated, rationally hating animal'). The 'social tragedy of the human animal', for Reich, was the outcome of the authoritarian inhibition of direct contact between the socially co-operative surface layer and the biologic core of the human being: in a Fascist (or capitalist or Stalinist) social order, the natural libidinal and social energies, Reich maintained, were 'distorted' by the intermediate character layer – the 'cruel, sadistic, lascivious, rapacious and envious impulses', which, 'in the language of sex-economy ... represent[ed] the sum total of all so-called "secondary drives"'.[60] An 'unfortunate structuralization' meant that 'every natural, social or libidinous impulse that wants to spring into action from the biologic core has to pass through this distorting layer'. The result was that individuals' sexual energies were not only repressed, but repressed in a way which made them easy prey to a Hitler or Stalin. Indeed, for Reich, such a personality type was the usual outcome of 'the basic emotional attitude of the suppressed man of our authoritarian machine civilization and its mechanistic-mystical conception of life'.

Thomas cannot have read Reich, but the similarity of the post-Freudian models reached by dissident sensibilities in the 1930s to those discernible in his poems is striking (Georges Bataille's ideas are another example). Thomas's 'odes' on the complexity and disillusioning aspects of sexual relationships have much in common with Reich's model of the self, which replaces Freud's fixed psychic categories with historical, processual and potentially changeable ones, positing the indivisibility of political and orgasmic energy as the only effective form of resistance to repression.[61] Thomas grasps this in 'All all and all', but the poems of the late 1930s are incomparably more dynamic and fluid in their treatment of the subject. 'How shall my animal', for example, almost demands to be read in terms of Reich's 'layers', with its 'animal' drawn up from a deep 'biologic core' to the surface, having to deal with the 'perverse, sadistic character layer' figured in 'brute' masculine terms:

> How shall it magnetize,
> Towards the studded male in a bent, midnight blaze
> That melts the lionhead's heel and horseshoe of the heart,
> A brute land in the cool top of the country days
> To trot with a loud mate the haybeds of a mile,
> Love and labour and kill
> In quick, sweet, cruel light till the locked ground sprout out,
> The black, burst sea rejoice,
> The bowels turn turtle,
> Claw of the crabbed veins squeeze from each red particle
> The parched and raging voice? (*CP*, 75–6)

Although it concerns the impossibility of fully translating an inner creative impulse into a poem in the external world without killing it, this poem is equally about the nature of the self and its relationships with others. The 'perverse drives' the anima(l) must deal with are those of the 'studded male' (a macho, even sadistic, image); s/he must also 'melt' the ferocious-sounding 'lionhead's heel' and a hardened 'horseshoe' heart and endure the violent buffeting necessary to make the 'locked ground' of the 'personality layer' 'sprout out'. 'Lionhead' is a Thomas coinage, possibly alluding to Revelation 9:17: 'The heads of the horses were like lions' heads'. But it also recalls the lion-headed, Napoleon-like hero of 'Le Lion de Belfort' – the first tale in Max Ernst's surrealist collage masterpiece *Une Semaine de Bonté* (1934).[62] In Ernst's work, we follow the heroic early career and subsequent meteoric social rise of the 'lion' through various phases, before it comes to a sudden end when he murders his mistress. Tried and guillotined for his crime, one of the final plates shows the lion's head, now that of a man, being held up by the executioner – who himself has the head of a lion! Critical of male pomposity and violence as it is, Ernst also underscores the point that phallocentrism invariably reproduces itself as a system, however severely the individuals who transgress its codes are punished. Like 'I make this in a warring absence' and 'Into her lying down head', 'How shall my animal' struggles, at one level, against interpellation within such a system. The several possible senses of 'studded male', in particular, focus on this – as a verb neologised from 'stud' farm, as leather 'studded' armour (where 'male' puns on chain-'mail') and also as *studied* – masculinity as acquired behaviour. Changing the gendered and sexualised self requires thorough rewriting, and, if the narrative of death-in-victory shows this to be a near-impossibility, the language in which it is told nevertheless assumes a self which is fundamentally metamorphic and androgynous.

The fluid body: Freud, foetuses, androgyny and feminism

'Morality should be understood as the precise opposite of ethics (it is the thinking of the body in a state of language).'

– Roland Barthes, 'Roland Barthes par Roland Barthes'.

I began this chapter by suggesting that Thomas's embrace of the materiality of language and the body was, for a masculinist modernist aesthetic and its Leavisite and Movement successors, negatively 'feminine' and 'decadent'. Neoclassicist, empirical and realist in their allegiances, those adopting these positions deplored the blatancy of the body in, and of, Thomas's work. However, as I have argued, Thomas's corporeal insistences are the opposite of the mindlessness or pure instinctualism so often attributed to them. Rather, he seems to consciously exploit Blakean ambiguities and draws on attitudes to the body by writers as different as Lawrence and Huxley, as well as mediating various contemporary anxieties and non-literary discourses concerning public and private bodies. The most important of these is, of course, Freudianism. Thomas consciously played the role of 'Freudian exemplar', as Stuart Crehan has noted, in his early poems and stories, which dramatise his struggles with social, religious and sexual repression. He may only have admitted, in the *New Verse* questionnaire, to reading *The Interpretation of Dreams*, but Thomas grasped that Freud's model of the human subject was a processual one and that it could be used as part of his own hybrid self-performance. In describing his poems' 'policeman rhythms' and 'mad doctor's bag' stanzas, in a letter of April 1936 to Vernon Watkins, he chose images which reflected an engagement with Freud at both a formal and genetic level in struggles between complex constraining forms and immense verbal energies (*CL*, 249). The battle between id, ego and superego is enacted in Thomas at many levels in split selves, polysemy, pararhyme and syllabic schemes, parapraxis, associative chains, dream-logic and so on, while the open-ended, irresolvable nature of inner conflict is frequently figured in paradox.

Revealingly, however, specific Freudian scenarios and motifs are harder to trace. There is certainly a strong element of castration anxiety on display in poems such as 'When, like a running grave'. 'My world is pyramid' seems to offer a version of the primal scene of parents surprised in the act of sex, one resulting in the conception of the poem's speaker ('Rotating halves ... horning as they drill / The arterial angel'), and its title may, in fact, allude to the Oedipal triangle (*CP*, 27), Certainly, we can see how this, and other poems, such as 'My hero bares his nerves', represent a speaker locked in a round of auto-erotic sexual selving, seeking empowerment through the exercise of the pen-as-penis. On occasions, this search seems at the expense of a father who is both minatory sky-god (the Jupiter Pluvius figure of 'Before I knocked', swinging his phallic 'rainy hammer') and the near-pitiable ghost already passing into ancestral memory of 'I fellowed sleep' ('An old, mad man still climbing in his ghost / My father's ghost is climbing in the rain') (*CP*, 11, 25). There are even autobiographical traces: Thomas works his own name into some poems, and 'Jack my fathers' must refer to D. J., 'Jack', Thomas (*CP*, 55). However, as Elder Olson noted as early as 1954, Thomas resists even as he incorporates elements of the Freudian model. While his symbolism, for example, can at times be Freudian (genital towers, worms, candles, rods and womb-tombs), it is inconsistently so and often contradicts Freud (ladders symbolise spiritual ascent, not intercourse; fruit symbolises children, not the breast).[63] Above all, the Oedipal struggle is muted in Thomas's work, partly, as I have suggested, because the son's fantasy of killing the father and gaining access to the mother has already been achieved, with the poem's linguistic materiality and *jouissance* appearing as a realisation of the plenitude of her body. The parricidal impulse is more likely to appear as aggression towards God on behalf of his 'doublecrossed' Son, albeit he is a version of Everyman and Thomas himself (*CP*, 12).

While he is then, in certain ways, the most Freudian poet of the 1930s, Thomas's relationship to psychoanalysis is partial and opportunistic, even parodic. Freudian scenarios are broached, only to be modified or dismissed. 'Do you not father me', for example, begins with a speaker who has the identity of a 'tall tower' – a Thomas symbol for adolescent solipsism – who asks his parents to confirm their responsibility for his conception and birth:

> Do you not father me, nor the erected arm
> For my tall tower's sake cast in her stone?
> Do you not mother me, nor, as I am,
> The lovers' house, lie suffering my stain? (*CP*, 42)

These are standard Freudian anxieties, although it is worth noting the gendering of the tower as 'her'. This complication now increases in a series of questions: did his parents not also 'sister me' and 'brother me', he asks? This increases further, when the parental and sibling identities are claimed by the speaker: 'Am I not father too, and the ascending boy, / The boy of woman and a wanton starer ... Am I not sister too ... Am I not all of you ... ?' (*CP*, 42). His parents reply that 'You are all of these', but this hardly settles the narrative. The tower speaks in its own voice to tell of the 'raz[ing]' of its 'wooden folly', followed by 'man-begetters ... ris[ing] grimly from the wrack'. In the final stanza, the 'seaweedy' shore tells him he is 'your sisters' sire', before there is a final assurance – if that is what it is – that 'Love's house ... and the tower death / Lie all unknowing of the grave sin-eater'. Oedipus was the 'sire' of 'sisters', yet this is followed by the assertion that the speaker is also 'The salt sucked dam', female and a mother. The punning 'dam' suggests that the narrative is obeying a verbal 'working from words' logic, as much as any Freudian schema, just as in stanza three, when the tower is razed / raised by a 'stroke' or stroking. In the last stanza of the poem, the emphasis is squarely on the liminal location of 'love's house' on the 'destroying sand' of the shore, rather than on land or sea. In short, Freudian elements – the phallus, narcissism, castration anxiety, incest – are sampled, but never cohere, subordinated as they are to the 'ascending boy' and his process-oriented interrogation of origins beside 'the directed sea'.

This is not only because of Thomas's well-known aversion to systems, but also because his interest in the body often lay in areas which Freud largely ignored; namely, the female body, the foetus and the neonate. In the 1930s, Thomas was particularly fascinated with the unborn; indeed, they are the main subject in a dozen of the ninety-one poems in the *Collected Poems*, and another dozen have antenatal references. Partly, this was because such a plastic phase of human development was amenable to the process poetic. Not only was foetal phylogeny then believed to recapitulate the ontology of the species, passing in nine months through the course of human evolution, but it allows for numerous links and parallels with the ancestral past, with the adolescent's 'birth' into adult sexuality and, as a pre-birth stage, with sleep and death. What do the unborn dream about? What do they know? Do they foresee those who will love them, their lives to come and their deaths? In 'Before I knocked', the embryo already '[smells] the maggot in [its] stool'. Similarly, in 'Then was my neophyte', a foetus sees a film of its own death projected onto the womb-wall (*CP*, 58).[64] There are familiar elements of the avant-garde fantasy of self-authoring, of *couvade*, and of the outsider's attempt to be born in a smothering national culture in this strain of Thomas's work. But to trace its development from, say, 'Where once the twilight locked' to 'If my head hurt a hair's foot' and 'Vision and Prayer' is to see how, as in his treatment of sex, development and birth, disgusted relish gives way to empathy, while nevertheless maintaining the earlier respect for the sheer difference and otherness of life in the womb.

Thomas's interest in this subject culminates with the seven of sixteen poems in *The Map of Love* devoted to it.[65] They are notable for an imaginative variety and ingenuity that was probably fostered by the imminence of the Second World War and the birth of his first child (Llewelyn) in January 1939. Perhaps the most remarkable of the poems, 'A saint about to fall', was written in September 1938 – the month of the Munich Agreement. Like other such poems, it conflates the child's birth-to-be with the orgasmic moment which made its conception possible in one of Thomas's most astounding lines – 'Glory cracked like a flea'. Unlike them, however, it addresses the child directly, punningly asking it to 'wake in' its father by bearing witness to 'The skull of the earth ... barbed with a war of burning brains and hair' (*CP*, 79). For as the child falls into life from the ruined heaven of the womb, the poem says, it will find the rubble of the already warring world below rising up to meet it. Virtuosically, but movingly, Thomas weaves together both womb- and world-scapes, the elemental terms of the former with the latter's 'carbolic city', bombed towns, annexations, poverty and almost-defeated Spanish Republic:

> Strike in the time-bomb town,
> Raise the live rafters of the eardrum,
> Throw your fear a parcel of stone
> Through the dark asylum,
> Lapped among herods wail
> As their blade marches in
> That the eyes are already murdered,
> The stocked heart is forced, and agony has another mouth to feed.
> O wake to see, after a noble fall,
> The old mud hatch again, the horrid
> Woe drip from the dishrag hands and the pressed sponge of the forehead,
> The breath draw back like a bolt through white oil
> And a stranger enter like iron.
> Cry joy that this witchlike midwife second
> Bullies into rough seas you so gentle
> And makes with a flick of the thumb and sun
> A thundering bullring of your silent and girl-circled island. (*CP*, 79–80)

Plummeting to its sublunary existence, the 'saint' flies the defiance of its first cry to 'strike' and 'raise' the world and those in it and may deceive the Saturn-like, offspring-devouring fear of the time that it enters, 'wail' injustice at those whose loss of selfhood has turned into things (their I / 'eyes' 'already murdered'). The desperate ambiguity of 'wake in' is now intensified in 'raise' / raze, 'lapped' (protected / devoured) and 'stocked' (well-prepared / put in the stocks), as the birth is imagined, a sponge at the sweating forehead of the mother in labour. The big question that the poem asks is: how can one bring a child – 'Bull[y]' it – into the 'rough seas' of a world of such misery and violence? There is no answer apart from the brilliant enactment of the interconnectedness of historical trauma and joy at birth (Thomas told Watkins that the words 'Cry joy' were the most important in the poem): even the 'iron' exit from the womb, with its oiled 'bolt' and 'flick of the thumb', approximates the readying of a gun for firing (*LVW*, 45).

The 'saint' so powerfully realised for its paralysed epoch strangely resembles another agonised, not-quite-redemptive, otherworldly visitant

– the 'Angel of History' of the ninth of Walter Benjamin's famous 'Theses on the Philosophy of History', a work finished just over a year later in spring 1940.[66] Their similarity is not only figurative and philosophical – like Benjamin's angel and Paul Klee's 'Angelus Novus', the saint, too, is caught in a 'storm … blowing from Paradise' and views a 'catastrophe', which hurls wreckage at his feet, unable to 'make whole what has been smashed' – but rests in the poem's extraordinary fusion of terror with rhythmic buoyancy and linguistic richness to create an equivalent of Benjamin's glimpse of potential messianic light in historical darkness – the 'strait gate', through which, even now, hope may enter to overcome pessimism and defeat. It is this residual possibility which informs 'If my head hurt a hair's foot' and 'Twenty four years', the poems which follow 'A saint about to fall' in *The Map of Love*. Both grant the power 'beyond choice in the dust-appointed grain' to biological determinism, as in the first two collections, but the first poem allows the foetus an incongruous, yet noble and moving offer to sacrifice itself, in order to spare its mother the pangs of labour, while in the second, the embryo (notably, the twenty-four-year-old Thomas, too) exuberantly embraces the 'meat-eating sun' and 'In the final direction of the elementary town … advance[s] for as long as forever is' (*CP*, 81).

One of the most distinctive aspects of Thomas's presentation of the foetus is its emphasis on its fluid identity as a 'sea hermaphrodite' (*CP*, 57). The embryo is, of course, basically female: maleness is a later complication, which increases vulnerability to disease and degeneracy. Thomas's concern, here, is not simply with a symbol for the androgynous nature of the artist's imagination: if the mother of 'If my head' addresses the child in her womb as 'my daughter or son', it is not only because she does not know its sex, but because Thomas wants to stress sexual and gender uncertainty and inbetweenness. When the speaker of 'Before I knocked' claims 'I … Was brother to Mnetha's daughter / And sister to the fathering worm', he, too, is underlining what Andrew Lycett calls Thomas's 'fascination with hermaphroditism'.[67] And in 'My world is pyramid', which puns on the Latin root of 'bisect' from *sectare*, meaning sex, the speaker, as Jean-Michel Rabaté points out, is fundamentally bisexual.[68]

The hermaphrodite qualities of the embryo, like the 'polymorphous perversity' of desire that Freud attributed to the infant, are taken by Thomas to apply to the human condition generally. This follows the logic of process, according to which the qualities of each separate stage of development are present in all others; as we have seen, Thomas often queries the ego-armour of the male self and, with it, the masculine, cerebral outlook of dominant critical discourses. Indeed, it is possible to see in his writing, broadly speaking, a form of *écriture féminine*, subversive of what Hélène Cixous, in 'The Laugh of the Medusa', mockingly dubbed 'glorious, phallic monosexuality'.[69] This is not to say, of course, that Thomas's writing is free from misogyny; lines such as 'Sin who had a woman's shape' and 'Frogs and satans and woman-luck' spring to mind (*CP*, 129, 111). Nor is it to claim, either, that Cixous's own formulae, which tend towards Romantic essentialism, are unproblematic. Nevertheless, Thomas's celebration of the female amounts to more than simply identifying, in a vaguely positive way, women with nature and nurture. One of the major reasons for this is his work's unrelenting oppugnancy to any, and all, binaries. Even very early poems, such as 'I see the boys of summer', involve confounding the binary systems which Cixous and others have shown are the basis of patriarchy. Another is Thomas's taste for linguistic excess, grotesquerie and gender ambiguity, which undermine masculine self-possession and self-presence and reveal the anxieties it masks and the repressions which maintain it.

This is clearest in the early fictions. In 'The Vest', for example, the climactic moment occurs when the madman who has murdered his wife enters a pub bar populated solely by women and reveals his crime by pulling out the blood-stained vest. Elsewhere, as in 'The Dress', male violence against women is presented as insanity, with woman as a healing force. Even Gwladys, the leader of the coven in 'The School for Witches', and Mrs Owen, in 'The Enemies', are the dominant characters in those fictions and, to some extent, operate critically upon a patriarchal, dualistic concept of women. In his letters, Thomas could reveal a period anxiety about his masculinity and even the perceived threat of homosexuality to it.[70] But this rarely took either a sexist or homophobic form, and, as Katie Gramich notes, he showed a dislike of socially prescribed gender roles and identities, and often shows his dissatisfaction with the burden of shouldering a singular, 'pure', heterosexual, male identity.[71] Insofar as the gothic-grotesque formula allowed it, the early fiction tends to question the female stereotypes created by Nonconformism repression and critically examines male complicity in them. In 'The Mouse and the Woman', for example, the protagonist believes he has written a woman into existence – 'Out of him had come another. A being had been born not out of the womb but out of the soul and the spinning head'. But when she appears and loves him, he is seized by puritanical fear and so un-writes her, because her nakedness 'was not good to look upon'. He, too, is driven mad. Not only is the inability to countenance female sexuality shown to be deranging, but the female character is made to present the Blakeian case for nakedness and the free expression of desire which Thomas makes in his letters of the time (*CS*, 77, 82). The tale also, significantly, mocks the fantasy of male self-authoring or 'womb envy'. Still more subversively, in 'The Peaches' (in which Aunt Annie is referred to as 'Mrs Jesus'), 'The Mouse and the Woman' and 'The Orchards', Thomas hints at the possibility of a female Christ.

This acknowledgement of male incompletion and association of the masculine with misogyny and deathliness propelled Thomas towards a more positive representation of women in *A Portrait of the Artist as a Young Dog*. 'Patricia, Edith and Arnold' and 'One Warm Saturday' describe female solidarity and empowerment in a recognisably realist and social milieu. Women also get to speak or are sympathetically ventriloquised in poems of this period. 'If my head hurt a hair's foot' is a dialogue of mother and child, while in 'After the funeral (For Anne Jones)', a poor and insignificant woman is named and granted her own royal bard. Thomas wrestles with the constraints of masculinity, particularly in the form of sexual jealousy and possessiveness (as we have seen) in poems of the early 1940s, such as 'Into her lying down head'. If the populist nature of his radio writing meant that it sometimes insuffi-ciently problematised the stereotypes it used, the later work is better represented by the self-mockery of 'Lament' and *Under Milk Wood*. As Gramich puts it: '"Little Willie Wee" ... [has a] presumably modest endowment ... [but is] ... preferred by Polly Garter to Tom, "strong as a bear and two yards long"'.[72] The most explicit expression of empathy is the passionate and elegiac identification of the speaker with the dead, childless women in 'In the White Giant's thigh', the final poem in the 1952 *Collected Poems*.

Feminist ideas inform the revaluation of Thomas and the body that I have attempted in this chapter, linking the thematics of female represen-tation to Thomas's radical and subversive poetic practice, the 'female' aspects of his writing *style*, in its linguistic materiality and 'narcissism'. Yet I am aware that my attempts have raised many more cruxes and questions than I have been able to answer. To take just one: can the 'female Jesus' be seen as an aspect of the wound symbolism and imagery found more generally in Thomas's work? And, if Thomas conflates Christ's wound with the female genitalia in his writing, does this amount to a positive feminisation of the oppressively patriarchal aspects of

Christianity? Or does it merely reinforce a traditional patriarchal typing of the vagina as a wound – a site of castration? My own sense is that the answers lie in Thomas's use of Oedipal and castration symbolism, which several critics have identified without linking to the wound imagery. That symbolism begins, conventionally enough, in the image of the *Struwwelpeter* of 'When, like a running grave'. It appears more glancingly in 'My world is pyramid' and 'Altarwise by owl-light', with 'braiding adders [loosed] from ... hairs' and a 'black medusa' – allusions to the snaky coiffure which Freud read as a multiple phallic symbol, petrific because representing the castration threat that women posed as castrated males. (*CP*, 27, 60)

Thomas increasingly revised the prioritisation of the male in this castration scenario in a way which anticipates later, post-feminist theorists.[73] As Angela Carter argues in *The Sadeian Woman*, the function of imaginary castration in the hands of Freud and his followers had been to type women as wounded creatures, who were born to bleed; in the symbolic economy of patriarchy, it thus plays a crucial role in denying them full human status. Thomas's work reverses this move; refusing to deny the wound *qua* wound, it nevertheless presents it as the mark of the human, rather than of the not-quite-human. In Thomas, the mark of the human – whether male or female – is a wound, the capacity to bleed, to be a 'sufferer with the wound' (*CP*, 113). Life is a movement towards 'the ambush of [one's] wounds', 'the woundward flight of the ancient young' and a 'whole pain [that] / Flows open' (*CP*, 145, 119). Hence, the special nature of Christ's wound; it is the sign of his humanity, which is, in turn, synonymous with his or her dual gender and, as the 'Thief' of 'In country sleep', s/he finds a way to steal innocence as the winged / Apple seed glides, / And falls, and flowers in the yawning wound at our sides' (*CP*, 140). (The wound is even given to Mary in 'Altarwise', going beyond sympathy to solidarity against the 'imaginary fact' that 'pervades the whole of men's attitudes towards women and women's attitudes to themselves'.)[74] Finally, the wound is writerly, allowing Thomas's own identification with Christ and the female – the rupture between word and self being a wound from which wordshed flows.

In conclusion, while the 'death-sex-time trap' continued to 'epitomize the human condition' for Thomas at the end of the 1930s, the female body – previously the site of many of the terrors that the 'trap' induced – became a site of resistance to it.[75] This is one of the themes of the tormented uxoriousness of the 'odes' of 1938 and 1940 ('How shall my animal', 'Into her lying down head', 'Unluckily for a death' and 'A saint about to fall'), as heralded by 'I make this in a warring absence'. If the stylistic shift of 1938 was largely the result of Thomas reaching certain absolute stylistic limits, it was also accompanied by this switch from phallic anxiety to wounded solidarity. The switch matched a more general surge in British culture in the currency and use of positive female images and archetypes in the later 1930s (often the earth itself was presented as regeneratively female). David Jones's *In Parenthesis* (1937) – its 'Queen of the Woods' sequence in particular – reflected a crucial step away from earlier representations of the earth as a devouring bitch-goddess in writing about the Great War. (Thomas was a reader of the BBC radio broadcast of the poem in 1938.) This was of a piece with the biomorphic trend in British culture, which Thomas pioneered in poetry and which had been present and increasingly marked in visual art throughout the decade. Finally, it is worth noting that Jungian (archetypal) psychology was beginning to displace Freudianism; the wartime New Apocalypse and neo-Romantic poets, for example, would take their cue from Jung, as well as from Thomas.

The rootedness of Thomas's poetry in the body and his refusal to separate mind / spirit from the flesh leads to a definition of selfhood which is sexual, but increasingly orientated towards the other, whether as female or, through the increasing humanisation of the foetus, as child. The bodily materiality of its language and its ability to resist easy consumption are what allow it to resist the false universals of gender stereotypes and sexual archetypes, even as it explores them, thus abstracting, rather than mystifying, sexual relationships and yielding to a mutable sense of identity at odds with the prison of rigidly bounded male selfhood found in much mid-century poetry. It moves from the anatomical to the erotic – meaning, by 'erotic', the overcoming of inhibited, superego-dominated aspects of the poetic of 'exuberant loss'.[76] By the outbreak of the war, as we shall see in Chapter 5, this procreative sexual body could offer to counter the coming slaughter a 'soft, / Unclenched, armless, silk and rough love that breaks all rocks' (*CP*, 103, 105).[77] Before we can fully understand Thomas's response to the war, however, it will first be necessary to look at the specifically Welsh dimensions of his writing of the body, religion and surrealism.

Notes

1 W. H. Auden, *The English Auden*, ed. Edward Mendelson (London: Faber, 1989), p. 261.

2 Thomas's intransigent physicality is apparent, even in his defence of the right to write about it. Asked to censor of some of his early stories, he invoked a public body, by way of asserting the rights of individual ones, stating: 'I'd rather tickle the cock of the English public than lick its arse' (*CL*, 371).

3 Peter Nicholls, *Modernisms: A Literary Guide* (London: Macmillan, 1995), pp. 195–6.

4 Peter Nicholls, *Modernisms: A Literary Guide*, pp. 201–2.

5 Peter Nicholls, *Modernisms: A Literary Guide*, p. 195.

6 Revealingly, it was Holbrook – Thomas's most persistent assailant – who published one of the first book-length studies of Plath, *Sylvia Plath: Poetry and Existence* (1976). As Jacqueline Rose notes, this is 'supremely representative of the [chauvinistic] sexual imaginary precipitated by Plath's work' and 'reveals … starkly the sexual fantasy which underpins one form of attack on feminism by the Right.' Jacqueline Rose, *The Haunting of Sylvia Plath* (London: Virago, 1992), p. 19.

7 Geoffrey Grigson, 'How Much Me Now Your Acrobatics Amaze', ed. E. W. Tedlock, *Dylan Thomas: The Legend and the Poet* (London: Heinemann, 1963), p. 160.

8 Graves also noted that: 'While Dylan Thomas may not actually have had syphilis, *philosophically* he was riddled with it'. Martin Seymour-Smith, *Robert Graves: His Life and Work* (London: Paladin Collins, 1987), p. 373. But see my Introduction for Graves's ambivalence on Thomas.

9 Sylvia Plath, *Collected Poems* (London: Faber, 1990), p. 254.

10 Richard Kearney, *Modern Movements in European Philosophy* (Manchester: Manchester University Press, 1986 [repr. 1987]), pp. 73–4.

11 William T. Moynihan, *The Craft and Art of Dylan Thomas* (Ithaca, NY: Cornell University Press, 1966), p. 163.

12 Embodied cognition brings together body and mind after their separation by Skinnerian behaviourism. As it is now understood, cognition does not consist of a consciousness capable of detachment from its physical habitus, so making affect unquantifiable and meaningless. Rather, it appears that body and mind constitute a continuum, that emotions, inextricably binding both, are central to cognition, rational decision-making and species survival, while consciousness can only perceive and construe the world through its embodiment. As Lakoff and Johnson have argued, this can be shown to extend to language, which is fundamentally shaped by 'conceptual metaphors' stemming from cognition's inescapably physical dimension. See George Lakoff and Mark Johnson, *Metaphors We Live By* (Chicago, IL: University of Chicago Press, 1980). For a full account of the senses of 'embodiment', see Tim Rohrer, 'The Body in Space: Dimensions of Embodiment'. See http://zakros.ucsd.edu/~troher/thebodyinspace.pdf. For a more general account of the scientific reversal of behaviourism and Cartesianism, this can be found in Anthony Damasio's *Descartes' Error* and *The Feeling of What Happens*.

13 Cited in http://www.nytimes.com/2003/04/19/books/i-feel-therefore-i-am. html?pagewanted=all&src=pm. This article – a summary of research – cites Jonathan Bate on 'the key neurophysiological insight of our time for students

of the humanities', namely the new opposition to the split between corpus and cogito and the consequent disdain for the body as machine or sink of corruption in Cartesian science and Judaeo-Christian theology.

14 John Barnie, editor of the Welsh journal *Planet*, has argued that: 'all [Thomas's] ... stuff about sex and death, and so on, was part of growing up in a world where sex was a taboo subject. It seemed daring to refer to it obliquely ... in modernist or symbolist imagery. But it's really the worst kind of provincialism masquerading as international modernism'. However, as Patrick Crotty trenchantly noted, this inverts the reality. Thomas's resonance shows that he overcame provinciality by forging a pioneering modernist poetry of the body out of the miseries of repression in a religiously fearful culture: 'his success in identifying universal implications in the contingencies of his native environment, that is to say, place him at the furthest possible remove from provincialism'. See Patrick Crotty, 'Falling off the Edge', *Planet*, 129 (June / July 1998), p. 14.

15 The poem, slightly misquoted by Thomas, is Ezra Pound's 'Fratres Minores'. The full text reads:

With minds still hovering above their testicles
Certain poets here and there in France
Still sigh over established and natural fact
Long since fully discussed by Ovid.
They howl. They complain in delicate and exhausted metres
That the twitching of three abdominal nerves
Is incapable of producing a lasting Nirvana.

Ezra Pound, *Collected Shorter Poems* (London: Faber, 1968), p. 168. Pound's poem stayed with Thomas: the verses beginning 'O Chatterton and others in the attic', within in a letter to Henry Treece of 16 June 1938, include the line 'Love's a decision of 3 nerves' (*CL*, 353).

16 Tim Armstrong, *Modernism, Technology and the Body: A Cultural Study* (Cambridge: Cambridge University Press, 1998), pp. 2–3.

17 It is worth adding that, as Tim Armstrong points out (citing Jean-Luc Nancy), 'the field which recent theory has labelled "writing the body" often occludes and dehistoricizes' the relationship between body and texts, ignoring modernity's own thinking on embodiment, and 'there is an incommensurability between the body and discourse ... mention of "the written body" obscures the fact that the body is not the locus of writing'. See Tim Armstrong, *Modernism, Technology and the Body*, p. 6.

18 Thomas's opposition to New Country revealingly found expression in bodily terms. Thus, his claim that: 'the emotional appeal in Auden wouldn't raise the corresponding emotion in a tick', for example, insinuates poetic anaemia and lack of passion, while Spender's alleged inability to 'get into contact with society' is attributed to his inability to 'get into contact with himself', because '[he] has only tickled his own outside with a feather' (*CL*, 121, 328).

19 Martin Dodsworth, 'The Concept of Mind and the Poetry of Dylan Thomas', ed. Walford Davies, *Dylan Thomas: New Critical Essays* (London: Dent, 1972), p. 112.

20 William Blake, 'There is No Natural Religion [First Series]', ed. Geoffrey Keynes, *The Poetry and Prose of William Blake* (London: Nonesuch Press, 1927 [repr. 1946]), p. 147.

21 William Blake, 'There is No Natural Religion [Second Series]', ed. Geoffrey Keynes, *The Poetry and Prose of William Blake*, p. 148.

22 Martin Dodsworth, 'The Concept of Mind and the Poetry of Dylan Thomas', p. 113.

23 William Blake, 'The Voice of the Devil', *The Marriage of Heaven and Hell*, ed. Geoffrey Keynes, *The Poetry and Prose of William Blake*, p. 182.

24 D. H. Lawrence, *The Plumed Serpent* (Harmondsworth: Penguin, 1961), p. 196.

25 Angela Carter, *The Sadeian Woman and the Ideology of Pornography* (London: Virago, 1987), p. 11.

26 Dorinda Outram, *The Body and the French Revolution: Sex, Class and Political Culture* (New Haven and London: Yale University Press, 1989), p. 1. In what follows, I am indebted to Outram's lucid study, particularly Chapter 1, 2 and 9.

27 Dorinda Outram, *The Body and the French Revolution*, p. 8.

28 Martin Dodsworth, 'The Concept of Mind and the Poetry of Dylan Thomas', p. 121.

29 Neil Corcoran, *English Poetry since 1940* (London: Longman, 1993), p. 45.

30 Thus, 'the world of a large part of Thomas's poetry is one in which the body narcissistically delights in its own sexuality' simply seems to mean that Thomas should focus more on an empirical external world, it being deemed improper to self-analyse (or play with oneself). Neil Corcoran, *English Poetry since 1940* (London: Longman, 1993), p. 43. However, the loose usage leads to a lack of critical nuance. Merely to deal with Freud's definition of narcissism, as I do here, leads us to the important distinction between primary and secondary narcissism. Each has a bearing on Thomas. On the one hand, primary narcissism is not only essential to human self-worth, but, as Peter Nicholls observes, it was deployed as a tactic by marginal writers, such as Mina Loy, Hilda Doolittle (H. D.) and Dorothy Richardson, to counter the phallocentric aesthetic of the male high modernists, since it can provide a legitimate route towards 'an ideal construction of the self, one which might free her from the "whirling" and "swirling" of hysteria'. Peter Nicholls, *Modernisms: A Literary Guide*, pp. 201–2. On the other hand, secondary narcissism may take megalomaniac, but also abject, forms, and the latter, explored by Freud in *Mourning and Melancholia*, offer crucial insights into the Blitz elegies that Thomas was to write, as I discuss in Chapter 5.

31 Geoffrey Grigson, 'Recollections of Dylan Thomas', ed. John Malcolm Brinnin, *A Casebook on Dylan Thomas* (New York, NY: T. Y. Crowell, 1961), p. 256. According to the terms of Grigson's article, if you surrender to such compulsions, you become a baby or 'suckling', 'inhuman' and 'out of humanity' – that is, nothing *but* gland (this is how I understand 'the Disembodied Gland' – one of his names for Thomas).

32 Thomas's friend Daniel Jones claimed that Thomas lacked interest in any systematic study 'with names ending in -ology, -onomy, -ography, osophy, -ic, -ics, or even, to a large extent, just -y (history, botany)', and the standard view of him is of someone who was technologically and scientifically illiterate. As I note in the Introduction, however, Thomas had read popular science books on physics and cosmology, as well as psychology and biology and was also aware of the concepts that we associate with modernist ideas about time and space. See Daniel Jones, *My Friend Dylan Thomas* (London: Dent, 1977), p. 55.

33 Ernest Henry Starling (1866–1927), a British physiologist, coined the word 'hormone' (from the Gk. *hormo* = I arouse to activity) in 1902. He was, with William Bayliss, the first person to identify and name a hormone (secretin). In 1912, Edward Sharpey-Schafer discovered the role of hormones in regulating bodily activity. The 1920s and 1930s saw the identification and use of insulin (in 1921 and 1926); the description of thyroxin (1926); the gonadtrophin (that is, hormonal) pregnancy test

(1927); the isolation of a pure female sex hormone – estrone (1929) – and of a pure male sex hormone – androsterone (1931); the isolation of progesterone (1934); and the synthesis of testosterone (1935).

34 In 1920, Eugen Steinach had concluded that unilateral vasoligation (severing and knotting) of the *ductus deferens* (sperm duct), or vasectomy, produced an increase in testicular hormonal production. His 'auto-plastic' treatment for 'middle-aged, listless individuals' became a popular surgical operation over the next two decades. The most publicised form of surgery was animal gland implants (the so-called 'monkey-gland' treatment), pioneered by Sergei Voronoff and popularised in the US by the Kansas quack 'Goat Gland Brinkley'. (The addition of soundtracks to silent films that had been completed, but overtaken by the invention of the Talkies before they could be released, was also known as 'goat-glanding', so it is a term that Thomas may have encountered as a film buff.)

35 It was also clear that physiological and hormonal identities did not always match. The richest source of oestrogen, it turned out, was the urine of a stallion; and both female and male hormones were present in the bodies of each sex. It was also found that the balance of male and female sex hormones present depended upon a range of glands, not just the ovaries and testes, all controlled by the little-understood pituitary. Similar uncertainties are reflected in Thomas's work, in which, as I show below, gender is frequently indeterminate, fluid or androgynous.

36 Aldous Huxley, *Brave New World* (London: Chatto, 1984). The general importance of Huxley's novel to Thomas's writing has, like other science-related texts, hitherto been overlooked.

37 See Donald J. Childs, *Modernism and Eugenics: Woolf, Eliot, Yeats, and the Culture of Degeneration* (Cambridge: Cambridge University Press, 2001), p. 11. As Childs notes (p. 4), eugenics was: 'positioned by writers from the 1880s to the 1930s to assume responsibility for a creation recently orphaned by the death of God'.

38 The Nazis passed their Eugenic Sterilisation Law on 1 January 1933.

39 Norbert Elias, *The Civilizing Process: Sociogenetic and Psychogenetic Investigations*, transl. Edmund Jephcott, eds. Eric Dunning, Johan Goudsblom and Stephen Mennell (London: Blackwell, 2000), p. 472.

40 Norbert Elias, *The Civilizing Process*, p. 472.

41 Norbert Elias, *The Civilizing Process*, p. 480.

42 William York Tindall, *A Reader's Guide to Dylan Thomas* (New York, NY: Syracuse University Press, 1962 [repr. 1996]), p. 43.

43 Ivan Phillips, 'I Sing the Bard Electric', *Times Literary Supplement* (19 September 2003), pp. 14–15.

44 It is less sombrely treated in the letters. To Trevor Hughes in the spring of 1934, he wrote: 'Our words – "give me a half-pint, a Hovis, a book by Paul de Kock, and thou, thou old lavatory chain" – are spells to drag up the personified Domdaniel pleasure. Everything we do drags up a devil' (*CL*, 144–5). The details of this are echoed in 'My hero bares his nerves', which was probably revised at this time.

45 Following Ralph Maud, I read the 'unborn devil' of the preceding stanza as speaking in this final stanza of the poem – a Thomas-persona conceding the deathliness of his world. That deathliness includes his 'salt unborn' self, which I also take, following Thomas's characteristic conflation of adolescent and foetal states, to be semen. See Ralph Maud, *Where Have the Old Words Got Me?*, pp. 183–8. In light of the poem's Egyptian imagery and Thomas's interest in recent discoveries about

ancient Egypt, it is also worth noting that, as Northrop Frye observes: 'Egyptian mythology begins with a god who creates the world by masturbation'. Northrop Frye, *Anatomy of Criticism* (London: Penguin, 1990), p. 156.

46 Ralph Maud cites Eric Partridge's *A Dictionary of Slang and Unconventional English* – as his authority and notes, also, 'the male nerve was pulled alone' in the short story 'The Holy Six' and 'cistern sex' in the third notebook. Ralph Maud, *Where Have the Old Words Got Me?*, pp. 82–3. There are Shakespearean precedents in *Macbeth* ('the cistern of my lust') and *Othello* ('a cistern for foul toads').

47 The 'hunger's emperor', the penis hanging between the two testicles, those 'sad knaves of thieves' is also the 'castrated Saviour' that Thomas referred to in a letter of the week of 11 November 1933 to Pamela Hansford Johnson (*CL*, 72).

48 Jacques Derrida, *Of Grammatology*, transl. and intro. Gayatri Chakrovorty Spivak (Baltimore, MD: The Johns Hopkins University Press, 1976), p. 155.

49 Thomas W. Laqueur, *Solitary Sex: A Cultural History of Masturbation* (Cambridge: MIT Press, 2003).

50 Thomas W. Laqueur, *Solitary Sex*, p. 4.

51 Dorinda Outram, *The Body and the French Revolution*, p. 41.

52 John Goodby and Chris Wigginton eds., *Dylan Thomas: New Casebook*, p. 68.

53 Thomas's defenders do his work no favours by diminishing its auto-erotic dimension. There is bravery in this aspect of his work, but Ralph Maud's claim that 'The process poems, which one expects to be merely morbidly descriptive, turn out to be, on the whole, moral and manly' achieves the peculiar distinction of making him sound like some *Boys' Own Paper* hero (*NP*, 38).

54 The 'sea' is invariably Darwinian – the evolutionary source of life – in Thomas (as well as, variously, the unconscious, a symbol of 'masculine' roughness and 'female' fecundity, a source of poetry and a place of imprisonment). 'On no work of words' , for example specifically relies on our knowledge of Darwin's hypothesis that seawater is the evolutionary origin of blood in fish and land animals, since its speaker calls on his own blood to de-evolve, should he deny his poetic gift: 'Ancient woods of my blood dash down to the nut of the seas / If I take to burn or return this world which each man's work' (*CP*, 78). As Clark Emery notes: '[Thomas] sees the history of man in scientific terms; as a slow development from primitive sea-born simplicity to its present land-locked complexity … recapitulated in each individual'. Clark Emery, *The World of Dylan Thomas* (Coral Gables, FL: University of Florida Press, 1962), p. 24. More bluntly, Maud asserts: '[A grief ago'] is not about sex, it is about DNA'. Ralph Maud, *Where Have the Old Words Got Me?*, p. 10.

55 In letters to Hermann Peschmann and Desmond Hawkins of January 1938 and August 1939, respectively, (*CL*, 313–14; 449–50). Into the Hawkins letter, Thomas also copied a passage from his explanation, written in March 1938 for Henry Treece, of the 'breeding' nature of his imagery.

56 Linden Huddlestone, 'An Approach to Dylan Thomas', *Penguin New Writing, Vol. XXXV* (1948), p. 143.

57 'The poem may look very sprawly', he told Robert Herring, 'but it's really properly formed' (*CL*, 519). Each of the three stanzas has 23 lines of 7, 7, 8, 11, 9, 6, 7, 7, 11, 8, 11, 7, 7, 11, 9, 11, 11, 8, 8, 20, 15 and 16 syllables, rhyming [with variations] *aaabcbcccdbbbdbefggdfhh*.

58 According to Caitlin, John – a family friend – raped her while she was modelling for him. She described their subsequent relationship as a form of prolonged sexual

harassment. Andrew Lycett's comment that 'she was coquettish and perfectly capable of seducing the priapic artist [who was] clearly more a sugar daddy with whom she slept than the rapist she later portrayed' seems to me a rather dubious attempt to mitigate this basic fact. See Caitlin Thomas (with George Tremlett), *Caitlin: A Warring Absence* (London: Secker & Warburg, 1986), pp. 26–7; Andrew Lycett, *Dylan Thomas: A New Life* (London: Weidenfeld & Nicolson, 2003), pp. 129–30.

59 See Jacob Korg, *Dylan Thomas* (New York, NY: Twayne Publishers, 1972), pp. 104–5: '[T]he final stanza testifies most convincingly to Thomas' capacity for submerging his resentments by withholding blame and for seeing the wife's infidelity of spirit as a fact of nature. ... it transmutes [these] into a ... testimonial to the impossibility of the perfect union lovers desire'.

60 Wilhelm Reich, *The Mass Psychology of Fascism*, transl. Vincent R. Carfagno (Harmondsworth: Penguin Books, 1975), p. 13.

61 Wilhelm Reich, *The Mass Psychology of Fascism*, p. 15.

62 Max Ernst, *Une Semaine de Bonté: A Surrealistic Novel in Collage* (New York, NY: Dover Publications, 1976), pp. 1–37.

63 Elder Olson, *The Poetry of Dylan Thomas* (Chicago, IL: University of Chicago Press, 1954), p. 6.

64 The fertilised egg is known as an embryo until about eight weeks after fertilisation; thereafter, it is designated a foetus.

65 'I make this in a warring absence', 'When all my five and country senses', 'It is the sinners' dust-tongued bell', 'How shall my animal', 'A saint about to fall', 'If my head hurt a hair's foot' and 'Twenty-four years'.

66 Benjamin's thesis takes the form of a meditation on the angel depicted in Paul Klee's painting 'Angelus Novus', who 'look[s] as though he is about to move away from something he is fixedly contemplating. His eyes are staring, his mouth is open and his wings are spread. This is how one pictures the angel of history. His face is turned toward the past. Where we perceive a chain of events, he sees one single catastrophe which keeps piling wreckage on wreckage and hurls it in front of his feet'. He adds: 'The angel would like to stay, awaken the dead, and make whole what has been smashed. But a storm is blowing from Paradise; it has got caught in his wings with such violence that the angel can no longer close them. This storm irresistibly propels him into the future to which his back is turned, while the pile of debris before him grows ever skyward. This storm is what we call progress'. Walter Benjamin, *Illuminations*, ed. Hannah Arendt, transl. Harry Zohn (Glasgow: Collins, 1979), pp. 259–60.

67 Andrew Lycett, *Dylan Thomas: A New Life* (London: Weidenfeld & Nicolson, 2003), p. 205.

68 Rabaté cites the opening stanza of the poem, noting that Thomas's use of 'bisect' points up the bisexual nature of a child created equally from mother and father: 'Paternity and motherhood similarly seem to divide a fundamentally bisexual being, born from the thunder of a neutral orgasm'. See Jean-Michel Rabaté, *Joyce Upon the Void: the Genesis of Doubt* (London: Palgrave Macmillan: 1991), p. 163.

69 See Katie Gramich's pioneering '"Daughters of Darkness": Dylan Thomas and the Celebration of the Female', in eds. John Goodby and Chris Wigginton, *Dylan Thomas: New Casebook*, p. 66. Gramich's essay is the first feminist reading of Thomas's work.

70 Thus, a letter of December 1933 to Pamela Hansford Johnson describes homosexuality as: 'the only vice that .... revolts me', following a passage in which he speaks of acting the part of Witwoud in a forthcoming production of *The Way of the World* ('... the second consecutive effeminate part. Any more of this type of playing and I shall be becoming decidedly girlish') (*CL*, 88). The impression given is of Thomas reining in his 'effeminate' self-presentation, in order to assert his heterosexual credentials to a woman with whom he wanted a sexual relationship. The comments may be set beside his warm friendship (which included 'sexual encounters') with Oswell Blakeston and Max Chapman – a gay couple, who were part of his circle in London. The surviving letters to Blakeston are friendly and generous-spirited. Chapman commented that Thomas was not homosexual, but rather vaguely bisexual: 'more just generally warm and sexual than disposed one way or another' (*CL*, 236, 254, 266). See also Paul Ferris, *Dylan Thomas* (London: Penguin, 1978), pp. 129–30.

71 As he put it in a letter of March 1934 to Glyn Jones, who wrote to him after reading his poem 'A Woman Speaks' in *The Adelphi* (but did not know whether Thomas was a he or she): 'The woman speaks but the young *man* writes, and your doubt as to my sex was quite complimentary, proving (or was it simply my uncommon name?) that I do not use too masculine a pen' (*CL*, 120).

72 Katie Gramich, '"Daughters of Darkness": Dylan Thomas and the Celebration of the Female', p. 81.

73 See, for example, Walter J. Ong, *Fighting for Life: Contest, Sexuality and Consciousness* (Ithaca, NY: Cornell University Press, 1981). Ong argues that male identity is driven by a fundamental insecurity, rooted in the fact that, from the embryo, a male foetus must secrete combative androgens to offset maternal hormones that do a female no harm. Male restlessness and desire for agonistic struggle stem from the fact that masculine identity is acutely problematic, in a way that female identity is not. After initial identification with the mother's body, the male secures his identity by growing away from it; he must separate, test himself against others like himself, without ever breaking the bond with the feminine sources of his confidence (his mother, lovers, muse). If, at some point, either nature or women are seen as adversaries, the consequences can be catastrophic. Male sexism is thus rooted in the fear of being absorbed by the other sex: men intuit that they are the 'expendable sex' and that 'Nature's first impulse is to create a woman'. In contrast, the woman's sexual identity crisis is brought on, Ong maintains, by the abiding crisis of the male.

74 Angela Carter, *The Sadeian Woman and the Ideology of Pornography*, p. 23.

75 William T. Moynihan, *The Craft and Art of Dylan Thomas* (Oxford, Oxford University Press, 1966), p, 257. The 'trap', as Moynihan describes it, becomes, after 1938, a way in which we 'prepare for our own death' through 'loving ... and ... reproduction', although this is not a simple switch, and there is a resistance to it, both at the level of style (which is why the poems of 1938–41 mix the older, gnarled style with the more 'transparent' one, which Thomas would finalise in the poems of 1944–45).

76 William Walton Rowe, *Three Lyric Poets: Harwood, Torrance, MacSweeney* (Tavistock: Northcote House, 2009), p. 7.

77 Georges Bataille's definition of eroticism as 'assenting to life up to the point of death' is suggestive of how Thomas's work moves from fear of sex as death to a reshaping of the links between them, in order to embrace process through sex. In words that might have been written to describe Thomas's development, Bataille notes: 'the first turbulent surge of erotic feeling overwhelms all else, so that gloomy considerations

of the fate in store for our discontinuous selves are forgotten. And then, beyond the intoxication of youth, we achieve the power to look death in the face and to perceive in death the pathway into unknowable and incomprehensible continuity – that path is the secret of eroticism and eroticism alone can reveal it'. Georges Bataille, *Eroticism*, transl. Mary Dalwood (London: Penguin, 2001), pp. 11, 24.

CHAPTER FOUR

'My jack of Christ': hybridity, the gothic-grotesque and surregionalism

Do you know the experience of sitting in a corner of a darkened room, a little light coming in through the window, and staring, fixedly and unmovedly, at the face of another in an opposite corner, never taking the eyes off the lines of the other's face? Slowly the face changes, the jaw droops, the brow slips into the cheeks, and the face is one strange white circle, utter darkness around it. Then new features form on the face, a goat's mouth slides across the circle, eyes shine in the pits of the cheeks. Then there is nothing but the circle again, and from the darkness around it rises, perhaps, the antlers of a deer, or a cloven foot, or the fingers of a hand, or a thing no words can ever describe, a shape, not beautiful or horrible, but as deep as hell and as quiet as heaven. ... It's all optical illusion, I suppose, but I always call it the invoking of devils.

– Dylan Thomas, letter to Pamela Hansford Johnson, 21 December 1933.

Monsters and borders

Like much poetry of the 1930s, Dylan Thomas's traced the contours of the *zeitgeist* in its concern with borders and the menace that they portended in a Europe fragmented into new nation-states and jittery with rumours of impending war. Thomas, however, had a head start, in this respect, on the English New Country poets, for, as Tony Conran notes, 'Anglo-Welsh is a description of a frontier as much as a culture', and Anglo-Welsh poets were adept at 'mov[ing] across this shadowy no-man's land in both directions'.[1] In Thomas's case, his English contemporaries' interest in being 'on the frontier' was written across a concern with border-zones and boundary-crossings, which derived from a far deeper, centuries-old condition. As I've argued in previous chapters, boundaries in Thomas's work were inscribed at the level of the body and in language, too, where they were treated as constitutive of the self in ways beyond the reach of programmes of rational analysis or therapy. Oscillation between the states of the living and the dead, inner and outer 'weathers', utterance and inarticulacy and a fixation on those times – gestation, birth, infancy, adolescence, orgasmic release, death – which resemble others or seem to overlap – are the very stuff of the early poems. The result is a series of overdetermined, intersecting borders and liminal zones, which traverse and constitute the subject, as well as figuring its uncertain place within larger social, national and international structures.

It is the way in which the many boundaries in Thomas's work produce its impure, mongrel, miscegenatory and hybrid qualities that I wish to investigate in this chapter. His early poems, as we have seen, possess these qualities in a formal sense, fusing modernist and New Country elements, while their style is distorted by swollen syntax, perverse puns, mutilated similes, catachretic metaphors and surrealist provocations. But they are also concerned with bodies, as I've also argued, and are therefore notable for physical monsters, too – doppelgangers, mermen, mummies, a Cadaver figure, sirens, scissor-men, vampires and mandrakes. This is the gothic and grotesque Thomas – the poet who, in Kenneth Rexroth's words 'hits you across the face with a reeking, bloody heart, a heart full of worms and needles and black blood and thorns, a werewolf heart'.[2]

Many of Thomas's monsters and much of his grotesquely slippery lexis came from his prolific, heterogeneous reading and promiscuous mingling of texts – of Beddoes, Blake, Webster, the Metaphysicals, Caradoc Evans and Arthur Machen – and from watching horror films – German Expressionist, the first Hollywood versions of *Frankenstein*, *Dracula*, *The Mummy's Curse*, and others.[3] Similarly, his reviews of horror fiction and thrillers for *The Morning Post* during 1935 and 1936 (under such headings as '"Frequent, Gory and Grotesque"' and 'Grand Goose Flesh Parade') reveal a taste for writing, which, as definitions of the Gothic have it, is constituted at the point where high taste and low culture meet – one source of his later work's confident populism.[4] But it was not just a personal matter, as noted in Chapter 1: the so-called realistic fiction of the 'mannerist modernist' moment 'displays a taste for … grotesquerie and self-parody', and the gothic-grotesque, much like the concern with crossing the boundary between 'high' and 'low', also had much to do with Thomas's Welshness.[5]

In *18 Poems* and *Twenty-five Poems*, monstrosity and the gothic-grotesque, with their ceaseless (usually negative) changes of state, are the perfect generic vehicles for process. Although the intensity of these usages faded and became less frequent from the late 1930s onwards, they continued in more dispersed and subtle forms. In 'How shall my animal' (1938), grotesque mutability dramatises the struggle between the poet and his inner 'animal' / anima in a series of zoomorphic metamorphoses (as snail, octopus, horse, lion, turtle, fish, crab and bird). What Thomas himself called its 'grotesque contrast[s]' enact the paradox of writing, in which setting living energy down in words fixes and kills it, even though, in an answering paradox, the finished poem vividly embodies the animal that is said to have been 'buried under the spelling wall' (CL, 376). Similarly, 'Unluckily for a death' (first written in 1939 and rewritten in 1945) uses the grotesque, to figure the violations in the natural order that would occur if the speaker's beloved left him, in terms of a miscegenatory menagerie: 'I see the tigron in tears / ... The she mules bear their minotaurs, / The duck-billed platypus broody in a milk of birds' (CP, 92). Elsewhere, Thomas's most ambitious feature film script, *The Doctor and the Devils* (1948), was an adaptation of the grisly story of the grave-robbers Burke and Hare, and ghosts feature both in 'A Child's Christmas in Wales' (1947) and 'The Followers' (1951).

Thomas's 'werewolf heart' is most blatant in the twenty-four short fictions that he wrote between 1933 and 1938. Alongside the process poetic, during 1933 and 1934 he forged its prose equivalent, densely associative and anti-realist, in which hallucination, vision, madness and dream displace almost all traces of the period's recording camera eye. Intense, gnomic and brief (their average length is just five pages), these tales inhabit, albeit with an expanded social dimension, the same universe as the poetry, sometimes verbally echoing them exactly.[6] Like the poetry, they push this early style to an extreme, while going even further in their use of taboo subjects. These include incest ('The Burning Baby'), vivisection ('The Lemon'), sexual violence ('The Dress'), madness ('The Mouse and the Woman'), murder ('The Vest'), crucifixion ('The Tree') and sexual-racial magic ('The School for Witches'). All are written in a visionary tone and contain gothic, doomy motifs – a locked tower ('The Tree'), a mad scientist ('The Lemon'), blood-stained vest ('The Vest'), a coven ('The School for Witches'), a dead baby ('The Burning Baby') and a bizarre potion made from sperm and blood (stirred with a dead man's finger, naturally) ('The Horse's Ha').

The Welshness of Thomas's gothic-grotesque is apparent in numerous examples. Thus, the many zoomorphic metamorphoses of 'How shall my animal' reflect those undergone by Gwion Bach in the process of becoming the *ur*-bard Taliesin in the fourteenth century *History of Taliesin* – a tale which allegorises the origins of poetic inspiration.[7] More significantly, his Freudian and revolutionary impulses, sexual and religious obsessions, dark wordplay and sardonic wit work through Nonconformist repressions and an abject social reality, as frankly acknowledged as they are darkly performed. Again, the early fictions provide the most obvious examples. The journey of Marlais – the protagonist of the 'The Orchards' – for example, derives from the 'folk-man walking' figure of Welsh lore, while 'The Dress' concludes with a madman resting his head in the lap of a woman whose dress is 'covered in flowers', an allusion to the tale of Blodeuwedd – the bride magically created from the blossoms of oak, broom and meadowsweet in *The Mabinogion*. Many of these stories are set in the Jarvis Valley, an imaginary West Wales location, and Thomas planned to use some of them as episodes in a novel, never completed, provisionally titled *A Doom on the Sun*. This would have been 'a kind of warped fable in which Lust, Greed, Cruelty, Spite, etc., appear all the time as old gentlemen in the background of the story' (*CL*, 160). In 'The Holy Six' (1937), the narrator sardonically notes at one point that 'the holy life was a constant erection to these gentlemen', and several of the stories intended for *A Doom on the Sun* indict a dying Welsh Nonconformist culture for continuing to repress sexual energy, forcing it to find expression in perversion, cruelty and 'sexually-tinged violence'.[8] It is no coincidence, given Thomas's and Wales's marginal, uncertain status, that these tales often turn on boundary-breaking moments – the child poised to crucify the idiot at the end of 'The Tree' and Rhiannon drawing the sheet over the face of Peter, who does not yet realise he is dead, in 'The Visitor'.

These 'satiric but elemental tales' most obviously link the monstrous, transgressive aspects of Thomas's 1930s poetry and his hybrid, Anglo-Welsh identity.[9] 'Gothic' is particularly useful as a way of defining this strain in Thomas; process committed him to a critique of New Country ratiocination, and the Gothic traditionally signifies a 'writing of excess', one which arose historically when the medieval, wild and primitive – excoriated by Enlightenment rationality, civility and self-restraint – were invested with a positive value, both in, and for, themselves.[10] Its taboo-breaking rationale makes it a kind of mocking mirror image of the classical 'sublime', shadowing the progress of modernity with a dark and subversive counter-narrative. In words by David Punter, which recall general descriptions of Thomas's work, it gives 'little or no access to an "objective" world ... [F]eelings of degeneracy abound. The worlds portrayed are ones infested with psychic and social decay, and coloured with the heightened hues of putrescence. Violence, rape and breakdown are the key motifs'.[11] For Angela Carter, the gothic has stylistic consequences, and these are also relevant to a consideration of Thomas: 'Characters and events are exaggerated beyond reality, to become symbols, ideas, passions. Its style will tend to be ornate, unnatural – and thus operate against the perennial desire to believe the world as fact. Its only humour is black humour. It retains a singular moral function – that of provoking unease'.[12] We need to supplement 'Gothic' with 'grotesque', it seems to me, because in this mode, distortion always borders on risibility and the ridiculous; it is through the juxtaposition of this 'low' material with the sublimity of horror that a story by Thomas that a creates its own version of Gothic's more homogeneous 'unease'. Thus, the grotesque informs Desmond Hawkins's attempt to define Thomas's penchant for telling gothic stories in company: 'He had a fund of stories about madness, lunatic asylums and strange symbolic possession – usually funny ... not solemn ... He certainly loved the "Gothic"'.[13] Crucially, for Thomas, both gothic and grotesque are rooted in the flesh. Gothic deals entirely with the profane, while the grotesque is central to the concept of the grotesque body. Both the frisson of terror and the seismic disturbance of laughter are bodily disturbances.

The gothic-grotesque is a perfect vehicle, of course, for the linguistic excess of Thomas's style and his representations of his own prodigious, monstrous person and the deformed society which shaped him – an aspect of his self-making wrongly ignored by many champions of his work, but picked up on by the many opponents who have monstered Thomas (as in Grigson's spiteful list of epithets and nicknames for him – 'cartilaginous', 'glandular', 'the Swansea Changeling', 'the Ugly Suckling', 'curious elf', 'Ditch', 'the snotty troll' and 'the Disembodied Gland').[14] These monstrous elements of his hybrid poetic identity fed the poetry of the mid-1930s after Thomas moved to London and was consolidating his reputation; indeed, the impact of London – the Dickensian, gothic-grotesque city par excellence – seems to have increased his use of them, as if he were asserting his difference from, and uncanny sympathy with, the City of Destruction. In parodic form, or under the period sign of the surreal in poems such as 'Altarwise by owl-light', he explored the monstrous and surreal *within* his Welsh inheritance, until, around 1937, this reached the expressive and formal limits of his process style. This point of development coincided with his marriage and was followed in 1938 by his move back to the Wales that he had tried to abandon. There he would settle, albeit for less than two years, and support the attempt to develop an indigenous group of Anglo-Welsh writers gathered around the journal *Wales*, revising the gothic-grotesque aspects of his writing accordingly.

Welsh Gothic: horror, the gothic-grotesque and the nation

The starting point for an exploration of Thomas's gothic-grotesque hybridity lies in Swansea – a town that, then as now, embodied many of Wales's internal divisions. Linguistically, it is at the western edge of the anglophone industrialised coastal strip of South Wales, bordering a Welsh-speaking hinterland in Carmarthenshire to the north and west.[15] As a busy port (in the 1930s), it was also both a place of cosmopolitan energies and, as a result of recent rural influxes and its proximity to the epicentre of the great 1904–5 religious revival, a centre for dissenting Nonconformism. But it was also noted for its sporting and theatrical energies; Andrew Lycett writes, with good reason, of the town's 'hybrid culture'.[16] These contrasts had their equivalents in Thomas's life, for the respectable 'jerry-villa'd, smug-suburbed' Uplands in which he grew up symbolised the class, cultural and geographical divides that his parents had crossed in travelling from Welsh-speaking, semi-rural, working-class backgrounds (*TB*, 3).[17] His parents had been raised as Welsh-speakers, but, like many of their generation, they saw the language as a handicap to advancement and did not teach it to their children. In religion, D. J. Thomas was a God-hating agnostic, while Florrie was a believer, who regularly took the young Dylan to the Congregationalist Paraclete chapel in Bishopston, where her brother-in-law was minister. He was also regularly sent to stay with his Welsh-speaking aunts, uncles and cousins in rural Carmarthenshire. His very name, 'Dylan' – then extremely rare – also embodied some of these contrasts, for if it expressed a residual pride in the origins that D. J. had suppressed, the family always pronounced it in the English way as 'Dillon'.[18]

Like many of the 'First Flowering' Anglo-Welsh writers, Thomas was powerfully shaped by his mixed working- and middle-class origins, for this interstitial social layer was particularly radicalised by the Depression. In fact, the factors which had produced a century of growth in South Wales's major industry, coal, had ended before the Wall Street Crash; a depression which began in coal in 1925 was the central happening in the history of twentieth-century Wales, and the General Strike and Depression simply turned crisis into catastrophe.[19] The Welsh economy was a victim of the fact that it had been developed lopsidedly –

grotesquely, one might say – to serve imperial needs, as a socio-economic monstrosity which was helpless before the Royal Navy's sudden switch from coal to oil in 1922 and a sudden influx of cheap European coal.[20] By 1933, male unemployment in Wales was over 30%, with some blackspots suffering levels of 70% or more. Recovery did not begin until late in the decade. The result was mass immiseration and population decline: half a million people (one-fifth of the entire population) left Wales during the 1930s, mainly from the south. Though it was one of the most advanced areas of the South Walian economy, 'even Swansea with its poets and musicians' fell into neglect and poverty.[21]

Thomas's social, historic and geographic liminality bore strongly on the strange and disturbing nature of his pre-1938 writing. It was the precondition for a complexly self-questioning subjectivity, one part of which was the *odi et amo* attitude to his country that was not uncommon among Welsh artists of his generation and which was starkly apparent in letters such as that of October 1933 to Pamela Hansford Johnson. In this, he complained about the rain and rural backwardness of Llangain, near Carmarthen, where he was staying, before bemoaning the 'industrial small towns', each 'a festering sore on the body of a dead country, half a mile of main street with its Prudential, its Co-Op, its Star, its cinema and pub', full of nothing but 'hideously pretty young girls … thin youths with caps and stained fingers holding their cigarettes, women, all breast and bottom' and 'little colliers, diseased in mind and body as only the Welsh can be …' (*CL*, 48). It is the big town boy's rather callow put-down of the hicks, unmingled with his usual sympathy for the poor, in order to create the maximum impact on Johnson, whom he wishes to visit in London. 'All Wales is like this', he concludes, 'It's impossible for me to tell you how much I want to get out of it all, out of narrowness and dirtiness, out of the eternal ugliness of the Welsh people, and all that belongs to them … I shall have to get out soon. I'm sick and this bloody country's killing me' (*CL*, 48). Typically, however, he immediately turns the comments against himself; they are 'melodramatic', he 'sound[s] like a third-rate play in which the "artistic" hero boasts of his superiority over his fellows' (*CL*, 48). Although there is no doubt that, for Thomas, there *is* a specific Welsh sickness, and Wales is, in many ways – as Tony Conran similarly described it thirty years later – 'a desperate little country', he incorporated his response to it within the dialogic inner drama of the 1930s poetry.[22] It is the fact that the Welsh situation is 'absurd', not that it is contemptible, which is crucial (*EPW*, 120).

Such liminality and ambivalence was enhanced by the literary contexts into which Thomas had emerged. In the early 1930s, Welsh literature was still absorbing the shock of the work of Caradoc Evans – the first anglophone Welsh writer of genuine achievement. Evans's first book, the short story collection *My People* (1915), broke irrevocably with the pious and formulaic fiction which preceded it; its tales, written in a pithy, distorted style, were fiercely antagonistic towards traditional rural Welsh culture and religion. Set in Manteg – a fictionalised version of Evans's own Cardiganshire village of Rhydlewis – they constituted a savage satire on the *gwerin* (peasantry, folk) valorised in nationalist discourse. Evans presents Welsh rural society as a brutal patriarchy dominated by peasant greed and low cunning, religious hypocrisy and the grinding oppression of women, the poor, the old and the weak. In this world, madness, casual violence and incest are all rife; and, while *My People* and subsequent fictions are clearly caricatural, they contained enough truth to hurt. At a time when the self-esteem of Liberal-Nonconformist Wales was reeling from the collapse of its socio-political hegemony, Evans had ripped open the scars inflicted by the Blue Books over half a century before.[23]

A tradition of Welsh gothic existed before Evans, but it was he who made it a model for a specifically Welsh, gothic-grotesque form of modernism. Thus, Tony Conran has argued that 'Modernism in Wales is most at home with the grotesque. It is there that modernism characteristically shows itself, in Saunders Lewis as much as in Caradoc Evans and Dylan Thomas. The nightmare of monstrosity underlies the middle-class rejection of the *buchedd* (rural way of life, culture), the sense of being suffocated by its hypocrisy and narrowness'.[24] *My People* used the device of purporting to be a literal translation from the Welsh to create innovatively grotesque verbal effects (although it is usually described as 'realist', its style is actually a mannerist exaggeration of Welsh English).[25] Exemplifying postcolonial hybridity, it subverts Standard English by incorporating 'Welshisms', yet simultaneously subverts Welsh by Englishing it. As John Harris puts it: '[Evans's] translations ... produce grotesque misreadings and, excited by their artistic possibilities, he incorporates a range of startling expressions purely of his own devising: they have no parallels in the Welsh language nor in the English language spoken in Wales'.[26] Even more pertinently, the style draws on the rhetorical authority of the Bible, while simultaneously reversing its direction. In Harris's words: 'Simple, often majestic and suggestive also of parable and myth', his language is 'turn[ed] ... devastatingly against' those 'Ministers and deacons [who] had made the Bible their "hateful weapon"', just as, more subtly, Thomas makes biblical rhetoric serve a relativistic vision of the universe in poems such as 'And death shall have no dominion'.[27] The relish for the grotesque is a reminder that, along with Joyce, for whom he also had deep affinities, Thomas's other favourite prose writer was Dickens.[28]

Evans's example, which widened the split between the Welsh language and Anglo-Welsh literature in Wales, was one of those which fed Thomas's more radical stylistic deviance, and he and Glyn Jones paid homage to Evans by visiting him in Aberystwyth in 1936. It was on this trip that Jones told Thomas the true story of Dr William Price of Llantrisant – a Unitarian minister and flamboyant, self-styled druid, whose pagan ceremonies and insistence on burning the body of his beloved infant son, Iesu Grist, had led to the repeal of the laws forbidding cremation in 1885 (*CL*, 172). As if to confirm his link with Evans, Thomas soon afterwards made this historical episode the basis of one of his most compelling anti-religious, gothic-grotesque stories, 'The Burning Baby'.[29]

If Evans is Thomas's source for style and setting, the themes and atmosphere of much of his early work often derive from another favourite Welsh author, Arthur Machen – an established Welsh writer, who praised and supported Evans.[30] Machen was a pioneering and hugely influential supernatural horror, Gothic and fantasy writer, whose work blended, among others, Rosicrucianism, Huysmans, Poe, Pater, Stevenson, *La Queste del Sante Graal* and Sherlock Holmes, and often made neo-Darwinian anxieties the basis for terror.[31] There are striking similarities with Thomas's early short stories. In Machen's novel *The Great God Pan* (1894), for example, a young girl mates with Pan, but her visionary power drives her mad. Helen Vaughan, their Welsh-named 'hell-child', dies by regressing through the stages of evolution. The fate of Professor Gregg in 'The Novel of the Black Seal' – a tale within Machen's other best-known novel, *The Hill of Dreams* (1907) – is to be similarly reduced to a 'primal slime'. Both are recalled at the conclusion of Thomas's 'An Adventure from a Work in Progress': 'She dangled there with bald and monstrous skull, bunched monkey face and soaked abdominal tail. Out of the webbed sea-pig and water-nudging fish a white pool spat in his palm' (*CS*, 123). Likewise, Thomas's quest-narratives, 'The Orchards' and 'A Prospect of the Sea', also owe much to *The Hill of Dreams* (1907) – an autobiographical novel about writing a novel.[32] The insistent biological emphases that Thomas shared with Machen extended to the older author's location of his exploration of these in Wales. Machen was fascinated by miscegenation and hybridity and by the notion that, beneath the surface of the modern world, there lurked sinister beings capable of interbreeding with modern humans. In 'The Novel of the Black Seal', the protagonist gradually uncovers evidence for a hidden pre- and non-human race hiding in the 'Grey Hills' between Carleon and Monmouth in a hybrid, idiot child that one of them has fathered with a local woman.

While the Welsh are distinct from the ancient race sought by Gregg in *The Hill of Dreams*, connections between them are repeatedly hinted at. The sibilant Welsh 'll' sound is linked to the reptilian speech of the *ur*-race, for example, and the dense forest of the Usk valley is likened to the Congo – this place must be backward in civilisational terms, it is implied, or it would not have been able to shelter pre-human survival from the gaze of science for so long. The suggestion is part of a wider discourse, in which the remoter parts of Wales were represented as harbouring primitive cultural survivals, such as witchcraft, Druidism and paganism. Gothic writers were naturally drawn towards the potential this offered. Gothic often has a political charge and has been used extensively to figure the experience of the non-English British nations (Scottish Gothic, for example, often does so in the form of the radically split self). It is usually reactionary; nineteenth-century Irish gothic fiction, for example, fed off Ascendancy fears of Catholicism and rebellion, and elsewhere Gothic was used as a vehicle for constructing non-whites and metropolitan-colonial whites as racially other. In Wales, anglophone writers were not divided from the population as the Anglo-Irish were from the Catholic masses, however, and were wary of entering into a metropolitan discourse which Othered their own. Because its authors could be both object and subject of their fictions, therefore, Welsh Gothic is ambivalent and uneasy, productive of self-division. In some cases, the solution was to cast the Welsh themselves in the role of a racial Other, largely out of a sense, albeit usually vaguely grasped, of solidarity.

This ambivalence may be seen in the context of a national self-image more impacted with England than any other constituent British nationality. Modern English stereotypes of the Welsh – as morbid, sexually repressed (yet lustful and 'Celtic' in their emotionalism), given to religious sectarianism and obsessed with genealogy – developed during the nineteenth century, both in fiction and on the stage, as a mockery of the deformities which imperial power had itself unwittingly inflicted over four centuries. Yet at the same time, and for all the profound ignorance of Welsh culture informing these depictions, the Welsh were indeed engaged in self-repression aimed at rebutting the centre's charges of immorality and backwardness; this was one of the results of the Blue Books scandal of the 1840s and after. The negative stereotypes were internalised, in order to be overcome, and so acquired great socio-historical force – in such cases, stereotypes are not necessarily 'unreal' simply because they simplify. They can be inhabited, performed and become lived realities. Moreover, this assimilation may have radical, self-empowering results, not just the reactionary ones that are usually associated with them.

Between late 1933, when he created the process style in his poetry, and 1938, when he subsequently modified it, Thomas used his biological-grotesque version of Welsh gothic as a vehicle for modernist experiment in his prose fiction, as I discussed in Chapter 2. Evans's Manteg became his own, less socially satirical, more primordially brooding Jarvis Valley. Rather than Evans's money, status and chapel oppression, Thomas's focus is on unbiddable processual forces – the 'old powers' of 'the worm in the earth ... the copulation in the tree ... the living grease in the soil' worshipped by Mr and Mrs Owen in 'The Enemies' (*CS*, 20). His experimental urge also gave his fictions a keener parodic edge; there is a hint of *Cold Comfort Farm* (1931) – a book that he enjoyed – that places them, in modern terms, closer to *The League of Gentlemen* than to such consciously literary treatments of rural deprivation and backwardness as, say, Bruce Chatwin's *On the Black Hill*. This is highlighted by the use of emblematic, playful names: Llareggub ('bugger all' backwards), Sam Rib, Dai Twice and Stul, Rafe and the other priests in 'The Holy Six'. In this, as in other ways, Thomas transforms his intertexts, adding modernist solipsism, while also mocking modernist pretension. The gothic-grotesque suited his Anglo-Welsh modernist needs, because it was fluid; within it, the disparate strains of adolescent sexual unease, historical crisis, outsider irreverence and belatedness could flourish and fuse.

The problem for the Welsh writer of gothic in English is how to mediate the effects of oppression and self-repression, without succumbing to the use of unreflective caricature and thus reinforcing national abjection. For Evans, it was the moral aim of exposing hypocrisy, cruelty and oppressiveness, which justified the attacks on his society. In typing rural Wales as a realm of visionary and chthonic powers, Thomas can be said to present an urban, anglophone, South Walian vision of rural Wales – one which nationalists would have regarded as a distortion of reality. But the qualities that Thomas identified in his Jarvis Valley stories, for all their more overt gothic elements – mad scientists, plague, incest and madness – are also those of his own process poetic. The caricature is a source of insight and constitutive of the creative self. Nor, while he undoubtedly intended to provoke a reaction, was he really interested in stigmatising any actual community – the fictions are too deeply embroiled within their gothic-grotesque representations to be satire proper. Rather, Thomas delves more deeply into the Nonconformist Imaginary than Evans does, in order to produce a paradoxically less ostensibly 'Welsh' result: his own gothic-grotesque modernism is a more autonomous, self-sufficient fictional realm than the older author's. Characters are alienated and driven mad in Evans's stories, but the minds of the alienated and the mad are the subjects of Thomas's 'The Vest' and 'The Mouse and the Woman'. Thomas's generic mix is more unstable, veering more readily between caricature and parody, melodrama and black humour, and this makes it more grotesque; 'disorienting and even frightening', it is also 'potentially comic', contradictorily exciting 'amusement and disgust, laughter and horror, mirth and revulsion'.[33]

In his early poetry, modernist monstrosity subordinates Thomas's self-dramatising, solipsistic, Hamletian soliloquists to its primordial, self-making medium. Hence the description of it to Johnson in December 1933, through allusion to the supreme gothic fiction, *Frankenstein*: 'So many modern poets take the living flesh as their object, and, by their clever dissecting, turn it into a carcase. I prefer to take the dead flesh, and, by any positivity of faith that is in me, build up a living flesh from it' (*CL*, 89). What Thomas attacks for its morbidity, he also understands to be the source of his creative self-division, and his abject subject matter is his own state of abjection. He revels, self-mockingly, in the construction of its brooding narcissism, lovingly referring to his poems as 'my wormy beasts' (*CL*, 153). The 'fascinated loathing', as Empson called it, fuses the sexual with conflicted roots to render an account of the struggle for selfhood more powerful than mere realism could arrive at. There is, however, a division of labour, for in the stories, the Welsh gothic-grotesque appears as manifest content, but in the process poems, it is subsumed by the more universal forces of process, outcropping more selectively in latent and condensed form, as just one factor in their apocalyptic temper.

In addition to the Welsh sources of the Gothic in Thomas's poetry, and the elements of the Gothic and grotesque, already noted, which he drew from Eliot and Joyce, it should be noted that the primary example for his gothic-inflected modernism was D. H. Lawrence. I use 'Gothic' here in the broad sense in which it is used by Tony Pinkney in his reading of Lawrence as a 'Northern' or 'Gothic Modernist', with a

Ruskinian emphasis on creaturely empathy and organic form, as opposed to the neoclassicist modernism of the 'Men of 1914' (a neoclassicism continued in the cerebral style of the New Country poets).In Lawrence, as in Thomas, the body-rooted grotesque and Gothic were the vehicles of a markedly different kind of social critique and style, rooted in their lower middle-class, non-metropolitan, Nonconformist upbringing. A comparison between Lawrence's essay 'Hymns in a Man's Life' and Thomas's comments on the 'great rhythms [that] rolled over me from the Welsh pulpits' in his 'Poetic Manifesto' reveals the similarity between them, just as Eliot's dismissal of the Nonconformist Liberal 'inner voice' in 'The Function of Criticism' reveals the stark difference between them and him (that Eliot's aside refers to Liberal and Nonconformist Swansea is serendipitous, but it could almost as easily be Eastwood): 'the possessors of the inner voice ride ten in a compartment to a football match at Swansea, listening to the inner voice which breathes the eternal message of vanity, fear and lust ... It is a voice to which, for convenience, we may give a name: and the name I suggest is Whiggery.'[34] In their attitudes to religion and sex in particular, Lawrence and Thomas represent a dissenting, visionary British modernism, one which can be traced back through Morris and Ruskin to Blake (not to mention Whitman), and ultimately to the writer-radicals of the seventeenth century. As Walford Davies rightly notes, the sexual assertiveness of both was clearly attributable to their reaction against 'a specific culture in which Bible-based fears of the Apocalypse enjoined retreat into 'social respectability'.[35]

Thomas, then, used Evans, Machen, Lawrence and others as models for constructing a grotesque critique of Wales and his own conflicted Welsh identity at the height of the Depression – the latest episode in a long history of Welsh defeat, self-repression and abjection. This is the source of his canonical anomalousness, but also of his greatness, because through it, the wider grotesquerie and horror of the 1930s was figured. Far from trying merely to generate a *frisson*, he limned his generation's fears and the decade's actual 'febrile grotesqueness'.[36] It is to the religious aspect of this 'febrile', gothic-grotesque inheritance that I now turn.

The blasphemer: 'my Jack of Christ ...'

Like Lawrence in his late story 'The Escaped Cock', Thomas was interested in a physical, sexualised Christ (in contrast to the desexualised Jesus of orthodox Christianity) and also shared Lawrence's urge to identify with him, as well as with his Old Testament types – Adam,

Samson and Noah. The language, stories and characters of the Bible (chiefly Genesis, Job, Ecclesiastes, John and Revelation and the 'great stories of Noah, Jonah, Lot, Moses, Jacob, David, Solomon') had been heard by Thomas 'from very early youth; the great rhythms had rolled over me from the Welsh pulpits', and he treated them as 'the common property of all who had been brought up in English-speaking communities' (*EPW*, 158). The habitual Christian frame of reference and tone of praise and invocation have led many to view him as a Christian poet, albeit an unorthodox one.[37] In doing so, the distinction is rarely drawn between whether Thomas was a Christian poet 'able to live Christianity in a public way', as Vernon Watkins believed, or whether he wrote Christian poems. This distinction is an important one to make.[38] When it is, it is often assumed that not to have faith and write about religion and the desire to believe, or to use religious references, is a kind of poetic bad faith. Thomas's 'Note' in the 1952 *Collected Poems* ran: 'I read somewhere of a shepherd who, when asked why he made, from within fairy rings, ritual observances to the moon to protect his flocks, replied: "I'd be a damn' fool if I didn't!" These poems, with all their crudities, doubts, and confusions, are written for the love of Man and in praise of God, and I'd be a damn' fool if they weren't' (*CP*, 173–4). Daniel Jones demurred at this: 'To him, Jericho might just as well have been a person as a place: but the addition of the Jericho ingredient to a poem, like the "Jack Christ" ingredient, could, he knew, induce a religious impression, in the same way as a mustard sandwich without ham can be imagined to be a ham sandwich with mustard'.[39] Yet the 'Note' has been read in diametrically opposed ways. R. B. Kershner sees the last few words as 'ringing affirmation' (albeit undercut by 'the ironic innuendo of "superstition"'), for example, while R. George Thomas sees it as the agnostic's 'truculent, face-saving clause'.[40] The ambiguity may reflect the difference between Thomas's 'Darwinian' attitude to religion in the 1930s poetry and a later, less dismissive one, which reflects awareness of the importance of the supernatural, without necessarily endorsing this as belief. Yet his review of an anarchist pamphlet for *The Adelphi* in 1935 praised the struggle for 'libertarian love' 'through the communism, the spiritual immediacy, of the Christ in man', and this early combination of politics and religion indicates something more considered than the purely reactive explanation of Bert Trick, who saw Thomas as the product of a revolt against 'his father's agnosticism' and 'the narrow Puritan conventions of his mother's Congregational background' (*EPW*, 177).[41]

Recent work by M. Wynn Thomas suggests, in fact, that in creating his poetic style, Thomas had in mind not only the 'process' of Alfred North Whitehead, but also the example of his great-uncle William Thomas.[42] This relative – the only one of note – was one of the boldest religious-political spirits of mid-nineteenth century Wales, a Unitarian preacher who campaigned for the secret ballot and resisted the discrimination against his flock of landless labourers and tenant farmers by a local absentee landlord. He was also in the Welsh tradition of preacher-poets, who followed this tradition in taking his bardic middle name, Marles, from the stream that flowed through his village. It was this name, anglicised as Marlais, which D. J. Thomas gave to both Dylan and his sister Nancy. Significantly, Gwilym Marles's Unitarian Nonconformism was of a radical and rare variety, existing in Wales only in the 'Black Spot', as it was known, of north Carmarthenshire. Unitarianism has a complex history within Welsh Nonconformism as a radical and minority tendency, which rejects the main Calvinistic tenets – the Trinity and incarnation in particular (which Unitarians regard as true not of Christ exclusively, but of Man universally), but also the resurrection in its literal sense, the divine nature of Christ, Original Sin, the Last Judgement and an afterlife.[43] For Unitarians, God is Love, and all human beings have the potential to be divine; the religious life consists of striving to realise it. Moreover, while Unitarianism was originally a post-Enlightenment sect, whose positivist rationalism would have been at odds with Thomas's post-Darwinian, processual worldview, it gained romantic-pantheistic inflections during the nineteenth century and it was in this form, heavily influenced the New England Transcendentalists (whose writings Thomas absorbed, along with those of the most important poet within their orbit, Walt Whitman) that it descended to him.

As I shall show in my reading of 'Altarwise by owl-light' later in this chapter, Thomas radicalised this radicalisation of Unitarianism to make the nature of faith itself an object of scrutiny and complicated it still further with elements drawn from Welsh Christian socialism, pacifism and anti-imperialism, as well as those religious, nominally Welsh Metaphysical poets, Herbert, Donne and Vaughan. All of the items of Unitarian belief, at least, can be traced in Thomas's metaphorised form of Christianity, in which Christianity is mined for structures, symbols and exempla in the same way that the New Country poets plundered Marx and Freud. This gave Welsh specificity to Thomas's exploration of subjectivity in psycho-linguistic terms and also accommodated the general modernist concern with the hunger for spiritual belief, following the blows dealt to Christianity by the First World War, science and secularism. In the unpublished tale 'Gaspar, Melchior, Balthasar' (1934), for example, we find that war and bombing have given rise to a bloody British revolution: amid the chaos, the narrator follows 'two ghosts' moving among 'the unburied fallen' to 'a dead woman, naked but for her shawl, with a bayonet wound in her breasts'. As 'her womb [of the dead mother] broke, lifted, through the flesh', the ghosts bow (brackets indicate deletions in the original):

> Gold, said [Gaspar] the first ghost, [holding] raising a golden shadow to the light of the moon.
>
> Frankincense, said [Melchior] the second ghost and his shadowy gift smoked from him.
>
> The noise of the guns grew nearer and still nearer.
>
> [Kneeling] I knelt where I stood [I] and felt the new joy of pain as a bullet drove into my [lung] breast. I fell upon the pavement near the two lifted arms, and [bitter as myrrh,] my [bitter] blood streamed bitterly on to the [mother's feet] emerging head. (CS, 367)

As in the poems, ghosts and solid bodies coexist, and revolution and revelation fuse in the climactic image, as Balthasar gives the 'myrrh' of his blood to the Christ of a dubious socialist apocalypse. As Thomas told Johnson, 'It's heaven on earth or no heaven', but this did not amount to a belief that some collective social transformation would occur (CL, 177). Yet Christian symbolism, particularly the cross, could be wrested from Christianity and put at the service of an existential self-making. 'I care not a damn for Christ, but only for his symbol, the symbol of death', Thomas told Johnson in late 1933, anticipating his use of 'cross' to represent rending contraries in 'I see the boys of summer' ('O see the poles are kissing as they cross') (CL, 82).

'God' is used interchangeably with the more agnostic 'spirit' in such letters, which rail against repression and the churches' complicity in the Great War, but leave the issue of a spiritual principle open: 'God is the country of the spirit, and each of us is given a little holding of ground in that country', which it is 'given to us to explore or neglect', he notes (CL, 103). The social context was mainstream Nonconformism's hijacking of Welshness in the second half of the nineteenth century and the thwarting of the emergence of a secular Welsh-language culture.[44] As the Irish critic Patrick Crotty has argued, this had a general effect on Welsh culture:

> One of the great paradoxes of Wales is that though the country embraced

a form of Calvinism it failed to develop the traditions of interiority and individual self-reliance elsewhere regarded as synonymous with Calvinism. Spirituality was conceived by the Nonconformists largely in communal terms … It is not to slight the democratic character of Nonconformist worship to observe that the theologically driven egalitarianism of the chapel resulted in the cultivation of a social conformity so thoroughgoing that Wales can seem in crucial respects the least Protestant country in Western Europe.[45]

Nonconformity was so strong a social glue, that it delayed the emergence, in both national literatures, of an 'existential drama of the soul', in Crotty's phrase. Thomas's writing, as I argued in Chapter 1, attempts to stage such a drama, wrestling the liberatory aspects of Christianity from its repressive aspects. The struggle involved is clear in the vehemence of his anti-chapel invective, such as the description in April 1934 of churchgoers passing his window wearing 'black suits, reddest eyes, & meanest expressions … all the starch, the thin pink blood, the hot salty longings and the respectable cream on top of the suburban scum'; they are hypocrites all, due to 'end up in the Sabbath well where the corpses of strangled preachers, promis[e] … a heaven they don't believe in to people who won't go there' (CL, 135). According to Thomas, they 'little realis[e] … how the eyes of men are abused by the town light, how the gasoline has crept under their nostrils like the smell of a new mechanical flower, how the stars have been counted for us … how the God of our image, gloved, hatted, & white, no longer sits playing with his stars but curving his Infinite length to the limits of a Jew's theory'. Einsteinian science has outstripped the cosy anthropomorphism of Nonconformity and accepting this is the only way for the 'dreadful passers' to realise their human potential as 'pagan houses of flesh and blood … creature-boned and sky-sexed' (CL, 135, 136). As in the writings of Alfred North Whitehead, spiritual aspiration has to be compatible with a material universe, even if the notion of spirit sometimes seems little more than the vitalist excess of a living-in-dying spending of the physical self.

As we have seen, the poetry often sets up an irresolvable tension between religious rhetoric and meaning-content, as in 'And death shall have no dominion'. At its most extreme in 'Vision and Prayer', this could involve imagining a conversion experience: 'I / Am found. / O let him / Scald me and drown / Me in his world's wound. … I am lost in the blinding / One. The sun roars at the prayer's end' (CP, 125). The stories occasionally expose the contradiction of having both a lack of faith and sense of Christianity's psychological and emotional validity; hence the boy in 'A Prospect of the Sea', who thinks that he 'does not believe in

God, but God had made this summer full of blue winds and heat and pigeons in the house wood' (*CS*, 89–90). It was in this paradoxical vein, that Thomas would tell John Malcolm Brinnin that his aim was to write 'poems in praise of God's world by a man who doesn't believe in God'; it is the culturally-constructed gap, and the oscillation that occurs within it and precisely what this does to language and notions of the subject, which interest Thomas, not some 'search for faith' or simple assertion of non-belief.[46] In exploring the paradoxes of religion in his early work, he inhabited the Nonconformist unconscious, in order to out its more grotesque, blasphemous and revolutionary forms, thereby critiquing a central paradox of Welsh identity. During the 1940s, this material became part of a more humanistic vision, as we shall see in Chapter 5, and seemed less unusual than it had been, because religiosity was more widespread in both poetry and public discourse during wartime.

To confound its patriarchal principle, Thomas would focus on the contradictions of the Bible, appropriating biblical figures and using – like Whitman – Christ as a vehicle for his poetic ego.[47] This is most marked in *Twenty-five Poems*: 'This bread I break', 'Incarnate devil', 'And death shall have no dominion' and 'Altarwise by owl-light' all have explicitly Christian themes. It is as if, having set out the process poetic in a pure form in *18 Poems*, Thomas then wished to test its ability to ingest orthodox faith and extend the relativistic stance of the first collection (in which pagan, pantheist, Hegelian-Marxist, classical, Egyptian and Christian belief systems, derived from high modernism's reading of *The Golden Bough*, all jostle together). In this second collection, the production and manipulation of faith effects and the fusing of anguished Victorian religious doubt and modern relativism to create a deadpan contradictoriness, at once secular and knowingly religiose, reached a climax; in its poems aimed at realising a new state of Christhood, whose law of libertarian love was directed against Nonconformity. Blake, Lawrence, Whitman, Marx, Freud and the Bible, were all mobilised for the purpose, often in parodic mode.

Thomas's own blasphemous identification with Christ meant identifying with his isolation, persecution and doubt, in order to stage dramas of masculine self-making and filial rebellion. As a proto-socialist rebel and author of the poetry of the Gospels, Christ was at once a role model and target for dissident energy. He was also the perfect figure for process, with its opposition to division and tendency to collapse chronology, because his birth / crucifixion were taken by Christians to '[synthesize] the duality of the body and soul and [make] history one timeless moment by his love'.[48] And as Logos, Christ was the ultimate signifier, who exceeded all social and psychic measure or control, allowing a poet, in his hybrid uncertainty, to identify with his abjection and resurrection in a material and grotesque body (which is also that of Wales). Poet and Christ merge in 'Before I knocked':[49]

> Before I knocked and flesh let enter,
> With liquid hands tapped on the womb,
> I who was shapeless as the water
> That shaped the Jordan near my home
> Was brother to Mnetha's daughter
> And sister to the fathering worm. (*CP*, 11)

This is Whitman's 'Man or woman as good as God' with a vengeance, for, even before conception, the Thomas-Christ protagonist tells of suffering and knowing 'the maggot in my stool' of mortality:

> I, born of flesh and ghost, was neither
> A ghost nor man, but mortal ghost.
> And I was struck down by death's feather.
> I was mortal to the last
> Long breath that carried to my father
> The message of his dying christ.
>
> You who bow down at cross and altar,
> Remember me and pity Him
> Who took my flesh and bone for armour
> And doublecrossed my mother's womb. (*CP*, 12)

As discussed in Chapter 2, this leads to a famous textual crux, in which the lowercase 'me' – the human speaker – accuses God, the Father, of a 'doublecross': by entering Mary as the Holy Ghost and leaving her in the form of the Son, God crossed the threshold of her womb twice (double-crossing), but also cheated ('doublecrossed') Mary, by depriving her of any sexual pleasure. But the main betrayal is God the Father's abandonment of his Son, 'Him', and, by extension, of all sons by their fathers. Moreover, since the 'dying christ' is lowercase (as in 'Vision and Prayer'), he also becomes – following the symbolism of poems such as 'My hero bares his nerves' – the father's tumescent penis after ejaculation and conception. This is the father's little death, the start of death for the son/Son; for once incarnate, he must die. The sexual act is imaged as crucifixion (another 'double cross'), because it fuses death and life (as symbol of the resurrection or res-*erection* perhaps). By making 'father', 'his' and 'christ' determinedly lowercase, the poem entangles God the

Father, Son and Holy Ghost in an Oedipal rivalry, pulling the divine down to a mortal level.

In this Oedipal sense, Thomas identifies not only with Christ, but also with his natural father, he who 'sw[ings] his rainy hammer' in stanza two. D. J. Thomas's nickname of 'Jack' is, usefully for Thomas, also an Everyman and slang for the penis – 'The jacks of frost they finger in the hives' – or, more specifically, the father as possessor of the phallus (*CP*, 7). Thus, in 'If I were tickled by the rub of love', the Christ-Thomas narrator is crucified on the phallic symbol of the cross, which thereby becomes emblematic of the suffering inflicted in acquiring adult sexuality and, more generally, the suffering inflicted by fathers on their sons:

> And what's the rub? Death's feather on the nerve?
> Your mouth, my love, the thistle in the kiss?
> My Jack of Christ born thorny on the tree?
> The words of death are dryer than his stiff,
> My wordy wounds are printed with your hair.
> I would be tickled by the rub that is:
> Man be my metaphor. (*CP*, 16)

These lines offer a shocking pun on 'stiff' as the dead Christ's body and his (and the speaker's) erection: there is no faith that Christ offers salvation, and stiffness takes us closer to death ('Death's feather' is 'on the nerve' of the penis, and there is an echo of Freud's notion in *The Psychopathology of Everyday Life* that: '[t]he two antithetical concepts of sex and death are frequently linked through the idea that death makes things stiff').[50] The 'little death' of orgasm, as a form of ego-dissolution, blasphemously figures a version of the selflessness of the great death endured by Christ, but sexuality and the promise of eternal life are overcome by 'The words of death'. 'Hair', as in the Surrealists, symbolises sex, here belonging to 'my love'; the 'wordy wounds' of the poems are 'printed' with sex, but it is 'your[s]'; there is at least some degree of mutuality, escape from the deathly and 'stiff[[ness]' of the in-turned self. But 'the rub that is' is inescapably sexual and cannot be reduced to humanistic comfort in the final line, as so many have claimed; 'would be' and 'be' are subjunctive, and the speaker remains torn by desire and desperately mortal.

Boldly rewriting Christian symbolism, using wordplay to deconstruct and expose the betrayals and contradictions of the tale of the incarnation and passion, Thomas imagines (male) human existence as suspended and crucified between sexuality and death in the same way that the penis – 'hunger's emperor' – hangs between the testicles, 'two sad knaves of thieves', in 'My hero bares his nerves' (*CP*, 14). The process is complex and contradictory and is intimately bound up with history, social crisis as detumescence. Thus, in a letter of November 1933, Thomas attacked the social order which produced the First World War: 'Civilisation is a murderer. We, with the cross of a castrated Saviour cut on our brows, sink deeper and deeper with the days into the pit of the West' (*CP*, 71–2).[51] The rhetoric comes from Nietzsche and Spengler, but it is directed against war and towards the wished-for socialist revolution – one which may realise Christianity's true ideals and, thus, restore its true potency. For the present, however, in the bitterest and most blasphemous of puns, Christ dies to become 'his stiff', to become, that is, the abstract, tyrannical father who crucified him and was responsible for the war, the possessor of a phallus which is potent only in its deathliness. In 'If I were tickled', as in 'Before I knocked', Thomas mixes complicity with, and critique of, phallocentrism, but he also extends it, via Christ-as-Logos, to 'words' and the 'wordy wounds' 'printed with' the 'hair' of his 'love'. Indeed, the poem allows for grammatical confusion between 'Jack of Christ' and 'my love', and this reminds us that, as well as being an instrument of death (cross as a 'cross' place of war and conflict) and maleness (the x chromosome), Thomas sometimes imagined the cross as a sign of Christ's femaleness (this would be a Freudian reading of 'castrated Saviour').

Through the figure of Christ, then, Thomas dramatised the predicaments of adolescent sexual identity, playing *lex talionis* off against New Testament loving-kindness. His work explores the nature of belief, not its truth-content: the evocation of presence is predicated on its absence. The 'negation of the negation' expresses spiritual hunger, but to say it incorporates religious language and typology in order to renew faith goes too far. For, while God might well be dead in a philosophical sense, Christianity continued to underwrite a repressive social order that Thomas had to resist. On the other hand, the idea of God remained inextricably bound up with ideas of truth, revelation, meaning and presence generally. Resisting this required immersion in the discourse to be subverted, and thus risked reinscribing Christianity in ghostly form. Or, as Barthes noted, 'God' is liable to infect all discussions of literary texts, especially where issues of truth are at stake.[52] Thomas's use of Christ – particularly as a figure for the struggling, persecuted and yet ultimately triumphant artist – therefore shows a deep ambivalence. In life, this entailed refusal of certain self-images of the writer as Author. For Adam Philips, by contrast with the 'Men of 1914': '[t]he game [Dylan Thomas] played was the game of not playing the game of the Christ-like artist' – a parody of the 'pieties of the bohemian writer's life'.[53]

Sympathy for the devil: the trickster and 'Altarwise by owl-light'

Disbelieving, yet marked, even wounded by religion, Dylan Thomas's work often sets up the eschatological schemas premised on its binaries – 'God' and 'Devil', 'Heaven' and 'Hell' and so on – with a grotesque intensity, which simultaneously undermines them. Its speakers sympathise or identify with Christ, but do so improperly. The supreme blasphemy is the suggestion that, to the extent that both are victims framed by an Old Testament-type Nobodaddy, Christ and Satan are kin. Thus, the very title of the poem, 'Incarnate devil', presents Satan in terms of Christ and exemplifies Thomas's interest in trickster figures, those who embody a blasphemous hybridity, young dogs who drag the old gods down into the heterogeneous flux and relativism of process.[54] Yet if Christ is treated transgressively, Satan is transgressivity as a principle, his serpent-like, hybrid aspect stressed above his usual role as the principle of pure evil.[55]

Trickster figures feature in most of the world's religions, and their function is to mediate between earth and heaven, god and man. Sometimes these figures are not wholly divine. Structurally, they introduce a degree of play into religious systems, preventing them from becoming over-rigid; as boundary-breakers, they share characteristics with the licensed fool or jester and act as carnivalesque escape valves. The outcomes of their actions are often mixed, even contrary to their intentions, and frequently grotesque. Satan – whose temptation of Eve backfires on him, because it leads to Christ's sacrifice and an augmentation of God's goodness – can be viewed as a figure of this kind. If he is, heresy may result; Christianity has regularly given rise to sects, such as the Gnostics, which, taking the Church's teaching on the fallenness of the material world to its logical conclusion, argue that Satan must have been responsible for the creation, acting as God's unwitting agent (the Manichaean or dualist heresy). On the other side of the *felix culpa* equation, Christ can also be seen as God's dupe, as in 'Before I knocked'.

Such heterodox thinking occurs in Milton and Blake and, via them, in Thomas's work, with its tendency to blur Satan, Christ and Thomas himself into a single trickster figure, often with a sexual twist: the speaker of 'If I were tickled by the rub of love' observes 'The world is half the devil's and my own / Daft with the drug that's smoking in a girl' (*CP*, 16). Thomas exploits the division between Old and New Testament morality and the paradox by which God *requires* Satan to bring about the Fall, so engineering human reliance on the Son for atonement. This manipulative Yahweh is the target of 'Incarnate devil':

> Incarnate devil in a talking snake,
> The central plains of Asia in his garden,
> In shaping-time the circle stung awake,
> In shapes of sin forked out the bearded apple,
> And God walked there who was a fiddling warden
> And played down pardon from the heavens' hill. (*CP*, 37)

Rather than endorsing the 'cloven myth' of the Bible tale, Thomas's serpent acts as a trickster who brings about the Fall, but who has also 'stung awake' the 'circle' of time, mortality and history, initiating the human struggle towards self-awareness. He is 'the fathering worm' of 'Before I knocked' – a central participant in cosmogony, rather than a belated intruder (*CP*, 11). Symbolically, as Don McKay has pointed out, this assumes that the flawed nature of existence is part of its essence, not some aberration, that diachronic energy has a place in the scheme of things at least equal to that of synchronic design and that creative activity is primarily a subversive exercise.[56] Yahweh, by contrast, is a 'fiddling warden' (that is, he 'fiddles' like Nero as Rome burns, even cheats or 'fiddles' Eden's inhabitants); a jealous god, he 'plays down pardon' or forgiveness. Satan, on the other hand, 'fork[s] out' (exposes division and pays for) the 'bearded apple', which will force God to grant 'pardon' in a brilliant, Magritte-like conflation of fruit, face and pubic hair, which suggests that bearded Christ and Freud are both fruits of the Fall into 'shapes of sin' (Freud, revealingly, described beards as a form of genital-display). *Felix culpa* is given a devilish slant, as the serpent enables not only Christ's sacrifice, but human progress, too, making him a necessary sharer of the divided world.

This trickster paradigm, as it might be called, finds its most dazzling elaboration in 'Altarwise by owl-light' – the sequence of ten inverted Petrarchan sonnets concluding *Twenty-five Poems*. This is one of Thomas's limit texts, pushing the early style to the verge of what he, himself, felt was self-parody and eliciting the most ingenious of all critical explications of his work.[57] The opening sonnet has been justly celebrated as the apogee of Thomas's mesmeric monstrosity. M. L. Rosenthal and Sally McGall nicely observe that its opening lines 'delight, intrigue, and puzzle us into becoming attuned to the metaphoric fling of associative and emotional movement', as they 'put Genesis and the genitals into manic alignment':

Altarwise by owl-light in the halfway-house
The gentleman lay graveward with his furies;
Abaddon in the hang-nail cracked from Adam,
And, from his fork, a dog among the fairies,
The atlas-eater with a jaw for news,
Bit out the mandrake with tomorrow's scream.
Then, penny-eyed, that gentleman of wounds,
Old cock from nowheres and the heaven's egg,
With bones unbuttoned to the halfway winds,
Hatched from the windy salvage on one leg,
Scraped at my cradle in a walking word
That night of time under the Christward shelter,
I am the long world's gentleman, he said,
And share my bed with Capricorn and Cancer. (*CP*, 58)

Given that the sequence opens with a mention of 'my cradle' and follows, in the second sonnet, with a 'child that sucketh long' and references to the pains of adolescence, death of faith, burial and resurrection, we are entitled to read 'Altarwise' as a species of *bildungsroman*, though one like no other. Introduced, as it is, by spoonerisms (on 'wise owl' and 'altar light'), an atrocious pun (Abaddon, the Angel of the Pit, or Satan, is 'A bad 'un') and a mixture of mythologies ('furies', a 'heavens' egg', 'fairies', the Bible and Freud), it is clear that this 'tale's sailor from a Christian voyage', as sonnet X calls him, will progress through verbal *jouissance* and conceptual metamorphosis, as much as through conventional character and narrative (*CP*, 63). Setting the tone for what will follow, the usual relational guideposts of syntax, theme and narrative are highly fluid in the opening sestet of the first sonnet. At the same time, however, the use of the definite article with several items increases the sense of their belonging to a stable structure, as well as their independent, symbolic importance. The growth of the speaker within this indeterminate, yet archetypal-seeming, context, it is suggested, will be a highly conflicted process of induction into the Symbolic Orders of religion, language and poetry.

Several identities, variously overlapping, can be discerned through the verbal pyrotechnics: the 'gentleman' of line two, who lies 'graveward' in the 'halfway-house' with his 'furies'; 'Abaddon' and 'Adam' in line three; the currish 'dog among the fairies' of line four; and the 'I' who refers to 'my cradle' in line eleven. The 'gentleman' facing East is likely to be Christ. 'Abaddon' is the Angel of the Bottomless Pit – a version of Satan. Anagrammatised 'God', the 'dog', was described in Thomas's explanation of the poem in a letter to Henry Treece, as '... the rip and cur among the myths, the snapper at demons, the scarer of ghosts, the wizard's heel-chaser' – a playfully inverted Christ-as-Satan (*CL*, 301).[58] 'Adam' and the 'I' of line eleven are probably related; if the speaker is a kind of Everyman, as he usually is in Thomas, then he is human – a 'son of Adam'. But the I-protagonist can also be identified with the 'characters' presented here, too: Adam is a type of Christ, and, insofar as the 'dog' has a 'jaw (nose) for news', he is also the *South Wales Evening Post* journalist. The dog vanishes after this sole appearance and may best be considered as having turned into the poem's subversive principle, rather than surviving as a 'character'.

As this suggests, the instability of identity and the problems it exposes within the very notion of character makes for difficulty in following the action. As ever, though, identifying the (often disguised) verbs is a good first move. 'Bit', in line six, is clearly a main verb, but 'cracked', in line three, and 'fork', in line four, both require careful consideration, too. Both initially appear to be something else – 'cracked' seems a past participle, describing Abaddon within an appositive clause, thus making 'bit' the main verb of the sentence, while 'fork' seems to be a noun (Adam's groin). But if 'cracked' is a main verb, then Abaddon actively splits off from Adam (Man) and also 'cracks' from him the 'dog', who then 'bites' out Adam's genitals. 'Tomorrow's scream' is, then, that of the mandrake-genitals, so the dog is castrating Adam, but ambiguously: 'tomorrow's scream' is an anguished awareness of future mortality and turmoil, and it may be as well to be rid of it. The dog may be tearing away that form of mandrake which fears the future, the prohibitions placed on it by religion, and releasing the form for which sex is pleasurable.

As opposed to 'cracked', McKay emphasises 'fork' as the main verb, taking it to mean 'birth of a divided being', in the sense in which it is used in 'In the beginning', with the offspring being the child implied by 'my cradle' in line eleven. 'Abaddon' and the dog are thus construable as forms of the 'gentleman', making the mandrake both the gentleman's phallus *and* the body of the child: 'Hence the gentleman "bites out" the child's body in procreation, while the child being created bites out his phallus: the two acts are simultaneous imagistically and syntactically. Abaddon, the destroying angel, and Adam, infant man and the father of mankind, may then be seen to represent functions filled at once by the gentleman and the child / narrator, and not as the fixed symbolic identity of either one'.[59] This is plausible enough, too, and the blurring of gentleman, Abaddon and dog fits my sense of the poem as a mini epic of the trickster spirit. But, even more than this, perhaps, it also serves to illustrate the fact that the identities of the gentleman, Abaddon, dog and protagonist are thoroughly confused within the opening six lines of the poem.

In truth, Thomas ensured that the poem could not be fully resolved in terms of any singular narrative, nor could its characters be rendered wholly distinct from each other. The bleeding together of identities – usually an intermittent feature of his work – has become wholly pervasive in the 'Altarwise' sonnets, and character and action may be legitimately read in a number of ways. The 'gentleman', for example, may well be Christ, but he has several aliases and epithets – 'old cock from nowheres' (I, VI), 'penny-eyed' and 'gentleman of wounds' (I), 'the fake gentleman' (V), the 'long gentleman' and 'my gentle wound' (IX) – and can scarcely be construed as a single entity. He seems to create the child in the opening lines *and* be destroyed by it; the result is 'characters as moments in the ongoing process, beings upon which the actions of the poem work to wean them away from substance into energy'.[60] The integrating syntactic structures which batten down the anarchic verbal energies in Thomas's other poems are so weak in this one that we are carried along on the welter of appositive images and blurred identities, as we follow the dimly discernible protagonist.

Moments of stability flash by; in line ten of sonnet I, 'the windy salvage on one leg' suggests Christ, since a crucified man appears to be one-legged, and 'salvage' may be a synonym for salvation. On the other hand, it also conjures up the literally one-legged Long John Silver, 'the fictional trickster who hatches from windy salvages' – 'windy', in this case, meaning not so much the summit of Golgotha, but 'over-rhetorical' and 'cowardly'.[61] Yet these meanings cannot be separated from the 'Christian voyage' interpretation, either; if 'salvage' means something saved, it usually applies to ships or scrap metal, not souls. Nor is 'old cock' – a slang male greeting – the way to address Christ (you wouldn't want him 'scrap[ing]' at your cradle, either). Hailing from 'nowheres', *ex nihilo*, this figure is also 'hatched from the heaven's egg' – a divine birth like that of Castor and Pollux. But in the final two lines, he has left the 'Christward shelter'. Like the Satan of Dante's *Inferno*, he is frozen in the lowest circle of Hell, his body protruding *through* the centre of the Earth, so that it is in both northern and southern hemispheres, thus 'shar[ing] [his] bed with Capricorn and Cancer' (goatish lust and death).[62]

But it all depends on what we allow ourselves to read into a text, which so avidly and powerfully reads us. If we decide to search for continuity and coherence, there seems to be plenty of evidence for it. For example, the hemispheres of sonnet I anticipate sonnet II, whose references to the 'horizontal cross-bones of Abaddon' and 'the verticals of Adam' make a ladder of lines of longitude and latitude, by which the speaker can 'Jacob to the stars'. The hemispheric / mapping imagery is continued in sonnet III, which concludes: 'We rung our weathering changes on the ladder, / Said the antipodes, and twice spring chimed' (*CP*, 59). Satisfyingly, these lines sound like a characteristic assertion of process: spring does, indeed, 'chime' twice a year on the globe, once in the northern and once in the southern hemisphere. Yet this train of images soon peters out; like others, it is not allowed to impose a unifying narrative. It is an example of how, as readers, we are encouraged to hypothesise and project such structures, only to find that they are inadequate (the fact that its images are of mapping makes this point with even more force). Like the doubting Thomas who is the protagonist of the sequence, our attempts to discover order only work locally and provisionally, bringing us up against the constructedness and provisionality of all narrative and belief.

It is not just that 'Altarwise' is about craft or writing, then – although it clearly is in sonnets VI and VII, which refer to 'oyster vowels' and 'written woods' – but that it embodies the trickster principle itself, even though it cannot, because of its very nature, fix this in a single figure. Its mongrel energies (de)structure the story of the protagonist and the various appearances of the 'gentleman'. The 'I' is mortal, defined as such in sonnet II's 'Death is all metaphors, shape in one history', and we follow it ascending, childlike, like 'the lamb on knocking knees' (sonnet III), but 'manned by midnight' and subject, at all times, to the logic of process as articulated by the 'hollow agent' at II's close – 'Hairs of your head … Are but the roots of nettles and of feathers … hemlock-headed in the wood of weathers' (*CP*, 59). The trickster principle dominates: the description of creative-destructive process in sonnet III recounts the Fall, in which Adam's wether (a castrated ram, rather than the 'castrated Saviour') becomes the 'Butt' of the 'tree-tailed worm that mounted Eve' in a 'flock of horns' in a scenario which 'aggressively conflates Eden's two most subversive elements (sex and the Devil) and combines them with the phallus' (*CP*, 59).[63]

The very openness of the approach is the theme of sonnet IV – a series of trickster-type questions of the kind asked by young children, recalling the 'What colour is glory?' of 'My world is pyramid':

> What is the metre of the dictionary?
> The size of genesis? the short spark's gender?

Shade without shape? the shape of Pharaoh's echo? ...
(Questions are hunchbacks to the poker marrow). (*CP*, 60)

The child's questions concern sex ('Where do babies come from?').
Literally, they are question marks which are the shape of embryos in
the womb or 'hunchbacks'. More discursively, the questions themselves
are treated as deformed, bent or crooked by the straight 'poker marrow'
(phallic virility) of the sexually mature adult. Even so, they may achieve
what the Bible tells us is impossible, its 'camel's eye' 'needl[ing]' through
the shroud' to see the embryo as 'a hump of splinters' in the mother's
womb. On the other hand, 'through' may mean not just *bypassing* death,
but seeing the embryo *as a result of* death. The last four lines answer a
question which has not been asked, but which is at the heart of, and the
answer to, all those which preceded it: what is love? 'Love', we learn, is
'a reflection of the mushroom features' of the embryo, reflected on 'the
bread-sided field' of the womb-wall. That is, all love begins in self-love
in the womb, but the 'stills' of narcissism become an 'Ark-lamped' film
turned outwards to others, when the 'smiling' 'close-up[s]' of the self are
'thrown back upon the cutting flood', which comes with birth and life.

The autonomous tendencies of language – the 'metre of the dictionary'
– are present throughout. So the 'rip' in 'Rip of the vaults' in sonnet
III is also R.I.P. ('vaults' being tombs, as well as jumps), leading to 'Rip
Van Winkle' two lines later – an apt figure for the self who is dissolved
in death, re-fashioned and re-awakened by the round of process. In
the same way that 'hump' in 'hump of splinters' leads to 'camel', III's
'marrow ladle' leads to 'poker marrow' in IV and then punningly suggests
'poker', as the card game, in V. In this case, it provokes a full-blown
Wild West fantasy, in which the archangel Gabriel appears as a cowboy
card-sharping evangelist working in cahoots with 'Jesu' and 'trumping
up' (the last trump, as well as a trump card) the 'king of spots' or Satan:

> And from the windy West came two-gunned Gabriel,
> From Jesu's sleeve trumped up the king of spots,
> The sheath-decked jacks, queen with a shuffled heart;
> Said the fake gentleman in a suit of spades,
> Black-tongued and tipsy from salvation's bottle,
> Rose my Byzantine Adam in the night ... (*CP*, 60)

The 'gentleman' is now an imposter (and so may be a version of the
speaker himself) – a kind of black-garbed, drunken hellfire preacher-
cum-undertaker, whose linkage of sex to death makes the Adamic
protagonist rise 'in the night' in an erectile, as well as a spiritual, manner

('Said' is the main verb here, and 'rose' is used transitively as 'made to rise'). As a result of the 'loss of blood' or semen, the protagonist '[falls]' on 'Ishmael's plain', the sea, 'Ishmael' being the narrator of *Moby-Dick*, as well as the biblical prophet. The tendency to place the main verb at the wrong end of the sentence ('said') is a reminder that the sonnets are inverted, providing a pretext for convoluted syntax. More broadly, as McKay notes, this sonnet: 'speaks about, and demonstrates, the craft of illusions – sleight of hand in poker, tall tales in religion and the Wild West'.[64] '[M]y Byzantine Adam' is the 'old Adam', 'Byzantine' perhaps because of his impossibly complex and confused state, hormonally driven and all at sea, where 'Jonah's Moby snatched me by the hair'.[65] Moby (Dick) is the penis, and whales (Wales), as in 'Ballad of the Long-legged Bait', symbolise phallic activity. Here, however, 'salt [sexual] Adam' is 'cross-stroked', perhaps in masturbation, perhaps in crucifixion, towards the 'frozen angel', Satan, who is tricksterishly confused with the crucified Christ 'Pin-legged on pole-hills'. In one of the most surrealist-seeming and evocative conclusions of the sequence, the speaker is left: 'By waste seas where the white bear quoted Virgil / And sirens singing from our lady's sea-straw' (*CP*, 60).

This mid-point of 'Altarwise' articulates a crisis, if not quite a specific dark night of the soul as Ralph Maud believes.[66] The 'sirens' are those of sexual desire and writing itself, and suffering continues in sonnet VI, which details the pangs of composition, as the protagonist produces a 'Cartoon of slashes' from the tight-lipped 'oyster vowels' and 'sea silence' on his 'wick of words'. Like the young Thomas toiling over his notebooks, he is 'tallow eyed' through burning the midnight oil or wax (and possessing, accordingly, a molten tallow 'I'). Utterance, as in 'In my craft or sullen art', comes at a high price. Here, it involves the return of the creatures of earlier sonnets, medusa, stinging-nettle and 'old cock from nowheres', resembling the gothic-grotesque material of the pre-*18 Poems* period; so daunting are they, that utterance leads to silencing, as the 'minstrel tongue' is 'lopped'. The speaker is reduced to being 'time's joker'; the would-be card becomes mere filler in the pack – a supplement surplus to the requirements of the real game, within, and around whom, conflict and role-switching rages. At one level, then, this sonnet describes the crisis of the self as a stylistic impasse (and 'Altarwise' is a primary example of this dead-end) and the potentially catastrophic outcome of its 'voyage' at the hands of the 'bagpipe-breasted ladies in the deadweed' or Lorelei-like 'sirens'.

Sonnet VII can be read – to stay with this biographical thread – as a charting of the point at which Thomas hit upon the process poetic. It appears in the lines that Donald Davie famously found to be 'radically vicious', because their syntax appeared to abandon the 'intelligible structure of the conscious mind'.[67] Leaving aside the fact that the 'intelligible structure of the conscious mind' – even after the half a century of major neuroscientific advances since he wrote this – is nothing like as obvious a thing as Davie seems to assume, the difficulty may nevertheless be conceded:

> Time is the tune my ladies lend their heartbreak,
> From bald pavilions and the house of bread
> Time tracks the sound of shape on man and cloud,
> On rose and icicle the ringing handprint. (*CP*, 61)

Walford Davies convincingly argues that the effect of 'simultaneity and identification' that is created here is not, in fact, a vice, but a requirement of the theme of the poem; indeed, a different instance of precisely that unity of subject and form that Davie himself demanded. In the line 'Time tracks the sound of shape on man and cloud', Davies notes that: 'what is being mimed is … the simultaneity of time and space' – a crucial component of process. 'Time tracks the sound of shape on man and cloud' – a line which Davie finds 'completely void of meaning', is, for Davies:

> Thomas's way of expressing what Time is: … imaginable only in terms of the sound and shape of things – things that are not abstract, and that move ('cloud'), fade ('rose'), and melt ('icicle'). Time 'tracks' these things both in the sense of creating the sad music of their mortality (the sound or significance of their shapes) as on a *sound-track*, and also in the sense of *tracking them down*. The reality of abstract Time is simultaneous and identical with the physical things it destroys.[68]

The creative-destructive aspects of process are thus enacted in the lines' simultaneity effects, especially in the way in which the last line extends the subject of 'Time' of the penultimate one, hovering in a grammatical stasis. In a more radically mimetic way than even Davies would allow, sonnet VII also offers a language taken back to 'all the written woods' of books (via the metonymy with leaves), as previously mentioned in line two; one, incidentally, alluding to the ancient Welsh tree alphabet, or, as Thomas puts it in lines four and five: 'Genesis in the root, the scarecrow word, / And one light's language in the book of trees'. Having reached this point, VII can yield to the supreme moment of time-space simultaneity in sonnet VIII, when trees become the Tree, words the

Word and crucifixion becomes the logical outcome of the crossing fictions of 'Altarwise':

> This was the crucifixion on the mountain,
> Time's nerve in vinegar, the gallow grave
> As tarred with blood as the bright thorns I wept;
> The world's my wound, God's Mary in her grief,
> Bent like three trees and bird-papped through her shift,
> With pins for teardrops is the long wound's woman.
> This was the sky, Jack Christ, each minstrel angle
> Drove in the heaven-driven of the nails
> Till the three-coloured rainbow from my nipples
> From pole to pole leapt round the snail-waked world.
> I by the tree of thieves, all glory's sawbones
> Unsex the skeleton this mountain minute,
> And by the blowclock witness of this sun
> Suffer the heaven's children through my heartbeat. (*CP*, 62)

Again, as in the sestet of sonnet I, subjectivity is in radical flux, and, as Philip Lahey usefully suggests, cinema and visual art offer a particularly apt model for approaching it.[69] This is because the poem's narrative cuts between the different 'minstrel angle[s]' (punning on 'ministering angels') of several viewers, while its extreme distortion and intensity – embodied wincingly by 'Time's nerve in vinegar' – conjures up Expressionist paintings of the time (say, Max Beckmann's 'Departure' triptych of 1932–3) or Picasso's crucifixion prints and oil paintings of 1930–2, inspired by Grünewald's Isenheim altarpiece of a tortured, thorn-studded Christ.[70] In Picasso's violently-coloured, distorted painting, Christ, with a huge, gaping head, is surrounded by other 'monstrous heads', including those of the Virgin Mary and Mary Magdalen, his side being pierced by a picador, as soldiers dice for his robe on a drum.[71] The Gospel according to St John records the presence of another Mary at the crucifixion – Mary the wife of Cleophas – and this trio of Marys, 'bent like three trees' of the three crosses, matches the male trio of Christ and the two thieves and the Holy Trinity itself, 'creating a complex image of womankind in "God's Mary in her grief"'.[72]

The confusion of the speaker with other possible subject positions and of male and female is important in helping us to read the poem as an account of the creative act, with the crucified Christ as artist (just as Picasso's painting, despite its public theme, presents a private image of desperation). Like Christ, the artist is 'all glory's sawbones' – a doctor of glory, able to overcome mortality by defeating time in his work, thus opening the kingdom of the spirit to the 'heaven's children', humanity, even as he turns to seed by witnessing this 'sun'-like glory (a 'blowclock' being a seeded dandelion). The 'skeleton', Death, is 'unsex[ed]', has sex taken away from him, as fear of the death innate in sexuality – a perpetual Thomas concern – is removed by this sacrifice (the 'blowclock' is also the 'gentleman's genitals, and His potency is now spread among all men'). As McKay claims: 'Thomas is violating the integrity of the Christian myth by moving the redemptive function from the Christ-figure to the narrator and by superimposing a fertility rite on the crucifixion'.[73] Like Prometheus (or 'the Dog'), the poet-narrator steals power from authority, relativising it. Thomas also restores the Renaissance's sexual reading of Christ's crucifixion as the nuptials of God and Man – one which had recently been given visual form in David Jones's 1931 engraving 'The Bride', depicting a crucifix in which the wound in Christ's foot is vulva-like.[74]

All of which is in line with the poem's general tendency – in Rosenthal and Gall's words – to show 'sexual energy heroically contend[ing]' with 'sheer fatality' and 'time' in 'life's epic struggle to persist'.[75] The tree of words of sonnet VII has become the 'gallow' (shallow / gallows) grave of the cross; the poet's cruci*fiction* has been written in terms of the crucifixion; Thomas uses the crucifixion of Christ as a metaphor for his own immolation. Part of the price to be paid for this audacity is his entombment in sonnet IX. As we would expect, the embalming process is highly textualised, and he is consigned to the 'dusts and furies' of an Egyptian 'triangle landscape', as sterile as those of 'My world is pyramid'. 'My gentle wound' ('gentle' being a near-homonym for 'gentile' and 'genital') leads only to a 'World in the sand', with 'rivers of the dead [Egyptian for the Milky Way] around my neck', like a noose (*CP*, 62).

Sonnet X, in optative mood, like IX, presents a far more coherent self than VIII. It summarises the 'tale's sailor' or sailor's tale of the sequence, showing the speaker now to be 'Atlaswise' (or worldly-wise), rather than religiously 'Altarwise', and 'hold[ing] halfway off the dummy bay', which is the false ('dummy') haven once offered by belief:

> Let the tale's sailor from a Christian voyage
> Atlaswise hold halfway off the dummy bay
> Time's ship-racked gospel on the globe I balance:
> So shall winged harbours through the rockbirds' eyes
> Spot the blown word, and on the seas I image
> December's thorn screwed in a brow of holly. (*CP*, 63)

Following resurrection from the Christian sacrifice, which is also that of Christian belief, he seeks a new apocalyptic beginning, which is personal, phallic, of the body and socialistically 'red'. He understands the world now through non-supernatural representations, and his 'ship-racked gospel' is that of 'Time', to be balanced by him 'on the globe', like Atlas's burden. The individual must shoulder responsibility for his actions, rejecting religious justifications. 'Halfway' is crucial: looking back to 'halfway house', the protagonist registers his wary distance from, but lack of any complete break with, religion; he remains aware of it as a form, however distorted, of the 'country of the spirit'. Yet his own 'bay' or harbour – that of art – will be a 'winged' one, and so the sequence ends with a challenge to St Peter – founder of the Church – and an assertion of imaginative vision:

> Let the first Peter from a rainbow's quayrail
> Ask the tall fish swept from the bible east,
> What rhubarb man peeled in her foam-blue channel
> Has sown a flying garden round that sea-ghost?
> Green as beginning, let the garden diving
> Soar, with its two bark towers, to that Day
> When the worm builds with the gold straws of venom
> My nest of mercies in the rude, red tree. (*CP*, 63)

A former fisherman, Peter, it is claimed, holds the keys (quays) to the kingdom, and he is envisaged at the 'quayrail' of the harbour of faith (God's covenant in the rainbow), angling for Christ 'the tall fish'. The sailor-poet would have Peter ask Christ which 'rhubarb man' (this is the pink and phallus-shaped poet himself, full of poetical blather or 'rhubarb') has inseminated the 'sea-ghost's' 'foam-blue channel' – a rhetorical question, which has, in a sense, already been answered in the sequence, which is the rhubarb man's poetic fruit or catch. What does the Church have to offer by way of a 'flying garden'? In Thomas's double language, the sailor may also be asking for Christ to explain incarnation and sexuality: 'peter' is a term for penis, and the 'foam-blue channel' is a vagina ('foam-blue' makes it Mary's and, therefore, Thomas-Christ's mother's, too). But the main sense, I feel, lies in the call for the garden of the Fall and the pie-in-the-sky of Christianity's promises of atonement and redemption to (oxymoronically) 'diving / Soar'; that is, to realise that only by descending to this world will the garden be redeemed and the potential of the human spirit to 'soar' be realised. The 'bark towers' are the trees of life and the knowledge of good and evil, both of which are as necessary to a secular vision of society as a religious one.

The crucial element is the central role of the trickster worm (or serpent / Satan), who will build out of negativity, out of poison, the speaker's future 'nest of mercies in the rude, red tree.' Thomas invokes the notion of *pharmakon* – the homeopathic dosage of poison which cures – symbolised in the snake-twined caduceus of the medical profession. A true vision of utopia has to seek the 'gold straws' within the venom, in order to make the bricks that it will build with. This being Thomas, the final audacious image – Empson found it 'ragingly good' – is also 'rude', unvarnished and offensive, but it is also the Anglo-Saxon rood or cross, which fuses with the 'red tree' of the phallus and political radicalism in a visionary-utopian rewriting of Nonconformism and socialism to create one of the most astonishing conclusions of any twentieth-century English poem.[76]

Surre(gion)alism and parody

Many contemporaries regarded Thomas's early poetry and prose works – 'Altarwise by owl-light', above all – as evidence that he was influenced by the most recent avant-garde European movement in the arts, Surrealism. Indeed, Thomas had given some justification for this widespread belief; in his 'Answers to an Enquiry', published in *New Verse* in October 1934, he admitted to being influenced by Freud and spoke of poetry's role as using the light cast on the unconscious by Freud to 'drag further into the clean nakedness of light even more of the hidden causes' (*EPW*, 150). This sounded very much like the surrealist objective of tapping the sources of imaginative energy in the unconscious, in order to 'prosecute' the reality of the everyday world. Moreover, as I suggested in Chapter 1, the reading of *transition* and other surrealist materials was one of the catalysts of the process style. Yet Thomas viewed the surrealist label, if not the thing itself, as a public liability. By 1935, he was denying that he had even heard of it to Richard Church, chief editor at his new publisher, Dent. Admittedly, the circumstances were unusual – the fogeyish Church seemed to be getting cold feet about publishing *Twenty-five Poems*, because he detected in it the 'pernicious' presence of surrealism, for which he had a particular dislike, and Thomas was evidently pulling the wool over his eyes (*CL*, 231).[77] But even when writing to his contemporary, Henry Treece, in 1938, Thomas distanced himself from surrealism ('my own sane bee in a bonnet can never be a pal of that French wasp forever stinging itself to death with a tail of boiled string' – a reference to his own antics at the 1936 International Surrealist Exhibition in London, where he toured the galleries offering visitors boiled string with the query 'Weak or strong?') (*CL*, 349). Less colourfully, in his 'Poetic Manifesto' of 1950, he also separated himself unequivocally from 'super-realism', as he called it. Yet read carefully, these disavowals are clearly aimed not at surrealism *per se*, as much as at the dominant definition of it as automaticist. Despite the multiple denials to the contrary, the early prose and poetry exists in a fruitful dialogue with Surrealism.

The context of the letter to Treece on 16 May 1938, for example, concerns Treece's intention to write a study of Thomas's work, and Thomas's keenness to scotch claims, such as that made by Stephen Spender in 1935, that his poetry was 'turned on like a tap ... just poetic stuff with no beginning nor end, shape, or intelligent and intelligible control' (*CL*, 344). Yet, as his letter to Treece of just two months before demonstrates, Thomas explained that he accorded the involuntary and unconscious a role in composing his poems: 'I make, *or let be made in me*' (added emphasis). Similarly, the nub of denial in the 'Poetic Manifesto' is based on André Breton's definition in the First Surrealist Manifesto of 1924, as cited by David Gascoyne in *A Short Survey of Surrealism*: 'SURREALISM: Pure psychic automatism, by which it is intended to express, verbally, in writing, or by other means, the real process of thought. Thought's dictation, in the absence of all control exercised by reason and outside all aesthetic or moral preoccupation'.[78] Thomas noted in response 'I do not mind where the images of a poem are dragged up: drag them up, if you like, from the nethermost sea of the hidden self; but before they reach paper, they must go through all the rational processes of the intellect' (*EPW*, 159). But, like his definition of the 'dialectical method' for Treece, the 'Poetic Manifesto' renounces the possibility of full, conscious control of the writing process; in fact, the points of maximum creativity in it turn out to be those moments when conscious control over the poem is lost, and the unforeseen linguistic event is able to manifest itself in the 'holes and gaps in the works of the poem' (*EPW*, 160).

As we have seen, Thomas's main exposure to Surrealism is likely to have come from *transition*, which he was reading by December 1933, if not before, and even the circumstantial evidence for his fascination with it is considerable.[79] Far from being repelled by it, Thomas seems to have privately believed in the potentially transformative power of Surrealism; a sense of being let down by its doctrinaire impulses is surely what informed a letter of 14 August 1935 to Daniel Jones, in which he lamented that 'Even surrealism, which seemed to have hopes and promise, preaches the decay of reality' (*CL*, 224). Next year, however, Thomas attended the International Surrealist Exhibition in London (reputedly contracting gonorrhoea from the Surrealist Phantom, Sheila Legge, who wandered the halls of the exhibition masked with a meat-grille covered in roses, brandishing a leg of lamb) and gave a reading on 26 June 1936 with Paul Éluard.[80] In the same year, he contributed to *transition* and Roger Roughton's *Contemporary Poetry and Prose* (1936–7) – the only British-based surrealist journal.[81] As late as 1950, he was the Stage Manager Who Gives the Clues in a one-off production at the Institute of Contemporary Arts (ICA) of Picasso's Surrealist play *Le desire est attrapé par le cul* (genteelly rendered as *Desire Caught by the Tail*), and, on his second US reading tour in 1952, he and Caitlin Thomas were the guests of Max Ernst and Dorothea Carrington.[82] More importantly, Thomas's poems and early stories are replete with frankly Surrealist devices, imagery and themes.

More substantively, any list of surrealist concerns – madness, the unconscious, primitive art, dreams, childhood, conjunctions of the mechanical and biological, biomorphism and unnerving transitions between seemingly unrelated images – fits much of Thomas's work between 1933 and 1941 and even beyond (the last section of 'Ceremony After a Fire Raid', for example, published in a special Lorca issue of *Our Time*). The earlier poems are saturated with surreal imagery and even refer to specific Surrealist moments and icons: the line 'Splitting the long eye open' in 'I, in my intricate image' refers to the eyeball-slicing climax of Dalí and Buñuel's *Un Chien Andalou*, while the 'lionhead' of 'How shall my animal' conjures up the lion-headed protagonist of Ernst's *Une Semaine de Bonté*, as noted in Chapter 3 (a reminder that David Gascoyne's 'Charity Week' was based on the Ernst work and that Gascoyne and Thomas met and shared a publisher during this period). Thomas's claim that readers should take the 'literal meaning' of his poems matches Gascoyne's comment on Eluard's *La Rose publique* that: 'Every line means exactly what it says' and the literalism of Surrealism generally (*CL*, 348). The merging of inner and outer, too – one of Surrealism's favourite effects – is systematically brought about by Thomas's microcosmic discourse. Even at the level of grammatical mannerism – namely, the use of definite and indefinite articles – Thomas can be seen to match Surrealist practice. Take, for example, the final stanza of 'A process in the weather of the heart':

A process in the weather of the world
Turns ghost to ghost; each mothered child
Sits in their doubled shade.
A process blows the moon into the sun,

Pulls down the shabby curtains of the skin;
And the heart gives up its dead. (*CP*, 11)

Here, Thomas uses the definite (and possessive) article to gesture, disorientatingly, towards things as if the reader is familiar with them ('*the* weather', '*their* doubled shade'), while the indefinite article, in its unnerving refusal of specificity, creates a displacement from the world of the human that conveys a distinct menace ('*A* process'?). Elsewhere, Thomas's mixing of universalism and the particular – as in 'And drown the cargoed apples in their tides' – encompasses a specific, reprehensible activity with universal-mythic generalisation to produce what Peter Nicholls has called Surrealism's 'interlocking of the absurd and the everyday'.[83] Similarly, Thomas's habit of using end-stopped lines was also a Surrealist habit, while the uncanny transitions in scale and scene of a poem such as 'I, in my intricate image' or the Daliesque imagery of 'I make this in a warring absence', as well as in stories such as 'An Adventure from an Work in Progress', leave no doubt as to why he is cited under Surrealism in glossaries of literary terms.[84]

It is not merely Thomas's work's thematic and imagistic qualities that align it with Surrealism, as we have seen. Paul C. Ray and Peter Nicholls have rightly argued that the imagery of Gascoyne's Surrealist poems is over-visual, conventional and lacks self-reflexiveness: 'Gascoyne ... misses that aspect of Surrealism that is obsessed with the work of *interpretation*. For while the most notable aspect of Surrealist writing is at first sight its capacity to produce the striking image, we find also, from Lautréamont to Péret, a deeper fascination with the alternative logic of the dream and the art-work, a logic which is conceptual rather than visual'.[85] This 'interpretative' aspect and 'deeper fascination', the generation of a genuine frisson – one which does not rely merely on the whimsical juxtaposition of dissimilars – is precisely what we do find in Thomas, of course, where material propagates itself under our eyes and is convincing as evidence of psychic exploration, because it is allied to memorable rhythm and narrative drive. But it is also a key to the reason why Thomas has not been viewed as surrealist and also for misreading surrealism's place in British culture more generally.

To understand this, we need to recall that the difference between surrealism's 'striking image' and 'alternative logic' aspects, which were encoded within it from the start of the movement. Its founding document, André Breton's surrealist manifesto of 1924, offered two definitions – one centring on psychic automatism as a way of manifesting the repressed activities of the mind; the other, 'encyclopaedic', having to do with a more mediated practice, based on forms of association. This second variety was said to be immanent in dream states, sexual attraction and the free play of thought and language and is the definition that is most relevant to Thomas's Joycean, gothic-grotesque, hybrid-parodic practice. Breton's second manifesto placed less emphasis on automatism, but was, even so, criticised by Eugene Jolas in his essay 'The Revolution of the Word' (published in *transition* in 1929) for idealism and for the ambiguity that flowed from this dual definition. For Jolas, 'pure psychic automatism' was impossible: the conscious mind would always mediate (to some degree) material that had issued from the unconscious, however much artists tried to bypass it. It 'was not enough to whirl the unaccustomed realities of the dream-state together', therefore. Rather, what was required was 'a means of creating the a-logical grammar which alone can mirror the new dimension'.[86] In part, Jolas was redefining surrealism's potential to fit *transition*'s prize exhibit – instalments of Joyce's *Work in Progress* – but this hardly disproves his case. An area of convergence between the two positions can be glimpsed in Breton's amplification in 1932 of an aspect of surrealism which had also been present from the start, namely its claim to roots in a native British vein of fantastic, nonsensical and fabular writing, which included Swift, Gothic novels, the Graveyard School poets, Blake, Edward Lear, Lewis Carroll and Synge.[87] This nativising of surrealism was taken up by Charles Madge in 'Surrealism for the English' in *New Verse* in December 1933 and also by Herbert Read in a 1935 review of Hugh Sykes Davies's surrealist novel *Petron*: 'under another name, or no name at all, it [surrealism] is already indigenous … Webster, Peele, Donne, Young, Blake, Beddoes, Poe, Swinburne … might all be regarded as precursors'.[88]

The area of overlap between Breton's, Madge's and Read's list of forebears and the intertextual mulch that fed Thomas's process poetic practices (as discussed in Chapter 1) is extremely close and highly suggestive. There is also a parallel to be drawn between the specifically biomorphic component of process which Thomas was developing at the end of 1933 and during 1934. Discussions of biomorphism, surrealism, abstraction and their political contexts were rife at this time and not confined to visual or literary theorising. The term 'biomorphic' began as an etymologically logical term in late nineteenth-century anthropology, but it was Thomas's then-friend Geoffrey Grigson who first deployed it in 1935 to denote a new kind of abstraction in the visual arts – one which combined geometrical designs with an exercising of memory and the emotions. Grigson's aim was to promote a resynthesising of intellect with emotion, form with matter, and while he soon veered towards promoting neo-Augustan asperities himself, the terms of his advocacy certainly provide a context for, and may even reflect, the impact that Thomas's poetry was making at this time. Biomorphism also featured heavily in Read's defence of abstract art and surrealism in the name of an organicist, biocentric politics of anarchism, similar in many ways to Thomas's own heterodox socialism. Against Communist Party claims that realism was the only permissible revolutionary mode, in *Art and Industry* (1935), Read defended abstract art for keeping 'the formal essence of all art' alive, and, in *Art and Society* (1937), he claimed that surrealism's goal was to unify the psyche with social life in recognition of the current lack of 'organic connection' between the two. Read's high praise for Thomas's *18 Poems* and *The Map of Love* reflect his belief that it was Thomas who best exemplified a modernist, 'biocentric', organic poetry which attempted this unification, and it is telling that, in 1950, Thomas used Read's own word for surrealism, 'super-realism'.

Given this context, it is possible to see how, with only a few external hints and under the gothic-grotesque fusions of his process style, Thomas could forge a form of Anglo-Welsh modernism under the period sign of surrealism – or, for want of an existing label, something that might be termed 'surregionalism'. Like Jolas, Read and Madge, but unlike Gascoyne, Thomas pragmatically rejected the programmatic and automaticist aspects of French surrealism and exploited its 'encyclopaedic' and Joycean aspect. This has been the source of difficulty in placing and understanding his relationship to surrealism. The general British perception of the movement has been a caricature version of the automaticist strand; surrealism equals the dream-like landscapes of Dalí, it involves drugs, insanity, sexual perversion and is little more than a synonym for 'weird'. Against this, sections of the British cultural élite, always fretting at the country's backwardness vis-à-vis European art and embarrassed by this vulgarised version, has difficulty in endorsing any native response to surrealism which does not comply closely with French practice.[89] Peter Nicholl's treatment of the subject, excellent in many ways, nevertheless claims that: 'English "neo-surrealists" were constantly falling short of their continental model', finding in surrealism 'an instigation to return to an older, deeply engrained romanticism while at the same time appearing to do something new and of the time'.[90] This reflects a too easy assumption of Parisian practice as normative, it seems to me, and overlooks the innovative aspects of a *British* biomorphic-surrealised 'romanticism' (Nicholl's chapter title, 'Surrealism in England', is revealing in this sense). Thus, he can write approvingly of 'Joyce discovering the movements of the unconscious not in visual images but in the workings of language itself. Dream and language … were intersecting worlds we inhabit rather than merely vehicles of self-expression', and yet fail to connect this with the Joycean Thomas's working 'from', rather than 'towards' words.[91] Against the evidence, Thomas's tactical denials of involvement with surrealism are taken at face value, as are Breton's own comments, and Thomas is deemed to have been 'more influenced by the English romantics than Breton'.[92] The superficiality of his engagement with surrealism is still maintained by certain avant-garde poet-critics, but the assertion is never accompanied by a discussion of just how poems like 'When, like a running grave' work if not surrealistically:

> When, like a running grave, time tracks you down,
> Your calm and cuddled is a scythe of hairs,
> Love in her gear is slowly through the house,
> Up naked stairs, a turtle in a hearse,
> Hauled to the dome,
>
> Comes, like a scissors stalking, tailor age,
> Deliver me who, timid in my tribe,
> Of love am barer than Cadaver's trap
> Robbed of the foxy tongue, his footed tape
> Of the bone inch,
>
> Deliver me, my masters, head and heart … (*CP*, 19)

This is one of many poems in which Thomas's method of setting disparate items within a standard syntax (but of suspended, simultaneous-seeming clauses) matches surrealism's deadpan presentation of incongruous and monstrous material in banal contexts. 'Running grave' (literally chasing, but also running like a sore), 'scythe of hairs', 'dove', 'hearse', 'stalking' scissors and 'foxy tongue' all seem arbitrary, but closer attention reveals associative logic and wordplay; thus, 'turtle' initially seems only the animal, but then in the context of 'calm and cuddled' and 'Love in her gear', it also becomes a turtle-dove: the sense of the inevitable death of love bizarrely enriches that of the very slow creature in the slowest of all vehicles, although, at another level, 'Love in her gear' is Delilah-like – a thief of energy, even as she is 'hauled to the dome', cerebralised or idealised in the starry dome of the mind or night sky. It is not that Thomas wants us to be able to rationalise the surrealist *frisson* away;

rather, he wants to multiply the narrative possibilities in a parenthesis between lines two and five, before the main verb 'comes' in line six. We can see how wordplay develops the narrative, with puns on 'gear' (clothing, differential), and we can feel the impact of surreal metaphor in the scythe (love and Time's) made from human hair. In surrealist metaphor, two simple terms are juxtaposed to create a third more potent than the sum of its parts.

As Geoff Ward has it: 'a Surrealist metaphor is a collage in miniature ... Strength comes from the shock-effect of encountering in poetic language something we could never meet elsewhere'.[93] No-one will ever see a 'scythe of hairs'; thus, it displays the militant literalism of surrealist metaphor mentioned earlier – that is, it behaves as if its attachments were not metaphorical, but metonymic. It is impossible to tell whether the 'scythe' is the girlfriend with scissors, a scythe made from hair, or hairs which cut like a scythe (castration fear, as well as the Grim Reaper, is implicit in the surrealist association of hair with female genitalia). Thus, the third term which is the metaphor 'forces an equality of attention onto the two originating terms ... by the equal weighting of the component nouns'.[94] It is also, of course, another of Thomas's cybernetic tropes fusing organic with inorganic. It is as far as it could be, then, from Gascoyne's inert, visual surrealism, although it is certainly in accord with Eluard's and Aragon's belief that surrealism had more to do with 'free play of ... language' than images.[95] Because his surrealism is one of the reasons for Thomas's international reputation, it is important to insist on this fact (he was, among other things, the most important surrealist poet in English before the New York School poets of the 1950s, albeit of a very different, less 'pure' variety). And if his hybrid or mannerist surrealism differs from European kinds, there are nevertheless some striking parallels to be drawn between it and that of Lorca, early Mandelstam and the Paul Celan of *Mohn und Gedächtnis* (as I argue in the Conclusion).

Thomas's surre(gion)al surrealism, then, availed itself of the materials available from his hybrid Anglo-Welsh origins, linking these to the dream, madness and visionary aspects of surrealism, as he discovered in *transition* and elsewhere, drawing sustenance for his process style from surrealism's 'gargoyle thinking'.[96] The operation was closely related to his taste for parody; Annis Pratt has claimed that in 'The Orchards', Thomas: '*parod[ies]* the surrealist method as a style which drives the hero, Marlais, to despair that "the word is too much with us"'.[97] Yet it might be better to say that such writings, like the poetry, reflect the way in which avant-garde practice required parody as part of a protective colouration in a culture inimical to innovation and experiment. Answering Glyn Jones's claim in a review of *Twenty-five Poems* that he had 'begun Guying himself', Thomas confessed, bullishly, that 'I'm not sorry that, in that Work in Progress thing ['Altarwise'], I did carry "certain features to their logical conclusion". It had, I think, to be done; the result had to be, in many of the lines & verses anyway, mad parody; and I'm glad that I parodied these features so soon after making them, & that I didn't leave it to anyone else' (*CL*, 272).[98] By this date, however, as he undoubtedly knew, a parody of 'Altarwise' part VIII had actually appeared in the journal *Comment*, and he was, in any case, parodying 'Altarwise' to amuse his friends. William Sansom's mid-1930s memoir 'Coming to London' recounts a meeting with Thomas: '"'I am the short world's shroud', he said" – said Mr. Thomas, I remember – "I share my bed with Finchley Road and foetus" ...'.[99] Self-parody, one might say, was inescapably an aspect of Thomas's surregionalist mannerist modernism, and, in some ways, it resembles what Nicholls identifies as English neo-surrealism's 'domestication' of surrealism.[100] Yet that should not distract from its achievements. Thomas's version of surrealism did not simply *invert* passive realism, as Gascoyne's did, or merely transcribe images, but explored and enacted the ceaseless trafficking between language and the conscious and unconscious mind. The closing of the period of his most intense engagement with this phenomenon is marked by 'How shall my animal' – a meta-poem, which makes the process of writing and its relationship to the linguistic unconscious its explicit theme and draws a line under his recent immersion in states close to the pre-linguistic. It reflects elegiacally yet with astonishing linguistic vigour on Thomas's understanding that, if an attempt to replicate French surrealism was impossible in English literary culture, a parodic, gothic-grotesque critique of those attempts made from the Anglo-Welsh margins could nevertheless produce much of the shock of dragging the 'animal' up from the recesses of the self: 'Lie dry, rest robbed, my beast. / You have kicked from a dark den, leaped up the whinnying light, / And dug your grave in my breast' (*CP*, 76).

'A border case like myself': Welsh Thomas, hybridity and postcoloniality

At the outset of his career, Dylan Thomas had a keen sense of himself as a Welsh writer. Despite later aspersions, he was always at least interested in the possibility of being part of a self-sufficient cadre of writers based in Wales. As early as 1931, his letters to young fellow writers from Swansea show that he made substantial progress towards assembling the first issue of a 'highbrow' literary journal, to be called *prose & verse* (lowercase in emulation of *transition*), before being defeated by a lack of subscribers. A review of Scottish poets for *The Adelphi* in September 1934 claimed that: 'The true future of English poetry, poetry that can be ... read aloud, that comes to life out of the red heart through the brain, lies in the Celtic countries where the universities are establishments for obtaining of degrees and the instruction in school-mastering, and where the artistic coterie is no more dictatorial an affair than the local John O' London's Society or the amateur theatre. Wales, Ireland, and, in particular, Scotland, are building up ... a poetry that is as serious and genuine as the poetry in Mr. Pound's Active Anthology ...' (*EPW*, 165–6). This links a certain kind of non-Audenesque poetry to a meritocratic, rather than class-based, higher education system and democratic cultural structures in the non-English British nations; like Thomas's non-metropolitan poetic style, it anticipates later developments in the shape of the Regionalist movement. However, the Depression meant that there was no material basis for such a grouping in Wales until the late 1930s. As Tony Conran notes, the emergent 'First Flowering' generation 'either stayed in Wales and festered in isolation or ... offered themselves as international or colonial recruits to the London intelligentsia'.[101] This was Thomas's situation after 1934; he would establish temporary footholds in London, but be forced to return regularly to Swansea or, after his marriage, to his mother-in-law's in Hampshire. From the first, the strength of his work compelled metropolitan recognition on its own terms, although it was too experimental to permit him to overcome poverty. But by 1937, economic circumstances were changing, and Thomas changed tactics. Regionalist and nationalist currents were at work, and the dream of developing a critical mass of writers working in Wales found a focal point with the launch in summer 1937 of the journal *Wales* by Keidrych Rhys.[102]

Wales would become one of the liveliest journals of the period, hospitable to experimental writing and inscribed with Rhys's own brand of cultural nationalism in its punchy editorials and slogan-decorated covers. It was pacifist and anti-imperialist, following an honourable Welsh tradition, opposed to Westminster, critical of London's literary 'establishment' and the 'sclerotic National Eisteddfod' equally, determined to forge links between anglophone and Welsh language writing.[103] The general upsurge in Welsh culture at this time was reflected in the appearance of other new journals, among them Gwyn Jones's *Welsh Review, Tir Newydd (New Ground)* and *Heddiw (Today)*. *Wales*'s own iconoclasm was reflected in the cover of the first issue, which bore the opening sentence of Thomas's story 'Prologue to an Adventure', which was continued inside: 'As I walked through the wilderness of the world, as I walked through the wilderness, as I walked through the city, with the loud electric faces and the crowded petrols of the wind dazzling and drowning me that winter night before the West died, I remembered the winds of the high, white world that bore me and the faces of a noiseless million in the busyhood of heaven staring on the afterbirth' (*CS*, 106). The 'city' is London, the 'world that bore me' is Wales: the tale is the last episode in Thomas's planned novel, *Doom on the Sun*, which was to reverse Christian's journey away from the City of Destruction in *Pilgrim's Progress*, and it follows the narrator and his companion, Daniel Dom, through the fleshpots of a London which, as depicted in the final sentences, is slowly inundated by 'the sea of destruction' (*CL*, 110).

Thomas's attitude to London is summed up in a letter to Watkins of December 1938: 'I've just come back from three dark days in London, city of the restless dead. It really is an insane city, & filled me with terror. Every pavement drills through your soles to your scalp, and out pops a lamp-post covered with hair. I'm not going to London again for years; its intelligentsia is so hurried in the head that nothing stays there; its glamour smells of goat; there's no difference between good and bad' (*CL*, 392–3). The same descent into a comic-nightmarish underworld ends the four-chapter fragment of Thomas's incomplete novel, *Adventures in the Skin Trade*, written over the summer of 1941, which is similarly poised between a critique of the corrupt metropolis and his own provincialism. This is reflected in the way that the exotic capital soon comes to be seen in terms of the Swansea that its protagonist has 'escaped': the people who adopt him are replicas of his family, the streets are 'like the streets at home' and even the women in the clubs 'whom he had seen as enamouring shapes ... were dull as sisters' seen close up; they 'might have lurched in from Llanelly on football night' and 'would sneeze when you kissed them and say Manners in the dark traps of hotel bedrooms' (*CS*, 265, 293, 294). Thomas's self-mocking description of the novel's style as 'a mixture of Oliver Twist, Little Dorrit, Kafka, Beachcomber, and good old 3–adjectives-a-penny belly-churning Thomas, the Rimbaud of Cwmdonkin Drive' underscores the point (*CL*, 548).[104] The short story reads as a declaration of intent to leave the capital, just as the novel reads as an attempt to capture the full cycle of flight-and-return.

In 1938, the Thomases moved to Laugharne, where they would live, intermittently, until July 1940. Laugharne is just across the Towy estuary from Llanybri, where Rhys had recently settled with his wife, the poet Lynette Roberts, after marrying in nearby Llansteffan in October 1939 (Thomas was best man at the wedding).[105] Thomas joined Rhys's effort to '[make] an influential group of writers in Wales' for the first time and came to act as an editorial advisor (*CL*, 400). Critiquing Welsh puritanism, as well as London-centredness, the positioning of 'Prologue to an Adventure' in *Wales* made it a declaration of modernist and (limited) separatist intent. Rhys's ambition in *Wales* was to provide a place where young Welsh language and Anglo-Welsh writers could come together. However, in a well-publicised lecture of 1938 'Is There An Anglo-Welsh Literature?', the response to the first issue and Thomas's story by Saunders Lewis – the leader of Plaid Cymru and a leading Welsh language writer – showed just how wide the gap between linguistic culturalist Welsh-Wales and the Anglo-Welsh writers was. For Lewis, there could be no such thing as 'Anglo-Welsh' literature; it was impure and, hence, for an essentialist politics, an intolerable contradiction in terms. Of the Welsh anglophone writers, he claimed, only a handful – those who wrote about Wales in a narrowly defined way – were truly 'Welsh', and in attacking 'that lively little quarterly called *Wales*', it was notable that Lewis identified the threat to his cultural apartheid in Thomas. Quoting the first sentence of 'Prologue to an Adventure', he noted:

> It is a tip-top sentence. But you will recognize that it belongs to the main stream of the English literary tradition. It is not only a deliberate echo of Bunyan, but that way also have gone Ezra Pound and Gertrude Stein, and perhaps the Frenchman, André Breton. Mr Dylan Thomas is obviously an equipped writer, but there is nothing hyphenated [i.e.: Anglo-Welsh] about him. He belongs to the English.[106]

Despite such scepticism, often descending to outright hostility, intercultural exchange took place in *Wales* between the two literary cultures for several years; Euros Bowen, Kate Roberts, Alun Llywelyn-Williams and Pennar Davies all learnt from Thomas's modernism, while the anglophone writer Glyn Jones was influenced by Welsh *hen benillion* and Llywelyn-Williams would, attack leading Welsh artists for refusing to face the problems of South Wales and treating the industrial regions as 'unWelsh phenomena'.[107] Meurig Walters, who wrote in both languages, was championed by Thomas himself, who made it clear that he was keen for *Wales* to succeed on Welsh terms, but preferred a non-essentialist definition of what these were. Thus, he berated Rhys at one point for 'dragg[ing] into your magazine all the little waste names ... that belong in the London rags & not, in thought or action or feeling, to anything connected to Wales', but queried his belief in 'racial' Welshness: 'I've never understood this racial talk, "his Irish talent", "undoubtedly Scotch inspiration", apart from whisky. Keidrich ... [is] an ardent nationalist, and a believer in all that stuff about racial inspiration, etc.' (*CL*, 400–1, 349).

Saunders Lewis really did believe in 'racial inspiration', however, to the point of being a racist. His (and Plaid's) politics at the time were profoundly reactionary, seeing, in the Depression, a sign that modern industrial, democratic society had failed and of the need to return to an agrarian, feudal society, presided over by aristocrats and the Catholic Church, bound to the British monarchy, but not its Parliament. In this view of things, urban South Wales was a gigantic error, and the English-speaking South Walian working-class were no more than a 'greasily civilized' mass, a 'halfpenny populace / Children of the dogs' deformed in body and spirit, the passive recipients of the dole, a debased foreign culture and the language of the oppressor, as Lewis puts it in what is agreed to be his greatest poem, 'The Deluge, 1939'.[108] Lewis's cultural politics owe much to those of the Irish Literary Revival; they match Yeats's peasant-aristocrat ideal with Daniel Corkery's thesis of a 'Hidden Ireland' and literary litmus test of land, nationality and religion, while his linguistic policy is an extreme version of D. P. Moran's and Douglas Hyde's schemes for de-anglicisation. Irish nationalism, however, which had compromised over the English language, was not extreme enough for Lewis, and, in many respects, the blood-and-soil nationalism of Maurice Barrès and Charles Maurras's right-wing *L'Action Francaise* group were more to his taste. In 1936, Lewis would call the English Government the 'new Anti-Christ' and mock 'Welsh socialists [who] cry out against the terrible cruelties of Hitler', unable to 'distinguish between propaganda and evidence'.[109] Anti-Semitism was part of the unsavoury blend; 'The Deluge, 1939' holds 'foul usurers' with 'their Hebrew snouts in the quarterly statistics' responsible for the Wall Street Crash and Depression.[110] It is with good reason that Mr Roberts, in Thomas's story 'Where Tawe Flows', uses the mocking challenge 'Heil, Saunders Lewis!' and little wonder that today's linguistic culturalists are torn between the need to register his status as the most important Welsh writer of the twentieth century and to say as little about his actual political beliefs as possible (*CS*, 186).[111]

For it was Lewis, as Darryl Jones has rightly noted, who was responsible more than any other figure for 'the predication of a distinctively Welsh cultural identity solely on linguistic grounds', for asserting it to be 'the *sina qua non* of Welsh*ness*'.[112] In terms of Lewis's cultural and racial absolutes, it was not enough for anglophone Welsh writers to have 'Welsh interests' if these were 'only incidental or accidental or just social'.[113] Merely being born in Wales and writing about your life there would not make you a truly Welsh writer: only a few deemed, in some unspecified way, to 'speak to Wales more than to England' qualified as Welsh writers. Faced with the incontrovertible richness of Anglo-Irish writing in English, Lewis attributed it to the qualities of Hiberno-English and argued that such a movement could not occur in South Wales, because the dialect there was 'the horrible jargon of men who have lost one tongue without acquiring another ... no feebler stuff is spoken in these islands'.[114]

Even more despised than the English Other was that which had a mongrel, miscegenatory and 'hyphenated' condition. It is because Lewis desired so ardently to eradicate this dissolute, unfixed and threatening aspect of his work that he has Dylan Thomas 'belong to the English'. Like the 'dregs' and 'slime' of the 'greasy' working classes in his poem, Thomas poses a threat, in terms of what Mary Douglas calls the 'interstitial'; that is, like those substances which metaphorically and metonymically violate clear liquid / solid, internal / external boundary distinctions.[115] 'Purity', as Douglas notes, 'is the enemy of change, of ambiguity and compromise' – of that which, in short, is 'hyphenated' – which is why Thomas's transgressive impurity is denied a share in Lewis's Welshness. And yet, in a self-contradiction common in such cases, Lewis unwittingly exposes his own misunderstanding of the Welsh identity from which he barred Thomas. For Lewis believes that imitating Bunyan makes Thomas 'English'; yet, to English ears in 1938, the opening sentence of 'Prologue to an Adventure' would have had (and still has) a distinctly Welsh ring to it. By 1938, Bunyan could not have been a model for any modern English writer; only in Wales, in fact – a country which had witnessed a mass religious revival as recently as 1904–5 and in which many households still owned a copy of Bunyan – would he be a usable model. With a convert's clumsy zeal and insensitivity to nuance, Lewis the aristocratic Catholic, with his strenuously-acquired Welshness, utterly misreads what would be obvious to the average chapel-goer.

Ironically, the howler points to the parallels that *did* exist between Thomas and his Welsh language peers. Gothic-grotesque writing, if not Thomas-like hybridity, is rife in much of the greatest Welsh language writing of the twentieth century. In poems such as Gwenallt's 'Y meirwon' / 'The dead', we enter a world of the pre-process poems of the third notebook: graveyard, mine-gas, rotten lungs, 'Bibled parlours, and … cinders of flesh in the coffin, and ashes of song, / [where] we learnt … Collects of red revolt and litanies of wrong'.[116] Similarly, the greatest of all modern Welsh language novels, Caradog Prichard's *Un Nos Ola Leuad* / *One Moonlit Night*, deals with deprivation, insanity and sexually motivated murder, reminding the reader of nothing so much as the world of the Jarvis Valley and Thomas's early fictions.[117] For the best twentieth-century Welsh writers in both languages, monstrosity flows, not so much from Wales's actual, but its *imaginative*, experience of its impacted, metropolitan colonial subordination within the British state. In the nation's greatest writing, this is manifested less as a straightforward protest against 'colonialism', than as an exploration of the distorting effects of internalised stereotypes of inferiority and superior apartness.

Yet Thomas's hybridity was a major source of his energy and originality in ways which clearly *do* anticipate current postcolonial theory. Without fully endorsing the postcolonial paradigm (which would be to appropriate the victimhood of countries and groups oppressed far more savagely), the work of Homi K. Bhabha, and his contestation of Edward Said's case that power and discourse are fully possessed by the coloniser, seems particularly apposite here. Rather, as Bhabha argues, a split in enunciation, caused by the ambivalent functioning of relations of knowledge and power, constitutes a dispersed and variously positioned native, who, by (mis)appropriating the terms of the dominant ideology, is able to intercede and resist co-option, through irony, mimicry and subversion. This breaks down monolithic identities and the stand-off between coloniser and colonised, allowing for the exploitation of marginal areas, where the discourses of power and appropriation are most vulnerable. That is, it shifts the debate, as the Irish critic Colin Graham has noted, into areas in which the ethically loaded dichotomy of coloniser / colonised (or metropolitan colonised) is less fixating.[118] Thomas's amusing and self-mocking representation of himself as a 'border case' in an address he made to Scottish P.E.N. in 1948 is a good example of this and of Mary Louise Pratt's more ethnographic concept of 'transculturation', by which subordinated cultures appropriate and re-use materials taken from dominant ones:[119]

I am a Welshman who does not live in his own country, mainly because he still wants to eat and drink, be rigged and roofed, and no Welsh writer can hunt his bread and butter in Wales unless he pulls his forelock to the Western Mail, Bethesdas on Sunday, and enters public houses by the back door, and reads Caradoc Evans only when alone, and by candlelight ... Regarded in England as Welsh and as a waterer of England's milk and living in Wales as an Englishman, I am too unnational to be here at all. I should be living in a small private leper-house in Hereford or Shropshire, one foot in Wales and my vowels in England, wearing red flannel drawers, a tall witches' hat and a coracle tiepin, and speaking English so Englishly that I sound like a literate Airedale, who has learned his 'a's and 'e's by correspondence course, piped and shagged and tweeded, but also with a harp, the look of all Sussex in my poached eye, and a whippet under my waistcoat. And here are Scotch writers at home, and greeted by writers of England and France, and a border case like myself ...[120]

This plays up to, and plays with, stereotypes of Wales (and England) to dramatise liminal inbetweenness – Englishness in Wales, Welshness in England and at-home-ness nowhere. The claim about forelock-pulling is metaphorical, of course, while the 'private leper house' is an amusing fantasy about where the absurd logic of binary thought might lead. But, at the same time, as with all of Thomas's manipulations of stereotype, there is a serious point – it is understood that one can actually be victimised by the puritanical Welsh press (as Caradoc Evans was), and there is real, as well as mock, envy of the 'Scotch writers'. Thomas is aware that whether stereotypes are objectively true is not the whole point; it is whether they are *felt* to be true that matters. His sense of their ideological function is signalled by the placing of invisible quote marks around caricature versions of Wales and England, so as to mock the ways in which the two essentialisms simplify in order to regard each other. The resultant 'leper-house' and 'border case' embody, in comic terms, the 'transcultural zone' or 'interstitial space'. In more serious mode, Thomas would, after reminiscing about Swansea in a letter of 1935 to Bert Trick, add: 'But I wouldn't be at home if I were at home. Everywhere I find myself seems to be nothing but a resting place between places that become resting places themselves' (*CL*, 218).

Thomas's desire, then, is for a Welshness which is distinct and assertive, but is not essentialist, and is inclusive and pluralist, rather than inward-looking and reactionary. He breaks up the positivist projections of a certain kind of nationalism (i.e. colonisation > resurgence > nationalism > liberation > the integral nation), attempting to make a virtue of operating between two fixed identities, riskily (for the danger of misunderstanding is real) playing their preconceptions against each other. Treading a narrow line between the cathartic and creative use of stereotype, identity is presented as a set of shifting positions, rather than some hungry Hegelian essence in search of fixed borders. In refusing the pure, Welsh-Wales forms of Welshness or Welshness *as* purity, his work is paradoxically most nationally representative, refusing to elide the monstrous, even abject dimension of Welsh history and tricksterishly hinting that a mongrel self is a truer image of the nation. Hybrid writings, as I have argued already in the Introduction, do not simply invert or balance between binary terms, but produce a more exorbitant, unnerving questioning of authority – that which is prodigious, grotesque and unconcerned with a grounded identity, rejecting the self-identical concept as a form of irrationalism. This hybrid sense is not a compromise between identities, but holds several versions of it in play at once; indeed, it is the 'multiplicity of personality' noted by Constantine Fitzgibbon.[121] In this sense, Thomas redefined Welshness by placing metamorphosis and role playing, rather than some fixed essence, at its heart. This was not the stage-Welshman (although he makes the odd appearance), but rather a refusal of definition; to use a phrase of Bhabha's which could have been coined with Thomas in mind, he exemplifies an attitude of 'sly civility' towards authority.[122] There are, of course, difficulties involved in such a reading, including the need to be aware that, in postmodern cultures, older forms of repression may have evolved into more elusive ones. But it suggests why critical attacks on Thomas so often try to cast him as an imposter and at how his blend of the intimate and of imitation (of religion, bardic *hwyl*, romanticism, modernism, Welshness or whatever) mocks fixed identities. By the same token, it shows how, far from shirking responsibility, he could be said to have articulated, more effectively than 1930s social realism, the cultural opacity of those belonging to subordinate components of the British state.[123]

'A monstrous image blindly / Magnified'

Thomas's return to Wales in 1938–40 saw the period of stylistic changes in his poetry and prose, already discussed in Chapter 2 and elsewhere. The gothic-grotesque and hybrid extremes of his early style were eased, markedly in his prose (the break between the experimental stories and those in *A Portrait of the Artist as a Young Dog* is almost absolute), but less so in his poetry. The poetry maintained the processual and verbal energies of the earlier work, but opened out its convoluted syntax and packed imagery. The boundaries within the different phases of both poetry and prose can be observed in *The Map of Love* and between it and *A Portrait*. *The Map of Love* is a heterogeneous work, which contains seven experimental fictions, but whose sixteen poems included examples of the most unyielding process style, relatively plain-style rewritings of notebook poems and examples of the more mobile and varied post-1938 style, including the poem which announces the change, 'Once it was the colour of saying'. By contrast, *A Portrait* is a homogeneous quasi-*bildungsroman* made up of short stories à la *Dubliners*, which charts the progress of a Dylan-figure from childhood to the point at which he is about to leave for London.

For the first time in his published work, the Thomas of the letters is recognisable in *Portrait*. Its stories involve quotidian scenarios in recognisable Swansea settings, and mingle pathos and observational acuity with comedy. Thomas clearly draws on some of his favourite popular authors, such as the children's writer Richmal Crompton, aiming at the general reading public for the first time. Yet *A Portrait* also combines its enhanced appeal with serious purpose, turning away from modernist prose, but remaining linked to it through its complex critique, both of it and Thomas's earlier self. As M. Wynn Thomas shrewdly notes, it 'mix[es] "high" culture with "low" life and popular appeal ... nicely suggested in the casual, throwaway title ... [which] combines a teasing reference to Joyce, a mockery of the high solemnity of Modernism's sanctification of "the artist", a knowingly modish narcissism (an artistic portrait of the artist), a promise of ... "laddishness" ... and a hint of that underworld of fantastic metamorphosis (comical, farcical, plangent and Circean-sinister by turns) into which the stories lead us, and where, at the end, they disturbingly abandon us'.[124] Similarly, certain poems written between 1938 and 1941 continue the gothic-grotesque in almost unabated vein, as my analysis of 'I make this in a warring absence', 'How shall my animal' and 'Into her lying down head' in Chapter 3 demonstrated. These poems illustrate Isobel Armstrong's point that 'ludic intellectual complexity and a disruptive libido' live together in the grotesque, as 'the related forms in which the oppressed consciousness both responds to and resists its condition'.[125] The macho 'studded male' and his 'lionhead's heel and horseshoe of the heart', and their conflict with the female energies of the anima/l in 'How shall my animal', for example, dramatise in ways which are not simply post-Freudian, but informed by the complexities of Thomas's marital strife with his 'golden, loathing wife' Caitlin, how the grotesque manifests itself 'not

only in libido and desire but also frustration and aggression' (*CL*, 859).[126]
However, *The Map of Love* also reflects the populist-critical swerve of
Portrait and does so most completely (and anticipating the post-1944
poetry most fully) in 'After the Funeral' (April 1938) – a staging-post
between the 'green fuse' of 1933 and the later pastoral mode.

'After the funeral' is also the first poem that Thomas addressed to a
specific individual – his aunt, Ann Jones. It therefore complicates the
distancing and dramatic staging of the self, the performance of sincerity,
which had been crucial to Thomas's poetic breakthrough in the notebook
poems. Its origins in that formative period reflect this fact. Even at
the time he wrote its first, very different version during February 1933,
Thomas expressed his surprise at his 'foul' lack of emotion at his aunt's
death and admitted that an attempt at an elegy had turned against
his 'egotistic preoccupation' with satirising her mourners (*CL*, 31). In
reworking this failed poem five years later, he kept the grotesque critique
of Nonconformism, but also turned it back on his younger self:

> After the funeral, mule praises, brays,
> Windshake of sailshaped ears, muffle-toed tap
> Tap happily of one peg in the thick
> Grave's foot, blinds down the lids, the teeth in black,
> The spittled eyes, the salt ponds in the sleeves,
> Morning smack of the spade that wakes up sleep,
> Shakes a desolate boy who slits his throat
> In the dark of the coffin and sheds dry leaves. (*CP*, 73)

The hypocritically exaggerated displays of grief 'shake' the boy, who,
sincerely but melodramatically, usurped his aunt's coffin in imagination
to make a suicidal gesture against religious hypocrisy. This produced
only 'dry leaves', however, in 1933. And yet the trope also symbolises an
awakening of conscience in the Thomas of 1938 to his earlier inadequate
response; he is woken from his moral 'sleep', and the suicide now becomes
the elimination of the morbidly romantic, self-centred pose of his younger
self. As in 'And death shall have no dominion', the poem moves towards
realising that a more adequate form of sincerity can only take a radically
ambiguous form. The adult self now mourns in a way which is also
exaggerated, but more broadly and ironically, responding to the 'dry leaves'
with images of wetness and fertility, keeping a vigil in Ann's parlour:

> … I stand, for this memorial's sake, alone
> In the snivelling hours with dead, humped Ann
> Whose hooded, fountain heart once fell in puddles
> Round the parched worlds of Wales and drowned each sun. (*CP*, 73)

The incipient bardic abandonment is checked by a parenthesised passage
of self-cautioning, occasioned by remembrance of Ann's own modesty:

> (Though this for her is a monstrous image blindly
> Magnified out of praise ...
> She would not have me sinking in the holy
> Flood of her heart's fame ...
> And need no druid of her broken body). (*CP*, 73)

Like other subjects of elegy (Lycidas and Adonais), Ann is not just
resurrected, but made into a fertility figure – 'a Welsh rural working class
Fisher Queen', as Barbara Hardy calls her – the solemnity leavened by
'snivelling' and the pun on 'parched'.[127] Thomas does not become Ann's
'druid', but a non-religious 'bard', like those of the Medieval Welsh
courts, acting on her behalf to summon 'all the seas' to an alternative,
non-Christian 'service', in which her formerly 'wood-tongued virtue' will
'babble like a bellbuoy' (the voices of bard and mistress are indistinguishable at this point). At this point, Ann appeals over the 'hymning
heads' of the congregation and 'bow[s] down the walls of the ferned
and foxy woods' in a pagan-Celtic ceremony worship of green nature.
Language has inflated, become 'monstrous' again, and the 'skyward
statue' of the poem dramatises the difficulty of both praising Ann and
respecting her 'spirit ... meek as milk'. It is both 'carved from' and for
her, and the delicate balance between letting Ann speak and usurping
her speech is contained in the pun on 'lie' in the lines 'I know her
scrubbed and sour humble hands / Lie with religion in their cramp'.
Religion is a lie, but it is also, for many, the heart of a heartless world;
Ann's hands' suffering – synecdoche for her life of drudgery – hold a
suffering truth, and their long labour, retrospectively empathised with,
symbolically recharges the trappings of her dead, domestic front parlour
with the force of process:

> These cloud-sopped, marble hands, this monumental
> Argument of the hewn voice, gesture and psalm
> Storm me forever over her grave until
> The stuffed lung of the fox twitch and cry Love
> And the strutting fern lay seeds on the black sill. (*CP*, 74)

At its close, the poem's linguistic surplus enacts an inundation of love
for Ann, which exceeds the poet's control and for which he cannot
claim credit. The ambiguous phrasing conveys this; the lack of a
comma after 'psalm' prevents a straightforward bracketing of 'gesture
and psalm' as nouns in an appositive clause, giving both something of

the status of verbs, suggesting 'storm' might be transitive, a request ('let them storm me'), as well as a statement ('they are storming me'). The poem is poised, that is, between declaration and expectation, and the speaker suggests that he might well be carried away by his own rhetoric (it is his own 'monumental / Argument' which may be storming him). Process and renewal is implicit in the pagan energy of the last two lines, confirming the green faith of the 'ferned and foxy woods', now virile and vivid intruders into the parlour, while at the same time the passage is intertextual with Prospero's calm and agnostic 'Our revels now are ended' (in 'cloud-sopped' / topped) in a renunciatory, anti-religious, even anti-poetic way. It is a verbal 'hewn' statue, which is both marmoreal and insubstantial, in accordance with the way it has put clichés of Welshness to powerful emotional use, while making us aware of itself as a rhetorical structure, a set of sincerity effects, aimed at achieving this end. But it also reveals, for the first time, the unlocated regional sense of the later poems; surre(gion)alism is swapped for something less radical, but more strictly patterned – an intertwining of 'summoned' seas, elegy, suburb and green countryside, all of which is thrown into relief by rituals of uncertain efficacy and the certainty of war.

Notes

1 Tony Conran, *Frontiers in Anglo-Welsh Poetry* (Cardiff: University of Wales Press, 1997), p. 12.

2 Kenneth Rexroth, ed., *The New British Poets: An Anthology* (New York, NY: New Directions, 1948), p. xix.

3 Among his favourites, as he informed Pamela Hansford Johnson, were *Dr Mabuse*, *The Cat and the Canary* and *The Cabinet of Dr Caligari* (*CL*, 115). Thomas is reported to have known by heart much of the dialogue of James Whale's comedy-horror gothic masterpiece *The Old Dark House* (1932).

4 Dylan Thomas, 'Frequent, Gory and Grotesque', *The Morning Post*, 11 October 1935, p. 15 (A review of *The Hollow Man*, *Mystery at Olympia*, *Murder in College* and *Murder in Midsummer*).

5 Marjorie Perloff, '"Barbed-Wire Entanglements": The "New American Poetry" 1930–32', *Poetry On & Off the Page: Essays for Emergent Occasions* (Evanston, IL: Northwestern University Press, 1998), p. 63.

6 Compare, for example, 'So fast I move defying time, the quiet gentleman / Whose beard wags in Egyptian wind', from 'Should lanterns shine' (*CP*, 52), with 'The Mouse and the Woman': 'Consider now the effigy of time, his long beard whitened by an Egyptian sun, his bare feet watered by the Sargasso Sea' (*CS*, 86).

7 See Dafydd Johnston, *The Literature of Wales* (Cardiff: University of Wales Press, 1994), p. 16: 'As a result of his high bardic status the figure of Taliesin became associated with a folk tale concerning the origin of poetic inspiration, known as *Hanes Taliesin* (*The History of Taliesin*), which probably evolved in the ninth or tenth

century … After accidentally swallowing three drops from the magic cauldron of the witch Ceridwen, Gwion Bach goes through a series of [animal] transformations before being reincarnated as the poet Taliesin imbued with the gift of prophecy'. Thomas's use of Welsh legend is a case of identification with what Johnston calls Taliesin's 'shamanistic persona'.

8 Lyndon Peach, *The Prose Writing of Dylan Thomas* (Houndmills: Macmillan, 1988), pp. 18–19. As Peach notes: 'The early stories are not simply delineations of sexual violence nor do they equate violence with sexual repression according to a simple formula. They betray a serious concern to try and understand the psychic origins of sexual violence. … The killer [in 'The Vest'] … tries to excuse his actions: "when he hurt her, it was to hide his pain. When he struck her cheek … it was to break the agony of his own head"'.

9 John Ackerman, *A Dylan Thomas Companion: Life, Poetry and Prose* (Houndmills: Macmillan, 1991), p. 173.

10 Fred Botting, *Gothic* (London: Routledge, 1996), p. 3.

11 David Punter, *The Literature of Terror: A History of Gothic Fictions from 1765 to the Present Day. Volume 1: The Gothic Tradition* (London & New York, NY: Longman, 1996), p. 43.

12 Angela Carter, *Fireworks: Nine Profane Pieces* (London: Quartet, 1974), p. 122.

13 Cited in Andrew Lycett, *Dylan Thomas: A New Life* (London: Weidenfeld & Nicolson, 2003), p. 112.

14 Geoffrey Grigson, 'Recollections of Dylan Thomas', *The London Magazine* (September 1957), p. 41. This was reprinted in John Malcolm Brinnin, ed., *A Casebook on Dylan Thomas* (New York, NY: T. Y. Crowell, 1961), p. 259.

15 According to Cecil Price, who attended Swansea Grammar School with Thomas: 'The town stands as a frontier and has all the vitality of its position. A mile from its centre [i.e.: in the 1920s], the Welsh-speaking area begins and a very different habit of mind and culture'. Cecil Price, in Miron Grindea, ed., *Adam: International Review*, 238 (1953), p. 39.

16 Andrew Lycett, *Dylan Thomas: A New Life*, pp. 8, 150–2.

17 See James A. Davies, *Dylan Thomas's Swansea, Gower and Laugharne* (Cardiff: University of Wales Press, 2000), for a wittily evocative account of the Swansea of Thomas's youth.

18 The name's ultimate source is *The Mabinogion* – the greatest of Medieval Welsh texts. In the tale of 'Math, Son of Mathonwy', Aranrhod, daughter of Dôn, is given a virginity test, as a necessary condition of becoming foot-holder to Math, Lord of Gwynedd. This involves stepping over Math's willow wand. As she does so, however, Aranrhod gives birth to two children, one of which Math arranges to be baptised Dylan: 'The boy was baptised, whereupon he immediately made for the sea, and when he came to the sea he immediately took on its nature and swam as well as the best fish. He was called Dylan son of Ton for no wave ever broke beneath him'. See *The Mabinogion*, transl. Jeffrey Gantz (London: Penguin, 1976), p. 106. However, D. J. Thomas is more likely to have been prompted in his choice of name by the dramatic poem *Dylan, son of the sea wave* (1908) by Thomas Evelyn Scott-Ellis – Baron Howard de Walden – which was set to music in 1910 by Joseph Holbrook, and the opera had been performed as recently as June 1914 at the Theatre Royal, Drury Lane, under the baton of Thomas Beecham. Gantz glosses Dylan as

meaning 'sea' and 'Ton' as 'wave'. This is a perpetual source of verbal play and sea imagery in Thomas's writing.

19 John Davies, *A History of Wales* (London: Penguin, 1993 [repr. 1994]), p. 549.

20 See Gwyn A. Williams, *When Was Wales?* (Harmondsworth: Penguin, 1985 [repr. 1991]), p. 253. In Swansea, 28,000 of a total population of less than 200,000 were registered as out-of-work by the early 1930s.

21 Gwyn A. Williams, *When Was Wales?*, p. 253.

22 Tony Conran, *Frontiers in Anglo-Welsh Poetry* (Cardiff: University of Wales Press, 1997), p. 253.

23 The 'Blue Books' is the name given to a notorious Parliamentary report on Welsh education of 1847, which reflected English Anglican contempt for Nonconformism and a Tory fear of Welsh political radicalism. The report branded the Welsh rural population idle, ignorant, dirty and promiscuous and claimed that the eradication of 'vice' was hampered by education in Welsh. The response, to what was seen as slander on the nation, galvanised attempts to construct a heroic, independent past and a virtuous *gwladwr* (peasant) and *gwerin* (noble Welsh folk). However, as noted in the Introduction, the *kulturkampf* which followed was largely aimed – with great success – at shaping policymaking at Westminster, rather than independence. Although Welsh Liberal Nonconformism had a marked pacifist and anti-imperialist strand, the benefits accruing to Wales from the British Empire meant the link with England was rarely questioned.

24 Tony Conran, *Frontiers in Anglo-Welsh Poetry*, p. 113. Arguably, the penchant for fantasy, the macabre and the grotesque (and wordplay) is also part of a self-defined Celtic literary tradition, as the Irish critic Vivian Mercier argues in his influential *The Irish Comic Tradition* (Oxford: Oxford University Press, 1962). Conran echoed Mercier in 1982, arguing that Evans: 'activated for our time a very ancient and persistent strain in the Celtic temperament … a delight which is at the same time serious and humorous, aggressive and fearful, in what is monstrous, grotesque, physically and morally freakish and even vile'. Tony Conran, *The Cost of Strangeness* (Llandysul: Gomer, 1982), p. 136.

25 The model for his calculated translationese was the Hiberno-English and Irish language hybrid forged in the early years of the century by J. M. Synge. This suggests that Evans should be aligned with a 'Celtic' tradition of grotesque obscenity, revived by modernism, as described by Vivian Mercier (see above).

26 Caradoc Evans, *My People*, ed. and intro. John Harris (Bridgend: Seren, 1987), p. 11.

27 Caradoc Evans, *My People*, p. 10.

28 See Patrick Parrinder, *James Joyce* (Cambridge: Cambridge University Press, 1985), pp. 1–13.

29 The story concerns the widowed vicar Rhys Rhys, whose incestuous coupling with his daughter in an attempt to produce 'the second coming of the son of man' produces a stillborn infant, whose body he burns on a hill above their home. (*CS*, 37) For a revealing discussion of this story and the 'burning baby' motif in Thomas's work, see M. Wynn Thomas, *In the Shadow of the Pulpit: Literature and Nonconformist Wales* (Cardiff: University of Wales Press, 2011), p. 249.

30 Arthur Machen (1863–1947) was born Arthur Llewelyn Jones in Carleon, Monmouthshire. He has been described as the greatest Welsh writer of gothic horror. However, given the lack of competition, this considerably underrates his achievement. His work has been hugely influential on writers, from H. P. Lovecraft

to Stephen King, and his contemporary devotees include Mark E. Smith of *The Fall*. His change of name, career in London and orientation towards non-Welsh audiences, as well as his ambiguous use of Welsh material, has led to his neglect by WWE critics.

31 See David Punter, *The Literature of Terror: A History of Gothic Fictions from 1765 to the Present Day, Volume 2: The Modern Gothic* (London: Longman, 1996), pp. 22–5. See also Walford Davies, *Dylan Thomas* (Milton Keynes: Open University Press, 1986), p. 55. Davies notes Thomas's use of Machen's *Autobiography* (1922) in *Under Milk Wood*.

32 Once described as 'the most decadent book in English', it is an autobiographical novel about writing a novel. See Annis Pratt, *Dylan Thomas' Early Prose: A Study in Creative Mythology* (Pittsburgh, PA: University of Pittsburgh Press, 1970), pp. 12–13.

33 Philip Thomson, *The Grotesque* (London: Methuen, 1972), p. 24.

34 D. H. Lawrence, 'Hymns in a Man's Life, ed. A. A. H. Inglis, *A Selection from Phoenix* (Harmondsworth: Penguin, 1979), pp. 19–24; Dylan Thomas, 'Poetic Manifesto', EPW, pp. 157–8; T. S. Eliot, 'The Function of Criticism', *Selected Essays* (London: Faber, 1932), pp. 27, 29.

35 Tony Pinkney, *D. H. Lawrence* (Hemel Hempstead: Harvester / Wheatsheaf, 1990), p. 73. Pinkney argues that Lawrence incorporated classicism within gothic's host of small details, overcoming its either / or binaries in a way which recalls Thomas's process, for only Gothic: 'deconstructs [classicist modernism's] rigid model of inside / outside'. For the 'specific culture' point, see Walford Davies, *Dylan Thomas* (Cardiff: University of Wales Press, 1972 [repr. 1990]), p. 21. See also D. H. Lawrence, ed. Mara Kalnins, *Apocalypse* (London: Penguin, 1995).

36 R. George Thomas, 'Dylan Thomas and Some Early Readers', *Poetry Wales*, 9: 2 (Autumn 1973), p. 11.

37 Interpretations of Thomas's attitude to, and use of, religion in his work range from Maud's sense of him as an outright unbeliever, through to Aneirin Talfan Davies's belief that he was a quasi-Roman Catholic by the end of his life. For a thorough summary and analysis, see R. B Kershner Jr., *Dylan Thomas: The Poet and His Critics* (Chicago, IL: American Library Association, 1976), pp. 66–105.

38 Gwen Watkins, *Dylan Thomas: Portrait of a Friend* (Talybont: Y Lolfa, 2005), p. 155.

39 Daniel Jones, *My Friend Dylan Thomas* (London: Dent, 1977), p. 57.

40 R. B. Kershner Jr., *Dylan Thomas: The Poet and His Critics* (Chicago, IL: American Library Association, 1976), pp. 67–8; R. George Thomas, 'Dylan Thomas and Some Early Readers', *Poetry Wales: Dylan Thomas Special Issue*, 9: 2 (Autumn 1973), p. 16.

41 David N. Thomas, ed., *Dylan Remembered: Volume One (1914–1934)* (Bridgend: Seren, 2003), p. 166. However, Trick is likely to have read Karl Kautsky's Marxist interpretation of Christianity, *The Foundations of Christianity* (1908), which interprets Christ's life and teachings in light of the primitive communism of, and said to have been influenced by the Essenes. Thomas was also a friend of the Reverend Leon Atkins – a Nonconformist minister and radical socialist minister in Swansea.

42 William Thomas (1834–1879), better known by his bardic name of Gwilym Marles, was born in Brechfa, near Llandysul, studied at the Presbyterian College in Carmarthen and won a scholarship to Glasgow University in 1856. He became a follower of the ideas of Theodore Parker, espousing Unitarianism as a minister at Llwynrhydowen. He published hymns, stories and a novel, as well as poems, opened

a grammar school, campaigned for the Liberal Party and supported local farmers in the tithe war against the Church of Wales. He was evicted from his chapel by landowners in 1876 because of his activism. For details, see M. Wynn Thomas, *In the Shadow of the Pulpit*, pp. 227–55. My thanks to Professor Thomas for allowing me to read this chapter before publication; what follows owes much to his work in this area. See also Andrew Lycett, *Dylan Thomas: A New Life*, pp. 9–10, 69.

43 As James Keery has observed, Thomas's position on atonement and redemption is generally that adopted in 'A Refusal to Mourn the Death, by Fire, of a Child in London' and resembles William Empson's in *Milton's God* (1955): 'his constant exploitation [in his work] of the crucifixion as a poetic *trope* culminates in [this poem's] contemptuous dismissal of the *doctrine* of atonement'. See James Keery, 'The Burning Baby and the Bathwater', *P.N. Review*, 33: 1 (September-October 2006), p. 58.

44 John Davies, *A History of Wales*, p. 501.

45 Patrick Crotty, 'Falling off the Edge', *Planet*, 129 (June / July 1998), p. 15.

46 John Malcolm Brinnin, *Dylan Thomas in America: An Intimate Journal* (New York, NY: Viking Press, 1957 [repr. 1964]), p. 128.

47 Whitman's democratic identification with Christ went beyond Blake's and was more secular; he combined frank corporeality and sexual openness, together with a belief in the Emersonian 'over-soul' linking body and cosmos in a manner resembling Thomas's vision of process. Whitman, for example, styled himself as the 'Wandering Messiah', holding that: 'The human being, made in God's image, and the God, made in human image, are potentially identical and morally equal', writing: 'What do you suppose I should intimate to you in a hundred ways, but that man or woman is as good as God?' See Gregory Woods, *Articulate Flesh: Male Homo-Eroticism and Modern Poetry* (London: Yale University Press, 1987), p. 47.

48 Linden Huddlestone, 'An Approach to Dylan Thomas', *Penguin New Writing*, Vol. XXXV (1948), pp. 148–9.

49 For a suggestive reading influenced by Julia Kristeva, see Chris Wigginton, *Modernism from the Margins*, pp. 36–9.

50 Sigmund Freud, *The Psychopathology of Everyday Life: Penguin Freud Library vol. 5*, transl. Alan Tyson, eds. James Strachey and Angela Richards (London: Penguin, 1991), p. 90, fn. 1.

51 Thomas adds: 'the churches are wrong, because they standardize our gods, because they label our morals, because they laud the death of a vanished Christ, and fear the crying of the new Christ in the wilderness' (*CL*, 72).

52 Cited in Andrew Bennett and Nicholas Royle, *An Introduction to Literature, Criticism and Theory* (Hemel Hempstead: Prentice Hall / Harvester Wheatsheaf, 1995), pp. 121–9. Bennett and Royle note that modern literary studies arose out of a need to find a substitute for religion during the nineteenth century, and the act of criticism – whatever the strength of the desire to desacralise literature – contains strong elements of the religious. In setting aside (*sacrare*) any text for special study, we confer on it special value, recognising 'its demand that it be translated and its insistence on being untranslatable'. Thomas's concern with religion should be considered in light of the way reading and critical activities which are supposedly secular and demystified habitually embody elements of the religious, citing authority, valorising 'Literature' (or its deconstruction) and seeking transcendent or chiliastic certainties.

53　Adam Phillips, 'A Terrible Thing, Thank God', *London Review of Books*, 26: 4 (4 March 2005), p. 24 (review of Andrew Lycett, *Dylan Thomas: A New Life*).

54　Donald McKay, 'Crafty Dylan and the Altarwise Sonnets: "I build a flying tower and pull it down"', *University of Toronto Quarterly*, 55: 4 (Summer 1986), p. 378.

55　God-dog is a typical Thomas-style anagram, but it also derives from *The Waste Land* and the Circe episode of *Ulysses*. *The Waste Land*'s image of the exhuming dog in 'The Burial of the Dead' ('O drive the Dog from hence that's foe to men, / Or with his nails he'll dig them up again') 'provokes', as Rainer Emig points out, 'interpretation as an anagram. Dog equals God, i.e. Christ nailed to the cross'. Rainer Emig, *Modernism in Poetry: Motivations, Structures and Limits* (London: Longman, 1995), p. 147.

56　Don McKay, 'Crafty Dylan and the Altarwise Sonnets', p. 378.

57　As noted in the Introduction, Elder Olson notoriously read the sequence as an elaborate allegory based on the legend of Hercules, which was informed in every detail by a detailed knowledge of astronomy and astrology. See Elder Olson, *The Poetry of Dylan Thomas* (Chicago, IL: University of Chicago Press, 1954), pp. 63–89. This is one reason why 'Altarwise' has been a particular target for Thomas's critics, among them Holbrook, for whom it is the epitome of everything he dislikes about Thomas: he speaks of 'disgusting image[s] of recoil from life ... pretentious nonsense ... the posturing as of a child convinced of his importance'. *Dylan Thomas and Poetic Dissociation* (Carbondale, IL: Southern Illinois University Press, 1963 [repr. 1964]), p. 82.

58　The (young) dog as 'atlas-eater' may also be compared with the child of Baudelaire's 'Le Voyage', who is 'amoureux de cartes' and for whom the world 'est égal a son vaste appetit'. *Charles Baudelaire: Selected Poems*, transl. Carol Clark (London: Penguin, 1995), p. 136.

59　Don McKay, 'Crafty Dylan and the Altarwise Sonnets', p. 388.

60　Don McKay, 'Crafty Dylan and the Altarwise Sonnets', p. 388.

61　Don McKay, 'Crafty Dylan and the Altarwise Sonnets', p. 389.

62　Thomas may also be alluding to the classical belief that the human soul 'came down [from heaven] by *Cancer*' at birth and, after death, 'ascended by *Capricornus*', as given in Browne's *Hydriotaphia*. See Sir Thomas Browne, *The Major Works*, ed. C. A. Patrides (London: Penguin, 1977), p. 300.

63　Don McKay, 'Crafty Dylan and the Altarwise Sonnets', p. 378.

64　Don McKay, 'Crafty Dylan and the Altarwise Sonnets', p. 390.

65　'Jonah's Moby' brilliantly conflates the Old Testament and Melville to suggest the speaker's literary-cum-religious quest. In *Moby Dick*, Queequeg saves Tashtego from falling into the jaws of Moby Dick by seizing him by his hair.

66　See Ralph Maud, *Where Have the Old Words Got Me?*, pp. 23–4.

67　Donald Davie, *Articulate Energy: An Enquiry into the Syntax of English Poetry* (London: Routledge & Kegan Paul, 1955), p. 126.

68　Walford Davies, *Dylan Thomas*, p. 104.

69　Philip Lahey, 'Dylan Thomas: A Reappraisal', *Critical Survey*, 5: 1 (1993), pp. 53–65. Even at this stage, as William York Tindall notes, subject position(s) remain uncertain: 'the speaker ... sometimes seems Mary, sometimes Jesus, and sometimes both together. Jesus "wept", but Mary seems to say His words'. William York Tindall, *A Reader's Guide to Dylan Thomas* (New York, NY: Syracuse University Press, 1962 [repr. 1996]), p. 139.

70 That 'time's nerve' (Christ and his crucifixion) are 'in vinegar' is also, of course, a punning reference to the way that they have been preserved or pickled in scripture and art.

71 See 'The Crucifixion' (1930) and 'The Crucifixion (After Grünewald)' (1932) in Carsten-Peter Warnke *Picasso*, ed. Ingo F. Walther (Köln: Taschen, 2002), pp. 337, 369.

72 Philip Lahey, 'Dylan Thomas: A Reappraisal', p. 62.

73 Don McKay, 'Crafty Dylan and the Altarwise Sonnets', p. 392.

74 See Thomas Dilworth, *Reading David Jones* (Cardiff: University of Wales Press, 2008), p. 186.

75 M. L. Rosenthal and Sally McGall, *The Modern Poetic Sequence*, p. 478.

76 William Empson, *Argufying*, p. 393.

77 Thomas pretended to pander to Church's reactionary objections and sent them up as he did so. It is still difficult to see how Church could have swallowed the mixture of fibs, mock-surprise and egregious flattery served up to him. Thus, Thomas claimed: 'I never have been, never will be, or never could be for that matter, a surrealist'; he had not even read any modern French poetry, he declares, 'either in the original or in translation', and 'never, to my knowledge ... a paragraph of surrealist literature'. Furthermore, 'I must confess that I read regrettably little modern poetry, and what "fashionable" poetry I do come across appears to be more or less communist propaganda. I am not a communist'. He added: 'I hope you won't mind, but I took the liberty, soon after receiving your letter, of writing to a very sound friend of mind [sic] and asking him what surrealism was, explaining, at the same time, that a critic whose work we both knew and admired had said that my own poems were themselves surrealist ... in his reply ... he quoted some dreadful definition about "the satanic juxtaposition of irrelevant objects etc."'. Thomas then professes to abhor 'experimental absurdities I hardly knew existed' and apportions the blame for any obscurity in his poems to his 'immaturity' and 'muddleheadedness' (*CL*, 22–3). Though it would have been easy to check Thomas's claims, Church did not bother, as his condescending acceptance letter shows: 'Still I cannot understand the meaning of the poems, but in this matter I have decided to put myself aside and let you and the public face each other'. If this was a private game conducted to determine just how gullible and self-deluding Church was, it succeeded. See Paul Ferris, *Dylan Thomas* (London: Penguin, 1978), p. 145.

78 Gascoyne was also the translator of Salvador Dalí's *Conquest of the Irrational* (1935), Breton's *What is Surrealism?* (1936), co-translator of Benjamin Peret's *Remove Your Hat* (1936) and contributor to a volume of translations of Éluard, *Thorns of Thunder* (1936). These publications give a good idea of the intensity of the encounter with surrealism at this time.

79 Daniel Jones claimed that Thomas was reading *transition* from 1930; Thomas's own correspondence proves his familiarity with it in December 1933. Thomas contributed 'The Mouse and the Woman' and 'Then was my neophyte' to the autumn 1936 issue. See Dougald McMillan, *transition: The History of a Literary Era* (London: Calder and Boyars, 1975).

80 Thomas was friendly with Roland Penrose, Henry Moore and several other organisers of this most important of all British surrealist events, held at the Burlington Gallery in the summer of 1936.

81 The stories Roughton published were 'The Burning Baby', 'The School for Witches'

and 'The Holy Six'; the poems published were the 'Altarwise' sonnets XIII, IX and X and 'Foster the light'. See Ralph Maud, *Dylan Thomas in Print: A Bibliographical History* (Pittsburgh, PA: University of Pittsburgh Press, 1970), p. 110.

82 See 'Pablo Picasso – Playwright', *Picture Post* (4 March 1950), pp. 20–1.

83 Peter Nicholls, 'Surrealism in England', eds. Peter Nicholls and Laura Marcus, *The Cambridge History of Twentieth Century English Literature* (Cambridge: Cambridge University Press, 2005), p. 400.

84 See, for example, M. H. Abrams, *A Glossary of Literary Terms* (Ithaca, NY: Harcourt, Brace, Jovanovich, 1985), p. 205.

85 Peter Nicholls, 'Surrealism in England', p. 401.

86 C. Ray, *The Surrealist Movement in England*, p. 78.

87 The essay was 'Surrealism Yesterday, To-Day, and To-Morrow', published in September 1932. See Paul C. Ray, *The Surrealist Movement in England* (Ithaca, NY: Cornell University Press, 1971), pp. 80–1.

88 C. Ray, *The Surrealist Movement in England*, p. 93.

89 This is a recurring problem in visual and musical, as well as literary, art in Britain. See, for example, the recent campaign, led by Ian McKellen, for the Tate (London) to display its collection of work by L. S. Lowry, as well as, say, the rather brittle and imitative modernist work of Ben Nicholson, reported in *The Guardian* in April 2011 (see http://www.guardian.co.uk/artanddesign/2011/apr/18/ls-lowry-tate). As Jonathan Jones notes there, the exclusion of Lowry has at least as much to do with class and snobbery towards popular art, than it does with a dislike of 'the provinces'. All of these factors operate in Thomas's case.

90 Peter Nicholls, 'Surrealism in England', p. 409.

91 Peter Nicholls, 'Surrealism in England', p. 414.

92 Peter Nicholls, 'Surrealism in England', p. 412. Nicholls claims that Thomas's work 'often radiates a sweaty over-excitement' and that it seeks 'a knowingly archetypal language of "clay" and "shroud"' also show a lapse into the stereotypes of the legend at certain points (would an 'unknowingly archetypal language' be better?).

93 Geoff Ward, *Statutes of Liberty: The New York School of Poets* (London: Palgrave, 2001), pp. 73–4.

94 Geoff Ward, *Statutes of Liberty: The New York School of Poets*, p. 74.

95 J. B. Kershner, *Dylan Thomas: The Poet and His Critics*, p. 145.

96 Annis Pratt, *Dylan Thomas' Early Prose: A Study in Creative Mythology* (Pittsburgh, PA: University of Pittsburgh Press, 1970), p. 137.

97 Annis Pratt, *Dylan Thomas' Early Prose: A Study in Creative Mythology*, p. 136.

98 Glyn Jones's claim is cited in Constantine FitzGibbon, *The Life of Dylan Thomas* (London: Dent, 1965 [repr. Plantin Paperbacks, 1987]), p. 221.

99 Signed 'Benjie', the *Comment* parody was titled 'After a Poem in (on) Progress by Thomas Dillon'. It read:

This was the oyster-cocktail in the salad,
The tail of space in oil, the solemn cow
All furred with hemlock, as slow eagles broke
To hybrid slumber. Mrs. Mary climbed,
Twisted like six o'clock, shark-finned and all,
With bills for ribbands in her roystered vest.
The limit grew, Tom God, each vacant rock
Blushed in impulsive loam of reaching crocks

Until I stayed the tankling from my chink,
When roof and roof met in a tortoise-brain.
I, by the pent-house door, all sawny-cowled,
Unveil the carrot of slopped after-time,
And by this flaunted flipwhack strike the shock,
Ripping the sand-bagged Summer for dry proof.
'Benjie', *Comment* (19 September 1936), p.95. For Sansom, see Constantine
Fitzgibbon, *The Life of Dylan Thomas*, p.187.

100 Peter Nicholls, 'Surrealism in England', p.403.

101 Tony Conran, *Frontiers in Anglo-Welsh Poetry*, p.111.

102 Keidrych Rhys (1913–1987), born William Ronald Rees Jones in Carmarthenshire,
was a poet, cultural activist, anthologist and editor of *Wales* (1937–9, 1943–9,
1958–60). Rhys was a friend of Dylan Thomas and most of the Welsh poets of his
generation. His Faber anthology, *Modern Welsh Poetry* (1944), brought together
the riches of recent Welsh anglophone and Welsh-language poetry in translation,
including work by David Jones, Dylan Thomas, Vernon Watkins, Saunders Lewis
and Lynette Roberts. His work has recently been collected and edited. See Keidrych
Rhys, *The Van Pool: Collected Poems*, ed. Charles Mudye (Bridgend: Seren, 2012).

103 See M. Wynn Thomas, *Corresponding Cultures: The Two Literatures of Wales*
(Cardiff: University of Wales Press, 1999), p.84.

104 In autobiographical terms, *Adventures in the Skin Trade* opens where 'One Warm
Saturday', the final story of *A Portrait of the Artist as a Young Dog*, leaves off, with
its protagonist, Samuel Bennet, destroying cherished objects belonging to his
family before departure and, once on the train, jettisoning all his London contact
addresses, except that of a girl he has never met. He attempts, that is, to render
the past and the future equally impossible: he has departed, but does not want to
arrive. The picaresque adventures of the title come to him, for he is unable to get
beyond the buffet at Paddington Station, until being adopted and compelled to
move on by Mr Allingham, a stranger. Sam, meanwhile, has got an empty Bass
bottle stuck on his little finger – a symbol of his regression. As Mrs Dacey observes:
'He's only a baby'; and his bottle is less a phallic symbol, than a sign that he is
unweaned. The plot, Thomas explained, would have had Samuel, at seven points in
the novel, 'look back and find he had shed a skin'. It would end with him finding
himself literally naked, back on the platform at Paddington, arrested for indecent
exposure. Samuel never arrives there, possibly because Thomas may have felt that
there was a moral dissonance between a picaresque-satiric comedy set in peacetime
London and London at war (*CS*, 273); Dylan Thomas, *Adventures in the Skin Trade*,
foreword by Vernon Watkins (London: Putnam, 1955), p.10.

105 Lynette Roberts (1909–1995) was a poet and writer of Welsh descent. Roberts was
born and brought up in Argentina and educated in London, where she moved in
literary circles that included Eliot and Wyndham Lewis. In Llanybri, she wrote
Poems (1943) and the late modernist masterpiece *Gods with Stainless Ears* (1951),
both published by Faber, and pursued other projects based on her study of local
dialect, crafts, customs and flora. She was a close friend of Alun Lewis and advisor
to Robert Graves for *The White Goddess*. See Lynette Roberts, *Collected Poems*,
ed. Patrick McGuinness (Manchester: Carcanet, 2005); Lynette Roberts, *Diaries,
Letters and Recollections*, ed. Patrick McGuinness (Manchester: Carcanet, 2008).

106 Saunders Lewis, 'Is There an Anglo-Welsh Literature?' (Cardiff: Guild of Graduates of the University of Wales, Cardiff Branch, 1939), p. 6.

107 M. Wynn Thomas, *Corresponding Cultures*, p. 129.

108 Saunders Lewis, 'The Deluge, 1939', transl. Tony Conran, *Welsh Verse* (Bridgend: Seren, 2003), pp. 275, 277.

109 Cited in Darryl Jones, '"I Failed Utterly": Saunders Lewis and the Cultural Politics of Welsh Modernism', *The Irish Review*, 19 (Spring / Summer 1996), p. 29.

110 Saunders Lewis, 'The Deluge, 1939', transl. Tony Conran, *Welsh Verse*, p. 276.

111 Menna Elfyn and John Rowlands, eds., *The Bloodaxe Book of Modern Welsh Poetry* (Highgreen: Bloodaxe Books, 2003), pp. 78–9.

112 Darryl Jones, '"I Failed Utterly": Saunders Lewis and the Cultural Politics of Welsh Modernism', p. 31.

113 Saunders Lewis, 'Is there an Anglo-Welsh Literature?' (Cardiff: Guild of Graduates of the University of Wales, Cardiff Branch, 1939), p. 12.

114 Tony Conran, transl., *Welsh Verse*, p. 87. Conran notes elsewhere that the chief conduit for the transmission of such attitudes to the present has been R. S. Thomas, conceived of as a kind of anti-Dylan: 'to the more extreme followers of R.S.', he writes, 'Dylan Thomas has often seemed little more than a traitor, or at best an irrelevance'. A less extreme cultural nationalism has attempted incorporation, rather than exclusion, as in, for example, M. Wynn Thomas's excellent account of the richness of the anglophone culture of industrial Glamorganshire. These efforts are signalled by the replacement of the category 'Anglo-Welsh literature' by 'Welsh Writing in English'. See Tony Conran, *Frontiers in Anglo-Welsh Poetry*, p. 187; M. Wynn Thomas, 'Writing Glamorgan', *Internal Difference: Literature in 20th-Century Wales* (Cardiff: University of Wales Press, 1992), pp. 25–48.

115 Mary Douglas, *Purity and Danger: An Analysis of the Concepts of Pollution and Taboo* (London and New York, NY: Routledge, 1966 [repr. 2000]), pp. 30–41, 163.

116 Gwenallt (David James Jones) (1899–1968) was one of the most powerful lyrical poets of the first half of the twentieth century. He was brought up in the industrial Swansea Valley, was a conscientious objector in the First World War and reacted strongly against Nonconformism, embracing Marxism for a time. Later, he became a Christian nationalist. See *The Bloodaxe Book of Modern Welsh Poetry*, eds. Menna Elfyn and John Rowlands, transl. Tony Conran (Newcastle-upon-Tyne: Bloodaxe Books, 2003), p. 98.

117 Caradog Prichard (1904–1980) was a poet, novelist and journalist in both Welsh and English. This novel is his major work, but he was also a National Eisteddfod Crown and Chair winner. See *Un Nos Ola Leuad / One Moonlit Night*, transl. Philip Mitchell (London: Penguin Books, 1999).

118 Colin Graham, '"Liminal Spaces": Post-Colonial Theories and Irish Culture', *The Irish Review*, 16 (Autumn / Winter 1994), p. 41.

119 Mary Louise Pratt, *Imperial Eyes: Travel Writing and Transculturation* (London: Routledge, 1992), p. 6.

120 Dylan Thomas, 'Address to the Scottish Society of Writers in Edinburgh', ed. Miron Grindea, *Adam: International Review*, 238 (1953), p. 68.

121 Constantine Fitzgibbon, *The Life of Dylan Thomas*, pp. 51–2.

122 Homi K. Bhabha, *The Location of Culture* (London: Routledge, 1994), p. 90.

123 I hesitate to apply the term 'subaltern' to Thomas, given Gayatri Spivak's attacks on its too-loose usage. However, in light of Thomas's notorious 'obscurity', I think

it is at least worth noting Edouard Glissant's description of (formerly) colonised cultures' 'refusal to become transparent or to be understood by the (former) colonizer ... the insistence on transparency being regarded as an insistence on Western hegemony'. Edouard Glissant, *Caribbean Discourse: Selected Essays*, transl. and intro. J. Michael Dash (Charlottesville, VA: University of Virginia Press, 1989), p. 22. See also Gayatri C. Spivak, *The Post-Colonial Critic* (London: Routledge, 1990). Not that this idea is exclusive to postcolonial criticism; Wolfgang Iser, for example, claims that 'mutuality' (his term for the interrelationship of cultures) is always accompanied by an element of opacity.

124 M. Wynn Thomas, *Corresponding Cultures: The Two Literatures of Wales* (Cardiff: University of Wales Press, 1999), pp. 75–6. See also R. George Thomas, 'Dylan Thomas and Some Early Readers', *Poetry Wales: Dylan Thomas Special Issue*, 9: 2 (Autumn 1973), p. 11.

125 As Isobel Armstrong notes, 'the Grotesque is not a unifying mode', and this is part of its value for Thomas, who wishes to preserve distortions, discrepancies and temporal discontinuities in his work of this period. Isobel Armstrong, *Victorian Poetry: Poetry, Poetics, Politics* (London: Routledge, 1996), pp. 288, 290.

126 Isobel Armstrong, *Victorian Poetry: Poetry, Poetics, Politics*, p. 291.

127 Barbara Hardy, *Dylan Thomas: An Original Language* (Athens and London: University of Georgia Press, 2000), p. 9.

CHAPTER FIVE

'Near and fire neighbours':
war, apocalypse and elegy

A screaming comes across the sky. It has happened before, but there is nothing to compare it to now. It is too late. The Evacuation still proceeds, but it's all theatre.

– Thomas Pynchon, *Gravity's Rainbow*.[1]

New Apocalypse?

The Map of Love, Thomas's third collection, was published on 24 August 1939. It contained sixteen poems and seven of the experimental short fictions written between 1933 and 1936. Like *Twenty-five Poems*, but in a rather different way, it was a transitional collection, containing poems from either side of the stylistic turn of 1938. The timing was not propitious. War broke out just ten days later on 3 September, completely displacing any notice the book might have attracted. It also sent Thomas into something of a tailspin; on 25 August, he wrote to Vernon Watkins confessing that 'This war, trembling even on the edge of Laugharne fills me with such horror & terror & lassitude' (*CL*, 453).[2] The war, moreover, had the effect of weakening Thomas's tentative footing on the ladder of a literary career and financial security. Applications for funding from the Royal Literary Fund over the next year were turned down, and many of the journals which had provided an income from casual reviewing vanished, victims of wartime restrictions on paper use and a changed literary climate. With a wife and child to support, Thomas's attempts to borrow money and make a living became ever more desperate. As they sank into poverty, the Thomases were driven out of Laugharne in 1940 by lack of money and the debts they owed to local tradespeople. Finally, in September 1941, Thomas got a job writing scripts for propaganda films

302

at Strand Films in London, earning a regular wage for the first time since his job as a teenage reporter.

Poor physical fitness, temperamental and ideological aversion to fighting, not to mention a sense of the absolute priority of his writing, helped Thomas avoid conscription. One result was that he and his family led a semi-nomadic wartime existence, often billeted on in-laws and friends, in Chelsea in London, as well as in Gloucestershire, Sussex, Talsarn, Llangain and New Quay in West Wales. But scriptwriting, as well as work for the BBC from 1943 onwards, meant that Thomas was continually in and out of London, often caught up in a Fitzrovia bohemian lifestyle, while his family lived in the country, away from the bombs. One result was that his marriage, always somewhat stormy, was punctuated by infidelities and rows. Moreover, despite remaining a civilian, Thomas was not exempt from the war's violence. He was caught up in many London raids, and his film work (he was involved in production, as well as writing) took him to recently bombed cities, such as Bradford and Coventry. His practical pacifism and 'mental militarism', scriptwriting and poetry conflicted, feeding a complex dynamic of defiance, self-hatred and resentment towards the war and his involvement in it (*CL*, 39). He would pick fights with total strangers, often servicemen, in pubs; on one occasion, the 'Majoda incident' at New Quay in 1945 (for which Thomas was not to blame), this escalated to the point of his bungalow being machine-gunned by an off-duty S.O.E. officer.[3]

Yet despite these difficulties the war years were good ones for Thomas's development and recognition as a writer. In April 1941, he agreed to sell the 1930–4 notebooks, which he had been mining throughout the 1930s.[4] His dependence on the notebooks has been much exaggerated by critics keen to cast him as a perpetual adolescent, but it was a symbolic moment, nonetheless. If this marked a shift in Thomas's relationship to his past and a confidence in his ability to create a new poetic idiom (which he succeeded in doing over the three years following the sale), the major change as regards his place in British poetry had already occurred three years before. Following the Munich Agreement in September 1938, it had become impossible for anyone – including, at last, the Government – to deny that war was inevitable. The political panaceas and positivism of the New Country poets suddenly seemed irrelevant and its hegemony crumbled. Auden's emigration to the US in January 1939 appeared as 'a symptom of the failure of social realism as an aesthetic doctrine', and *New Verse* and *Twentieth Century Verse* – the journals most closely associated with it – folded in the same year.[5] Later in 1939, *The New Apocalypse* anthology, edited by Henry Treece and J. F. Hendry, and offering a style consciously opposed to that of the New Country poets, was published. The advent of New Apocalypse marked a shift in British poetry as a whole, from politics to myth, cerebral irony to intuition and collective struggle to a re-fashioning of the subject at bodily, psychic and linguistic levels. From it, the new poetry of the 1940s would develop.

The New Apocalypse group of young poets associated with the anthology were all, in fact, Thomas's contemporaries and were the junior branch of the response to the crisis of 1929–33 (as I argued in Chapter 1, this was coeval with the Audenesque style, although it is often presented merely as a reaction against it).[6] Grouped around the journal *Seven* (founded in 1937), New Apocalypse had effectively arrived in 1938 at the poetic position held by Thomas since late 1933. Alex Comfort, another Apocalyptic, would note in 1944: 'The socialist poets [of the 1930s] attempted to deny the awareness [of the Tragic Sense] and to turn to society, but in Spain the face of the unpleasant black figure was unveiled ... Dylan Thomas knew it early in life, long before the Spanish defeat'.[7] In the introduction to *The New Apocalypse*, Thomas's pioneering role was acknowledged, with Hendry describing him as 'the most organic of modern English [sic] poets' and a central inspiration.[8] Treece had already published an essay on Thomas by October 1937, began corresponding with him in 1938 and was working on a book-length study of his work (the first of its kind, it finally appeared in 1949). For both editors, Thomas was the prime example of how poets could shape material from the unconscious into an organic mythology, based on somatic drives and cyclical processes, which was both personal and universal in its symbolism. Crucially, Thomas's language use also accorded, in its more complex and subtle way, with Treece's belief that, in order for myth to perform its work, poetry had to reclaim its archaic musical powers, such that 'at times ... music may take control of poetry'.[9]

The relationship between New Apocalypse and Thomas has been considerably muddied over the years, and it is only in the last decade that – thanks largely to the research of James Keery and one or two others – it has started to become clearer.[10] We know that Thomas declined, in late 1938, to sign the New Apocalypse manifesto, 'Apocalypse, or, The Whole Man' ('I agree with and like much of it, and some of it, I think, is manifestly absurd ... organic reality is all my cock') (*CL*,

397). The Manifesto, which probably went unpublished as a result, was not rediscovered and published until 2003. It is a collage of quotations (including one from a Thomas letter to Treece) and fleshes out the group poetic as a rejection of mechanistic thought, including the 'ethereal [abstract] rationalism' of New Country, along with 'Marxism's claim that human mastery of the natural world would eliminate myth', and of the 'deliberate irrationalism' of surrealism.[11] It proposed that material from the unconscious be subjected to conscious shaping through the use of fundamental and organic myths – these alone being capable of reinte-grating the fractured modern subject with society to create the 'Whole Man' – and used to pose questions, which (unlike the narratives of New Country poets) 'could not be neatly summarized or given fable-like clarity'.[12] Reading it, one can see why 'organic' was such an honorific term for New Apocalypse and how much it meant when Hendry applied it to Thomas. As Keery rightly maintains, however, despite his refusal and his frequently waspish comments about its members, the manifesto shows how deeply Thomas (who had contributed to *New Apocalypse* and would go on to promote the careers of some New Apocalypse poets) was 'the centre around which the movement cohered'.[13] However reluctant he was to join literary groupings, he was inescapably the origin and exemplar of the New Apocalyptic 'mode of visionary modernism', as Peter Riley has called it – a 'densely metaphoric poetry in a heavily stressed metrics and a tone of staged personal declaration over a fictive arena' – and, even in his refusal to sign their Manifesto, he 'emerged as a leader' for them.[14]

Far from being a malign presence, as post-Movement criticism has insisted, Thomas's influence on the New Apocalypse poets was largely beneficial, particularly in the case of W. S. Graham – the best of the group. Furthermore, as Keery shows, by the middle of the war, the New Apocalypse poetic had spread to the extent that it informed a broader neo-Romantic movement, which included the Oxford poets Philip Larkin, Sidney Keyes, Drummond Allison and John Heath-Stubbs, as well as the work of Vernon Watkins, Kathleen Raine and Alun Lewis. More established poets, including even MacNeice, Spender, Eliot and Edith Sitwell, were drawn into its force field. Critical orthodoxy maintains that the apocalyptic element vanished from British poetry with the dispersal of the group during the war, taking a BBC broadcast of 7 April 1942 by Herbert Read, which championed 'The New Romantic School', as the moment of its dissolution. But, to the contrary, as Keery argues, the two terms were understood as synonymous; Read's was an exercise in rebranding, not re-definition, one agreed with by Hendry and Treece and intended to hitch New Apocalypse to neo-Romanticism in the other arts (in which it succeeded).[15] The high-water mark of the New Apocalypse tide occurred after, not before, *Deaths and Entrances* (1946) and it reverberated on well into the early 1950s.

Returning to the late 1930s, we can grasp something of Thomas's talismanic power for the Apocalyptics in two poems published in *Delta* and *Seven* in 1939. These were, respectively, 'Because the pleasure-bird whistles' and 'When I woke'.[16]

As its original *Delta* title ('January 1939') hints, the first of these poems looks back over the political and moral disasters of the previous year – the Moscow Show Trials, the *Anschluss*, Franco's triumphs and Munich. It opens with a question – 'Because the pleasure bird whistles after the hot wires, / Shall the blind horse sing sweeter?' This alludes to the common belief that song-birds sang better if they were blinded, and to a recent dream, or nightmare, of Thomas's, in which a horse stood in a cage made of red-hot wires while a bystander observed: 'He sings better now'.[17] The 'bird and beast', the poem goes on to say, are merely 'convenient', created to suffer the poet's mood. But the question they pose is serious enough: in Thomas's words to Desmond Hawkins in August 1939 'because [the bird] is made to sing sweeter through suffering what it doesn't understand, does that mean everything is sweeter through incomprehensible, or blind, suffering?' (*CL*, 448).

The poem answers this in its presentation of the poet first as an 'enamoured man alone', who 'Savours the lick of the times through a deadly wood of hair ... Nor ever, as the wild tongue breaks its tombs, / Rounds to look at the red, wagged root'. But Thomas then challenges this unwilling self to 'spin and stare' back at the 'old year / Toppling and burning' and to feed its dead with 'the meat of a fable', to overcome his 'antipodean' distance from them as 'an upright man', in order to provide at least some nourishment and 'grace' to history's victims. Indeed, what has injured them injures him (*CP*, 67). This answers the indifference of the 'enamoured man'. But the dead, here, are also words themselves, released from the 'tombs' broken by the 'wild tongue': the poet can make suffering sing, but understands that it is not simply a matter of enumerating agonies; historical crisis is a crisis of language, and poetry must embody that, too.

'When I woke' also tells of a moment when personal nightmare coincides, or collides, with breaking apocalypse in the world of public events. It tells of waking to the sounds of bells, sea and birds, which, at first, drive out the 'coiling crowd' of images left over from a nightmare. However, a 'man outside with a billhook, / Up to his head in his blood, / Cutting the morning off' shows that the nightmare has infected the world. The speaker counters this by declaring that he subjectively 'make[s] ... / Everybody's earth' by perceiving it anew each morning (*CP*, 111). But the nightmare is confirmed by his hearing 'Crossly out of the town noises / A voice in the erected air'; this is very likely to be the radio broadcast of Sunday 3 September by Neville Chamberlain, which announced that Britain was at war. In the version of the poem published in *Seven*, that voice is said to be 'Shaking humanity's houses', the morning 'breaking / Bulls and wolves in iron palaces: / Winds in their nests in the ruins of man'. The bulls and wolves (and possibly eagles' 'nests') may or may not be nation-specific (Spain / Italy, Russia, Germany), but this doomily prophetic close was replaced in *Deaths and Entrances* with the more ambiguous image of a sheet drawn 'over the islands' and 'coins on my eyelids' singing 'like shells'. Like 'Because the pleasure bird whistles', it is not one of Thomas's best poems – the alteration is not a great improvement – but it does unnervingly fuse personal and public fears, archetypes coexisting with the contemporary in Thomas's own surreal-organic terms ('erected air', for example, is a brilliant epithet for radio waves – one that undermines the phallic sabre-rattling of speech-makers and anticipates the extraordinary importance of the radio to the forthcoming propaganda war: the world of Churchill, Lord Haw-Haw, J. B. Priestley and Tokyo Rose). Both poems enact what seemed, by this stage, to be the unstoppable slide towards war, linking it to the unnerving power of dream, the animal and the irrational.

Under the conditions of war, two currents, which had been secondary and separate during the 1930s – apocalyptic vision in mainstream poetry and social reconstruction in mainstream politics – would come together to shape national life by the early 1940s. Both crossed in Thomas's poetry. The Beveridge Report of 1942 – the blueprint for the Welfare State, which was used to mobilise the population to fight – contained the pledge that future governments would care for all citizens 'from the cradle to the grave', translating the womb-tomb coordinates of Thomas's poetry into the language of the Social Democratic New Jerusalem (like Thomas, too, Beveridge's language could be Bunyanesque; he described the obstacles on the road to reconstruction as five 'Giant Evils' – 'Want, Disease, Ignorance, Squalor and Idleness').[18] 'Womb' and 'tomb', however, effectively ghost a sight rhyme with 'bomb' in much of Thomas's work, and it is no coincidence that the two wartime periods in which he wrote poems, 1939–41 and 1944–5, coincided almost exactly with the Blitz and the 'Little Blitz' of the V-weapons – the two periods of greatest civilian suffering.

There was a poetry boom during the war.[19] Some of the reasons for this were as mundane as a paper shortage, which gave lyric poems an advantage over novels, as well as the lack of time available to read longer works. Moreover, poetry, particularly New Apocalypse poetry, spoke directly of first and last things, addressing the basic existential issues raised by the war, thus addressing the hunger for meaning, which often took religious form, as I discuss later. But poetry's popularity – as of the arts more generally – also reflected wartime goodwill and solidarity, the desire to discover a common culture, particularly after the National Government, led by Churchill, replaced Chamberlain's Tories in May 1940. The greater sense of collective struggle helped narrow the gap between artists and the rest of the population and led to an attempt to impart a popular dimension to 1930s modernism.[20] Yet the war's blurring of private and public spheres and the kinds of ethical questions raised by propaganda work also led to a conflict between imaginative freedom and government exhortations to communal resolve. This meant resistance to official attempts to convert private fantasy into 'public spirit', to turn soldiers and citizens into 'actors-out of [the State's] historical drama'.[21] Thomas's habitual poetic self-performance unavoidably grew more public in such circumstances. From being a Hamlet-like trickster, he became a celebrant of the procreative body and grieving memorialist of the Blitz dead. Initially, his poetry continued the trend begun in *The Map of Love*, humanising the bitter intensities of the 1930s process style, while retaining much of its metaphysical, worked quality. Then, after a gap in which Thomas wrote no poetry, between 1941 and 1944, an even greater acceptance of the cycle of birth, supersession and death was apparent, aligning the triumphs and betrayals of marriage with those of the war and pitching sexual regeneration and pastoral escapism against the threat of some final silence.

'Fight not my enemies': Thomas and the war

With his usual knack of being in the right place at the right time, Thomas found himself caught up in the first raid of the London Blitz.[22] A few days later, he wrote to Vernon Watkins:

> I had to go to London last week to see about a BBC job, & left at the beginning of the big Saturday raid. The Hyde Park guns were booming.

Guns on the top of Selfridges. A 'plane brought down in Tottenham Court Road. White-faced taxis still trembling through the streets, though, & buses going, & even people being shaved. Are you frightened these nights? When I wake up out of burning birdman dreams – they were frying aviators one night in a huge frying pan: it sounds whimsical now, it was appalling then – and hear the sound of bombs & gunfire only a little way away, I'm so relieved I could laugh or cry. What *is* so frightening, I think, is the idea of greyclothed, grey-faced, blackarmletted troops marching, one morning, without a sound up a village street. Boots on the cobbles, of course, but no Heil-shouting, grenading, goosestepping. Just silence. That's what Goebbels has done for me. I get nightmares like invasions, all successful. (Ink gone). (*CL*, 524)

Striking in its grotesque blend of normalcy and terror and in the sheer theatricality of the event (the black taxis dusted white, as if with make-up), this is air-raid as spectacle. Near-surreal images from the real world ('Guns on the top of Selfridges) jostle with comic-book style ones as if from a dream. As Ivan Phillips has noted, Thomas moves from a jittery scene of physical threat full of the 'heady disruption of culturally fraught signs (Hyde Park, Selfridges, the BBC)', and the strange equivocation of 'relieved', to the more unambiguously menacing imaginative threat – 'a petrification rather than a shake-up of the sign-systems'.[23] Near-hysterical loquacity tries to stave off the ultimate threat of 'just silence' and the writer's equivalent: '(Ink gone)'. The final image of 'blackarmletted troops marching … up a village street' sounds like an anticipation of the 1942 film *Went the Day Well*, based on Graham Greene's story 'The Lieutenant Died Last', which told the story of the village of Bramley End being captured by Nazi paratroopers.[24] All of these aspects, from fears of silencing to surreal nightmares about invasion, loom large in the wartime poems.

Thomas's response to the war was chiefly shaped by its most appallingly novel aspect – the aerial bombardment of cities. This placed civilians on what had once been a distant front line. The changed relationship between civilian and combatant in the Second World War represented, for Thomas, as for many, an ethical regression of huge proportions, even compared to the First World War (when the civilian inability to grasp the horror of the slaughter had been a major subject for soldier-poets). The inevitability of such bombardment had been growing in the 1920s and 1930s and had vigorously exercised the imaginations of novelists, poets and filmmakers, as well as military planners and scientists (Orson Welles's famous hysteria-producing *War of the Worlds* radio broadcast exploited the same sense of threat). As Leo Mellor has argued: 'an enormous range of popular novels in the interwar period portrayed London being destroyed by various gases, bombs, heat rays and even more exotic armaments'; a novel like Joseph O'Neill's *Day of Wrath* (1936) projected a future war as 'a limitless horror', while 'Patrick Hamilton, George Orwell, Louis MacNeice, Henry Green and … Virginia Woolf – all experimented with different forms of representation to capture the outlines of aerial-borne dread and threat'.[25] At the same time, military experts, such as J. F. C. Fuller, claimed that a single raid might cause 200,000 minor casualties and throw the whole city into a panic within half an hour. Certainly, official thinking was based on the belief that 'the bomber will always get through'. One calculation was that the Germans would drop 100,000 tons of bombs on London in the first two weeks of bombing, 211,000 civilians would be killed and 422,000 wounded (in the event, less than one-third of this number was killed in the bombing of all British cities throughout the entire war).[26] So great was the fear, that, as soon as war was declared, the evacuation of children from the cities was immediately organised; although this was voluntary, a million had been sent to the countryside by the end of 1939.

Following the fall of France in May 1940, most of Britain came within range of the Luftwaffe, and British cities awaited in trepidation the fate of Guernica, Warsaw, Rotterdam or worse. Anxiety increased after Dunkirk in May 1940, and the once-firm division between the Front and the Home Front began to crumble. With the beginning of the Blitz proper in September that year, it dissolved. The casualties of the raids seemed shocking, precisely because the danger at home 'was random, not restricted to the young and able, and far less a matter of choice or obligation imposed upon certain members of the population by the state', and 'civilians felt an intensity of experience close to that of front-line soldiers'.[27] The invasion threat of autumn 1940 also intensified an island-fortress mentality, as did the fact that, until 1942, the war was an almost unbroken succession of defeats. Few troops fought during the early war years, billeted in rural (and, therefore, safe) locations. As the nation turned in on itself, enduring and waiting, civilians bore the brunt of the enemy assault; not until 1941 were their casualties exceeded by those of the armed forces.[28] Indeed, while soldier poets, such as Keith Douglas, lamented their lack of subject matter – 'Rosenberg I only repeat what you were saying' – civilian poets were, paradoxically, in a better position to write about the war than those in uniform.[29] The Blitzed city swiftly became iconic: as Stephen Spender noted in a catalogue for a 1942 exhibition of wartime paintings 'In this war, by "War Pictures" we mean, pre-eminently, paintings of the Blitz ... The background to this war, corresponding to the Western Front in the last war, is the bombed city'.[30]

The 'background' was often described most memorably by non-English writers, perhaps because they were naturally more alert than natives to the strangeness of the Blitzed capital. When we think of Blitz poetry, we remember the work of non-English poets: 'Little Gidding' by Eliot, *Trilogy* by H. D., 'The Trolls' and 'Brother Fire' by MacNeice and Thomas's Blitz poems, which, as V. S. Pritchett put it 'caught the screams in the mind's confusion as certainly as Picasso's *Guernica* had done a few years before'.[31] Such work best captures the febrile, uncannily charged atmospheres and landscapes, simultaneously libidinal and repressed, of wartime London, with its blackouts and blinding searchlights, its common purposes and individual suspicions, its propaganda and espionage, and its surreal landscapes of destruction – a zone in which the normal barriers between public and private selves might suddenly rear up or collapse. In it, as in fiction of the time, such as Elizabeth Bowen's 'The Demon Lover' and 'Mysterious Kôr', the boundaries between the worlds of the living and the dead were eroded, threatening ontological seepage; doubles, revenants and phantoms abounded. Thomas's 1930s poetry, full of 'doubles' and spectres, had anticipated such 'familiar compound ghosts' and now added figures such as the girl of 'Love in the asylum', living, but '[a]t large as the dead', to its hoverers between worlds (*CP*, 90).

Thomas's attitude to the war was the product of many factors: the initial distrust of the Chamberlain Government, widespread on the Left; the Welsh traditions of anti-imperialist pacifism ('My great horror's killing', he told Sir Kenneth Clark in April 1940); his initial failure to get congenial war work; the desire to be left alone, often expressed through a mixture of despair and strained jocularity ('[I shall] declare myself a neutral state, or join as a small tank'; 'What do I want for Xmas ...? A war-escaper ...') (*CL*, 461, 494, 508).[32] He was unwilling to support the war, however indirectly: the Army Medical Corps meant 'patch[ing] poor buggers up to send them out again into quick insanity and bullets', while a munitions factory entailed 'Clocking in, turning a screw, winding a wheel ... to help to kill another stranger, deary me I'd rather be a poet anyday and live on guile and beer' (*CL*, 540). He was dismissive of media-generated community spirit: 'the matey folk-warmth of the trenches can only make for hysterical friendships, do or die companionships, the joking desperate homosexual propinquity of those about to die: the joy of living and dying with a Saturday football crowd on an exploding ground'. The need to 'go on with our out-of-war life' was imperative, he argued. The fact that the 'folk-warmth of the trenches' was based on the 'fostering of hate against a bewildered buggered people [the Germans]' simply made it worse (*CL*, 481, 469, 471).

To call these protestations purely selfish, politically motivated or moralistic would be to both overstate and understate the case, as well as to indulge in ahistorical hindsight; it is important for a start to note that many shared Thomas's lack of enthusiasm. Reprehensible *sauve qui peut* sentiments *and* quixotic high-mindedness mix in shifting measures from letter to letter. If, in July 1939, he could cynically observe that he would let his country 'rot', an article gathering writers' objections to the war, planned for *Life & Letters* later that year, reveals a different attitude. It was a naïve venture, for, while long expectation of the coming war had left British culture strangely empty, drained of credulity and commitment, most people, including the Left, still felt that it was right to fight. But, for Thomas, this fudged certain ethical issues, and, when Rayner Heppenstall replied that he couldn't contribute, because he felt that it was a writer's duty to join up, in order to experience the reality of his times, Thomas rounded on him: 'If to undergo contemporary reality to its most extreme is to join in a war – the evil of which is the war itself & not the things it is supposed, wrongly, to be attempting to exterminate – against people you do not know, and probably to be killed or maimed, then one can only say flippantly that the best poems about death were always written when the writer was alive, that Lorca didn't have to be gored before writing a bullsong ...' (*CL*, 480).[33] The argument is both unanswerable and inadequate. It exposes the contradiction in Heppenstall's logic, which valorises empirical individual experience as 'reality', but accepts the word of the state concerning the need to turn other individuals into an abstract Other, the better to 'exterminate' them. Heppenstall's response is pragmatic, that of C. Day Lewis's well-known riposte to the fatuous question posed in *The Times*, 'Where Are the War Poets?': 'It is the logic of our times ... That we who lived by honest dreams / Defend the bad against the worse'.[34] But in the most fundamental terms, total war was to be destructive of all human values. As a British M.P. asked the American journalist Ed Murrow on the eve of war: 'Are we to be the first to bomb women and children?'[35] If another of Thomas's claims – that fascism was 'here already' – was clearly erroneous, there was nevertheless a logic in his anger, which was that of an ethical absolutist confronted by the bogus universality of liberal humanism (*CL*, 469).[36] In this sense, Thomas's explanation to Heppenstall – 'I wanted to know what my friends ... are going to do when they are told by the State to fight not their enemies' – is a revealing kind of literalism, an archaic-sounding challenge to turn the other cheek issued in the characteristic form of a double negative.

The same sense of 'the enemy' as 'people you do not know', 'not [our] enemies' and 'strangers' and resistance to, as well as penetration by, the myth of collectivity is central to 'Deaths and Entrances' – a public, but also self-addressed, poem, which probes the ethical issues raised by violence and blurs both psychic and public-private boundaries between ourselves and others, friends and foes. This poem is about the 'nightmares of invasion' and was completed during November 1940. Its eponymous title is derived from John Donne's last sermon, 'Death's Duell', which presents birth as an entrance from the womb, one kind of tomb, into this world, another kind of tomb: 'deliverance *from* that *death*, the death of the *wombe*, is an *entrance*, a delivering over to *another death*', our mortal existence being nothing but 'dying Life, and living Death'.[37] (As Thomas put it, throughout the collection, the two terms 'keep their individualities and lose them in each other') (*CL*, 396). The poem addresses those on the 'eve' of being killed in the 'incendiary' raids, as well as the self of the speaker, in these paradoxical and con-fused terms:

On almost the incendiary eve
    Of several near deaths,
When one at the great least of your best loved
    And always known must leave
Lions and fires of his flying breath,
    Of your immortal friends
Who'd raise the organs of the counted dust
    To shoot and sing your praise,
One who called deepest down shall hold his peace
    That cannot sink or cease
    Endlessly to his wound
In many married London's estranging grief.

On almost the incendiary eve
    When at your lips and keys,
Locking, unlocking, the murdered strangers weave,
    One who is most unknown,
Your polestar neighbour, sun of another street,
    Will dive up to his tears.
He'll bathe his raining blood in the male sea
    Who strode for your own dead
And wind his globe out of your water thread

> And load the throats of shells
>   With every cry since light
> Flashed first across his thunderclapping eyes.
>
> On almost the incendiary eve
>   Of deaths and entrances,
> When near and strange wounded on London's waves
>   Have sought your single grave,
> One enemy, of many, who knows well
>   Your heart is luminous
> In the watched dark, quivering through locks and caves,
>   Will pull the thunderbolts
> To shut the sun, plunge, mount your darkened keys
>   And sear just riders back,
>   Until that one loved least
> Looms the last Samson of your zodiac. (*CP*, 97–8)

As narrative, this concerns 'you' (who may also be the speaking self); the first stanza is concerned with the 'near deaths' of its 'best loved' and 'always known', while the second stanza deals with those known to it, but not personally (perhaps the 'murdered strangers' fighting the Battle of Britain, who 'weave' contrails in the skies above and whose planes plummet down into the North Sea): and, finally, in the third stanza, the 'one' of stanza one – now 'one enemy', the 'one loved least' – arrives with destructive force, like a Luftwaffe pilot dropping his bombs. Following its title, in which two terms form a quasi-oxymoron or paradox ('deaths' are only superficially not 'entrances'), the poem works through a self-deconstructing paradox. For example, the 'polestar' of the second stanza is distant, making 'polestar neighbours' a kind of contradiction in terms. But if 'polestar' is taken in its navigational and broader metaphoric sense, too (it is adjectival) – as meaning 'reliable' – then we get the more complex sense of a dependable neighbour, who is at the same time distant from the 'you' of the poem. The same goes for 'near and strange wounded' in stanza three, in which 'strange' is both 'unusual' (and so not in opposition to 'near', although things which are 'near' are usually not 'strange' to us), but also 'strange' in the more archaic sense that we find in 'estranged', or distant, which is oxymoronic.

'Deaths and Entrances' appeared in May 1940, and these phrases anticipate 'near and fire neighbour' from 'There was a saviour' of September 1940, as the 'fear' / 'far' pun suggests. In 'There was a saviour', the context is clearer: an indictment of 'we who could not stir ... when we heard / Greed on man beating near and fire neighbour' – an attack, that is, on the lack of compassion, social conscience and international justice which has led to war (*CP*, 104). In 'Deaths and Entrances', it is likely that Thomas was thinking of complex love-hate relationships, too (the 'great least of ... best loved'); the addressee is an aspect of the speaker himself – a lover or wife. The self, the war and relationships with others are inextricably mingled, and definitions of friend and foe are blurred; he who is 'most unknown' seems an intimate figure, who 'strode for your own dead' and will 'wind his globe out of your water thread' (*CP*, 98). As with the two phrases discussed above, this is not a simple oxymoron – the sense is that anonymous pilots, 'suns [sons] of another street', both defend and are attacking 'you'. That 'you' is complicit and intimate with these 'suns' / 'sons', who are its lovers; 'Your heart is luminous / In the watched dark' means it breaches the blackout, treacherously leading the bombers towards their target (the 'dark' is 'watched', because it is fearfully observed, divided into 'watches' by ARP wardens, and because the luminous dials of wrist*watches* are still visible in the blackout darkness). 'The last Samson of your zodiac' is a German pilot crashing in the act of bombing you, with 'your zodiac' roughly meaning 'your fate'. The 'One enemy, of many' who will finally reach you may be the personified figure of Death himself (signalled by the way in which Thomas capitalises 'One' in all three stanzas); Death is, simultaneously, also the pilots – both friend and foe – to whom the poem refers. And yet, the uterine imagery of the second stanza, with its 'globe' and umbilical 'water thread', also allows us to read the 'polestar neighbour' as making an entrance of another kind – as an embryo entering / exiting into the world of the war during a bombing raid, perhaps, with its light 'thunderclapping' the child's eyes.[38] In this way, then, the poem literalises the birth of deaths, although it resists any singular narrative through its slippery pronouns and ambiguous syntax, for the blurring of identities – inner and outer, friend and foe – is a crucial part of its meaning.

Robin Skelton has claimed that 'The theme of lost or threatened identity gave rise to much poetry of the time', and Elizabeth Bowen would write of living 'with every pore open': 'Sometimes I hardly know where I stopped and somebody else began ... Walls went down'.[39] But in Thomas's poems, this is deliberately courted.[40] If the 'he' of the final lines is death, for example, the relationship between him and the speaker / addressee is paradoxical: he is both an 'immortal friend', who is 'always known' and who 'call[s] deepest down' – Thanatos, the death-wish – and one who is 'most unknown' – '[an] enemy'. Death's known / unknown and friend / enemy quality is captured in the opening description of the 'one' as 'at the great least of your best loved'. Because 'one' is followed by 'at', rather than 'of', we are encouraged to construct this as 'One [who is] at the great least …', with the emphasis being on a single figure, not one who is representative of some collective of the 'best loved'. The twisting of the idiom 'very least' by the substitution of 'great' also literalises the meaning of 'very' as quantity, rather than as merely rhetorical intensifier, making us consider the singularity of the 'one' referred to. The effect of these sleights is to put the sense of 'very least' (most worthless) in jeopardy; doesn't this mean, somehow, the *greatest* of the 'best loved'? We get the sense that this is someone that the 'you' thinks is not terribly important, but who actually (perhaps unconsciously) is – a common attitude to death, which is inescapable, but difficult to face. It means almost-deaths (ones which haven't yet happened), but also 'deaths of those *near* to me', as it does in 'near and strange wounded', where it appears to adapt the idiom 'near and far', until we realise that 'strange' also has the archaic, root meaning of 'far'. This sends us back to 'estranging grief', where this physical sense is present, and also to the proleptic 'murdered strangers'. Similarly, the 'estranging grief' is of 'many married London', another union juxtaposed with a separation. Oscillation between terms for distance and proximity, union and disunion and varying subject positions occurs throughout. Clarke Emery and Ralph Maud, for example, think 'Deaths and Entrances' addresses a different figure in each stanza: a close friend, a 'stranger' who is an enemy bomber (or Christ-figure) and, finally, Thomas.[41] Yet, as we have seen, the 'stranger' inhabits the 'friend', as the 'near' inhabits the 'far' at every point. The poem is 'about' the war, but complicated by the fraught relationship that we have with death, our selves and others. Its paradoxical quality stems from the fact that the speaker is someone who would rather be killed, than 'murder' 'not my enemies', and who dissolves into the others over the course of exploring this condition.

A related strain of self-sacrifice existed in the wartime Christian poetic revival that associated with Charles Williams, T. S. Eliot, Edith Sitwell and Anne Ridler.[42] The threat of sudden death created a widespread desire to be reassured about permanent human values and this, combined with a heightened sense of the irrational, led to an upsurge of religious belief and religious poetry, reflected, for example, in a first Penguin *Anthology of Religious Verse* (1942). As Louis MacNeice, hardly a believer himself, put it in September 1940: 'To both the question of pleasure and to the question of value the utilitarian has no answer. The faith in the *value* of living is a mystical faith'.[43] But there were more and less orthodox versions of religious or religiously aware poetry; that of Kathleen Raine, Mervyn Peake, David Gascoyne and Thomas stressed Christianity's prophetic-apocalyptic aspects, as those which made it relevant to the times and capable, even to non-believers, of evoking a deep collective echo.[44] He responded to Eliot's *Four Quartets*, the main work of this revival, in 'A Winter's Tale' (1944), which alludes to 'Little Gidding''s 'unimaginable / Zero summer', 'Burnt Norton''s intersection of the timeless and temporal and 'East Coker''s vision of the past. But Thomas matches the 'dauncers signifying matrimonie' of the latter with 'wanton' dancers, offering a natural, rather than historical, context and a dionysiac, rather than ecclesiastical emphasis.[45] Elsewhere, Thomas's mood is closer to the Blakeian, even Dostoyevskian, extreme of Gascoyne's 'Ecce Homo', in which the 'Christ of Revolution and Poetry', 'the rejected and condemned become / Agents of the divine'.[46] The war rekindled Thomas's interest in religious imagery in the form of radical, inter-subjective sympathy created through a signifying excess, as a response to the impending death of the others, which is always, as in Donne, one's own death. The fluidity of 'Deaths and Entrances' simultaneously visualises the life and death drives, the speaker's fear of death and his complicity with it. His inability to shut out sympathy for the Other in the dark will attract his nemesis – the bomber pilot – who is his destructive selves, all to be reunited in his 'single grave'.

Thomas was aware of the risk of self-aggrandisement in such gestures, and his general scepticism towards wartime myths helped inoculate him against 'matey warmth' deriving from the much-touted 'Blitz spirit'. Yet, in a more radical sense of dissolution, a poem like 'Deaths and Entrances' emerged from precisely the area – where collective fantasy breached the border between private and public, allowing 'a disconcerting and seductive merging of one person with another, of insides with outsides' – in which such myths of solidarity were fostered.[47] Writing to Vernon Watkins in March 1940, Thomas confessed his tendency in 'dirty, weeping, expansive moments' to 'slip, in grand delusions of all-embracing humanitarianism, everyone into himself' (*CL*, 505) – a point which was made again in the satirical-surreal poem of summer 1940, 'The Countryman's Return':

> I propped humanity's weight
> Against the fruit machine,
> Opened my breast and into
> The spongebag let them all melt. (*SP2*, 58)

In this piece, which he never collected, the 'seductive merging' is all the more potent in often having a sexual dimension, as in the 'quivering' heart of 'Deaths and Entrances', the Freudian 'locks and caves' and 'keys' and the action of 'he' in 'plung[ing], mount[ing] your darkened keys'. Its threatened invasions are mapped across sexual jealousy within marriage, the husband imagining the air raids as Death cuckolding him. The 'just rider' seems to want his faithless partner violently subjugated, to the extent of imagining himself as Samson bringing the pillars of the marriage temple down on their heads. If the speaker will 'hold his peace' about their strife, he nevertheless must speak it in some 'deepest' way, through the 'wound' of his poetry; thus, he is both a victim of infidelity and 'one' with his wife's lover, like the Luftwaffe pilot dropping his bombs and crashing into the 'many married' city. Rooting abstract concerns in the body, Thomas offers a 'key' to the dilemmas of war in terms of vengeful, yet masochistic, anxieties in his betrayed, self-cancelling Samson – a figure who recurs in 'Into her lying down head' and 'Ballad of the Long-legged Bait' and who may also symbolise the nation 'on the eve' of trying to save its honour and self-respect, by bringing the temple of the old order down about its own ears. In such ways, Thomas both resisted and indulged in personal fantasies, which were also simultaneously collective ones, offering himself as both analyst and symptom of the crises of individual subjects and the nation at war.

'Freudian apocalypse': the Blitz sublime and the erotic public sphere

Thomas's poems of the 1930s had explored 'the radical equilibrium that exists between death and sex, the way in which they "exchange their energies and excite each other"', to use Jean Baudrillard's phrase – an equilibrium, in short, that could only exist in extremes, not in some golden mean.[48] As foreshadowed in 'I make this in a warring absence' and confirmed by the reference to Samson in 'Deaths and Entrances', this 'exchange' and 'excitation' of the energies of Eros and Thanatos is traced in Thomas's own drama of married fidelity and betrayal, desire and jealousy, in *Deaths and Entrances*, where it is additionally read in terms of the war, with public and private events constantly melding and overlapping each other. The imbrication of the marital and martial is clear in 'On a Wedding Anniversary', in which marriage is a blitzed house – 'The windows pour into their heart / And the doors burn in their brain' – but this short lyric is atypical in its clumsy symbolism (Thomas, himself, did not like it) (*CP*, 103). More satisfying and challenging are those poems, such as 'Deaths and Entrances' and 'Into her lying down head', in which Thomas was able to bring together paradoxical and often painful states in a less blatant, more exploratory way.

Thomas's writing of his own life through the collective life of the war was a strategy that was adopted by many writers, of course. Like several of them, for example, he experienced the Blitz in a Freudian-surreal, apocalyptic way or in terms of what Stuart Sillars calls 'the Blitz sublime', by which the raids appeared as a manifestation of repressed psychic energies. Material from the Mass-Observation project (itself a spin-off of surrealism's valorisation of the uncanniness of the everyday) shows that 'an element of exhilaration [was] very common' among those witnessing the Blitz bombing, with 'initial fear giving way to an awareness of the beauty of the night sky lanced through by searchlight beams'.[49] Thomas's Blitz poems reflect the way that many took the responses to the destruction as proof of Freud's model of the human subject and theories concerning its workings – that is, as the breaking-out of its destructive, often surreal, fantasies, from the obscurity of its deepest desires. For them, the inferno inflicted on the city matched its inhabitant's own engulfment in conflicted desire and rage for liberation from both psychic and sexual impasse. Louis MacNeice's poem 'Brother Fire', for example, addressed its subject as 'O enemy and image of ourselves, / Did we not ... Echo your thoughts in ours? "Destroy! Destroy!"'. Similarly, David Gascoyne's 'Inferno' spoke of 'Bottomless depths of roaring emptiness', which were also the poet's own.[50] Figuring this liberation or outbreak as an escape of animal energy became something of a cliché. A lone horse gallops through the burning, blitzed London streets in Humphrey Jenning's film *Fires Were Started*, and was soon followed by others in *No Direction* and *Caught*, novels of the Blitz by Henry Green and James Hanley. There was a political dimension to these apocalyptic, almost nihilistic outbreaks of energy; many on the Left, George Orwell among them, initially viewed the bombing with a sense of *schadenfreude*. One New Apocalypse journal was revealingly called *Arson*, and MacNeice addresses 'Brother Fire' as a 'dialectician' (although whether ironically or in sympathy is not clear). . As capitalist Babylon-London reaped the whirlwind of appeasement, it was imagined that it would provoke a revolt against the ruling class, and, in a way, this is exactly what came to pass.

This was because, as Stuart Sillars and Leo Mellor note, many artists glimpsed a regenerative aspect in the destruction: '[Henry] Moore, Thomas and Eliot all see ... the blitz as a kind of renewal, a literal and terrible ordeal and transformation by fire'.[51] More impurely, the threat of extinction exacerbated the sexual impulse: *carpe diem* was a common poetic theme, as unmarried couples disregarded pre-war codes of conduct and slept together before they were separated by war; one-third of all wartime births were illegitimate. The Blitzed city was a place, a state of mind, which – due to the disruption of the raids, the breaking of daily routines, encounters in shelters, trains and hospitals, often under the cover of the blackout – facilitated sexual encounters, as well as those of spies and spivs. As Lyndsey Stonebridge notes: 'Surreally particular to the British Home Front was the uncanny way in which the anxious space of a nation under siege, ghosted by phantoms half-glimpsed in the black-out, exteriorized the unconscious, made fantasy look like reality', fuelling an 'erotically-charged public sphere'.[52] Revolutionary and regressive, political, psychic and sexual energies ran together and were inextricably bound up, too, with death, in a dynamic and 'radical equilibrium', in which exultant release coexisted with loss and grief.

'Into her lying down head', as we saw, is alert to this charged atmosphere in its 'colossal intimacies of silent / Once seen strangers or shades on a stair', with living and dead inhabiting the same space and in which 'Man' is 'the burning England', where the beloved is 'sleep-walking', evoking the male body as Blitzed national territory (*CP*, 94, 95). The ambiguity of the poem's title ensures that its sexual fraught narrative oscillates between two poles, innocence and betrayal, with the speaker's ambivalence about the war matching his ambivalence concerning his partner. The redemption of the couple, like their apocalyptic tribulations, is conceived in sexual form, and this is both curative and punishing. In the contemporary 'Love in the asylum', marriage is figured both as a refuge from the violence of war and as a lunatic asylum, whose wards open out onto padded cells with their straitjackets. Erotic energy in wartime seems to be even more unstable than in peace, capable of aggravating or providing a haven from war's destructive power. The difference with the pre-war poems is that Thomas's new submission to process now led him to place a higher value on human life and be less equivocal about the body, which he came to sanctify using the religious material previously used to dramatise a trickster *bildungsroman*. By 1944 and 'Holy Spring', religious language had been harnessed to sanctify the 'bed of love' at a time of war, making of it the 'immortal hospital' to cure the war-distraught body and spirit (*CP*, 133).

Like Blake, Thomas was particularly concerned with the exploitation of patterns of sexual repression in the public sphere, most obviously in

'There was a saviour', another poem, like 'Deaths and Entrances' and 'Into her lying down head', of the Phoney War. It weaves together the uncertainties of adolescent sexuality and later insight into these concerns, in order to explore the responsibility for war at both a national and personal level. It opens with a meek and mild Sunday-School type figure of Jesus:

> There was a saviour
> Rarer than radium,
> Commoner than water, crueller than truth;
> Children kept from the sun
> Assembled at his tongue
> To hear the golden note turn in a groove,
> Prisoners of wishes locked their eyes
> In the jails and studies of his keyless smiles. (*CP*, 104)

However, the positive associations conjured up by 'rarer', 'golden' and 'smiles' are undermined from the start. 'Kept from the sun' (at a Sunday School, perhaps) puns on 'Son' and so implies the opposite of 'assemb[ling] at his tongue', unless 'tongue' here is metonymic for 'one who speaks on behalf of the saviour' and inverts his message. Likewise, 'rarer than radium' is mellifluous, and radium is used medically (as it was to treat Thomas's father's cancer of the throat), but it is also highly dangerous, and, as the source of X-rays, it allows others to see into and through you. Together with the proverb-style coinages 'commoner than water' and 'crueller than truth', the saviour, as presented to the children, is thus a kind of omnipresent, omniscient and caustic invigilator. His voice may be a 'golden note', but it 'turn[s] in a groove' – that is, it is stuck in a rut like a gramophone needle. The last two lines establish a pattern, repeated in the next two stanzas, of building and imprisonment imagery used analogously, in which a human term is followed by a building metaphor. A human turn is followed by another human one: '[t]he "we" of the poem and the "saviour" of the poem are presented in human terms but between them there intervene buildings'.[53]

Rephrasing this, we might say that the first occurrence of the pattern tells us that those who manage to 'lock' the 'eyes' of the 'children' in the 'jails' and 'studies' of the saviour's 'smiles' (with all the Blakean associations of 'eyes' and sight) are, themselves, the prisoners, not of the smiles, but 'of wishes': it is the imprisonment of desire, which eternally and groundlessly traverses human subjectivities, that leads to the transforming of the smiles into jails. 'Prisoners of wishes' cuts both ways, in fact, since it can mean *im*prisoners; thus, those who are caught will, in turn, imprison others. This is repression, as Freud defined it; the 'prisoners' expend so much energy repressing their desire, that they cut themselves off 'from the sun' – life as it might be enjoyed. They connect the process of repression with the 'smiles' of the 'saviour' (arbitrarily, since there is no real link) and make the smiles into 'jails and studies'. 'Keyless' applies to the 'jails and studies' – there is no way out once inside – and to institutional Christianity, likewise to churches, which can no longer show the way to 'the sun', (alluding to Matthew 16:18–19: 'Thou art Peter, and upon this rock I will build my church ... And I will give unto thee the keys of the kingdom of heaven'). 'Keyless' also echoes 'clueless': the saviour himself may not realise the cycle of repression that he has inadvertently started.

The stanza outlines the mechanisms by which repression reproduces itself, inducting new subjects. But religion is only the start: the following two stanzas extend the critique in more broadly ideological terms applicable to the 1930s and the war. Thus, stanza two articulates the confusions of the 'safe unrest' of adolescence and its complex feeling towards a father figure, in whose 'murdering breath', the speakers 'hid [their] fears', in order to 'do' 'silence ... when earth grew loud / In lairs and asylums of the tremendous shout'. The building metaphors now suggest ferocity and concealment, on the one hand, and madness and sanctuary, on the other; the metaphor 'is becoming both ambiguous and ambivalent ... much nastier ... and yet more pitiful'.[54] The saviour has changed, from placid smiles to 'the tremendous shout', which may be the cry from the cross, but also hints at the shouts of obedience and defiance at a political rally. This, in turn, could be read as Fascist (or Stalinist), just as 'lairs' and 'asylums' have a double meaning.

The Christian-fascist duality is continued in stanza three: here, the building metaphor of 'glory' in 'the churches of his tears / Under his downy arm you sighed as he struck' describes a delight in suffering – first, masochistically, of the self, and then, as a result, of others: 'O you who could not cry ... when a man died / Put a tear for joy in the unearthly flood' (CP, 104). Winifred Nowottny notes that the 'shock' of conflating Christianity and fascism stems from the 'argument of the poem that an ethos of suffering may become involved with a displacement of aggression that finds its release in militarism, and that the worshippers of the Father, travestying His image into a mirror of their own conflicts, execute the same psychological manoeuvre as those who identified themselves with the strength of Hitler'; that is, the Versailles Treaty as the crucifixion and subsequent aggression of Germany.[55]

The fourth and fifth stanzas describe a cure to this, but also unveil the horrors to which repression has brought the now-adult 'children' of stanza one. 'Now in the dark there is only yourself and myself', the poem asserts, because radical self-alienation has produced the callous indifference to the exploitation and suffering which led to war; the 'you' of stanza three is now us: 'O *we* who could not stir / One lean sigh when we heard / Greed on man beating near and fire neighbour' (added emphasis) (*CP*, 104). As Edgell Rickword put it in 1941: 'war is the result of the same will that condemns the people to a low and precarious standard of life whether engaged with an external foe or not ... The true poets of this war ... see the war not as a temporary disease, but as the culminating criminality of a system'.[56] 'There was a saviour' proves Thomas to be a 'true poet of this war' in this sense, and in its dense implication of psychic, social and even economic structures in conflict. The 'Two proud, blacked brothers' of stanza four, who find themselves caught in the 'inhospitable hollow year' of the Blitz, are now forced to admit that, in the past, they selfishly 'wailed and nested in the sky-blue wall' of pie-in-the-sky religion and ideology, instead of accepting kinship with the oppressed, and must now show themselves capable of 'break[ing] a giant tear ... For the drooping of homes / That did not nurse [their] bones'.

'Drooping' and 'nurse' reinforce the point that, for Thomas, ethics invariably has a physical, sexual-nurturing dimension; 'unclenching', un-estranging themselves, the brothers will allow strangers (who are also their unknown selves) to enter the 'unentered house' of the repressed love, which had been 'exiled in [them]':

> Now see alone in us,
>   Our own true strangers' dust
> Ride through the doors of our unentered house.
> Exiled in us we arouse the soft,
> Unclenched, armless, silk and rough love that breaks all rocks. (*CP*, 105)

In these extraordinary final lines, Thomas makes healing sexuality androgynous, with the emphasis on traditional feminine qualities: love must be 'silk and rough', 'soft' and untumescent, anti-phallocentric and 'armless' – a paradoxical gift of Venus (as in the Venus de Milo, which is damaged, but also un- or dis-armed). What could have been simply sexual is richly erotic, has a strange and yet familiarly proverbial power: dripping water wears away the hardest rock. The dissolving of the *homo clausus* or 'armoured man' of the war may yet lead to release from ideological imprisonment; recognition of shared human sexual nature is the poem's true 'saviour'.

'Prosecuting reality': neo-Romanticism, surrealism and modernism

By the late 1930s, the shock value of surrealism – the last international vernacular style of pre-war modernism – was beginning to fade. However, the outbreak of war, and the Blitz, in particular, suddenly made it a widespread reality. Effects which could be called surreal now unavoidably pervaded everyday existence, or stared out from newspapers, photo-journals and newsreels. Mantelpieces, with trinkets and pictures still intact, dangling three storeys up on the sides of blasted-away terraces; barrage balloons looming above street-ends like gigantic Magritte torsos; Hans Bellmer-like jumblings of department store mannequins on pavements; thousands of Londoners sleeping on the platforms of Underground stations; city skylines altering daily to reveal new perspectives – all of these everyday sights led Dunkirk survivors and civilians, just as much as writers, like Spender and Evelyn Waugh, to view the new reality as one in which it was 'as if the war were not so much creating its own effects as bringing weird peacetime imaginings to life'.[57] In particular, the Blitz reproduced surrealism's uncanny aspect – its melding of organic and inorganic and the disturbing interplay between private and public spheres. Albeit in diluted form, a version of the surreal was renewed by events and absorbed by a mass audience.

In visual art, as in Thomas's poetry, this had been going on for some time. Graham Sutherland's paintings of the late 1930s combine referential form and purely abstract relationships, developing this breakthrough, in Stuart Sillars's words, into 'something we can more properly call biomorphic because the "object" is referential in a deliberately confused, unclear manner. Sometimes the confusion is vague and threatening, as familiar natural objects becomes sinister, imprecisely suggesting an evil which is never made explicit; sometimes it is positive in an unexpected and moving way, showing a new natural relationship, a kind of twentieth century visual *discordia concours* which offers us some way out of the immediate physical and moral impasse'. As Sillars argues, this is far more than stylistic mannerism: 'it is a suggestion, through the use of figures which combine animal and human [and vegetable] features, of the commonality of the created, organic world which develops and extends the Romantic notion of the place of humankind within the living world. ... Lacking explicit moral statement, it rests on the uncertainty of a time when the "humane-ness" of humanity as both everyday reality and moral concept is seriously in doubt'.[58] Pre-war studies of rocks and tortured tree trunks, often made in Wales, reappear in Sutherland's paintings of the effects of the Blitz in London's East End, which refigure twisted girders and lift-shafts into organic, vegetable-like growths rearing from their blasted streetscapes.[59] The same can be said of the paintings of John and Paul Nash, John Minton, John Craxton and Ceri Richards, as it can of the drawings and sculptures of Henry Moore and the photography of Bill Brandt and Lee Miller. Sillars's account of what was happening in visual art seems to me as good a description as any of the stance that we find in Thomas's wartime poetry, and a reminder that biomorphism was a form of surrealism, in which the artist reaffirmed the non-random meaning of imagery. Seeking eternal values amid the insanity of war, it found these in the human body – its fibres, fluids, neurones, vascular system and so on – as well as in the organic world which is demonstrably reborn in each generation.

The similarities of this fusion of Romanticism, surrealism and modernism in British art with Thomas's early writing are not difficult to discover, and they underscore the fact that his wartime poetry cannot be fully understood apart from a larger artistic context, which included film and music, as well as visual art. Many of the artists involved were friends of Thomas, and it is possible to discern in the work of all of them the wartime artistic project of democratising modernism – one which led to a renewed version of high 'modernism beyond the Blitz' of the sort noted by Marina MacKay, but which also involved the Blakeian-visionary, existential-biomorphic, surrealist-inflected strain of Thomas, the New Apocalypse poets and many visual artists.[60]

This can be seen by the extent to which the neo-Romantic, modernist-surrealist shift was also a regionalist revolt – one which had a specifically 'Celtic' edge, as noted in Chapter 4. In visual art, it meant a 'remaking of British topography', which began in the mid-1930s, as witnessed by the apparently mundane *Shell Guide to Dorset* (1936) by Paul Nash. This was the first in a series covering England and Wales, which, in their muted but unique way, were part of the British avant-garde. Devoted to subject matter that was seemingly opposed to the experimental, the Guides were modernist in appearance and utilised features of both surrealism and photomontage.[62] They are evidence of what David Mellor has called the 'theatricality' of British landscapes of this period, particularly as regards their fascination with the 'Celtic', biomorphic and marginal.[61] Sutherland and Minton, as well as Lucien Freud and

John Craxton, made a point of painting in Wales during these years, while John Piper was heavily influenced by what he called the 'Celtic supremacy' of 'linear and rhythmical' styles in Celtic art between the eighth and thirteenth centuries. In the same spirit, as David Jones noted, James Joyce claimed that the intricacies of *The Book of Kells* lay behind the verbal convolutions of *Finnegans Wake*. Mellor observes: 'An "Expressionist", "visionary" genealogy was being constructed for a British visual culture in troubled times, a genealogy independent of Continental forces, drawn from seemingly indigenous criteria. By the time of Read's *British Contemporary Art* (1951) this cultural nationalism is assumed and self-supporting'.[63] So it was that, as war broke, artists acted as if England had already been invaded, such that 'Britishness' was to be relocated in Celtic fastnesses (quite literally in the case of the National Gallery's stashing of its old masters in slate quarries in North Wales). At the same time, the emphasis on outsiderness and the move to the peripheries, which consequently made Wales the heart of Britishness, was part of the resistance to a centralising state, for Britain's geographical extremes 'were in opposition to London, to the centre, to the habitual hegemony of fine buildings and institutionalized rites. Along with the paternalistic desire to appropriate ... there co-existed the egalitarian aspect of a new humanism'.[64]

The ambiguity of these developments was crucial, because it extended their appeal. Regionalism and many shades of nationalism were rarely opposed to national unity, which might be strengthened by a keener sense of internal difference. But they were in favour of an appreciation of local landscape, custom and tradition and the Celticising and pastoral-surrealist strain in British culture, and this involved a continual contest between self-assertion and co-operation. There was, at times, undoubtedly, an element of English aggrandisement and blindness to cultural difference to this. But to see wartime English interest in Wales as no more than metropolitan condescension is to risk letting a purist nationalism occlude the real significance of the radical shift which occured.[65] Such attitudes were not common at the time, except among extreme nationalists, partly because beating Nazism soon became inextricable from the chance to implement Beveridge. In their contemporary form, they run the risk of being anachronistic and missing the 'egalitarian aspect' of the 1940s – one which largely benefitted Welsh art and writing. Wartime requirements and artistic currents came together in an overarching, common British sense of solidarity. However much the government encouraged this, largely in the form of the forerunner of the Arts Council, CEMA (Council for the Encouragement of Music and Art, for which Thomas himself scripted a film in 1942), it was following, not leading, a growing trend – one which meant nationwide tours by orchestras, musicians, drama companies and art exhibitions, often in venues such as factory canteens, church and village halls and barracks. There was resurgence of poetry, not just in Wales and Scotland, where it predated 1939, but also in Northern Ireland and the various regions of England. Thomas's example, as a successful non-metropolitan poet succeeding on his own terms in the London literary world, had helped crystallise the movement which lay behind these developments: in turn, their success emboldened him. This was to be reflected, as I discuss in Chapter 6, in the way in which his poetry performed a form of 'Britishness' from 1944 onwards.

Reflecting the new currency of neo-Romantic modernism and what Stuart Sillars calls the 'paradoxically surreal elements of actual experience', Thomas's wartime poetry also changed in its metaphoric vocabulary.[66] In 1938–41, its gothic-grotesque elements were ousted by images which reflected a fusion of his concern with psychic constraint and the cityscape of the Blitz. This, too, was part of his attempt to gain purchase in the public sphere. Jail, asylum, menagerie, church, theatre, nursery, hospital, kennel, nunnery, zoo and houses (also as 'slum', 'lairs' and 'hovels') and their urban locations (park, street and pavement) all make an appearance, although Thomas's trademark mythic resonance is retained. Likewise, inner spaces and points of ingress and egress (studies, rooms, corridors, stairwells, doors and windows) and the mechanisms of securing these (locks, bolts, wards and keys) create a potent poetics of built space. 'Death's Duell', with its architectural metaphors conveying a medieval sense of the body as the soul's prison, is one intertext at play here. But it is chiefly Blake, for whom rock, stone and the buildings which are made of these materials are associated with the material manifestations of the forces which produce earthly hell (the 'satanic mills' of the factories, churches, prisons and barracks of industrialism, religion and tyrannical government), who informs Thomas's new practice. Blake is Thomas's guide beside the 'charter'd Thames', and he is the main source of an increasingly dynamic symbolism of the self – its confinement, struggle and escape from bondage.[67]

It may be limiting to read these poems purely in Freudian terms, of course. As with the Apocalypse poets, the extensiveness of Thomas's use of images of buildings, like his extended exploration of sea symbolism in 'Ballad of the Long-legged Bait' or snowscapes in 'A Winter's Tale', can be fruitfully read, like much of his poetry, in relation to Jung. Jung's depth psychology, with its idiom of fantasy and archetype, had become current by the 1940s, and this enabled poets to explore in novel and fluid, but structured ways, as Thomas was doing, the violence of the war. For the New Apocalypse poets, it was not so easy; as Peter Riley argues, in their work, Thomas's 'disruptive, declamatory mode' was led increasingly to a poetry of 'anguish and fear', with human existence viewed as malign, to a much greater degree than in Thomas.[68] Unlike him, most were unable to develop styles distinctive enough to resist being dragged into solipsism and abstraction by the pressure of the war. But this is not to say that they were all weak poets. J. F. Hendry's *The Bombed Happiness* (1942) and *The Orchestral Mountain* (1943) (mourning his wife, who was a Blitz victim) stand comparison with all but the very best poetry of the war. Indeed, the basic Apocalypse achievement of reinventing surrealism as myth-creation and 'myth "as a mode of release from the object-machine, whether state, system or rationalism"' was impressively continued by John Heath-Stubbs and W. S. Graham, among others.[69] More broadly, these developments fostered and reflected the general radicalisation of British culture. Modernism gained a level of mass acceptability, while, at the same time, modernist artists demonstrated wartime solidarity by devising more popular modes. As early as 1940, as Tolley notes: 'the clear cut antagonism between traditionalists and moderns had begun to blur' and, by 1950, 'the acceptance of a contemporary idiom … was widespread among literate people'.[70] The success of *Deaths and Entrances* in its publication in 1946 was central to that development.

'The tiered and hearing tide': war as performance and ritual resistance

Having considered Thomas's relationship to Apocalypse and his Freudian-surreal and religious-erotic rendering of the Blitz, I now return to the way in which life on the 'Home Front' was lived 'as if in a theatre' and the corresponding theatricality in self-perception and poetic self-performance.

The first year of the war was experienced as a kind of unreal representation or simulacrum – the Phoney War – in which the dreaded Nazi onslaught continually threatened, but failed to materialise. Later, after the Battle of Britain and the Blitz, 'the war moved from the horizon to the map' and became distanced once again. This phrase is from Elizabeth Bowen's *The Heat of the Day*, which opens in an open-air theatre in Regent's Park. In this novel, the concert being performed is an image for the 'artificial memory system' covering a 'deeper [national] emptiness', which is Britain's wartime culture and arguably the novel's real theme.[71] Likewise, the title and tenor of Virginia Woolf's *Between the Acts*, set in the first summer of the war, suggests a radical theatricality. This sense of deep unreality, vacuity and unease persisted, even when the bombs started falling.

As we have seen, Thomas's breakthrough as a poet in the third and fourth notebooks had been, in part, due to the distancing that he achieved from his subject matter, through the construction of space of his poems as a kind of imaginary stage. Equally, his work throughout the 1930s, both before and after 1938, was self-consciously rhetorical, and self-dramatising. Thomas spent much of the war in London, where many dramatic masks were expected of him and where he revelled in presenting a multiplicity of personalities. This is not to say merely that he was more of a self-performer than most. Rather, it is to observe that the nature of his poetry was such that theatricalised dissonance between different realities and selves, which wartime demanded, was unusually exacerbated in his case. This is bound up with aspects of the war poems I have already discussed, and some of its implications can be traced in the first of his three elegies for victims of the Blitz, 'Among those Killed in the Dawn Raid was a Man Aged a Hundred', published in August 1941:

> When the morning was waking over the war
> He put on his clothes and stepped out and he died,
> The locks yawned loose and a blast blew them wide,
> He dropped where he loved on the burst pavement stone
> And the funeral grains of the slaughtered floor.
> Tell his street on its back he stopped a sun
> And the craters of his eyes grew springshoots and fire
> When all the keys shot from the locks, and rang.
> Dig no more for the chains of his grey-haired heart.
> The heavenly ambulance drawn by a wound
> Assembling waits for the spade's ring on the cage.
> O keep his bones away from that common cart,
> The morning is flying on the wings of his age
> And a hundred storks perch on the sun's right hand. (*CP*, 112)

The poem originated in a newspaper article about a centenarian killed in a bombing raid on Hull. By using the headline as a title, Thomas was not just breaking with his general practise, but he was also linking this to the debate about the war and its media representation. The death is viewed through the lens of his process vision, initially in a bare, monosyllabic vocabulary, but then in images, which are increasingly bizarre, even disturbingly flippant, given the subject matter. The ostensible 'message' is the rejection of the 'heavenly ambulance' of Christian consolation as no more than a 'common cart', but this is presented in Dalíesque fashion, drawn through the sky by 'a wound', and the final image is cartoon-like. Is the piece a heartless *jeu* concocted at the old man's expense? Or is it a witty mockery of the futility of war (all this firepower to kill such an old man)? Criticism, as a result, has been divided: it is 'an angry report from the battlefront', or 'light-hearted', or 'a most excellent jest', or 'fanciful ... pure trifling [with] no imagination'.[72] Certainly, there is a conceited refusal of seriousness; epithets ('slaughtered') are transferred, euphemisms are coined ('he stopped a sun'), religion (as 'sun' / 'son' or 'heavenly ambulance') is manipulated for effect and puns are indulged in ('waking' has a dual meaning, making 'mourning' a pun, too). The language of mourning is destabilised and made playful, and any normal elegiac appeal to the authentic – as suffering or loss – is undermined and implicitly denied. Instead, a brilliantly brittle tonal undecidability is offered as a substitute rite by this linguistic performance (what Steve Vine calls 'a language of celebration that parodically compounds irony with affirmation', an 'ironic imagism whose metaphoric potentiality floats free of any attempt to grasp the event' as mimetic representation).[73] The irreverently grotesque incongruity of such linguistic display and images such as 'craters of ... eyes [that] grew springshoots and fires' lead to the final image of regeneration: each one of the 100 years becomes a baby brought by a stork, as in the tale told to curious children who ask where babies come from.[74]

If 'There was a saviour' is an analysis of the psychosexual roots of war in selfishness and unlove, 'Among Those Killed' uses an absurd occasion to offer a positive, yet deliberately contrived, image for the life force continually working against war's destructiveness. As the two elegies of 1944–5 would also declare, Thomas's basic carnivalesque urge was to proclaim that '[m]ilitary power and strength are helpless against the material bodily procreative principle', in Mikhail Bakhtin's words.[75] As well as embodying a more demonstrative and public expression of process, this carnivalesque, seriously playful and often ritualistic element was also a response to the theatrical, simulacra-like aspect of the war. The 'Phoney War' threw this into relief; the interim between the declaration of war and Dunkirk and the Battle of Britain was characterised by neurotic anticipation, and it fed a more general sense that the war was, at some level, simply an illusory, staged event. Even when the Blitz did begin, it was regarded as peculiarly theatrical: the blackouts, like the lights dimming in an auditorium, prepared the audience for the night's performance. For those directly involved in the Forces or the war economy, 'the gigantic slapstick of modern war' involved complete surrender to it, as to a kind of theatrical production, whose disciplines – costume-like uniforms, routines, codes, scripts, rehearsals and role play – effectively constituted the war.[76] This inaction and the ironically staged internalisation of Army jargon is the subject of one of the best (and best-known) of all wartime poems, Henry Reed's 'Naming of Parts'. But combat, too, was often seen as a violent version of performance. In Keith Douglas's North African poems, for example, soldiers caught between a Cairo furlough and desert combat seem 'mimes', treading the 'boards of the stage' of war, their destinies played out in front of 'scenery' (Douglas described himself as a 'figure writhing on the backcloth').[77] On the Home and military fronts, it was not just that war was dramatic; rather, something of the essence of war was felt to reside in its theatrical nature. As the idiom had it, there were 'theatres of war'; mobile, spectacular and all-pervasive, Total War's theatricality had an ontological force, which came to pervade and define existence.[78]

This theatricality is implicit in the primary source of the phrase 'deaths and entrances', as already noted: Donne's conceit in 'Death's Duell' that 'this *exitus a morte* [birth], is but *introitus in mortem*, this *issue*, this deliverance *from* that *death*, the death of the *wombe*, is an *entrance*, a delivering over to *another death*, the manifold deathes of this *world*'.[79] However, the echo of Jaques's 'seven ages of man' speech in *As You Like It* is also unmistakable: 'All the world's a stage / And all the men and women merely players; / They have their exits and their entrances'.[80] 'Exits and entrances' informs *Deaths and Entrances*; deaths are 'exits' from life. Shakespeare has inverted the rightful order of his pairing for the sake of euphony (entrances have to precede exits), although this accords with the simultaneity of event of Thomas's process poetic. Donne, by contrast, doctrinally insists on the paradoxical equivalence of his pairing ('death' as an 'entrance' into true, everlasting life). The relationship between the sources is asymmetric, and the resultant overde-termination prevents a simple metaphorical equivalence or an allegorical reading of the title.

The theatrical cue is taken up elsewhere in the collection: the girl in 'Love in the Asylum' who walks the 'madhouse boards', a 'savagely young King Lear', performances on 'middle moonlit stages / Out to the tiered and hearing tide' and a 'strut and trade of charms / On the ivory stages' (*CP*, 91, 94, 95, 106). However, these references are less significant in themselves, than in their hinting towards the consciously performed and staged quality of the poems in a broader sense. Theatricality, rather than 'the theatre' as such, pervades *Deaths and Entrances*. This is linked to anxiety about the entrance of personal rhetoric into the public realm. The language of exhortation, slogan, censorship and euphemism enter the private sphere; the government controls and shapes language (thus, the 'theatre of war' sanitises a bloody actuality by conflating combat with surgery, as in the contemporary 'surgical strike'). Unravelling such language recalls Thomas's debate with Heppenstall; in war, he suggested, the (humane) individual self must be made strange to itself, through acting a military role sanctioned by a communal myth or fantasy, in order to play its part; the enemy, by the same token, must be dehumanised. Violence against the Other always begins with violence against oneself and one's empathic capability; in this way, people can commit acts of aggression against 'those not [their] enemies' – deeds they would be horrified to commit against known or imaginable individuals. The war poems respond to such a fear of acting out of character, but grasp the unavoidable and deadly theatricality of warfare. 'Deaths' always accompany Thomas's entrancing dramatic 'entrances', just as actors who forget their lines are said to 'die' on stage or those who make other actors forget their lines are said to 'corpse' them, and the poems' sense of the theatricality of the wartime self is charged with foreboding.

Theatricality also flowed from the erosion of distinct zones of war and peace and the newly mechanised nature of warfare, which distanced military personnel from the consequences of their actions, and dissolved personal responsibility in the collective. Alan Ross's poem 'Radar', about a naval operative tracking and destroying U-boats, recounts 'Control is remote; feelings, like hands, / Gloved by space. Responsibility is shared, too. / And destroying the enemy by radar / We never see what we do'.[81] The self, as a result, is dispersed, flattened and decathected. Thomas resisted officialdom's harnessing of language to instrumental ends, by turning the theatricality of war and his own ambivalent performance as both a writer and citizen towards forms of ritual. Theatricality, in this sense, is not a mockery of the war-dead; rather, it is a way of trying to come at an appropriate form of ritual, often by making the fire of the Blitz part of what Leo Mellor calls a 'redemptive or phoenix-yielding dynamic'. It involves, in Thomas's war poetry, a more pantheistic and consolatory version of the monism of process – a tracing of a belief system out of violence and desire using the elemental forces of the earlier writing, such that 'the rituals in Thomas can be read theologically – if not under the sign of any conventional religion', since, in Mellor's words, 'the mediation of spiritual beliefs into performative forms, and the types of failure when such a movement is made, allows an understanding of why ritual reaches such importance – and why fire has a part to play'.[82]

This ritualistic emphasis is strikingly apparent in the visual appearance of certain poems, such as 'Poem in October', which are centred on the page to give them a symmetrical, mandala-like appearance. The best known example is 'Vision and Prayer'; its first six stanzas are diamond-shaped, the final six bobbin- or quincunx-shaped. The shape-poem alludes to modernist experimentation, but more to the Metaphysical poets, reinforcing the religious, celebratory tone of much of the collection. It also draws on the Welsh praise poetry tradition, as I discuss in Chapter 6, and its reverent, even rapt, attitude before nature. The threat of biomorphic mutation alters, such that the threatening, hormone-driven body of the 1930s becomes a source of plenitude, a locus of ethical value, in resisting the depredations of war. Ceremonies, sermons, conversions, baptisms, visions, prayers, marriages and other rituals dominate, reflected in the elaborate address of numerous poems. There are, for example, apostrophic addresses in eleven of the twenty-six poems, varying from vocative interjection ('O / Out of a bed of love ...') to ambiguous resignation ('Oh as I was young and easy ...') (*CP*, 133, 134). Many poems rely on frameworks which might be called ceremonial; the separate, carefully nested temporalities of 'A Winter's Tale', for example, or the continual retwisting of phrase in 'The conversation of prayers' ('By ... the man on the stairs ... From the man on the stairs ... the man on the stairs ... Dragging him up the stairs') (*CP*, 85). All these effects yield a ritualistic, performed utterance and are set against the ever-present threat of silencing.

The poems in Thomas's fourth collection, then, reflect a heightened awareness of the theatricality of wartime existence. They mediate the war as a theatrical dissonance between increasingly multiple selves and the disjunctive realities surrounding them. In their formality, these poems aim at an audience which is broader than the avant-garde coterie readership of the 1930s, occupying the space of ritual and the power to grant meaning which is usually occupied by power. It was not just a case, for Thomas, of 'exposing' the terrible fact that war 'hollowed and emptied out the private mind, transforming it into a scene of lies, artificial dreams and fabricated emotions', as one critic describes the task of wartime writers (what else do writers do, if not create 'artificial dreams and fabricated emotions', in order to arrive at truth by indirection?).[83] Rather, because it was no longer possible to separate the 'private mind' from public and collective pressures, the question shifted to how to dramatise the encounter between them. This was the question that Thomas wrestled with during the mid-war break in his poetry writing.

Deceptively doubled: Thomas, film and stylistic change

The poems written between May 1944 and September 1945 (twelve of the twenty-six included in *Deaths and Entrances*) have a greater verbal limpidity and apparent structural clarity than those dating from June 1939 to August 1941, with their dense, often jittery and conceited verbal textures.[84] This change is usually linked to the fact that, in September 1941, Thomas began work as a scriptwriter for Donald Taylor's Strand Films.[85] He wrote at least fourteen scripts for Strand and its successor, Gryphon Films, all of which were war-related. They ranged from recruitment shorts (*Balloon Site 568* [1942]), doses of imperial propaganda (*The Battle for Freedom* [1942]) and attacks on Nazi leadership (*These Are the Men* [1943]) to films about reconstruction and peacetime planning, such as *New Towns for Old* (1942) and *A City Reborn* (1945). The best of these scripts were two lyrical, quasi-experimental celebrations of national variety-within-unity – *Wales – Green Mountain, Black Mountain* (1942) and *Our Country* (1944). From 1943, Thomas also began working as a radio broadcaster, regularly performing and writing for the BBC. Over the ten-year period from 1943–53, he would take part in a total of 145 separate programmes, with 'Reminiscences of Childhood' (1943 and 1945), 'Quite Early One Morning' (1944) and 'Memories of Christmas' (1945) being wartime productions. In common with poems such as 'The hunchback in the park', 'Poem in October' and 'Fern Hill', the wartime radio scripts drew on childhood memories, although their nostalgia is less complex.

The films about reconstruction reflected Thomas's own political outlook and were part of government attempts to mobilise the population for the war effort, by promising major social reform once victory had been won. *Wales – Green Mountain, Black Mountain*, which lyrically explores wartime Welsh rural and urban landscapes, uses iconic older footage of closing colliery gates, dole queues and the destitute grubbing for coal on spoil-heaps shot for Taylor's documentary *Today We Live* of

1936.[86] Linking the destitution of the 1930s to lack of planning, it exhorts viewers not to forget:

> ... the procession of the old-young men
> From dole queue to corner and back again,
> From the pinched, packed streets to the peak of slag
> In the bite of the winters with shovel and bag ... (*CFS*, 31)

The British Council, who had commissioned the film, rejected it as too Left-wing to be shown abroad; however, the Ministry of Information (MOI) were happy to snap it up. Such films were part of the political shift to the Left, which took place during the war – a reminder of Lord Boothby's famous quip that: 'The MOI did not win the war, but it certainly won the election for Labour'.[87]

Our Country – Thomas's best script – is the only one in which his words followed the visual imagery, rather than vice versa. An atmospheric film of great visual beauty, it allegorises national unity by following the peregrinations of a merchant seaman, around the various parts of Britain, before he eventually boards an Aberdeen trawler. Within the journey, the musings of a factory girl he meets in Sheffield (the only prose in the script) act as a kind of still central point. What makes the piece significant is its verbal invention – 'the owl sound of the dry wind in the tube tunnels' – its resemblance to the wartime poetry (it echoes all three of his elegies, as well as other poems), its allusions to Eliot's *Little Gidding*, Auden's 'Look, stranger' and 'The Night-Mail' and its anticipation of the pastoral tone of the last poems:

> Take any direction any road up or down
> the island alters round every village corner
> at every turn of a town.
> Take to the woods
> or the slow lanes drenched with quietness and leaves
> or to the climbing roads above the valleys
> where the bright plaits of the rivers weave:
> the weaving island leads all ways
> calls a man down from the windblown sky-touching island height
> to the towns in the bowls of smoke
> the clamorous galleries and metalscapes of mechanised night. (*CFS*, 71–2)

Such passages have been taken to support the claim that the new demands of film and radio led Thomas to poetic clarity. Andrew Sinclair, for example, argues that 'his stint as a documentary writer ... taught him economy, precision, and simplicity of expression. His major post-war poems … seem to have benefitted from that workaday wartime need to communicate with the people of Britain in as clear a voice as possible'.[88]

It is certainly true that the pre-film poems of 1939–41 are mainly in the denser, impacted style of *The Map of Love* and that many of those that were to have the largest impact on his enlarged audience date from the 1944–5 period. There is no doubt, too, that the more grotesque aspects of process, already modified after 1938, almost disappear in the 1944–5 poems. We can trace the change by comparing Thomas's two long narrative poems of the time, 'Ballad of the Long-legged Bait' (1941) and 'A Winter's Tale' (1944). 'Ballad' is Thomas's most virtuoso treatment of the sea as symbol and physical–psychic state; in it, 'a young man goes out to fish for sexual experience' using his bride as bait. She enjoys promiscuous sexual adventures beneath the waves, luring him, Lorelei-like, down into the depths, where he 'catches a family, the church, and the village green', and is dragged through the seabed to a land of normality on the other side of passion (*CP*, 247). Although it is difficult to summarise neatly, the poem suggests that sexual abandon leads us back to the quotidian existence we sought to escape in it (as in *Adventures in the Skin Trade* – the novel that Thomas was also working on in 1941). In 'A Winter's Tale', a speaker in the present tells the tale of a hermit in the past, who is inspired by meditation to pursue a 'she-bird' through the snowscape of the surrounding countryside. His faith in her thaws a frozen past of 'departed villages', dancers, nightingales and 'centaur dead' horses, finally drawing her to him for a union and consummation that is both ecstatic and death-like. The war lurks in both poems – the Battle of the Atlantic in 'Ballad' and the Russian front's 'white / Inhuman cradle' in 'A Winter's Tale' – and both have an encounter with 'the long dead':

> One by one in dust and shawl,
> Dry as echoes and insect-faced,
> His fathers cling to the hand of the girl
> And the dead hand leads the past,
>
> … And the old men sing from newborn lips:
>
> *Time is killing another son.*
> *Kill Time! She turns in her pain!*
> *The oak is felled in the acorn*
> *And the hawk in the egg kills the wren.* (*CP*, 130)

This passage from the central section of 'Ballad' matches the central part of 'A Winter's Tale' in describing the awakening of a frozen fossilised past. Yet the conjunction of 'insect' – a process word from the early poetry – together with an explicit (spoken and italicised) account of the inextricability of birth and death marks this out as a transitional work. In 'A Winter's Tale', the residual 1930s vocabulary has vanished; its log, pot, bird, vale, snow, bread and bride are elemental in a fable or fairy-tale sense drawn from the world of archetype, and its rhythms are less jagged and demanding. Comparison of the two, then, reveals a switch from an intensive style, which has already shed some of the gnarledness of the 1930s work, to an extensive one, which is more relaxed and pared-back, in some ways resembling the simple lyricism of *Our Country*.

Yet Sinclair is wrong to attribute this to the direct influence of Thomas's film and radio work, and not only because a phrase such as 'communicate with the people of Britain' strikes a false, pompous note. Thomas was capable of 'economy, precision and simplicity of expression' before the war, nor is this always evident after 1944, as a poem such as 'In country sleep' shows. Although the majority of the clearer poems in *Deaths and Entrances* are post-1944, 'The hunchback in the park' – to take just one example – dates from 1941. Assuming that the purpose of poetry is a narrowly defined 'communication', Sinclair misses the point of the early work's difficulty and the logic of the evolution of Thomas's style. In reality, something like the opposite of his account was the case. Thomas was deeply disturbed at 'writing recruiting literature or broadcasting appeals for warm bodies to become cold' and had been dragooned into it by poverty (*CL*, 465). Like many writers, he felt resentful at the irony of his skill being put at the service of power; the fact was that the better that he did his job, the more plausible government became and the deeper his complicity with its workings. Guilt and a sense of self-betrayal turned to real alienation for many writers, who were painfully aware that their co-operation was swiftly turned into co-option.

Thus, George Orwell, who had endorsed a manifesto published in *Horizon* in October 1941 calling on writers 'to interpret the war so that cultural unity is re-established and the war-effort emotionally co-ordinated' was soon observing bitterly that: 'To compose a propaganda pamphlet or a radio feature needs just as much work as to write something you believe in with the difference that the finished product is worthless'. Eventually, Orwell resigned from the BBC's Indian section, because of duplicitous broadcasts on Indian independence, claiming 'we are all drowning in filth'.[89] Thomas's response to a similar dilemma was subversion, rather than resignation.[90] *Our Country*, the one film in which he was given free rein, is the exception that proves the rule. Phrases like 'weathers of her eyes' and 'capsising sea' show its proximity to his poetry and what Ackerman calls its 'heroic lyricism' is tempered at one point by the air-raid memories of the girl in Sheffield: 'you never knew if there wouldn't be a whine and a scream and a noise like the whole town blowing up and then suddenly all the houses falling down on you and everybody you knew lying all dead in the street. And suddenly the lights would be out, and then, this is the end of the world I would say to myself ... And you were dead as well' (*CFS*, 72). At this point, arguably, the film briefly offers a populist version of the Apocalyptic territory covered by the poetry. But the clarity, even of this script, is different to the artfully contrived kind of even a short lyric, such as 'In my craft or sullen art', and the concessions that Thomas did make to transparency have to be considered together with the other kinds of difficulty, which he multiplied to offset the loss of his denser textures. Arguably, film writing left its mark on the poems in *Deaths and Entrances* just as much in the way that their plethora of directional articles mimics filmic movement; like a tracking camera, the poems shift their viewpoints ceaselessly 'up', 'under', 'above', 'down', 'over' and 'below'.

While film work was congenial to him in certain ways, Thomas certainly felt, as Empson claimed, that he had 'been tempted to write war propaganda [in his film-scripts] ... and then felt that this would be disgusting'; even the films of reconstruction, which suited his politics, he resented having to write.[91] This fed his ambivalence towards the war, his sense of acting out a role and selling out his poetic talent. While he undoubtedly aimed for more clarity in moving away from the stylistic impasse of 1936–7, he sought to devise a kind that created different kinds of complex effects. The struggle to do this is reflected most obviously in the least successful poems in the book, such as the two that I considered at the opening of this chapter, 'When I woke' and 'Because the pleasure-bird whistles', or 'To Others than You' and 'Once below a time'. As ever with Thomas, the larger uncertainty is reflected at a formal level in the poems' choppy lineation and awkward rhythms (and even 'The hunchback in the park' suffers from this, to some extent). A new combination of unemphatic, yet convincing, rhythm, and defamiliari-sation through repetition, had yet to appear; and I discuss this more fully in Chapter 6. For now, however, I shall touch on its operation in 'In my craft or sullen art', which contains the tension between the wish to be more widely heard and the anti-social aspect of writing between 1930s and 1940s writing selves as its theme ('sullen' has both its modern sense and the medieval one of 'unique, isolated' from the Latin *solus*, alone).

The speaker of the poem claims not to write for conventional rewards – 'ambition or bread / Or the strut and trade of charms / On the ivory stages' – but for what he calls the 'common wages' of the 'most secret heart' of the lovers, who 'lie abed' at the late hour of writing (*CP*, 106). The poem's paradox is that, despite this, the lovers 'pay no praise or wages / Nor heed my craft or art'. Characteristically, it states by indirection, using negatives ('not', 'nor'), a list of those that the poet does not write for and who more or less make up the public sphere – authority, tradition or academia ('ivory' in stanza one finding its more usual collocation in 'tower/ing' in stanza two). The poem seems to be too short and straightforward to resist explication, but it nevertheless manages to frustrate it. Why craft *or* (sullen) art? And why is 'sullen' omitted in the final line, which otherwise almost repeats the opening one? How does the poem move from the lovers 'with all their griefs in their arms' in stanza one to 'arms / Round the griefs of the ages' in stanza two? War has something to do with this, for although the scenario seems archetypal and remote from the modern, this is deceptive. The key terms – 'labour', 'wages' and 'trade', for example – are drawn from modern economics, and hackneyed bourgeois–romantic notions about 'inspiration' are undermined by the contemporary, negative sense of 'sullen'. This unobtrusive yet insistent terminology obliquely refers to art's commodification and the plight of the lyric poet in the era of late capitalism, forced to 'strut and trade' his 'charms' in the marketplace. The poem rejects this, but is marked by it, too, as it is by the war: the 'raging moon' is the *furor poeticus*, but also a bomber's moon, as the repeated 'arms' suggest, and this is in opposition to the lovers and poetry. As elsewhere in *Deaths and Entrances*, part of Thomas's solution is to oppose killing with new life. Diana, the moon goddess, is also the goddess of childbirth, presiding over the 'labour' of the poet, as also over the labour that is the purpose of the biological forces driving the lovers. Nevertheless, the downbeat conclusion places a question mark over the possibility of lyric, and it marks a shift from the old idea of the necessary isolation of the poet to a deeper isolation, in which the fact that writing is unrewarded must be its own reward. The traditional scenario – that poets are misunderstood by an unfeeling world, but embraced by lovers – no longer holds. In fact, since the poet sees his rejection in advance, he writes for the lovers, not because he thinks they'll understand him, but because he understands that they, with nothing to give each other but themselves, do so utterly. In a world in which only 'sullen' love and lyric seem to have no exchange-value, it is the absoluteness and the purity of their gesture which he praises. The guarantee of their integrity is that they cannot be exchanged for each other; separate isolation becomes a final, irreducible form of solidarity. And in admitting his isolation, the poet's art loses its 'sullen'-ness by recognising his need for a human link, even as this is denied him. Paradoxically, perversely, the lovers' ignorance of the poet is the reason why he feels compelled to write 'for' them.

Mourning, elegy and wounds

'Deaths and Entrances' is a proleptic elegy; 'Among Those Killed' shows how, during the Blitz of 1940–1, Thomas initially tackled the task of writing an elegy for the civilian war-dead with an excitable blend of anxiety and affirmation in a decidedly poetic *performance*. In the final section of this chapter, I concentrate on the two later elegies, 'Ceremony After a Fire Raid' (1944) and 'A Refusal to Mourn' (1945), which were written for child victims of the 'Little Blitz' – that is, for human beings at the other extreme of the life cycle from a centenarian – and conclude by returning to the 'silence' mentioned at its outset.

The elegies again tackle the ethical issue of how suffering can be represented, without it being appropriated in a self-aggrandising way by the lyric self. Thomas's moral shock at the war made it impossible for him to shirk the task, but, as we have seen, he was keenly aware that all public utterance risked co-option by the discourses of power. His response was not to downplay the rhetorical aspect (which ran the risk of mock-humility or appearing casual anyway), but to paradox-ically intensify the poetry's performative aspect, invoking ritual, using extensive apostrophe and sacralising the human body, as both the focus of the suffering that the war caused and the source of overcoming its destruction and hatred. Elegy is, of course, already a paradoxical lyric genre. It ranges from impersonal commemoration of public figures, through the different gradations of sorrow represented in mourning a friend, parent, spouse or lover; from neoclassical restraint to 'grief fettered by numbers' and rhapsodic derangement. Traditionally, elegy also expresses doubts about the very capacity of language to figure loss – the 'reluctant submission to language', in Peter Sacks's phrase, seeming to involve relinquishment of the lost object to the 'substitutive labours of signification', as if to engage in such mourning were 'in some sense to *collude* with loss'.[92] Elegy has, then, a wide and potentially unstable range of subject positions and a tendency to foreground linguistic betrayal, incapacity and silencing. These tendencies were exacerbated in the twentieth century, a period of technologised mass death, during which poetry and the elegy have become inextricably linked. Jahan Ramanzani has argued that this has occurred despite poetry's tendency to subvert the impulse of redemption in elegy – which is often 'anti-consolatory and anti-encomiastic ... anti-conventional and sometimes even anti-literary' – because modern poetry draws so much of its energy from the traumas of war, the death of God and the weakening of mourning rites.[93] Perhaps the biggest danger that this poses comes through the elegist's necessary identification with the object of mourning. While 'Lycidas' or 'Adonais', for example, are also elegies for their authors, in the face of modern atrocity, such empathic identification requires extraordinary tact and alertness if it is not to seem self-aggrandising.

Like other wartime poets, Thomas's desire to fashion a more wide-reaching form of modernism meant that he was particularly sensitive to the dangers of inadvertently appropriating suffering to the lyric ego. This is one of the reasons for the performative, artificial quality of 'Among Those Killed', which exacerbates the gap between its headline-style title and non-realist style in its refusal to co-opt death to a journalistic mode. Elsewhere, Thomas's work also refuses, as much modern poetry does, to translate grief into consolation, corresponding to Freud's 'melancholic' variant on the normal process of mourning, offering 'fierce resistance to solace' instead of recuperation, immersion in loss rather than transcendence of it (insofar as it neither abandons the dead, nor heals the living, melancholy matches one of Thomas's most-used symbols – that of the open wound, as discussed in Chapter 3). In this situation, as Steve Vine notes, 'the subject's narcissism is exploded, and no substitutive object or meaning comes to fill the void ... [it is left] perpetually bereft'.[94] Yet, while alert to such voiding, Thomas's war elegies are typical of his other work in confronting melancholic withdrawal with forms of affirmation.

A poem which may be read as a companion piece to the elegies, 'Lie still, sleep becalmed', offers the most comprehensive wartime reconfiguration of the central symbol of the wound. It centres on a 'sufferer with the wound / In the throat', who is urged to 'lie still', to not disturb the 'silent sea' on which 'we' are 'trembl[ing] listening / To the sea sound flowing like blood from the loud wound' – a wound whose bandage breaks 'in a storm of singing', releasing the 'voices of the drowned' (*CP*, 113). The poem conflates the various wounds of writing, D. J. Thomas's cancerous throat, and sex with a discernible, though never naturalistically described, wartime scene, namely that of the torpedoed

sailor adrift on wreckage 'under the mile off moon'. The sestet turns in
fear from the siren-like call of the abandoned, wounded one, asking it
to 'sleep becalmed', lest 'we' are forced to obey it 'and ride with you
through the drowned'. The final lines, then, open out into melancholy
– an unappeasable wound that threatens to 'empty the ego until it is
totally impoverished', in Ramazani's words, a form of mourning, by
which loss enters the subject and drains it utterly.[95] One of the tensions
in Thomas's wartime poetry arises from the awareness of how bereftness
and the rejection of the collusions of utterance may threaten language
itself, undermining his instinct to confront melancholic withdrawal with
forms of affirmation. Above all, for Thomas, any affirmation had to
forego what he saw as the abhorrent Christian doctrine of redemption
for suffering in this world in some afterlife.

Burning babies

The question of redemption is particularly pertinent, given the centrality
of children and the concept of childhood to the elegiac mode of *Deaths
and Entrances*. As Jacob Korg notes: 'the spectacle of a child consumed
by fire ... impressed Thomas as the formulation of an ultimate question,
for it involved the greatest imaginable suffering inflicted on the greatest
imaginable innocence'.[96] This is the most important component of
Thomas's moral shock at the war, from which Vernon Watkins would
claim he never recovered, and it is at the heart of, and literally delimits,
a collection which is framed by two poems, 'The conversation of prayers'
and 'Fern Hill', that contrast the adult and the child self. A child's
burning body had been the final eerie image of his story 'The Burning
Baby' (1934). But in the mid-1930s, the dead child became an international symbol for the brutality of fascism and the merciless nature of
the impending world war. One of the defining images of the era was a
Spanish government poster of late 1936, in which the image of a child
killed by a Nationalist bombing raid on Madrid is superimposed against
a sky filled with bombers. The text above the image reads 'Madrid –
The "Military" Practice of the Rebels', while beneath, it reads: 'If You
Tolerate This Your Children Will Be Next'. As Leo Mellor describes it:
'The child's hair is blown back and away from the body and appears
clotted with blood. The eyes are ruptured and the mouth is open. It
still retains its power as an icon of pain, and as a dramatic representation of the horror of war'. The image had its effect on British poetry;
Auden described it, with rather heartless insouciance, as 'a bombed baby

couchant upon a field of aeroplanes' in the *New Statesman* and *Nation* in January 1937, while George Barker's book-length poem *Elegy on Spain* (1939) reproduced it and carried the explanatory subtitle 'Dedication to the photograph of a child killed in an air raid on Barcelona' (sic) when it was republished, without the image, in his *Lament and Triumph* (1940). The poster also prompted 'Proud Motherhood (Madrid, AD 1937)' by Thomas's friend Edgell Rickward. Picasso's 'Guernica', with its central image of a mother holding her dead child, was soon equally well-known. Attacks on defenceless civilian populations in Abyssinia and China were also taking place and registering themselves on the public consciousness. As Mellor notes, the photographs from these conflicts 'return again and again to the dead child as an ultimate horror'.[97]

Thomas, who had helped entertain a group of Basque refugee children at Sketty Hall in 1937 and recently become a father, followed the temper of the times, by re-using the image, but now in an existential and elegiac register. In the poems of *Deaths and Entrances*, however, defenceless childhood innocence and adult Total War are not simply starkly juxtaposed, but overlap at numerous points and in various ways. Children will be born to replace the war-dead, as the title of the collection suggests, but, at the same time, the war had insinuated itself into memories of childhood, as far as Thomas was concerned, robbing them of their ability to offer refuge. The childhood self of 'Poem in October' is described ominously as a 'long dead child', who sings 'burning / In the sun' and whose 'tears [burn] my cheeks' from out of 'the listening / Summertime of the dead' (*CP*, 88). The concept of childhood itself had been irreversibly damaged by the violence that humanity had shown itself capable of inflicting upon children; Thomas's recalling of its utopian pleasures, as in 'Fern Hill', is, paradoxically, prompted by its violation through war. Kathleen Raine, in 'New Year 1943', viewed London as populated by ghostly-seeming people, living partly in the present and partly in their childhoods; like such figures, Thomas records in his wartime writing the urge to recapture a lost childhood, as well as the haunted awareness that this is futile. Thus, his 1946 radio feature 'Return Journey', about a visit to blitzed Swansea in search of a younger self, ends with the park-keeper pronouncing that self to be 'Dead ... Dead ... Dead ... Dead ... Dead ... Dead'.

In the war elegies, the dead child specifically symbolises an outraged humanity and draws on predecessors, including Robert Southwell's 'The Burning Babe' and Blake's 'A Little Boy Lost' ('burned ... in a holy place'). It may also be informed by the pathos of the case cited in

Freud's *Interpretation of Dreams* (the one work by Freud that Thomas admitted to reading), in which a father dreams that his beloved dead son appears to him and 'whisper[s] to him reproachfully: "Father, don't you see I'm burning?"[98] Such materials shaped Thomas's poetic contribution to contemporary discourse about the Blitz, the Tube shelterers and the 'Blitz myth'. Angus Calder, in *The Myth of the Blitz*, notes: 'That civilian "morale" survived exposure to conditions often as frightful as those of battle is what came to guarantee, mythically, that the British people, as a whole, deserved to save Europe and defeat Hitler'.[99] He interprets this myth negatively, yet, as David Ashford has pointed out, counterfactual assaults on the myth's more naïvely communalist aspects seriously misrepresent its significance and wrongly diminish the achievement of collective struggle, in order to elide its political import and outcomes; namely, the rejection of Churchill, Attlee's landslide victory and the founding of the Welfare State (similarly, recent histories have sought to bury its achievements under the label 'Age of Austerity'). Ashford argues that the myth of the Tube shelterers is also 'a folk myth of regeneration driven by an underlying dualism' – a 'richly suggestive', rather than reductive, myth, at the heart of which is 'the figure of the child asleep in the Tube'.[100] If children represented past memories and a present which frequently involved child-like vulnerability and dependence, they also symbolised the future which was being fought for. It is in this context, rather than in the light of, say, Valentine Cunningham's sneer that 'Thomas didn't mind, in fact he rather liked, writing about burning babies', that the elegies need to be read.[101] The image of the burnt or dead child, like the sense of national self-sacrifice, was not sensationalist; on the contrary, its apocalyptic dimension derived from material circumstances, and its use by Thomas was rooted in collective, as well as personal, sorrow and outrage.

Thomas's stylistic shift in the poetic silence that extended from (roughly) August 1941 to April 1944 can be viewed as, in part, a response to the way in which the figures of the child and the mother and child had become central to the emergent myth of the Blitz and the war more generally. As war continued, the figure of the child served as a universal motif, by which modernist artists tapped into the popular sense of collective struggle, bridging the split between high and low, abstract and realist art. One of the greatest musical compositions of the war, for example, Michael Tippett's *A Child of Our Time* (1939–41, first performed 1944) centres on a threatened child (Tippett's libretto – Jungian, paradox-ridden, centred on wholeness and sacrifice with a mother-child relationship at its heart – is an important New Apocalypse text in its own right).[102] As with similar works, the child and the mother-child bond are treated as sacrosanct and constitutive of the human in a war that slaughtered millions of children.

The most enduring and compelling visual images of the war made in Britain are Henry Moore's drawings of the Londoners, largely working-class women and their children, who began to use Tube stations as shelters in defiance of the authorities in late 1940. Drawings such as 'Mother and Child among Underground Sleepers' were widely acclaimed, and Thomas – a friend of Moore's – pinned reproductions of several of them from the photojournal *Lilliput* to the walls of his flat.[103] Everything said so far about the effects of the Blitz as registered in literature – its sublime dissolution of distinctions and its surreal contrasts – applied to the shelterers, whose 'private [family] life was lived in public' and whom well-heeled sightseers would go to visit, gawping at the 'fantastic look' of people eating, washing, dressing, breastfeeding, cleaning their teeth and sleeping on platforms in a place, to use Moore's words, of 'drama and strangeness'.[104] The rapprochement between popular and elite taste is signalled in Kenneth Clark's comment that Moore's 'abstract-looking style of the 1930s' was modified, 'without any loss of completeness' in the pictures; Moore, too, noted that the works 'humanised everything I had been doing ... [they] represented an artistic turning point for me'.[105] Several of the drawings centred on the figure of a mother holding a child ('a kind of apocalyptic, enduring madonna and child') and became the basis of his greatest wartime sculpture, the Northampton *Madonna and Child* of 1943–4, 'unmistakably derived from the shelter drawings of mothers and children' and widely understood as 'a statement of the values for which the war was professedly being fought'.[106] This work was the turning point in Moore's public reputation, just as *Deaths and Entrances* was in Thomas's. Crucially, Moore's style, like Thomas's, 'humanises', without being realist. Moore, indeed, shied away from naturalistic reportage, feeling the scrutiny that it required would violate the shelterers' privacy. A similar blend of monumentalism and tact distinguishes Thomas's elegies.

Yet, if this answers the mimeticist criticism that the elegies are insufficiently 'realistic', the significance of the children in Thomas's poems, as in Moore's drawings, is as contradictory as it is profound.[107] The return to childhood leads to irrational fear, regression and a resurfacing of buried trauma, as much as to saving illusory or escapist worlds and the retrieving of private space. To introduce personal material in a regimented, identity-submerging, centralised society is, in itself, to regress to a simpler, more universal state of being; this paradoxical sense that the personal cry was the best way of accessing the general subconscious, rather than a simple desire for personal expression, lies behind the use of childhood memories in some of Thomas's war poems.

It is a reminder that the concept of the collective unconscious and the wartime understanding of the role of childhood owed something to Carl Jung's influential essay of 1940, 'On the Psychology of the Child-Archetype', which claimed that 'The "child" is all that is abandoned and exposed and at the same time divinely powerful, the insignificant beginning and the triumphal end'.[108] The child can stand both for an individual past and a 'collective pre-conscious past'. In wartime, the child is, above all, 'potential future'. As with biomorphic imagery, artists often used the child as an emblem of regeneration, both political and metaphysical, insofar as it could be made to symbolise renewal, without requiring assent to the doctrine of redemption in an afterlife. The child–mother bond, in turn, also transcended both territory and history, because it was seen as biologically inviolable and exemplary of self-sacrifice. Thomas and Moore accept the risk of sentimentality, which the use of such motifs inevitably courts, treading a fine line in celebrating stoicism and displaying tenderness for the vulnerable and dispossessed. Moore's images, like Thomas's of the 'dark veins of the mother' of London, have a monitory power derived from Egyptian tomb art, Etruscan funeral sculpture and, by the very end of the war, the piled bodies of the Nazi death camps. Certain figures in the Moore drawings, as Stansky and Abrahams note, 'have an extraordinary combination of horror and magnificence' – a collocation which calculates incommensurability, in order to mark the unspeakableness of the event, and echoes Thomas's 'majesty and burning' in 'A Refusal to Mourn'.[109]

Ceremonies of innocence

Like 'Among Those Killed' of 1941, the titles of Thomas's elegies of 1944–45 announce their public status. 'A Refusal to Mourn the Death, by Fire, of a Child in London' (March 1945) adapts the earlier poem's strategy, by rejecting the expected response to an event described in newspaper headline terms, while 'Ceremony After a Fire Raid' (May 1944) signals that it takes the form of a public ritual (and part II of 'Ceremony' also originally bore the headline-style title 'Among Those Burned To Death Was A Child Aged A Few Hours'). In doing so, and at the risk of seeming religiose or of an equally conventional ironic rejectionism, they read an atrocity within the regenerative context of process, in order to resist its appropriation by Church encomium and government slogan ('Your Britain – Fight For It NOW!'). 'Ceremony' is a defiant outfacing of death, which invokes what Mikhail Bakhtin called the 'generative principle', while 'A Refusal' is a more ambiguous 'rob[ing]' of the child 'with the long friends' in Henry Moore-like monumental abstraction (*CP*, 86). Each poem performs its linguistic recuperation differently – the first in the oxymoronic, provocative language of the Blitz sublime; the second in a more chastened mode threatened by silence; and both are disturbed by the linkage of the sublime with such deaths, to the extent that 'A Refusal' may be read as a palinode or apology for the sublime aspect of 'Ceremony'.

'Ceremony' has a ritual-like tripartite structure. Part I sets the terms of that ceremony's ritualistic energies and ethical concerns or, as Leo Mellor puts it, offers 'notes for its performance', by setting the scene of a bombed street and the dead child in a jagged stanza form, reduced, at points, to single word lines, which enacts the blasted cityscape and the convulsive nature of grief, yet nevertheless suggests a ritual antiphon of chant and response:[110]

Myselves
The grievers
Grieve
Among the street burned to tireless death
A child of a few hours
With its kneading mouth
Charred on the black breast of the grave
The mother dug, and its arms full of fires. (*CP*, 107)

'Myselves' (the word is repeated in stanzas two and three) and 'among' are at the wrong grammatical angle, verbal equivalents of the twisted planes of a face in, say, Picasso's 'The Weeping Woman', conveying radical shock, but also dissolving a first person singular into plural, communal grieving. This stanza, like the three which follow it, works 'from words', riskily, given its subject; from 'grievers' to 'grieve', then decomposing their vocables into 'grave' and 'kneading', proliferating internal, as well as end, rhyme and punning agonisingly (on 'kneading' and 'dug') to intensify the awful actuality of the child's death. Syntactical violation announces violation of the natural order, as the nurturing mother becomes the 'black breast' of death. Stanza two laments the loss of the child's future progeny (the 'centuries of the child') calling for the singing of 'Darkness kindled back into beginning', since 'miracles cannot atone'. Then, breaking the traditional bounds of elegy, the child is asked both to 'forgive' the 'we' – adult witnesses – and then, as 'forgive' becomes 'give for', to 'give' her death as the basis for a pantheistic, process-based faith, which 'myselves the believers / May hold ... in a great flood'. Finally, in the fourth and final stanza, the 'we' 'Crying / Your dying / Cry':

> ... chant the flying sea
> In the body bereft.
> Love is the last light spoken. Oh
> Seed of sons in the loin of the black husk left. (*CP*, 107)

'Chant' has something of the power of 'enchant'; a 'flying sea' or 'great flood', somehow latent in the child's 'body bereft', is being invoked.

Part II has to escape the negativity of the 'black husk', and it does so by considering available forms of ritual. It seems uncertain ('I know not whether / Adam or Eve, the adorned holy bullock / Or the white ewe lamb / Or the chosen virgin ... Was the first to die') in the face of the enormity of 'the cinder of the little skull' of the dead child. But the hesitancy is really beside the point, I think. The main point is that all these symbols of religion *did* 'die'. The reiteration of properties generates a religious aura, but, as in 'And death shall have no dominion', attentive readers will notice that the spirit and letter of the text pull in different directions. Religions are 'lying' (in both senses), and the stanza continues in the 'lull' of the child's death and what it tells us about their sacrificial impulse (*CP*, 108). But without these, we might ask, how is the child to 'give' the 'great flood' of her lost offspring – her regenerative potential?

'I know', opening stanza two, seems to contradict the first stanza by answering its hesitancy – 'I know the legend / Of Adam and Eve is never ... silent in my service'. Yet the *literal* sense is merely that the speaker 'knows' that the discourse of Christianity will inevitably inform any counter-ritual or 'service' that he can perform. Again, the rhetoric is self-undermining; what is recognised is that one can only conceptualise an alternative to religion using the language it has bequeathed. However, this is not merely rhetorical juggling; Thomas continued to view Christ as a negation of punitive Old Testament doctrine and as a valid symbol of human potential. Hence, the rest of the stanza develops the hints given in part I that the dead child is a type of Christ; both are 'the one / Child who was priest and servants ... the serpent's / Night fall and the fruit like a sun' (*CP*, 108). Christ / the dead child is understood to have erased all post-lapsarian 'legend' and led us back to a 'Beginning crumbled back to darkness', reversing the terms in the line quoted above in stanza two of part I. Having arrived at a ground zero of biological origin, 'darkness' does not burn down to beginnings; rather, 'beginning' now emerges from the primordial darkness. On this realisation, a regenerative, alternative ritual can be rebuilt.

As a result, in part III, fire returns, but with a fiercely refining action, ahead of the 'flying sea' of part I, which will douse it and complete the apocalyptic preparation necessary for a new beginning – spiritual, sexual and social – which has more than a hint of Attlee's New Jerusalem about it:

Into the organpipes and steeples
Of the luminous cathedrals,
Into the weathercocks' molten mouths
Rippling in twelve-winded circles,
Into the dead clock burning the hour
Over the urn of sabbaths
Over the whirling ditch of daybreak
Over the sun's hovel and the slum of fire
And the golden pavements laid in requiems,
Into the cauldrons of the statuary,
Into the bread in a wheatfield of flames,
Into the wine burning like brandy,
The masses of the sea
The masses of the sea under
The masses of the infant-bearing sea
Erupt, fountain, and enter to utter for ever
Glory glory glory
The sundering ultimate kingdom of genesis' thunder. (*CP*, 108–9)

As Thomas told Watkins: '[the poem] really is a Ceremony, and the third part ... is the music at the end', and this astonishing stanza is a single unravelling sentence with now-you-see-it-now-you-don't punctuation, long-delayed main verbs and choric and Hallelujah chorus-like power (*CL*, 580). It begins with 'Into', but the nature of that which is going 'into' the 'organpipes', 'steeples', 'cathedrals', 'weathercocks', 'clock' and 'over' the 'urn', 'daybreak', 'sun', 'pavements', 'statuary', 'bread' and 'wine' – namely, 'The masses of the sea' – is not known until line thirteen. The Blitz fires are shown consuming the fabric of institutional Christianity – imagined as the city's Wren churches, whose devastation was lamented by Eliot and instantly memorialised in print – and the inner-city 'slum' and 'hovel', which Beveridge, and the propaganda films scripted by Thomas, were proclaiming would soon be swept away.[111] (Indeed, 'Golden pavements' alludes to Golden Square in Soho, where

Strand Films had its offices.) But this fire and flood are ritualistic and visionary, fusing baptism, mass, burial ('requiems') and the body incarnated in its apocalyptic Mass; the 'great flood', invoked in part, is sexual and spiritual, as well as socialistic.

At one level, then, the 'masses of the sea' are the radicalised populace surging up as they would in the election of 1945, for 'Ceremony' reinscribes the New Country's abstract lexicon of social change in its processual apocalyptic terms, invoking the 'refining fire' of Eliot's *Little Gidding*, but stripped of its Anglican conservatism. Crucially, however, the social dimension is subsumed within a vision of death and life as inseparable within the continuity of existence. Birth, therefore, unstoppably 'fountains' out of death and proclaiming this is a fit response to the child's unnatural death. Burning London is quenched by the 'erupting' sea, and what it 'enter[s] to utter' is propelled by liturgical repetition through its main verbs to shower spectacularly in the last two lines. The liquefying release of a pantheistic process follows a series of directional switches (three 'intos', three 'overs' and three more 'intos'), which concludes in the 'thunder' of a new, non-biblical creation (a lower case 'genesis') – a regeneration through the birth of all the generations that were denied their future by the death of this specific child.

In these lines, the simultaneous occurrence of conception, as well as birth, baptism and death by drowning produces a sacred, yet sexual, climax. The sea is an amniotic *tsunami*, dousing the Blitz fires that killed the child, just as the new births will counter its death. The reiterated 'glory' comes from 'The Lord's Prayer' ('For ever and ever, the power and the glory'), as Thomas signals in his use of 'utter for *ever*', and the deluge 'glories' the 'sundering ultimate kingdom' of separation of child from mother – the expulsion from the womb, which is a happy fall, recapitulating the expulsion from Eden. But the sacred is unashamedly sexual, for 'glory' is also a Thomas word for orgasm (as in 'Glory cracked like a flea' in 'A saint about to fall'). 'Utter' is thus an ejaculation in both senses; death is translated by the 'little death' into the mass birth of the poem's ending. Rather than offering a traditional form of consolation ('miracles cannot atone'), Thomas calls for copulation to thrive. Inverting the fierily purgative narrative, the child's vanished 'centuries' are the 'sea', which is summoned to punish the sinful city in a paradoxical renewal through drenching sex and birth. The poem has moved from a brief moment of insight into human community and continuity, granted by the child's death, to the 'sundering' discontinuity of new lives, which will make good that death. Overcoming it involves an exultant public witness

to essentially private acts, as Thomas offers himself as the prophet of
the baby-boomer generation – if in a somewhat ambiguous mode, since
after the continuity created by orgasm and conception, a birth, however
joyful, is a reminder of the 'sundering' of our discontinuous existences.

Refusing to mourn

'A Refusal to Mourn the Death, by Fire, of a Child in London', written
nearly a year after 'Ceremony After a Fire Raid' in March 1945, is more
concerned with the generic problem of elegy – how to speak of the dead,
without appropriating their suffering and avoiding self-aggrandisement –
and may be read as a palinode for the exuberant outfacing of death in
'Ceremony', with its anti-headline of a title offering a dignified refusal
of the public discourses that would use civilian deaths for propaganda
purposes. But the terms of the refusal are shaped by other texts, more
than by Thomas's own poetry. The most important is Wilfred Owen's
'Dulce et Decorum Est'.[112] In a broadcast on Owen that he made in
1946, Thomas would cast him as the embodiment of the self-sacrificial
'position-in-calamity', taken by the true poet caught up in modern
war – that is, as an Apocalyptic poet.[113] Owen's poem was directed at,
and was to have borne an ironic dedication to, a civilian poet (Jessie
Pope), whose complacently patriotic verses had angered him. It is this
circumstance of the earlier poem, which cued Thomas's rejection of the
propaganda capital that might be made out of the victims of the V1 and
V2 attacks. Of course, in the Second World War, propaganda tended to
be relatively low-key, knowing full well the distrust in which jingoism
and hate-mongering against the enemy was held, because of its use
during the First World War. As a result, 'A Refusal' does not denounce
'the old lie', as such. It begins by creating an unstable zone of negative
meaning, which seems to defer any kind of mourning at all:

> Never until the mankind making
> Bird beast and flower
> Fathering and all humbling darkness
> Tells with silence the last light breaking
> And the still hour
> Is come of the sea tumbling in harness
>
> And I must enter again the round
> Zion of the water bead
> And the synagogue of the ear of corn
> Shall I let pray the shadow of a sound

Or sow my salt seed
In the least valley of sackcloth to mourn

The majesty and burning of the child's death. (*CP*, 85)

The poem's opening word, 'Never', indirectly conjures up Winston Churchill's two most famous wartime speeches: that of 5 June 1940, with its reiterated 'never' ('We shall fight them on the beaches ... we shall never give in ... we shall never surrender ...'), and that which celebrated victory in the Battle of Britain later that summer in the lapidary phrase: 'Never, in the field of human conflict, has so much been owed, by so many, to so few'. It introduces an even more elaborately unspooling period, however – one which replaces Churchill's human history defined by 'conflict' in a vaster cosmic context. This does not simply critique political discourse or 'propaganda'. The parallel between the politician and propaganda-writing poet makes it simultaneously ironic and indicative of an uncanny doubling, and Churchill's rhetoric is given an erotic–anarchistic makeover at various points in *Deaths and Entrances*.[114] Beyond this, 'Never until' is, of course, a solecism: 'never' means 'not ever', and there can be no 'until' about it (one may say 'never' or 'not until', but not 'never until'). The double negative sets up the possibility of an affirmation, but refuses, at this point, to make it. Instead, the reader is led through a set of minimally punctuated clauses and unhyphenated compounds, as the speaker tries to define the conditions under which mourning may take place. Those conditions are extreme – that is, they involve the death of the speaker (his 'entering again' the continuum of the 'all humbling darkness') or the death of creation (the failure of the organic continuum itself) or, more likely, both at some unspecified future point. Indeed, they are impossible conditions: whether they mean individual death or the death of the world (through war or cosmic disaster), the mourning will not be fulfilled in any meaningful, public sense. This seems excessive at first, given the desire simply to 'not murder' with 'a grave truth' or 'Elegy' 'the mankind of [the girl's] going'. The speaker then states the grounds of his refusal: a wish not to 'blaspheme down the stations of the breath' – that is, to tritely memorialise the agonies of life and death. 'Stations of the breath' plays on Stations of the Cross and alludes to the Tube stations used as shelters, as I mentioned in the Introduction. But, like 'erected voice' in 'When I woke', it is also a synonym for the radio (we speak of radio 'stations', and the radio carries sound waves made by 'breath') and so takes issue with government-controlled media. 'Zion', 'synagogue' and 'sackcloth' in stanza two reinforce a Judaeo-Christian frame of reference; as in 'Ceremony', however, Thomas uses this, before rejecting it and turning to his own:

> Deep with the first dead lies London's daughter,
> Robed in the long friends,
> The grains beyond age, the dark veins of her mother,
> Secret by the unmourning water
> Of the riding Thames.
> After the first death, there is no other. (*CP*, 86)

The final stanza pantheistically asserts the girl's incorporation within the mother earth of London (she is 'London's daughter'), renewed as part of the natural cycle. In doing so, it reflects a final stage in the shift in Thomas's attitudes away from the grotesque and ironic sense of unity with the earth, derived from such First World War poems as Owen's 'À Terre', to one in which the earth is seen as maternal, embodying procreative and nurturing forces (in this he was reflecting a general shift in British art, noted by Stuart Sillars, over the twenty years after 1918).[115] The refusal to mourn ('unmourning') is still present, but nature's indifference is 'riding', sexually active and thus regenerative (as in 'Fern Hill', this post-Freudian aspect is one of the things which ensure that the child is not merely 'a twentieth century equivalent of the object of the Lucy poems').[116] The final line appears to confirm the pantheistic rejection of religious orthodoxy; spared a second death in the form of official 'elegy', which would 'blaspheme' against the awfulness of her actual death, the girl will not have to face judgement and the 'second death' of Revelation either. This, in itself, is a consolation, and so the poem seems to be having its cake and eating it, too – refusing to mourn, yet managing to lament and memorialise.

This is one reason why, at certain points, 'A Refusal' alludes to the historical contexts of the death, as I argued in the Introduction. As well as sympathizing with the Holocaust victims and Tube shelterers, a specifically male militarism is being indicted (the contrast between '*man*kind of her going' and 'man*kind* making' heightens this).[117] More, the refusal to individuate the death in a realist way is a refusal to kill the girl a second time with 'a grave truth' (in this, it follows the point made more bluntly in 'This side of the truth' that the 'unminding skies' know nothing 'Of innocence and guilt'). Interpretation must begin with this ethical 'refusal' to betray the girl's death in this way, even as it acknowledges that the concluding lines seem to offer consolation. But the real tact of 'A Refusal' lies in its creation of an undecidable verbal space, which allows for mourning, without moralising. Its two opening words tell us that something will not happen *and* that it will, and its last line is equally enigmatic; 'first death' logically predicates another one, but we are told that there is 'no other' (Thomas chose not to write, say, 'After the only [or 'one'] death, there is no other' and thus eliminate ambiguity). Between these, the narrative time frame is unorthodox, switching from Doomsday to the present of the child's death to the historical progression of London and the Thames, conferring a mythic aura on each of these scenarios. The leap between them thwarts the construction of a coherent or framing narrative, chronology or context, despite the authoritativeness of tone. This prevents us from grounding the poem's meaning, which has to hover in a paradoxical zone between 'never' and 'until' and 'first death' and 'no other' – that is, in a place where the limits of language have been made manifest. This is the gap between the rhetoric of the stated 'refusal to mourn' and the consolation that seems somehow to be offered. But this does not gesture to some pure space beyond elegy; it shows, rather, that, if driven to extremes, language will not let us do anything other than oscillate between these (im)possibilities. In the terminology of deconstruction, it might be said, what Thomas does is identify 'the language trap', seem to fall into it, and then undermine that too, disturbing even the pantheistic consolation that the poem ostensibly offers.[118]

The famous last line is therefore more problematic than it seems in several ways. The 'first death' refers to the death which is birth in 'Death's Duell'; it is a 'first death', because, for Donne and orthodox Christian believers, actual death is birth into life everlasting. However it is also a reference to the trope of the 'second death' of the apocalyptic biblical Book of Revelation, which promises the Final Judgement and a 'fiery lake' of eternal torment for sinners after the death of the body.[119] In this sense the line is a rejection of orthodox Christian doctrine, a denial of the doctrine that dead sinners face eternal punishment – a doctrine which Thomas, like the Empson of *Milton's God* (1955), felt to be abhorrent, because it predicated a god who was a 'torture monster'. In refusing to murder the child by conventionally elegising her, the line offers consolation, of course, in a pantheistic creed, but although 'all deaths are the same in that they represent a return to nature', as David Kennedy puts it, and this is more tenderly expressed here, than in 'And death shall have no dominion', it is not simple or sentimental; the poet is deferring mourning, until his own experience is adequate to the child's own (in other words, until the point of his death or Doomsday).[120] It

partly undoes the anti-elegiac gesture, the double negative producing a
positive, but not in a hypocritical way; the refusal to mourn is simply
shown to be a kind of purism, which eventually has a limit ('never until').
Yet even this does not exhaust the rich ambiguities of this enigmatic
line, which, as Keery notes, it is not only intertextual with the Bible
and Thomas himself, but with numerous other poets, from Hardy to
Hendry.[121] There are bleaker possibilities, too. If a strong emphasis is
placed on the denial that the child will be killed in the poem, that
is *textually*, then the line can be taken to mean that that there is *only*
death. This point is made by Steve Vine, when he notes that the line –
broken by the punctilious comma at the caesura, as if to draw attention
to this possibility – may also mean 'not "there is no other death"', but
"there is no other *but* death"', that 'death is admitted absolutely rather
than denied utterly'.[122] In this reading, even as it allows for mourning,
the line revolts against the attempt at mourning's symbolic compensation, opening up the radical and unassuagable wound of melancholia.
The Thames, in this case, is 'unmourning', because this loss cannot be
mourned, its 'water', an endless flow of tears ('Thames', suggestively, is a
near-anagram of 'Thomas'). Having generated an implicit elegy, moving
against the grain of the elaborate 'refusal', Thomas suddenly destroys it.
But however it is read, grief for the death of the child and the children
we all are in the face of death is expressed in a fitting, moving and
memorable fashion.

From elegy to pastoral

The war provoked Thomas to elegise, not just its child victims, but also
childhood itself – innocence, as well as innocents. However, his two
elegies are paralleled by poems about living children, such as 'This side
of the truth' (dedicated to Llewelyn) and the boy of 'The conversation
of prayers', or about childhood memories, such as 'The hunchback in the
park', 'Poem in October' and 'Fern Hill'. They accord with the complex
wartime figuration of the child and childhood in British art, which
was drawn both by the urge to escape into childhood (as pre-adult and
Edenic, but problematised by a Freudian awareness of infant sexuality)
and by a projection of utopian political expectation onto childhood (but
haunted by a fear that the concept of childhood had been destroyed).
Such poems are as much 'about' the war as the elegies themselves, and
those which use Thomas's own childhood are not realist representations
of the past, so much as reflections of the moral shock of the war. This

moral, structural and relational aspect is hinted at in Thomas's insistence in a letter to his publishers that space be found for 'Fern Hill' in *Deaths and Entrances* after they had received the final manuscript: 'I am enclosing a further poem, "Fern Hill", not so far included in the book, which I very much *want* included as it is an *essential* part of the feeling and meaning of the book as a whole' (*CL*, 633).

'Poem in October', written the year before 'Fern Hill', is – like 'Especially when the October wind', 'Twenty-four years' and 'Poem on his Birthday' – one of the birthday poems which mark Thomas's different stylistic phases. Recounting a morning walk through a Welsh seaside town on the day of his 'thirtieth year to heaven', like 'Fern Hill' it also recalls childhood, but radically distances and buries it. The tactile, quasi-naïve immediacy of detail ('the sea wet church the size of a snail / With its horns through mist and the castle / Brown as owls') and the lyrical, quasi-confessional tone, encourage us to read the poem as a circular, Romantic paean to the healing powers of memory. Yet the first stanza's strange form of (main) verb, 'beckon', 'sets forth' a recently woken, still-fuddled consciousness, hinting at disturbances to come, such as the strangely existential boundary of 'the road / Over the border' that the speaker takes when exiting the town through 'gates [that] closed as the town awoke', more a Miltonic expulsion than a country stroll. This is followed by the meteorological freak of stanza three, in which the speaker stands on the hill in sunshine, while the town below him is in cloud, leading him to fancy that 'all the gardens / Of spring and summer were blooming in the tall tales / Beyond the border and under the larkful cloud'. (*CP*, 87) But although 'There could I marvel my birthday away', the weather 'turn[s] around' again, replacing this vision with one of childhood:

> It turned away from the blithe country
> And down the other air and the blue altered sky
>   Streamed again a wonder of summer
>   With apples
>   Pears and red currants
> And I saw in the turning so clearly a child's
> Forgotten mornings when he walked with his mother
>   Through the parables
>   Of sun light
>   And the legends of the green chapels
>
> And the twice told fields of infancy
> That his tears burned my cheeks and his heart moved in mine.

These were the woods the river and sea
    Where a boy
   In the listening
Summertime of the dead whispered the truth of his joy
To the trees and the stones and the fish in the tide. (*CP*, 87–8)

We are not being offered a simple binary 'now' and 'then', adulthood
and childhood memory. Rather, the speaker glimpses 'all the [Edenic
or Hesperidean] gardens' before the 'turn' replaces this 'blithe country'
with the vision of childhood. There are two 'turns', and three states, or
landscapes: the present, on the hill, a 'blithe country' of lost faith or
utopian belief, and the childhood vision. The weather turns '*down* the
other air' into the childhood 'mornings', suggesting a fall. And although
'forgotten mornings' can mean that the forgetting was done by the
child or the adult, the implication of either is that the adult memory
is actually a *recreation*, rather than a remembering as such. 'So clearly'
refers not to a memory, but to the vividness of the adult's imagining of
what he was. Although ecstatic-seeming, then, the 'wonder of summer'
is something to 'wonder' about. This vision is pantheistically written
into the natural, reconstituted in 'the legends of the green chapels', but
its landscapes are 'twice told'. Thomas isn't denying that we remember
childhood; what he is saying is that we more often create, or are told, or
imagine that we remember things. This differs from a Romantic sense of
the nurturing, healing power of childhood memory and the sense of a
continuous selfhood which it sustains – the child as father to the man.
Indeed, the poem inhabits, in order to undermine, the tropes of the
Romantic childhood pastoral. The contrasting weather does not trigger
memories, but reminds the speaker of the hiatus between himself and
the past, which he then tries to fill.

What is being identified here is the nostalgia that we have for our
childhood. There is no unmediated access to childhood, but rather
a contrast between it and 'tall tales'. The 'parables' and 'legends' are
undone, but lamented. It is not simply that the usual Romantic nostrums
are upset or that the link between past and present is shown to be neither
causal nor simple; rather, the 'tall tales' of the 'blithe country' refer to
the idealising impulse itself – they are 'Beyond the border' between
childhood and adulthood, which the speaker senses is unbridgeable,
even as he feels impelled to try to cross it. As he does so, his perception
of the present is upset by the knowingly idealising 'turn' – a word used
in its different forms four times. Figurative, as well as weather-related,
the repeated 'turn' turns out to be a series of re-'turns', which enact the

activity of remembering as a folding over of recreations of the child's 'mornings' within the idealising impulse. That impulse is placed under suspicion, even as it is indulged; there is no direct bridge from the brief October sunshine to the 'tall tales' or the glowingly faked-up memory, whose belated recreation the poem records.

As I argued earlier, 'the long dead child' that 'sang burning / In the sun' suggests that its 'joy' went up in the Blitz fires. War has killed off the idea of childhood and an organic continuity between it and the adult; it is now recalled only as 'the listening / Summertime of the dead', the past childhood as yet another uncanny wartime 'shade'. Memory is destructive, as well as recuperative: it is not an achieved outcome of the 'turning' of internal 'weather', but is 'in' – that is, happening *within* or during – the actual process of turning.[123] Rather than an idealisation of childhood, then, the poem explores how childhood is idealised as a form of fantasy – a process common in the war years, when it became a form of indirect mourning for the self and others, both a consolation for, and an evasion of, loss. When the speaker prays in the poem's final lines we should hear echoes of Calvary in the hill and town 'leaved with … blood'. Ambiguous as the changeable weather, the speaker projects a future, while seemingly hypnotised by a vision of the past, and while 'O may' might be calm prayer, it could equally be a desperate plea.

The same kind of painful ambiguity is realised in Thomas's best-loved poem, 'Fern Hill', by even more lyrically persuasive means. This plunges more immediately and deeply into the imagined paradise of childhood than 'Poem in October':

> Now as I was young and easy under the apple boughs
> About the lilting house and happy as the grass was green,
>> The night above the dingle starry,
>>> Time let me hail and climb
>> Golden in the heydays of his eyes … (*CP*, 134)

Here, adult becomes child, and, as in 'A refusal to mourn', this is conveyed in a solecism – the temporal incompatibility of 'Now' and 'was'. We initially read 'now' as a colloquial introduction, but it is soon clear that it is an uncanny fusing of present and past tenses. While the poem is technically in the past tense, a plethora of connectives ('And … and … and') give rise to a run of continuous present participles ('lilting … singing … shining') and a levelling of event, while the use of the non-specific pronoun 'it' blurs the self with its actions ('All the sun long it was running, it was lovely, the hay / Fields high as the house, the tunes from the chimneys, it was air / And playing'). All of these devices contribute to the utopian stasis of the child's experience of time. Stewart Crehan, disputing the charge that the poem ignores its historical moment of 1945 and is 'as political as a mountain goat', rightly underscores the poem's creation of a timeless 'anarchic paradise of play', a 'libidinous, joyous ... amoral and decidedly unsentimental Eden' and its memorable re-enactment of 'an unrepressed, unashamedly self-centred freedom'.[124] For this reason, as he notes, it is 'not essentially a nostalgic poem', but one which allows for the realisation of the id (in which there is nothing that corresponds to the idea of time).

From being a collaborator in creating this world, Time slowly asserts itself and the 'Now' / 'was' union starts to unravel with the penultimate stanza's admission of the unknowingness of the earlier self: 'nothing I cared, at my sky blue trades, that time allows ... / so few and such morning songs / Before the children green and golden / Follow him out of grace // Nothing I cared ...' (*CP*, 135). This stanza is grammatically incomplete; its final comma leads, as if the unravelling of stasis can no longer be held up, to a repetition of 'Nothing I cared' at the opening of the final stanza, which lends to 'nothing' the force of a capitalised noun – an absent presence. The speaker recalls waking 'to the farm forever fled from the childless land' (in a typical confusion of subject and object, both farm *and* the speaker have 'fled'; each grows strange to the other.) The final lines recapitulate the poem in concentrated form; 'green' (as colour) finally leads to the comparison of the child (and poet) with the sea, the lines of the poem imaged as the 'chains' of gravity, which impel the stanza-like, to-and-fro tidal movements of the waves:

> Oh as I was young and easy in the mercy of his means,
>   Time held me green and dying
>   Though I sang in my chains like the sea. (*CP*, 135)

'Held' is brilliantly double; although it means 'arrested', in the context of chains, it means 'cradled', too, both 'green and dying' at the same time, returning us to the rocking movement of the poem's opening lines, in which, as Crehan notes, 'Thomas makes the signifiers themselves mouth what the lips of infancy need and do ... The pleasures of the breast are re-enacted; and in the real word, a boy on a swing may subconsciously recall the pleasure of being rocked ... both actions happen together in mutual identification'.[125] The lines also introduce a sense of childhood sexuality and its blurring with adult desire. The poem's title, 'Fern Hill', revises the actual name of the farm ('Fernhill'), thus emphasising the allusion to the *mons veneris* – the poem as an infantile yearning for breast or womb. Likewise, the nursery rhyme 'horn' that the boy blows (like 'Little Boy Blue') is also the phallus. Here, as elsewhere in *Deaths and Entrances*, Thomas brings together social and psychological movements and gives shape to the complexity of wartime questionings concerning regression and utopian advance; apolitical, he certainly is not. To what extent is solitude possible or permissible during war? And how does one distinguish between a necessary and an imposed silence? What is the relationship between the artist and the mass media? Did the wartime state infantilise the population, as was so often claimed? And would this be increased by a Welfare State? These are all questions relevant to our own time, as that most enduring legacy of the war is finally privatised.

For Thomas, singing in one's chains only ambiguously defied the silencing with which war threatened poetry, as I discussed at the start of this chapter, temporarily reversing the etymological meaning of infant, from *infans*, Latin for 'without speech', but not wholly stilling fears which would re-emerge after the war in the form of the 'cyclone of silence' threatened by nuclear weapons. As already noted, his friend Vernon Watkins claimed that: 'the war ... was a nightmare from which [Dylan] never completely recovered' (*LVW*, 19). Even so, it saw history and biology swap the roles that they had in his 1930s poetry; history became determinism, while the biological–unconscious drives became a reservoir, albeit precarious, of healing and renewal. In this sense elegy, for children and childhood, led Thomas back to its origins in the pastoral – the subject of my final chapter.

Notes

1 Thomas Pynchon, *Gravity's Rainbow* (London: Jonathan Cape, 1973), p. 3.
2 Although Thomas lived in Laugharne from 1949 until his death, he first lived there with Caitlin Thomas for six months in 1938, then for another ten months in 1939, with intermittent visits in 1940 and 1941.
3 See Constantine Fitzgibbon, *The Life of Dylan Thomas* (London: Plantin Publishers, 1987), p. 292. The machine-gun attack was by William Killick, husband of Vera Killick (née Phillips) – a friend of the Thomases. William Killick had returned from dangerous guerrilla combat in Nazi-occupied Greece in early 1945 and was aggrieved to find that his wife had been pooling her financial resources with the more meagre ones of the Thomases. On a drinking spree in New Quay on 6 March, William Killick was offended at being ignored by Thomas and is alleged to have directed anti-Semitic abuse at Fanya Fisher – a Russian-Jewish member of a group of friends from the London film world, then visiting Thomas. Killick is said to have hit Fisher in the face and to have been restrained by Thomas. Later that evening, Killick went to the Thomases's bungalow, 'Majoda', where there were four other adults apart from Thomas and two sleeping children. William Killick

fired into it using an illegally held sten-gun and threatened the occupants with a hand-grenade. Miraculously, no-one was injured or killed. This event was the basis for John Maybury's film *The Edge of Love* (2008), which starred Sienna Miller, Kiera Knightley and Matthew Rhys. The script, written by Killick's granddaughter, omits the attacks on Fisher and wrongly has Thomas perjure himself at the subsequent trial, in order to get Killick imprisoned (in fact, both Thomas and Fisher gave testimony which mitigated Killick's culpability). See David N. Thomas, *Dylan Thomas: A Farm, Two Mansions and a Bungalow* (Bridgend: Seren, 2000), pp. 115–41.

4 The bookseller Bertram Rota approached Thomas and acquired them on behalf of the Lockwood Memorial Library of Buffalo University in 1941. He paid $140.00 for them (£25.00 of which went to Thomas). See Dylan Thomas, *The Notebook Poems: 1930–1934*, ed. Ralph Maud (London: Dent, 1990), pp. xi-x. Also Paul Ferris, *Dylan Thomas* (London: Penguin, 1978), p. 185.

5 Cyril Connolly in *Horizon* (February 1940) cited in Robin Skelton, ed., *Poetry of the Forties* (Harmondsworth: Penguin, 1968), p. 18. Or, as Thomas had observed on the outbreak of war: 'Auden is in America isn't he? And the very best place, too, for a militant communist at this time' (*CL*, 410).

6 Like Thomas, New Apocalypse's influences included Yeats, surrealism, Jung, Picasso, Kafka, Herbert Read, Eliot and Lawrence (whose *Apocalypse* (1931) gave them their name). Among others, the New Apocalypse poets included Nicholas Moore, Dorian Cooke, Norman MacCaig and G. S. Fraser; others, such as W. S. Graham and Alex Comfort, would identify with the grouping in the early 1940s.

7 Alex Comfort, 'Art and Social Responsibility', *New Road* (1944), cited in A. T. Tolley, *The Poetry of the Forties* (Manchester: Manchester University Press, 1985), p. 43.

8 J. F. Hendry, 'Writers and Apocalypse', *The New Apocalypse* (London: Fortune Press, 1939 / 1940), p. 15. *The New Apocalypse* included Thomas's short story 'The Burning Baby' and his poem 'How shall my animal'.

9 Cited in Robin Skelton, ed., *Poetry of the Forties*, p. 23.

10 As Keery notes, the 'apparent isolation and real neglect' is to be found in a 'critical Act of Oblivion' passed after the rise of the Movement: 'By its provisions, the poetry of the 1940s was effectively expunged from the canon and serious appraisal of the period became an offence'. James Keery, 'James Burns Singer and the Act of Oblivion', *Angel Exhaust*, 11 (Winter 1994), pp. 101–2.

11 The manifesto was published by Giles Goodland – the son of John Goodland, one of its authors – in *P. N. Review*, 154 (November-December 2003), pp. 22–5.

12 Robin Skelton, ed., *Poetry of the Forties*, p. 26.

13 *The White Horseman* (1941) and *The Crown and the Sickle* (1944) were the second and third New Apocalypse anthologies. Thomas's symbiotic relationship with the Apocalypse poets resembled the one that he had with surrealism – flippant, bantering, and deniable when challenged, but real nevertheless.

14 Linda M. Shires, *British Poetry of the Second World War* (London: Macmillan, 1985), p. 42. James Keery, 'The Burning Baby and the Bathwater', *PN Review* 154, 3: 2 (November-December 2003), p. 28.

15 As an art critic, anarchist theorist, poet and publisher, Herbert Read was a crucial figure in shaping the New Apocalypse poetic and, as poetry editor at Routledge, in publishing New Apocalypse poets. His intellectual relationship to them has been likened to that of Godwin to the Romantic poets. He had been promoting an

anti-classicist, neo-Romantic case since the publication of *Reason and Romanticism* (1926), while his 'What is Revolutionary Art?' (1935) and *Poetry and Anarchism* (1938) were key texts for almost all 1940s poets. As discussed in Chapter 4, Read argued for the existence of a native proto-surrealism and heaped high praise on Thomas's poetry; his review of *The Map of Love* led to Thomas thanking him for: 'the best [review] I have ever had' (*CL*, 477).

16 'Because the pleasure bird whistles' (as 'January 1939') appeared in the Paris-based journal *Delta* in Easter 1939; 'When I woke' was published in *Seven*, 6 (Autumn 1939) with 'To Others Than You' and 'Paper and Sticks'. The issue also carried the review of *The Map of Love* by Read, as referred to in fn. 15.

17 Gwen Watkins, *Dylan Thomas: Portrait of a Friend* (Talybont: Y Lolfa, 2005), p. 75.

18 *The Beveridge Report* (1942) – a government White Paper, which became a bestseller – was arguably the single most important publication of the war. It was largely because it was felt that Labour would implement Beveridge that it won its historic victory in 1945. See Sir William Beveridge, *Report on Social Insurance and Allied Services* (HMSO, December 1942); cited in *Modern History Sourcebook*, see www.fordham.edu

19 The 'poetry boom' saw published poetry titles rise from 210 in 1940 to 249 in 1942, 329 in 1943, and 328 in 1944. New poetry journals included Tambimuttu's *Poetry* (London), Wrey Gardiner's *Poetry Quarterly* and Cyril Connolly's *Horizon*, all three of which were outlets for Thomas's poetry and that of the Apocalypse poets. See A. T. Tolley, *The Poetry of the Forties*, pp. 1–8.

20 The Apocalyptic mood had a rejuvenating effect on several members of the high modernist generation, such as Eliot, H. D., David Jones and Edith Sitwell, who all arguably produced their best work in the 1940s. Modernism was also renewed for younger poets under wartime conditions, as the work of Lynette Roberts, W. S. Graham and Thomas himself testifies. See John Goodby, 'Dylan Thomas and the Poetry of the 1940s', ed. Michael O'Neill, *The Cambridge History of English Poetry* (Cambridge: Cambridge University Press, 2010), pp. 858–78.

21 Adam Piette, *Imagination at War: British Fiction and Poetry 1939–1945* (London: Macmillan, 1995), p. 2.

22 London was bombed for fifty-seven nights from 7 September 1940 to 1 January 1941, during which time 13,339 people were killed and 17,937 injured. Frequent raids occurred thereafter until 16 May 1941, with heavy bombing resuming in March. In total, there were 1,386 raids on the Port of London. 'The Blitz' is generally understood to refer to this September 1940 to May 1941 period; the 'Little Blitz' refers to the V-weapons attacks of 1944–45.

23 Ivan Philips, '"Death is all Metaphor": Dylan Thomas's Radical Morbidity', eds. John Goodby and Chris Wigginton, *Dylan Thomas: New Casebook*, p. 131.

24 There was a long tradition of counterfactual history books and films imagining a German invasion of Britain, from George Chesney's *The Battle of Dorking* (1870) to efforts contemporary with Thomas's letter, most notably Douglas Brown's and Christopher Serpell's *Loss of Eden* (1940). Humphrey Jennings's 1943 film, *The Silent Village* – about an Ouradour-sur-Marne style massacre of the population of the Welsh village of 'Cwmgiedd' – is also in the spirit of Thomas's 'Just silence'.

25 Leo Mellor, *Reading the Ruins: Modernism, Bombsites and British Culture* (Cambridge: Cambridge University Press, 2011), p. 14.

26 Peter Stansky and William Abrahams, *London's Burning: Life, Death and Art in the Second World War* (London: Constable, 1994), p. 33.

27 Peter Stansky and William Abrahams, *London's Burning*, pp. 104, 129.

28 Richard M. Titmuss, *Problems of Social Policy* (London: Longmans, 1950), p. 335. During the war, approximately 60,000 were killed in the bombing of England alone, half of them in London. 86,000 were seriously injured, 149,000 were slightly injured and two-and-a-half million made homeless (in a population of thirty-nine million). Swansea's 'Three Nights Blitz' of 19–21 February 1941, which devastated forty-one acres of the centre, killed 230, injured 409 and made 7,000 people homeless, is a central feature of Thomas's radio feature 'Return Journey' of 1947.

29 Keith Douglas, 'Desert Flowers', ed. Desmond Graham, *The Complete Poems* (Oxford: Oxford University Press, 1995), p. 102.

30 Peter Stansky and William Abrahams, *London's Burning*, p. 50.

31 V. S. Pritchett, 'A Bit of a Smash', *New Statesman* (24 February 1967), p. 259.

32 Thomas had a genuine and long-standing interest in pacifism. He expressed a desire to join the 'No More War' movement with Bert Trick on 8 August 1934, when he described himself to the Secretary of the Welsh branch of the Movement as 'an active propagandist' alarmed by 'the present militarist trend of national politics' (*CL*, 192). After 1945, he was involved in the Peace Movement, signed the Stockholm Peace Petition and actively supported the Authors World Peace Appeal. See Jack Lindsay, *Meetings with Poets* (London: Frederick Muller, 1968), pp. 35–7.

33 Thomas approached D. S. Savage, Hugh MacDiarmid, Herbert Read, Glyn Jones, Nicholas Moore, Keidrich Rhys, Lawrence Durrell, George Barker, Rayner Heppenstall and Desmond Hawkins. Several of them contributed statements. His sensitivity to the language in which rationalizations of contributing to the war effort were couched is evident in his letter to Heppenstall: 'I am not "making a stand against war" – which I doubt was the expression I used; if I did use it, it was for convenience ... not to be offered as an expression of my own thinking or for you to put into inverted commas and throw back to me; certainly not as a militant priggishness ... (I too can recognize a cliché & must let you know, as you let me know, that I recognise it as one)' (*CL*, 480).

34 Robin Skelton, ed., *Poetry of the Forties*, p. 19.

35 'Origins', *The Guardian*, September 2009, p. 32 ('This Was the Second World War' pamphlet series).

36 Writing to Kenneth Patchen three weeks later, Thomas called Heppenstall's explanation a 'pernicious misreasoning'. He added: 'At a recent London tribunal for conscientious objectors, the presiding Judge refused to register one man as an objector because he refused to fight "only on *moral & ethical* grounds"' (*CL*, 491).

37 John Donne, 'Death's Duell, or, A Consolation to the Soule, against the dying Life, and living Death of the Body', ed. John Hayward, *Complete Poetry and Selected Prose* (London: Nonesuch Press, 1930), pp. 742–3.

38 The second stanza recalls Paul Nash's celebrated painting *The Battle of Britain* (1941), which gives a pilot's-eye view of the 'water thread' Thames winding to the 'globe' of the North Sea, the surface of which is broken ('entered' and 'bath[ed] ... in') by shot-down aircraft. While there is no question of 'influence', this is a good example of the way that artists in different media responded in similar ways to the war and its myths.

39 Elizabeth Bowen, *The Mulberry Tree: Writings of Elizabeth Bowen*, ed. Hermione

Lee (London: Vintage, 1999), p. 33. Cited in Heather Ingman, *A History of the Irish Short Story* (Cambridge: Cambridge University Press, 2009), p. 152.

40 Robin Skelton, ed., *Poetry of the Forties*, p. 20.

41 See Clarke Emery, *The World of Dylan Thomas* (Coral Gables, FL: University of Miami Press, 1962), pp. 180–2; Ralph Maud, *Where Have All the Old Words Got Me?* (Cardiff: University of Wales Press, 2003), pp. 72–6.

42 Adam Piette notes, in the essay 'The Redeemed City' (October 1941), that Williams wrote of 'the law of bearing one another's burdens' in the necessary struggle between the Allies (representing the City) and the Axis (the Infamy) and how '[t]his Tolkien-style combat needed soldier conscripts ready to sacrifice themselves in an act of interchange, an offering of imaginations and bodies as substitutes for the souls of brethren and enemies', adding that this had its poetic outcomes in 'medievalising, Rilkean, Yeatsian, Lawrentian and Jungian symbolism dwelling on the necessary death wish'. Adam Piette, *Imagination at War: British Fiction and Poetry 1939–1945*, p. 12

43 Louis MacNeice, *The Poetry of W. B. Yeats* (London: Faber, 1941), p. xviii. Similarly, in one of his 'London Letters' written for a US journal in July 1941, MacNeice acknowledged that what was 'being forced upon people' was 'the religious sense', for, under nightly bombardment, 'we need all the senses we were born with; and one of those is the religious'. Louis MacNeice, *Selected Prose of Louis MacNeice*, ed. Alan Heuser (Oxford: Clarendon Press, 1990), p. 136.

44 'Unluckily for a death', published as 'Poem (to Caitlin)' in 1939 and then rewritten in 1945, exemplifies the shift in Thomas's work towards establishing a religious tonality. The second version more explicitly praises the 'true love' and her 'prayed flesh' for saving him from deaths at the hands of an ascetic lover and destructive passion; his 'lucky burly body' becomes 'my holy lucky body', the temptress turns into a 'saint', who will fail to seduce him as long as he refuses to bow to the 'blessing' of the beloved and refuses to walk 'in the cool of her 'mortal garden / With immortality at my side like Christ the sky' – a paradoxical truth told by the 'young stars … Hurling into beginning like Christ the child' (*CP*, 91–2). These references are, however, part of a refusal to devalue the life of the flesh in the hope of immortality. 'Christ the child' tells this, because he exposes the pie-in-the-sky of 'Christ the sky's afterlife.

45 John Ackerman, *A Dylan Thomas Companion* (London: Macmillan, 1991), p. 127.

46 David Gascoyne, *Selected Poems* (London: Enitharmon Press, 1994), p. 80.

47 Neil Reeve, 'Surrealism, William Sansom and the London Blitz', eds. Àngela Santa and Marta Giné, *Surrealismo y Literatura en Europa* (Lleida: Edicions de la Universitat de Lleida, 2001), p. 193.

48 Ivan Phillips, '"Death is all metaphor": Dylan Thomas's Radical Morbidity', eds. John Goodby and Chris Wigginton, *Dylan Thomas: New Casebook*, p. 128.

49 Stuart Sillars, *British Romantic Art and the Second World War* (New York, NY: St Martin's Press, 1991), pp. 96–7. David Jones, for example: 'took a childish delight in the red and green flares that soared into the sky at the start of an air-raid: in January 1940 he observed that London had "the feeling of a besieged town and a very real feeling and it's nice that all the advertisement signs and all the commercial electrical displays have vanished". He was living in circumstances not much removed at some moments from the Front Line [of 1914–18]'. Jonathan Miles and Derek Shiel, *David Jones: The Maker Unmade* (Bridgend: Seren Books, 2003), p. 186.

50 Louis MacNeice, *Collected Poems*, ed. E. R. Dodds (London: Faber, 1979), p. 196; David Gascoyne, *Selected Poems*, p. 82.

51 Stuart Sillars, *British Romantic Art and the Second World War*, p. 182.

52 Lyndsey Stonebridge, '"Bombs and Roses": The Writing of Anxiety in Henry Green's *Caught*', eds. R. Mengham and N. H. Reeve, *The Fiction of the 1940s: Stories of Survival* (Palgrave: London, 2001), cited in Neil Reeve, 'Surrealism, William Sansom and the London Blitz', p. 193.

53 Winifred Nowottny, *The Language Poets Use* (London: Athlone Press, 1962 [repr. 1975]), p. 194. The phrases 'locked their eyes / In the jails and studies / of his keyless smiles', 'silence to do ... / In lairs and asylums / of the tremendous shout' and 'glory to hear / In the churches / of his tears' each run according to the formula: '*something human* / In the *buildings* of [*some expression of*] *human feeling*'. As in 'Deaths and Entrances', this refrain-based formula helps the reader overcome the high degree of uncertainty concerning tenses and pronouns: '[i]t would be a reasonable inference ... that "we" and "you" [in the poem] are somehow the same and yet somehow different ... [i]t would seem ... that it is being forced upon our notice that this is a poem about continuous identities with a changing outlook, taken at various points in a continuum running through the poem'.

54 Winifred Nowottny, *The Language Poets Use*, p. 119.

55 Winifred Nowottny, *The Language Poets Use*, p. 213.

56 Charles Hobday, *Edgell Rickword: A Poet at War* (Manchester: Carcanet, 1989), p. 224.

57 Neil Reeve, 'Surrealism, William Sansom and the London Blitz', p. 191. Spender noted: 'The immense resources of all the governments of the world are now being devoted to producing surrealist effects. Surrealism has ceased to be fantasy, its "objects" hurtle round our heads, its operations cause the strangest conjunctions of phenomena in the most unexpected places, its pronouncements fill the newspapers. The youngest and newest school of English poets signified this occasion by calling themselves "Apocalyptics". Instead of being prophets, they were now witnesses in a world which had been overtaken by prophecies'. Those who had prophesied so acutely were, he added, not the New Country poets, but 'Barker, Thomas and Gascoyne'. See 'Some Observations on English Poetry Between Two Wars', eds. Lindsay Drummond, Henry Treece and Stefan Schimanski, *Transformations*, 3 (n.d., c. 1945), p. 176. Cited by James Keery, 'The Burning Baby and the Bathwater', Part 9, '"Muddying Inclusivity"', *PN Review* 156, 30: 4 (March-April 2004), p. 42.

58 Stuart Sillars, *British Romantic Art and the Second World War*, p. 155.

59 Sutherland's wartime paintings were much influenced by visits that he made to Wales, both before the war and as a war artist; the natural, biomorphic forms that his paintings used and fused with inorganic shapes were derived from observations made of seaside objects, such as rocks, driftwood, birds and plants, to which he gave 'totemic significance'. His first encounter with the Blitz landscape occurred during a visit to Swansea: 'Swansea was the first sight I had of the possibilities of destruction as a subject ...'. Peter Stansky and William Abrahams, *London's Burning*, pp. 52–3.

60 See Marina MacKay, *Modernism and World War II* (Cambridge: Cambridge University Press, 2007), pp. 1–21.

61 David Mellor, *A Paradise Lost: The Neo-Romantic Imagination in Britain 1935–55* (London: Barbican Art Gallery, 1987), p. 34.

62 See http://www.creativereview.co.uk/cr-blog/2008/february/the-shell-guides-a-very-british-surrealism Piper's own approach was to accentuate the 'theatricality of nature'. He spent most of the 1940s in Snowdonia, and this was part of a 'wartime mapping out of an "other" Britain', as Mellor notes. For a full discussion, see Clare Morgan, 'Exile and the Kingdom: Margiad Evans and the Mythic Landscape of Wales', *Welsh Writing in English: A Yearbook*, 6 (Winter 2000), pp. 89–118.

63 David Mellor, ed., *Class Culture & Social Change – A New View of the 1930s* (Sussex: Harvester, 1980), pp. 37–8.

64 Clare Morgan, 'Exile and the Kingdom', p. 92.

65 Thus, M. Wynn Thomas claims that: 'During the war, Wales became suddenly and briefly attractive [to] such as Dylan Thomas ... [it was a] time of the temporary glamorizing of Wales and its writers'. . In fact, Thomas had moved to Laugharne from London in 1938, calling London 'an insane city' and vowing not to return 'for years' (*CL*, 392). That is, he moved to Wales *before* the war and was forced *by the war* to leave it in 1940. M. Wynn Thomas, *Corresponding Cultures: The Two Literatures of Wales* (Cardiff: University of Wales Press, 1999), pp. 123–4.

66 Stuart Sillars, *British Romantic Art and the Second World War*, p. 83.

67 Thus, the 'hunchback in the park' drinks from a 'chained cup' and is tethered to his fantasies of 'a woman figure without fault', although 'nobody chained him up'; 'One voice in chains declaims' in 'Into her lying down head'; 'Love and his patients' 'roar on a chain' in 'On a Wedding Anniversary'; 'chains' trail from the centenarian's 'grey-haired heart' in 'Among those Killed'; the child in 'Fern Hill' 'sang in [his] chains like the sea' (*CP*, 93–4, 103, 112). This particular strand of the imagery of imprisonment is, like the others in the collection, ambiguous: the boys follow the hunchback to his 'kennel in the dark', while the child of 'Fern Hill', will turn the repression imposed by a growing sense of Time's bondage into poetry.

68 '[T]he impression is of a move towards a tone of menace, which could be put down to the war but aims itself further and deeper. "My mind's rat gnaws / Down to the singing stone my soul my flower / Clutched in the claw, ground in the jaw of living" (Henry Treece). ... Rather than a passionate incantation compounding mind and body, birth and death, these secondary poets again and again construct a scenario of threat, the horror beneath the surface obliquely indexed through metaphors implicating mind, body, landscape and polis in a declamation of revelatory and frequently incisive anger'. Peter Riley, 'Thomas and Apocalypse', *Poetry Wales*, 44: 3 (Winter 2008–9), p. 14.

69 See 'Apocalypse, or The Whole Man', in *P. N. Review*, 154 (November-December 2003), pp. 22–5.

70 A. T. Tolley, *The Poetry of the Forties*, pp. 176–7.

71 Elizabeth Bowen, *The Heat of the Day* (London: Penguin, 1990), p. 92; Adam Piette, *Imagination at War: British Fiction and Poetry 1939–1945*, p. 4.

72 Andrew Lycett, *Dylan Thomas: A New Life* (London: Weidenfeld & Nicolson, 2003), p. 191; Paul Ferris, *Dylan Thomas* (London: Penguin, 1977 [repr. 1978]), p. 187; Clark Emery, *The World of Dylan Thomas* (Miami, FL: University of Miami Press, 1962), p. 175; Elder Olson, *The Poetry of Dylan Thomas* (Chicago, IL: University of Chicago Press, 1954), p. 26.

73 Steve Vine, '"Shot from the locks": Poetry, Mourning, *Deaths and Entrances*', eds. John Goodby and Chris Wigginton, *Dylan Thomas: New Casebook*, p. 141.

74 Steve Vine, '"Shot from the locks": Poetry, Mourning, *Deaths and Entrances*', eds. John Goodby and Chris Wigginton, *Dylan Thomas: New Casebook*, p. 141.

75 Mikhail Bakhtin, *Rabelais and His World*, transl. Helene Iswolsky (Bloomington, IN: Indiana University Press, 1984), p. 314.

76 Karl Shapiro in Oscar Williams, ed., *The War Poets* (New York, NY: John Day, 1945), p. 27.

77 See Keith Douglas, 'Landscape with Figures 2', ed. Desmond Graham, *The Complete Poems* (Oxford: Oxford University Press, 1995), p. 103.

78 The earliest usage of theatre of war is given in the *OED* as 1920, which is attributed, appropriately, to Winston Churchill; although the metaphoric sense of a battle as a 'show' or spectacle was current in the First World War ('The Show' is the title of one of Owen's last poems).

79 John Donne, *Complete Poetry and Selected Prose*, ed. John Hayward (London: Nonesuch Press, 1930), pp. 742–3.

80 Gwen Watkins remembers that, in May 1940, 'Dylan quoted to Vernon the first two lines of a new poem ['Deaths and Entrances'] ... He said that he was going to call his next book by the same title "because that is all I write about or ever want to write about"'. Gwen Watkins, *Portrait of a Friend*, p. 92.

81 Robert Hewison, *Under Siege: Literary Life in London 1939–45* (London: Methuen, 1988), pp. 136–7.

82 Leo Mellor, *Reading the Ruins: Modernism, Bombsites and British Culture*, p. 82.

83 Adam Piette, *Imagination at War: British Fiction and Poetry 1939–1945*, p. 4.

84 Following Vernon Watkins, A. T. Tolley claims that the war had an immediate impact and that, 'between 1939 and 1941', there was a 'new clarity, a greater naturalness of rhythm and imagery', evidenced in 'There was a saviour' and 'On a wedding anniversary'. A. T. Tolley, *The Poetry of the Forties*, p. 90. This pairs two utterly unlike poems, however. 'On a wedding anniversary' is an unambitious piece in an atypically straightforward style, while 'There was a saviour' is, as we have seen, complex, verbally dense and often rhythmically *un*natural. The impact of the war, as I try to show, occurred in a much patchier, complex and mediated way than Tolley suggests.

85 Strand was the largest documentary filmmaker contracted to the Ministry of Information (MOI); it made seventy-five films for them in 1942 alone. As Desmond Hawkins noted, radio not only began a rapid expansion at the beginning of the war, but eroded the traditional forms of writing as it absorbed resources and labour previously channelled into print literature, initiating: 'the multi-media world that we know today, with its instant coverage, its eyewitness testimony, its documentary verisimilitude'. Desmond Hawkins, *When I Was: A Memoir of the Years Between the Wars* (London: Macmillan, 1989), pp. 212–13.

86 Taylor learned his trade from John Grierson – the leading British Left documentary filmmaker of the 1930s.

87 John Ackerman, *A Dylan Thomas Companion* (London: Macmillan, 1991), p. xv.

88 Andrew Sinclair, *Dylan Thomas: No Man More Magical* (New York, NY: Holt, Rinehart and Winston, 1975), p. 118.

89 Adam Piette, *Imagination at War: British Fiction and Poetry 1939–1945*, p. 160. Thomas broadcast on Orwell's India programme, and his film-script for *Battle for Freedom* (1942) gives the official government line in opposing Indian demands for full self-rule.

90 For example, Thomas made a short satirical film, now lost, with the director Oswald Mitchell, entitled *Is Your Ernie Really Necessary?*, poking fun at the wartime government slogan 'Is your journey really necessary?' It was suppressed, predictably enough, by a horrified Ministry of War transport authority after a first viewing. See Andrew Lycett, *Dylan Thomas: A New Life*, p. 206.

91 William Empson, 'To Understand a Modern Poem: "A Refusal to Mourn the Death, by Fire, of a Child in London"', by Dylan Thomas', *Argufying*, p. 385 (see also *CL*, 465).

92 Peter Sacks, *The English Elegy: Studies in the Genre from Spenser to Yeats* (Princeton, NJ: Yale University Press, 1985), p. 2.

93 Jahan Ramanzani, *Poetry of Mourning: The Modern Elegy from Hardy to Heaney* (Chicago, IL: Chicago University Press, 1994), pp. 1–2.

94 Steve Vine, '"Shot from the locks": Poetry, Mourning, *Deaths and Entrances*', p. 149.

95 Jahan Ramazani, *Poetry of Mourning: The Modern Elegy from Hardy to Heaney*, p. 4.

96 Jacob Korg, *Dylan Thomas* (New York, NY: Hippocrene Books [repr. 1972]), p. 165.

97 Leo Mellor, *Reading the Ruins: Modernism, Bombsites and British Culture*, p. 26.

98 Sigmund Freud, *The Interpretation of Dreams*, Penguin Freud Library Vol. 4, transl. James Strachey and ed. Angela Richards (Harmondsworth: Penguin, 1983), pp. 652–5.

99 Angus Calder, *The Myth of the Blitz* (London: Pimlico, 1991), p. 142.

100 David Ashford, 'Children Asleep in the Underground: The Tube Shelters of Brandt and Moore', *The Cambridge Quarterly*, XXXVI: 4 (Winter 2007), p. 297.

101 Valentine Cunningham, *British Writers of the Thirties* (Oxford: Oxford University Press, 1988), p. 65, cited by James Keery, 'The Burning Baby and the Bathwater', *P. N. Review* 156, 30: 4 (March-April 2004), p. 41.

102 See, for example, the booklet accompanying the 1986 André Previn / Brighton Festival Chorus / Royal Philharmonic recording (IMP Carlton Classics Series, LC 8747).

103 See Constantine Fitzgibbon, *Dylan Thomas*, p. 289. The drawings in *Lilliput* appeared in December 1942, juxtaposed in collage-fashion with photographs by Bill Brandt. That year, some of the drawings had also appeared in *Poetry (London)*; 'The sketches of sleeping children are particularly loving; perhaps the most magnificent are the two sketches of children covered with blankets sleeping in bunks ... found in the *Poetry London* publication'. Peter Stansky and William Abrahams, *London's Burning*, p. 47.

104 Peter Stansky and William Abrahams, *London's Burning*, pp. 35–6.

105 Peter Stansky and William Abrahams, *London's Burning*, p. 48.

106 Stuart Sillars, *British Romantic Art and the Second World War*, p. 180. Peter Stansky and William Abrahams, *London's Burning*, pp. 60, 67.

107 Neil Corcoran claims that the 'lack of individuation' of the child's death is 'questionable' and that this places it in the 'realms of consolatory inevitability' and robs it of its 'disturbing and even deranging' character. This only applies if one insists on a limited mimetic definition of poetry. Moore's drawings of shelterers are non-'individuated', but they certainly 'disturb' and are no more 'questionable' than realist portraits would be. Thomas likewise refuses to turn a collective experience into anecdote or individual case-history, aiming at mythic solidarity, rather than a demonstration of empathy, which would risk self-aggrandisement and

the appropriation of the girl's suffering. See Neil Corcoran, *English Poetry since 1940* (London: Longman, 1993), p. 46.

108 C. G. Jung, 'Zur Psychologie des Kind-Archetypus', *Das göttliche Kind* (1940), cited in David Ashford, 'Children Asleep in the Underground', p. 313.

109 Stuart Sillars, *British Romantic Art and the Second World War*, p. 181. Peter Stansky and William Abrams, *London's Burning*, p. 47. The phrase is characteristic of the Blitz sublime – compare it to Henry Green's Mr Jonas in the novel *Caught*, who thinks of the 'wide-eyed magnificence of the fires'.

110 Leo Mellor, *Reading the Ruins: Modernism, Bombsites and British Culture*, p. 80.

111 Cecil Beaton, *History under Fire: 52 Photographs of Air Raid Damage to London Buildings, 1940–41*, commentary by James Pope-Hennessy (London: B. T. Batsford, 1941).

112 Thomas counted Owen as one of the four most influential poets of his generation (with Eliot, Yeats and Hopkins). The pantheism of 'À Terre' informs the process poetic, and he regarded Owen as an honorary Anglo-Welsh poet, describing him in his broadcast 'Welsh Poetry' of 1946 as the author of 'sensuous and pitiful elegies on the great *undying* dead of the massacred world about him ... the *pleader* of the sufferings of men; he writes *as* the articulate dead: murdered manhood is given a great and dark golden tongue' (*TB*, 39).

113 Citing Thomas's radio piece 'Wilfred Owen', broadcast 19 June 1946 – 'He buries his smashed head with his own singed hands, and is himself the intoning priest over the ceremony, the suicide, the sunset. He is the common touch. He is the bell of the church of the broken body' – James Keery convincingly argues that Thomas presented Owen as a 1940s Apocalyptic poet *avant la lettre*. See James Keery, 'The Burning Baby and the Bathwater', *P. N. Review* 171, 33: 1 (September-October 2006), p. 58.

114 Compare, to take just one example, the phrase 'scythes of his arms' and the island and beach imagery of 'Into her lying down head' – a poem finished and sent to Vernon Watkins a day after Churchill's 5 June speech, in which he described how 'the German eruption swept like a sharp scythe' through the Low Countries into France.

115 Sillars draws a comparison between the 'pessimistic and static' vision of the relationship between man and earth found in Owen, who seeks in the natural world 'only a refuge from suffering by becoming insensate' and that offered in Part 7 of David Jones's *In Parenthesis* (1937), in which the earth offers not only refuge, but tenderness and spiritually enriching qualities, which: 'merge human and natural processes in a continuum of care and renewal'. ... [T]he timelessness of the Jones passage is also important ... It is the growing, nurturing earth which endures'. Stuart Sillars, *British Romantic Art and the Second World War*, pp. 142–5.

116 Stuart Sillars, *British Romantic Art and the Second World War*, p. 175.

117 The allusion to the holocaust seems to have been noticed by just one critic, Laurence Stapleton, in *Some Poets and Their Resources: The Future Agenda* (Lanham: University Press of America, 1995), p. 46: 'I like to think that ... "the round / Zion of the water bead / And the synagogue of the ear of corn" implies a solidarity with the Jews whose destruction in Germany was a denial of all that humanity means'. Thomas's wartime philosemitism led to him being made an 'honorary Jew' by the Polish painter Jankel Adler (see also fn. 3 above).

118 I draw here on the reading of 'A Refusal to Mourn' offered as illustrative

of the deconstructive method by Peter Barry. It first identifies paradoxes and contradictions (as in 'Never until'), then reads the poem as narratively, tonally, contextually and chronologically ungrounded, then identifies moments of linguistic inadequacy, of the gap between the 'refusal to mourn' and consolation (this taken to 'prove' that the speaker cannot stand in a pure space beyond elegy) and finally decides whether the poem proposes such a 'pure space' or if, having identified 'the language trap', it dismantles it. See Peter Barry, *Beginning Theory* (Manchester: Manchester University Press, 1994), pp. 73–7.

119 The 'second death' is mentioned in Revelations 2: II; 20, VI and XIV; 21, VIII.

120 David Kennedy, *Elegy* (London: Routledge, 2007), p. 73.

121 James Keery's virtuoso exposition of the complex intertextuality of this famous line can only be briefly sketched here. Keery notes Thomas's primary challenge to Revelation: 'there is no second death. There is no lake of fire or Christian hell'. Following this, he convincingly argues that a number of other texts are invoked. Lionel Johnson's 'The Dark Angel', as he points out, is one case of the persistence of the doctrine ('The second Death that never dies'). In Hardy's 'The To-Be-Forgotten', 'the second death' refers to 'predestined oblivion', although his 'In Tenebris I' contradicts John of Patmos, like Thomas. Keery notes that 'first dead' appears in Swinburne's 'The Triumph of Time' and, finally, it is a rare case of a New Apocalypse poet returning the Thomas influence in J. F. Hendry's 'The Toy Soldier' ('This was the first death. There were many others'). As he concludes: 'It is not the case that "Mr Thomas's imagery is neither precise nor deliberate" … A more precisely *specific* line would be far to seek'. James Keery, 'The Burning Baby and the Bathwater', *P. N. Review* 171, 33: 1 (September-October 2006), pp. 57–8.

122 Steve Vine, '"Shot from the locks": Poetry, Mourning, *Deaths and Entrances*', p. 150.

123 This fluid, ungraspable aspect of 'turn/ing' has something of the minatory charge it has in Yeats's 'The Second Coming'. The threat is conveyed by the internal rhyme: 'turned' and 'turning' are matched by 'burned' and 'burning', evoking the image of the burning children of other poems in *Deaths and Entrances*.

124 Stewart Crehan, '"The Lips of Time"', eds. John Goodby and Chris Wigginton, *Dylan Thomas: New Casebook*, p. 62. The 'mountain goat' comment is Russell Davies's dismissive description of 'Fern Hill' in 'Fibs of Vision', *Review* (Autumn / Winter 1971–2), p. 69.

125 Stewart Crehan, '"The Lips of Time"', eds. John Goodby and Chris Wigginton, *Dylan Thomas: New Casebook*, p. 62.

CHAPTER SIX

'That country kind': Cold War pastoral, carnival and the late style

[H]e writes a poem. It is, of course, about Nature; ... a decorous pantheist, he is one with the rill, the rhyming-mill, the rosy-bottomed milkmaid, the russet-cheeked rat-catcher, swains, swine, pipits, pippins. You can smell the country in his poems, the fields, the flowers, the armpits of Triptolemus, the barns, the byres, the hay, and, most of all, the corn.

– Dylan Thomas, 'How to be a Poet: or, the Ascent of Parnassus Made Easy' (*QEOM*, 196).

Success, 'disillusion and experiment'

The success of *Deaths and Entrances*, published in February 1946, marked the beginning of Thomas's popular reputation as a poet, building as it did on his reputation as a broadcaster, which had been steadily growing since 1943. A first print run of 3,000 copies sold out within a month, and sales were matched by widespread critical acclaim.[1] In his fourth collection, the visionary modernist strain of British poetry that Thomas had pioneered achieved an apocalyptic and neo-Romantic apotheosis. Its variousness – a mixture of war elegy, pastoral, love lyric and childhood reminiscence – perfectly expressed the conflicted post-war mood of loss, trepidation and hope on the eve of the peaceful social revolution represented by the vote for Attlee's Labour Party against the war leader, Churchill, and the subsequent creation of the Welfare State. Not long afterwards, in the autumn of 1946, the BBC launched its cultural network, the Third Programme. The demand for Thomas as both an actor and writer increased, and he displayed a natural affinity for the medium in both capacities.[2] He became a household name, and his appeal continued unabated until the time of his death in 1953.[3]

Against this, by late 1945, life in London's Fitzrovian bohemia had brought Thomas close to the point of physical collapse.[4] After a brief period of hospitalisation, in early 1946, he moved with his family from London to rural Oxfordshire, where they lived until moving to Laugharne in rural Carmarthenshire in May 1949. Although based in the country, Thomas continued to make his living in radio and film – work which entailed regular sorties to the capital. (And, in addition to the US, Thomas also visited Ireland in 1946, Italy in 1947, Prague in 1949 and Iran in 1951.) The rural–urban tensions which ensued undoubtedly played some part in the pastoral turn that I examine in this chapter; pastoral is an urban creation – a stylised representation of rural life, devised by city-dwellers to reflect upon their own existences (although, in Thomas's case, it also subsumed the Nonconformist trope of London as the City of Destruction and Dreadful Night). But if non-urban life was a relief in some ways, it was not an escape from Thomas's problems – marital disintegration, the problems caused by impecuniousness, the demands of scriptwriting and growing family responsibilities. It would, therefore, be wrong to think that he treated the genre as merely compensatory, as an escape into Romantic scene-painting, especially since he soon came to regard Laugharne ambivalently, as 'this wet, idyllic tomb on the coast' (*CL*, 969). Rather, pastoral's traditional generic role of presenting the complex within the simple, with its movement of retreat and return and its manipulation of stereotypical representations, made it a vehicle for exploring the new demands of life in the post-war world.

The late poems' generosity of spirit and celebratory, if often anguished, tone is a reminder that this time of partial retreat was also one of rapidly changing cultural and social conditions. Scriptwriting, broadcasting and the four US reading tours of 1950–3 were responses to the drastic reduction of a pre-war literary scene that had included coteries which encouraged experimentation and journals which were tolerant of more than one poetic style and offered review work (after the war, literary criticism and journalism was increasingly professionalised and academicised).[5] The expanding mass media made up some of the shortfall, but it had different demands and its audiences were less inclined to accept on trust a writer's claims of justifiable difficulty. The stylistic gap between the poems of 1939–41 and *Under Milk Wood* reflects not only Thomas's increased stylistic range, but also his awareness of the fragmentation of literary culture during the 1940s. As the possessor of great comic gifts and a natural populist instinct, this fragmentation was something that he benefitted from more than most. Nevertheless, he remained essentially a 1930s lyric poet, whose most important work was of an intensity that required to be 'hammered out ... in an almost prison-like solitude', and this was at odds, in significant ways, with the more profitable role of public entertainer, into which he entered in the mid-1940s.[6] On this, it should be said that, despite being, to some extent, the prisoner of his personal myth, he was far from being the 'Bubbles who fell among literary touts', in John Wain's patronising phrase. Thomas was, at all times, aware of the perils of populism and popularity and guarded against them. Returning from the US, he wrote of 'ranting poems to enthusiastic audiences that, the week before, had been equally enthusiastic about lectures on Railway Development or the Modern Turkish Essay' (CL, 969). In his attempt to explain the figure of the Thief of 'In country sleep' to a journalist in New York in 1950, he observed: 'alcohol is the thief today. But tomorrow he could be fame or success or exaggerated introspection or self-analysis. The thief is anything that robs you of your faith, your reason for being'.[7]

If, then, the later poems 'healingly [register] ... optimistic pantheism' and celebrate the flesh and the natural world, they are also often suffused with new anxieties.[8] As David Daiches cautions: 'Thomas did not rush towards the celebration of unity in all life and all time which later became an important theme of comfort to him: he moved to it through disillusion and experiment'.[9] This is nowhere clearer than in his response to what the 'Prologue' to his *Collected Poems 1934–1952* calls the 'poor peace' of the Cold War, precariously underwritten by atomic weapons (CP, 1). The regenerative fire of 'Ceremony After a Fire Raid' and the fathering sun / son of 'Holy Spring' were soon overshadowed by the possibility of global conflagration. The 'shadow of a hand', which takes that of the child in 'Fern Hill' – a poem completed just after VJ Day – ominously recalls the silhouettes of those vaporised at Hiroshima and Nagasaki. The secrets which powered the sun, as origin of all natural life, were now harnessed to annihilation. As one of the few British poets who maintained the intensity of his 1930s socialism and a signatory of the Stockholm Peace Petition, the Rosenberg Petition and the Authors World Peace Appeal, as well as a vehement defender of the new NHS (though he grumbled about the taxation that it required), Thomas was acutely sensitive to East-West tensions and the threat of war.[10] His application for a visa for his first visit to the US was delayed, as a result of his Left-wing sympathies, and he remained an outsider in establishment terms (the BBC, for example, decided not to offer him a permanent job). But the potential rewards in America encouraged persistence. The publication of *In Country Sleep* – a chapbook – on the eve of his second tour there, in 1952, and in an exclusively US edition, reflects the growing importance of this audience and market.

In Country Sleep contained the six poems written during 1947–51 – 'In country sleep' (1947), 'Over Sir John's hill' (1949), 'In the White Giant's Thigh' (1950), 'Lament', 'Do not go gentle into that good night' and 'Poem on his birthday' (all 1951) – but not his very last poem, 'Prologue'. Of these, 'Lament', 'Do not go gentle' and 'Prologue' are occasional pieces. However, 'In country sleep', 'Over Sir John's hill' and 'In the White Giant's Thigh' are substantial works. They were intended, Thomas claimed, to be sections of a larger, incomplete project called *In Country Heaven*, and they show his poetry developing in new and fruitful directions, largely as a result of the pastoral turn (this project is discussed later in this chapter).[11] 'Poem on his birthday' is also a substantial poem; Thomas had not written it when he described *In Country Heaven*, but it is possible that it, too, belongs to this larger work.

It is important to state exactly what Thomas wrote in his final years at the outset of this chapter, because, despite its widespread appeal, the later work – including most of the more popular pieces in *Deaths and Entrances* – is still the source of considerable critical differences. John Ackerman once said that 'It sometimes seems as though there are two ways of disliking [Dylan] Thomas: one is to dislike him, the other to disparage the later poems', and while this is not quite true (the early poems get plenty of disparagement, too), the later work does attract praise and blame which is qualitatively different to that attracted by the 1930s writing or the more difficult poems of *Deaths and Entrances*.[12] For many, this work, with its childhood themes and rural and seashore settings, is the soft underbelly of Thomas's *oeuvre*. Thus, for Russell Davies, 'Fern Hill' is simply diluted Wordsworth, while, for John Fuller it is 'emotionally dishonest' to boot.[13] More recently, Seamus Heaney claims that 'A Winter's Tale' 'is meant to be a visionary projection, but … rather suggests a winter-wonderland in the Hollywood mode. It is too softly contoured, too obligingly suffused with radiance and too repetitive – the verbal equivalent of a Disney fantasia'. (In a similar vein, Heaney finds *Under Milk Wood* 'symptomatic of a not irreprehensible collusion with the stereotype of the voluble Taffy'.)[14] Against this, Derek Mahon, in a Faber-published selection marking the fiftieth anniversary of Thomas's death, claimed that 'In country sleep', 'Over Sir John's hill' and 'In the White Giant's Thigh' 'represent his crowning achievement' and form a trilogy, which 'moves from a vision of peace and refuge … to the menacing external world … and concludes in an ecstasy of rhapsodic resolution and celebration'.[15] Many of Thomas's Welsh champions, as we have seen, see the work as the outcome of a hard-won struggle for clarity and communal locatedness. Rather differently, Barbara Hardy values it for its extension of the 'green' or ecological aspect, which she sees as a consistent concern of Thomas's poetry from *18 Poems* onwards, while Richard Chamberlain has argued that the work's pastoral aspect makes manifest the opposition to dominative instrumental logic, which is latent in the earlier poetry.[16]

In developing the case made by Hardy and Chamberlain, I shall argue that the clarity of the poetry written from 1944 onwards is deceptive. Walford Davies, for example, claims that Thomas became a 'Romantic' poet following a 'decisive ... retreat from the techniques of Modernism', his earlier 'techniques of indirection' replaced by 'a direct descriptive style ... convey[ing] ... a strong sense of the poet's own confessional presence' and the 'early imagined worlds' rejected, in favour of 'the strong continuity of a realistic landscape'.[17] But Davies, it seems to me, allows relief at what is taken to be an embrace of lyrical autobiography to blind him to the innovative aspects of the later work. Thomas undeniably tried to communicate more directly in his poetry after 1938. In 1952, he said: 'I am trying for more clarity now. At first I thought it enough to leave an impression of sound and feeling and let the meaning seep in later, but since I've been giving these broadcasts and reading other men's poetry as well as my own, I find it better to have more meaning at first reading'.[18] But this does not mean that he opted for poetry of the unified, stable self, wielding language in a largely instrumental way, in order to express its relation to a world described in 'realistic' terms.

As my reading of 'Poem in October' in Chapter 5 showed, the clarity of the 'Romantic' later poems is illusory in several ways. For one thing, they exhibit a blithe disregard for realism. For example, the opening of part II of 'In country sleep' nominally lists many of the properties of the 'realistic landscape' that Davies claims to find:

Night and the reindeer on the clouds above the haycocks
And the wings of the great roc ribboned for the fair!
The leaping saga of prayer! And high, there, on the hare-
       Heeled winds the rooks
Cawing from their black bethels soaring, the holy books
Of birds! Among the cocks like fire the red fox

Burning! Night and the vein of birds in the winged, sloe wrist
Of the wood! Pastoral beat of blood through the laced leaves!
The stream from the priest black wristed spinney and sleeves

Of thistling frost
Of the nightingale's din and tale! The upgiven ghost
Of the dingle torn to singing and the surpliced

Hill of cypresses! (*CP*, 141)

This is clearly very different to the visceral–cosmic territory mapped out by the early process poems. Yet, despite the 'rooks', 'haycocks', 'fox', sloes, 'leaves', 'stream' and 'spinney', it would be absurd to call the passage realistic; it is clearly at odds with the empirical pastoral or landscape tradition of Wordsworth, Clare, Hardy and Edward Thomas, within which Davies would place it. Rather than modest description, the passage flaunts the materiality of its signifiers and flags its construct-edness and artifice; it anthropomorphises nature to a degree which is flagrantly excessive for poems in the English nature poetry tradition. The metaphoric activity is incessant, and 'surplice' surely hints at its 'surplus' quality (not to mention that 'cypresses' are surplus to any Carmarthenshire landscape requirements). The same goes, to varying degrees, for all the later poems. Even the most Hardyesque of them, 'In the White Giant's Thigh', grants sonic patterning an unusual degree of equality with, and sometimes precedence over, discursive sense ('in the dowse / Of day, in the thistle aisles') and has its grotesque pun ('brides in the hawed house' [whorehouse]) to puncture realist illusion, as surely as 'After the funeral' does in 'parched' (*CP*, 151). Although 'the poet's own confessional presence' is relatively stable, it is ceaselessly disrupted by patterning, symbolism, personification, allegory, pun and repetition. Moreover, these poems can scarcely be regarded as 'confessional'; rather, the occasions of biography (the references to the writing shed as a 'seashaken house' and the view from it, etc.) are used by Thomas as the vehicles for a particular kind of linguistic and tropic display. As Tony Conran rightly argues, biography is 'a technical problem' in these works, a vehicle for poems which are not confessional, for 'to express his personal feelings – if we mean, by that, the finding of exact words for the empirical situation that he was in – is quite clearly not what he was trying to do'.[19]

Their elaborate artifice, and his suspicion that these are not conventionally expressivist poems, are what inform Fuller's jibe, with the assumption that 'emotion' and artifice are incompatible and 'emotion' can be unproblemat-ically present in a text; that Thomas tried, but failed to write late Romantic poems. Yet Fuller is at least alert to the artifice; Davies either minimises this or views the poems as deficient for being inadequately communal and relying 'more on atmosphere than on relationships'.[20] Even so, both he and Fuller share a Movement-derived view of what poetry should be. To Thomas's detractors, the late poems fuel an anglocentric dislike for his bardic-rhapsodic qualities, while, for his champions, it is central to the effort to normalise his work as a totality – to make him the prodigal son, who whored after modernism, saw the error of his ways and, just in time, returned to the fold, in order to celebrate his roots. But as I will try to show, the main continuity between these poems is stylistic, not that of any 'realistic landscape'. Their romanticism is in quotation marks, as it were; the new powers of destruction that Thomas discerns in the natural world he praises, and the apocalyptic ambiguity the poems attain, reveal greater continuity with the early poems than is acknowledged. The conjunctions of opposites in a line like 'O see the poles are kissing as thy cross' in 'I see the boys of summer' is no more forceful and undecidable than the journey 'sail[ing] out to die' at the close of 'Poem on his birthday', eighteen years later, in which rhapsodic transfiguration and atomic extinction are inseparable (*CP*, 7, 147).

In offering 'more meaning at first reading', then Thomas by no means offered full sense or the only sense. There are gestures evocative of 1940s neo-Romanticism's re-annexing of the natural world, a more limpid style and some unravelling of autobiographical material from the condensed textures of the process poetry. But this signifies less the complete abandonment of modernism, than the reshaping of some of its concerns in a new guise. That guise is a paradoxically complex clarity – a new style based on repetition, verbal exfoliation and a miscegenatory incorporation of the English poetic canon. In his 'Poetic Manifesto' of 1951, Thomas listed 'paragram' among his 'technical paraphernalia', and it is the term that I shall use in what follows to describe the peculiarities of the later style (*EPW*, 158). I shall argue that increased 'presence' and sense of place are there for the sake of the verbal web, rather than being existential givens, and that the disagreement over the value of the late poems reflects the queasy blend of sincerity and detachment, Anglo-Welsh and English, Romantic and modern (if not fully modernist), which this brought about. I shall discuss its vehicle, the pastoral, before broaching specific questions of style.

Placing the pastoral

Writing to Princess Caetani in October 1951, Thomas described the First Voice and Eli Jenkins of *Under Milk Wood* in this way: '[they] never judge nor condemn but explain and make strangely simple & simply strange'

(*CL*, 906). 'Strangely simple & simply strange' is a good definition of pastoral as a genre, which, while capable of varying interpretations, is fundamentally about putting the complex into the simple. Thomas uses and fuses several of its many different kinds in his late works, from its original status as a form in which a rural retreat returns 'insights relevant to [an] urban audience', to writing which is 'about' the countryside, and even writing which idealises the reality of the countryside and those living there. This latter pejorative, escapist sense was the usage applied by radical critics in the 1970s and 1980s – those who saw pastoral as a form of false consciousness. But this overlooked its carnivalesque and utopian possibilities, and the animus diminished with the rise of ecocriticism and Cultural Studies in the late 1980s and the discovery of pastoral's capacity for oblique critique.[21] Indeed, its pluralism was seen to have an innate ideological charge; so Terry Gifford's study *Pastoral* (1999) could describe a genre, which, by then, included 'Freudian pastoral', a 'pastoral of childhood', 'proletarian pastoral', 'urban pastoral' and 'revolutionary [lesbian-ecofeminist] pastoralisms', even as the response of ecocritics to pollution and global warming promoted a more general revival of interest.[22]

Today, more than ever before, pastoral's distinctive ability is seen as that of both containing and appearing to evade tensions between country and city, art and nature, the human and the non-human, our social and inner, and masculine and feminine, selves. This aptitude for encompassing contradictions is what most appealed to Thomas – a poet whose work often attempts to push paradoxical, problematic states to the highest possible pitch. So 'In Country Sleep' is an ecological pastoral ('the country is holy'), 'Poem in October' is a 'pastoral of childhood', 'In the White Giant's Thigh' has a proto-feminist pastoral aspect, and so on. In response to the shock of the war, two works – 'Fern Hill' and *Under Milk Wood*, in particular – are 'Freudian pastoral', insofar as they explore the hankering after a prelapsarian, pre-sexual subject and acknowledge the impossibility of this, given Freud's identification of childhood sexuality. Finally, and primarily within 'Poem on his Birthday' and 'Over Sir John's hill', the threat of atomic weapons to humanity and nature produced an ecological perspective, in what might be called, to add to Gifford's list, 'Cold War pastoral'.

Thomas's pastoral reminds us of his affinities with an earlier, more oblique radicalism than that of the 1970s and 1980s, namely William Empson's in *Some Versions of Pastoral* (1935). In this text, Empson applied the promiscuous forms of close reading developed in *Seven Types of*

Ambiguity (1930) to a highly unconventional exploration of the grounds on which utopias are constructed. According to Empson, the pastoral in English had migrated under pressure from Puritanism into other kinds of writing, including Newgate pastoral, writing for children and – being provocatively up-to-date – proletarian literature. Proposing that fictional idealisations of the working class were descended from Sidney's shepherds and shepherdesses did not endear Empson to socialist realist orthodoxy, but the whimsicality of his thesis was only apparent. His real aim was to champion pastoral as a critical category, because it was inherently heterogeneous, formally loose and resistant to fixity. Rather than being simply about pastoral or about the pastoral as a 'simple' genre, *Some Versions* was an imaginatively indirect attempt to theorise the nature of literature itself – a defence of its humane role in the polarised climate of the 1930s. As in Thomas's work, the emphasis that Empson laid on pastoral's paradoxicality and pluralism, in opposition to false totalities and resolutions, affirmed the generation of life-affirming untidiness from apparently simple antinomies.

These ethical and stylistic implications of pastoral were later emphasised by Veronica Forrest-Thompson, a critic heavily influenced by Empson, who noted in *Poetic Artifice* (1978) the permission that it gave the poet to 'simplify and exalt', 'but also, and by the same token, parody'.[23] In Thomas's later poems, the use of paragrammatic variation-in-repetition and a near-parodic interweaving of canonical allusion in unprecedentedly elaborate poems fulfils pastoral's generic obligation to unify the natural with the highly artificial. As well as making the point that pastoral has to do with style and structure as much as theme, both Empson and Forrest-Thompson stress that it is open-ended and not obliged to be rural or territorially rooted. Thomas's sense of the pastoral is, likewise, miscegenatory and ungrounded; his countryside (like Keats's, but unlike Wordsworth's) is a suburbanite's, usually related in some way to the interstitial zone of the seashore, as in the ending of 'Fern Hill' – a poem about a farm, whose last word is 'sea'. It is the shore – that now-you-see-it-now-you-don't tidal zone, an unstable non-location of risk, voyaging and mutable selves – that is ultimately home to Thomas's hybrid, liminal subject, and it is defined against the kind of territoriality which underwrites self-possession.[24] Its impropriety is evident in the language used by critics, who feel that rural life is a repository of timeless national values, as witness Holbrook's sneering description of Thomas's appeal to the 'half-educated audience of English suburbia' and the 'suburban semi-intellectual, middle-class, conservative audience of the BBC'.[25]

Thomas, I shall argue, used the 'counterforce' of complexity, which so often undercuts the idyll of pastoral, exploiting its 'multiple frames' and the fact that it is essential to pastoral's effects that the reader: 'is conscious of its status as a [literary] device, so that she ... can see what the writer is doing with the device'.[26] The ultimate form of this distancing from the pastoral vision as reality is the pastoral as allegory. Thomas's pastorals tend towards allegory, but they temper escapism with the genre's inherent doubleness – its capacity to assume oppositional forms. They affirm a new acceptance of the cycle of procreation, birth, procreation, supersession and death, along with techniques and subjects allied to the pastoral (such as childhood) that permit a potential reconciliation of the patterns of life and death in terms of the past and present. This tempers the fierce simultaneity of the process poetry. But, on the other hand, the shadow of the bomb falls across them; as early as 18 June 1946, Thomas alluded to 'this ... apparently hell-bent earth' (B, 62) at the end of a radio broadcast. Whether, as a result, it is possible to maintain faith in life is typically posed in the language of religious faith, but the dilemma is a secular one, and the poems oppose annihilation with sensual verbal excess and carnivalesque gusto. This is tinged with something of the quality of the medieval Welsh *gorhoffedd* genre ('boast' or 'praise' poetry) and ranges from the phallically deflating self-mockery of the pen/is-with-a-swagger of 'Lament' and *Under Milk Wood*'s exuberant mining of oral and popular culture – seaside postcards, radio comedy, music hall bawdy, children's play-rhyme, drinking songs and newspaper verses – to the proto-feminist celebration of female sexual pleasure in 'In the White Giant's Thigh'. As this suggests, unlike most rustic visions of the 1940s, Thomas's pastoral has little place for either stability or tranquillity.[27]

'Fond climates': place and pastoral belonging

If, as has been claimed, a pastoral note was 'curiously instinctive' from the first and apparent in 'early actualizations of Eden', the sense of specific location and scene-painting are nevertheless among the least significant things about the later poems.[28] Of course, they reflect affection for West Wales and say something about where Thomas was writing. 'Prologue', in particular, mentions Wales by name, and contains 'bryns' ('hills'), a 'Welsh and reverent rook', 'stars of Wales' and 'Dai mouse'.[29] But this is an atypical, introductory-summatory poem. Hybrid, slightly unfixed forms of place and attachment to them are the norm. So, sending

'Poem in October' to Vernon Watkins in 1944, Thomas described it as 'a Laugharne poem, the first place poem I've written', and, sure enough, the poem's 'harbour and neighbour wood', its hill, church, 'gates' and 'castle / Brown as owls' can all be found in Laugharne itself, where he had begun an earlier version of the poem in 1939 (*CL*, 580). Yet the town's name, which had featured in a first draft of 1939, had disappeared by 1944, and the poem's topography had become calculatedly inaccurate. There is no place in Laugharne itself, for example, from which it is physically possible to view church, castle and harbour, as the poem's speaker does. Nor could the church be 'sea wet', as it stands about a mile inland.[30] As in other poems of the final period, Thomas deliberately avoids specifics and proper names. Like Llareggub, the town in *Under Milk Wood*, the town of the poem is not an actual place realistically recalled, but a composite created for imaginative purposes (Thomas described *Under Milk Wood* as 'a more or less play set in a Wales that I'm sad to say never was') (*CL*, 962).

Much the same can be said of the other later 'poems of place'. While 'Over Sir John's hill', 'Poem on his Birthday' and 'Prologue' conjure up the views of the Towy estuary that Thomas enjoyed from his writing shed in Laugharne, the scenes that they present incline towards the abstract and emblematic. 'Over Sir John's hill' takes the name of the hill above Laugharne as its title. It is mentioned again within the poem, as is the river Towy, three times. Even so, the poem's speaker calls himself 'young Aesop', and the landscape is strictly subordinate to the poem's aim of unravelling its pathetic fallacy along allegorical lines. With 'In country sleep', this tendency is even clearer, for the countryside is rendered in a timeless, placeless, conventional folk- or fairy-tale lexis ('hearthstone', 'hamlet', 'greenwood', 'homestall', 'hobnail') (*CP*, 144, 139–40). The belief that Thomas's Carmarthenshire surroundings inspired such poems in any causal way seems equally naïve. 'Poem in October' was written in New Quay, while 'In country sleep' was written in Italy in 1947 (the poem includes 'cypresses', as if to drive the point home). Research on *Under Milk Wood* reveals that '[t]here is nothing ... to support the view that the magic of Laugharne was at the heart of the Llareggub project. The town provided little in the way of inspiration or motivation ... At most, only some three hundred lines, or seventeen percent, of the play had been written [there], and some of these could well have been written in London'.[31] Thomas, it should go without saying, did not need to be living in a place to write about it, nor did he represent it realistically. But it is possible to argue that Laugharne, like New Quay, was 'inspiration' in its anomalous neither-Welsh-nor-Englishness; when Thomas described Laugharne before WWII as 'a little Danzig', he was referring to the attractiveness of its radical inbetween, unlocatable quality (*CL*, 454).

We should therefore be very wary of trying to ground Thomas's later work in any specific West Wales landscape. The Reverend Eli Jenkins, affectionately depicted though he is, recites a 'morning hymn', which is not only a parody of county newspaper verse, but also more broadly of the place-name poem and the poem of place. Nevertheless, Thomas did not simply indulge in a reflex gainsaying of truisms about place and belonging. Rather, he aimed to scrutinise and deconstruct the truisms and stereotypes that surround the urge to be rooted and specify territorial allegiance, in order to reveal its hidden contradictions and complexities. There is a good example of this in the opening lines of 'In the White Giant's Thigh':

> Through throats where many rivers meet, the curlews cry,
> Under the conceiving moon, on the high chalk hill,
> And there this night I walk in the white giant's thigh
> Where barren as boulders women lie longing still
>
> To labour and love though they lay down long ago.
>
> Through throats where many rivers meet, the women pray,
> Pleading in the waded bay for the seed to flow
> Though the names on their weed grown stones are rained away,
>
> And alone in the night's eternal, curving act
> They yearn with tongues of curlews for the unconceived
> And immemorial sons of the cudgelling, hacked
>
> Hill. (*CP*, 150)

At the risk of appearing to do the opposite of what I have been arguing by trying nail the poem to the 'real world', the model for the 'giant' is likely to be the chalk figure carved into a hillside at Cerne Abbas in Hampshire, not far from Blashford, where Thomas's in-laws lived (there are no such figures in Wales). The giant is endowed with a club (hence the 'cudgelling' hill) and a large phallus (his 'thigh'). The poem is based on a folk belief that hitherto childless women who are impregnated within the giant's phallus would conceive. Crucially, however, the Cerne Abbas giant predates the Anglo-Saxon invasions. It is a Romano-Brythonic (that is, proto-Welsh) structure, which survived in what later became an English landscape. From the outset, then, the poem problematises stable 'English' and 'Welsh' identities. But it takes this a stage further by mapping the miles-inland Hampshire landscape of the giant onto the womb-like estuarial 'waded bay' of Laugharne (formed by two rivers). This hybrid effect is further complicated, since the town of Laugharne is an anglicised outpost in a Welsh-speaking area – an 'Englishry' (while Thomas's writing place looked across the estuary to the Welsh-speaking area, where he had relatives and holidayed as a child). Wales-in-England is overlaid on an England-in-Wales in a double problematisation of Welshness and Englishness. Similar discreet, yet disturbing effects occur throughout the work. Thus, in the short story 'Old Garbo', Swansea is referred to as 'Tawe, South Wales, England'. M. Wynn Thomas calls this 'a classic instance of colonial disorientation', indicating a place which 'exists interstitially as Homi Bhabha would say … between the Welsh language culture of the past and the … sophisticated contemporary world'.[32] Yet there is not really anything 'disorientated' about it; Thomas is signalling his irreducible hybridity by playing two kinds of misappropriation – the Cymrophone linguistic culturalist one ('Tawe' for 'Swansea') and the anglocentric one ('England' for 'Wales') – off against each other. His attitude to both essentialisms is of a plague-on-both-your-houses kind. The same subversive attitude informs the modification of his best-known proper name, 'Fern Hill', from 'Fernhill', as I noted in Chapter 5, as it does for the one proper name used to metonymically stand in for a town in Wales, the highly English-sounding 'Sir John's hill'. In this context, it is revealing that the seven post-war poems share just three place names – 'Wales', 'Sir John's hill' and 'Towy' – and just one local dialect word – 'gambo' (a farm cart) – between them (CP, 2, 142, 143, 144, 151).

For all this, Thomas undoubtedly creates an *effect* of locatedness, albeit an ambiguous one, and this is what causes critics with an axe to grind to see a greater or lesser amount of it than is actually the case. Seamus Heaney's attack shows that he thinks Thomas is trying and failing to create locality in some realist sense, and, although we might wonder why a 'Disney fantasia' might be so inappropriate in 1944 (the snowscapes of the Russian front and the Battle of the Bulge adjoin those of Disney and Thomas's hermit, too), his comments do reflect Thomas's refusal to keep fantasy and realism apart. For Heaney, himself a poet in the anti-pastoral tradition, Thomas's poem lacks the detail that would establish a consistent sense of locatedness; it therefore does not 'earn' the right to its 'visionary projection'. Heaney's critical model is Patrick Kavanagh, whose opposition of parochial to provincial was directed at poets who peddled their peasant Irishness: 'The provincial has no mind of his own; he does not trust what his eyes see until he has heard what the metropolis – towards which his eyes are turned – has to say on any subject ... The parochial mentality on the other hand is never in any doubt about the social and artistic validity of his parish'.[33] This leads Heaney to the rather laboured joke that 'A Winter's Tale' is 'more a case of "vended Wales" than "wended vales", so like a tourist board landscape is it'.[34] This ignores what the title pointedly tells us – that the poem is a fable – and its avoidance of Welsh locational indicators (we get 'minstrels', not 'bards', for example). Heaney fails to see that the repetition signals not weakness, but an innovative, paragrammatic, quintessentially pastoral style. At times, this can seem to resemble the kind of mimetic realism that Heaney favours – that is, the autotelic sound-patterning subserves a 'real world' scene enlivened by conceits, naturalistic detail and judiciously chosen adjectives and adverbs:

> ... the dung hills white as wool and the hen
> Roosts sleeping chill till the flame of the cock crow
> Combs through the mantled yard and the morning men
>
>   Stumble out with their spades,
> The cattle stirring, the mousing cat stepping shy,
> The puffed birds hopping and hunting, the milk maids
> Gentle in their clogs over the fallen sky,
> And all the woken farm at its white trades ... (CP, 99)

Even in this passage, however, the verbal patterning is so rich as to verge on displacing the realist description-plus-tropes formula for poetic writing and, hence, a 'grounded' relationship between the lyric 'I' and a specific territory. Of course, there is value in asserting a marginal territory's identity in realist terms against the centre. But, in and of itself, this has limited critical power; indeed, such assertions may easily mystify a place's relations with power through their reliance on blood-and-soil categories. To simply invert the centre-versus-periphery model, especially where 'region' is shorthand for an essential, fixed identity, is usually to confirm its terms; escaping it requires more devious deconstructions of self and place (ironically Heaney's own poetry, which grounds selfhood and cleaves to a dubiously territorialised sexual politics, enjoys its own cosily 'vended' relationship with metropolitan British poetic taste and on precisely these essentialist terms).

Heaney's 'vended' can be considered in relation to Thomas's prose writing of the 1940s and 1950s, in which he uses markers of Welsh location and Welshness, but signals their inadequacy by presenting them in the form of the stereotypes discussed in Chapter 4. Thus, in the broadcast 'Living in Wales' of June 1949, concerning his return to Laugharne that same year, the truth value of each stereotype is activated and problematised at the same time. Thomas writes from the buffet car of a train near Oxford and applies English stereotypes of its colonial populations to the English passengers that he finds around him; he will never, he claims, understand them: 'hearing, everywhere, the snobcalls, the prigchants, the mating cries, the tom-toms of a curious, and maybe, cannibal, race', living in a 'dark and savage country', which oppresses his Welsh sensibility and 'sickens' him with its 'cultural witch-doctors', 'ritual pomp', 'odorous courts' and 'periodic sacrifice of the young' (*TB*, 201–2). What keeps him going in England are his memories of Wales, he adds, listing several of them. But then he turns upon this gesture and confesses that 'all this was easy stuff, like settles in the corners, hams on the hooks, hymns after stop-tap, tenors with leeks ... What was harder to remember was what birds sounded like and said in Gower; what sort of a sound and a shape was Carmarthen Bay; how did the morning come in through the windows at Solva; what silence when night fell in the Aeron Valley' (*TB*, 205). It is the hyphenated hybrid aspect of his being, Thomas seems to be saying, that makes the psychologically nuanced memory of realism impossibly fugitive. But, although condemned to use them, he refuses the stereotypical dismissal of stereotypes, too. He adds that a repellent 'tailwag of rich tweedy women babytalking to their poodles. ... [i]s no more England than a village cricket match is', yet, as Walford Davies points out, this undercuts the apology; village cricket matches actually *are* quintessentially English.

The conflicted sense of not-belonging in England applies to his sense of belonging in Wales: 'I know that I am home again because I feel just as I felt when I was not at home, only more so. And still there are harps and whippets on the castled and pitheaded hills' (*TB*, 206). The stereotypes do not disappear when the prodigal son returns. When he wonders if, returned to Wales, he is the same person that he was in England, 'trundling under the blaring lights ... [my] beautiful barrow of raspberries', he acknowledges that he has 'peddled' stereotypes, but, characteristically, barbs the admission: raspberries are not just a fruit (and they are certainly not a fruit associated with Wales), but also a rude riposte (*TB*, 205). While stereotypes can dangerously oversimplify things, they can also be twisted to signal the basic alienation which should be fundamental to the writer, wherever s/he happens to reside. As in the later poetry, identity which claims to be equal to itself or to a given place, is distrusted and made subject to differential play. Simple means, again, produce complex results, and, however dated the discourse that Thomas manipulates now seems ('witchdoctor', etc.), his attack on southern middle-class English smugness has a prophetic, postcolonial dimension too.

Still, if Walford Davies's assessment of Thomas's success is diametrically opposed to Heaney's, Heaney would agree with his assertion, that: 'As a convincing artist [Thomas] needed a background ... a full look exacted at the best suggests an atmospheric and locational rootedness of a convincing kind'.[35] The terms of the claim reflect the mainstream poetic requirement of a biographical drama ('convincing' as a synonym for sincerity) rooted in a given location; poetry as a transparent window on 'reality'. Both miss the unrootedness of Thomas's littoral locations. The later poems are involved with Wales, we might say, and seem to invoke places, but they are not 'poems of place'; rather, they make us consider the place of 'place' in poetry. Rather than being vulnerable because of their 'unearned final-stanza-optimisms' – which accepts too readily the terms of a restricted poetic economy – Thomas's excessive poetic freely spends itself in symbolic-visionary landscapes of the mind that border on those of Marvell and Traherne.[36] It is to these canonical and stylistic dimensions of the pastoral scene that I now turn.

'Strangely simple & simply strange': pastoral and paragram

Having tried to define Thomas's thematics of pastoral, I now wish to extend it in what I take to be its more significant, stylistic sense; meaning, by this, the alteration in the verbal textures of his poetry towards repetition and mellifluousness and away from the clashing sounds and crowded, muscular syntax of the preceding work. Thomas lightened his verbal palette from 1944, developing more spacious rhythms and making stresses lighter, with lilting anapaests and dactyls substituting for heavier-footed iambs and spondees, and minimising punctuation. Sentences might still be long and complex, but their appositive clauses are not simply heaped up, as before, making the unfolding sense easier to follow. Yet if the sonic patterns convey less emotional urgency at a local level, they are nevertheless more intricately and conscientiously worked out on the larger scale of elaborate stanza patterns (the forerunner of these are the 'odes' of 1938–41). The change is appropriate to pastoral: the poems' movement, music and metrical schemes create an air of relaxation within complexly inter-involved patterning – what I am calling here 'paragrammatic'. Davies and Heaney regret and deplore, respectively, Thomas's refusal to yoke his 'natural descriptive talent' to the 'challenge' of realising 'the mundane'. For Davies '[t]oo often the later poems breed celebration only out of celebration, without establishing a sufficiently contrasting ordinariness over against which affirmation can appear an exciting (because vulnerable) challenge to our sense of reality'.37 The trouble is that this assumes that the poem subserves a non-linguistic 'sense of reality', always reflecting on, and defined by, 'sufficiently contrasting ordinariness'. For Thomas, on the contrary, the poem is itself the necessary 'reality' and 'ordinariness'. It 'excites' as a language event, not as conceited language, in contrast to the mundane world that it 'establishes'. Rather than moving imperfectly towards realism, as Davies's claim implies, between mid-1941 and mid-1944 Thomas was incubating a transition from one kind of writing of excess to another. Steve McCaffery writes of the late Barthes's shifting from 'a utilitarian understanding (including a readerly production of meaning) towards a pleasure or "jouissance" of texts', in which a linguistic surplus is generated beyond any mimetic-utilitarian requirement.38 This kind of new emphasis on 'pleasure', it seems to me, is what we find in Thomas's poetry after 1944.

Thomas balanced the gains of this style against the loss of overt difficulty and the irreducibility which he felt was constitutive of poetry. As we have seen, he had foreseen the dangers of the merely expressive utterance of the historical self, rather than the quarrying of its linguistic substrate, in 'Once it was the colour of saying'. These are anticipated again by 'The hunchback in the park' (July 1941) – the poem which immediately preceded the gestation period of 1941–4 and was also, significantly, the last poem with its origins in the notebooks.

Its subject is the poet, split into the 'truant boys' – imaginers of the 'loud zoo of the willow groves' – and the hunchbacked social misfit of the title, who creates as his muse 'A woman figure without fault' (*CP*, 93). The spare simplicity of the poem and its repetitions (of 'made', 'straight', 'dark', 'trees', 'water', 'bell', 'birds', 'mister', and so on) look forward to the later style. So, too, does the fact that the notebook version uses an outrageous pun ('mister' / 'mistier'), which was ignored in the act of rewriting (*NP*, 110).39 What is not yet present is the mellifluous fluidity of the post-1944 poems – the rhythm, like several other poems of the period, is slightly choppy, forcing the reader to make unusual placements of stress. That mellifluousness signals a thematic and canonical or intertextual shift, as Thomas evolved his version of the dominant Virgilian line of the English poetic tradition – that is, the one running from Chaucer through Spenser, Milton, Wordsworth, Keats, Hood, Tennyson and Hardy to Yeats – with its emphasis on the pleasing liquidity of sound, polish and tonal elevation. This also included a shift in the subset of Thomas's favoured Metaphysicals, from Donne to Vaughan, Marvell and Traherne. The break, then, is with the rugged line of Skelton, the Elizabethan lyricists, Jacobean drama, Blake, Beddoes and Browning – that which is associated with the grotesque. (This is a very general description, of course, with numerous exceptions: Spenser and Hardy can be rugged, and Hopkins became more, not less, prominent in Thomas's work.)[40]

The new style places less immediate weight of meaning on individual words. Not only pun, but unusual syntactical forms become rarer, while ductile, unhurried lines offer less resistance to the act of reading. Musical effects are no longer only local and may extend over the entire fabric of a poem, playing across the waveringly symmetrical stanza forms, while the saturation of similar and related sounds creates a sense of stasis – a different version of the simultaneity effects of the earlier poetry. The subtlety of the effects is evident in the *abacabcbac* assonantal end-rhyme scheme of 'Poem in October' (the first stanza uses 'heaven', 'heron', 'beckon', 'second'; 'wood', 'rook', 'foot'; 'shore', 'wall' and 'forth'). The striking shape of this poem, like many others, serves to emphasise its materiality and its shape on the page in a different, but equally effective, way to that of the earlier poetry. Seemingly at variance with the 'natural' flowing rhythms, form throws the poetry's artifice into greater relief. This is most evident in 'Vision and Prayer', with its alternate hourglass or bobbin- and diamond-shaped stanzas, but the same could be said of 'Fern Hill' or 'Over Sir John's hill'. Even more than before, Thomas is interested in the effect of the total shape, or *gestalt*, of the poem, looking back to Herbert's 'Easter Wings' and 'The Altar', but forward, too, to concrete poetry.[41]

'Poem in October' is also the first Thomas poem in which syllabic metre is dominant. While many of the earlier poems have a regular syllable count, they also display a regular stress pattern in 'The force that through the green fuse', for example, the syllable count for each five-line stanza is 10, 10, 4, 10, 10 (with two minor exceptions). The 10–syllable lines are all iambic pentameters, and the 4–syllable lines are all trimeters with three stresses: although the syllable count is regular, stress is the poem's organising principle. In 'Poem in October', however, while the syllable-count pattern is constant (9, 12, 9, 3, 5, 12, 12, 5, 3 and 9 syllables per line), the stress-count within lines of the same length varies. English poetry is largely stress-based, but in these poems, syllable-, not stress-, count is the backbone – though 'backbone' is the wrong term for the kind of fluidity-in-fixity which these stanza shapes embody.

The most complex stanza form among these later poems is that of 'Over Sir John's hill':

> Over Sir John's hill,
> The hawk on fire hangs still;
> In a hoisted cloud, at drop of dusk, he pulls to his claws
> And gallows, up the rays of his eyes the small birds of the bay
> And the shrill child's play
> Wars
> Of the sparrows and such who swansing, dusk, in wrangling hedges.
> And blithely they squawk
> To fiery tyburn over the wrestle of elms until
> The flash the noosed hawk
> Crashes, and slowly the fishing holy stalking heron
> In the river Towy below bows his tilted headstone. (*CP*, 142)

It is revealing that it is difficult to say precisely where the stresses ought to go; there might be no stress at all on 'wars' – the sixth line (the emphasis being on the fact that they are '*play* wars', not the real thing) – whereas in the second stanza ('There / Where the elegiac fisherbird …'), where the same line begins a sentence, it undoubtedly has a stress – a strong one. Thomas, however, does not just vary stress patterns in lines of the same syllabic length so much as weaken stress throughout. These poems (and despite Thomas's own recorded performances of them, it should be said) eschew emphatic, regular rhythms and distribute meaning more equally among their words, giving a levelling effect, both at the level of signification and the sonic web.

'A Winter's Tale' – perhaps because the snowscape is a metaphorical wiping clean of the poetic page – is nicely illustrative of the complexity of the sonic web in its interweaving of the different soundings of just one vowel; here, the 'o' sounds in the opening stanzas ('snow', 'over', 'floating', 'frozen', 'smoke'; 'folded', 'cold', 'folds', 'told'; 'of', 'flocked'; 'among'; 'owl', 'cowl') push musicality to tongue-twisting, but mesmerising, limits:

> It is a winter's tale
> That the snow blind twilight ferries over the lakes
> And floating fields from the farm in the cup of the vales,
> Gliding windless through the hand folded flakes,

The pale breath of cattle at the stealthy sail,

>   And the stars falling cold,
> And the smell of hay in the snow, and the far owl
> Warning among the folds, and the frozen hold
> Flocked with the sheep white smoke of the farm house cowl
> In the river wended vales where the tale was told. (*CP*, 99)

Sound has a larger structural function, since each of the poem's four-time zones is scored by different sound-clusters, while a set of repeated phrases – 'cup of the vales', 'hand folded flakes', 'wended vales', 'bride bed', 'floating fields', 'glided … wide', 'the spit and the black pot in the log bright light', 'home of prayers', 'centaur dead' – binds these zones in an intricate, self-referential, complexly self-modifying network. One could posit a mimetic purpose for this; the soft barrage of sounds and words enacts the continuous descent of snowflakes, accumulating and modifying the 'shape of sound' and the 'sound of shape', but this is secondary. The play of sound for its own sake is more important in a work which is an extended lyric, as it constructs more than a narrative in the usual sense. Near the end of the hermit's trek through the snow on his quest, the poem halts to enumerate its properties:

> Listen and look where she sails the goose plucked sea,
>
>   The sky, the bird, the bride,
> The cloud, the need, the planted stars, the joy beyond
> The fields of seed and the time dying flesh astride,
> The heavens, the heaven, the grave, the burning font. (*CP*, 102)

The appositional pile-up of the poems' themes creates an overdetermined knot, which exemplifies the way that the later poems use terms that seem to be clearly understood to generate problems of interpretation that are almost as great as those found in the earlier work. In narrative terms, this constitutes a heaping-up of the allegorical ideals represented by the she-bird, but, stylistically, the attempt at simultaneity collapses the narrative in linguistic overplus, Barthesian *jouissance* or Bataillian general economy. Under it, the compartmentalisation of the poem ruptures, enacting the inadequacy of language to the visionary 'joy beyond' of the hermit.

These verse textures are part of the broader stylistic shift towards patterns of repetition, which extend the measured, predictable recurrence-as-refrain of the earlier poetry to something less insistent and more pervasive; a reminder that Thomas's 'strangely simple & simply strange' is itself an example of polyptoton – a figure of repetition. Rather than detonating several meanings simultaneously through pun, we get a continuous, subtle modification of key words and phrases; the effect is metonymic, rather than metaphoric, creating transference, rather than condensation. 'The conversation of prayers', based on the shared etymology of 'conversation', 'converse' and 'conversion', is a good example, with 'conversation' signifying 'conversion' into an opposite quality – this being the source of the poem's paradox:

> The conversation of prayers about to be said
> By the child going to bed and the man on the stairs
> Who climbs to his dying love in her high room,
> The one not caring to whom in his sleep he will move
> And the other full of tears that she will be dead,
>
> Turns in the dark on the sound they know will arise
> Into the answering skies from the green ground,
> From the man on the stairs and the child by his bed.
> The sound about to be said in the two prayers
> For the sleep in a safe land and the love who dies
>
> Will be the same grief flying. Whom shall they calm?
> Shall the child sleep unharmed or the man be crying?
> The conversation of prayers about to be said
> Turns on the quick and the dead, and the man on the stairs
> Tonight shall find no dying but alive and warm
>
> In the fire of his care his love in the high room.
> And the child not caring to whom he climbs his prayer
> Shall drown in a grief as deep as his true grave,
> And mark the dark eyed wave, through the eyes of sleep,
> Dragging him up the stairs to one who lies dead. (*CP*, 85)

Two prayers – the man's and the child's – are 'about to be said', and the poem projects the convers/ation of the two, as they cross in the ascent towards the 'answering skies'. After establishing the child's 'not caring' prayer and the man's fear that his love will die, the twists of sense begin (as in 'Poem in October') with 'turns' at the beginning of stanza two. The 'sound about to be said in the two prayers' 'will be' the 'same grief flying'. Most commentators take this to mean that the substance of the two prayers – the unselfish wish of the man and the selfish wish of the child – are judged, with the child found wanting: the 'conversation' 'turns on the quick and the dead' (that is, the man's prayer is for someone living, while the child's is for a selfish 'dead' security). Hence, the man receives the security the child had taken for granted, while the child receives the man's death-haunted vision. As a narrative, the poem can be taken as autobiographical, with the 'dying love' as a reference to that of Dylan and Caitlin and the 'child' being Llewelyn – it was written at the same time as 'This side of the truth' – or Thomas himself, as a 'not caring' child (he runs his 'heedless ways' in 'Fern Hill').

However, there are several problems with trying to assign such definite meanings. For a start, while Thomas may be emphasising the arbitrariness of fate, as in 'This side of the truth' with its 'unminding skies', it is hard to see him punishing the child with 'a grief as deep as his true grave', given his revulsion at the suffering of children, as shown in the elegies. Second, the standard reading of the poem requires that one of the two figures has his prayer answered, while the other does not, but the poem's central question – 'Shall the child sleep unharmed *or* the man be crying?' (emphasis added) – does not support this either / or interpretation. If the child 'sleep[s] unharmed', the man will most certainly 'be crying' for his 'dying love'; for the either / or choice to operate, the 'or' should be an 'and'. This is just one of several cruxes. For example, is it the child who 'marks' the 'dark eyed wave' in the last stanza or are we, the readers, being asked to? Again, the ostensible logic of the poem supports a 'conversion' narrative only at first glance. It is as if Thomas is trying to catch us out to challenge the assumptions that we create in the process of interpretation.

Other possible narratives therefore have to be entertained for progress to be made. It might, for example, also be read as an example of a lyric of the divided self: psychoanalytically, the child within the adult, as in 'Poem in October' (this is enhanced by the ambiguity of 'his bed' in line eight, which may be the child's or the man's). More obliquely, the child may represent the wartime infantilisation of adults, with their nostalgic search for, and idealisation of, childhood memories (and, conversely, the way that the war forced children to become adults). The repetitions of the poem – the scattering of its key terms throughout in a mesmeric, always-altering weave of sense and sound – means that these possibilities are all available. And we need to remember that the second stanza warns us, twice, that it is not the meaning content of the prayers that 'turns' and converses / converts, but '*The sound*' of them. This has to be taken literally, to some extent. And, in addition, the 'sounds' are only ever 'about to be said', they are never actually uttered. The poem, then, is one verbal event anticipating another – it is only ever a speculation, a potential suspended in its verbal web. 'Sound' refers the reader to this web, to the elaborate phonic and rhetorical parallelism, criss-crossing rhyme scheme (mid-line / end-line rhymes), the rhyming of the middle and final words of the last line of each stanza with the corresponding words in the first stanza, the circularity by which the final line's 'stairs' and 'dead' rhyme with 'prayers' and 'said' of the opening line in the same order for the first time and to the extraordinary amount of repetition, something which is reinforced by the preponderance of monosyllables – 189 of the poem's 202 words.[42]

Critics point to the mimetic purpose of such details, and clearly some of them do reflect the poem's 'conversation' theme. Yet the repetition (as in 'A Winter's Tale' or 'In country sleep') is far in excess of any mimetic requirement. The recycling bespeaks a poetic which is at once both minimalist and excessive (This also applies to imagery and metaphor. Jacob Korg notes that the poem: 'is typical of the late style, in that the richness of repetition is matched by a paucity of imagery').[43] Any mimetic function arises from the pared-back nature of the style, which courts monotony only to thwart it. Indeed, the intricacy of the verbal weave is a substitute for rich imagery and metaphor: an end in itself, it offers parodic intensification of repetition as a fundamental quality of poetry.[44] Far from being clumsy, it exemplifies Jakobson's famous axiom defining the poetic function as the projection of the principle of equivalence from the axis of selection to that of combination. Reiterative richness and imagistic paucity creates a tension between clarity and ambiguity, in which the densities and deformations of the process poetic have not so much been jettisoned, as transmuted.

Similarly, in 'Fern Hill', the simple-seeming key words 'green' and 'gold(en)' are repeated to create complex shifts of meaning. Green occurs in all six stanzas: it means the colour; 'youthful, growing'; 'naïve, unknowing' (the child has to appear in both senses to the adult speaker); and – on its last appearance ('green and dying') – 'gangrenous, subject to corruption'. 'Golden', which appears in stanzas one, two and five, means both idealised in the memory of the adult speaker and ripe for harvest (Thomas shifts meanings by maintaining an ambiguity about whether 'time' has a lowercase or uppercase 't' – mere temporality or personified Time as a kindlier counterpart to the early poetry's 'Cadaver'). The first meaning of 'gold' indicates the limitations of the adult's viewpoint, just as the first meaning of 'green' indicates those of the child's, for there is no ultimate narrative authority here, unless it is that of 'Time' himself. So, in stanza one, the child is 'Golden in the heydays of his eyes' (with a pun, however, on 'hay-(making) days'), while, in stanza two, he is 'green and golden', because he is gradually becoming subject to 'the process of natural growth, corruption and mortality'. This, in turn, anticipates stanza five, in which all of the 'children green and golden follow him [time] out of grace', as if he were the Pied Piper.

Repetition in 'Fern Hill' also includes cliché, distorted idiom, proverb and nursery rhyme. Thus, the phrase 'heydays of his eyes' comes from 'apple of his eye' – the child being the apple of Time's eye and the overseer of orchards and apple-wagons (the 'apple towns'). 'Young and easy' adapts 'free and easy', making 'young' mean 'free' and thus 'only the young are free', revised by the final line's sense of the invisible 'chains' of time, which held the speaker 'green and dying'. 'Happy as the grass was green' likewise has its source in 'happy as the day was long'; a chilling irony, for, in Alastair Fowler's words, 'the day of grass is not long, and "as for man, his days are as grass"'.[45] The 'golden' warmth of the poem is continually being qualified; it both 'contains and appears to evade' its various tensions and contradictions, between youth and age, innocence and experience, and it does so in the 'inherently double form' of pastoral.

Thomas's later poems often avail themselves of Renaissance models, whose highly wrought, stylised forms endorse such paragrammatic patterning. In 'Fern Hill', the multiple repetitions (of 'green', 'gold' and analogies and tropes [each stanza contains, for example, a musical sound]) offer a tight, circular structure, which, together with the fact that it has six stanzas, give it more than a passing resemblance to a sestina. The similarity is hinted at by the echo in the phrase 'morning songs' of Sidney's double sestina 'Ye Goatherd Gods' and the fact that the last three lines, introduced by a repetition of 'young and easy', separate themselves from the rest of the poem and so resemble a sestina's three-line recapitulatory coda.[46] The best-known example of this kind of model is, of course, the villanelle form of 'Do not go gentle into that good night'. Typically, Thomas exploits the strictness of the form to create a gap between the poem's denotative content and its effect as a speech act. Thus, while its reiterated 'message' is that the father should 'rage' against his fate, showing the cantankerousness with which he lived his life, the poem's rhythms and music are those of a lullaby. This tension appears in the opening lines. 'Do not go gentle into that good night / Old age should burn and rave at close of day', we learn, but the first tercet concedes that: 'wise men ... know dark is right', even though they 'Do not go gentle into that good night'. The successive examples of old men, defined by their qualities in life

– as 'good', 'wild' and 'grave' – resist in the same way, asserting their individual qualities at the end, true to the poem's Yeatsian terms of tragic gaiety and rage; resignation would be a betrayal. Even so, the repetition of 'go gentle' reminds us of the common wisdom, which is that of the 'wise men', that 'dark is right'. 'Good night' does not only mean farewell, but acknowledges that the 'night' of death is ultimately a 'good' – a natural and fitting conclusion to life. The son's use of the phrase betrays his understanding of its rightness. His plea that his father ought not to 'go gentle' is shown to be an understandable, but unnatural, one, rooted in his own fear of death and a desire to see it outfaced. His final plea to 'Curse, bless, me now with your fierce tears' brings the doubleness of the poem to a climax; a 'curse' would be a 'blessing', because the speaker wants his father to 'rage', but its oxymoronic quality brilliantly enacts a loss of poise and bewilderment in the face of death. Despite its apparent simplicity, 'Do not go gentle' creates complex linguistic and emotional cruxes by worrying at simple material – in this case, the cliché of the good or peaceful death.

Leon S. Roudiez's definition of the paragram cited by Julia Kristeva in *Revolution in Poetic Language* runs: 'A text is paragrammatic … in the sense that its organization of words (and their denotations), grammar and syntax is challenged by the infinite possibilities provided by letters or phonemes combining to form networks of significance not accessible through conventional reading habits'.[47] Or, as Steve McCaffery puts it: 'The percolation of language through the paragram contaminates the notion of an ideal, unitary meaning and thereby counters the supposition that words can "fix" or stabilize in closure. Paragrammatic wordplay manufactures a crisis within semantic economy, for whilst engendering meanings, the paragram also turns unitary meaning against itself'.[48] The seemingly fluid, but actually highly restrictive, forms of the later poems generate networks of 'contamination', but they do so unassertively, through repetition, rather than explosive metaphoric, paronomasic and appositive densities. The poems exploit 'paragramatic path[s] … determined by the local indications of a words' own spatio-phonic connotations', creating a 'centrifuge in which the verbal centre is itself scattered', but Thomas's 'scattering' is incremental and subtle, as in the repetition of 'Thief' in 'In country sleep', or the way that 'child', 'sound', 'bed', 'care', and so on function as the paragrammatic 'flow-producing agents' in the syntactic economy of 'The conversation of prayers', preventing standard grammar from asserting full control by 'inscribing themselves among that other economy whose notion of word (as a fixed, double articulation of signifier / signified) upholds the functional distributions of a presentation'.

Canonical miscegenation and pastoral

Before looking in more detail at these final works, I wish to briefly examine the sense in which Thomas's use of reference, allusion and citation might be said to follow his pastoral turn and his spatially dispersed, seemingly more transparent, style. Trying to describe the later poetry's texture, G. S. Fraser spoke of a 'rapid and muscular fluency that puts one in mind sometime of a more relaxed Hopkins, sometimes of a more concentrated Swinburne'.[49] But rather than identifying any dominant 'influence', it might be better to call the effect 'anthologistic'; it is rather like reading a radically boiled down and reduced Palgrave's *Golden Treasury*. Unlike the early poems, in which intertexts are buried deep, we get full-on allusions, which are intended to be picked up at once or almost at once. Reading 'Fern Hill', for example, thoughts of the 'Immortality Ode' and 'Tintern Abbey' are unavoidable. Thomas also quoted Lawrence's little-known 'Ballad of Another Ophelia' when discussing the poem in a letter to Oscar Williams, but they have only apples in common; and Lawrence's are either 'bitter' or 'brackish' (*CL*, 622). Typically, he says nothing about 'swallow thronged loft' alluding to 'To Autumn's 'gathering swallows' or how his sun and 'lilting house' recall Hood's 'I remember, I remember'. Thomas has made 'dingle' seem Welsh, so well-known is his usage in 'Fern Hill', but his source is probably Arnold's pastorals 'The Scholar Gypsy' ('listen with enchanted ears, / From dark dingles to the nightingales') and 'Thyrsis' ('many a dingle on the loved hill-side'), as well as W. H. Auden's 'Doom is darker and deeper than any sea-dingle'. This is to say nothing of Metaphysical intertexts, which include Thomas Traherne's *Centuries of Meditations* and Henry Vaughan's 'The Retreat', or allusions to nursery rhymes and works of children's literature, such as Kenneth Grahame's *The Golden Age*. Invoking and echoing such multifarious sources, Thomas nevertheless effortlessly absorbs them all within his own idiom, dissolving any potential anxiety of influence into fluent praise and lament.

This tactic is closely related to the talent for mimicry and pastiche.[50] 'In my craft or sullen art' and 'Do not go gentle', for example, are almost-but-not-quite Yeats; the old men and their 'raging' against the 'dying of the light' recall the wild and wicked old men of Yeats's late lyrics, as does their lexis. 'In my craft' uses a Yeatsian short-line lyric form and its indifferent young lovers recall those of Yeats's 'Politics', purloining its final word, 'arms', for use in a wartime context. Further evidence of Thomas's efforts to inhabit, in order to write out of, and away from, Yeats is found in archive materials held at the University of Austin in Texas, which include convincing imitations of Crazy Jane period lyrics:

> An old man or a young man,
> And I am none of these,
> Goes down upon the praying mat
> And kneels on his knuckled knees
> Whenever a fine lady
> Does his poor body good.
> And if she gives him beauty
> Or a cure for his hot blood,
> He weeps like one of the willow trees
> That stands in a grave wood. (*SP2*, 99)

The ability to get so close to the original enabled Thomas, unlike Vernon Watkins or the young Philip Larkin, to use Yeats's style without being swamped by it; 'sullen' deftly deflates the Yeatsian tone from within, by signalling a maturely self-deprecating consciousness alien to its heroic posturing. As well as Yeats in Thoor Ballylee, 'In my craft' alludes to other canonical tower-dwelling antecedents, including Shelley's solitary Platonist and the scholar of Milton's 'Il penseroso'. All the later poems deliberately court charges of imitation at some point; thus, lines from 'In country sleep' ('And high, there, on the hare-/Heeled winds …') and from 'Over Sir John's hill' ('the gulled birds hare / To the hawk on fire … / In a whack of wind') both ask to be compared with Hopkins's 'The Windhover'. A particularly complex example occurs in the final stanza of 'Over Sir John's hill', in which 'Only a hoot owl / Hollows, a grassblade blown in cupped hands, in the looted elms'. This absorbs Wordsworth's 'There was a boy!', in which the boy, 'both hands / Press'd closely, palm to palm … Blew mimic hootings to the silent owl / That they might answer him'. The boy, we learn at the end of the poem, is dead, and the allusion deepens the elegiac tone of Thomas's poem. But also, in reversing the call by making it come from the owl and imagining the owl itself blowing a 'grassblade', Thomas offers a paradigm of the mimic methods of the later poems. 'Over Sir John's hill' mimics a poem about mimicry; it is art that seems to be imitating nature (the owl), by representing it imitating art (Wordsworth's boy) imitating nature (the owls in Wordsworth's poem). In this *mise en abyme*, as in the syntactical contortions of 'In country sleep', it is difficult, if not impossible, to tell who is mimicking who, what is 'real' and what is a copy (*CP*, 141, 143, 144).

'A Winter's Tale', of course, borrows the title of a Shakespeare play, which is both a canonical instance of pastoral and similarly concludes with a woman bringing a man back to life. Thomas, however, literalises the title in his snowy landscape (Shakespeare's usage is more proverbial than seasonal) and makes the main canonical presence not Shakespeare, but Keats, commonly regarded as the most Shakespearian English poet (and thus another kind of mimic). The landscape or snowscape of the poem is Keatsian from the outset: that of the 'Bright star' sonnet, with its 'new, soft-fallen mask / Of snow upon the mountains and the moors' and, above all, 'The Eve of St Agnes'. Thomas unabashedly shepherds Keats's owl ... a-cold, 'flock in woolly fold' and 'patient, holy man' into the opening of his poem.[51] Later, in Thomas's 'nightingale ...[that] flies on the grains of her wings', Keats's supreme symbol of poetry is winged by process, as cliché is given an uncanny aspect and the complex is put into the simple (*CP*, 100). The fate of Thomas's hermit blends those of Keats's 'beadsman' and lovers – the hermit's union with the 'she-bird' is an expiration 'among ... ashes cold' *and* a sexual 'solution sweet'.[52]

Both unions are ambiguous, nevertheless: Keats's, notoriously, verges on rape, while it is left unclear whether the transfiguring fusion with the she-bird in 'the whirl-/ Pool at the wanting centre' is hypothermic delusion or mystic vision (it is both of these at once, too).[53] It is at this point that the most striking parallel, with Yeats's 'Leda and the Swan', is drawn, but reversed:

> And through the thighs of the engulfing bride,
> The woman breasted and the heaven headed
>
> > Bird, he was brought low,
> Burning in the bride bed of love, in the whirl-
> Pool at the wanting centre, in the folds
> Of paradise, in the spun bud of the world.
> And she rose with him flowering in her melting snow. (*CP*, 103)

Zeus, the descending swan-rapist, is turned into the ascending and 'heaven headed / Bird', whose vulva's 'bud' and 'folds' overcome Yeatsian phallogocentrism, this being recast in a verbally expansive, redemptive vision of an empowered and active feminine principle.

It was by such means that Thomas set up a new kind of relationship with canonical predecessors in the English and Anglo-Welsh traditions.[54] I have used terms such as 'allusion' and 'echoing' to describe this, but neither is quite right. Thomas does not ironically (or reverently) frame quotations or mimic the *topoi* or verbal formulations of other poets in a straightforward way. Rather, his new paragrammatic style is used to contain and simultaneously diffuse the material he alludes to. The results are neither pastiche nor parody, neither outright tribute nor critique, although elements of all of these occur. Success is measured by the degree to which such potent material can be incorporated, without being swamped.

But why do it in the first place? Like 'Fern Hill' in James A. Davies's reading, the later poems are 'interstitial' in Homi Bhabha's sense; located by Thomas at the interface between one literature and another and defining themselves in relation to external texts and canons. By embedding Anglo-Welsh poetry in the English canon and vice versa, and deconstructing the pretensions of both to be discrete entities, Thomas, in effect, forges a new hybrid – a public poetry based on the pastoral of wide and enduring appeal. In 'A Winter's Tale', Keats, Yeats and Eliot contradictorily conjure up lush Romanticism and anti-Romantic modernism, paganism and Christianity, florid and spare styles, feminine softness and masculine hardness. As a result, the reader's footing is uncertain; s/he is forced to understand the poems comparatively, in relation to overlapping traditions that exist 'on what might be called poetical marches, like the Welsh Marches ... a site of cultural forces which are often in tension yet which combine and create as much as they compete and cancel out'.[55] This 'marcher' quality is one of the reasons why critics have been nonplussed by it, particularly in recent years, when internal British borders have been drawn with increasing sharpness.

For some Welsh critics, these poems sell out Wales, because they make Anglo-Welsh literature subservient to the English tradition. James A. Davies, in contrast, endorses the idea that 'Fern Hill' 'draws its main positive strength ... from its links with the greater tradition, with English literature's version and Eliot's "ideal order"'.[56] But both positions ignore Thomas's rejection of 'tradition' in these fixed senses and his playful exposure of the heterogeneity of the 'English' canon's wholeness and continuity, as well as the Anglo-Welsh lack of 'greatness'. Thomas's love of English canonical poetry is clear enough, but his semi-assimilated display of it is intended to signal the extreme impactedness of Wales and England. Difference, underwritten by Thomas's unique style, is set beside uncanny mimicry, for if he draws on English poetry's ideal order, he suffuses it with bardic *hwyl*, Celtic lyricism and a simulacrum of the medieval Welsh tradition of the praise-poem, with its quasi-visionary apprehension of the created world. Performing elements of English *and* Welsh 'identity', the result is a non-assertive regionalism or, in Bakhtinian terms, poetry which 'has no sovereign internal territory, [being] wholly on and always on the boundary' – a miscegenation of English and Anglo-Welshness, which mischievously hints at their inseparability.[57]

Cold War pastoral: *In Country Heaven*

Thomas's pastoral turn reflects the threat of nuclear war and the possibility of the annihilation of all life on the planet, for by 1947, the 'still hour' of 'A Refusal to Mourn' had become an imagined post-World War Three 'whirlwind silence' in 'In country sleep'. Thomas was by no means alone among post-war British poets in developing some kind of 'Cold War pastoral' or ecological-ruralist response to this threat. Lynette Roberts, for instance, noted that: 'basic rural cultures, earth rhythms ... [are] what we will be forced back to if that atom war arises'.[58] The 'Prologue' that Thomas wrote to introduce his *Collected Poems* in 1952 may be seen as an apocalyptic form of such a pastoral; in it, the narrator presents himself as a 'moonshine / Drinking Noah', offering his book as an 'ark' to ride out the flood of 'molten fear' created by the 'cities of nine / Days' night whose towers will catch / In the religious wind / Like stalks of tall, dry straw' (*CP*, 1). Such changes are one of the contexts for the splendidly mixed, ambitious and canonically miscegenatory *In Country Heaven* sequence which, as Walford Davies and Ralph Maud have shown, developed from an uncompleted pastoral *ur*-poem, titled 'In Country Heaven', which Thomas wrote in March mid-1947, but which he abandoned and quarried for the three completed poems we now have (*CP*, 259–63). This is how Thomas presented them in a broadcast of 25 September 1950:

> These three poems will, one day, form separate parts of a long poem which is in preparation ... The poem is to be called 'In Country Heaven'. The godhead, the author, the milky-way farmer, the first cause, architect, lamplighter, quintessence, the beginning Word, the anthropomorphic bawler-out and blackballer, the stuff of all men, scapegoat, martyr, maker, woe-bearer – He, on top of a hill in Heaven, weeps whenever, outside that state of being called his country, one of his worlds drops dead, vanishes screaming, shrivels, explodes, murders itself. And when he weeps, Light and His tears glide down together, hand in hand. So, at the beginning of the projected poem, he weeps, and Country Heaven is suddenly dark. Bushes and owls blow out like sparks. And the countrymen of heaven crouch all together under the hedges

and, among themselves in the tear-salt darkness, surmise which world, which star, which of their late, turning homes, in the skies has gone for ever. And this time, spreads the heavenly hedgerow rumour, it is the Earth. The Earth has killed itself. It is black, petrified, wizened, poisoned, burst; insanity has blown it rotten; and no creatures at all, joyful, despairing, cruel, kind, dumb, afire, loving, dull, no creatures at all shortly and brutishly hunt their days down like enemies on that corrupted face. And, one by one, these heavenly hedgerow-men, who once were of Earth, call one another, through the long night, Light and His tears falling, what they remember, what they sense in the submerged wilderness and on the exposed hairsbreadth of the mind, what they feel on the trembling on the nerves of a nerve, what they know in their Edenie hearts, of that self-killed place. They remember places, fears, loves, exultation, misery, animal joy, ignorance, and mysteries, all *we* know and don't know ... The poem is made of these tellings. And the poem becomes, at last, an affirmation of the beautiful and terrible worth of the Earth. It grows into a praise of what is and what could be on this lump in the skies. It is a poem about happiness...

The remembered tellings, which are the components of the poem, are not all told as they are remembered, are not all told as though they are remembered; the poem will not be a series of poems in the present tense. The memory, in all tenses, can look towards the future, can caution and admonish. The rememberer may live himself back into active participation in the remembered scene, adventure, or spiritual condition. (*TB*, *224–26*)

The blend of pastoral, secular religiosity, sci-fi and anticipatory memory (its tense is the future anterior: 'will have been') is typical of the unstable generic mix of Thomas's later writing. Haunting it is the very real possibility, with the nuclear arms race in full swing, of the world being 'blown rotten'.[59] The late 1940s saw tension between the Soviet Union and the US ratcheting up, with potential flashpoints in Berlin, Greece, China and elsewhere. In the US, the House Un-American Activities Committee and MacCarthyite red-baiting and witch-hunting were in full swing. In 1950, the Korean War started, with Thomas describing liberty as 'something to do with what Our Side gives to people after it has napalmed them' in a letter to the American poet Oscar Williams in 1952 (*CL*, 938). His correspondence echoed the paranoid international climate, darkly (as at the time of the execution of the Rosenbergs, for example) or with a self-protective flippancy (he dismissed an unproductive period as 'two months when there was nothing in my head but a little Nagasaki, all low and hot') (*CL*, 1005, 639). Even rural West Wales offered no escape, as nearby Pendine became a missile-testing range,

with its explosions audible in Laugharne. Thus, 'Poem on his birthday'
is also a self-elegy; it 'celebrates' *and* 'spurns' the anniversary, surrounded
by devouring nature, which 'tast[es] the flesh of [its] own death', just as
the speaker is 'afraid' of the same process among humanity, with 'his
own fiery end in the cloud of an atomic explosion', '[h]is death lurk[ing]
for him, and for all, in the next lunatic war' (*CP*, 254). '[T]omorrow
weeps in a blind cage / Terror will rage apart / Before chains break to
hammer flame', because:

> ... the rocketing wind will blow
> The bones out of the hills,
> And the scythed boulders bleed, and the last
> Rage shattered waters kick
> Masts and fishes to the still quick stars ... (*CP*, 145, 146)

And yet, at the same time, this poem and *In Country Heaven* are 'about
happiness'. In the midst of the possible annihilation of all sentient
beings that inhabit it, the planet continues to have a 'beautiful', as well
as a 'terrible', worth, and it is the unnerving blend of the two which
constitutes the sublime in these later poems. As a sequence *In Country
Heaven* explores the paradoxical pitch to which their contradictions push
the process poetic, its future anterior setting framing and justifying
an unembarrassed celebration of the natural world – something only
possible as an idealised, post-atomic memory. All three poems reflect the
impossible conditions of their existence by dramatising both a desire to
believe *and* the simultaneous impossibility of believing.

'In country sleep' uses the bedtime stories told by a father to his
daughter as its occasion. 'My father would often read to me', Aeronwy
Thomas recalled, 'We both favoured *Grimm's Fairy Tales*. He would
enact the main characters becoming the wolf or ... child, giving credible
characteristics of evil and good. We both relished the thrill of horror and
fear'.[60] The father draws on fairy tale imagery at first, in order to offer
adult reassurance against such fears:

> Never and never, my girl riding far and near
> In the land of the hearthstone tales, and spelled asleep,
> Fear or believe that the wolf in a sheepwhite hood
> Loping and bleating roughly and blithely shall leap,
>   My dear, my dear,
> Out of a lair in the flocked leaves in the dew dipped year
> To eat out your heart in the house in the rosy wood. (*CP*, 139)

The 'girl' learns that the pastoral world of the tales is unthreatening, even holy: the 'fables graze / On the lord's table of the bowing grass', and she is told to 'Sleep spelled at rest'. But the father has already asked the apparently rhetorical question 'For who unmanningly haunts the mountain ravened eaves / Or skulks in the dell moon ...?' In his excessive wish to reassure his daughter, he now lets slip that she should 'Fear most / For ever not the wolf in his baaing hood ... but the Thief as meek as the dew' (CP, 140, 139, 140). This shadowy, ambiguous figure echoes the warning of I Thessalonians 5:2 ('For yourselves know perfectly that the day of the Lord so cometh as a thief in the night'), the use of the term 'meek' ('gentle Jesus meek and mild') suggesting that he is Christ. However, the insistence on 'Thief' seems more Satan-like, and he seems more like a natural force than either, likened at the end of the first of the poem's two sections to falling dew, apple-seed, snow and stars. Before this point, the father has moved from his suggestion that acknowledging that 'the country is holy' will deter the Thief, to a recognition of the inevitability of his coming: 'Yet out of the beaked, web dark and the pouncing boughs / Be you sure the Thief will seek a way sly and sure ... This night and each vast night ... my own, lost love'; indeed, that 'Ever and ever he finds a way' 'since ... you were born'. The final image of part I of the poem is of the Thief 'finding a way ... As the world falls, silent as the cyclone of silence' (CP, 140).

Part II, quoted at the beginning of this chapter, consists of a series of no less than sixteen exclamatory statements – a list of fairy tale and pastoral properties, which 'All tell, this night, of him / Who comes as red as the fox and as sly as the heeled wind' (CP, 141). Pastoral and child's tale, earlier a kind of bulwark against the Thief, are now confessing that they bear witness to him and his inevitable coming. The speaker senses that, in some way, the sleeper draws the Thief to her, in a passage in which the tortuousness enacts the difficulty with which he arrives at this conclusion:

Earth, air, water, fire, singing into the white act,

The haygold haired, my love asleep, and the rift blue
Eyed, in the haloed house, in her rareness and hilly
High riding, held and blessed and true, and so stilly
                    Lying the sky
Might cross its planets, the bell weep, night gather her eyes,
The Thief fall on the dead like the willy nilly dew,

Only for the turning of the earth in her holy
Heart! (CP, 141–142)

Here, the main condition of what is being recounted, the clause beginning 'Only', disorientatingly falls at the very end of the sentence: it means 'If it were not for …' or 'but for'. If we place it at the start of the sentence, we get a subordinate clause, which runs from 'Earth, air, water …' to 'Lying' and states how the natural world 'lies' 'in' the 'rareness' of the girl' in her keeping. (This clause has its own subordinate clause: 'my love asleep … and so stilly lying'.) The object of the opening clause is what follows after 'Lying'. It therefore runs: 'If it were not for the earth turning in her holy heart, earth, air etc., "held" in her "rareness", then "the sky might cross its planets", the stern death-knell would weep, the night would "gather her eyes", and the Thief might "fall on the dead like the willy nilly dew"'. That is, without the girl's care, the natural order would be overturned. It isn't, though, and, as a result, the Thief can hear 'the wound in her side' and comes to her. Her care for the world has drawn the Thief to her.

Yet he 'Comes designed to my love to steal not her tide raking / Wound, nor her riding high, nor her eyes, nor kindled hair' (that is, to steal neither her sexual innocence, nor her attributes of beauty), but:

> … her faith that each vast night and the saga of prayer
> He comes to take
> Her faith that this last night for his unsacred sake
> He comes to leave her in the lawless sun awaking
>
> Naked and forsaken to grieve he will not come. (*CP*, 142)

This explanation of what the Thief actually *does* come to take emerges from an extraordinarily self-modifying, Russian doll-like concatenation of negatives.[61] We learn – or, rather, it now dawns on the speaker – that the girl has 'faith' in the Thief coming to take her faith – that 'faith' being that he comes to make her grieve that he will not come. Thus, the core of her faith is in the Thief's ability to make her grieve for him not coming, and, unravelling this, we realise that the key word in the passage is one at its opening, which initially seemed superfluous: 'designed'. It means 'has designs on', but the speaker now sees that the Thief's predation is desired by his daughter and that this is part of a 'design' of her own, whereby faith can only exist through the process of being threatened, in which the daughter has to collude. It is in the nature of perfection and innocence, we might say, to attract that which wants to steal or spoil it. More, it actively encourages or creates that agent. The Thief is not malicious, then, so much as part of the natural (unnatural) order of things, and that order is paradoxical. The result is another *mis en abyme* moment. Christ, as thief, and the Devil, as saviour – the unwilling and willing victim – predator and victim exchanging places. The inter-involvement is complete. By the end of the poem, the speaker's fear has come to be that the girl will lose her fear. There are some notes summarising this final section in the mss held in Texas:

> If you believe (and fear) that every night, night without end, the Thief comes to try to steal your faith that every night he comes to steal your faith that your faith is there – then you will wake with your faith steadfast and deathless.

> If you are innocent of the Thief, you are in danger. If you are innocent of the loss of faith, you cannot be faithful. If you do not know the Thief as well as you know God, then you do not know God well. Christian looked through a hole in the floor of heaven and saw hell. You must look through faith and see disbelief. (*CP*, 251–2)

If you wake without having had your faith tested, then you really are bereft, naked in the 'lawless sun'. As long as the Thief keeps coming to try to steal her faith, and she has faith in the fact that he will keep coming and keep trying to do so, so she will keep her faith in life. In the prose passage, like the poem itself, Thomas's punctuation and patterns of repetition are chosen in order to make it difficult to grasp the thought ('comes to try to steal your faith that every night he comes to steal your faith that your faith is there'), thus enacting its paradoxical quality. 'In country sleep', then, sees life as only fully realised when deliberately jeopardised.

The paradoxicality of 'In country sleep' has a source in the overlap between classical pastoral, Christ's dual rôle as both the Good Shepherd and the sacrificial Lamb of God. He protects the lamb, is father to his flock – humanity – but is, at the same time, himself a lamb-like victim. Thomas uses this image cluster a good deal in the later poems. The exalted and apocalyptic last lines of the first part of 'In country sleep' evoke Christ-in-Man ('the yawning wound at our sides'), and the fiery judgement he seems about to visit upon himself suggests one of the meanings of the 'Thief' is atomic war falling upon the sleeping child as ineluctably

> ... as the star falls, as the winged
> Apple seed glides,
> And falls, and flowers in the yawning wound at our sides,
> As the world falls, silent as the cyclone of silence. (*CP*, 140)

At the end of the second section – the conclusion of the poem – the child is told: 'you shall wake, from country sleep, this dawn and each first dawn, / Your faith as deathless as the outcry of the ruled sun' (*CP*, 142). This contrasts with 'the lawless sun' of five lines before, indicating the sun's ungovernability. 'Lawless' and 'ruled' operate in an ambiguous relationship to each other, telling of the ungovernability of the sun as such (it is outside human law), but of human mastery of its processes, which have recently been harnessed ('ruled') for destructive ('lawless') ends. The sun's response is an 'outcry' against such perversion of its natural activity of *fostering* life on earth (*CP*, 142). The 'sun' is also the 'son' of a non-existent God – Christ is 'ruled' by God, but among his last 'outcries' ('Father, father, why hast thou forsaken me?') is a protest against divine 'ruling' (the sentiment of 'Before I knocked'). The allusion emphasises that this is a world in which man's powers have become god-like, while supernatural control or sanction over them has ceased to exist.

The other major late poems employ similar exalted, yet annihilatory, apocalyptic imagery. In the 'mansouled, fiery islands' of the last stanza of 'Poem on his birthday', we see not just cockle-pickers silhouetted on the mudflats of the Towy estuary, but those other 'fiery islands' (*CP*, 147) – Bikini, Eniwetok, Elugelab, Monte Bello – of the Pacific test ranges. And, following its long inventory of Hardyesque rural properties, 'In the White Giant's Thigh' also ends with an ambiguous image, which is at once transcendence and immolation: 'And the daughters of darkness flame like Fawkes fires still'.

The paradox of faith in humanity, which takes the form of negation of a negation, is illustrated most dramatically in 'Over Sir John's hill', which is both doomily and playfully eschatological. It is saturated with religious terms and alludes to Matthew 10:29's assurance of God's knowledge of even the death of a sparrow. More than the other poems of *In Country Heaven*, it seems a posthumous remembrance according to Thomas's schema, with its apparently blatant religious dimension framed as an issue of faith in the vitalism of the natural world. It originates in the conceit of the small 'gulled birds' seeming to will their own deaths, because they fly upwards, out of safety, when the hawk appears above them. From this anthromorphising observation derives the 'hangman' hawk, who executes 'sparrows and such', on which the 'just hill', wearing its 'black cap of jack- / Daws', has passed sentence. In turn, an allegorical landscape unfolds, within which the 'leaves of the water' can be opened 'at a passage / Of psalms and shadows', and 'Death' may be 'read in a shell' (*CP*, 143, 142, 143). Christian pantheism beckons, but 'shadows' qualify 'psalms', and the 'young Aesop' narrator offers something more like process in the form of elaborate pathetic fallacy – a *paysage moralisé*.

One source for Thomas's interest in faith was the 1940s Christian revival, as discussed in Chapter 4. Thomas, I argued there, did not modify his focus on first and last things, and actually intensified his use of religious imagery; yet this was at odds with the revival's conservatism. In 'Over Sir John's hill', it could be argued that the perpetual destruction of the natural cycle naturalises the threat of nuclear extinction that we detect in the poem and that this reflects on man's inherent wickedness. However, this is contested to the degree that man himself is part of nature. Man's problem is that he projects his crises onto the natural world and so, falsely, naturalises them. Thus, the hawk resembles a bomber with a payload – 'his viperish fuse hangs looped with flames under the brand / Wing' – and nature is both menaced and suffused by the threat. God, too, dwells in a 'whirlwind silence', which is that of the Bomb, like the 'cyclone silence' of 'In country sleep'. Nature and God are both anthropomorphic constructs. But the ethical conclusion which is drawn is not that they are subordinate to a dominative logic or should be rejected; on the contrary, both, as aspects of the fully human, require care. Against destruction, in 'Prologue' Thomas offers his 'flock' of poems rescued, Noah-like, from the rhetorical 'flood ... Of fear, rage red, manalive', in all after it; his Cold War apocalyptic pastorals he 'toils towards the ambush of his wounds' and an aspirational 'blessed, unborn God and His Ghost' in 'young Heaven's fold' (*CP*, 2). God is 'fabulous' and 'dear', awe-inspiring, but a fable, cherished, but costly, whose light is at once 'unknown' and 'famous'. This is a paradoxical reworking of Unitarianism, in which the speaker prays 'Faithlessly unto Him', confusing himself with God by referring to both in the third person – an unbelieving believer among pagan 'druid herons' (*CP*, 146).

Thus, the 'dilly dilly' that the birds sing in 'Over Sir John's hill' echoes 'Dylan' and thereby implicates him as with the unheeding prey, as well as the predator. But he is more accurately, we come to see, the heron, a mourner given to 'grieve' and 'tell-tale the knelled / Guilt' of the birds 'for their souls' song' – 'guilt', because of their ignorance and complicity – and it is this 'tell-tale' activity, necessary in an amoral universe, which is the true subject of the poem, and which supplies its conclusion:

> Through windows
> Of dusk and water I see the tilting whispering
>
> Heron, mirrored, go,
> As the snapt feathers snow,

Fishing in the tear of the Towy. Only a hoot owl
Hollows, a grassblade blown in cupped hands, in the looted elms,
And no green cocks or hens
Shout
Now on Sir John's hill. The heron, ankling the scaly
Lowlands of the waves,
Makes all the music; and I who hear the tune of the slow,
Wear-willow river, grave,
Before the lunge of night, the notes on this time-shaken
Stone for the sake of the souls of the slain birds sailing. (*CP*, 144)

The claim, untrue in a salvational sense, but true in an aesthetic one, is that he makes the 'grave[d] stone' (gravestone) of the poem out of the 'elegiac' heron's cry 'for the sake of the souls of the slain birds'. The heron is the mourner of the victims of the natural world from within it – an intermediary, who leaves the speaker to passively record his 'music' as a lyrical-elegiac trace in a universe which neither heron, nor heron-identified poet, can do more than 'fable' in a superannuated religious language. 'Over Sir John's hill' is a 'swansing' for the singing of swansongs – an elegy for the elegiac, as well as an elegy proper.

The self-sacrificial stance that Thomas adopted in WWII is no longer tenable. Even as a cipher for faith, the Son has been overshadowed by the manmade sun of the nuclear fireball. All humanity has become a potential sacrifice to the same energy, which is the source of all life on earth, and pastoral offers itself in these conditions as a traditional way of integrating, without harmfully assimilating, opposed forces, and so, of absorbing threat. But it has a desperate edge, because the natural world's red in tooth-and-claw Darwinian cycle now seems to point to, even belong to, a holocaust which would far exceed it. The pastoral juxtaposition of celebratory, healing art and the violence of war erupt most glaringly at the opening of part II of 'In country sleep', with its 'dingle torn to singing'. There is nothing meliorist or conventional about the balance this presents; the nuclear threat poses a violent challenge to the poem's pastoral logic, but there is also the suggestion that the natural properties enumerated here celebrate the violence and drive towards self-killing. Nature anticipates, may even strain towards, a post-human, post-pastoral, in which the worst has happened. Yet Thomas's style now offers nature as a construct, embodying our sense of its vulnerability to human destructiveness, exacerbating an ecological awareness. Sentiment, pastoral plenitude and violent threat are brought together in a manner that forces us to: 'confront [our] own implication in humanity's disastrous aesthetic attraction to dominative thought'.[62]

According to this reading, the stylised violence of the later poems is an attempt to both incorporate human violence. In Richard Chamberlain's words, the natural world and reveal it as unnatural; 'the natural world thus appears as a source of connective epiphanies, yet also as a dangerous bower which tempts us to embrace mystifying political ideologies'.[63] This engagement with the Cold War, then, is not merely thematic. The poems trace the contours of a larger crisis in post-war writing; namely, how literature, as previously conceived, can happen at all. Both the atrocities of war and the fact that humanity was now capable of destroying itself had undermined traditional humanist values. Although its verbal lushness, makes it very different from the pared-back minimalism of Samuel Beckett, Louis MacNeice and William Golding,' Thomas's later work joins theirs in its use of allegory and negative theology to reflect a crisis in writing and representation.

The Blitz anti-elegies had attempted to find ways to represent the unrepresentable or, more accurately, to represent its unrepresentability. From its inception, then, the late style was a search for ways of saying the new forms of the unsayable. As Thomas noted in a radio broadcast on the poetry of Wilfred Owen recorded 19 June 1946:

> At this time, when, in the words of an American critic, the audiences of the earth, witnessing what may well be the last act of their own tragedy, insist upon chief actors who are senseless enough to perform a cataclysm, the voice of the poetry of Wilfred Owen speaks to us, down the revolving stages of thirty years, with terrible new significance and strength. We had not forgotten his poetry, but perhaps we had allowed ourselves to think of it as the voice of one particular time, one place, one war. Now, at the beginning of what, in the future, may never be known to historians as the 'atomic age' – for obvious reasons: there may be no historians – we can see, re-reading Owen, that he is a poet of all times, all places, all wars. (TB, 95)

Thomas's point foreshadows Jacques Derrida's argument, that there is no choice about the actual narration of nuclear apocalypse, since it is: 'a phenomenon whose essential feature is that of being *fabulously textual*, through and through'.[64] For Derrida, as for Thomas, literary responses to the threat are always deeply ambiguous, reluctant to represent annihilation, not so much out of unwillingness to confront it, but because of a desire to contain it. For many, even more reluctant than Thomas, it was as if, having become historical, such horror had to be kept silent, in order to prevent habituation to it. Furthermore, the very idea of a nuclear war was, in a profound sense, simply unwritable; there will be nowhere to write from, no-one to write *to*, no-one to write in such an eventuality – and so the unspeakable demands representation by other means.

The paradoxical aspect of nuclear holocaust arises from the fact that it can only be adequately represented in fable and fiction. Because it will destroy all records by which it might persist or come into being in the future, it can only ever be known in advance 'in projections, predictions, and premonitory narratives', in Steven Connor's words. A terminal event, which stands outside the continuum of history and narrative, insofar as it signals the obliteration of these, it can paradoxically only ever be signalled by, and within, narrative itself; thus, 'The intimate proximity of the end of the world which has characterised life since the end of the Second World War, making this period of history qualitatively different from that of any other ... means the habituation of a double-bind in which we simultaneously must and must not narrate a kind of absolute ending that we anyway both cannot and cannot not narrate'.[65] Though Thomas's response was pastoral, rather than parabolic, verbal exfoliation, rather than minimalism, it complemented, rather than contradicted those of his contemporaries; his poems of excess, artifice and repetition generate anxiety about the fact of writing and the limits of language, around which narrative organises itself, dramatising the desire to believe and the impossibility of believing ('cannot and cannot not narrate').

Thomas and the culture industry

Thomas's relation to the canon, like his style, changed during wartime and with his own increased canonical prominence. His 1930s audience had consisted of small, self-constituted elite of poetry readers, who were trained in the exacting techniques of close analysis demanded by modernist writing. Most were not only accustomed to, but demanded, a degree of formal and linguistic innovation, and he had ably fulfilled (and exploited) such expectations. Although war brought about a temporary convergence between modernism and tradition in the form of neo-Romanticism, this audience and its milieu ebbed away during the later 1940s. Moreover, as the war ended in 1945, revelation of the horror of the modern barbarism of the Nazi death camps undermined the European avant-garde's self-confidence in modernity and its sense of a pioneering role.[66] The pretensions of the project of modernity, for many, ended in the ashes of Auschwitz and Belsen. Donald Davie used the example of Ezra Pound to link a dehumanised concern with formalism and inhuman totalitarianism in *The Purity of Diction in English Verse* (1952), and to advocate his native, empirical, conservative 'tradition'.

From 1944 on Thomas tried to forge new means by which to figure poetry's linguistic excess, as well as accommodating an audience both shocked and sensitised by the war. One of his responses to the fragmenting literary sphere was to move away from strictly literary genres, and this propelled him towards a degree of media involvement which would be unmatched by any other British poet of the period. Thomas would write radio features, film scripts and television pieces, while his US readings also led to him making recordings for the just-founded Caedmon Records during his 1952 tour. These became hugely successful after his death, effectively laying the basis for the spoken word LP industry in the US. The degree of Thomas's involvement in various mass media forms makes his writing particularly susceptible to readings based on the analyses of mid-century popular culture by Theodor Adorno, Max Horkheimer and, somewhat later, Marshall McLuhan.

Adorno's work of the late 1930s and *Dialectic of Enlightenment* (1943), co-written with Horkheimer, analyses the baleful effects of modernity, identifying the emergence from Enlightenment attempts to demystify nature and myth of an unreasoning, positivist will to power. While technological rationality led 'from the slingshot to the megaton bomb', according to their study, there was no equivalent history leading from savagery to humanitarianism. In Nazi Germany, as a result, perverted rationality had led to a totalitarian administered society and the catastrophe of war and holocaust; in the liberal democracies, an equivalent repressive integration was accomplished, not politically, in fascism, but through the 'culture industry' – a consummation of kitsch and degraded technical rationality, by which leisure time was absorbed and administered, and the masses manipulated and pacified with the products of Hollywood, commercial radio and television and Tin Pan Alley. This repressive unification of 'free' time, along the same lines of exchange and equivalence that reigned in the sphere of production (where one of its contemporary forms is 'micro-management'), increased the domination of the values of consumer capitalism.[67]

For Adorno, however, the relationship between modernist high art and industrially produced consumer art was a dialectical one, in which neither side was wholly 'right' or 'wrong'. Both kinds of art, he famously pronounced, 'bear the stigmata of capitalism, and both contain elements of change (though never, of course, the middle term between Schönberg and the American film). Both are halves of an integral freedom, to which, however, they do not add up'.[68] What are central are the 'dialectical entwinement of high and low art' and the way that they form a 'broken unity', consisting of 'the illusory universality of mass art and the abstract, restricted particularity of autonomous art'. It is within the force field of this 'broken unity' that such different works as *Deaths and Entrances* and *Under Milk Wood* have to be viewed, in order to make more complete sense as the products of one writer, and to grasp the nature of the predicament that Thomas faced, balancing, as he did, between an earlier habit of solitary poetic composition and the more profitable role of public entertainer.

This was not an easy balance to strike, although Adorno's baleful reading of mass culture has to be set against more positive ones, such as that offered in Walter Benjamin's 'The Work of Art in an Age of Mechanical Reproduction', in which more credence is granted to the democratising potential of technical innovation. It is important not to exaggerate the difficulties facing Thomas, who exploited all the electronic media he encountered with such aplomb, or to assume that the attempt to negotiate the two poles of his writing *was* doomed to failure. Arguably, in fact, he was beginning to successfully balance them by the time of his death; although minor in comparison with the best of his poetry, *Under Milk Wood* is a masterpiece of its kind, and Thomas had been contracted to work on other, even more genre-crossing works, including a libretto for an opera by Stravinsky. He had also nearly reached the point at which his impecuniousness would not have been an insurmountable problem – the *Collected Poems* sold well, and the royalties from *Under Milk Wood* and LP recordings were soon to flow abundantly. It is a cruel irony that, in the four years after his death, Thomas's work earned $2 million.[69] (Even in the early 1990s, it was still earning around £120,000 a year.)

Unusually, Thomas's work is not only highly susceptible to electronic media adaptation, but it has its own cybernetic qualities (as I noted in Chapter 3), suggestive of areas in which print and electronic media merge. It is no coincidence that Marshall McLuhan adapted two Thomas poems, 'The force that through the green fuse' and 'The hand that signed the paper', as pieces of experimental typography and slogans for the electric age in *The Medium is the Message* (1967) and *Counterblast* (1969). For McLuhan, Thomas exemplified to perfection his claim that pre-Gutenberg oral culture had been revived by electronic media as the medium of the global village, fusing primitive phonocentrism and modern technological sophistication. Thomas had anticipated developments only which only became fully apparent in the 1960s: 'The ease with which he took to microphone and phonograph was equal only to his joyous storming over his audience with an eloquence which owed more to the bardic than the literary tradition. But it is precisely the microphone, the phonograph and radio that have readied our perception again for enjoyment as speech and song'.[70] McLuhan's sense of Thomas's cyborg energies draws attention to the 'thinning line between bucolics and cybernetics' in his work – the way that, in it, the pastoral and the wired-up post-industrial world go hand-in-hand. This is more than simply a professional writer's adaptation to circumstances. Thomas's acceptance of the new media stemmed from his (Welsh, lower-middle class) lack of elitist fear of technological levelling, his gift for entertaining and his journalistic past.

Mid-1940s radio features, such as 'Quite Early One Morning' and 'Return Journey', link an older oral culture to its modern manifestations in popular journalism, film and radio comedy. They show Thomas mixing the quaint aside and the shrewd insight, realism and stereotype-based comedy, wordplay and anti-authority sentiment, often using the frame of childhood memory or nostalgic reminiscence, satisfying both his own and popular tastes. *The Doctor and the Devils*, brings many of these qualities together in a final, gothic-tinged minor masterpiece. Still more suggestive of the confusion of high and low and the carnivalesque blurring of Leavisite demarcations is William Empson's recollection of a film on the life of Dickens, which Thomas planned to write at this time; as Empson noted 'it would have meant a considerable improvement of quality in the entertainment profession', because it would have been 'very profound and very box-office'.[71]

This conjunction is reflected in the way that those entranced by the anthology favourites and *Under Milk Wood* were not necessarily deterred by the tougher poetry, and frequently moved on to read it. For Karl Shapiro, the enigma of Thomas was that '[h]is audience was the impossible one: a general audience for a barely understandable poet', and that 'impossible' appeal came from the poetry's unmistakeable rhythmic urgency, primal themes and confessional tone.[72] Arguably, the obscurity of the poems could flatter a reader into believing that they could grasp difficult writing without much effort. But it would be cynical to dismiss the way that the verbal and emotive appeal of even the difficult work drew readers to extend themselves. By an irony which would surely have amused Thomas, this approach was encouraged by the eclectic formats and haphazard manner in which his work circulated for three or so decades after his death: his publishers, Dent, supplemented the

Collected Poems (1952), *Under Milk Wood* (1954) and prose anthologies *Quite Early One Morning* (1954) and *A Prospect of the Sea* (1955) with three 'miscellanies', published in 1963, 1966 and 1978 (an annotated *Collected Poems* appeared only in 1971). These lacked a named editor, notes or bibliographical apparatus, and seem to have been a market-driven repackaging exercise rather than an attempt to present the work coherently, but they nevertheless faithfully reflected Thomas's stylistic range (*Miscellany Two*, for example, includes 'Altarwise by owl-light' and 'A Visit to Grandpa's').[73]

By 1950, the gap between 'high' and 'low' culture was wider than it had been (and is in our own time), exacerbated as it was by an élite backlash against new forces of cultural democratisation. In Thomas's own work, a rapprochement between obscurity and transparency had been going on since 1938, and the pastoral-as-retreat aspect of the post-war poems was one way of managing this relationship – a form of balance between inclusivity and technical virtuosity, verbal lushness and a tone of apocalyptic foreboding. His involvement with mass culture was perhaps least successful in the LP recordings, which, while hugely popular, too obviously indulge in bardic *hwyl*. Thomas's own acknowledgement of this – as 'second-rate Charles Laughton', '[my] usual evangelistic trombone', and so on – has not, of course, spared it from being used as proof of the limitations of the poetry itself.[74] As a radio actor, however, Thomas had a varied technique, and a few recordings exist to prove this; one of 'If I were tickled by the rub of love' is charged with sardonic, stage-villain relish, and there is a moving, husky rendition of 'In my craft or sullen art'. The damage caused by the disparity between text and reading style is particularly marked in the later poems, whose quicksilver textures and shifting rhythms suffer most from monotony and thrasonical inflation. As a result, while the LPs did most to spread Thomas's fame, and are still weirdly impressive, it is arguable that, in the long run, they have contributed to the decline in his reputation.[75]

Of course, Thomas was never completely successful in marrying the different aspects of his work, and the attempt to do so certainly exacerbated the strains which contributed to his premature death. This feat was simply not as possible in mid-century as it might be today, where cultural crossover is the norm rather than the exception. The widespread use of categories such as 'highbrow', 'middlebrow' and 'lowbrow', and of terms such as 'scruple' and 'discrimination', reflected the growing polarisation of cultural debate a tendency to couch arguments in moralising terms. In part this reflected the influence of the followers of *Scrutiny* in the expanding higher education sector. For a Scrutineer, once one had attained the skills required to read, say, a lyric by Donne, it was simply not possible to go back to enjoying a thriller or BBC radio feature.[76] Thomas's practices made him appear suspect to traditional elitists, while to neo-modernists and avant-gardists, he seemed to be colluding with the culture industry; both would subsequently disapprove of his work. Yet Thomas was a pioneer of the more creatively eclectic aspects of our own culture. Like Sylvia Plath, a decade later, he was, in Jacqueline Rose's words, writing at a point of tension between high and popular culture 'without resolution or dissipation of what produces the clash between the two'.[77] It is with a consideration of the interrelationship of these in his best-known work, *Under Milk Wood*, that I shall conclude this chapter.

Satyr play and carnivalesque: 'Lament' and *Under Milk Wood*

Though seemingly a light-hearted, even whimsical work, the long gestation period of *Under Milk Wood* bespeaks the problems involved in its creation, difficulties which had to do with solving a series of technical, generic and thematic challenges (in this regard, it should be borne in mind that, although it had reached broadcastable form before his death, *Under Milk Wood* remains incomplete).[78] The idea for a 'day in the life of a community' piece came from *Ulysses*, though *Under Milk Wood* does not pretend to invite comparison, and can be traced from as early as 1932. In 1939, Thomas mentioned writing a play for, and about, the inhabitants of Laugharne. Its radio forerunners are 'Quite Early One Morning' (1944) (which contains the opening scenario and four characters of *Under Milk Wood*), 'The Londoner' (1946), 'Margate – Past and Present' (1946) and 'Return Journey' (1947). All four saw Thomas overcome specific technical challenges, leading him to the use of a narrator and the blind Captain Cat to act as the 'eyes' of the listener and thus give coherence in the absence of a plot. Similarly, in 1946, a thumbnail-sketched parody of T. F. Powys in the broadcast 'How to Begin a Story' noted the possibilities for a 'sophisticatedly contrived bucolic morality' and a set of paired characters, whose desires for each other are held in permanent stasis, never consummated or reciprocated, but never extinguished, either.[79]

The link with the poetry is largely tonal, but there are some revealing areas of thematic overlap and of originating impulse, too. *Under Milk Wood* does not directly reflect the Cold War, but it began life as a courtroom drama for radio, called 'The Town That Was Mad'. This had a tangential link to the post-war political situation; its premise was a Welsh nationalist election victory (like that recently scored by Attlee's Labour Party). The new government, based in Cardiff, disapproved of the eccentricity of Llareggub, and the drama was to have centred on the indictment and collective trial of the population of the town, with a view to cordoning it off, in order to prevent the rest of Wales being infected by its insanity (*UMW*, xxi). On trial, the inhabitants would have learnt the ways of the outside world which they had ignored for so long and ended up by declaring *it* mad, thus gladly embracing their quarantine (*UMW*, xxii). The manuscript shows that, even after dropping the 'Town That Was Mad' idea, Thomas considered incorporating references to 'tragedy', 'sadness', 'poverty', 'idiocy' and 'incest' to explain the zaniness of some of the inhabitants of Llareggub (*UMW*, xxxviii).

Rather than the poems of *In Country Heaven*, the poem that has most in common with *Under Milk Wood* is the slighter 'Lament' (1951). This takes the form of a deathbed confession by a speaker who sums up a life of sexual pursuit – a phase in each stanza – from his escapades as 'a springtailed tom in red hot town' and 'bright, bass prime' to being 'only half the man I was' and marrying a 'sunday wife' to save his soul, with the attendant 'deadly virtues' of 'chastity', 'piety', 'innocence' and 'modesty'. The poem's knockabout sexual humour is that of Llareggub, a 'place of love', and it is clearly intertextual with the play's Donkey Street, with an 'owl fl[ying] home past Bethesda' and the 'grassgreen gooseberried double bed of the wood' (*UMW*, 8):

> When I was a windy boy and a bit
> And the black spit of the chapel fold,
> (Sighed the old ram rod, dying of women),
> I tiptoed shy in the gooseberry wood,
> The rude owl cried like a telltale tit,
> I skipped in a blush as the big girls rolled
> Ninepin down on the donkeys' common … (*CP*, 148)

'Lament' is cruder than *Under Milk Wood*: 'coarse and violent' and 'not quite clean, and worked at, between the willies, very hard' in Thomas's punningly sexualised description (*CL*, 881). It also evokes Welsh praise poetry and the swagger poems of the fifteenth century *bardd* Dafydd ap Gwilym. Yet both works attack Nonconformist repression and rely on cartoon-like exaggeration; moreover, the poem's comic deflation of phallocentrism has much in common with the play's genial mockery of male desire and delusion. Polly Garter might easily mistake the speaker of 'Lament' for Mr Waldo on a dark night in Milk Wood.[80]

This (self)critical aspect was missed by those who saw the radio 'play for voices' as a slight on the national character. Indeed, critics generally failed to see that something of the critique and the *univers concentra-tionnaire* aspect of 'The Town That Was Mad' persisted. Constantine Fitzgibbon rightly observed that the original spirit of the work – that 'the village is the only place that is left free in the whole world, for … the rest of the globe is the camp, is mad' – survived in the form of Llareggub's insouciant disregard for the outside world, and this became the true basis of its enormous popularity.[81] This is apparent, to some degree, in the fact that the Welsh Home Service 'initially resisted attempts to broadcast the "lusty" play, which it thought unsuitable for family listening'. (As a result, Thomas's most 'Welsh' work was broadcast in England, before Wales.) More broadly, *Under Milk Wood* (like 'Lament') has been one of the pieces taken to confirm his incorrigible lechery and treachery and has attracted nationalist and Nonconformist opprobrium as a result. It has often been read as Thomas once said the *Spoon River Anthology* was read: 'Many people read it in order to deny that it was true; many, discovering that in essence it was, denounced it even more loudly' (*TB*, 256). Not only Welsh critics felt this. Dent's chief editor considered it pornographic, and certain episodes – such as Mae Rose Cottage's circling of her nipples with lipstick – were omitted from the first edition. As M. Wynn Thomas has noted, *Under Milk Wood* is a key text in the ideological manoeuvring between Welsh anglophone and Cymrophone cultures, spawning, among other responses, Marcel Williams's *Diawl y Wenallt* (*The Devil of Milk Wood*), in which the pieties of Welsh Dylanites and his Welsh-Wales opponents are satirised in a novel which has Dylan resurrected in Llareggub, with orgiastic results.[82] Yet, as Williams's work suggests, the most subversive aspect of *Under Milk Wood* is not so much any specific critique of Nonconformism, as its status as comic, carnivalesque pastoral.

Dylan Thomas had moved, in the late 1930s, from a focus on the youthful, glandular body to a celebration of existence – 'the time dying flesh astride', as 'A Winter's Tale' put it. The omission of the hyphen between 'time' and 'dying' turns some of the force of 'dying', as applied to 'flesh', back onto 'time'; sexual love and procreation – as in 'Ceremony After a Fire Raid' – become not a threat, but a means of briefly tempering the bitterness of mortality. In this, *Under Milk Wood* can be read as an extension of the carnivalesque potential of the later poetry, a comic pendant or satyr-play to their cosmic tragedy. According to Peter Stallybrass and Allon White in *The Politics and Poetics of Transgression* (1986), one of the most influential critical deployments of the concept, carnival is to be seen 'as a world of topsy-turvy, of heteroglot exuberance, of ceaseless overrunning and excess where all is mixed, hybrid, ritually degraded and defiled'. They add that 'as well as the emphasis on the possibility of subversion through bodily functions and bodily parts, attention is also drawn to the subversive potential of language'.[83] Moreover, as Bakhtin puts it, the carnivalesque generates 'festive laughter' – a laughter which is universal, does not spare the mocker himself and is ambivalent; it is triumphant *and* mocking, trangressively shaking bodily propriety and self-possession and traversing the limits of social forms.[84] Far from being calendrically fixed, the carnivalesque is a mobile set of symbolic practices and textual forms, which establish a 'life ... subject only to its own laws ...; it is a special condition of the entire world'.[85] As such, it has a utopian, affirmative and political power, embodying the awareness of the masses of their own 'immortality' ('time dying' as time-defying) and the relativity of all officially constituted truth and authority.[86] And, as Terry Gifford observes, the carnivalesque has a particular affinity with pastoral and the trickster figure.[87]

There are many ways in which *Under Milk Wood* both fits and adapts these criteria to create a carnivalesque pastoral for the mid-century age of radio. Crucially, as its surtitle declares, it is not a play or drama for radio, but 'a play for voices' and also *of* 'voices'.[88] In its reliance on sound effects and the listener's imagination, it has more in common with sound poetry and radio comedy – a genre which reached its zenith in the period in which it was conceived, between the end of the war and the mid-1960s, in such shows as *ITMA* (*It's That Man Again*), *The Goons* and *Round the Horne*.[89] The purely aural dimension in which *Under Milk Wood* exists frees up by foregrounding its heteroglossic aspect – its lyric descriptive passages, guidebook parody, newspaper verse, use of dialect and exuberant mining of oral, musical and popular culture, from bawdy end-of-the-pier routines, music hall double entendre and puns (Mrs Ogmore Pritchard as big-'besomed', for example) to children's skipping rhymes, drinking songs and newspaper verse. The exploitation of stock situations and characters also reminds us of its resemblances to radio soaps, the first of which – *The Archers* – began in January 1951. (It may be no coincidence that *Coronation Street*, the first British television soap, has the same name as one of the two main streets in Llareggub.)

Under Milk Wood's medium also facilitates, precisely through not having to present it in visual terms, carnival's grotesque exaggeration of the body, particularly the sexual body. This has a Freudian dream element in Gossamer Beynon's fantasies of Sinbad Sailors ('all cucumber and hooves') and Rose Mae Cottage's desire for a 'Mr. Right', who leaps 'like a brilliantined trout', and has more obvious comic-malign aspects in Butcher Beynon's assertion that he butchers moles, otters, shrews, 'dogs' eyes, manchop' or Mr Pugh's daydream of poisoning Mrs Pugh using 'a venomous porridge unknown to toxicologists which will scald and viper through her until her ears fall off like figs, her toes grow big and black as balloons, and steam comes screaming out of her navel' (*UMW*, 46). Thomas can push this to surreal extremes ('dogs bark blue in the face'; 'before you let the sun in, mind it wipes its shoes'), and the self-generative aspects of language are given their head. This extends from the famous opening, with its parody of Genesis ('To begin at the beginning') and puns and paragrams ('the sloeblack, slow, black, crowblack, fishing boat-bobbing sea') to its swollen and comically sinister lists ('custard, buckets, henna, rat-traps, shrimp nets, sugar, stamps, confetti, paraffin, hatchets, whistles') and riffs on vocables and wordplays. Although this can seem to verge on indulgence, especially if the piece is realised only in reading, the fact that *Under Milk Wood*'s central character might be language itself should suggest that verbal play ought not to be perceived as a weakness as such.

Under Milk Wood also, of course, presents a 'topsy-turvy world', both in relation to the placing of Llareggub and Milk Wood and in its treatment of sex. Milk Wood itself functions symbolically as Llareggub's night-time Other – its libido – but it is not located *below* the town, in the way that the unconscious is commonly conceptualised as lying below, and being subject to, the conscious mind. On the contrary, we are told that Llareggub lies 'under' the wood, and it does so in a topographical and psychosexual sense. The life of the town, libidinous in dreams and under the trees of Milk Wood, is, in daytime, a relatively painless idyll. Llareggub's web of unconsummated relationships form a genially repressive structure, charged to an unusual degree, if not animated by, the libidinous night-time id. The punitive superego, at least, is not much in evidence, and the reality principle is defied without too much suffering, because Llareggub is autonomous and timeless; its 'symbolic practices and textual forms' establish a 'life ... subject only to its own laws' and form an 'entire world'. (Temporality, as defined by the world and authority, is arrested like the clock stuck 'at half past eleven' in the Sailors' Arms.)

From its hill above Llareggub, Milk Wood oversees, as well as overlooks, the population. The town's schoolchildren are inducted into its upside-down values by a playground game, which involves the forfeiting of kisses to be claimed later in the wood:

> GIRL: Kiss me in Milk Wood Dicky
> Or give me a penny quickly. (*UMW*, 44–5)

The sexual symbolism is both blatant and innocent, in accordance with Llareggub's emotional economy, poised between infant and adult sexuality, between voyeuristic desire and physical enjoyment. 'Dicky' is blatantly phallic, but a childish diminutive. This is all implicit in the title, since 'milk' invokes a nurturing breast, while 'wood' is a bushy pubic zone and slang for an erection. Children visit the wood, and it is also where Polly Garter nightly ties up the town's sexual loose ends. If the adult characters are child-like in their nostalgia and naïvety, the children are knowing, though still innocent. As in 'Fern Hill' and 'In country sleep', Thomas tempers nostalgia for childhood, by reminding us of the sexual nature of children, as revealed by Freud, although here this is not accompanied by menace or trauma. The darker material of earlier drafts outcrops briefly on this child–adult border, when a girl tells her mother that 'Nogood Boyo gave me three pennies yesterday but I wouldn't', but we never learn what it is that she 'wouldn't' (*UMW*, 53). Whether or not this is a textual fossil, it serves to mark a point, beyond which Thomas cannot go, without undermining Llareggub's utopian suspension between states.

Thus, while the childhood world will submit to the sway of the patriarchal Symbolic Order elsewhere, it will never fully do so in Llareggub. The conflict between the semiotic and Symbolic orders at the heart of Thomas's poetry is more passively and dilutedly present in the interplay of the comic-erotic and a melancholic awareness of mortality around which *Under Milk Wood* plotlessly circles. It is a work which comically defines happiness in terms of the frustrations which are paradoxically essential to the preservation of that happiness, and it makes a point of ending in the night out of which it sprang. Polly Garter's song provides an un-ignorable leitmotif, as well as the work's final words: 'But I always think as I tumble into bed / Of Little Willie Wee who is dead, dead, dead …' (*UMW*, 62).[90] Polly's love beyond the grave (for a man whose small penis is defined by urination – its sole childhood function) is matched by Captain Cat's earthier desire for Rosie Probert, although both link sex and death, desire and its unattainability. Their colloquy – Thomas's favourite part of the work – is another reminder that *Et in Llareggub ego* and is the closest that the play gets to poetry. Asking to 'Let me shipwreck in your thighs', Captain Cat is answered 'Knock twice, Jack, / At the door of my grave / And ask for Rosie':

ROSIE PROBERT
Remember her.
She is forgetting.
The earth which filled her mouth
Is vanishing from her.
Remember me.
I have forgotten you.
I am going into the darkness of the darkness for ever.
I have forgotten that I was ever born.

CHILD
Look ...
Captain Cat is crying. (*UMW*, 52–3)

Yet, for all this, it is not graveyard wisdom that we are finally left with. Even the deathly hygienic, glacial Mrs Ogmore-Pritchard has expressed sexual desire (much to the terror of the ghosts of her two husbands), and this is in accord with the work's carnivalesque aspect. While Rosie's final speech is an act of self-erasure, it is contradictory ('I have forgotten that ...'), and her last word is 'born', immediately followed by a child's voice. The pathos of Thomas's last pastoral creation opposes annihilation with sensual excess and comic gusto, leavened with carnival's sense of inevitable, vulgar renewal. Although he recasts it for an electronic age and his sense of the grotesque and carnivalesque subversion hardly embraces communal solidarity, *Under Milk Wood* nevertheless resembles more traditional carnival in evincing a 'sheer delight in Heraclitean flux' and an 'understand[ing of] the human body not as the mortal husk of an individual ... but as the collective great body of the people'.[91] In doing so, it realises some of the populist potential, which might, had Thomas lived, have also emerged in the poetry.

Conclusion: 'astonished delight' and 'esoteric salutation'

Thomas's early work acknowledged an explosive oneness with nature, but also an inability to address it or speak on its behalf and a refusal to sentimentalise or essentialise it. At that point, he separated the 'green' aspect of process from the Romantic and rural associations of pastoral. In 'After the funeral', however, the green world acquired its own pagan, anti-puritan force, and, in the war elegies, the dumbness that Thomas had felt in the presence of the 'green fuse' became a more active refusal to integrate perceptions of the war-dead into a falsely coherent 'poetic' resolution. The later poems finally take the paradoxical logic of pastoral into the countryside. There, it is clear what a new war might mean: man's destruction of the planet, all life, nature and 'greenness'.

At a point in history where it only exists on human sufferance, nature is even more a vulnerable human construct than formerly. As a result, the ecological resistance to destruction occurs in a manner which foregrounds its own anthropomorphised, allegorical and artificial rendering of nature, not in some celebration of rootedness, chthonic powers or even process in its earlier, impersonal sense.[92] The desire to 'create the illusion of nature emerging from alienation' is resisted by the sense, exacerbated by the threat of nuclear weaponry, of the unthinking human exploitation of nature and a desire to not be part of it. One climax of this desire appears in the lines already quoted from 'In country sleep' at the opening of this chapter. For Richard Chamberlain, the sudden irruption of violence (reflected in thirteen exclamation marks in seventeen lines) shows how the late poetry 'at once advertises [nature's] permeation by society' or its anthropomorphic, 'Disneyesque' aspect and, at the same time, 'resists the idea that it is "culturally constructed" as the simple opposite of society or merely its conceptual remainder'.[93] Nature is dependent upon man, but still resists appropriation in its stubborn otherness.

Put another way, this is an affirmation of the deep ecological impulse of such work, emphasising the mechanisms by which it responds to the ethical demands of pastoral. As Barbara Hardy observes 'there are very few of Thomas's poems which do not offer a meditation on nature'; he is what we would now call a 'green poet' – one who 'fully understands the politics of greenness, anticipating our present wishes and efforts to care for the globe, our polluted environment, and to displace the human animal from a still prevailing arrogant centrality'.[94] In this regard, his work compares favourably with most post-Wordsworthian revisions of the genre. These have tended to be anti-modern, drawing on countervailing notions of 'organic community' (as in Leavis) or still more atavistic strategies for asserting 'dwelling', groundedness and blood-and-soil belonging (often bolstered by the more reactionary notion of late Heidegger). Thomas's response to nationalism meant that he instinctively opposed territorial possessiveness of a Romantic-reactionary kind, such as we find in the work of R. S. Thomas or Seamus Heaney. Thomas celebrates his locale, but in a way which is indirect, abstract and unmilitant, opposed to both nation and metropolis and trusting to the verbal performance of a sense of place, rather than the assertion of specific territorial pieties. His solution to the paradoxes of pastoral involves empathy without identification and is ethical, rather than ethnic.[95] Living at a time when the full destructive consequences of both nationalism (however 'minor') and a stance of domination over nature are writ large in the crises that beset our planet, from Iraq and Afghanistan on the one hand, to global warming on the other, such a modest, yet far-reaching, poetic has obvious relevance and appeal.

The issue of what Thomas would have done, had he lived, tends to distract from the fact that his death was an accidental event. However rhapsodic and accepting of mortality his later work was, it did not build towards or anticipate that end. Yet it seems appropriate, even so, to end this final chapter with a glimpse of what we know of his plans beyond the fatal fourth tour of the US. There are two possibilities hinted at which I would like to sketch in concluding this chapter. One of them is raised by a libretto, which Igor Stravinsky asked Thomas to write for him (money from the readings of *Under Milk Wood* in New York were to have funded his travel onwards to California to live and work with the composer for several weeks in the winter of 1953). As Thomas envisaged it, the opera would be set in a world devastated by nuclear war: 'Almost all life had disappeared. The scene was to be a cave in completely barren surroundings. Miraculously two young people had survived, and they had to find life again in an almost total absence of it'.[96] The boy was to have had 'groping recollections of life before the destruction', and 'the incident that made Dylan's imagination glow was when the boy tried to remember and explain to the girl what a tree was'. Painfully and slowly, at first, the two were to be shown rediscovering the world around them, devising a new language and new theories about the origins of the universe, in order to explain their situation. It would have been an extraordinary conception of a post-atomic, Eve-and-Adamic, *ur*-language word-world and would have marked another original development in yet another art form.

Extraordinary though it would have been, however, the opera was in the vein of writing that includes *Under Milk Wood* and the later poems – a pastoral projection of the potentially posthumous existence of humanity. The second work I will mention is very different, although it also has to do with the imaginative opening up of new worlds. Although it is only a short newspaper article, it is, in certain ways, even more radical than the opera. Thomas's now almost-forgotten review of the Nigerian novelist Amos Tutuola's novel, *The Palm-Wine Drinkard*, titled 'Blithe Spirit', was carried in *The Observer* on 6 July

1952 and consists chiefly of a recounting of the novel's 'narrative': 'This is the brief, thronged, grisly and bewitching story, or series of stories, written in young English by a West African, about the journey of an expert and devoted palm-wine drinkard through a nightmare of indescribable adventures, all simply and carefully described, in the spirit-bristling bush' (*EPW*, 203). Thomas's energetic account is true to Tutuola's Rabelaisian excess and some of his emphases remind us of his own poetry and fiction: a journey to a city of dreadful night, fusions of the 'convenient features of civilized life' with folk-surrealism and cod primitivism and the mingling of the worlds of the living and the dead (*EPW*, 204). Thomas concludes: 'The writing is nearly always terse and direct, strong, wry, flat and savoury; the big, and often comic, terrors are as near and understandable as the numerous small details of price, size, and number; and nothing is too prodigious or too trivial to put down in this tall, devilish story' (*EPW*, 204). To describe this overwhelmingly laudatory review as 'primarily a spirited synopsis' – as it has been in the best article on the subject to date – is understandable.[97] But it nevertheless misses the point that, as in his efforts to explain his own work, Thomas is letting the novel speak in its own terms, precisely because its style is of a kind, like his own, which actively resists prosaic exposition. It should be remembered that, in 1952, African writing in English was entirely unrecognised in Britain. What Thomas did – and, however unintentional, it is an astonishing achievement – was, quite simply, to put such writing on the map of world literature. In 1972, the Ghanaian poet and novelist Kofi Awoonor traced the value 'placed on African writing in England' back to 'Dylan Thomas's reception of Amos Tutuola's *Palm-Wine Drinkard* in 1952'. In 1998, Chinua Achebe said much the same thing: Tutuola's novel had 'led the way for modern West African writing in English' and the first reviewer to recognise its importance had been:

> the celebrated Welsh poet Dylan Thomas … It was a brief essay, but Thomas wasted no time and seemingly no effort getting right into the spirit of Tutuola's tale. He also captured the letter of it and gave a masterful, joyous summary of the plot such as no one … has ever bettered, for its comprehensiveness, accuracy and humour … As far as I know, Dylan Thomas never went to Africa; his recognition of Tutuola's merit … was … the spontaneous recognition of one blithe spirit by another, like the esoteric salutation given by one ancestral mask to another in Igbo masquerade.[98]

Bernth Lindfors, editor of *Critical Perspectives on Amos Tutuola* (1975), made the same point, attributing the British response of 'astonished delight' to the novel to Thomas's positive response. Moreover, Thomas's comments, incorporated on the dust jacket of the novel, were repeated by American reviewers. We should, of course, resist the urge to sentimentalise at this point and recognise Thomas's habitual tonal doubleness; the last sentence of his review rings a little like his thirtieth birthday tribute to Auden, as described by Linden Huddlestone in a 1953 tribute to Thomas: 'we are never sure exactly when a tongue is in cheek or hat is in hand, bonnet over the windmill or sober as a judge'.[99] Even so, it is proper, I feel, to note Thomas's clairvoyance with regard to the most significant new movement in English-language literature of the last half century – that of the former Empire 'writing back' – and permissible to imagine how, writing with such unashamed brilliance out of his own liminal origins, he would have relished such comradeship, had he lived to enjoy it.

Notes

1 The book went into four impressions in its first year. It continued to appear as a separate volume after the publication of the *Collected Poems 1934–1952* and was still in print in 1970 after several editions.

2 In 1946, the peak year of his involvement in radio, Thomas appeared in forty-nine BBC radio broadcasts, eleven of which he had written himself. The next largest number of radio appearances was twenty-four in 1947. Overall, during 1943–53, Thomas appeared in 156 broadcasts, of which twenty-eight were self-penned (see *TB*, 287–91, for details).

3 Thus, Thomas's friend Jack Lindsay: 'I recall noting the very moment of his reputation's expansion. He was one of several of us who read verse at the Ethical Society's rooms in Bayswater [in early 1946] ... There was only the usual small audience. Then, a few months later, with his first important BBC renderings having intervened, he gave a reading (somewhere in Kensington, I think) at which there was an overflowing and rapturous audience of young people'. See Jack Lindsay, *Meetings with Poets* (Frederick Muller: London, 1968), p. 22. The most recent poems made the greatest impact; 'Poem in October', for example, was included in two anthologies of 1946. In 1949, Thomas's poems appeared in five anthologies, *A Portrait of the Artist as a Young Dog* was reprinted in a 50,000–copy Guild paperback impression, and Henry Treece published the first monograph on his work. The 1952 *Collected Poems* won the 1952 William Foyle Poetry Prize and sold 30,400 copies in its first year. See Ralph Maud, *Dylan Thomas in Print*, p. 16.

4 See Paul Ferris, *Dylan Thomas* (London: Penguin, 1978), p. 216: 'In February or March 1946 he was in St Stephen's Hospital, London, for four days, with "alcoholic gastritis"'.

5 See R. George Thomas, 'Dylan Thomas and Some Early Readers', *Poetry Wales*, 9: 2 (Autumn 1973), p. 15.

6 R. George Thomas, 'Dylan Thomas and Some Early Readers', pp. 14–45

7 Paul Ferris, *Dylan Thomas*, p. 227.

8 John Ackerman, *A Dylan Thomas Companion: Life, Poetry and Prose* (London: Macmillan, 1991), p. 129.

9 David Daiches, 'The Poetry of Dylan Thomas', *Dylan Thomas: A Collection of Critical Essays*, ed. C. B. Cox (Englewood Cliffs, NJ: Prentice-Hall, 1966), p. 17.

10 See Jack Lindsay, *Meetings With Poets* (London: Frederick Muller, 1968), p. 35. During his first American tour in March 1950, Thomas got into an argument about the NHS with a doctor's wife at the house of Robert Baldwin, chairman of the English faculty at Kenyon College: 'She described it as a Marxist front, which annoyed him intensely. He exploded with rage, reducing her to tears …'. See Andrew Lycett, *Dylan Thomas: A New Life* (London: Weidenfeld & Nicolson, 2003), p. 292.

11 Notes for a poem titled 'In Country Heaven', which was intended to link together the other poems, were found among Thomas's papers after his death.

12 Cited in Roland Mathias, *Poetry Dimension 2* (London: Abacus Books, 1974), p. 61.

13 Russell Davies, 'Fibs of Vision', *Review* (Autumn / Winter 1971–2), p. 69; 1954; Seamus Heaney, *Dylan the Durable? On Dylan Thomas* (Bennington, VT: Bellitt / Troy Chapbooks Series, 1992), pp. 23–4.

14 Seamus Heaney, *Dylan the Durable? On Dylan Thomas*, p. 23; also the chapter of the same name in *The Redress of Poetry* (London: Faber, 1995), pp. 124–45.

15 Dylan Thomas, *Dylan Thomas: Poems Selected by Derek Mahon* (London: Faber, 2003), p. xvi. Mahon likes 'A Winter's Tale', too. The opinions quoted here are representative of the general attitudes of these two poet-critics to Thomas's work.

16 See Barbara Hardy, *Dylan Thomas: An Original Language* (Athens, GA: University of Georgia Press, 2000); Richard Chamberlain, 'Fuse and Refuse: The Pastoral Logic of Dylan Thomas's Poetry', Dylan Thomas Boathouse at Laugharne, see www.dylanthomasboathouse.com

17 Walford Davies, *Dylan Thomas* (Milton Keynes: Open University Press, 1986), p. 119.

18 Marjorie Adix, 'From Dylan Thomas: Memories and Appreciations', ed. John Malcolm Brinnin, *A Casebook on Dylan Thomas* (New York, NY: T. Y. Crowell, 1961), p. 285.

19 Tony Conran, *Frontiers in Anglo-Welsh Poetry* (Cardiff: University of Wales Press, 1997), p. 119.

20 Walford Davies, ed., 'The Wanton Starer', *Dylan Thomas: New Critical Essays* (London: Dent, 1972), p. 164.

21 As Terry Gifford has argued: there are 'complex and sentimental kinds of pastoralism – one escapist, one in which the pastoral design circumscribes the pastoral ideal', for example. Equally, pastoral may involve: 'a critique of present society, or … be a dramatic form of unresolved dialogue about the tensions in that society, or it can be a retreat from politics into an apparently aesthetic landscape that is devoid of conflict and tension'. Terry Gifford, *Pastoral* (London: Routledge, 1999), p. 10.

22 Terry Gifford, *Pastoral*, p. 4.

23 Veronica Forrest-Thompson, *Poetic Artifice: A Theory of Twentieth Century Poetry* (Manchester: Manchester University Press, 1978), pp. 113, 120–1.

24 Writing to Vernon Watkins from Cornwall in 1936, Thomas asserted that he preferred 'the bound slope of a suburban hill … to all these miles of green fields' and was 'not a country man': 'I stand for, if anything, the aspidistra, the provincial drive, the morning café, the evening pub' (*CL*, 248). It is worth noting that the

Welsh suburb was a rare thing in the interwar years. As James A. Davies has pointed out: 'Only in the larger places – the Radyr, Rhiwbeina and Roath Park areas of Cardiff, the Mumbles, Sketty and Uplands parts of Swansea, possibly in Newport – was it possible for that suburbia to emerge'. James A. Davies, *Dylan Thomas's Swansea, Gower and Laugharne* (Cardiff: University of Wales Press, 2000), pp. 3–4. In Richard Chamberlain's interpretation of Thomas's explanation of the *In Country Heaven* sequence: 'places are in-betweens or irrevocably lost from the perspective these poems will be made to adopt. Poems, just as provisionally or unattainably, are not now but "to be". The final words can be read with a general application, as well as Thomas's primary meaning, to the poems collected as "In Country Heaven". Poetry is in the process of becoming. It is located, as "Over Sir John's hill" suggests, in the non-moralising, non-industrious, non-Aesopian pastoral persona of the observing heron, and in the coast as a pastoral location, between land and sea, between the known and the unknowable …'. Richard Chamberlain, 'Fuse and Refuse: The Pastoral Logic of Dylan Thomas's Poetry', p. 4.

25 Cited by Laurence Lerner, 'Sex in Arcadia: "Under Milk Wood"', ed. Walford Davies, *Dylan Thomas: New Critical Essays*, p. 278.

26 Terry Gifford, *Pastoral*, pp. 11–12.

27 See David Masters, 'Going Modern and Being British: Art in Britain 1930–55', ed. Gary Day, *Literature and Culture in Modern Britain, volume 2 1930–55* (London: Longman, 1997), p. 204.

28 Walford Davies, 'The Wanton Starer', p. 154.

29 Thomas deliberately uses the anglicised form of the plural of 'bryn'; the Welsh is 'bryniau'.

30 Because of his belief that Thomas was committed to realism, Walford Davies is forced to adopt an either / or stand on this point: 'Laugharne's own ancient church, the other side of the rise of the village, is not visible from Sir John's hill; therefore, either it is imagined or Thomas is describing the church at Llanybri across the estuary' (*SP2*, 147).

31 David N. Thomas, '*Under Milk Wood*'s birth-in-exile', *New Welsh Review* 52, 13: 4 (Spring 2001), pp. 51, 53.

32 M. Wynn Thomas, *Corresponding Cultures: The Two Literatures of Wales* (Cardiff, University of Wales Press, 1999), p. 78.

33 Patrick Kavanagh, 'Parochialism and Provincialism', ed. Antoinette Quinn, *A Poet's Country: Selected Prose* (Dublin: Lilliput Press, 2003), p. 237.

34 Seamus Heaney, *Dylan the Durable? On Dylan Thomas*, Bennington Chapbooks on Literature (Bennington VT, Chapbooks in Literature Series, no publisher given, 1992, p. 22.

35 Walford Davies, 'The Wanton Starer', p. 149. It should be noted that this assertion was made in 1972. Neither it, nor the sometimes negative attitude to Thomas of that essay, recurs in Davies's subsequent work.

36 Walford Davies, 'The Wanton Starer', p. 163.

37 Walford Davies, 'The Wanton Starer', p. 162.

38 Steve McCaffery, *North of Intention: Critical Writings 1973–1986* (New York, NY: Roof Books, 2000), p. 202.

39 For a discussion of the 'mistier' / 'mister' pun, see Jon Silkin, *The Life of Metrical and Free Verse in Twentieth Century Poetry* (London: Macmillan, 1997), pp. 257–61.

40 Thomas ambiguously informed Vernon Watkins that his favourite modern poet was Hardy, but that the greatest was Yeats.

41 It seems to misleading to argue that the shapes of these stanzas are mimetic. For example, it has been claimed that 'Vision and Prayer's diamond shapes represent prayer and its hourglass shapes represent Thomas's obsession with mortality. But it makes at least as much sense to think of each shape as determined by the other's absence, existing as testimony to the arbitrary and abstract starkness of the patterning impulse.

42 Thus, the definite article occurs twenty-four times, 'his' seven times, 'who(m)' five times, 'child', 'man', 'will', 'stair(s)', 'sleep' and 'prayer(s)' four times, 'about', 'love', 'said', 'dead', 'care / ing', 'shall' three times and 'dark', 'conversation', 'sound', 'room', 'one', 'dying', 'climbs', 'turns', 'high' and 'bed' twice. Lines eight and nine almost exactly reverse lines one and two; thirteen and fourteen revert again to the original order of lines one and two, keeping the rhyme but altering one phrase; lines three and four are echoed in lines ten and eleven and so on.

43 Jacob Korg, *Dylan Thomas* (New York, NY: Hippocrene Books, 1972), p. 112.

44 'Repetition of sound, syllable, word, phrase, line, strophe, metrical pattern, or syntactic structure lies at the core of any definition of poetry. The notion that too much literal repetition is tedious, dull, or just plain bad runs counter to the most widely perceived fundamentals of verbal art and its ubiquitous use by poets'. Alex Preminger and T. V. F. Brogan, eds., *The New Princeton Encyclopaedia of Poetry and Poetics* (Princeton, NJ: Princeton University Press, 1993), p. 1035.

45 Alastair Fowler, 'Adder's Tongue on Maiden Hair: Early Stages in Reading "Fern Hill"', ed. Walford Davies, *Dylan Thomas: New Critical Essays* (London: Dent, 1972), p. 231.

46 Alastair Fowler, 'Adder's Tongue on Maiden Hair: Early Stages in Reading "Fern Hill"', pp. 235–6. Thomas's radio talk of 1947 on Sidney indicates familiarity with his poetry. See 'Sir Philip Sidney', *QEOM*, p. 142.

47 See Julia Kristeva, *Revolution in Poetic Language*, translated by Margaret Waller, New York, Columbia University Press, 1984, p. 256.

48 Steve McCaffery, *North of Intention: Critical Writings 1973–1986* (New York, NY: Roof Books, 2000), pp. 63–4.

49 G. S. Fraser, 'Dylan Thomas', ed. John Malcom Brinnin, *A Casebook on Dylan Thomas*, p. 50.

50 The choice of the villanelle for 'Do not go gentle into that good night', for example, was probably influenced by the extensive use of it by Empson. In 1942, Thomas wrote a truncated pastiche Empson villanelle 'Not your winged lust but his must now change suit' for a special Empson issue of *Horizon*. It also features in the novel *The Death of the King's Canary*, which Thomas co-wrote in 1942 with John Davenport. The novel also contains parodies of Eliot, Auden, Day Lewis, Roy Campbell, Spender and other contemporaries and testifies to Thomas's skill at parody and pastiche (his ability to improvise these is widely noted in memoirs of the time).

51 John Keats, *The Complete Poems*, ed. John Barnard (London: Penguin, 1988), p. 312.

52 John Keats, *The Complete Poems*, ed. John Barnard, pp. 324, 322.

53 'Eve of St Agnes' is Keats's most Shakespearean poem, and Thomas's use of both is no coincidence. Keats's theory of the 'chameleon poet' arose from his Oedipal *agon* with Milton and Wordsworth and led him to posit Shakespeare as the supreme poet

of non-identity. Keats's simultaneously bold and derivative method of resistance is followed by Thomas in appropriating a predecessor who renounced appropriation.

54 What matters here, of course, is not the actual 'Welshness' of these poets in some blood-and-soil sense, so much as the perception of these poets as Welsh in criticism of Thomas's time. As usual in his later poetry, Thomas is manipulating perceptions, rather than essentialist-defined 'realities'.

55 James A. Davies, 'Questions of Identity: The Movement and "Fern Hill"', eds. John Goodby and Chris Wigginton, *Dylan Thomas: New Casebook*, p. 169.

56 James A. Davies, 'Questions of Identity: The Movement and "Fern Hill"', p. 169.

57 James A. Davies, 'Questions of Identity: The Movement and "Fern Hill"', p. 169.

58 Lynette Roberts, *Diaries, Letters and Recollections*, ed. Patrick McGuinness (Manchester: Carcanet, 2008), p. 150.

59 Following the two atom bombs dropped on Hiroshima and Nagasaki in 1945, the US began a series of tests on Bikini Atoll in the Pacific in 1946 and soon amassed a nuclear arsenal. The USSR, which detonated its first atom bomb in 1949, responded in kind.

60 Aeronwy Thomas-Ellis, *Christmas and Other Memories* (London: Amwy Press, 1978), p. 14.

61 In Maud's words: 'Thomas presents this in a triple negative. She has this fear that each night he will come to eliminate her fear that this is the night he will come only to leave her forsaken, feeling that he will not come: the threat is that this belief will be stolen from her. Each night his presence negates the fear that he will not come. ... In this way a poem of Experience emerges from the poem of Innocence that "In country sleep" would have been if its theme had simply been protection of the loved one'. Ralph Maud, *Where Have the Old Words Got Me?*, p. 152.

62 Richard Chamberlain, 'Fuse and Refuse: The Pastoral Logic of Dylan Thomas's Poetry', p. 4. See www.dylanthomasboathouse.com

63 Richard Chamberlain, 'Fuse and Refuse: The Pastoral Logic of Dylan Thomas's Poetry', p. 4.

64 Jacques Derrida, 'No Apocalypse, Not Now (Full Speed Ahead, Seven Missiles, Seven Missives)', transl. Catherine Porter and Philip Lewis, *Diacritics* 14 (1984), pp. 20–31.

65 Steven Connor, *The English Novel in History 1950–1995* (London: Routledge, 1996), pp. 202–3.

66 This is not to say that the dissemination of 'high' culture, often defined in modernist terms, did not become public policy in many areas: 'the "heroic" era [of modernism] came crashing to an end in WWII' and was succeeded by its stylistic institutionalisation', as David Harvey notes. In certain spheres, modernist styles: 'became hegemonic after 1945 [and] exhibited a much more comfortable relation to the dominant power centres ... a corporate version of the Enlightenment project of development for progress and human emancipation held sway as a political-economic dominant'. David Harvey, *The Condition of Postmodernity: An Enquiry into the Origins of Cultural Change* (Oxford: Blackwell, 1992), p. 35. Harvey's statement holds for architecture, music and the visual arts. In British literary culture, however, a strong traditional empirical bias led to the Movement's anti-modernist backlash from the mid-1950s onwards.

67 The basic coordinates of Adorno's argument are charted in his essay 'On the Fetish

Character in Music and the Regression of Listening' (1938) and are developed further in *Dialectic of Enlightenment*.

68 Letter of 18 March 1936: Ernst Bloch et al., *Aesthetics and Politics*, transl. and ed. Rodney Taylor, Afterword by Fredric Jameson (London: NLB, 1977), p.123. For Adorno, high modernist art, through its dissident and creatively distorted formal structures, was alone able to register the deformations of the spirit created by existence under late capitalism, but was increasingly choked off by the products of the culture industry.

69 Martin E. Gingerich, 'Dylan Thomas and America', *Dylan Thomas Remembered* (Swansea: Dylan Thomas Society, 1978), p.34.

70 Cited in Ivan Philips, 'I Sing the Bard Electric: Dylan Thomas, A Poet for the Age of Mass Media', *Times Literary Supplement* (19 September 2003), p.14.

71 William Empson, *Argufying*, p.392.

72 Karl Shapiro, 'Dylan Thomas', ed. C. B. Cox, *Dylan Thomas: A Collection of Critical Essays* (Englewood Cliffs, NJ: Prentice-Hall, 1966), p.176.

73 The miscellanies are structured only by rough chronological logic and an attempt at some generic mixing. For example, *Miscellany One* (1963) comprises six poems from *18 Poems*, five from *Twenty-five Poem*, none from *The Map of Love*, two from *Deaths and Entrances*, plus 'Prologue', 'Do not go gentle', and Vernon Watkins's completion of 'Elegy'. The prose pieces included are three very early stories, the late 'The Followers', and three 1940s broadcasts.'

74 Andrew Lycett, *Dylan Thomas: A New Life*, pp.286, 291, 297.

75 From the outset of his career, Thomas opposed speech-based, casual reading styles. As he noted, their 'naturalness' was often loaded, an attempt to convey: 'by studious flatness, semi-detachment, and an almost condescending undersaying … the impression that what [the poet] really means is: Great things, but my own' (*QEOM*, 167). This attacks the false modesty informing the treatment of language as transparent, and a healthy reassertion of its opacity. Nevertheless, it is also a reminder that: 'the concept of breath [in poetry] is tinged by ideological mysticism'. See Hazel Smith, *Hyperscapes in the Poetry of Frank O'Hara* (Liverpool: Liverpool University Press, 2000), p.138.

76 '[For Leavisites] [t]he distinction between art and mere entertainment is personified in terms of a distinction between the active and autonomous reader and a mere member of a readership. … This idea is both contradicted and, in an intriguing sense, complemented by the modernist construction of the ideal reader of the future … In its way, the modernist ideal reader is an exact counterpart to the idealised reader of mass fiction; though each is defined against the other, each is also imagined as a wholly self-identical category, with no possibility of traffic or fraternisation between the two kinds of reader or readership. The central principle of Leavisite close reading [i.e. that of an "ideal reader of the future"] and the educational practices founded upon it is that of irreversible evolution; having become a sensitive and flexible reader, one is supposed to be incapable, except in the case of pathological relapse, of reverting to one's earlier condition'. Steven Connor, *The English Novel in History: 1950–1995*, p.22.

77 Jacqueline Rose, *The Haunting of Sylvia Plath* (London: Virago, 1992), pp.3, 10.

78 Its subsequent history, as Peter Lewis rightly observes in his account of its gestation, amounts to 'one of the greatest literary and dramatic success stories of [the twentieth] century, and [unique] for something conceived as a radio play'. Peter

Lewis, 'The Radio Road to Llareggub', ed. John Drakakis, *British Radio Drama* (Cambridge: Cambridge University Press, 1981), p. 75.

79 This offers a kind of blueprint for many of *Under Milk Wood*'s scenarios: 'Mr Beetroot, that cracked though cosmic symbol of something or other, will, in the nutty village with dialect, oafs, and potted sermons, conduct his investigation into unreal rural life. Everyone, in this sophisticatedly contrived bucolic morality, has his or her obsession: Minnie Wurzel wants only the vicar; the vicar, the Reverend Nut, wants only the ghost of William Cowper to come into his brown study and read him "The Task"; the Sexton wants worms; the worms want the vicar ... Cruel farmers persecute old cowherds called Crumpet, who talk, all day long, to cows ... it is all very cosy in Upper Story' (*TB*, 124–5).

80 Although it has been read, rather naïvely, as a confessional poem (by Seamus Heaney, among others), 'Lament' originally had the title 'The Miner's Lament' and was possibly conceived as a song for a play set in a Welsh mining village. This is reflected in its punning references to a 'ram rod', 'black spit' and the repeated phrase 'coal black' and its account of the tension between the libido and Nonconformist propriety.

81 See Constantine Fitzgibbon, *The Life of Dylan Thomas* (London: Plantin, 1987), p. 269.

82 M. Wynn Thomas, '"He Belongs to the English": Welsh Dylan and Welsh-language Culture', eds. Glyn Pursglove, John Goodby and Chris Wigginton, *The Swansea Review: Under the Spelling Wall*, 20 (2000), pp. 122–34.

83 Peter Stallybrass and Allon White, *The Politics and Poetics of Transgression* (Ithaca, NY: Cornell University Press, 1986), p. 8.

84 Mikhail Bakhtin, *Rabelais and His World*, transl. Hélène Iswolsky (Bloomington, IN: Indiana University Press, 1984), p. 8.

85 Mikhail Bakhtin, *Rabelais and His World*, p. 7.

86 Mikhail Bakhtin, *Rabelais and His World*, p. 10.

87 See Terry Gifford, *Pastoral*, pp. 23–4: '[P]astoral is carnivalesque in Bakhtin's sense of playfully subverting what is currently taken for granted; the hegemony of the urban establishment'; 'The trickster figure ... in the English folk tradition ... is the Guiser, the Fool, or the Clown, Shakespeare's shepherds often perform the role of the Clown, and in doing so insinuate a humorous critique of court behaviour ... Thus the pastoral can "enforme morall discipline", either by recovering values located in the Golden Age, or by a comic critique of the present through the "vaile" of Arcadia'.

88 For years, as Peter Lewis notes, many critics misjudged *Under Milk Wood*, because they viewed it as a dramatic work, which happened to be presented on radio. Its static quality and 'flat' characters were thus seen as a flaw. In truth, it is closely tailored to its medium and is only fully effective in it. David Holbrook in particular, in his typically humourless way, shows himself to be guilty of requiring what Thomas never promises: 'There is nothing essentially dramatic about the work, because the embodiments have no moral existences, and there is no conflict, development, or synthesis: everything is equally of amusing interest, as to a child, and this lack of essential drama makes [it] a tedious piece of verbal "ingenuity", "redeemed" only by its innuendoes and salacious jokes.' David Holbrook, 'Metaphor and Maturity: T. F. Powys and Dylan Thomas', in *The Pelican Guide to English Literature*, vol. VII (Harmondsworth: Penguin, 1961), p. 417.

89 Just how close Thomas himself came to writing radio comedy is shown by a letter of 1951 to Ted Kavanagh, the *ITMA* scriptwriter, mooting a co-authored series with the provisional title of *Quid's Inn* (*CL*, 880).

90 As Lerner notes, it is significant that Polly Garter's song, which recurs throughout the work and concludes it, is a nursery rhyme: '[t]his says to us what [Thomas] nowhere says explicitly, that what she has lost is childhood'. Laurence Lerner, 'Sex in Arcadia: "*Under Milk Wood*"', p. 275.

91 Gary Saul Morson and Caryl Emerson, cited in Julian Wolfreys, *Critical Keywords in Literary and Cultural Theory* (Basingstoke: Palgrave Macmillan, 2004), p. 29.

92 As in Adorno's more general explanation of the workings of lyric: 'The "I" whose voice is heard in the lyric ... is not immediately at one with the nature to which its expression refers. It has lost it ... and attempts to restore it through animation, through immersion in the "I" itself. It is only through humanization that nature is to be restored to the rights that human domination took from it'. Theodor W. Adorno, 'On Lyric Poetry and Society', ed. Rolf Tiedemann, transl. Shierry Weber Nicholsen, *Notes to Literature, Vol. 1* (New York, NY: Columbia University Press, 1991), p. 41.

93 Richard Chamberlain, 'Fuse and Refuse: The Pastoral Logic of Dylan Thomas's Poetry', p. 3.

94 Barbara Hardy, *Dylan Thomas: An Original Language*, p. 132.

95 Hardy argues that: '[Thomas's] Welshness ... is admirably unmilitant, antinationalist, unpartisan, humorous and pacifist'. Barbara Hardy, *Dylan Thomas, An Original Language*, p. 1.

96 Philip Burton, 'Seventeen Further Memoirs', ed. Miron Grindea, *Adam: International Review* (Dylan Thomas Memorial Number), 238 (1953), p. 37.

97 Daniel Williams's pioneering article on the Tutuola review errs in claiming that, by quoting Thomas on the dustcover of *The Palm-Wine Drinkard*, Tutuola's American publishers: 'were allowing one "true primitive" to espouse another'. The *New York Times* review of *A Palm-Wine Drinkard* by Selden Rodman, which Williams quotes to bear this out, in fact says the opposite: 'If you like ... the poems of Dylan Thomas the chances are you will like this novel, though probably not for reasons having anything to do with the author's intentions. For Amos Tutuola is not a revolutionist of the word, not a mathematician, not a surrealist. He is a true primitive'. It is clear from this that Rodman is contrasting Thomas – the more calculating 'revolutionist of the word ... mathematician ... [and] surrealist' – with the 'true primitive', Tutuola. The misreading of Rodman stems from an over-eagerness to demonstrate that Thomas was read as a 'primitive' in America – as I argue in the Conclusion (fn. 22), this belongs to a discourse in WWE that seeks to exaggerate Thomas's primitivism and thereby undermine his true Welsh credentials. See Daniel Williams, 'Beyond National Literature? Dylan Thomas and Amos Tutuola in "Igbo masquerade"', *New Welsh Review*, 60 (Summer 2003), pp. 5–10.

98 Daniel Williams, 'Beyond National Literature?', pp. 5–6.

99 Linden Huddlestone, 'To Take to Give is All', ed. Miron Grindea, *Adam: International Review*, p. 47.

CONCLUSION

'The liquid choirs of his tribes': Dylan Thomas as icon, influence and intertext

Tristan Tzara: I don't know much about contemporary literature in England. Could you tell me about it?

Lee Harwood: It's difficult. The only poets that are published aren't poets. They're just intellectuals who write clever lines. The only poet we've had this century is Dylan Thomas.

Tristan Tzara: Yes, recently I was offered an Italian literary prize and I accepted it for the sole reason that Dylan Thomas had received it once.

– Lee Harwood interview with Tristan Tzara, 1963.[1]

By Dylan Thomas Square his statue fidgets, turning from
the English chain-house steak bar and the new marina
to the sunset, where no wave breaks over his fame.
He sees through me as if I was America,
which grew a culture of his death under glass.

– 'Aeronwy's Story', Ian Duhig.[2]

'The death of Dylan Thomas', as Karl Shapiro put it, 'was the cause of the most singular demonstration of suffering in modern literary history. One searches the memory in vain for any parallel to it'.[3] The mourning was on an appropriately mythic scale, and it crossed social and cultural boundaries; not only were there two *Times* obituaries, but one by the popular columnist 'Vicky' in *The Daily Mirror*. It was most intense in the US, where guilt and the sense that Thomas symbolised the charisma missing from post-war society intensified the response. But everywhere, he was seen as a rebel against modern, mass society's 'control, complacency and deliberation' and as one who, 'magnificently ill-equipped to deal with the modern world', in Cyril Connolly's phrase, had become a 'victim of the organization man'.[4] Indeed, for some, it was lyric poetry itself, or even a certain kind of human possibility, which had been lost. He was seen as 'the first modern romantic ... who offered himself up as a public, not a private, sacrifice', exemplifying the point made by Jacqueline Rose of Sylvia Plath – that one of the things that the reception of such poets reveals about our 'general culture' is the 'perverse component (voyeurism and sadism) of [its] public acclaim'.[5]

At the same time, Thomas's appeal was contradictory, and this reflected his unique position within the conflicted, shifting set of relationships between elite and mass culture: he was very popular, but self-deprecating and without pose or literary pomp. Nevertheless, he also seemed an unreconstructed representative of the bardic sublime and was a genuinely difficult modernist poet. Paradox was the essence of his significance, for, despite the personal charm, his poetry was 'not a civilizing manoeuvre, a replanting of the gardens; it was a holocaust, a sowing of the wind', and so it seemed as if he had lived and been destroyed by the amoral 'force' celebrated in his poetry.[6] For some, the gap between the different kinds of reputation, reflected in what they saw as Thomas's refusal to take himself and his work sufficiently seriously, had informed the desire to please, to perform, and hence the sense of himself as a fake which had ultimately proved killing.[7] Theories and memoirs poured forth, the two most substantial – *Dylan Thomas in America* (1956) by John Malcolm Brinnin and Caitlin Thomas's riposte in *Leftover Life to Kill* (1957) – replicating the debate which had marked his life over the kind of poet he had been and the significance of his work.

To a large extent, the self-immolating Thomas was a myth within the myth, his primitivism almost entirely the creation of an America which required a counterbalance to the fact that it was the place 'where the full force of technological culture is felt'.[8] Much has been said about whether America, as a result, was responsible for his self-neglectful, ultimately self-destructive, behaviour. Elizabeth Hardwick felt that it had been guilty of a 'murderous permissiveness' in allowing scope for the exercise of the 'real doom' behind Thomas's undoubted taste for theatricalism and scandal.[9] Thomas was, of course, as aware of what was going on as much as anyone else; the bad-boy behaviour was part of the deal – an integral part of a routine he could no more escape than could his audiences. This is why, in accounts of the misbehaviour and suffering, there is always the suggestion of someone acting a part already prepared for him. Even so, there is truth in Hardwick's observation that, while Brinnin's book was priggish, it was most astonishing of all in revealing 'the wild and limitless nature of his devotion to his subject ... Thomas was an addiction'.[10] The hyperbolic response to Thomas and his passing was something more than just shock at 'genius' being destroyed (or confirming its self-destructive nature) or the mere articulation of wider anxieties concerning modernity.[11]

We might describe this 'something more' as a turning point in the negotiation of the relationship between 'low' and 'high' culture, in which the former gained ground at the expense of the latter. The Movement's version of it was to blokeishly define 'low' as empirical, prosy down-to-earthness, as part of their decoupling of poetry from risk-taking – that is, from the investigation of the nature of the self, both in, and through, language. The rejection of Thomas which went with this required that he be presented as a 'high' cultural figure, with the excesses of his life commonsensically and damningly linked to the general economy or excess of his style. This reconfirmed the trend (interrupted in the 1940s) whereby, in David Gervais's words, 'much of the art of our post-symbolist poetry since early Auden has consisted in finding ways of smuggling prose sense back into the equation. So much so that a full-blooded Romantic like Dylan Thomas has come to seem an anomaly'. However this description of Thomas might be qualified, Gervais is surely right in seeing this as the reason why, in much contemporary British poetry, 'inspiration never dips below the conscious mind', it having largely dispensed with the notion that 'moral and psychological insight might be enshrined in the beauty and force of the verse itself, rather than serving simply as a rider to it'.[12] Initially a style of ironic ordinariness for a new meritocracy, it now has to do with institutionalised slanginess, pluralism and 'accessibility'. In both Movement and New Gen phases, as I argued in my Preface, this tendency has been a self-denying ordinance that has deeply damaged British poetry, even if late modernism's linkage to youth and counterculture helped ensure that Thomas's work remained critically highly valued until the mid-1970s and fixed his popularity and popular image. This was the period in which, as Derek Mahon put it, Thomas became 'the hero of a million solitary teenage bedrooms ... a subversive folk-rock Dionysian celebrity before the concept was co-opted and institutionalized, [one who] struck an immediate chord with the young: a proto-feminist and radical pacifist, he talked the talk and walked the walk'.[13] This Thomas anticipated and surfed a sociocultural revolution, becoming the figure for the doomed poet, enshrined on the cover of The Beatles's *Sergeant Pepper's* album and in Bob Dylan's adopted name. As LPs carried his voice around the world, other artists, particularly those working in popular cultural forms, were energised by his example. In music, for example, Thomas's cross-generic appeal attracted jazz and classical composers, while his adoption by folk and rock, in particular – King Crimson's 'Starless and Bible Black' is just one example of scores of similar tributes – signified his incorporation into Marshall McLuhan's electronic 'global village'.[14] Much the same goes for cinema's love affair with Thomas, from a film of *Under Milk Wood* (1972) starring Richard Burton, Elizabeth Taylor and Peter O'Toole to Pierce Brosnan's taste for Thomas memorabilia, George Clooney's recitation of 'And death shall have no dominion' in *Solaris* (2002) and the biopic, *The Edge of Love* (2008).[15]

Artists in popular cultural forms recognise, in Thomas, a rare 'high' art figure with mass appeal, a virtuoso public performer and bohemian, who anticipated the vicissitudes that they feel they face themselves. This foreshadowing of contemporary celebrity is what lies behind Thomas's transfiguration from cultural icon to an icon of culture – as when, while the credits roll on a *Crompton World Encyclopaedia* CD-ROM, Nehru's declaration of Indian independence segues into Thomas reading 'Do not go gentle into that good night'. The consumerist aspect of this power to signify culture is well-illustrated by a television advert of Spring 2007 for Volkswagen's new Golf model. Sampling Richard Burton's rendition of the opening of *Under Milk Wood* as the voice-over for an atmospheric small-hours' drive through inner-city Los Angeles, this says a great deal about Thomas's value as cultural capital.[16] Such uses of the legend deserve a study in their own right and might usefully extend current discussions about the role of poetry in 'the age of media'.[17] The Volkswagen case, in particular, raises the question of the relationship between literature and consumerism. Is the former simply appropriated by the latter? Or is there a more dialectical exchange, with the ad's sinister images critiquing what is cosy in Thomas, while the more barbed parts of *Under Milk Wood* undermine the advert's rather clichéd urban dystopia?

The problem with Thomas's larger cultural presence is that it is so often taken as a sign that his literary significance is of a minor kind (populist, emotive, adolescent and commercially biddable). As Pennar Davies – Thomas's Welsh-language contemporary – rather self-dramatisingly put it in 1954: 'To the votaries of the [Thomas] cult there is a suggestion of the sacrilegious in the boldness of those who would dare to describe him as, let us say, a gifted entertainer, a phenomenon in the history of twentieth century publicity, and as an interesting minor poet'.[18] And while many young poets underwent (perhaps, even now, some still do) an initiatory period of Thomas-enchantment, the idiosyncrasy of his style has always rendered it profoundly inimitable, unlike most models, and this perhaps makes it seem suspect. In many diagrams of 'career' development, a Thomas phase is usually presented as one equivalent to poetic self-abuse – necessary, an awakening to the possibilities of the medium, but eventually to be denounced if one wishes to move towards 'maturity'.

Immediately after his death, Thomas did 'capture the young poets' in America, at least, but this was born of instinctive brief sympathy and identification, rather than deep engagement.[19] As a result, the critical consensus that emerged in the 1960s was that he had had no lasting impact: 'Thomas's poetry is itself a kind of endpoint in its own direction, like *Finnegans Wake*, rather than a stimulus to further exploration, like the early work of Eliot', as R. B. Kershner put it.[20] This reinforced the idea of him as a retrograde figure, going against the inexorable demotic trend of twentieth century poetry: splendid, maybe, but Canute-like. This is certainly why, in recent literary journalism, he signifies little more than verbal exoticism (thus, a 2007 *Guardian* review of Daljit Nagra's *Look We Have Coming to Dover!* could claim, with no sense of absurdity, that: 'Like his stylistic forebear Dylan Thomas, Nagra's creative latitude with words lends the surfaces of his poems colour and movement').[21] Such a superficial appropriation is representative of the amnesia of mainstream poetry and its critical-academic outriders concerning Thomas's work, albeit of a fairly benevolent kind in this case; of the difficulty it has in locating him and defining his achievement, and hence of ascertaining just how real the 'endpoint' might be. In concluding this study, and against the belief in his lack of contemporary influence, I shall argue that Thomas's poetry has been a kind of secret, but powerful, leaven in US and British poetry over the last fifty years, and that he continues to haunt the fraught zone between traditionalist and alternative poetry in Britain.[22] Forgotten and denied though it generally is, his impact on the poetic landscape will be seen to resemble that of some huge Jurassic meteor – a vast, weathered crater, invisible at ground level, but unmissable from the air, and requiring a major rethink of the standard narrative of events.

* * *

In 1977, Eric Homberger claimed that: 'no British poet since Dylan Thomas has made a significant impact on American taste', and this remains true to the present day.[23] Certainly, the revivifying jolt that Thomas gave a schizophrenically sedate poetry culture of the early 1950s is well-attested. Unlike Auden, whose impact was predicated, in part, on the authority that English writing still possessed over US writing prior to the Second World War, Thomas made his impact because of his outsiderness and because of his arrival, in 1950, at a moment when reactionary attacks, symbolised by McCarthyism, had left the liberal intelligentsia cowed. His iconoclastic energy was a living refutation of mealy-mouthedness and self-censorship. It also helped that he was fascinated by US poetry and that his own work was indebted to Whitman and sounded something like Crane. A US selection of Thomas's work had appeared as early as 1940; he was respected by poets, publishers and anthologists there, and was well ahead of his British contemporaries in appreciating US poetry. In the mid-1940s, when his reputation was at its height, Thomas acted as a transatlantic conduit between American poetry and Oxford students; at a reading in 1947, for example, he started 'a great many budding [English] poets' reading Richard Wilbur, Allen Tate, Robert Penn Warren, John Crowe Ransom and Wallace Stevens.[24] If he was ambivalent about academic orthodoxy and the New Criticism, there was nevertheless admiration on both sides. Touring in America, Thomas met and befriended other poets, including Richard Wilbur, Robert Lowell, Elizabeth Bishop, Delmore Schwartz, Theodor Roethke and W. S. Merwin. Away from the academic circuit, he met Robinson Jeffers, Kenneth Rexroth, William Faulkner, Kenneth Patchen, Ray Bradbury and Henry Miller (and non-literary artists, such as Max Ernst, John Cage, Charlie Chaplin and Andy Warhol). It is significant that young African-American poets – Bob Kaufman, Clyde Hamlet, Steve Korrett and Al Young among them – also felt that Thomas spoke to them.[25] In a very real sense, and at the minor cost of being typecast as a Celtic *primitif,* Thomas came close to being an honorary American poet in the early 1950s.

   Thomas's immediate and most obvious contribution to the US poetry scene, however, was a revival of the poetry reading as a genuine cultural event. His mesmerically powerful performances, over 150 of them between 1950 and 1953, were major cultural events, reminding Americans of the strength of their own neglected bardic tradition and weakening the stranglehold of scholarly and clerical styles. But Thomas's chief significance lay in the fact of his influence on practitioners of both 'cooked' and 'raw' poetries. On the one hand he seemed to endorse Beat self-exposure (and Kenneth Rexroth's 'Thou Shalt Not Kill' [1954], a protest against Thomas's death, was the chief model for Allen Ginsberg's *Howl*]).[26] On the other, the travails exposed by Brinnin served as a model for the Confessionals' self-wounding honesty. Moreover Thomas's muscular lyricism is in Robert Lowell's 'The Quaker Graveyard in Nantucket' (1945) and John Berryman's *Homage to Mistress Bradstreet* (1953). This is especially noticeable in Berryman's empathy with his subject's labour pangs, in which Thomas can be seen helping Berryman engineer his delivery from the influence of Yeats and Auden: as, for example, in phrases such as 'One proud tug greens Heaven', 'Fireflies of childhood torch / You down' and 'O all your ages at the mercy of my loves / together lie at once, forever or / so long as I happen'.[27] The vegetable vein of 'The force that through the green fuse' likewise fuelled Theodore Roethke's break from Auden into the Freudian and plant-life imaginings of his great 'greenhouse poems'.[28] More obliquely, the New York poets, bringing surrealism to US poetry in the early 1950s, were treading a path Thomas had taken, almost alone, twenty years before. Frank O'Hara skipped hearing Thomas read, allegedly because he couldn't stand 'all that Welsh spit', but was, in fact, a great admirer of the early work; as John Ashbery noted, 'the more abandoned side of Dylan Thomas' was one of the very select number of bases for his freedom of expression.[29] Even the older William Carlos Williams conceded that some of Thomas's lyrics were 'far and away beyond the reach of any contemporary English or American poet' (although he added that: 'he cannot be of much use to us [American poets]').[30]

The scope of Thomas's impact on US poetry is remarkable, and it testifies to his characteristic hybrid ambivalence. This permits other, more tentative analogies to be advanced, particularly with regard to Thomas's anticipation of, and amenability to, certain avant-garde practices and discourses. If his 'hewn' forms seem far removed from the 'composition by field' advocated by Charles Olson in 'Projective Verse' (1950), more than a shared *zeitgeist* links Thomas with Olson's claim that 'not the eye but the ear' should be the 'measurer' of poetry, that poets should 'take speech up in all its fullness' and go 'down through the workings of his throat to that place where breath comes from, where breath has its beginnings, where drama has to come from, where, the coincidence is, all act springs'.[31] As noted earlier, from the mid-1930s on, Thomas emphasised poetry's roots in the physiology of sound production, insisting on 'poetry that ... comes to life out of the red heart through the brain', attacking conversational reading styles as 'this lack of aural value and ... debasing of an art that is primarily dependent on the musical mingling of vowels and consonants' (*EPW*, 166). While Thomas was no proto-Projectivist, both he and Olson share a concern with the materiality of language and valorise 'voice' to a near-mystical degree.

This stress on utterance, physiology, flux and linguistic materiality suggests other parallels between Thomas and radical American poetics, based on a shared rejection of realism and belief in linguistic experiment. Robert Duncan's essay 'Equilibrations', for example, sounds very much like Thomas describing how poems should work 'from', not 'towards', words: 'The poem is not a stream of consciousness, but an area of composition in which I work with whatever comes into it. Only words come into it. Sounds and ideas. The tone leading of vowels, the various percussions of consonants. The play of numbers in stresses and syllables. ... Rimes, the reiteration of formations in the design, even puns, lead into complexities of the field. ... A word has the weight of an actual stone in his hand. The tone of a vowel has the colour of a wing'.[32] It is as if Duncan recalls 'Once it was the colour of saying', here, and its 'stone[s] [wound] off like a reel'. In his odder manner, John Cage, too, echoes the spirit, if not the letter, of Thomas. 'Coexistence of dissimilars; multiplicity; plurality of centers; "Split the stick, and there is Jesus'''; 'Unimpededness and interpenetration; no cause and effect' – such aphorisms thematically remind us of the process poetic, but also that Thomas's craftedness was merely, as with Cage, the means to an arbitrary grace, to a verbal entity 'so constructed that it is wide open at any second to receive the accidental miracle which makes a work of craftsmanship a work of art' (*QEOM*, 152).

The poets mentioned might reasonably object to being associated with Thomas, but they nevertheless share his resistance to 'realist & mimetic ideas about poetry'. So, more recently, Charles Bernstein's poem-essay, 'Artifice and Absorption', champions 'using antiabsorptive techniques / (nontransparent or nonnaturalizing elements) / (artifice) / for absorptive / ends' as did Thomas, and as does critical work by Lyn Hejinian, Steve McCaffery and other North American avant-garde and L=A=N=G=U=A=G=E poets, very different though their poetic practices are from his.[33] When McCaffery attacks the 'referential fallacy', for example, he is targeting working 'towards' words, while his case for 'let[ting] the direct, empirical experience of a grapheme replace what the signifier in a word will always try to discharge: its signifier and referent' is anticipated in works such as 'Altarwise by owl-light', which forces readers to consider words as material print and sounds, before realising their sense-content.[34] Like Thomas, such poets reject conversational 'voice' and stress the artificiality and rhetoricity, unique to poetry, by which the political implications of the assumed compact between word and thing, syntax and reasonableness, is exposed, in order – as another American critic said of Thomas's work as early as 1945 – 'to free poetry from the strictures of paternity, from religion and from death' and to 'establish the unique individual not merely as the victim, but as the agent of choice; not alone *created by history* but *creative in history*'.[35]

Thomas's impact on Welsh poetry matched his ambiguous reputation there, which was compounded by the fact that the poet who had so adroitly manipulated Welsh stereotypes, swiftly and inevitably became one himself. Following his death, there was genuine sadness and a widespread sense of national loss. The subsequent career of Vernon Watkins was conducted in Thomas's shadow, and the early work of Leslie Norris, John Ormond, Dannie Abse and other emerging poets of the 1950s was haunted by Thomas's voice. Welsh language poets, too, paid tribute on his death: Saunders Lewis rescinded his harsh judgement of 1938, for example, and there was a notably positive tribute from Euros Bowen. In general, however, Welsh language culture and the anglophone poets and critics swayed by it opted, as I noted in the Introduction, to treat Thomas warily. There is no denying, of course, that the pervasiveness of Thomas's work often had an oppressive effect on his successors. For Peter Finch in 1967, 'To live in Wales, / Is to be mumbled at / by re-incarnations of Dylan Thomas / in numerous diverse disguises'.[36] By the 1960s, young poets rejected those reincarnations, because they distorted external expectations of Welsh poetry and limited their own poetic potential. They sought to distance themselves from the sentimentalised and sensationalised legend and to write differently.

This they achieved, primarily by turning to themes accredited by the role of the *bardd gwerin*: history, place, family, religion, the land and the fraught relationship with the Welsh language and literary tradition. To begin with, such work performed the useful function of distinguishing Welsh poetry in thematic terms from other poetries in the United Kingdom. By the mid-1970s, however, with its empirical poetic and limited subject matter, this 'Second Flowering' had become a more insular, even claustrophobic, Welsh version of the English poetry that it wished to define itself against. The trend was exemplified by R. S. Thomas, its one practitioner of stature, whose Anglophobia and denunciations of Welsh self-betrayal reflected guilt and anger at the predicament of the Welsh language and a national identity understood in essentialist terms.[37]

What distinguishes Anglo-Welsh poetry from other national traditions of anglophone poetry in these islands is the extreme belatedness of its emergence (not until the 1930s), a circumstance attributable to the intimidating prestige of a continuing vigorous tradition of poetry in Welsh. By contrast with the likes of Swift, Goldsmith, Moore and early Yeats in Ireland or Burns, Scott and Thompson in Scotland, Anglo-Welsh poetry registered a near three-hundred year silence after Henry Vaughan in the seventeenth century. When modern poetry emerged, it was at the moment of modernism's maximum prestige, and there was little mainstream canonical ballast, from which a status quo might be asserted against modernism's influence. As a result, Dylan Thomas, David Jones and Lynette Roberts, modernists all three, are Anglo-Welsh poetry's founding figures. The work of the best mainstream poet of this 'First Flowering' – the Housmanesque Idris Davies – is markedly less impressive than that of his modernist-influenced contemporaries. So it was that when a non-modernist Anglo-Welsh poetry made another attempt to establish itself in the 1960s and 1970s, it was more successful, but rested upon a Movement-influenced aesthetic and a canon constructed so as to marginalise the modernists.[38] As a result, the official Anglo-Welsh poetry world, including its academic-critical superstructure, has ever since been subject to destabilising pressure from an originating moment it must disavow (one reason why Thomas's later work is prized and the earlier poetry is avoided by WWE academics is because it allows for discussion of him in more conservative critical terms). Ironically, the high relative preponderance of the alternative poetic tradition Anglo-Welsh poetry is what gives it its unique excellence and distinction; indeed, it is arguably Wales's most original and significant contribution to twentieth century culture.

Robert Lowell and John Berryman, two of the US poets championed by Thomas, were among the chief models for post-Movement English poets held up for emulation by A. Alvarez in his Introduction to *The New Poetry* (1962). Alvarez's anthology marked the end of the overt influence of the Movement, and it singled out Ted Hughes for particular praise, while noting (if rather patronisingly) that Thomas 'in his early poems, had something rather original to say'. Alvarez, though, dismissed the Apocalyptic Forties and missed the extent to which Hughes developed out of Thomas as well as D. H. Lawrence.[39] As James Keery has argued: 'much of [Hughes's] rewiring of English nature poetry is implicit in a single electrifying line' – 'The force that through the green fuse drives the flower'.[40] Anti-Apocalypse orthodoxy has made it difficult to trace the continuity between it and the energies and ambition of Hughes, but this is the true context of his work, and in truth his poetry has few qualms about displaying it. 'Over Sir John's hill' alone supplies *Gaudete*'s 'The lark sizzles in my ear / Like a fuse', 'the drills of his eyes / On a short fierce fuse' in 'Jaguar', and the 'black- / Back gull' of 'Wind'.[41] In this case, Hopkins is a common ancestor, although, as Keery notes, Thomas's line 'To the hawk on fire ... In a whack of wind' sounds more like Hughes than Thomas himself.[42] More generally, many of Hughes's poems insist that foreknowledge of death gives the human predicament a metaphysical dimension, and they often attempt to unravel the fusion of the inner and outer worlds of Thomas's process poems, intrigued by, but critical of, the self-consciousness which separates man from the natural world, as Thomas does in 'The force that through the green fuse'. 'Egg-Head', for example, from *The Hawk in the Rain* (1957), seems to take its cue from the line 'As sunlight paints the shelling of their heads' in 'I see the boys of summer' and the Donnean conceit behind *Deaths and Entrances*. In it, the unborn child of the Thomas poem, deaf and blind in the womb, is the central image for human beings after birth, and their development of 'a staturing "I am"' and 'feats of torpor', which are aimed at filtering out the wonders and terrors of the universe.[43]

Yet because Thomas is involved, critical denial and avoidance, in one form or another, remains strong: thus, Keith Sagar claims that Hughes, in 1954, was 'too much under the influence of Dylan Thomas', but fails to explain how or why, while on the other hand Thomas West claims that 'the closer one looks [at early Hughes] the more one is struck by the absence of direct literary influence'.[44] They can't both be right. The main point at issue, however, is more a chronological one – to do with the ingrained prejudice against the 1940s. This is because Hughes didn't 'revolt against' the Movement any more than Thomas 'reacted against' Auden. Rather, as a keen follower of Thomas and Apocalypse poetry in his formative years, he preceded the Movement and carried on regardless of it – a point, Keery observes, 'both made and missed' by one of his biographers, Elaine Feinstein: 'His supervisor [at Cambridge] ... confessed that she had learned more from him about Dylan Thomas than he had learned from her about John Donne'.[45]

One poet that Hughes would have introduced to Thomas's work, of course, had she not already known it as well as he did himself, was Sylvia Plath. In high school, Plath had 'imitated and idolised' Thomas. At college, she wrote a paper on him and won an honourable mention in a writing contest named after him. If *The Bell Jar* is any indication, she also spent much of her free time reading his work, too. Indeed, she 'loved Dylan Thomas ... almost more than life itself' and put an end to her engagement to a long-term boyfriend, because of 'a knock-down-drag-out argument ... over whether Thomas's death had been the fault of [Brinnin]' or not.[46] Commentators have made the point that Plath saw Ted Hughes as 'a second Dylan Thomas', albeit a better-looking one, and that this constituted not a little of his appeal; one game that the pair played involved Hughes calling out 'a line of Thomas or Shakespeare' and Plath completing the passage. As in the case of Hughes, the fascination was non-intimidating and highly productive. Plath's poems are densely intertextual with Thomas's; in fact, according to Gary Lane, 'Dylan Thomas is the vocal colossus of Plath's *The Colossus*' – the first collection that she published after meeting Hughes. In one of the more extreme cases, 'The Snowman on the Moor', Thomas's style breaks in at the poem's mid-point to correct the 'pretty poeticisms' of its first part, dubiously representing a desired masculine power for the female speaker in a welter of allusions to 'A Winter's Tale', 'In the White Giant's Thigh' and 'Into her lying down head'.[47] The very title of 'All the Dead Dears' adopts *Under Milk Wood*'s 'all my dead dears' and exemplifies Thomas's process philosophy in its inter-involvement of the living and the dead and the usurping of one generation by the next. Its undersea details derive from Captain Cat's undersea interlocutors: 'How they grip us through thick and thin / The barnacle dead! ... until we go, / Each skulled-and-crossboned Gulliver / Riddled with ghosts, to lie / Deadlocked with them, taking root as the cradles rock'.[48] More important still is Plath's inheritance and development of Thomas's poems of gestation, birth and dialogues with embryos in her pregnancy poems 'The Manor Garden', 'You're' and 'Nick and the Candlestick'.

It can also be argued that Thomas was a model for Plath of the 'serious' poet who engaged with mass culture. Like Plath, who published chick-lit fictions in *Mademoiselle* and *Seventeen*, as well as poems in the *TLS*, Thomas was not embarrassed by writing for the market. In relation to the institutions of culture, she, like Thomas, was a hybrid 'crossing over the boundaries of cultural difference with an extraordinary and almost transgressive ease'.[49] Both, as already noted, suffered as a result. It is noteworthy that commentators in the 1950s routinely gendered mass culture as 'female', in order to dismiss it, and this sheds light on Plath's and Thomas's legends and the way that they subsequently developed. The fact that they were both singled out for book-length attack by David Holbrook on similar grounds (their poetry assumed to be fluid, 'hysterical', destructive of qualitative distinctions, etc.) is thus more than mere coincidence and underlines the fact that they both chose to write at a point of tension between high and popular culture, even if Plath offers less 'resolution or dissipation of what produces the clash between the two', than the more genial Thomas.[50]

Other examples of the persistence of Thomas's influence are highly significant in terms of developments in British poetry over the last half-century. Geoffrey Hill's earliest poems were written at Oxford, where Thomas lived until May 1949, and, in their more intellectual vein, both 'Genesis' and 'God's Little Mountain' take their cue from him: 'By blood we live, the hot, the cold, / To ravage and redeem the world: / There is no bloodless myth will hold'.[51] Edwin Morgan, too, has claimed: '[the Anglo-Welsh / New Apocalypse] interested me when I was starting off to write, people like Dylan Thomas and David Gascoyne'.[52] The engagement of the most important pioneer of post-war British neo-modernist poetry, Roy Fisher, went deeper still:

> What is interesting … is that it was reading Dylan Thomas that enabled me to start [writing poems]. It was like one of those astronomical events where a body is struck by another and kicked out of its familiar orbit into a new one … I came across *The Burning Baby*, then read, along with the gang of surrealist and neo-romantic things I was hunting out, the first two collections of poems and *The Map of Love*. It was simply the spectacle of something quite primal … a sort of linguistic / imaginative magma, unsuspected innards, the breaking of taboos one hadn't known existed, that shook up my innocence. That was all. I've not returned to those Thomas texts for years, but they remain an extraordinary phenomenon, which won't quite factorize out into the visible elements – Welsh, the Bible, drink, testosterone and so forth – there's still something that resists explanation, however difficult it might be to find a place for it.[53]

The most powerful of Fisher's early poems, 'The Lemon Bride' (1954), which James Keery reads with Larkin's 'Deceptions' and Yeats's 'Leda and the Swan', owes at least as much to Thomas's 1934 short story, 'The Lemon', which supplies several of the poem's properties: lemon, wax, frost, tree, acid, knives and the Thomas phrase 'outside weather'. Thomas's story involves a mad scientist, a boy, and a girl with a lemon containing an acid which kills and resurrects, while Fisher's poem presents the 'rage' and intactness of a violated girl who is a figure for the poet, beset by 1950s culture, but both are mythopoeic constructs, with Fisher indebted to Thomas's figuring of sexual anxiety and gothic-grotesque menace in a poem said to be his 'authentic point of departure'.[54]

The continuation of Thomas's Blakean, existential-visionary strain of modernism, absent from most histories, is nowhere more apparent than in the case of W. S. Graham. Graham, who began his career as a New Apocalypse poet, has become an exemplary figure for several contemporary late-modernist poets, including Tony Lopez and Denise Riley. He is crucial to the case that I am making here, because he has also been, for some mainstream critics, the one poet most worth salvaging from what they judge to be the stylistic shambles of the 1940s.[55] In order to do this, however, it has been necessary to write off his New Apocalypse poetry and dispute its continuity with the later, more admired work. However, Graham refused to endorse this process and insisted, until the end of his life, that his early poetry was not at all cast into the shade by the later writing, increasingly powerful though that was. As he put it to Michael Schmidt in 1977:

> It is not like that [growing out of the Thomas influence]. I was disappointed you writing the old cliché about me ... I am getting better I hope. But it is not like a graph saying 'he started out not knowing what he was doing and then went through his Dylan Thomas phase (Which I got a great deal out of) and now he [is] refining himself' ... It was you belittling, too much, for the sake of the last books, the early poetry. Of course I think there is an advance, but if I put out 'Here Next the Chair I Was' [*Cage Without Grievance*, 1942], now, I would be proud and 'THEY' would like it well.

Lopez convincingly argues that the even earlier poem, *The Seven Journeys*, 'contains in embryo almost all the subjects of his major works' and that 'Graham's development ... was prefigured at the outset of his writing ... not something that occurred to him after getting clear of youthful influence'.[56]

Graham's bond with Thomas, who encouraged and promoted him and visited him in Glasgow, as well as meeting him in Fitzrovia (he was probably the first fellow writer to whom Thomas read 'Fern Hill'), was strong.[57] In *Poetry Scotland* in 1946, he followed Thomas's claim that a poem had to work 'from', rather than 'towards', words, to be 'made out of words' first and foremost, rather than subserve an expressivist or sociological poetic:

> The most difficult thing for me to remember is that a poem is made out of words and not of the expanding heart, the overflowing soul, or the sensitive observer. A poem is made of words. It is words in a certain order, good or bad by the significance of its addition to life and not to be judged by any other value put upon it by imagining how or why or by what kind of man it was made.[58]

The Seven Journeys shows Graham systematically externalising and extending those aspects of Thomas's poetry to do with linguistic play, textualised landscapes and verbal embodiments of the erotic and the unconscious, pushing towards a more explicit questioning of the relationship between language and the self or being. This is apparent in the way that poems such as 'Ballad of the Long-legged Bait', for example, feed into *The Nightfishing* (1955), the first section of which opens in the same metre as Thomas's 'Prologue' and includes gulls, fishing, a boat-journey, 'the dead / Of night and the dead / Of all my life' and ends by echoing Thomas's 'To Wales in my arms' with 'The present opens its arms' (*CP*, 1, 2).[59] Much the same could be said of the polar white-out and Arctic explorers of *Malcolm Mooney's Land* (1970), which take off from the line 'Cold Nansen's beak on a boat full of gongs' ('Once below a time') and the snowscape-text of 'A Winter's Tale', as much as from real-life tales of polar exploration (*CP*, 110). But while these verbal echoes and thematic similarities could easily be multiplied, it should be said that Graham's use of Thomas is very rarely derivative in a bad sense; he actively incorporates him, even as the debt is acknowledged. At one point in the late piece 'What is language using us for?' from *Implements in Their Places* (1977), the speaker encounters another traveller in the waste, describing him as the 'King of Whales', and notes:

> The King of Whales dearly wanted
> To have a word with me about how
> I had been trying to crash
> The Great Barrier.[60]

He tells of being unable to answer him very well 'in the white / Crystal of art he set me in.' The poem then asks who the king of Whales might be, and we learn that he is 'a kind of old uncle of mine /And yours' who sledges across the ice-cap 'Shouting at his delinquent dogs'. The speaker adds that he will only discern the purpose of this figure by 'going / Out of my habits which is my name / To ask him how I can do better.'

I do not see that there can be much doubt that Graham's 'King of Whales' is an affectionate, comic-archetypal rendering of Dylan Thomas, given his status as mentor, the nature of the 'word' he wants, the use of Thomas's favourite 'whales / Wales' pun, and the presence of the 'delinquent dogs', an allusion to the 'dog among the fairies' of 'Altarwise by owl-light' and *A Portrait of the Artist as a Young Dog*.[61] But despite this the notes to the recent *New Collected Poems* miss the allusion, nor is Thomas listed in its 'People' appendix or mentioned in the Introduction by the editor, Matthew Francis.[62] The silence would seem to arise more from embarrassment than hostility, but the result is the suppression of one of the more important lines of succession in mid-twentieth century British poetry.

Although, like Thomas's, Graham's style became more transparent over time, this clarity was not reached by making concessions to the empirical and mimetic, as is so often claimed. Rather, he worked his way through the 'Celtic' subjects of plant, season, and sexuality and the Blakean urban pastoral of the Greenock poems, as part of a logical process of isolating and focusing on a stripped-back version of language, the self and landscape. The everyday world in this work is often considered from a perspective which is non-specific and metaphysical, influenced by Graves's *The White Goddess* and late Heidegger. Hence the claim sometimes made that Graham is Dylan Thomas plus Heidegger or, as 'What is the Language Using Us For?' might rephrase it: 'Man acts as though he were the shaper and master of language, while in fact language remains the master of man'.[63]

This kind of misreading of Thomas's influence has its equivalent on the other side of the poetic fence. In a pioneering essay on Lynette Roberts of 1994, Nigel Wheale damned Thomas's 'hopelessly private obscurity', accusing him of 'writing with no recoverable patterns of any interest' – an odd position for someone seeking to rehabilitate Roberts.[64] However, appreciation of Thomas's importance has been growing in recent years. Tony Lopez's 1991 study of W. S. Graham strove rather desperately to distance Graham from Thomas's influence; however, his later *Meaning Performance* (2006) offers some redress and usefully rebuts a few Thomas stereotypes.[65] In fact, most of the recent attempts to critically rehabilitate the 1940s and Thomas have been made by critics who are also late modernist poets, like Lopez himself, such as James Keery and Andrew Duncan. Thus, while none of Duncan's five studies to date on alternative poetry discuss Thomas, they all assume his centrality.

Equally, British avant-garde *poetry* probably owes more to Thomas than it is prepared to admit. Drew Milne's sonnet sequence 'Foul Papers' opens:

Clamour for change, with this to plough on
even though fresh mint, under a flat
climate, borders on wisteria
buoyed and flushed in a slogan too far,
or wills no attempt to portray what palls
as in every body flirts, don't they?
So minting, some feel like death over it

whose only sin is unlikely grist,
wit and wag this sizzling raunch bears all,
wailing wall to boot, and now we're told
due more to Herod's engineering,
nature not withstanding, as a fly
passes on withering western winds,
and all the bold sedge goes hand in fist,
spent in forage round other and earth.[66]

Sheet Mettle was praised on its appearance as the best first collection since Auden's *Poems* (1930); but the cliché invites more than the usual scepticism, given that 'Foul Papers' evidently owes at least as much to the kind of 'dialectical method' behind 'Altarwise by owl-light' as it does to the chiselled neoclassical syntax we find in 'Sonnets From China'. The literalisation and twisting of cliché ('plough on', 'borders on', 'hand in fist'), pun ('fresh mint', 'bears all'), word separation ('every body', 'not withstanding'), echo-bounce ('wisteria' / 'hysteria'), deep-buried allusion ('The sedge is withered from the lake') and straining of syntax through heaped-up appositive clauses; these are all Thomas's methods, not Auden's. Milne's poem is deeply involved in working *from*, not simply *towards*, words, and its techniques for subverting a means-end view of language are a far cry even from the Auden of *The Orators*. There is no disputing that the Auden comparison is applicable at the level of socio-political purview (although Thomas's 'dialectical method' means that his work, too, has political implications). Which is to say that Auden may be a presiding spirit, but only up to a point; indeed, Milne's style hints at a fusion of Thomas and Auden, a bringing together of the 'two halves' of the great successor to Eliot which Gabriel Pearson claimed English poetry failed to throw up in the 1930s. Thomas's mediated presence within this kind of writing, often associated with Cambridge, may stretch back several decades, despite the disclaimers of some. It is worth remarking, perhaps, that the Acknowledgements to *Poet in the Making* (1968) include Ralph Maud's thanks to one 'Jeremy Prynne, whose eyes I have used on the manuscript … at various times'.[67] And whether or not Prynne has himself acknowledged an interest in Thomas, other experimental poets – Geraldine Monk, Maggie O'Sullivan and David Annwn, for example – have done so.

Finally, we might consider Thomas's presence and influence in the non-anglophone world. The Welsh poet Euros Bowen made the point that 'Thomas was not, as commonly supposed, a Welsh poet writing in an English tradition, but rather a Welsh poet whose work was European in character', and while he was wrong about Thomas's use of 'English tradition', as I showed in Chapter 6, he was right about his work's 'European' qualities.[68] As opposed to 'the English tradition' stemming from Hardy, Thomas's sense of poetry as the language art matched that found in most non-English-speaking cultures. This is reflected in one of the most striking facts about his reception; namely, the extent to which he has been translated. Not only are there translations in all the major European languages – French, Italian, German, Spanish and Russian – and often more than one – but in most of the smaller nation languages, too, including Bulgarian, Catalan, Rumanian, Czech, Serbo-Croat, Polish, Dutch, Greek, Latvian, Danish, Polish, Swedish, Norwegian, Finnish, Portuguese and, of course, Welsh. Thomas has also been translated into several non-European languages, among them Arabic, Japanese and Chinese. One reason for this range is the fact that his work was favoured in the former Soviet Bloc. Although no research has yet been done on the reasons for this, it is unlikely that it was solely because of his political ideals (although they surely helped) since Thomas's socialism had marked anarchist and Christian qualities. Rather, it would seem that, like Robert Burns – another Western poet favoured in the Soviet Union – petit-bourgeois deviancy and bohemianism were set aside, because he was a comparatively lower-class rebel against, and victim of, capitalist hypocrisy and materialism. It is likely, then, that there was an element of licensed dissent in this display of official tolerance. The preference of translators in all languages is, as one would expect, for the poems and *Under Milk Wood* (which, by 1967, had been rendered into over fifty languages), but the stories and radio features have often been translated, too.

The Thomas legend has, of course, played a role in attracting so many translators and foreign publishers. However, it is unlikely that this would have been sufficient on its own to account for his extraordinary pulling power. Along with the mix of post-Symbolist coordinates, Celticity and nostalgic appeal, Thomas's universal themes and the lack (in the poetry at least) of easily dated, specific sociocultural details may also have helped. And while Thomas's notorious obscurity makes him very difficult to translate, it may, paradoxically, have added to the appeal; he has often, like Joyce, been taken as a useful limit-case writer – one who can be used to test the boundaries of the translatable. In this capacity, his work – perverse as it must seem to some – is taken to exemplify the genius of the English language. Moreover, as a particularly challenging case, he has frequently featured in theoretical discussions concerning the nature of translation.[69]

Although it is difficult to quantify Thomas's influence on non-anglophone poets, one example – that of Paul Celan – deserves particular mention here. As James Keery has argued, Celan, Thomas and the New Apocalypse poets arise out of the same 'matrix of European visionary modernism' and share a vocabulary and thematics. The frequency with which they arrive at similar verbal formulations is striking; thus, the 'black milk' of Nicholas Moore's 'My Little Monster' is re-coined in Celan's 'Todesfuge', while Celan's 'Epitaph for Francois', to take another example, echoes in phrasing, wordplay, sentiment and focus upon first and last things, such Thomas lyrics as 'The force that through the green fuse' and 'Twenty-four years':

> The two doors of the world
> stand open:
> opened by you
> in the twinight.
> We hear them slam and slam
> and carry the thing that's uncertain
> and carry the green thing into your Ever.[70]

These parallels are more than mere coincidence. Amy Colin notes, in her study of Celan, that Celan read about, and was influenced by 'Thomas's idea of poetic images as bearing the seed of their own destruction' – that is, the crucial passage in his letter to Henry Treece of 1938 – and he certainly also read Thomas's poems.[71] Keery rightly observes that: 'there is ... an intimate link between Thomas's "seedy shifting" and "gold tithings" and a "Celanian chain of metaphors derived from alchemy: gold-seed / semen-grain, etc". ... Celan pursued the quintessentially Apocalyptic theme of (im)mortality by means of the same blasphemous image-complex ("the exultant psalmist's sexual member bears the mark of God")'. Quoting Celan's 'Spasms', Keery adds: 'The last line ["I sing the scarscore of the bone-staff"] sounds like an out-take from "I dreamed my genesis"!'[72] This, of course, sheds a particularly ironic light on the mainstream critical consensus concerning Celan, who is widely regarded, rightly, as probably the greatest of post-war European poets, and the denigration of 1940s poetry, New Apocalypse and Thomas himself.

'That's the point innit?': some conclusions

Reassessed with an eye to his occluded palpable intertextual presences and his numerous haunting absences, Thomas appears far more central than is usually allowed to modern English, Anglo-Welsh and British poetry, not least in challenging the compartmentalised thinking that these terms represent. In this book, I have tried to explain why I think his work mattered to almost all of his contemporaries and why it continued to matter at the highest critical level for two decades after his death. I have also tried to explain why, although it retained its appeal for a general audience, it fell out of favour in academic criticism and literary journalism in the 1970s and remains unplaceable but un-ignorable today, continuing to enchant, baffle and antagonise. As a contribution to ending the impasse in Thomas studies, I have rearticulated the claims it makes on our understanding of the poetry of the last eighty years, suggesting fresh approaches in the hope that these will be taken up, argued with, expanded and improved upon. I have done so, because it seems to me that bringing Thomas into better focus is not just a matter of historical redress, but of understanding the moment in which poetry finds itself right now.

I've argued, further, that the failure to deal with Thomas is the result of his interstitial, impure and hybrid nature: variously, and in varying proportions, his poetry has been considered too avant-garde by the mainstream, too mainstream by the avant-garde, too Welsh by the English, too English by the Welsh, too popular by a cultural elite, although not too elite by the general public. Thomas's representation today by a few anthology favourites, which do not fully evince his full development as a poet, is also part of the problem. Currently, his work is spread between different poetic camps, its several parts seemingly incompatible with each other and the totality of his achievement hard to define or categorise. For now, it remains, above all, a nagging reminder of what Keith Tuma, in his study of British experimental poetry, *Fishing by Obstinate Isles* (1998), describes as the 'faultlines' opened up in British poetry by *The Waste Land*, which British poetry still struggles to deal with. The faultlines are, tacitly, recognised by many and often deplored; but if there is some desire to overcome them, there is not yet much will to do so. So, in an interview of 2007, the then-editor of *Poetry Review*, Fiona Sampson, answered the question 'what place [do] you think the avant-garde has in the current British poetry scene' by replying 'I think they [mainstream and avant-garde] don't talk to each other at all ... I think that people whose practice, in one way or another, tries to bridge the two streams do badly, because neither can quite tolerate it. They both see it as a lack of intellectual loyalty.[73] The trouble is that Tuma, like Sampson, as a representative of the mainstream that he criticises, sees just one fault line, with Auden alone bestriding it and sheep 'retreat[ing] from modernist poetry' and the goats, such as Basil Bunting and Joseph Macleod, 'extending and revising' it.[74] Thomas, who was both sheep and goat (to say nothing of dog), the hybridiser of Eliot and Auden, Lawrence and Joyce, disrupts this schema and so is rarely mentioned.

Even so, his status as the ghost at the banquet of today's self-proclaimed pluralist poetry culture is increasingly reflected in the way that so many British poets felt (and still feel) the need to confront the fact of his marginalisation. Some, such as John Hartley Williams and Derek Mahon, have made the case for reinstating him. Most, however, are defeated by the legend after an initial bout or two. Michael Donaghy, for example, is representative in admitting to being 'intoxicated' by Thomas as an adolescent, but later concluding that he had failed to develop.[75] Equally Thomas's continuing entanglement with the 'dire decade' myth can be traced in a review in 2004 of W. S. Graham's *New Collected Poems* by Don Paterson, who argued that the 1940s had been a bad time for beginning poets, because 'the high camp of Dylan Thomas and Wallace Stevens left almost a whole generation mincing in their wake, all with that mangled syntax and hysterical rhetoric that made the modernist drag-artist only too easy to spot'.[76] It's yet another example of Thomas outing a critic's prejudice – here, a Scottish macho fear of effeminacy and queerness – but it also reveals the size of the obstacles that stand in the way of reassessment.

Much of the problem remains an unspoken resistance to the implications of Thomas's language use, best articulated by Seamus Heaney – the most influential British mainstream poet since Larkin. As Jeffrey Side has noted recently, Thomas was the fly in the ointment of the upgraded Movement poetic that Heaney inherited from Philip Hobsbaum, his earliest mentor. While Heaney has acknowledged that poetry 'cannot afford to lose its ... joy in being a process of language as well as a representation of things in the world', the extent to which his own poetry allows for 'process' is limited by any measure of it that Thomas would have recognised, and Heaney's criticism, for all its sonorous phrase-making, displays an ingrained empirical distrust of ingenuity, artifice and play. His essay on Thomas in *The Redress of Poetry* (and *Dylan the Durable*) shows, Side points out, the 'discomfort'

Thomas causes him as a prime offender against Hobsbaum's dictum that 'language is never arbitrary'; for him, Thomas 'place[s] a too unenlightened trust in the plasticity of language'. At the same time, however, Heaney feels compelled to pay tribute to poetry's autotelic and visionary dimensions; this is unconvincing, but it is at least arguable that his engagement with Thomas mediates the limitations placed on his own poetic practice by post-Movement orthodoxy concerning language as 'unequivocal communication'.[77] Thomas was a favourite poet of the Belfast Group in the early 1960s, and he has a conflicted meaning for Heaney, the struggle with his example arguably encoded in *Death of a Naturalist* (1966) – his first collection – which reads as an extended reaction against 'Fern Hill' (this is how *real* farms work) and a grudging tribute to the mimetic power and pastoral vision of Thomas's late poetry more generally.

My point, to be clear, is not that mainstream poets necessarily dislike Thomas – they are generally more receptive to him than academics – but that they have a distorted image of him. There is a recurrent impulse to try to 'place' his poetry and the phenomena that he represents, which amounts to a return of the repressed, nagging at and undermining the mainstream's self-image, because it reminds it of its self-imposed restrictions and self-denying stylistic ordinances. This anxiety, it should be added, is an improvement on the neo-Movement 1980s and reflects the rise of pluralism signalled by *The New Poetry* (1993) and the New Generation poets promotion of 1994.[78] Yet that new heterogeneity did not, unfortunately, open up the mid-century for significant reconsideration (the commonest 'influences' that the twenty New Gen poets cited were Elizabeth Bishop, Robert Lowell and W. H. Auden).[79] Although there was some widening of mainstream poetry practices, this was less evident in criticism, as I noted in my Introduction, and Thomas continues to be represented in terms of the clichés of the legend, leaving his radical and disruptive hybridity unacknowledged.

This is evident in the continuing failure to re-evaluate the 1930s or 1940s. Gabriel Pearson's notion that the styles of Auden and Thomas originate in a shared 'apocalyptic' response to the crisis of 1929–33, developing neo-Augustan and neo-Blakeian / Romantic versions, respectively, of a native modernism (in short, that they are 'complementary') remains un-investigated: 'each over-developed what the other neglects', Pearson suggests, 'crudely, thought as against feeling. Auden handles language from the outside, like a craftsman or sportsman, while Thomas burrows into the body of the language itself from which he delivers oracles from the heat of its decomposition'.[80] Poets and critics badly need to address this crucial moment in English and Anglo-Welsh poetry (which has its Irish and Scottish dimensions, too) and to embrace the possibility of a *British* poetry, which is not only more at ease with its different geographical identities, but with its different traditions and modes. That this has not happened is a measure of the limitations of the pluralist turn. In this sense, as John Matthias has wryly noted, ideas of pluralism have been extended 'to race, religion, class, language, gender, sexual preference – to everything, in fact, except poetics'.[81]

Any real consideration of Thomas's poetry exposes the superficiality of this version of the 'democratic voice', as an anthology edited by Simon Armitage and Robert Crawford called it, because it confounds the two-dimensional dichotomy of mainstream versus alternative, centre versus periphery, making it clear that poetry is an active, creative exploration in the act of submitting to, and struggling with, language, the self, the body and the world; that it is not merely a means for expressing where the already defined self locates itself in relation to these things.[82] However, as we approach the centenary of Thomas's birth, the argument against monolithic traditions bearing national essences has been partly won. Some of the fissures and fault-lines, which link as well as dividing, are at least being rendered visible and made available for critical scrutiny.

At some point, the dialogue will have to turn to Thomas, who holds the answers to so many of the questions which need answering. At a conference on Thomas that I helped organise in 1998, I overheard one of the older generation of Thomas scholars observing to another that the only thing now left to do was to track down the few remaining unrecognised allusions in 'Altarwise by owl-light'. It seemed to me, at the time, that, on the contrary, criticism's task with regard to Thomas had scarcely begun. Since then, sufficient steps have probably been taken to prevent the centenary in 2014 becoming simply a retelling of the stale clichés of the legend (as Thomas once said, interrupting himself in conversational mid-flow, 'Someone is boring me. I think it's me'). But far more is required. Poets and critics interested in overcoming the divisions might do worse than start seriously considering what the linguistic dynamism of *18 Poems* says about 1930s writing, or examining the implications for poetic language of the four 'odes' of 1938–40, or exploring the ethical issues raised by the war elegies and Cold War pastorals. If they are feeling particularly brave, they might even consider analyzing Thomas's most notoriously forbidding and famously alluring work, a Degree Zero of twentieth century English language poetry. Or, as the late Richard Caddel put it on the British poets list, responding to the question 'Who likes Dylan Thomas?':

> I like DT. I admire the push of what he did, when he did it – an attempt to lift the art above the drab aural flatness into which it had (for the most part) sunk, and to ground that on technique – rhyme, shape, invention. The criticisms, that it's 'artificial' ... that it's 'overblown' (of course it's overblown, that's the point innit? Memories of my counterpoint tutor who said, Well, Rick, I'm an organist, and I just like a bloody big noise all around me ...) and so on, well they seem pretty nimminy to me. That he's 'uneven' too is self-evident – nevertheless I'd rather have 'prentice poets bang their heads on 'Altarwise by owl-light' as an object to emulate than much of the middlepace stuff which takes up so much time and space.[83]

Notes

1 Lee Harwood, 'The Parable of Tristan Tzara and the Callow Youth', *Poetry Wales*, 47: 2 (Autumn 2011), p. 28. Harwood interviewed Tzara in the year of his death, 1963.

2 Ian Duhig, 'Aeronwy's Story', *Nominies* (Newcastle-upon-Tyne: Bloodaxe, 1998), p. 37.

3 Karl Shapiro, 'Dylan Thomas', ed. C. B. Cox *Dylan Thomas: A Collection of Critical Essays* (Englewood Cliffs, NJ: Prentice-Hall, 1966), p. 169.

4 Alfred Kazin, 'The Posthumous Life of Dylan Thomas', *Atlantic Monthly* (October 1957), pp. 166–7. Kazin's is the most sympathetic and penetrating assessment of Thomas's impact upon the US, and of the US upon him. Connolly's obituary in *The Times* (15 November 1953) overlooks the fact that Thomas actually managed to cope with most aspects of the 'modern world' well enough.

5 Karl Shapiro, 'Dylan Thomas', p. 170. Jacqueline Rose, *The Haunting of Sylvia Plath* (London: Virago, 1992), p. 3.

6 Karl Shapiro, 'Dylan Thomas', p. 171.

7 Alfred Kazin, 'The Posthumous Life of Dylan Thomas', *Atlantic Monthly* (October 1957), p. 165. Kazin claims: 'He had no philosophy or belief that could express for him ... the burden of love and terror before the natural world that is the subject of all his poetry. ... he was left with his fantastic linguistic gift as if it were something to read from ... but not, in the artistic sense, to practice as a criticism of life. ... Being an utterly accessible and friendly and idle-feeling man, he couldn't help seeing himself as a faintly comic version of that universally respected legend, "The Poet"'.

8 Alfred Kazin, 'The Posthumous Life of Dylan Thomas', p. 167.

9 Elizabeth Hardwick, 'America and Dylan Thomas', ed. John Malcolm Brinnin, *A Casebook on Dylan Thomas* (New York, NY: T. Y. Crowell, 1961), p. 151. Hardwick's moving and insightful sense of Thomas in America, like Kazin's, bears repeated reading. Like other American accounts, it highlights the risky self-expenditure

which informed Thomas's performativity: 'He was both immoderately available and, in the deepest sense, unavailable too. His extraordinary gregariousness was a sign of his extremity. He knew everyone in the world, but for a long time he had perhaps been unable to know anyone'. In Britain, of course, the adulation and personal availability were not present to the same potentially dangerous degree.

10 Elizabeth Hardwick, 'America and Dylan Thomas', p. 156.

11 I refer here to how, in popular notions of 'the genius', the gift of the artist is given at the expense of a terrible, often fatal, flaw – alcoholism, personal sorrow, disfigurement and disease. This belief that great gifts exact a high price, including destruction, is an ancient one. Those who confront the supernatural in order to gain their powers always bear the mark (often hidden) of their encounter. In Western culture, the archetype is Oedipus, whose name conceals / reveals the possession of a deformed foot.

12 David Gervais, 'On French and English Poets', *P.N. Review* 145, 28: 5 (May-June 2002), pp. 30, 31, 33.

13 Dylan Thomas, *Selected Poems*, ed. Derek Mahon (London: Faber, 2003), p. xviii.

14 Thus, *Under Milk Wood* inspired the most celebrated British jazz composition, Stan Tracy's *Under Milk Wood Suite* (1958); John Cale and Robin Williamson have recorded albums of Thomas songs; Mick Jagger, Patti Smith and Jim Morrison were, and are, devoted fans; and Thomas was John Lennon's favourite writer. Igor Stravinsky set 'Do not go gentle into that good night' as an elegy for Thomas, and Milton Babbitt, Louis Andriessen and Udo Kasemets are just some of the dozens of modern classical composers who have followed suit. See Lily Chia Brissman, 'In All His Tuneful Turning: Song Settings of Dylan Thomas's Poetry For Solo Voice and Piano', eds. Glyn Pursglove, John Goodby and Chris Wigginton, *The Swansea Review: Dylan Thomas Special Issue*, 20 (2000), pp. 150–66.

15 In an amusing example of conflict between the musical and filmic currents of Thomas-adulation, it was reported in the late 1990s that Mick Jagger and Pierce Brosnan (whose son is named after Thomas) were bidding against each other for possession of the double bed Dylan and Caitlin shared in Laugharne: see http://www.independent.co.uk/news/arts-battle-breaks-out-over-dead-poets-final-resting-place-1137706.html

16 The ad, created by DBB London, directed by Noam Murro and using the Cliff Martinez song 'Don't Blow It', lasts for 1 minute 31 seconds. It follows a man driving his VW Golf through the early morning, eerily traffic-free LA. We see (voyeuristically, like *Under Milk Wood*'s listeners) blazing, empty skyscrapers in the central district, exhausted cops in an all-night diner, a burning van on waste ground, a bedroom with a strange stag-headed coat-rack and a solitary prostitute (or is she?) among other things. See http://www.vw.nightdrive.com

17 For an illuminating discussion of this question, see Marjorie Perloff, *Radical Artifice: Writing Poetry in the Age of Media* (Chicago and London: University of Chicago Press, 1991), particularly Chapter 6, 'How It Means: Making Poetic Sense in Media Society'.

18 Pennar Davies, 'Sober Reflections on Dylan Thomas', *Dock Leaves*, 5: 15 (1954), pp. 13–17.

19 Karl Shapiro claimed in 1955 that 'Thomas has more imitators today than any other poet in the literature'. Karl Shapiro, 'Dylan Thomas', p. 172.

20 In the same spirit, David Daiches noted '[he] had no lessons to teach others as Pound and Eliot had'. See Kershner, *Poet and His Critics*, p.128.

21 Sarah Crown, 'A Flighty Mix-Up Country', *The Guardian Saturday Review*, 24 February 2007, p.18.

22 Of 'British' poetries, I only have space for a discussion of English and Anglo-Welsh here, although I touch on Thomas's importance to the Scottish W. S. Graham. Work in this area has only begun; for one recent case study, see my '"Bulbous Taliesin": MacNeice and Dylan Thomas', in eds. Fran Brearton and Edna Longley, *Incorrigibly Plural: Louis MacNeice and his Legacy* (Manchester: Carcanet, 2012), pp.204–23.

23 Eric Homberger, *The Art of the Real: Poetry in England and America since 1939* (London and Totowa, NJ: Dent and Rowman and Littlefield, 1977), p.180.

24 John Wain, *Sprightly Running: Part of an Autobiography* (London: Macmillan, 1962), cited in James Keery, 'Menacing Works in my Isolation: Early Pieces', eds. John Kerrigan and Peter Robinson, *The Thing about Roy Fisher* (Liverpool: Liverpool University Press, 2000), p.79.

25 Kenneth Rexroth, for example, improbably likened Thomas to Charlie 'Bird' Parker, claiming that both used their unsurpassed technical mastery to make their art appear spontaneous and were 'two ruined Titans … two great juvenile delinquents – the heroes of the post-war generation …'. M. Wynn Thomas and Daniel Williams suggest that Thomas was 'Americanised' by being cleansed of his 'English designations … Bohemian Marxist; Symbolist; one of the Apocalyptic poets', and by being isolated from 'foreign traditions … [such as] the Metaphysical poets, the Welsh language *cynghanedd* tradition', though a trace of his Welshness was preserved, because it was 'his passport to America … [as] a … "primitive"'. Useful as this is, it is unclear why 'Metaphysical' is 'foreign' and not 'English', or how the 'English' terms came to be so designated (many other Welsh poets were 'Bohemian Marxist', 'Symbolist' and 'Apocalyptic'). The aim seems to be to exaggerate Thomas's 'Englishness' without dispensing with 'Metaphysical' – the one unimpeachably canonical quality. See M. Wynn Thomas and Daniel Williams, '"A Sweet Union?": Dylan Thomas and Post-War American Poetry, eds. Gilbert Bennett, Eryl Jenkins and Eurwen Price, *I Sang in My Chains: Essays and Poems in Tribute to Dylan Thomas* (Swansea: The Dylan Thomas Society of Great Britain, 2003), p.57.

26 It was in 1954, at one of Rexroth's weekly seminars, that Ginsberg first heard the poem, which claimed, as *Howl* would in 1956, that bourgeois attitudes and capitalist values were responsible for murdering artists. For a tribute to Thomas by one of the leading Beat poets, see Lawrence Ferlinghetti, 'Palinode for Dylan Thomas', *These Are My Rivers: New & Selected Poems 1955–1993* (San Francisco, CA: New Directions Books, 1994), pp.42–3.

27 John Berryman, *Collected Poems 1937–1971* (London: Faber, 1991), pp.138, 146–7. See Philip Coleman, '"An Unclassified Strange Flower": Towards an Analysis of John Berryman's Contact with Dylan Thomas', eds. Glyn Pursglove, John Goodby and Chris Wigginton, *The Swansea Review*, pp.22–33.

28 Louis Simpson, *A Revolution in Taste* (New York, NY: Macmillan, 1978), p.38.

29 O'Hara's dismissal is reported in James Schuyler's 'The Morning of the Poem'. See James Schuyler, *Collected Poems* (New York, NY: Farrar, Strauss and Giroux, 1998),

p. 286. For Ashbery, see *The Collected Poems of Frank O'Hara*, ed. Donald Allen (Berkeley, CA: University of California Press, 1995), p. viii.

30 Cited in R. B. Kershner, Jr., *Dylan Thomas: The Poet and his Critics* (Chicago, IL: American Library Association 1976), p. 125.

31 Charles Olson, 'Projective Verse', ed. Paul Hoover, *Postmodern American Poetry: A Norton Anthology* (New York, NY: W. W. Norton, 1994), pp. 613–21.

32 Paul Hoover, *Postmodern American Poetry*, pp. 621–8.

33 Among the relevant issues touched on in Bernstein's fascinating work are the restrictions of 'the abstract / closed sentence', which deflects attention to 'an abstracted, or accompanying "meaning"', as opposed to 'the imploded sentence', in which 'the reader stays plugged in to the wave-like / pulse of the writing'; the way 'a surface disruption of syntactic ideality / can expand the total prosody of the poem'; poetry's need to 'resist rested definition'; the claim that 'a radical ambivalence / … lies at the heart of writing'; the way 'repetitions … create a kind of disabsorptive charm'; and the way that the visible and aural impermeable obtrusion of words into the world 'makes a reader's absorption / in words possible', their physicality ensuring that 'Writing is not a thin film / of expendable substitutions that, when reading, falls / away / like scales / to reveal a meaning' and hence the 'thickness' of writing as something 'ineradicable, yet mortal'. Bernstein draws on Merleau-Ponty and Bataille to explain poetry's 'thickness of words' and the way that it can lead 'to the same place as eroticism'. Charles Bernstein, *A Poetics* (Cambridge, MA: Harvard University Press, 1998), pp. 9–89.

34 Steve McCaffery, 'Diminished Reference and the Model Reader', *North of Intention: Critical Writings 1973–1986* (New York, NY: Roof Books, 2000), pp. 13–29. The point is not, of course, to deny that signification matters, but rather to interfere with the ideology by which the signifying process, and, thus, language itself, is rendered invisible.

35 Robert Horan, 'In Defense of Dylan Thomas', *The Kenyon Review*, VII: 2 (Spring 1945), p. 305.

36 Peter Finch, Selected Poems (Bridgend: Poetry Wales Press, 1987), p. 15.

37 Mainstream Anglo-Welsh poetry became dull and repetitive in the 1970s. The 'New Gen' moment of 1994, initially promised renewal, but led chiefly to market-defined pluralism and the aping of English fashions, symbolised by the huge burden of expectation heaped on the modest talent of Owen Sheers. See John Goodby, '"Deflected Forces of Currents": Mapping Welsh Modernist Poetry', *Poetry Wales*, 46: 1 (Summer 2010), pp. 52–8.

38 A relatively recent example of this tendency is Meic Stephens's anthology *Poetry 1900–2000* (Cardiff: University of Wales Press, 2007). It enshrines the backward look and excludes such important poets as John James, Wendy Mulford, Philip Jenkins, David Annwn and David Greenslade. The most recent critical work on Anglo-Welsh poetry contains an essay on Peter Finch – unavoidably, given his public profile – but frustratingly refers to 'John James … and others' in passing only, continuing the tradition of neglect. See Daniel G. Williams, ed., *Slanderous Tongues: Essays on Welsh Poetry in English 1970–2005* (Bridgend: Seren Books, 2010), p. 12.

39 A. Alvarez, *The New Poetry* (London: Penguin, 1962 [repr. 1966]), p. 23.

40 James Keery, 'The Burning Baby and the Bathwater', *P. N. Review* 171, 33: 1 (September-October 2006), p. 59.

41 Ted Hughes, *Collected Poems*, ed. Paul Keegan (London: Faber, 2003), pp. 359, 19–20, 36.

42 James Keery, 'The Burning Baby and the Bathwater', *P. N. Review* 171, p. 59.

43 Ted Hughes, ed. Paul Keegan, *Collected Poems*, p. 34.

44 Cited by James Keery, 'The Burning Baby and the Bathwater', *P. N. Review* 171, p. 59.

45 James Keery, 'The Burning Baby and the Bathwater', *P. N. Review* 171, p. 59.

46 John Gordon, 'Being Sylvia Being Ted Being Dylan: Plath's "The Snowman on the Moor"', *Journal of Modern Literature*, 27: 1 / 2 (Fall 2003), p. 188.

47 As John Gordon notes, in this poem: 'Plath's relation to Thomas goes beyond the usual questions of poetic influence. It is rather a matter of willed identification, a subsuming of self into other, of the "I am Heathcliff" stamp, effected through the appearance of a Thomas surrogate's surrogate and authenticated with an act of ventriloquy'. John Gordon, 'Being Sylvia Being Ted Being Dylan: Plath's "The Snowman on the Moor"', p. 191.

48 Sylvia Plath, 'All the Dead Dears', ed. and intro. Ted Hughes, *Collected Poems* (London: Faber, 1991), pp. 70–1. For the other three poems, see Plath, *Poems*, pp. 125, 141, 240–2.

49 Jacqueline Rose, *The Haunting of Sylvia Plath*, p. 167.

50 Jacqueline Rose, *The Haunting of Sylvia Plath*, pp. 10, 169.

51 Geoffrey Hill, *Collected Poems* (Harmondsworth: Penguin, 1985), p. 16.

52 Interview with Edwin Morgan, *Angel Exhaust*, 10 (Spring 1994), p. 53.

53 James Keery, '"Menacing Works in my Isolation": Early Pieces', ed. John Kerrigan and Peter Robinson, *The Thing About Roy Fisher: Critical Studies* (Liverpool: Liverpool University Press, 2000), p. 51.

54 James Keery, 'Menacing Works in my Isolation', pp. 50–1.

55 Thus, for Neil Corcoran, although at first 'helplessly parasitic on Thomas', Graham's is 'arguably the finest contribution to post-war [British] poetry by a poet who began publishing in the 1940s'. Neil Corcoran, *English Poetry Since 1940* (London: Macmillan, 1993), p. 47.

56 See 'His Perfect Hunger's Daily Changing Bread', *P.N. Review*, 27: 1 (September-October 2000), pp. 35–8. This review by James Keery of *The Nightfisherman: Selected Letters of W. S. Graham* is the source from which many of my comments are taken.

57 This event was commemorated by David Wright in his poem 'Incident in Soho', which describes this 'unlike making of history' at a time when 'History – big word – [was] being made … in Normandy'. Wright saw, but could not (being deaf) hear, Thomas reading a poem to Graham in a Soho pub and asked him afterwards if he could see it: 'He gave it me, then turning to the other: / "Well Sydney?" The first reading of "Fern Hill"'. See Tony Lopez, *Meaning Performance* (Cambridge: Salt, 2006), p. 92.

58 *The Nightfisherman: Selected Letters of W. S. Graham*, eds. Michael and Margaret Snow (Manchester: Carcanet, 1999), pp. 379–83. See W. S. Graham, *New Selected Poems*, ed. Matthew Francis (London: Faber, 2004), pp. xvi, xviii.

59 W. S. Graham, *New Collected Poems*, pp. 106–7.

60 W. S. Graham, *New Collected Poems*, p. 202.

61 W. S. Graham, *New Collected Poems*, p. 127.

62 W. S. Graham, *New Collected Poems*, p. 202–3.

63 Martin Heidegger, *Language, Poetry, Thought*, transl. Albert Hofstadter (New York, NY: Harper & Row, 1975), p. 215.

64 Nigel Wheale, 'Lynette Roberts: Legend and Form in the 1940s', *Critical Quarterly*, 36: 3 (Autumn 1994), p. 13.

65 Tony Lopez, *Meaning Performance* (Cambridge: Salt, 2006), pp. 92–4. Citing Philip Larkin's enthusiastic description of Dylan Thomas and his reading at the Oxford English Club in November 1941, Lopez adds: 'Notice that Thomas is portrayed … as an ordinary "bloke" and also as a very worldly poet who is, as we learn from the jokes he makes and the parodies he reads, keenly aware of the dangers involved in the public role of the poet. He is in Larkin's sketch really the opposite of the bardic poet that the Movement writers later made him out to be'.

66 Drew Milne, *Sheet Mettle* (London: Alfred David Editions, 1994), p. 73.

67 Ralph Maud, *Poetry in the Making*, p. 43.

68 Cited in Nathalie Wourm, 'Dylan Thomas and the French Symbolists', ed. Tony Brown, *Welsh Writing in English: A Yearbook of Critical Essays*, vol. 5 (1999), p. 27.

69 See, for a recent example, the "In Your Translating Eyes" event of 25 March 2013: http://www.cardiff.ac.uk/europ/newsandevents/events/dylanthomastranslation. html

70 Paul Celan, *Selected Poems*, transl. Michael Hamburger (London: Penguin, 1990), p. 79.

71 Amy Colin, *Paul Celan: Holograms of Darkness* (Indiana, IN: Indiana University Press, 1991), p. 99. As noted by Keery (see fn. below).

72 James Keery, 'The Burning Baby and the Bathwater', *P.N. Review*, 31: 6 (July-August 2005), p. 59.

73 '"The Practice of Poetry: Fiona Sampson interviewed by Simon Jarvis", *English: The Journal of the English Association*, 56:214 (Spring 2007), pp. 73–88.'

74 Keith Tuma, *Fishing by Obstinate Isles: Modern and Postmodern British Poetry and American Readers* (Evanston, IL: Northwestern University Press, 1998), pp. 108–9. Those in retreat included 'the Auden circle', Empson and such Americans as Ransom and Tate, while the extenders of 'the modernist practice of Pound, Williams, Eliot, Stevens, and Moore, as well as of Europeans', included the Objectivists, Charles Henri Ford and Myriel Rukeyser and, in Britain, Auden, Bunting, Charles Madge and Joseph Gordon Macleod. The trouble with this is not just that the lack of discrimination between very different figures makes the categories too unwieldy to be useful, but also they are too starkly antinomian: extenders (who include such unlikely bedfellows as Pound and Stevens) or retreaters, but no intermingling.

75 For Donaghy, see http://www.poetrymagazines.org.uk/magazine/record.asp?id=3297

76 For Paterson, see 'Prism Visitor', *The Observer Review*, 2004. Paterson sympathises with, and identifies, the reason for Graham's neglect – 'What happened was the Movement … *The Less Deceived* was published in the same year [as *The Nightfishing*, which] set the tone – quiet, ironic, self-deprecating, unmistakably English – for the next 20–odd' – but does not see that the philosophical and aesthetic presuppositions of the Movement poem are still more or less standard for most British poetry, including his own.

77 Jeffrey Side, 'The Influence of Wordsworth's Empiricist Aesthetic on Seamus Heaney's Criticism and Poetry', *English*, 59: 225 (Summer 2010), p. 157. Side concludes: 'This is not to deny what is to be found in Heaney's poetry that is valuable, only to emphasize that such aspects should not be regarded as solely

sufficient for the purposes of poetic composition as I believe has become the case in Britain'.

78 See *Poetry Review: New Generation Poets*, Special Issue, 84: 1 (Spring 1994). New Gen was a publisher-generated promotion of twenty youngish and 'different' poets, which reflected larger social trends towards tolerance of minorities and economic ones towards consumerism and niche marketing. It ably reflected the widening of the mainstream poetry spectrum since the Motion and Morrison Penguin anthology of 1981, but its self-proclaimed variousness excluded all late modernist small press-published poets. It did, however, initiate debates about the extent of the overlapping of 'High Street' and more experimental poetries (poets taken to belong, to some extent, to this interstitial zone included Pauline Stainer, Ken Smith, Geoffrey Hill, Roy Fisher, Paul Muldoon, Glyn Maxwell, Edwin Morgan, John Ash, Denise Riley, Peter Didsbury, James Fenton and Ian McMillan). These debates have continued. Significant contributions include those by Ian Gregson (*Contemporary Poetry and Postmodernism: Dialogue and Estrangement* [1996]), David Kennedy (*New Relations: The Refashioning of British Poetry 1980–1994* [1996]), Peter Barry (*Poetry Wars: British Poetry of the 1970s and the Battle of Earl's Court* [2006]) and Andrew Duncan (*The Council of Heresy: A Primer of Poetry in a Balkanised Terrain* [2009] and *The Long 1950s: Morality and Fantasy as Stakes in the Poetic Game* [2012]). See the Preface, and Preface fn. 11, for a related discussion

79 See *Poetry Review: New Generation Poets* (A *Poetry Review* Special Issue), 84:1 (Spring 1994), pp. 8–112. However, one should be wary of inferring too much from these preferences; it may be a salutary warning against preconceptions (as well as against the value of a term like 'influence'), for example, that Carol Ann Duffy's 'Three influential 20th C. books' are Neruda's *Twenty Love Poems and a Song of Despair,* Césaire's *Cahier d'un retour au pays natal* and W. S. Graham's *Implements in their Places.*

80 Gabriel Pearson, 'Gabriel Pearson on Dylan Thomas', *The Spectator Review of Books,* 20 November 1970, pp. 731–2. Pearson concluded by stating that: 'Of the two, I believe, against the grain of current prejudice, Thomas denied less of himself than Auden and emerges from a reading of his poetry and prose as the richer, more humanly grounded artist'. It is possible to demur at this, but nevertheless see that the Auden-Thomas weighting requires major rebalancing.

81 John Matthias, 'British Poetry at Y2K', p. 30. See http://www.electronicbookreview. com/

82 'The Democratic Voice' is the Introduction to *The Penguin Book of Poetry from Britain and Ireland* (London: Penguin, 1998).

83 Caddel's post is dated 24 June 1998. See British poets archives, 'Re: Who likes Dylan Thomas', http://www.mailbase.ac.uk/lists/british-poets/1998–06/0281.html

84 'The Practice of Poetry: Fiona Sampson interviewed by Simon Jarvis', *English: The Journal of the English Association,* 56:214 (Spring 2007), pp. 73–88.

SELECT BIBLIOGRAPHY
Books by Dylan Thomas

Poetry

18 Poems, London, Parton Press, 1934.

Twenty-five Poems, London, Dent, 1936.

The Map of Love, London, Dent, 1939.

The World I Breathe, Norfolk, CT, New Directions, 1939.

New Poems, Norfolk, CT, New Directions, 1943.

Deaths and Entrances, London, Dent, 1946.

Twenty-Six Poems, London, Dent, 1950.

In Country Sleep, New York, NY, New Directions, 1952.

Collected Poems 1934–1952, London, Dent, 1952.

The Notebooks of Dylan Thomas, ed. and intro. Ralph Maud, London, New Directions, 1967 (repr. *Poet in the Making*, London, Dent, 1968).

The Notebook Poems 1930–1934, ed. and intro. Ralph Maud, London, Dent, 1990.

Dylan Thomas: The Poems, ed. and intro. Daniel Jones, London, Dent, 1971.

Collected Poems 1934–1953, eds. Walford Davies and Ralph Maud, London, Dent, 1989.

Letter to Loren, ed. Jeff Towns, Swansea, Salubrious Press, 1993.

Prose

Portrait of the Artist as a Young Dog, London, Dent, 1940.

Selected Writings by Dylan Thomas, New York, NY, New Directions, 1946.

Quite Early One Morning, ed. Aneurin Talfan Davies, London, Dent, 1954.

Adventures in the Skin Trade and Other Stories, New York, NY, New Directions, 1955 (repr. *Collected Stories*, 1983).

A Prospect of the Sea and Other Stories and Prose Writings, ed. Daniel Jones, London, Dent, 1955.

A Child's Christmas in Wales, Norfolk, CT, New Directions, 1955.

Dylan Thomas: Early Prose Writings, ed. Walford Davies, London, Dent, 1971.

The Death of the King's Canary, with John Davenport and intro. Constantine Fitzgibbon, London, Hutchinson, 1976.

Collected Stories, ed. Walford Davies and intro. Leslie Norris, London, Dent, 1983.

Dramatic, film and radio writings

The Doctor and the Devils, London, Dent, 1953.

Under Milk Wood, London, Dent, 1954 (repr. ed. Ralph Maud and Walford Davies, intro. Walford Davies, 1995).

Dylan Thomas: The Broadcasts, ed. Ralph Maud, London, Dent, 1991.

Dylan Thomas: The Complete Screen Plays, ed. John Ackerman, New York, NY, Applause Books, 1995 (includes previously published *The Doctor and the Devils*,

London: Dent, 1953; *The Beach of Falesá*, New York, NY, Stein and Day, 1963; and *Twenty Years A-Growing*, London, Dent, 1964).

Correspondence and critical writing

See also *Quite Early One Morning* and *Dylan Thomas: The Broadcasts* (above).

Letters to Vernon Watkins, intro. Vernon Watkins, London, Dent, 1957.

'Poetic Manifesto', *Texas Quarterly*, 4 (Winter 1961), 45–53.

'Replies to an Enquiry', *New Verse*, 11 (October 1934), 8–9.

The Collected Letters, ed. Paul Ferris, 2nd edn., London, Dent, 2000.

Critical works on Dylan Thomas

Critical studies

Ackerman, John, *A Dylan Thomas Companion: Life, Poetry and Prose*, London, Macmillan, 1991.

——— *Welsh Dylan: Dylan Thomas' Life, Writing and his Work*, London, John Jones, 1979.

Davies, Aneurin Talfan, *Dylan: Druid of the Broken Body*, London, Dent, 1964.

Davies, James A., *A Companion to Dylan Thomas*, Greensborough, University of Kentucky Press, 1997.

Davies, Walford, *Dylan Thomas*, Cardiff, University of Wales Press, 1990 (repr. 1972).

——— *Dylan Thomas*, Milton Keynes, Open University Press, 1986.

Fraser, G. S., *Dylan Thomas*, London, Longmans, 1957.

Hardy, Barbara, *Dylan Thomas: An Original Language*, Athens and London, University of Georgia Press, 2000.

Holbrook, David, *The Code of Night*, London, Athlone, 1972.

——— *Llareggub Revisited: Dylan Thomas and the State of Modern Poetry*, London, Bowes and Bowes, 1962 (repr. *Dylan Thomas and Poetic Dissociation*, Carbondale, IL, Southern Illinois University Press, 1964).

Jones, T. H., *Dylan Thomas*, Edinburgh and London, Oliver and Boyd, 1963.

Kershner, R. B. Jr., *Dylan Thomas: The Poet and His Critics*, Chicago, IL, American Library Association, 1976.

Kidder, Rushworth M., *Dylan Thomas: The Country of the Spirit*, Princeton, NJ, Princeton University Press, 1973.

Kleinman, Hyman H., *The Religious Sonnets of Dylan Thomas: A Study in Imagery and Meaning*, Berkeley, CA, University of California Press, 1963.

Korg, Jacob, *Dylan Thomas*, New York, NY, Twayne, 1965 (repr. Hippocrene Books, 1972).

Maud, Ralph, *Entrances to Dylan Thomas' Poetry*, Pittsburgh, PA, University of Pittsburgh Press, 1963.

Moynihan, William T., *The Craft and Art of Dylan Thomas*, Oxford, Oxford University Press, 1966.

Olson, Elder, *The Poetry of Dylan Thomas*, Chicago, IL, University of Chicago Press, 1954.

Pratt, Annis, *Dylan Thomas' Early Prose: A Study in Creative Mythology*, Pittsburgh, PA, University of Pittsburgh Press, 1970.

Treece, Henry, *Dylan Thomas: 'Dog Among the Fairies'*, London, Lindsay Drummond, 1949.

Wardi, Eynel, *Once Below a Time: Dylan Thomas, Julia Kristeva, and Other Speaking Subjects*, New York, NY, SUNY Press, 2000.

Wigginton, Chris, *Modernism from the Margins: The 1930s Poetry of Louis MacNeice and Dylan Thomas*, Cardiff, University of Wales Press, 2007.

PhD theses

Bubear, Rhian, '"The World of Words": A Post-Freudian Rereading of Dylan Thomas's Early Poetry', unpublished PhD thesis, University of Swansea, 2011.

Hornick, Lita, 'The Intricate Image: A Study of Dylan Thomas', unpublished PhD thesis, Columbia University, 1958.

Golightly, Victor, '"Two on a tower": the influence of W.B. Yeats on Vernon Watkins and Dylan Thomas', unpublished Ph.D thesis, University of Wales Swansea, 2003.

Parkinson, Siobhán, *Obscurity in the* Collected Poems *of Dylan Thomas*, unpublished Ph.D., University College Dublin, 1981.

Essay collections

Bold, Alan, ed., *Dylan Thomas: Craft or Sullen Art*, London / New York, NY, Vision Press, 1990.

Brinnin, J. M., ed., *A Casebook on Dylan Thomas*, New York, NY, T. Y. Crowell, 1961.

Cox, C. B., ed., *Dylan Thomas: A Collection of Critical Essays*, London, Prentice-Hall, 1962 (repr. Englewood Cliffs, NJ, Prentice-Hall, 1966).

Davies, Walford, ed., *Dylan Thomas: New Critical Essays*, London, Dent, 1972.

Goodby, John and Chris Wigginton, eds., *Dylan Thomas: New Casebook*, Basingstoke, Palgrave, 2001.

Tedlock, E. W., ed., *Dylan Thomas: The Legend and the Poet*, London, Heinemann / Mercury Books, 1963.

Special journal issues

Glyn Pursglove, John Goodby and Chris Wigginton, eds., *The Swansea Review: Under the Spelling Wall*, 20 (2000).

Les Années 30. Dylan Thomas (Université de Nantes), 12 (Juin 1990).

Poetry Wales: Dylan Thomas Special Issue, 9: 2 (Autumn 1973).

Adam International Review, Dylan Thomas Memorial Number, 238 (1953).

Book chapters and journal essays

Aivaz, David, 'The Poetry of Dylan Thomas', *The Hudson Review*, VIII: 3 (Autumn 1950) (repr. Tedlock, 1963), 382–404.

Balakiev, James J., 'The Ambiguous Reversal of Dylan Thomas's "In Country Sleep"', *Papers on Language and Literature*, 32: 1 (1996), 21–44.

Bayley, John, 'Dylan Thomas', ed. John Bayley, *The Romantic Survival*, London, Constable, 1957.

Conran, Tony, '"After the Funeral": The Praise-Poetry of Dylan Thomas', *The Cost of Strangeness: Essays on the English Poets of Wales*, ed. Tony Conran, Llandysul, Gomer Press, 1982.

——— '"I saw Time Murder me": Dylan Thomas and the Tragic Soliloquy', *Frontiers in Anglo-Welsh Poetry*, ed. Tony Conran, Cardiff, University of Wales Press, 1997.

Crehan, Stewart, 'The Lips of Time', ed. Alan Bold, *Dylan Thomas: Craft or Sullen Art*, London / New York, NY, Vision Press, 1990; Crehan, Stewart, 'The Lips of Time', eds. John Goodby and Chris Wigginton, *Dylan Thomas: New Casebook*, Basingstoke, Palgrave, 2001.

Goodby, John, '"The Rimbaud of Cwmdonkin Drive": Dylan Thomas as Surrealist', in *Dada and Beyond: (Vol. 2) Dada and its Legacies*, eds. Elza Adamowicz and Eric Robertson, Amsterdam/New York: Rodopi Press, 2012.

——— 'Bulbous Taliesin': Dylan Thomas and Louis MacNeice, in *'Incorrigibly plural': Louis MacNeice and his Legacy*, eds. Fran Brearton and Edna Longley, Manchester: Carcanet Press, 2012.

——— 'Djuna Barnes' as a source for Dylan Thomas, *Notes & Queries*, 58: 1 (March 2011), 127–30.

——— 'Dylan Thomas and the poetry of the 1940s', in *The Cambridge History of English Poetry*, ed. Michael O'Neill, Cambridge: Cambridge University Press, 2010.

——— 'Dylan Thomas's sources in Whitman and the use of "sidle" as noun', *Notes & Queries*, 52:1 (March 2005), 105–7.

Goodby, John and Chris Wigginton, '"Shut, too, in a Tower of Words": Dylan Thomas' Modernism', eds. Alex Davis and Lee Jenkins, *The Locations of Literary Modernism*, Cambridge, Cambridge University Press, 2000.

Heaney, Seamus, 'Dylan the Durable? On Dylan Thomas', *The Redress of Poetry*, London, Faber, 1995 (orig. published as *Dylan the Durable? On Dylan Thomas*, Bennington, VT, Chapbooks in Literature Series, no publisher, 1992.

Horan, Robert, 'In Defense of Dylan Thomas', *The Kenyon Review*, VII: 3 (Spring 1945), 304–10.

Keery, James, 'The Burning Baby and the Bathwater', *P.N. Review* 151, 29: 5 (May-June 2003), 49–54; *P.N. Review* 152, 29: 6 (July-August 2003), 57–62; *P.N. Review* 154, 3: 2 (November-December 2003), 22–25 (by Giles Goodland), 26–32 (by James Keery); *P.N. Review* 156, 30: 4 (March-April 2004), 40–42; *P.N. Review* 159, 31: 1 (September-October 2004), 45–49; *P.N. Review* 164, 31: 6 (July-August 2005), 57–61; *P.N. Review* 170, 32: 6 (July-August 2006), 59–65; *P.N. Review* 171, 33: 1 (September-October 2006), 56–62.

Korg, Jacob, 'Imagery and Universe in Dylan Thomas's "18 Poems"', *Accent*, XVII: 1 (Winter 1957), 3–15.

Lewis, Peter, 'The Radio Road to Llareggub', ed. John Drakakis, *British Radio Drama*, Cambridge, Cambridge University Press, 1981.

McKay, Don, 'What Shall We Do with a Drunken Poet?: Dylan Thomas' Poetic Language', *Queen's Quarterly*, 93: 4 (1986), 794–807.

——— 'Crafty Dylan and the Altarwise Sonnets: "I Build a Flying Tower and I Pull it Down"', *University of Toronto Quarterly*, 55 (1985/6), 357–94.

McNees, Eleanor J., *Eucharistic Poetry: The Search for Presence in the Writings of John Donne, Gerard Manley Hopkins, Dylan Thomas, and Geoffrey Hill*, Lewisburg, TN, Bucknell University Press, 1992.

Mathias, Roland, 'Lord Cutglass, Twenty Years After', ed. Danny Abse, *Poetry Dimension 2*, London, Sphere Books, 1974, 61–89.

Miller, J. Hillis, 'Dylan Thomas', ed. J. Hillis Miller, *Poets of Reality: Six Twentieth Century Writers*, Cambridge, MA, Harvard University Press, 1966.

Morgan, George, 'Dylan Thomas's "In the Direction of the Beginning": Towards or Beyond Meaning?', *Cycnos*, 20: 2 (2003), 1–17.

——— 'Dylan Thomas and the Ghost of Shakespeare', *Cycnos*, 5 (1989), 113–21.

Nowottny, Winifred, 'Symbolism and Obscurity', ed. Winifred Nowottny, *The Language Poets Use*, London, The Athlone Press, 1962 (repr. 1975).

Riley, Peter, 'Thomas and Apocalypse', *Poetry Wales*, 44: 3 (Winter 2008–09), 12–16.

Scarfe, Francis, 'Dylan Thomas: A Pioneer', ed. Francis Scarfe, *Auden and After: The Liberation of Poetry 1930–41*, London, Routledge, 1942 (repr. 1945).

Silkin, Jon, 'Dylan Thomas', ed. Jon Silkin, *The Life of Metrical and Free Verse in Twentieth-Century Poetry*, Basingstoke, Macmillan, 1997.

Simpson, Louis, 'The Color of Saying', ed. Louis Simpson, *A Revolution in Taste*, New York, NY, Macmillan, 1978.

Thomas, M. Wynn, '"Marlais": Dylan Thomas and the "Tin Bethels"', ed. M. Wynn Thomas, *In the Shadow of the Pulpit: Literature and Nonconformist Wales*, Cardiff, University of Wales Press, 2010.

——— '"He belongs to the English": Welsh Dylan and Welsh-Language Culture', eds. Glyn Pursglove, John Goodby and Chris Wigginton, *The Swansea Review: Under the Spelling Wall*, 20 (2000).

——— 'Portraits of the Artist as a Young Welshman', ed. M. Wynn Thomas, *Corresponding Cultures: The Two Literatures of Wales*, Cardiff, University of Wales Press, 1999.

Thurley, Geoffrey, 'Dylan Thomas: Merlin as Sponger', ed. Geoffrey Thurley, *The Ironic Harvest: English Poetry in the Twentieth Century*, London, Edward Arnold, 1974.

Tolley, A. T., *The Poetry of the Thirties*, London, Victor Gollancz, 1975.

——— *The Poetry of the Forties*, Manchester, Manchester University Press, 1985.

Williams, Daniel, 'Beyond National Literature? Dylan Thomas and Amos Tutuola in "Igbo masquerade"', *New Welsh Review*, 60 (Summer 2003), 5–12.

Young, Alan, 'Image as Structure: Dylan Thomas and Poetic Meaning', *Critical Quarterly*, 17 (1975), 333–45.

Guides and Bibliographies

Emery, Clark, *The World of Dylan Thomas*, Miami, FL, University of Miami Press, 1962.

Gaston, George M. A., *Dylan Thomas: a reference guide*, Boston, Mass., G. K. Hall & Co., 1987.

Maud, Ralph (with Albert Glover), *Dylan Thomas in Print: A Bibliographical History*, Pittsburgh, PA, University of Pittsburgh Press, 1970.

———— *Where Have the Old Words Got Me?*, Cardiff, University of Wales Press, 2003.

Rolph, J. Alexander, *Dylan Thomas: A Bibliography*, London, Dent, 1956.

Tindall, William York, *A Reader's Guide to Dylan Thomas*, New York, NY, Farrar, Strauss and Giroux, 1962 (repr. 1996, Syracuse University Press).

General context, literary history and critical theory

Adamowicz, Elza, *Surrealist Collage in Text and Image: Dissecting the Exquisite Corpse*, Cambridge, Cambridge University Press, 1998 (repr. 2005).

Adorno, Theodor W., *The Culture Industry: Selected Essays on Mass Culture*, ed. J. M. Bernstein, London, Routledge, 1992.

———— 'On Lyric Poetry and Society', *Notes to Literature*, Vol. *1*, ed. Theodor W. Adorno, New York, NY, Columbia University Press, 1991.

Armstrong, Tim, *Modernism, Technology and the Body*, Cambridge, Cambridge University Press, 1998.

Ashford, David, 'Children Asleep in the Underground: The Tubes Stations of Brandt and Moore', *The Cambridge Quarterly*, vol. XXXVI, no. 4 (2007), 296–316.

Babha, Homi K., *The Location of Culture*, London, Routledge, 1994.

Bakhtin, Mikhail, *Rabelais and His World*, transl. Helene Iswolsky, Bloomington, IN, Indiana University Press, 1984.

Bataille, Georges, *Eroticism*, transl. Mary Dalwood and intro. Colin McCabe, London, Penguin Books, 2001.

Benjamin, Walter, *Illuminations*, transl. Harry Zohn, Glasgow, Collins, 1979.

Caesar, Adrian, *Dividing Lines: Poetry, Class and Ideology in the 1930s*, Manchester, Manchester University Press, 1991.

Childs, Donald J., *Modernism and Eugenics: Woolf, Eliot, Yeats, and the Culture of Degeneration*, Cambridge, Cambridge University Press, 2001.

Corcoran, Neil, *English Poetry since 1940*, London, Longman, 1993.

Culler, Jonathan, ed., *On Puns: The Foundation of Letters*, Oxford, Basil Blackwell, 1988.

Cunningham, Valentine, *British Writers of the Thirties*, Oxford, Oxford University Press, 1988.

Davie, Donald, *Articulate Energy*, London, Routledge and Kegan Paul, 1955.

———— *Purity of Diction in English Verse*, London, Chatto & Windus, 1952.

Davies, John, *A History of Wales*, London, Penguin, 1994.

Eagleton, Terry, *Literary Theory: An Introduction*, Oxford, Basil Blackwell, 1983.

Easthope, Anthony, *Poetry as Discourse*, London, Methuen, 1983.

Elias, Norbert, *The Civilizing Process: Sociogenetic and Psychogenetic Investigations*, transl. Edmund Jephcott, Oxford, Basil Blackwell, 2000.

Emig, Rainer, *Modernism in Poetry: Motivations, Structures and Limits*, London, Longman, 1995.

Empson, William, *Seven Types of Ambiguity*, Harmondsworth, Penguin (repr. 1977).

——— *Some Versions of Pastoral*, Harmondsworth, Penguin (repr. 1995).

Foucault, Michel, *The History of Sexuality, Vol. 1: An Introduction*, transl. Robert Hurley, London, Penguin, 1990.

Freud, Sigmund, *The Interpretation of Dreams*, Vol. 4 Pelican Freud Library, eds. James Strachey, Alan Tyson and Angela Richards, transl. James Strachey, Harmondsworth, Penguin, 1983.

——— *The Psychopathology of Everyday Life*, Vol. 5 Penguin Freud Library, ed. Angela Richards and transl. Alan Tyson, Harmondsworth, Penguin, (repr.) 1991.

——— *Jokes and their Relation to the Unconscious*, Vol. 6 Penguin Freud Library, ed. Angela Richards and transl. James Strachey, Harmondsworth, Penguin, 1991.

——— *On Metapsychology*, Vol. 11 Penguin Freud Library, ed. Angela Richards and transl. James Strachey, Harmondsworth, Penguin, (repr.) 1991.

Gantz, Jeffrey, transl. *The Mabinogion*, Harmondsworth, Penguin, 1976.

Hartley, Jenny, *Millions Like Us: British Women's Fiction of the Second World War*, London, Virago Press, 1997.

Hewison, Robert, *Under Siege: Literary Life in London 1939–45*, London, Methuen, 1977 (repr. 1988).

Hopkins, David, *Dada and Surrealism: A Very Short Introduction*, Oxford, Oxford University Press, 2004.

Hynes, Samuel, *The Auden Generation: Literature and Politics in England in the 1930s*, London, Bodley Head, 1976.

Larrissy, Edward, *Reading Twentieth Century Poetry: The Language of Gender and Objects*, Oxford, Basil Blackwell, 1990.

Lecercle, Jean-Jacques, *The Violence of Language*, London, Routledge, 1990.

MacKay, Marina, *Modernism and World War II*, Cambridge, Cambridge University Press, 2007.

McMillan, Dougald, *transition: The History of a Literary Era 1927–1938*, London, Calder and Boyars, 1975.

Mellor, Leo, *Reading the Ruins: Modernism, Bombsites and British Culture*, Cambridge: Cambridge University Press, 2011.

Mengham, Rod and N. H. Reeve, eds., *The Fiction of the 1940s: Stories of Survival*, New York, NY, Houndmills, 2001.

Milne, Drew, 'Modernist poetry in the British Isles', in Alex Davis and Lee M. Jenkins eds. *The Cambridge Companion to Modernist Poetry*, Cambridge, Cambridge University Press, 2007.

Nichols, Peter, *Modernisms: A Literary Guide*, Basingstoke, Macmillan, 1995.

Ong, Walter J., *Fighting for Life: Contest, Sexuality and Consciousness*, Ithaca and London, Cornell University Press, 1981.

Outram, Dorinda, *The Body and the French Revolution*, New Haven and London, Yale University Press, 1989.

Penhallurick, Rob, *Studying the English Language*, Basingstoke, Palgrave, 2010.

Piette, Adam, *Imagination at War: British Fiction and Poetry 1939–45*, London, Papermac, 1995.

Plain, Gill, *Women's Fiction of the Second World War: Gender, Power and Resistance*, Edinburgh, Edinburgh University Press, 1996.

Punter, David, *The Literature of Terror: A History of Gothic Fictions from 1765 to the Present Day*, vol. II, *The Modern Gothic*, London, Longman, 1996.

Rawlinson, Mark, *British Writing of the Second World War*, Oxford, Oxford University Press, 2000.

Ray, Paul C., *The Surrealist Movement in England*, Ithaca and London, Cornell University Press, 1971.

Reich, Wilhelm, *The Mass Psychology of Fascism*, London, Pelican, 1975.

Sheppard, Richard, *Modernism – Dada – Postmodernism*, Evanston, IL, Northwest University Press, 2000.

Sillars, Stuart, *British Romantic Art and the Second World War*, New York, NY, St Martin's Press, 1991.

Stallybrass, Peter and Allon White, *The Politics and Poetics of Transgression*, Ithaca, NY, Cornell University Press, 1986.

Thomson, Philip, *The Grotesque*, London, Methuen, 1972.

Tuma, Keith, *Fishing by Obstinate Isles: Modern and Postmodern British Poetry and American Readers*, Evanston, IL, Northwestern University Press, 1998.

Wilde, Alan, *Horizons of Assent: Modernism, Postmodernism, and the Ironic Imagination*, Philadelphia, PA, University of Pennsylvania Press, 1987.

Williams, Gwyn A., *When Was Wales?: A History of the Welsh*, London, Penguin, 1985 (repr. 1991).

Young, Alan, *Dada and After: Extremist Modernism and English Literature*, Manchester, Manchester University Press, 1981.

Biography

Brinnin, John Malcolm, *Dylan Thomas in America*, Boston, MA, Little, Brown and Co., 1955.

Davies, James A., *Dylan Thomas's Swansea, Gower and Laugharne*, Cardiff, University of Wales Press, 2000.

Ferris, Paul, *Dylan Thomas*, Harmondsworth, Penguin, 1978.

Fitzgibbon, Constantine, *The Life of Dylan Thomas*, London, Dent, 1965 (repr. Plantin Paperbacks, 1987).

Hawkins, Desmond, *When I Was: A Memoir of the Years between the Wars*, London, Macmillan, 1989.

Heppenstall, Rayner, *Four Absentees*, London, Barrie and Rockliff, 1960.

Holt, Heather, *Dylan Thomas: The Actor*, Llandebie, Dinefwr Press, 2003.

Jones, Daniel, *My Friend Dylan Thomas*, London, Dent, 1977.

Lycett, Andrew, *Dylan Thomas: A New Life*, London, Weidenfeld and Nicholson, 2003.

Sinclair, Andrew, *Dylan Thomas: No Man More Magical*, New York, NY, Holt, Rinehart and Winston, 1975.

Thomas, Caitlin, *Leftover Life to Kill*, London, Putnam, 1957.

Thomas, David N., *Dylan Thomas: A Farm, Two Mansions and a Bungalow*, foreword by Paul Ferris, Bridgend, Seren Books, 2000.

———— ed., *Dylan Remembered: Interviews by Colin Edwards, Vol. 1 1914–1934*, Bridgend, Seren Books, 2003.

———— ed., *Dylan Remembered: Interviews by Colin Edwards Vol. 2 1935–1953*, Bridgend, Seren Books, 2004.

Watkins, Gwen, *Dylan Thomas: Portrait of a Friend*, Talybont, Y Lolfa, 2005.

INDEX